ISBN 978-0-483-02577-6
PIBN 10721230

THE FORUM.

VOL. XXXVII.

JULY, 1905—JUNE, 1906.

NEW YORK:

THE FORUM PUBLISHING COMPANY.

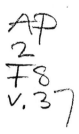

PRESS OF
THE PUBLISHERS' PRINTING COMPANY
82, 84 LAFAYETTE PLACE
NEW YORK

CONTENTS.

THE FORUM.

VOL. XXXVII, NO. 1.

JULY—SEPTEMBER, 1905.

NEW YORK:

THE FORUM PUBLISHING COMPANY.

PRESS OF
THE PUBLISHERS' PRINTING COMPANY
82, 84 LAFAYETTE PLACE
NEW YORK

The Forum

JULY, 1905.

AMERICAN POLITICS.

ORDINARILY the adjournment of Congress is followed by a long period of dulness in the field of politics. This year is an exception to the rule. Events of profound interest and significance have followed each other in rapid succession since Congress adjourned on the fourth of March. It is my purpose to use these events as texts for suggestive comment, avoiding, as far as possible, the repetition of well-known facts.

First of all, the municipal election in Chicago, when Judge Edward F. Dunne was chosen mayor by a plurality of 24,248, upon a platform which committed the victorious candidate to the principle of municipal ownership of street railroads, must be regarded as one of the most interesting political happenings of recent years. My article in the last issue of THE FORUM called attention to the popular drift toward federalism or governmental control of almost every industry. The election in Chicago was only another manifestation of this almost universal feeling. The people are becoming weary of contributing to the wealth of great corporations without sharing in the profits. The large dividends paid upon street-railroad stock, for instance, come from the pockets of the individuals who ride upon the cars. It is useless to argue with them that they enjoy rapid and safe transportation for the nickel which they pay. From their point of view, if there is large profit in a multitude of nickels, there is no reason why the municipality should not operate the railroad system as a public institution and not as a money-making corporation, and thus reduce the cost of a ride to three cents or even less.

In other words, the people are thinking for themselves. The voting population in the United States is the most intelligent in the world. The time is past when men go to the polls like dumb, driven animals. They are reasoning and figuring, and, as might be expected, they take a very selfish and practical view. The sentimentality of party devotion has almost entirely disappeared. The presidential election of 1896 was a triumph of material interests. Thousands upon thousands then drifted away from ancient ties of party fealty and obeyed the instincts of self-preservation, fearful lest their accumulation, large or small, might be adversely affected. The same feeling was paramount in 1900 and 1904. The municipal election in Chicago was a logical result of those campaigns. Elections in the future will be determined by the same cause. The voters will consider, first of all, their own interests. They will give little heed to platforms and candidates, except as these appeal to personal and practical considerations.

There is truth in Judge Dunne's statement that the movement in favor of municipal ownership of all public utilities has taken deep root among the intelligent people of this country. "It is no passing sentiment," he says. "It is here to stay. Municipal ownership and operation of these utilities and governmental ownership of railroads, telegraphs, and express transportation are practical questions, upon which the people must pass within a very short time; and the politicians and parties who ignore these questions must be prepared for a short-lived career before the people." The movement is based upon the popular belief that municipal ownership of public utilities means that the people, and not a few fortunate stockholders, will share the profits. Curiously enough, the United States Government has done more than any other single agency in instilling this belief into the population. During the past two or three years, the United States consuls abroad have contributed an interesting and valuable series of reports upon the various phases of municipal ownership in Great Britain; and, almost without exception, these reports have been arguments in favor of the system. These documents have been widely circulated throughout this country, and they have stimulated the idea of municipal ownership to an extraordinary degree.

Take, for instance, the report of United States Consul Hamm, upon the success of the experiment of city-owned cars in Hull. He emphasizes the cheapness of the fare, namely, one penny on all lines for all distances; and he discusses the financial phase with evident approbation. During the twelve months preceding his report, the gross income was about $445,000; the cost of operation was about $223,000. "This," he says, "left a gross profit of $212,000, and, deducting interest on the investment and the sinking fund, left a net profit of $122,000, or an average of $12,000 a mile of double track, which went into the city treasury." He admits that wages are lower than in the United States, but he points out that the cost of living is less; and the employees, he adds, are of an excellent class, fully equal in intelligence and efficiency to those employed on any street-car line. He finds many other points of favorable comparison, and then he concludes as follows:

These are the results of the municipalization of city transit in Hull. They give American cities a striking proof of the mistake they have made in surrendering their streets to private companies, that operate the lines for their private benefit and often to the detriment of the public. If the advocates of the municipalization of street-car lines in the United States wish a good object-lesson on their side of the question, they cannot do better than to study the Hull tramway system.

If this report stood singly and alone, it might not be entitled to consideration. As a matter of fact, there are before me a series of similar publications issued by the federal Government, and all tending to prove, upon the evidence of United States consuls, that municipalization is a complete success. Mr. Frank W. Mahin, for instance, reports in regard to Leicester that for the first half of 1904 the net profits of the municipal gas-works were $110,000; of the electric-light works, $12,500; and of the water-works, $44,000. "All this surplus," he remarks significantly, "goes to reduce taxes or to benefit the public in other ways." From Leeds comes the statement that the operation of the tramways by the city authorities for twelve months showed a surplus of over $286,-000, "which was turned over to the city treasurer to be used in reducing the city taxes." Advances in wages were given to the employees, and every three months bonuses are allowed motormen who perform their duties without accident. "So the public," said the consul, "is benefited in two ways — by having low street-car fares and a reduction in taxation."

Nor is this all. Mr. James Boyle, the United States consul at Liverpool, has written most entertainingly and instructively concerning the development of municipal socialism in Great Britain. We learn from him that at the time he made his report there were in Great Britain 931 municipalities owning water-works, 99 owning the street railroads or tramways, 240 owning the gas-works, and 181 supplying electricity. Every one knows how far advanced Glasgow is in the matter of municipal ownership. It may not be so well known that Liverpool is also

one of the foremost cities in municipal socialism.   It owns the water-
works, one of the best systems in the world; it operates the street cars;
it supplies the electric light and power; it has one of the largest and
best public-bath systems anywhere, including one of the finest Turkish
baths in Europe; it provides public laundries for the poor districts; it
furnishes flowers and plants for the windows in the slums; it sells ster-
ilized milk for the children of the poor at cost price; it has a salaried
organist to play its famous municipal organ; it gives municipal lectures
— and all these in addition to the usual undertakings of municipalities,
such as parks with concerts, technical schools, etc.   The greatest work
accomplished in Liverpool, however, is that of providing dwellings for
the very poor in the place of unsanitary buildings, which are demolished
as fast as possible.

Further examination into the facts of municipal ownership in Great
Britain, as presented by our consuls, reveals a condition of affairs of
which an American public has probably only a most inadequate conception.   Several towns, such as Doncaster, Chester, and Lincoln, are the
owners of race courses, from which they derive considerable income —
sufficient, in the case of the first-named town, to enable the corporation
to do away with the borough rate.   The corporation of Bath owns the
hot springs, nearly all the cold springs, the famous Roman baths, and
the pump-rooms, and has recently expended $150,000 in a magnificent
promenade; Bournemouth owns the winter gardens and the golf links;
Brighton enjoys a large revenue from its pavilion and aquarium; Col-
chester owns the Colne oyster fishery; Birkenhead operates a municipal
ferry system between that city and Liverpool; St. Helen's supplies ster-
ilized milk; Southport possesses a municipal amusement park, which
brings in considerable revenue; and Nottingham, Wolverhampton, and
Birmingham maintain city sewerage farms, the latter city selling farm
stock, wool, crops, and milk to the value of $125,000 per year.   In
summing up the results of the experiment in Great Britain, Mr. Boyle
makes these pertinent suggestions:

The claim is made that the best-governed towns in Great Britain and the towns
that have the least taxes are those where municipal socialism prevails.   But this
claim is strongly controverted, especially as to ultimate results; and the opponents
of muncipial socialism charge against that system a tendency to extravagance, jobbery, official indifference, and lethargy; and the broader charge is made that the
system contracts and paralyzes individual effort and enterprise.   Yet it should be
kept in mind, in connection with this criticism, that municipal socialism has in some
cases been embarked upon almost out of necessity — as, for instance, in the case
of the housing of the poor in Liverpool, where private enterprise has not only

failed absolutely to solve the problem, but has not even alleviated its most crying evils.

Two observations are appropriate to be made in conclusion: Speaking generally, municipal government in Great Britain is honest, intelligent, and energetic; and, as a rule, politics has but little to do with the engagement or retention of civic employees.

Not only the United States consuls in England, but also those in Canada and Germany have been active propagandists of the municipal-ownership idea. The system is spreading in Canada, while in Germany, according to Mr. Ernest L. Harris, commercial agent, "there is a very strong tendency on the part of the state or municipal authorities, as the case may be, to secure control of all the works which contribute in any way toward the public welfare." Mr. Harris helps along the cause by remarking that "Government control of all such enterprises has led to a great rivalry among the large cities of the empire in striving to be first in the application of the newest methods and latest inventions known to science."

This presentation of the interesting facts concerning municipal ownership abroad is warranted by several considerations. In the first place, I do not believe that the American people have anything like an adequate idea of the extent to which the experiment has been adopted in other countries; nor do I think that we, as a nation, have appreciated the work which has been done by our consuls in fanning into a blaze the slumbering embers of American socialism. Most important of all, however, is the probability that this question of municipal ownership will become a great political issue in the future. There is already talk of a movement in New York City toward municipal control of public utilities, and the subject is certain to be uppermost in the minds of those who are seeking new rallying cries for the masses of the voters. It is already announced that Mr. Bryan purposes next fall to make a tour of the world for the express purpose of investigating this question. The newspapers, always on the alert for contributions upon the foremost topic, are discussing the subject from every point of view; and the Chicago "Tribune" has already sent abroad one of its most intelligent and accurate correspondents, Mr. Raymond Patterson, to gather every possible detail of information.

The leaders of the radical wing of the Democratic party will gladly welcome "social democracy" as a new issue. If they do no more, they can point to the spectacle of a Republican administration demanding from Congress federal control of railroad rates and to the federal ownership of transportation facilities in the case of the acquisition of the stock of the Panama railway and steamship lines. The cry for municipal ownership will be in harmony with the chorus of denunciation of trusts and corporations. It would not be surprising to see Mr. Bryan return from his contemplated trip an apostle of municipal and federal ownership, and prepared, through the accumulation of facts such as have already been presented in this article, to present the subject with the same eloquence and plausibility which marked his treatment of the silver question.

The tariff question bids fair to be the other principal political issue of the near future. During the session of Congress last winter, President Roosevelt called attention to the fact that, unless the federal authorities were expressly directed to purchase in the United States all the supplies necessary in the construction of the Panama canal, it would be more economical to make these purchases in the open markets of the world. Congress failed to heed the President's suggestion. With characteristic directness of purpose, however, he announced that, as Congress had ignored the problem, he purposed to deal with it in a way that appealed more forcibly to his sense of duty. In other words, he did not feel justified in limiting Panama Canal purchases to the United States and thus adding $20,000,000 to the cost of the enterprise. It is difficult to exaggerate the degree of sensation which this announcement created. The "stand-patters" stood aghast. The President had executed a flank movement which made tariff revision a certainty. His position was an official, authoritative declaration, from the highest possible source, that, through the operation of the tariff barrier, American citizens were being compelled to pay unnecessarily high prices for articles of American manufacture.

It will be remembered that during the last session of Congress, Representative Babcock, of Wisconsin, and other advocates of tariff revision, cited many products of this country which were sold more cheaply to the foreign purchaser than to the home consumer. The opponents of revision, following the late Senator Hanna's advice to "stand pat," prevented any legislation, and Mr. Babcock and his colleagues were temporarily hushed. It is easy to imagine, however, the confidence with which they will return to the assault when Congress meets in extra session next fall. They will have behind them every thoughtful American voter, regardless of party, who will want to know why the policy prescribed by the President for the rich nation is not also an excellent thing for the poor individual.

The next Congress will be overwhelmingly Republican. On all matters of party policy the majority will be so great that the Democrats will hardly deem it worth while to demand a call of the roll. At the same time, it is worth while to remember that an unusually large number of the members of the next Congress will be new men, who will be more apt to follow the leadership of the President than of the coterie which will attempt to dominate the attitude of the House upon the tariff question. These men will be fresh from the people, as the saying is, and they will look upon the subject from a point of view not altogether satisfactory to the anti-revisionists. The new members from the Western States may especially be expected to advocate reform.

So intense was the feeling created by the President's action, and so earnest was the protest from Speaker Cannon, Representative Dalzell, Representative Grosvenor, and other prominent "stand-patters," that it was finally agreed that the ships desired in the prosecution of the canal work should be chartered and not purchased, and that only supplies imperatively demanded should be secured. The ultimate determination of the Administration's position is to be left to Congress. This means a certain precipitation of a tariff debate in the next session. The President will, while this is in progress, stand aside, calmly awaiting the verdict. If Congress shall decree the purchase of all supplies in the American market, without regard to the increased cost thereby entailed, the President and the canal commission will accept that decision, but will, of course, be relieved from all responsibility.

In the mean time, we may expect that both revisionists and anti-revisionists will gird themselves for the contest. It will be a battle royal. For three or four years members of the reform element in the Republican party have been trying to secure action on the tariff. They have argued, and with considerable plausibility, that if the Republican party did not correct the manifest inequalities and abuses, the people would revolt and place the task of applying the remedy in the hands of the Democratic party. It was better, from the point of view of the reformers, to have the tariff dealt with in the house of its friends than in that of its enemies. All their arguments and efforts were unavailing until President Roosevelt, by his decisive action, brought his party face to face with the necessity for action. The introduction of a resolution in the next session, authorizing the canal commission to make its purchases in open market, will confront Congress with the issue which it has sought to avoid. No longer, like the ostrich, can it hide its head in the sand and vainly imagine that all is peace.

The discussion of the tariff question and the attempt to solve the problem of open-market purchases are, of course, fraught with grave danger. The President is not, however, one who believes in weak and indeterminate dealing with a vital question. He sees that with the growth and domination of the protected trusts a tariff struggle is inevitable. He would grapple with it firmly while a presidential election is still a distant event, and thus, if possible, remove a vexatious issue before it can do harm to his party. The wisest and most far-sighted Republicans agree with him. These men will, when the question comes before Congress for discussion next session, advocate a thorough revision of the tariff, believing that such action will result in intrenching the Republican party only the more strongly in popular favor. They will be opposed by the men who are wedded to the policy of the highest possible duties upon every item in the lengthy tariff schedule, and who assert that the higher the tariff the greater is the prosperity of the country. The nucleus of this opposition will be the Republican delegation from Pennsylvania, which has always stood for the principle of protection in its extremest form. The members from the Keystone State will find some support among their New York and Ohio colleagues, with the small delegation from West Virginia also in line. Where else can they count upon votes? Not in New England, which is honeycombed with revision sentiment. Not along the border States of the North, where McCleary, of Minnesota, and other leading Republicans have been preaching successfully the doctrine of a lower and more equalized tariff. Not on the Pacific slope, where the tariff-reform sentiment is well advanced. Not in the agricultural States of the Middle West, where the outcry against a protection that makes the trusts possible is especially emphatic.

It would seem, therefore, as if the result of the struggle for tariff reform would be a victory for those who do not regard the Dingley schedules as sacred. It is impossible to predict at this time the exact lines along which revision will come, but it is certain that it will not be radical, viewed from the standpoint of the free-trader. The people will be satisfied if the change prevents the accumulation of great fortunes at the expense of the individual consumer, which is the case at present. Nobody in this country, with the exception of a few extremists, wants the principle of protection abolished. Its record of accomplishment will always entitle it to consideration. Consequently, the revision of the tariff ought to affect comparatively few items. We can hardly expect, however, to be spared the usual juggling with the sugar schedule.

Any one who has been closely observant of the progress of tariff legislation in Washington knows that the moment the sugar schedule is touched is the moment when the door of flagrant stock speculation and consequent scandal is opened. That is true, no matter whether the Republicans or the Democrats are in power. Each rumor emanating from the Capitol is utilized by the speculators in Wall Street to advance or depress sugar stock, while around the national legislature there is an atmosphere of the most unhealthy character. No one would object if the profits of the sugar trust were diminished with corresponding advance to the consumer. The fact is, however, that, in the past, when a new tariff bill became a law, the trust was always the beneficiary. President Roosevelt is a strong, clean man. He must exercise all his strength and purity if he wants his party to emerge unscathed from a tariff discussion which includes a manipulation of the sugar schedule.

President Roosevelt has iterated and reiterated his refusal to be considered again a candidate for the Presidency. Despite his emphatic assertions, several newspapers, and notably the New York "World," persist in predicting that he will be renominated and re-elected. Inquiry in various cities reveals the fact that this feeling is quite prevalent. Mr. Roosevelt's enormous majority last fall, coupled with the all-important fact that he is stronger to-day with the people than ever before, places him in a peculiar position. A man with less courage and strength of character than he possesses would, in all probability, yield to the almost universal desire that he remain in the White House. His purpose is, however, so fixed, that it is not worth while, in discussing the future, to take his name into consideration.

Upon whom is his mantle to fall? The question is being considered in Washington, despite the fact that it cannot be decided for some time to come. It is now certain that there will be at least four active candidates in the field. Leslie M. Shaw, of Iowa, now Secretary of the Treasury; Joseph B. Foraker, Senator from Ohio; William H. Taft, of the same State, Secretary of War; and Charles W. Fairbanks, of Indiana, now Vice-President — these are the men who are to-day most prominent in the public eye as possible candidates. Secretary Shaw will, it is expected, leave the cabinet in time to direct his canvass for the nomination, and from present developments will align himself with the "stand-patters" upon the tariff question. He is a man of much force, and of pleasant personality; he is a good campaigner, and has considerable experience in organization. Senator Foraker is one of the best-known

Republicans in the United States, able, eloquent, and resourceful. Secretary Taft has had comparatively little to do with politics. His predilections have been for the bench, and, it will be remembered, he was a federal judge when he was appointed governor of the Philippines. In the latter capacity, as well as in his present position, he has developed much executive ability; and while it is well known that formerly his highest ambition was to become the Chief Justice of the United States Supreme Court, it is now recognized that events may make him turn toward the White House. It was significant that he was named as the presiding officer of the Ohio Republican State convention. His selection for this position brought him, for the first time in twenty years, into active relation with the politicians of the State, and there is a unanimous agreement as to the favorable impression which he created. He is a man of much magnetism and tactfulness, and is universally liked. Vice-President Fairbanks, who is, perhaps, the only avowed candidate, is closely identified with the agencies which brought McKinley into the White House, and it is expected that these relations will be of material assistance to him. In addition to these men, there are others who, like Elihu Root, of New York, are available and would make worthy candidates before the people. In fact, the Republican field is thick with Presidential timber.

Senator Henry Cabot Lodge once argued, when he was anxious to see Theodore Roosevelt nominated for second place upon the Republican national ticket, that the Vice-Presidency would in the future, as in the early days of the republic, be the stepping-stone to the Presidency. Most people would be apt to take issue with Senator Lodge in his assertion; but whether it be true or not, it is certain that the man who wins the nomination must work for it. In other words, the day has passed when any individual, not already President, can expect a nomination through the magic of his name. There must be organization of the most systematic and thorough character. Except in rare instances, where deadlocks have driven a convention hastily to select a hitherto unregarded candidate, the successful aspirant has had behind him a well-disciplined organization, which has withstood all attacks and by its inherent strength has become the nucleus of the requisite number of votes. Politics, like everything else nowadays, is a very practical business. The candidate who relies upon sentiment will find himself deserted, while honors are bestowed upon his opponent. Apparently not one of the candidates, unless it be Mr. Fairbanks, has as yet attempted any organization. All of them, however, are gradually advancing into the limelight. Mr. Taft, as already stated, was the pivot upon which revolved the Ohio State convention; Mr. Fairbanks was the central figure at the convention of Republican editors, and listened with evident pleasure to an indorsement of his candidacy; Secretary Shaw's name has been formally announced at a dinner attended by his admirers; and Senator Foraker is taking an active interest in the question of railroad freight rates, which is likely to be more or less political before it is finally decided. When the candidates eventually begin their work of organization, it will be interesting to watch their methods, and possibly, perhaps, to anticipate the result.

As for the outlook for the Democratic party, not even·the most partial observer can see any solidification of disunited factions. Judge Parker, erstwhile Democratic nominee for the Presidency, speaking at a dinner in New York, points in one direction, while Mr. Bryan, through his newspaper and in various addresses, is headed absolutely opposite. Judge Parker urges the Democrats to return to their old moorings. He wants "real and recognized principles — not a collection of fads, many of them useless and some of them dangerous and opposed to the historic position of our organization." Mr. Bryan, on the other hand, said, in a speech at Des Moines, that "the last election proved the folly of the attempt to make the Democratic party a conservative party or a competitor with the Republican party for the favor of the trusts and syndicates." Then Mr. Bryan made this interesting statement: "The aggressive and progressive element — the radical element, if you please — of the Democratic party is again in control of the party."

Mr. Bryan has supplemented this assertion with the announcement that his active participation in political matters of late is due to the fact that the radicals are once again in command, and that he is assisting them in making "the control of the radical and progressive element more complete." He has issued a plan for national organization, urging all Democrats to send to him their pledge to attend every primary and to use their influence "to secure a clear, honest, and straightforward declaration of the party's position on every question upon which the voters of the party desire to speak." This is his initial effort to array his forces around him. In an interview at Minneapolis, he said that "what is known as the radical wing of the party is, of course, in control now, and it is gaining strength every day, so that when the next election comes around it ought to sweep the country."

Upon the whole, there seems to be ample ground for the statement, which comes from Mr. Bryan's home, to the effect that he is laying plans for capturing the Democratic presidential nomination in 1908. In political circles in the national capital he is already regarded as the leader of the next Democratic national convention, and it is believed that even if he is not the nominee, he will be in a position to name the candidate. There is no indication, at present, of any action on the part of the conservatives to counteract Mr. Bryan's industry. Their wing of the party is apparently indifferent and is allowing Mr. Bryan to lay the foundation for the organization that will dominate the national convention. It is no wonder, therefore, that candidates for the presidential nomination are not numerous in the Democratic ranks.

The political upheaval in Philadelphia was one of those popular revolutions which are not unusual in this country and which may be expected when the burden of municipal corruption becomes too grievous to be borne. The people of New York will, for instance, drift along quietly for many years, indifferently accepting many abuses. Suddenly, however, the moment comes when patience ceases to be a virtue; a wave of resentment and indignation sweeps over the community; and the men who have prospered in power are carried into oblivion. This was the case with Philadelphia. Not long ago it was characterized by a magazine writer as "corrupt and contented." These adjectives have lost their application. Philadelphia is stirred by a storm of vast dimensions. This will have no effect upon national politics, for Pennsylvania's Republican majority is too great to be neutralized by any local condition; but there will be a moral effect in stimulating everywhere the movement for honesty in municipal administration.

It is worth while to reprint here a succinct statement of the facts connected with this remarkable political revolution:

In 1897, Philadelphia owned and was running its gas-works. The United Gas Improvement Company made an effort to lease and manage the plant, which was accepted. The lease was made and is still in operation. It expires in 1927, but the city has the right of buying it back in 1907. By the terms of this instrument, the company pledged itself to pay to the city all that was collected above 90 cents per 1,000 cubic feet of gas until 1912, all above 85 cents until 1917, and all above 75 cents until 1927, when the plant will revert to the city free of charge and incumbrance. At present, consumers are buying $1 gas, and the city last year received an income of $650,000 from this overcharge. Such was the "gas" situation in Philadelphia when the politicians in power sprung the proposition that the lease should be extended until 1980, with the right to charge $1 gas until 1927 and 90 cents thereafter, in consideration that the company pay to the city $25,000,000 in cash instalments before December 15, 1907. The excuse offered for the rather remarkable transaction was that the city was badly in need of money and could obtain it most quickly by this means.

The ordinance for the extension of the lease had already passed the city councils when the storm broke. Mayor Weaver severed himself from the local political "machine" and allied himself with the indignant citizens. He vetoed the proposed legislation. The newspapers, without exception, opposed the extension of the lease and indulged in almost hysterical appeals to the citizens to visit vengeance upon the councilmen who had voted for the gas trust. As a result of the storm, Philadelphia ought now to have a clearer atmosphere. To make complete the work of reform, however, it will be necessary for those who have led in the revolution to see that, at the next election, the candidates of the "machine" are not chosen by default. This has been one trouble in the past. Men who should have been vigilant in the protection of the city's good name have been indifferent, either refraining from voting or following blindly the leadership of a recognized "boss." Nor must the work be left to election day. In the primaries there must be an attendance of men determined that none but good candidates shall be nominated. There must be, in fact, a genuine change of conditions. It will take energy, perseverance, and courage, however, to keep forever broken the bonds which have enthralled Philadelphia in the past; but if these characteristics are shown and the results accomplished, the friends of good citizenship will universally rejoice.

The State campaigns this year are not many in number, but they are quite interesting. In Maryland, for instance, a constitutional amendment is proposed by the Democrats which will have the effect of eliminating the colored voter. It is proposed that Maryland, in other words, shall follow the course pursued by Virginia, North Carolina, and other Southern States, in disqualifying the negro. If this amendment is carried — and it would seem as if the Southern sentiment would bring about this result — Maryland will be a Democratic State beyond question for some time to come. Outside of this issue, the election will have little significance, being confined to the choice of members of the legislature and a few minor State officers. In Virginia, on the other hand, the interest in the contest centres around men and not principles. By the action of the State Democratic convention, the election of a United States Senator is now a matter of expression of individual views at the primaries. This is a new experiment for Virginia; and the two principal candidates for the position — Senator Thomas S. Martin, whose term is about to expire, and Gov. A. J. Montague — are now engaged in a personal canvass of the State. A governor, a lieutenant-governor, members of the legislature, and other officers will also be named at the primaries.   The issues are purely local; and, although the Republicans have effected a new organization and are talking optimistically, the result will be Democratic.

Massachusetts and Rhode Island will elect governors next fall.   The campaigns will not open until October.   Rhode Island has, of late, been noted for the narrow margins by which elections have been carried, and the election this year will be strenuously contested.   The situation in Massachusetts has been made somewhat uncertain by the announcement of the present Democratic governor, William L. Douglas, that he will not be a candidate for renomination.   It will be recalled that he won the governorship last fall by a majority of 56,000, in a year marked by a Republican landslide, and his reëlection was generally conceded.   It is hardly likely that the Democrats can nominate any one who will develop an equal amount of strength among the voters, and Mr. Douglas's successor is likely to be a Republican.   There will be some national interest in the election, owing to the fact that tariff revision will unquestionably figure in the campaign.

In Ohio a governor is to be elected, and the Republicans have already renominated Governor Herrick upon a platform indorsing protection. In Kentucky there is to be a contest over the United States Senatorship, Senator Blackburn, a veteran in national legislation, being opposed by Governor Beckham — a situation similar to that which exists in Virginia.   As the season advances there will be much interest in the mayoralty campaign in New York City, an event which always attracts national attention.

Up to the present time, none of the State Democratic conventions has been held.   The organization of these conventions will afford an opportunity to determine the truth of Mr. Bryan's remark that the radical wing of the party is in control.   After the election in 1900, the conservative faction of the Democrats began to organize in order to control the convention of 1904.   This situation is now reversed.   It is the radicals who, under Mr. Bryan, are now working for preliminary vietories.   They hope to control in Rhode Island, they will seek to dominate in Massachusetts, and they will make an effort to organize the Ohio convention.   In the Ohio convention, the two factions of the Democracy are led by men of considerable force, and their contests for supremacy are always picturesque.

                                        HENRY LITCHFIELD WEST.

FOREIGN AFFAIRS.

THE second quarter of the year 1905 has made history. It has seen the Russo-Japanese war brought to an end and the belligerents induced to discuss terms of peace through the efforts of the President of the United States; it has seen the great foreign minister of France forced out of the cabinet; it has seen a dissolution of the Scandinavian union. These are momentous events and will have far-reaching effects. In becoming the means whereby Russia and Japan were brought into contact, President Roosevelt has taken high rank with the foremost diplomatists of the world, and has immensely enhanced not only his own personal prestige, but also the position of the United States in world politics. He has done what no European Power has been able to do; what Russia's closest ally and her nearest friend found it impossible to do. He has again unmistakably demonstrated that the United States has relinquished the traditions of more than a century; that, from being a negligible quantity in international affairs it has become one of the most important elements in all that goes to make up the peace, progress, and civilization of the world. "I have called into being a new power," said Canning when he proposed the Monroe Doctrine as an offset to the Holy Alliance. Curiously enough it was Spain that called into being the latent power of the United States. In the space of seven years, Europe has seen the United States emerge from its isolation, its voice and assistance sought, its strength respected and desired, its counsel deferred to, until to-day Europe stands aside, while America brings warring nations to terms.

Russia's last hope that she could retrieve her losses and crush her opponent was destroyed when Admiral Rojestvensky's armada went to destruction at the hands of Admiral Togo in the Straits of Corea. There is a curious blend of sympathy in the character of the Slav and the Asiatic. Both to a certain extent are fatalists, but their fatalism takes different forms. The fatalism of the Slav is the fatalism of the gambler, to whom luck is a god, to whom science is nothing and chance everything, who defies mathematics to magnify an aleatory risk; while

2

the fatalism of the Asiatic is only another term for patriotism, cool courage, fanatical bravery, and, in the case of the Japanese, careful calculation of known factors and probable results. Russia sent her Baltic fleet to the Far East precisely as a gambler places his remaining dollars on the table that has swept away his fortune. Russia had seen her troops beaten on land — beaten, whether they fought on the offensive or defensive; beaten, whether they fought behind entrenchments or in the open; beaten, whether they outnumbered or were inferior to the enemy. Russia had seen her ships destroyed — destroyed by gun fire, destroyed by mines, destroyed by strategy; and yet, like the gambler, she was superstitiously convinced that the "luck" must at last change and the last coin in the purse must bring fortune. On Rojestvensky everything was staked, and the loss of Rojestvensky means the loss of all.

As a great military power Russia no longer exists, because a great military power under modern conditions must be powerful on sea as well as on land. Russia is the one great nation that now has no navy, which cannot have a navy for many years to come. The mere physical task of creating a navy is the work of years; but it is far easier to build ships than to make sailors, to train officers, to teach them to know their ships, to handle them under all conditions of weather, to make gunners of them. Russia can buy ships in the United States, in England, in France, in Germany, as well as build them in her own yards; but men are not to be bought or raised up at command. From being one of the arbiters of the world's destiny her destiny is now at the mercy of the world.

The current of history and progress has been turned from the West to the East by the battle of the Sea of Japan. It is one of the decisive battles of the world, fit to rank on sea with Salamis and Actium and the destruction of the Spanish armada; with Marathon and Waterloo and the Yalu on land. The decisive battles of history are not those in which the losses have been heaviest or the captures the greatest, but those which have affected the fate of the belligerents, and through them the entire world. Had Medina Sidonia routed Howard and Drake, England would have come under the rule of Spain; and what that would have meant not only to England but to all the world the history of the past three centuries tells us. Had Napoleon defeated Wellington at Waterloo, the entire Continent, possibly England as well, would have come under the dominion of the Corsican. Had Russia defeated the Japanese at the crossing of the Yalu, and driven them back as Hannibal did Sempronius at the Trebbia, and Suvaroff the French at the same place two thousand years later, the history of the past year would not have been written. Had Rojestvensky, and not Togo, been the victor in the Straits of Corea, all the valor and sacrifices of Japan would have counted as nothing.

The moral no less than the political effect of this victory is so tremendous that the world will not immediately realize all that it means. All Asia will be quickened by it. A new pride will be born in the Asiatic, who under a deep humility veils a consuming pride. The Asiatic can have no real sympathy for the Aryan; why should he? The white man has laid a heavy hand upon the yellow man and the brown man; he has treated him as an inferior, pillaged him, and bullied him. Against the might of the white man the Asiatic was powerless, and the invincibility of the white man on the sea was a conviction so firmly established that no Asiatic dared to believe that it could ever be overthrown. In India and in China, in the Philippines and the Malay Archipelago, the defeat of Russia at the hands of Japan will produce consequences as yet only faintly to be comprehended. Will they advance or retard the progress of the world? It is too early to say; but of one thing we may feel certain: if in the Asiatic a new pride is born, if there is infused in him a spirit of nationality, if he is no longer content to be a subjugated race and takes his place as an equal of the white, the world will have gained — gained enormously, even if England should lose India, and the United States the Philippines, and China should stand as the equal of the other nations. Independence, self-reliance, pride of race, courage — these are the qualities that make individuals as well as nations great; they are the only qualities that make a nation.

Japan already is being warned by her candid friends not to be too arrogant. Why should not Japan be as arrogant as she pleases? Was ever England restrained from a display of arrogance? Is modesty such a besetting sin of America? Did Germany shrink into obscurity after she had thrashed France? Japan may be as arrogant as she pleases, provided it is the arrogance of enlightened civilization, the same arrogance that has made England and the United States and Germany great. If she merely swaggers and is intoxicated by her own reflection, if she becomes the Narcissus among nations, she will go to perdition as surely as Russia has gone, that swaggerer among nations, the only one that was so enamored of her brute strength that she worshipped it and set it above intelligence.

"No wonder they thought him worthy of notice. Every original man of every magnitude is; nay, in the long run, who or what else is? But how much more if your original man was a king over men; whose movements were polar, and carried from day to day those of the world along with them?"

Thus Carlyle wrote of Frederick the Great, and thus can be written of the present head of the House of Hohenzollern, the central figure in European politics, whose movements are polar and carry the world with him. Although the German Emperor has been under the world's microscope for the last seventeen years, although all his words and actions have been dissected and analyzed, his motives examined into, and his purposes submitted to every known test, he is to-day as much as he ever was an enigma. His motives are more generally misunderstood than comprehended, and usually a wrong construction is placed upon his actions. The most extraordinary quality of the human mind is the lasting effect made by a first impression.

The first picture of William II projected on the world's screen was the figure of undisciplined irresponsibility. That was the first and most lasting impression. Malice and ignorance developed this picture. The young King, no longer under the hand of restraint, his own master at the time when most men are still serving their apprenticeship, called without adequate preparation to the highest place, knowing the mighty power he wielded and longing to use it, ambitious, reckless, daring — these represented the picture the world had of the successor of the first William, under whose iron hand had been forged on the anvil of war a nation, and of the gentle Frederick, who all too soon passed "unto the kingdom of perpetual night."

But how different has been the real from the imaginary! When the present Emperor came to the throne, Germany's position in the hierarchy of nations was not firmly established. She was too young, too new, too close to her own creation to command the respect that the world pays to age and tradition. She had won her place among the great Powers by a *coup ;* just as a great trader but yesterday ennobled may sit among the elect, who in the arrogance of ancestry treat him with impertinence tempered with fear; with superciliousness so that he shall not presume too much on his power, yet with fear that he may exercise that power. Germany had won her way into the council by sheer weight, by the one thing that the world has always respected — scientific force. When Moltke stretched forth his hand, and Prussian and Saxon and Bavarian moved forward shoulder to shoulder, crushing down the power of France; when Bismarck transmuted a score of petty principalities into an empire; when the King of Prussia was crowned emperor — the world was compelled to treat Germany with respect even if it denied her affection. William II, it was said, knowing that Germany was still looked upon as "new," would again show his strength, and once more strength would command respect. The world expected Germany to make war and waited.

It still waits. William has not made war, although at times the temptation must have been great to have set his mailed legions in motion. Without having fired a shot or moved a single soldier, Germany has taken her place as one of the great Powers of the earth, one to be reckoned with and consulted whenever the political pawns are moved. Naturally this has aroused the envy of other Powers.

The business of government at the beginning of the twentieth century is much like the business of trade. It is brutally selfish business all the way through. Every Government has its own interests to serve, precisely as every trader's end is to look upon a fair balance sheet at the end of the year. The proprietor of a great department store does not necessarily have to drive his competitor into bankruptcy to succeed. However, if competition becomes so keen that a competitor goes under, that is unfortunate, but one of the incidents of trade. Government is business, and it is the business of government to make its people rich and strong and prosperous. To enable them to win success, it must command respect and fear. The German Emperor, by great ability, far-seeing wisdom, and tremendous energy, has won for Germany both respect and fear, and has incurred the envy of rivals. The man who makes a failure of life runs no risk of being calumniated or envied. It is only the great and powerful nation that is disliked and abused. At the root of most national animosities is jealousy. The Kaiser has his own end to gain and cannot consider the feelings of England or of the United States or of any other country. He takes care of the interests of Germany; other countries must look out for themselves.

The world has been thrown into a mild panic because the Emperor refused to acquiesce in the Anglo-French agreement relating to Morocco without consultation with him, and it was said that this gave new evidence of the Kaiser's desire always to make trouble and to be in the lime-light. Is the Kaiser's action so entirely irrational, and does it argue such irresponsibility, as his enemies would try to make us believe? The Anglo-French agreement was a very satisfactory arrangement for England and France. By it they were able to establish cordial relations and settle numerous vexing questions — questions that not so long ago threatened the peace of both countries. France at last consented to legitimize England's position in Egypt, to end the irritation that came from the exercise of treaty rights in Newfoundland; England was willing to flatter French vanity and give her a free hand in Morocco. It was excellent statesmanship so far as the two high contracting Powers were concerned; but if it annoyed Germany which was unceremoniously pushed to one side and totally ignored while the earth was being partitioned, who can be surprised?

It is not at all improbable that the Kaiser has simply patterned his diplomacy after that of France, which has been effective. England was in possession in Egypt, Egypt·was England, and all the world knew it; but France covered her head with a blanket and imagined she had built a house of her own. Ever since it became manifest that England would never relinquish her control of Egypt — and it was for the benefit of the whole world that she should remain in possession — France deliberately set herself to work to annoy and embarrass the English administration. Chagrin was at the bottom of French resentment. When England bombarded Alexandria, which was the beginning of the English occupation of the land of the Pharaohs, England expected and invited France to join her. Had France accepted that invitation, had the combined Anglo-French fleets taken part in the engagement, France would have shared with England in all that followed. But France missed her great opportunity: to England alone was left the task of restoring order and instituting a new *régime;* and too late France realized the magnitude of her blunder.

France tried to dislodge England, and England refused to budge; France repeatedly asked England when she intended to retire, and England refused to commit herself. When England found it necessary to readjust the finances of Egypt, France, having a voice in the international financial control, refused to sanction the English plans, and England had to advance the requisite funds. The position of France, in a word, was that England had no legitimate standing in Egypt, and therefore she, France, would make her position as embarrassing as possible. The time came when France could surrender her imaginary rights for substantial gains, and England was willing to make a general settlement. So far as France was concerned her diplomacy.had not been unprofitable.

It is not at all unlikely that the Emperor intends to pursue exactly the same tactics in Morocco. The Emperor does not purpose to admit that France has any superior rights in Morocco, or that she is justified in regarding Morocco as her special sphere of influence. That he would make Morocco a *casus belli* seems to me too utterly preposterous to be worthy of consideration by any serious-minded person, much as it may appeal to the jaundiced imagination of sensational newsmongers; but that he will practise a studied policy of elaborate "pin pricks" is fully to be expected. To adopt a simile borrowed from patent law, he has filed an interference; he has given notice that he does not admit the broad claims set up by France. Wherever and whenever he can annoy and embarrass France he will do so, until at last the opposition of Germany may become so annoying that France may do in regard to Morocco what England did in regard to Egypt — that is, France may finally throw Morocco and all its alloys into the melting pot, and from the molten flux hammer out a new element.

Modern diplomacy makes nations cultivate friendly relations for so long as those relations can be turned to account. In this again modern diplomacy follows the methods of modern business. A merchant buys where he can buy cheapest. He is willing to trade for joint account so long as the account shows profit, but will transfer his trade to a rival if he can make better terms. Wedged in between France and Russia, with France unfriendly if not positively hostile, it is not only natural, but almost vital, that Germany should lessen her anxiety by keeping on good terms with Russia, a policy instilled into German statesmen by Bismarck.

Like all the rest of the world, Germany magnified the striking power of Russia. Of France, Germany entertained little fear; but Russia was a huge, unshapely mass, whose very bulk was appalling and who inspired terror because she was always a mystery. Although Russia was the ally of France — an alliance directed against Germany more than any other Power — Germany managed to keep on very good terms with her northern neighbor, and in a measure to deprive France of some part of the effectiveness of the alliance. The collapse of the Russian bubble has affected both France and Germany powerfully. It has suddenly cut from France the prop on which she has been leaning, believing it to be strong enough to support her; Germany had believed that she was facing a dragon spitting fire, but has now discovered that the fearsome beast is nothing more ferocious than a cat whose whiskers have been rubbed with phosphorus. Now that Germany has little to fear from Russia, she can face France with more courage, which perhaps in a measure explains why the Kaiser has deemed the time ripe to raise the Moroccan question.

The war in the Far East and the revelation of Russia's military inefficiency, corruption, and financial weakness have curiously changed the European equilibrium. While it has relieved Germany of the menace of Russia and brought France to a realization of the one-sided character of her alliance, it has caused both France and England to appreciate the importance of working in harmony. Undoubtedly the war made the understanding between England and France possible — as yet it is not a formal alliance, but that it may be an alliance in the strict sense of the term before long is not at all improbable — and convinced the statesmen of both countries that their interests are common rather than antagonistic. With Russia eliminated for the time being, and with England and France animated by the same motives, Germany finds herself both weaker and stronger — weaker, because there has virtually come into being an Anglo-French alliance; stronger, because her frontiers need fewer troops than formerly. Germany, however, has nothing to fear from the Anglo-French *entente*. Neither country wants war. On the contrary, both countries ask no greater boon than peace; and unless Germany assumes the position of the aggressor and wantonly provokes hostilities, she may feel secure from attack.

Germany's allies are Italy and Austria, the members of the Triple Alliance; and because of the shifting of the equilibrium it is only natural that Germany should seek to emphasize the solidarity of the Central European Powers. Several months ago I pointed out to the readers of this review the artificial nature of that alliance, and advanced the opinion that at least one of its members, Italy, was only lukewarm in its support. Recent events confirm the correctness of that belief. It is difficult to see what Italy gains by bolstering up Germany, while it is only too obvious that she has much more to gain by being on friendly terms with France; and now that France and England are in concord, the long and traditional friendship existing between England and Italy is an additional inducement to Italy to draw closer to France. The German Emperor, after his two hours' visit to Morocco, went to Italy, where, at Naples, as the guest of the King of Italy, he somewhat effusively referred to his ally. It did not escape the notice of European statesmen that the effusiveness was all on one side. The King, in his reply to the Emperor's toast, omitted all reference to the Triple Alliance; and, while cordial, was more studiously polite than affectionate. The Italian press, with the exception of the Catholic organs — which still rankle over the Combes-Rouvier policy of separation of church and state in France — did not avail itself of the visit of the Kaiser to grow enthusiastic over the Triple Alliance or to encourage the Emperor in his Morocco adventure, which, there is reason to believe, has met with no greater favor in Vienna than it has in Rome.

Only a few weeks ago the world was astounded by newspaper reports of a speech made by the Kaiser to his officers after a review, in the course of which he is alleged to have said that the Russian officers at Mukden were drunk, that the Japanese were the scourge of God, and that, as Russia had shown herself unable to cope with the yellow peril, Germany might have to deal with it. The Russian Government having asked whether the Kaiser had been correctly reported, a semi-official *démenti* was issued from Berlin, which was accepted as satisfactory in St. Petersburg, while the German press, with its tongue in its cheek, published additional details.

The Emperor spoke with an object. He ran the risk of being misunderstood and ridiculed by the world, and cared not in the least, because he was speaking to his own audience and with a definite object in view. The Emperor preached against immorality and proclaimed the virtues of the strenuous and abstemious life. The German officer and the German private, he is reported to have said, must work so hard and employ their time to such good advantage during the day that when night comes they are physically exhausted, and, instead of finding recreation in enervating pleasures, they have to go to bed early. Turning to the officers, he told them that the officers' corps was the soul of the army and must always be kept up to the mark, otherwise the army would suffer. From what we know of the German officer, from the life of a garrison town as portrayed by Lieutenant Bilse and other German writers, the German Emperor's words were not ill-timed, and undoubtedly met with the approval of the great mass of the German people.

That speech is quite in accord with a little talk — popularly known as the "bellyband" speech — which the Emperor made to the officers who were ordered to China to relieve the legations, and which all Europe thought excruciatingly funny. The meeting was supposed to be private, and the Emperor addressed the officers not in the capacity of Emperor or commander-in-chief, but as one comrade to another. Knowing the convivial habits of the German officer and the danger of the Chinese climate to unacclimatized Europeans he, in a fatherly sort of way, gave them much advice as to what they should eat and drink, and especially as to what they should avoid. Among other things he told them that the experience of the British military authorities in the Far East had shown the necessity of guarding against colds, and that there was no better protection than to wear a band of flannel around the lower part of the stomach, such as mothers all over the civilized world put on their new-born infants. Some of the opposition German papers, having obtained an inkling of the Emperor's remarks, attempted to make him ridiculous by putting him in the attitude of uttering platitudes upon infantile belly-bands; and the press throughout Europe poked fun at the German officer going out to fight the Chinese equipped with his little flannel band, like a baby fresh from his mother's arms. But if the press thought it was doing the Emperor an injury it overshot the mark, because the army saw in it only another evidence of the Emperor's intense interest in everything that pertained to its welfare, and the men in the ranks were grateful to him for his solicitude.

A sequel of the Morocco incident, the full effects of which cannot as yet be predicted, is the resignation of M. Delcassé, the French Minister of Foreign Affairs. Morocco gave rise to an acrimonious debate in the Chamber, in which the Nationalists and the Socialists, the enemies of the Government, played into the hands of Germany by seeking to discredit M. Delcassé, who was charged with being responsible for German anger because he had not notified Germany of the terms of the Anglo-French agreement. M. Rouvier, the Prime Minister, came to the defence of his colleague, and in the course of his speech indulged in this outspoken language:

With what are we reproached? With not having, on the morrow of the Anglo-French agreement, officially signified that agreement to Germany. It should have been said to the other nations, for no notification was made of the agreement which the Chamber has approved. Had not the speech of the Chancellor von Bülow all the value of acquiescence? Did he not declare himself satisfied on condition that Germany's commercial interests were not menaced? What has happened since? Military events have weakened our ally. Perhaps then the neighbors with whom we mean to live on good terms thought that they might — by raising a discussion and by reopening a question which we had the right to consider closed, owing to the language used beyond the Vosges — obtain certain commercial advantages.

Feeling, as he expressed it, that "he no longer possessed the necessary authority to manage the foreign affairs of France," M. Delcassé tendered his resignation as Foreign Minister, much to the delight of Berlin, and greatly to the annoyance of all the other capitals, where the ability, balance, and sanity of this really great statesman are fully recognized and appreciated. President Loubet, Prime Minister Rouvier, his cabinet colleagues, and the leaders of the republican party in the Chamber brought so much pressure to bear upon him that M. Delcassé was induced to withdraw his resignation and retain his portfolio. But a few weeks later he again resigned, this time for good, and his portfolio has been assumed by M. Rouvier, the Prime Minister. It is inconceivable that France should permit her most distinguished statesman to retire at a time when there was never greater need for the services of a man of breadth and experience. M. Delcassé made the Franco-Russian alliance possible, which, whatever else may be said about it, gave France confidence in herself and acted as a check on German aggressions. With the King and Lord Lansdowne, he shares the honor of having brought about the *entente* with England and having restored France to much of her old position. These were achievements that entitled him to the respect and gratitude of France. But, either M. Rouvier, for reasons purely personal and selfish, was willing to rid himself of his services, or else M. Rouvier believes that it is too dangerous for France to risk the hostility of Germany. M. Delcassé's policy was directed against Germany, and nothing caused Germany greater annoyance than the Anglo-French *entente;* his firm stand in regard to Morocco, in particular, causing additional irritation in the Wilhelmstrasse. M. Rouvier, on the other hand, dislikes Russia and admires Germany. He is a banker, brought up in the Paris branch of the house of Rothschild, and is one of the German "intellectuals." If the Rouvier policy means a *rapprochement* with Germany and a cooling of the recently displayed affection for England, we may look forward to some extremely interesting continental politics.

It has been frequently pointed out that the Russian alliance is no longer popular in France, in fact, that in certain quarters it is extremely unpopular; but it is to be doubted whether France would sanction cutting loose from Russia and jettisoning the English cargo to make room for the German consignment. The French ship of state is not big enough to carry the Kaiser as well as the King. Alsace and Lorraine have been neither forgiven nor forgotten, although France sensibly tries not to remember. The French statesman who at this day cherishes the belief that he can make Germany a friend of France is either amazingly far-visioned .or amazingly short-sighted; and one is inclined to think that M. Rouvier's statesmanship is too intellectual to be practical.

Typical of the disfavor in which the Russian alliance is held by the French press are the sarcastic references of "Le Courier Européen," a high-class Paris weekly, in its review of the work of the well-known Russian historian Ilowaisky. A portion of this veracious historian's narrative warrants translation:

At the beginning of the month of February, 1904, Japan, incited by England on the one side and Pope Pius X on the other, treacherously attacked the Russian fleet peacefully anchored in Port Arthur. . . . After the outbreak of the war France desired to come to the assistance of Russia, but the Emperor Nicholas II declined this generous offer. General Kuropatkin was appointed commander-in-chief of the Russian troops. After a series of bloody engagements on the banks of the Yalu, the Russians marched rapidly to the north of Manchuria, and after having executed a march lasting six months, without parallel in the military history of the world, arrived at the capital of Manchuria, Mukden. At the same time General Stoessel, who for eleven months had successfully withstood the attack of the great Japanese army under General Nogi, had recourse to a *ruse de guerre* and surrendered Port Arthur to the Japanese, thus enabling General Kuropatkin successfully to carry out his march to the north.

The Mikado, dismayed, demanded of England that she come to his assistance. England advised that the internal troubles in Russia be fomented, and to accomplish this end she sent two million pounds sterling to St. Petersburg, which was distributed among the evil disposed. The distribution of this money was made by a Catholic priest, Mecislas Ledochowski (falsely reported to have died in Rome in 1903), who obtained by fraud the Pope's blessing, and who by means of a fraudulent passport arrived in St. Petersburg under the name of Père Gaponne."

Thus is history made for the benefit of the rising generation in Russia.

Several months ago an anonymous author in the London "Quarterly Review" gave a vivid insight into the character of the Czar. The author was vouched for by the editor of the "Quarterly" as a Russian of high official standing, and it was evident that he had exceptional opportunities for studying the Czar and the ways of the court. In the London "National Review" for May the same author contributed an article on "The End of the Autocracy," and this is the picture he painted of the man who is responsible for the slaughter in Manchuria:

And the leader of the nation during this terrible crisis is a sickly youth of arrested development and a morbid will, whose inability to govern might perhaps pass unnoticed if he would but allow any man of intellect or will-power to grapple with the jarring elements. This, however, he refuses to permit, while allotting to obscure soldiers and seamen, tricksters and money-grabbers, a share of the supreme power to the detriment of the nation. The mental and moral impotency of this well-intentioned marplot, who cannot be said to have had even experience, unless ten years of uniform failure could impart it, is one of the commonplaces of conversation in town and country. Even the rough and ready droshky drivers say of him that he has been thrust among rulers like a pestle among spoons.

Yet, apprised of his impotence by the Boudoir Council, he wishes to will, and takes the volition for the deed. No occurrence, no event, makes a lasting impression on his mind. Abroad our armies may be scattered, our ships sunk, our credit ruined; he is serene in spite of it all. At home the whole framework of society may be going to pieces; Nicholas sits still and fondly annotates state papers — a very Narcissus of the inkpot. In our country, whenever the temperature grows too hot, the custom has been for ages to break the thermometer, not on any account to let in the cool air. And the Emperor keeps to it religiously. The results are now beginning to appear. The whole nation will feel them, has already begun to experience them, and is reeling under the blows. Hundreds of thousands of men, hundreds of millions of roubles, are being offered up at the shrine of the autocrat, who is still insatiate."

Russia is such an absolute anachronism — living in the present she breathes the spirit of the past — that to the Western world she is incomprehensible. The same writer with cynical levity shows how Russia is steeped to her eyelids in slavish superstition, with her faculties deadened by the overpowering fumes of incense:

The Japanese prepared for the campaign by despatching troops, and we answered by opening our folding icons and raising aloft our religious banners and crosses and bending pliant knees. Our commanders on being appointed went about to the holy places, from monastery to monastery, watching and waiting. Kuropatkin pilgrimaged thus for fourteen days, and garnered in a gallery of icons unto the destruction of the enemy. And the commander-in-chief, not yet satisfied with his piety and his collection of folded images, kept on pilgrimaging. Finally he started. And from many of the stations on the long way came telegraphic messages announcing the edifying tidings to all: "Arrived in Zlatoust. Heard mass. Received icons." And our people or press rejoiced exceedingly. At last, with a wagon-load of holy images, he set out hopefully.

Admiral Skrydloff also watched and prayed and collected images against the impious enemy. And yet our society, wise in its generation, says the enemy chose the better part. But the religious among the masses explain our reverses by saying that on the journey to the Far East the two consignments of holy images got mixed, and those which were to have helped the admiral on sea were exchanged for the icons meant for the general of the land troops. These simple-minded Christians add that Makaroff was the only commander who paid no attention to his religious duties, but took a special train and reached Port Arthur in ten days. And, "behold," they add, "how terribly he was punished for his irreligion! He went down with all on board. Every one of our generals and admirals remain safe and sound to this day, whereas he perished for his temerity."

The policy of Russia is so haphazard, so childish, so devoid of all sense, that it is practically impossible to follow or to understand it. Imperial rescripts and ukases, contradictory and meaningless, make up the diet fed to strong stomachs, as if men hungering and freezing could have their cravings appeased by crude pictures of seeds of corn and lumps of coal.

If the government of Russia had an intelligent purpose in view, from its actions logical deductions could be made. But the Russian government is not so constituted. With any other Government it would be perfectly proper to conclude that the transfer of Count Cassini from Washington to Madrid was indicative of the realization of the injury that Count Cassini had done to Russian interests in the United States and a desire to retrieve the past. Washington has become one of the most important diplomatic posts in the Russian service; Madrid is merely a relic of the past, when Spain was mistress of the seas and pioneer on the land. Between Spain and Russia there are neither commercial nor political relations, and no stretch of the imagination can conceive of Spain as holding a. position where morally or materially she might be able to advance or retard the progress of Russia. A transfer from Washington is no promotion, especially not in the case of an ambassador who aspired to be sent to Paris, the nerve centre of continental diplomacy. England, only a little more than a year ago, showed her estimate of the relative importance of the two capitals, when she transferred Sir Mortimer Durand, her present very capable representative, from Madrid to Washington; and England, as a Mediterranean power, has interests to serve in Madrid.

When common sense and liberalism replace bigotry and autocracy in Russia, the necessity for the friendship of the United States will be made apparent to Russia; and that friendship can be gained. Some men of advanced views already understand that, but as yet they are in the minority. Almost from the outbreak of the war Russia has endeavored to raise money in this country, but her efforts have been in vain; whereas Japan, bound by no "traditional ties," has found not only sympathy, but what has been of more value to her in a national emergency, namely, money, in America. Japanese bonds were bought because they were regarded as a profitable and safe investment; but the public would not have insisted upon being granted the privilege to subscribe if it had not felt that in helping Japan it would demonstrate in the most effective way its detestation of Russia. For many years to come, Russia must be financed from the outside so as to develop her internal resources; and the United States can take a prominent part in this work, which is for the benefit of all the world, if Russia will give pledge of her sincerity that henceforth she is to be animated by a spirit of enlightened civilization and religious and civil tolerance instead of a spirit of mediævalism and fifteenth-century oppression. If Russia will do her share in the world's progress she will not find the world turned against her; but so long as the world sees in her an enemy to advancement, the world will league against her and hold it a righteous act to stifle her ambitions.

It may be that the Czar has a more subtle sense of humor than he is generally credited with. It is in accord with the fitness of things that Count Cassini should close his diplomatic career in Spain; Spain sitting on the ruins of her former greatness, exactly as Count Cassini is surrounded by the débris of what was considered extraordinary achievement. With Alexieff, Brezabrazoff, and some of the grand dukes, Count Cassini shares the responsibility for the present plight of Russia and her decline from a Power of the first magnitude. As minister to China he negotiated the Cassini Convention, by which Russia fastened her grip on Manchuria and began her march "to universal domination," as the Russian "Forwards" fondly believed, and the rest of the world only too bitterly feared. With Li Hung Chang under the malign influence of Russia, with England and the United States too indifferent or too timid to interfere, with the other Powers believing that their profit lay in being on the side of Russia, it did not require extraordinary powers for Russia to gain a predominant position in China, and Count Cassini was hailed as a modern Metternich or Talleyrand. At that time he received a genuine promotion; from minister to China he was made ambassador to the United States — sent to the United States because the importance of the position of the United States in the politics of the Far East was beginning to be realized in St. Petersburg. In ten years Count Cassini has lived to see the dream of "universal domination" shattered: Port Arthur, the triumph of his diplomacy, for the second time in the hands of Japan, there to remain; the corpses of his countrymen bleaching on the plains and valleys and mountains of Manchuria; their commanders beaten or seeking safety in flight; her statesmen distraught; her financiers humbly beseeching all the world for money. *Stat magni nominis umbra!*

It is no secret that Japan is anxious to make peace, but it must be on such terms as will make for real peace and not merely for an armed truce. Whether we are approaching the end of this bloody tragedy no one can tell, because the decision rests not in Tokyo but in St. Petersburg; but the terms that Japan is willing to offer are not such that Russia can find incompatible with her dignity to accept, provided she is prepared to acknowledge that she has been defeated and must pay the penalty. Some time ago it was generally believed that Japan would demand an indemnity to recoup herself for the expenses of the war; but there is now reason to believe that, should Russia propose peace in the immediate future, Japan might be willing to forego the indemnity, or at least be satisfied with such a moderate sum that it would not strain Russian finances to meet it.

One of the important results of the war is the certainty of the extension of the scope of the Anglo-Japanese alliance, now limited in its effects. That alliance is defensive only, and to prevent either party from having to sustain unaided the attack of a hostile coalition, which in the case of Japan would mean annihilation. In England both the Government and the opposition are in favor of a new treaty in lieu of the existing one — which does not expire until 1907, provided neither of the contracting parties is at war, in which case, *ipso facto*, it remains effective until the conclusion of hostilities — the terms of which are only vaguely hinted at, but which it is believed will be offensive as well as defensive, differing from the present treaty in that if either party is attacked the other will come to the assistance of its ally without waiting for a hostile coalition to be formed.

Equally important will be its extension so as to embrace the Middle as well as the Far East. The present treaty was made to preserve the *status quo* in China and Corea, both of which are now sufficiently safeguarded by the military triumphs of Japan; but England has recognized that, with an end to Russia's ambitions in the Far East, she will turn her energies in other directions; and the pressure that was removed from India so long as Manchuria taxed Russian resources will once more be applied. The cardinal principle of Asiatic belief is the implacable hatred of England and Russia, a hatred that will last so long as the two nations exist. The Asiatic is always an opportunist. Nothing appeals to him so powerfully as success, especially success gained by force. Russia, once so greatly feared, has been stripped of much of her terror to the Asiatic mind; and as Russia has sunk in the estimation of the Asiatic, the prestige of England has steadily risen. An alliance between England and Japan, that should have for its purpose the keeping of Russia within her present boundaries, that would place at the disposal of Japan the British fleet, and at the command of England the Japanese army in case India was attacked, would make Russia pause before provoking conflict.

There is very good reason for believing that sinister influences are being brought to bear upon Japan to persuade her not to enter into a new treaty of such far-reaching scope. The pride of Japan has been appealed to; she has been told that she has vindicated her right to be considered a great Power, that she can stand alone and needs no assistance from any one. Her self-interest has been appealed to. She has been told that so long as Russia has free play for her energies in the Middle East, she is unlikely to try to regain her lost foothold in the Far East; and that as England is Japan's great commercial rival — the only rival she really has to fear — it would be folly for her to play England's game at her own expense and give proof to Russia of her irreconcilable hostility.

That Japan, however, is not likely to be influenced by these obviously specious arguments may be looked upon as quite certain. The end of the war will see her not exhausted, but tired out, and it will take her several years to recover from her wounds and be as strong as she was before the war. During these years she cannot afford to keep herself on a war footing, to live from day to day in nervous apprehension of the call to arms. She needs not only peace, but a feeling of security — a feeling that will inspire confidence among foreign nations, and especially in England and America, so that foreign capital will seek investment in Japan to develop her resources and enable her to engage in her industrial and commercial expansion. Everything points to Japan gaining by a broad treaty of alliance with England, the general provisions of which, I have no doubt, have already been discussed by the two cabinets.

This new treaty and the war itself perhaps furnish the explanation why Mr. Balfour continues to hang on to office. Virtually he remains in power by the grace of his opponents, who could destroy him at any time if they really wished to do so. Why they do not has been the mystery ever since it became obvious that the tide was running against the premier, who was forced to see constituency after constituency reverse its political complexion and his majority in the House crumbling away.

The belief exists that Mr. Balfour, who is really very weary of his task and would be only too glad to be relieved of the responsibilities of office, has been asked by the King to endeavor by every means in his power to stave off a dissolution until the conclusion of the war in the Far East. The theory of the British constitution is that the King does not interfere in politics and has no politics; he is neither Liberal nor Conservative, and is satisfied with any ministry that commands a majority of the electorate. But King Edward has shown himself to be the foremost statesman and diplomatist of England, if not of the world, and with great tact has made his personality felt. It is not unlikely that the King prefers not to risk the dangerous experiment of swapping horses while crossing a stream, and would rather have Mr. Balfour and Lord Lansdowne take part in the negotiations for peace — in which England as the ally of Japan will act as adviser and friend — than to have new men in power, who may not share the views of the present Government in regard to the alliance, or who may be less bold in executing their policy.

As Foreign Secretary, Lord Lansdowne has made a pronounced success. He has handled more than one dangerous situation with consum-

3

mate skill, and he has made his rivals respect him. He has not been a spectacular foreign minister; but he has been better than that: he has been a minister who has achieved results, who in playing the game of diplomacy has sacrificed a pawn in order to checkmate his opponent. It is not to be wondered at that the King would regard it as detrimental to the interests of the empire if at this time Lord Lansdowne should have to leave Downing Street. A suggestion from the King to Mr. Balfour would of course be all-sufficient and make him strive to keep his control of the Commons until such time as he could relinquish it with safety; and this Mr. Balfour would do without regard to his own inclination to drop the titanic load that grows heavier with each day.

Mr. Chamberlain has displayed a most unselfish spirit in his attempt to reunite the Conservative party by the adoption of a reasonable compromise on the fiscal question. In this he has subordinated his own strong personal views to a loyal desire to bring about harmony in the ranks. Everything depends on how far Mr. Balfour will go to meet him. It depends on Mr. Balfour whether the Conservatives shall go into the next campaign, which cannot now be much longer deferred, fighting shoulder to shoulder against the common enemy, or torn by internal differences, many of which are largely academic and relate to procedure rather than to vital principles. If the Conservative free-traders follow Mr. Balfour's banner, and the Conservative protectionists range themselves under the Chamberlain standard, they will be routed at the polls; but if they fight under one leader, while it is certain they will be defeated, they will be a compact, well-disciplined army hanging on the flanks of the victors, harassing them at every turn, and ready to take advantage of the first tactical blunder committed.

Mr. Balfour has many of the characteristics of his distinguished uncle, the late Marquis of Salisbury, one of whose traits was an almost alarming freedom of expression in the discussion of great questions and whose "blazing indiscretions" of oratory were famous. In the House of Commons, in discussing the work of the committee on national defence, which is the *imperium in imperio* of the cabinet, Mr. Balfour astonished the oldest members by the frankness with which he referred to Russia, and by the evident warning, in the nature of a threat, which he intended to convey. The possibility of an invasion of India by Russia, he said, without ambiguity or delicate diplomatic phrasing, "had long been a dream of military leaders." He calmly showed the difficulties that would confront Russia; but he warned the House that if Great Britain permitted the slow absorption of Afghanistan and allowed Russia to extend her strategic railways, Great Britain would, sooner or later, "be faced with some of the greatest military problems that ever confronted the British Government." Russia's march toward India, Mr. Balfour remarked, had from time to time caused great alarm. Great Britain had, by diplomatic means, he significantly added, endeavored to prevent Russia's expansion. The only inference to be drawn from this is that diplomatic means having failed — and Mr. Balfour acknowledged that Russia's expansion must be "taken as an accepted fact " — England would find herself compelled to use other means to escape "the greatest military problem " to which he had previously referred.

Whether Mr. Balfour was preparing the country to "take on " Russia after Japan had finished with her, or whether it was to make the newer and larger alliance with Japan more palatable, is, of course, not known; but his frank warning that Russia was always to be regarded as a foe and treated accordingly shows why England considers it good policy to pledge Japan the use of her fleet, in case of attack by Russia or any other Power, in exchange for the use of Japanese troops in India, in case the "dream of military leaders" ceases to be a dream and becomes a reality. If only a year ago the suggestion had been made that Japan would protect for England her Indian empire, the idea would have been scouted as a fantasy too grotesque to be worthy of serious consideration; but so great has been the development of Japan in the short space of a single year, so powerful has she proved herself, that, whereas a year ago England almost condescendingly admitted Japan as a junior partner, she now deals with her as an equal.

We may make up our minds to one thing. If, after the war is over, there is no change in the internal system of Russia, the bogey of English statesmen will be the march of Russia toward India. Whether Russia will provoke hostilities no man is rash enough to predict, and much will depend upon the turn of events. If Russia should find an ally that would leave England not entirely free in Europe, and if Russia believed that her army on the Afghanistan frontier was sufficiently large to afford her an even chance, she might take the risk; otherwise not. This is one of the reasons among many why English statesmen in all their calculations always consider Germany as a possible ally of Russia and therefore a foe to themselves, and why, whenever a new battleship is laid down in a German yard, British naval estimates are revised. The future of Germany, the German Emperor told his people, lies on the sea. Russia has no future unless she has a strong naval ally.

England is slowly recovering from the tremendous drain of the Boer War, and the budget speech of Mr. Austen Chamberlain, the Chancellor of the Exchequer, showed a surplus over the estimates for the fiscal year just closed of nearly $15,000,000.

A budget speech is usually too technical to be interesting except to financiers, but there was one portion of Mr. Chamberlain's speech that appealed to the sociologist rather than to the financier. Basing his calculations on the experience of previous years, Mr. Chamberlain had overestimated the amount to be derived from the duties on spirits and liquor; but he told the House that the excise receipts were far short of his expectations, and that the consumption of spirits and beer in 1904 was less than at any time during the last fifteen years.

In his opinion, the habits of the English people were changing. The money that was formerly spent in the public-house was going elsewhere, and the laboring man, instead of drinking when his work was finished, found his enjoyment in outdoor amusement. If this is true, while it may compel chancellors of the exchequer to enlarge the basis of taxation, it marks the beginning of a new era in England. The curse of England is drunkenness, to which can be laid most of the poverty and misery of the lower classes. The British workmen, even the best, spend entirely too much on beer. The man who works only at odd times is soddened by gin; the race is devitalized by alcohol; and money that should be spent for nourishing food goes for drink. Any decrease in the consumption of liquor and spirits is a marked change for the good, and its effects will be seen in a reduction of pauperism and an increase in productive capacity.

In dissolving the union with Sweden, Norway has brought to a head a long-smouldering discontent. The separation is a revolution, the most extraordinary the world has ever known. It is the first time that a revolution has been accomplished by act of Parliament; that it has been accomplished without the shedding of a single drop of blood; and that it was accepted, the moment it happened, as a *fait accompli* which both parties took quietly and almost without resentment. Norway has long been anxious to sever the bond of union. Now that she is independent, it is not unlikely that she will adopt a republican form of government. Both countries are too small to have any influence in politics; their only importance lying in their relation to some of the great Powers.

A. MAURICE LOW.

FINANCE.

In the domain of finance, the past three months may fairly be called a period of the unexpected. What has happened has been very largely what was neither foreshadowed nor counted on beforehand by the market. Those who are usually competent judges of a situation have been so thoroughly mistaken that it is very difficult for them to find an explanation of what has actually happened. They had predicted easy money, and money rates were higher than in the eighteen months preceding. They had looked for continued increase in trade activity and for continued maintenance of financial values; what the quarter has witnessed has been a definite halt in the industrial movement, and a fall of such violence on the Stock Exchange as to shatter for the time almost completely the visions of cheerful optimism. We shall see, in the course of our review, the reasons for these disappointments.

A structure of very ill-grounded speculation had been in progress on the Stock Exchange and elsewhere; it collapsed when the basis of fact underlying it was tested. But in going ahead too fast and too far, the stock market merely duplicated the action of industry in general. Dealers who had been buying merchandise, on a tacit belief that nothing could impair the strength of the situation, discovered all at once that for months ahead their needs had been provided for, and that the basic factors which were going to create the later demand were not yet assured. The result was a halt so abrupt as to cause much inconvenience and some alarm to those who had taken too much for granted. It will remain for our further study of the situation to discover how far, if at all, the status of real prosperity was impaired.

Unlike the preceding quarter, the past three months have been marked by many events of a nature to leave their mark on the financial situation. Of these there are three which stand out conspicuously and whose bearing on current finance it is impossible fully to determine, even at this writing. The first was the final dismantling of the $400,000,000 Northern Securities combination, which, setting free again the railway stocks over which the Wall Street battle of 1901 was fought, developed a very remarkable situation. The second was the Equitable Life Assurance scandal, which, toward the quarter's end, rose to proportions which caused, throughout the financial community, a feeling of genuine consternation. The third was the memorable victory of the Japanese fleet in the Corean Straits on May 28, which came on an unusual political and financial situation, and has been followed by negotiations for peace which promise to affect that situation still more curiously. Along with these occurrences came some significant incidents in banking circles. It is to these four episodes, in connection with the unexpected movement on the Stock Exchange, to which I shall chiefly direct attention.

We saw in our review of the situation three months ago that, although the financial markets had advanced at an extravagant rate during February and the greater part of March, there was nevertheless at least some ground for improving markets in the real conditions of the period. As a matter of fact, the distinctive down-turn on the Stock Exchange, which was not to cease until fifteen to twenty-five points had been lopped off from values, occurred at the very time when these tangible signs of promise were most in evidence. The story of that reaction, of its causes, and of the reasons which made it so severe, gives an unusually clear object-lesson on the nature of financial movements.

It was a common saying in financial circles, as the month of March drew to a close, that not a cloud could be seen in the financial sky. Abroad, the Japanese had just won the decisive battle of Mukden; Kuropatkin was retreating in disorder; the French bankers had refused further advances of capital to the Russian Government; and expectation was widespread that peace was near at hand. Responding to these developments in the Eastern situation, Europe's financial markets revived perceptibly. British consols rose to the highest point since the middle of 1903, and, with a general revival in all the foreign markets, there came a flow of foreign capital into this country.

At home, all financial signs pointed definitely to fair weather. Readers of these articles are aware that the familiar tests of financial health are bank exchanges, sales at the Stock Exchange, and iron production and consumption. As for exchange of checks at the country's clearing-houses, the record for last March was never paralleled by any month in our financial history. Up to that month, the highest record was the $12,831,000,000 in the month of May, 1901, when the greatest Wall Street speculation of our time culminated. The record for last March was $12,915,000,000, and it compared with only a trifle over $8,000,-

000,000 for the same month in 1904. Stock Exchange transactions during March rose to 29,138,000 shares, comparing with 11,440,000 in the same month a year ago. This showing, though it fell far short of the 42,148,000 shares of May, 1901, nevertheless exceeded, by over two million shares, the record of the month of March in that same year. Until the present year, the high record in American iron output was the 1,713,000 tons of May, 1903. In March of the present year this figure rose to 1,936,000, which was easily high record in our history. Nor was this all; for, despite such a huge production, iron supplies on hand declined in March 31,489 tons — this on the heels of a continuous decrease since July, 1904. In other words, current consumption ran beyond even the unprecedented output.

These signs of promise might have meant less had they been attended by uncertain or unfavorable indications from the crops. But the Government's estimate on wheat, published on April 10, was exceptionally favorable. Winter-sown wheat, which had gone into the colder weather with somewhat doubtful prospects, turned up in April with the best acreage estimate but one in the country's records, and with an estimate of condition exceeded during the past twenty years only by the April estimates of 1886, 1889, 1891, 1901, and 1903. The grain trade's interpretation of this Government return was that, barring accidents, we might expect the best winter crop ever gathered — the indicated yield being 470,000,000 bushels, which would compare with the 332,000,000 harvested last year, and with 429,600,000 in the famous "wheat year" of 1901.

So much, then, for the tangible signs of promise. It should be evident that such hopeful indications warranted at least a considerable rise in financial values — always provided that the favorable developments had not been already "discounted" by the advance in last year's markets. But this was the very proviso which Wall Street neglected to make. The truth appeared to be that the markets of this spring very soon exhausted their normal capacity for "discounting." Long before the upward movement culminated, it had been plainly recognized on the Stock Exchange that the real investing public had retired from the market. This did not check the activities of the speculating pools and cliques, who were forcing up prices on the basis of borrowed money. Very low rates for loans had provided abundant resources for such speculation. It was fostered further by circulation of Stock Exchange rumors, all of which went to show that intrinsic values were for one reason or another in process of swift enhancement. For instance, it was declared that Union Pacific stock would really be a vast beneficiary from the Northern Securities liquidation, and that all chance of further dispute between the rival railway factions was removed. On this basis Union Pacific stock rose 26 points. Similar rumors, affecting Northern Securities stock itself, put up the price from 130 at the opening of the year to 159 in March and 185⅜ in April.

Next, all Wall Street was informed that Union Pacific had bought up the New York Central and was about to absorb that property, at highly advantageous terms, to complete a through transcontinental line. New York Central stock rose 26 points on this report. Reading stock, it was next asserted, was being bought in increased quantities by connecting railways, and about 20 points were added to its price. Reports that a certain speculator had gained possession of the Tennessee iron properties, and was about to amalgamate them into a single corporation, sent up Tennessee Coal stock 38 points and Sloss-Sheffield Iron 58. These figures will give some conception of the Stock Exchange movement which preceded or accompanied the good news of March.

Now let us see what followed. The first discovery was that the very low money rates on which the speculators had been depending for their operation were an uncertain reliance. Early in March call money at New York, from its easy 2 per cent level, rose to 4 per cent. It went to 5 per cent in the middle of April, and touched 7 per cent for a moment on April 20. At the same time, recall of funds by interior banks and by the Treasury cut down the New York bank reserves some $34,000,000, forcing reduction of not less than $50,000,000 in the loans. Next it was seen that the battle of Mukden had not ended the Eastern war, but that Russia was fighting stubbornly on to the very last ditch. Rejected at the Paris money market, the Government managed, first, to borrow some $50,000,000 from its home institutions, and, next, during April, raised in the German market $50,000,000 more on nine months' notes at 5 per cent. While this was going on, the various Russian fleets, which had long tarried on the coast of Africa or in the Baltic, pressed forward to join their forces on the coast of Asia and approached the Japanese waters. The effect of this development on the European markets was the immediate blight of the promising movement of recovery. Europe's own markets fell and American securities held abroad were in large measure sold back to New York. The effect on Russian and Japanese securities may be judged from the following table of London quotations:

	Russian 4 per cents.	Japanese 4 per cents.
January	91¼	76¼
Week before Battle of Mukden	88¾	85¼
Week after the battle	86¼	88¼
End of May	88¾	83¼

Since American finance itself had shown no great sensitiveness to Eastern war developments, it might have been, and, indeed, was, argued that if all went well at home our financial markets had no reason for reaction. But disappointment was in store at home as well for the highly keyed optimism of March. We have seen what part was played in creating sentiment by the iron trade's monthly showing. From July, 1904, to April, 1905, there had been, as we have seen, not only a steady increase in monthly output, but a steady decrease in undelivered supplies in the hands of makers. Consumption, during nine successive months, was greater than production. In April this state of things was suddenly arrested. Supplies on hand increased from 439,000 tons on April 1 to 451,000 at the opening of May. The increase of itself was trifling, but it marked a turn. Such a turn occurred in October, 1895. It was followed by continuous increase in supplies and by further reaction in iron and other industries, which remained unarrested until September, 1896. Precisely such a turn in November, 1899, foretold protracted dulness in the trade until September, 1900. Another still, in June, 1902, went on until July, 1904, and that was a period of industrial reaction.

I do not say that an increase of 12,000 tons in such supplies, when the monthly consumption verges on 2,000,000, infallibly foreshadows prolonged reaction. But of the fact that such an increase has been a reasonably truthful forecast during a dozen years past, there is no doubt at all. If this were a mere coincidence, the coincidence was not pleasant. As a matter of fact, announcement of April's increased "visible supply" was shortly followed by news of a definite check to activity in steel and iron. What this failed to accomplish in the way of shaking the boundless optimism of a month or two before was effected by the reports of the crop outlook. To be sure, such reports present nothing new. A springtime enlivened by reports of drought, of excessive rainfall, and of damage over large areas to growing grain is as familiar on the eve of an abundant harvest as on that of a harvest failure. But the reports of the season just past were at least a reminder that harvests are never certainties until harvest-time.

So much for the general causes which had a part in what Wall Street described as the market's incomprehensible reaction.   But we have also seen that the excessively high March prices on the Stock Exchange resulted quite as much from rumors of what was to happen with the investment properties concerned as from general conditions.   Let us see how these "rumors" materialized.   First, there were the Stock Exchange tales, to which I have referred, of important influences at work in the New York Central, the Reading, and the Tennessee iron properties.   As regards New York Central, the story of the purchase by Union Pacific was denied outright in the strongest terms, and by people whose word was sufficient.   The stock as a consequence declined 24 points.   The "rumor" that Reading stock was being heavily bought by other companies was shattered still more effectively.   Early in May it came to light that the Lake Shore Railroad, which, in 1903, had bought 169,000 shares of Reading stock for purposes of control, had sold at the high March price 79,000 of these shares.   In other words, instead of buying more of the Reading stock, companies already owning an interest had sold half of what they had had; for it was assumed that, since the Baltimore and Ohio bought in 1903 a block of Reading stock equal to that of the Lake Shore, it had sold along with that company this year.

Such news was not only destructive of a foolish "rumor," but it caused some puzzled consideration over the whole "community-of-interest" theory.   That theory was based on the purchase and retention, by one railway corporation, of stock in a competing one.   Such buying pushed up prices, even when it was known that bonds would be sold to the public to raise the purchase-money.   But here were two such buyers selling for a speculative profit part of the stock acquired, yet not retiring the bonds issued to provide for it.   This action put the "community-of-interest" theory in a totally new light.   It became, at least potentially, a menace to Stock Exchange values.   Reading stock itself fell 13 points.   Meanwhile the efforts of speculators to get hold of the Southern iron properties broke down so disastrously that their own forced sales caused declines of from 30 to 45 points in the stocks concerned.

A still more impressive incident was to follow.   On April 3, the federal Supreme Court ruled finally against the Union Pacific's demand for the return of the stock as deposited by it in the Northern Securities merger.   A fortnight later that $400,000,000 concern began to distribute its Northern Pacific and Great Northern shares under the Supreme Court's order.   This liquidation began in the third week of April.

It was carried out on the *pro rata* basis, each shareholder getting his proportionate share of each of those two stocks.

It speedily appeared not only that the tales of mysterious profits to accrue on that liquidation had no basis, but that the distribution itself was leading to an awkward situation. On April 11, President Harriman of the Union Pacific, who had been a director in the Northern Securities, representing his company's $82,000,000 holdings of that stock, was summarily dropped by the shareholders and replaced by a follower of Mr. Hill. This did not seem to point to harmony, and it was followed by a development still more impressive. It was a reasonable assumption that if any immediate advantage was to accrue to Northern Securities shareholders on the liquidation, Union Pacific, with its large interest in that company, would have got some wind of it. Yet, in the middle of April, it was discovered that sales running to upward of $5,000,000 had been made in that very stock and on the open market by the Union Pacific's treasury. At almost the same time, the Union Pacific management had called a shareholders' meeting to approve the issue, in the board's discretion, of $100,000,000 new preferred stock of the company; and the shareholders duly gave authority. No explanation as to the use to which this immense fund would be put was made; and, in fact, since the company's preferred stock already outstanding brought less than par upon the market, and since the new stock could not be lawfully sold for less than par, it was obvious that no money would be raised for the latter immediately. Nevertheless, the announcement startled financial markets, both at home and abroad; the inference being promptly drawn that this was a "war measure," planned for a possible contest in the Western railway field.

In the middle of May, at the annual meeting of the Northern Pacific shareholders, came still another shock. It will be recalled that when the Union Pacific placed its holdings in the merger, in November, 1901, it held a majority of Northern Pacific's $155,000,000 stock. The plan of distributing *pro rata* Northern Securities assets — Northern Pacific and Great Northern stock alike — would, on the other hand, leave Union Pacific with a minority of Northern Pacific shares. This was the question fought out by Harriman in the federal courts during 1904. He lost the suit; the stock was distributed *pro rata;* Union Pacific was left, after the liquidation, with a minority of Northern Pacific stock; and at the Northern Pacific shareholders' meeting, May 18, the three Union Pacific representatives on the board — Messrs. Harriman, Stillman, and William Rockefeller — were dropped. The inference from this action was to some extent modified by the statement, given out along with it, that the law of Minnesota, whose charter Northern Pacific holds, provides not only that no railway corporation as such shall control a competing or parallel line running within that State, but that no officer of such railroad corporation "shall act as an officer of any other railroad corporation owning or having the control of a parallel or competing line." The federal Supreme Court, in dismissing the Harriman suit, on April 3, had expressly declared that "the Northern Pacific system, taken in conjunction with the Burlington system [which it owns], is competitive with the Union Pacific system" — which, along with the Minnesota statute, seemed to settle the status of the Harriman directors.

It is true that the same federal Supreme Court, in deciding against the Northern Securities merger, on March 14, 1904, had declared Great Northern also to be a "natural competitor for business" with the Northern Pacific, and that for this reason the Hill-Morgan party, controlling Northern Pacific, excluded not only Union Pacific directors from that board, on May 18, but debarred Great Northern directors also. In replacing all these retiring members of the board, however — and this was the real point of interest — not a single new director friendly to Union Pacific's interest was elected. James J. Hill did not appear on the new Northern Pacific board, any more than did E. H. Harriman; but every name on the list was that of a recognized Hill partisan.

Both factions presently gave out statements that their differences would now be waived; that, in the words of the announcement, henceforth "there will be strict observance of the rights of both parties"; and, to give force to this assertion, it was made known that a railway line, under construction into a territory claimed by both Northern and Union Pacific, would now be built under their joint auspices. But meanwhile the stocks which had risen with such great violence in March, on the report of some favorable situation to follow the great merger's dissolution, suffered such declines as 23 points in Northern Pacific, 22 in Union Pacific, and 25 in Northern Securities. The public was not shaken in its conviction that a feeling of bitter and possibly dangerous hostility still remained.

It is, in fact, hard to predict the outcome. From one point of view, the great railway fight of 1901 is settled. Northern Pacific and Great Northern bought the Burlington; Union Pacific, a close competitor of that railway, asked to participate in the control. The request was refused. Union Pacific itself then undertook to buy up Northern Pacific stock. The plan succeeded, but only at the cost of the Northern Pacific corner. To avert the consequences of that corner, the Northern Securities holding company was organized. Its forced dissolution, under orders of the court, left the Northern Pacific, as we have seen already, in the hands of the interests which controlled it before the fight began; and with that control went the control of the Burlington. Union Pacific had fought its fight and lost. Whatever it had to fear from the Burlington in those hands four years ago, it apparently has to fear to-day. This is the plain situation.

It may not lead to unsettling consequences; it is at least unlikely to do so in the very near future. Both rival factions are unquestionably honest in asserting that they want no "war of rates," which would injure both belligerents and in the end perhaps accomplish nothing. Such danger as exists of a contest of this sort will arise at a time when declining traffic leads to urgent quest of competitive business, or when some new expansion scheme, conceived by the one side or the other, revives all the jealousies of 1901 and provokes retaliation. Indeed, this whole four-years' fight is but one in a series of such conflicts between the same two parties. No longer ago than 1889, a bitter contest, oddly resembling in many ways the present quarrel, broke out between them. Then, as in 1901, both companies were bidding for a third, which controlled a line in competitive territory. The striking difference in the two famous conflicts is that in 1889 Northern Pacific won the fight on the Stock Exchange, only to lose it in the courts; whereas Union Pacific has had the same experience since 1901.

I have mentioned, as one of the potent influences in the season's finance, the entanglement of certain banks in unlucky speculations. The first of these disclosures had a profound influence in bringing to earth the past season's Wall Street cardhouse. This episode began with a bold attempt to corner wheat. In view of what we have already seen as to the high promise shown for the wheat crop in March and April, the fact that a corner operation was at that very time in progress may perplex the reader. But the earliest wheat of 1905 cannot come to market before July, and, in the interim, with last year's deficient crop and the enormous home consumption, supplies are running extremely low. Not to go into details, it was evident last autumn that if the outside world bought freely no margin whatever would remain. Basing its programme on these facts, a group of speculators started to get into a position where they could dictate prices. Wheat at Chicago ruled above one dollar from last August onward; it ranged around $1.12 when the "clique" was buying. What the speculators bought were contracts for delivery in May — a month when the new crop, however promising, could not affect supplies.

The corner manipulators were said to have held at one time such contracts to the extent of 20,000,000 bushels; and on February 16 they put up the price to $1.21½ per bushel. By April, though the price had relaxed a trifle, the grain trade leaned to the conviction that a genuine corner in May was probable, in the course of which $1.50 or more might easily be named as the price at which contracts must be settled. The "clique" would have practically all the wheat, and whoever had contracted to deliver it must buy from them.

Corners, however, are dangerous experiments; and it is an almost invariable rule that something which no one had reckoned in his calculations suddenly changes the situation. One development, this past season, was the virtual disappearance of the export trade. For the ten months after harvest began in July, 1904, the following very remarkable results were shown. The figures comprise all wheat exported, whether in grain or flour, as declared by the Government reports:

Ten months ending April 30.	Bushels.	Ten Months Ending April 30.	Bushels.
1905	36,700,000	1901.....................	172,500,000
1904	112,900,000	1900.....................	151,300,000
1903	176,000,000	1899.....................	194,000,000
1902	204,600,000	1898.....................	182,200,000

In the first three months of 1902, following a large wheat harvest here, England imported 12,152,000 hundredweight of wheat and flour from the United States; in the same months of 1905, she took only 1,544,000. But whereas, during this period of 1902, Russia, India, Australia, and the Argentine sent to England only 4,117,000 hundredweight, their contribution in 1905 was 20,668,000.

These bountiful outside supplies made needless any urgent bidding for American consumers — indeed, in the ten months ending April 30, we actually imported 2,600,000 bushels against only 6,800 a year before. What alarmed the corner managers rather more seriously, however, as the spring drew on, was evidence that the farmers had more old wheat to sell than had been supposed. This is what wrecked young Leiter's corner in 1898 and has wrecked a dozen others; for a time comes when corner operators, to sustain their market, must buy at top prices all the wheat presented. If they have made miscalculations as to how much may be expected, this may exhaust their capital. Up to the end of March there was a ten-per-cent decrease, as compared with the previous season, in wheat delivered at the city markets. With April the situation changed: the weekly record ran one to two hundred thousand bushels beyond last year. While this was happening, the price at Chicago, which normally should be several cents lower than at New York, was actually higher by thirteen cents per bushel. The market, in other words, was thoroughly fictitious; the farmers understood it; and the floor of every granary was sure to be scraped to make May deliveries at Chicago.

But April was not yet over when still another wholly unforeseen development shattered the corner undertaking. Even the so-called "Gates clique," who were managing the corner, had been puzzled by signs that some one besides themselves was in trouble because of these miscalculations. On Monday, April 26, the truth came suddenly to light. Frank C. Bigelow, president of the First National Bank of Milwaukee, an institution with $13,000,000 deposits, known as the largest Western bank outside of Chicago, was found to have defaulted to the extent of a million dollars, which he had sunk first in stocks, and then in the wheat-corner speculation.

The bank was saved through money advanced by Bigelow's fellow-directors, but the consequences elsewhere were profound. First, panic seized on the cornerers of wheat, as well it might. Their hurried sales, encountering on the market closing-out sales for Bigelow's account, broke the price for May delivery from $1.10 per bushel to 86½ cents. On the public mind the affair had larger consequences. It cannot be said that it aroused widespread doubt as to the solvency of other banks. It did not, for instance, at all repeat the panic of distrust in fiduciary institutions which followed the scandals of the Marine, Second National, and Metropolitan banks at New York City in 1884. But it unquestionably started a vague and unpleasant feeling of distrust; and in the minds of the reminiscent, it suggested some disagreeable analogies.

At a very similar juncture during the "boom" of the eighties, namely, in 1887, as in the present year, there first occurred a futile attempt to corner wheat, and next, on the downfall of that undertaking, it was discovered that the president of an important bank had robbed his institution to provide funds for the speculation. But the part of the parallel which was most unpleasant was the fact that the violent break in wheat during 1887 and the bank failure which accompanied it were followed by a series of bank suspensions throughout the United States, the

cause of almost every one of these failures being either speculation or
defalcation.

Then, as now, the true explanation was that a highly speculative
market and tales of enormous profits won by gambling operations in it
had turned the heads and demoralized the integrity of the culprits. To
an extent, the same unpleasant condition of affairs has followed the
Bigelow episode. No doubt the reason is that the Milwaukee episode
started directors of other banks into overhauling the books of their institutions. As was to be expected, they found, in many instances, quite
enough to justify their misgivings. Half a dozen little banks — chiefly
in Ohio and the younger Western States — suspended during May, most
of them having to confess that the free abandonment of their resources
to speculators was the cause. On May 23 the list fairly rounded out
with the scandalous confessions involved in the Merchants' Trust Company failure at New York — a small institution, to be sure, but which
had placed the whole of its deposit funds in foolish promotions which
made the concern in reality insolvent from the start.

These unpleasant developments did not prove a radically unsound
condition of American banking. They did, however, demonstrate very
clearly that the extravagant and prolonged speculation on our markets
had in large measure blunted the moral sense of the community. That
some such reckoning must be had for lowered standards of business integrity was the unqualified prediction, even in 1901, of every one conversant at all with financial history. It was precisely this question
which gave the keen edge to public interest in the Equitable Life developments of the past three months, which we have now to review. I
outlined, in the last number of THE FORUM, the situation which had
suddenly developed in that company's affairs as a result of President
Alexander's request for the retirement of Mr. Hyde. It will be recalled
that the gist of Mr. Alexander's position, as expressed in his formal
manifesto of last February, was this:

> The reëlection of Mr. Hyde as vice-president, with all the powers he has exercised
> in the absence of the president, would be most prejudicial to the welfare and
> progress of the society, and to the conservation of trust funds held for the benefit of
> our policy-holders.

I explained also the peculiar nature of the situation created by the
fact that Mr. Hyde was really the owner of the Equitable, through the
possession, by himself and his family, of fifty-one per cent of the com-

pany's $100,000 stock. The president of the company was in reality asking that its owner be removed from official participation in its management. In most corporations such a request would obviously have been preposterous; but the nature of life-insurance business — the fact that its essential nature is that of a coöperative and mutual undertaking by the policy-holders — made the case peculiar.

Mr. Hyde immediately recognized this; and, before the controversy was fairly under way, the Equitable directors voted, with his consent, that the society's charter should be so amended as eventually to confer on policy-holders the right to elect twenty-eight of the fifty-two directors, the remaining twenty-four to be named by holders of the stock. It soon became manifest, however, that this compromise would not settle the difficulty. What happened was the immediate bringing of a suit to enjoin this "mutualization plan," on the ground that stockholders' rights were sacrificed. This suit was brought in the New York courts, not by Mr. Hyde — who indeed intervened to oppose it — but by minority holders of Equitable shares. On May 26 Judge Maddox granted the injunction. The mutualization plan, the court affirmed, was contrary to both State and federal constitutions, and for a double reason: First, that by depriving a shareholder of the right to vote for the fifty-two directors, it violated the contract made by the company when the stock was issued; and, second, that "the right of stock to control the corporation, to the exclusion of every other interest, is a vested right," and that "to lessen or interfere with that right would violate the provision of the Constitution that life, liberty, and property shall not be taken without due process of law." The issues thus defined, unless settled outside of court beforehand, are bound to go forward on appeal to the federal Supreme Court. That would probably occupy two years, and in the mean time the present status must remain.

All these events brought the situation squarely back to the question how any capitalist, owning a company through its stock, could be dislodged from office save by his own consent. In Mr. Hyde's case that consent was formally refused, and under rather extraordinary circumstances. On April 18, more than two hundred general agents of the Equitable came to New York at the call of President Alexander, but promptly organized as an independent convention. After deliberation these agents, by a large majority, adopted a resolution as follows, addressed to Mr. Hyde:

We, the general agents and managers of the Equitable, assembled in convention, from all parts of the United States and Canada, are personally and through our agents in closer touch with the people, and, knowing the deep-seated convictions of the policy-holders, are deeply deploring the necessity for our action, therefore sincerely and earnestly appeal to you, on behalf of the Equitable, to the creation and upbuilding of which your father devoted his life, and for the sake of its policy-holders and its agents, to set aside all personal interests and now voluntarily retire from the vice-presidency.

This resolution was presented personally, and in person Mr. Hyde replied to it that he had no intention of resigning his office; that he regarded such a course as cowardly and disgraceful to the memory of his father; and that he deemed any further action or comment improper while the questions at issue were in the hands of the directors. After a month of futile compromises and aimless public bickering, the business of the company was so gravely affected by the broad inferences drawn from the insinuations of the quarrelling officers that the directors eventually met; and, at the opening of April, they appointed from among their number a committee to investigate the entire management and position of the society. It consisted originally of seven members, including Mr. H. C. Frick, of the steel corporation, Mr. M. E. Ingalls, of the "Big Four" Railway, Mr. E. H. Harriman, of the Union Pacific, Mr. Brayton Ives, of the Metropolitan Trust Company, Mr. James J. Hill, of the Great Northern Railway, and two well-known private capitalists, Mr. C. N. Bliss and Mr. D. O. Mills.

At the outset, the public was disposed to place no very great confidence in the results of their reports, more particularly so in view of the fact that Mr. Hill and Mr. Mills both resigned from the committee; Mr. Hill's withdrawal being explicitly on the ground that he could not have the scope he asked for in a personal investigation. In the second week of April, Mr. Frick, as chairman of the committee, gave out a public statement on the lines of investigation which it proposed to follow; and the programme there outlined was so thorough as to restore at once the confidence of the general public in the committee's purposes. Summed up in brief, Mr. Frick's communication — addressed, as it necessarily was, to the president of the society — called for information on the following points:

All salaries paid, by whom authorized, and for performance of what duties; compensation received by any officer or employee from any corporation connected with the Equitable; names of all individuals on the pay-roll who are connected by blood or marriage with its officers, and particulars as to their employment; investments of the Equitable in other banking corporations, and the full nature of its connection with them; all loans made to any officer or employee, with the circumstances of such loans; all transactions with banking or brokerage houses as to the company's investments; any case where officer or director received a profit on such transaction because of his office in the Equitable; contracts with the society's agents and the payments thereunder; real estate transactions; and, finally, the account of "commissions, advertising, postage, and exchange," and "all other disbursements," to which were charged, respectively, in the last annual report, $7,900,285 and $7,179,318, and as to which the committee asked for "all the items and vouchers" and complete information regarding them.

In order to make complete and sweeping the scope of the investigation, the following comprehensive paragraph was added:

If any one has any information or knowledge of any other act, matter, or thing done or permitted to be done by any officer, director, trustee, or employee of the society inconsistent with the best interests of the society or unfair toward any officer, director, trustee, or employee thereof, the committee will take up and investigate any such matter on being informed of the same by you or any other officer, director, trustee, or employee, or stockholder, or policy-holder.

The committee's questions were on their face bound to bring to light any scandal in the way of improper investments, improper use of official position, nepotism in appointments, or official irregularity of any sort. It was not long before the committee's call for information bore definite fruit. On April 15, Mr. Hyde made the following statement over his signature to the committee:

There had been a syndicate known as "James H. Hyde and Associates," including James W. Alexander, president of the society, whose participation was always equal to my own, and this syndicate had been underwriters of a number of banking issues of securities, and the Equitable Society purchased, in some instances, in the ordinary course of business, securities which had been underwritten by this syndicate. At the outset of this controversy, Mr. Alexander and I were both advised by counsel that as to any such syndicate transactions in which any officers of the Equitable Society had been interested, a full statement should be made up and laid before the board of directors, and whatever law and justice required regarding them should be done by the officers concerned. Following the advice above referred to, I examined all these syndicate transactions and deposited my check for $61,446.92 with the treasurer of the society as trustee.

In concluding this statement, Mr. Hyde added that he admitted no wrongdoing, and that the transactions referred to were "made with the sanction of universal precedent."

The law governing cases of this sort is entirely explicit. The New York Insurance act contains the following provision:

No director or other officer of an insurance corporation doing business in this State shall receive any money or valuable thing for negotiating, procuring, or recommending any loan from any such corporation, or for selling or aiding in the sale of any stocks or securities to or by such corporation.

Any person violating the provisions of this section shall forfeit his position as such director or officer, and be disqualified from thereafter holding any such office in any insurance corporation.

There is no need of intricate argument as to the meaning of this statute.   It is sweeping in terms and perfectly clear in language.   Without any question, it was inserted by makers of the law in order to prevent the use of insurance companies by their officers for the sake of "unloading" questionable securities in whose sale such officers had a private interest.   The law does not stop with forbidding merely the sale of bad securities under such circumstances, obviously because proof of such character might be extremely difficult.   It was presumed by the legislators that for any man to be both buyer and seller on an extensive scale, while trust funds of insurance policy-holders were the purchase money, would lead to a wholly unsafe position.   Hence the extremely comprehensive language of the law.   Its purport has been recognized in other companies by a standing agreement whereby a banker, holding office which gave him power to pass on investments of an insurance company, returned to that company all his profits from sales of securities made by his banking house to such company.   Thus explained, it will be obvious that Mr. Hyde admitted a violation of the law, his real apology being an appeal to precedent.   Mr. Hyde's intimation that the president of the Equitable had been engaged in all such syndicates drew forth an immediate denial from Mr. Alexander, and the matter remained in doubt pending the investigation of the committee.

So much was known before the Frick committee was ready to report. The date for that report had been fixed at May 31.   It was made to the directors on that day; but it turned out to be so frank and unsparing in its revelation of the disorders in the society that the board which received it was thrown into outright panic.   Apparently something of a "whitewashing" nature had been looked for.   Charges were angrily made, by implicated officers, that they had been "betrayed" by the committee — as if that committee's duty was to find them innocent.   The directors refused to receive the report, refused to order its publication, refused even to vote recognition of the committee's labors in preparing it.   As was to be expected, public indignation instantly flared up to white heat.   The committee's chairman resigned his directorship in the Equitable, and was followed by twelve other directors.   The committee itself boldly published the report which the Equitable board had repudiated.   The demand that Mr. Hyde surrender his control, and that both he and President Alexander resign their offices, was angry and determined; but both officers declared that they would not give way to it. The company's business came to an absolute standstill, and the public turned, with an urgency that bade fair to be irresistible, to the State

Insurance Department and the State legislature to do what the board had left undone.

All this was unnecessary. Fortunately events so moved as to force a solution of this seemingly hopeless dilemma in the quarter which had been no longer looked to. Grave legal doubts existed as to the society's power to buy up the Hyde stock at a premium, even if Mr. Hyde were to consent to sell. However this may be, it transpired that Mr. Hyde was very soon thereafter induced to sell his majority control, and the stock was then placed in the hands of three trustees — Ex-President Cleveland, Chief Justice Morgan J. O'Brien, of the New York State Supreme Court, and Mr. George Westinghouse; and it asked these trustees, in selecting a new board of directors, to allow the policy-holders to name twenty-eight of the total fifty-two. Mr. Alexander and Mr. Hyde resigned their offices, and Secretary Paul Morton, of the Navy Department, was made chairman of the company. In a more or less definite way pledges were made that the excessive balances in auxiliary companies should now be cut down, and that investment of the trust funds should be hereafter restricted to securities authorized for savings banks. This promised real reform; it is too early, however, to discuss such projects at this writing, when the new board and the new officers are yet to be appointed. There will undoubtedly be more to say at a future time of the bearing of the whole Equitable episode on life insurance generally. That recent practices in that field will be profoundly modified, and for the better, there is no doubt whatever.

At this writing, it is still impossible to say what the situation created by Admiral Togo's extraordinary naval victory means to the world's finance. It is certain that financial Europe had for weeks been asserting that the arrival of Rojestvensky in the China seas — with the possibility of a Japanese defeat which would open the coasts of Japan to the enemy and isolate the Manchurian army — was the main depressing influence on the markets. It was so regarded because of the general conviction that such a defeat would prolong the war and widen the opportunity for European complications.

The battle was fought and the Russian sea-power was annihilated with a completeness surpassing the epoch-making achievements of Themistocles, Don Juan of Austria, Sir Francis Drake, and Lord Nelson. But the Russian court still refused to treat for peace, notwithstanding that its ally, France, had refused it further money accommodation, that Germany was grudgingly lending on harsh terms, and that its last recourse, a domestic loan, was floated only by virtual compulsion of the Russian banks. How this deadlock was finally broken through President Roosevelt's bold and adroit move of mediation, and how, on the 10th of June, Japan and Russia consented to negotiate for peace, is a story that need not here be retold. The question, for the longer future, concerns the results that the return of peace will have on the financial situation. Certainly the removal of this danger-spot at the moment when the Equitable storm-cloud has passed away, and when underlying financial conditions are not unpropitious, gives just ground for optimism.

Recent experience has rather shaken the inferences commonly drawn, however, from the buoyant prosperity which followed the settlement of our Spanish war. That the United States was then on the eve of a real industrial "boom" unconnected with the war, and that the Treaty of Paris meant, to the defeated Power, release from a burdensome colonial entanglement and $20,000,000 cash, had been forgotten. The real meaning of the aftermath of war was not realized until the pacification of the Transvaal, in 1902, was followed by two years of financial exhaustion for the victorious state. The strain of the Eastern war has been as severe as that of the South African conflict. It remains to be seen how its consequences will be felt by the successful and the defeated Powers, and, in particular, what is going to happen to the huge political derelict, Russia, as well as to the European market, to which that country owes two billions of dollars, and to which it must owe much more if Japan imposes an indemnity.

ALEXANDER D. NOYES.

ARCHITECTURE.

THE record of architectural activity for the eighteen months which have elapsed since my last review in THE FORUM contains no items of startling interest. In the United States, the most notable features of the record are the continued activity in educational architecture along the whole line, from grammar schools to universities, including library buildings and museums; the increased vigor of the movement for municipal improvement; important railway terminal enterprises in various cities; and the widely published reorganization of the methods and administration of the School of Architecture of Columbia University.

Surveying the whole field of American architectural activity, one is impressed with the fact that fire has been and continues to be one of the sternest and most effective of schoolmasters to our people. Chicago and Boston, over thirty years ago, began a series of costly object-lessons, repeated on a smaller scale in many other American cities at various intervals since 1872, by which our people were forced to learn the lesson of solid and fire-resisting construction. But for these lessons we might still be erecting large and costly public buildings with wooden floor beams and stud partitions, and we certainly should never have learned the manifold uses of steel, terra-cotta, and concrete, which have made modern American methods of construction so efficient. An added stimulus to the development of new structural materials, processes, and methods is now supplied by the rapid diminution of the visible timber supply. The increasing cost of lumber must before long reach the point at which it will compel the invention and adoption, for country houses and cheap buildings, of materials and methods which, while cheaper than our present systems of using brick and steel, will be more durable and far less inflammable than wood. Whether reinforced concrete, concrete blocks, terra-cotta, or some new and as yet unknown material will furnish the final solution of the problem cannot now be prophesied. At present concrete has the lead, and is being experimented with by the architects, with results not yet sufficiently tested as to be definitely accepted.

A notable example of the successful use of a new plastic concrete composition is the extensive Jefferson Medical College at Philadelphia, by John T. Windrim. In France, the architectural use of *béton armé* has progressed much further than here, though no one but a blind enthusiast would claim for the buildings erected in the new material a high rank as models of architectural beauty. The color and texture of concrete are both against it, and no system of architectural forms has as yet been devised at once suited to the material and pleasing to a critical, æsthetic taste. The stuccoed buildings of the Old World and of Spanish America offer the most suggestive analogues to buildings of concrete; but the problem of imparting beauty and charm to structures of *ciment armé* will not be solved by any merely formal copying of stuccoed rubble.

The Baltimore fire has furnished ammunition to both the terra-cotta and the concrete camps, in their verbal battles in favor of one and against the other of these two very useful materials. The trade magazines of the two parties are amusing reading; each side arguing the complete failure of the material championed by the other and the triumphant success of its own. Careful students draw from the same data the general conclusion that both materials are valuable in fire-resisting construction; but that success or failure in any given test depends largely upon the workmanship, and is often affected by special conditions which do not warrant sweeping conclusions, certainly not such as would favor one material to the exclusion of the other.

Among recent extensions of the applications of fire-resisting construction to structures of a class heretofore too often built with complete disregard of the dangers of fire, a recent issue of a trade magazine describes and illustrates two examples in church architecture; the first, the Roman Catholic church of St. Paul, at Chicago; the second, the Broadway Tabernacle church in this city, already referred to in my last review of architecture in THE FORUM, but only recently completed and dedicated.

The interest in the first-named example lies chiefly in its construction, which is of brick and terra-cotta throughout. It is one of the few American churches having a genuine vault of masonry or brick, and is particularly noteworthy as an example of the modern application of the mediæval method of vault construction. The ribs were first built of moulded brick, and made to serve as supports for the centring, upon which the fillings were laid up. Following the true Gothic principle, the constructive materials and methods used are everywhere disclosed in the design, which, however, is far from being an archæological copy of any mediæval structure. This church is a valuable and encouraging illustration of the adaptability of historic methods to modern uses, and of intelligence in so adapting them. The parish that was willing to build so thoroughly and soundly deserves a compliment, as does the architect, Mr. H. J. Schlacks, who made so wise a use of his knowledge of architectural history. The second-named church differs from the first alike in materials and methods of design. It is interesting chiefly by its intelligent plan, in which was solved the difficult problem of combining a ten-story parish-house with a capacious church auditorium in a distinctly churchly *ensemble*. The Gothic style employed is here merely a dress for a distinctly twentieth-century construction of steel framework with concrete floor-fillings. The widely bruited rumor that the building comprises in its equipments a theatre, a swimming-tank, and a banquet-hall is a pure fiction.

While we are noting progress in ecclesiastical architecture, it is fitting here to mention the active resumption of work on the Cathedral of St. John the Divine, rendered possible by several large gifts during the past year. The great so-called "monoliths"—really *duoliths*—of the choir have been set up, and the masonry of the choir walls is slowly but visibly taking shape. The completion of the choir of this vast edifice is promised within a very few years. The Lady Chapel of St. Patrick's Roman Catholic Cathedral in New York (C. T. Mathews) is also progressing toward completion. It is a beautiful and scholarly piece of Gothic design in white marble.

The subject of discussion at the April meeting of the Architectural League of New York was the question of "the best type of the modern church." The speakers were all clergymen, excepting one, who is the editor of a church paper. The conclusions elicited by the discussions were perhaps not very definite, but some of the suggestions made were excellent. It was clearly brought out that there never can be *one* "best type," for there will always be at least two types of church: one designed with the altar as its focus of interest, the other with the pulpit; one kind being built to see in, the other to hear in; one for ceremonial, for ritual worship, the other for exhortation and exposition. But there was evident a strong prevailing sentiment of insistence upon architectural expressiveness, upon the importance of dignity and beauty in the design and equipments of the house of God, and upon the value of associations, whether with or without symbolism. This meeting is one of many evidences that religious architecture in the United States is on the threshold of a notable advance in quality and seriousness.

Any one who has studied the illustrations in recent magazines and architectural publications, not only of churches but also of educational buildings, can hardly have failed to be struck by the manifestations of a revival of Gothic forms and conceptions in these two classes of structures. This phenomenon, which has been made the subject of a series of articles in "The Craftsman," is an interesting one, especially when compared with the Gothic revivals in Europe in the middle of the last century. The difference between the two movements, both in their genesis and their spirit, is fundamental. That of the English Gothicists of 1825 to 1875 was the protest of an enlightened coterie against the philistinism and artistic destitution of their time. It was a movement of scholars and reformers; a propaganda in favor of the use of a "national" and "Christian" style, which it was sought at first to copy textually, and then to adapt to modern uses. It was, as it were, forced upon the architects from the outside. It produced some notable works and rescued ecclesiastical architecture from debasement; but it was never a spontaneous movement, and failed to develop the vital modern style that its advocates hoped to see.

The present movement in the United States is more spontaneous. It has originated among the architects, and has never been burdened or narrowed by the responsibilities of a propaganda. It is one of the natural developments of modern architectural eclecticism in a country which possesses no ancient traditions, and in which the endless variety of types, requirements, and systems of construction, all in a constant state of flux and change, is forever constraining its architects to seek, wherever they can find them, the forms in which they may dress their works and express their conceptions. Twenty-five years ago they imagined that the round-arched, mediæval styles of western Europe might furnish them with an apparel for all the varied forms of modern buildings; but an earnest and widespread experimentation through a dozen years demonstrated the limitations of the style. Then came the Chicago World's Fair, and for a while it seemed as though classic Roman models might suffice for our architectural needs, at least for the more monumental requirements of the art. Later, and particularly in those realms visited by the youthful enthusiasts who came every year from the ateliers of the Paris Ecole des Beaux-Arts, there was a splendid efflorescence of French architecture, varying from François Premier to Louis Quinze, and denominated collectively by the irreverent, "the Cartouche style." And now the field is being invaded by the mullioned windows and turrets of Gothic architecture.

The significant features about these rapidly succeeding "styles" have been: (1) that each has been introduced not as the result of an outside propaganda to which the architects have yielded, but by the architects themselves; and (2) that each movement or fashion or style, whichever it may be called, has come about in the effort to supply some element that was lacking in our architecture, to meet some demand for which the existing fashions were inadequate. As a result, each movement — at least since the passing of the Richardsonian Romanesque — has left a more or less permanent deposit; and it has become established as the best kind of architecture for certain classes of buildings. For great and monumental public edifices, such as State capitols, libraries, and museums, the dignity and stateliness, the ample scale, and the very formality of the various versions of classic architecture are now pretty generally accepted as the most appropriate form of design.

For buildings on city streets, especially for hotels and apartment-houses, Parisian models have quite deservedly found favor. Large country houses are quite generally designed in what we call the Colonial or Georgian style; while for smaller houses of wood a more intimate and picturesque style, distinctively American and modern, has been developed during the past twenty-five years. It is now more and more rarely that churches are built otherwise than in some version of Gothic design; and for schools and colleges, the English Tudor and Elizabethan collegiate buildings have furnished models both of composition and detail, which have been found admirably suited for the needs of our scholastic architecture. The evolution of design in tall buildings has produced certain types of treatment which are gradually crystallizing into a definite style, quite irrespective of the historic source of the details employed.

It seems, therefore, that we are in the presence of a somewhat novel phenomenon in the history of style — the development on eclectic principles of a number of quite distinct forms of architectural expression for distinct types of buildings. This is the natural result of modern conditions, which have steadily tended toward differentiation of types, while more and more we have had opened to our choice the whole range of forms developed by the varied experience of past ages. If we can manage to lay aside the old prejudice, assiduously fostered by literary critics of art, and decide in favor of a new, original, uniform, modern, "national" style, of which the critics have so long dreamed and declaimed, we shall recognize the fitness and reasonableness of the present state of style development, whose seeming confusion is really controlled by a certain common sense.   For we shall also recognize that, like all living movements in art, it is a movement of transition.

The freedom with which our architects handle, modify, and adapt the historic styles to the varied problems they have to solve is the despair of the purist, but it is the pledge of sincerity and progress.   The coming generation will see these several systems of treatment undergo successive gradual changes, by which they will depart further and further from the historic originals, and receive more and more the common stamp impressed upon them by the national taste.   But it may perhaps never again happen that a single system of forms and details, constituting a style as closely defined as, for example, the French Gothic style of the fourteenth century or the Roman Five Orders, will be applied alike to all sorts of buildings of all sorts of materials and systems of construction.   From this point of view, such an edifice as the new Times Building in New York is especially interesting.   It is called a Gothic building, and some of its details have been inspired by Gothic models; but the divergences from the Gothic style are more noticeable than the resemblances, and — whatever may be one's opinion of the merit of the details — it is a striking and original building, as distinctively Twentieth-Century American as Amiens is Thirteenth-Century French.   The same may be said of the new Trinity Building on lower Broadway, another so-called Gothic structure, less picturesque in mass, but equally modern and American.

In educational architecture the tendency becomes more marked each year to consider not merely the individual structure, but the group. Colleges and universities which have grown up in the haphazard American fashion, with ill-assorted buildings of various styles and colors grouped in a hit-or-miss way around a green or "campus," have begun or are now beginning to study plans for a symmetrical and harmonious architectural development.   Washington University in St. Louis has occupied the new buildings erected just before the Louisiana Purchase Exposition, as a part of the extensive and picturesque scheme planned by those gifted architects, the lamented Edward Cope and John Stewardson.   These are stone buildings in that adaptation of the English collegiate Gothic style which the same architects used so successfully in Blair Hall at Princeton.   Princeton University is about to erect a new recitation hall, in memory of President McCosh, from plans by Mr. Raleigh Gildersleeve; and this is to form one side of a new quadrangle in the rear of the Marquand Chapel, which will be the central feature of its western side.   This quadrangle will be in the English collegiate style; and thus, with the new dormitory recently built from plans by Mr. B. W. Morris, Jr., and with the new gymnasium and Blair Hall, all in the same general style, and the library, which is of stone in a slightly different version of late English Gothic design, a certain architectural harmony will in time dominate the once heterogeneous assortment of buildings in that most beautiful of American university towns.

The imposing group of Gothic buildings projected for West Point (Craim, Goodhue, and Fergusson) is another illustration of the serious study of the problem of artistic harmony and monumental grouping, though its realization is still in the future. The new buildings of the City College in New York — another Gothic group, in gray stone and white terra-cotta (George B. Post) — constitute another notable work of striking originality and vigor of design. In the South, the rebuilding and enlargement of the University of Virginia — the earliest example, by the way, of a monumentally planned university group in this country — and the measures taken by the University of the South to secure a comprehensive plan for future building, are evidences of the spread of this new conception of architectural propriety. Amherst College has meanwhile placed the future development of its beautiful grounds and buildings in the hands of a special committee of experts, among whom are Mr. C. F. McKim and Mr. Daniel Burnham.

The Gothicists, however, are not in control of all the universities; and Columbia, like the University of California, refuses to be diverted from the path of a more classical development. The Morningside Heights are at present a scene of great activity, and the students of the School of Architecture of Columbia University have about them obJcet-lessons in modern construction which should be of great practical value. Two great dormitories (McKim, Mead, & White), a noble chapel from plans by Howells and Stokes, and a building for the School of Mines, by A. W. Brunner, are now in process of erection, and ground has been broken for the much-needed building for the College. All these are of the most solid and thorough construction, and carry perceptibly toward realization the great *plan d'ensemble* of the architects for the whole university group. Plans have been drawn, though not yet finally adopted in detail, for the Barnard College group, to be erected on the property given to the college a year or two ago, south of the present building and adjoining Columbia University on the west. Union Theological Seminary is about to build close to Barnard on Claremont Avenue, and thus a most extensive and imposing group of educational buildings will soon cover a large part of the historic battlefield of Harlem Heights.

Meanwhile, Johns Hopkins University, of Baltimore, has adopted for its proposed new buildings an admirable plan by Parker and Thomas, with Manning Brothers as landscape artists; and the vast group of buildings for the new Carnegie Institute at Pittsburg has been entrusted to Mr. H. F. Hornbostel. Both of these awards were made as the result of important competitions. The designs in both cases will follow Renaissance precedents.

The good work of library construction goes on apace, thanks in large part to the Pactolian stream which issues from that wonderful migratory source located now at Skibo Castle and now at Fifth Avenue and Ninety-first Street, New York, and which pours its golden deposit now upon bookless wastes in town and country, and now into the empty treasuries of the smaller colleges. The architectural influence of Mr. Carnegie's admirable library benefactions has been considerable, and has been almost uniformly salutary. The modest size of the majority of the libraries recently erected, upon the principle of the multiplication of branches, which Mr. Carnegie agrees with most librarians in encouraging, has by no means prevented their receiving dignified architectural treatment; and there has been developed in their design a well-marked and interesting type of building, which is equally recognizable whether treated in the so-called Greek, Roman, or Renaissance styles; that is, with details suggested by or borrowed from those styles.

Among the more or less important central libraries recently opened may be mentioned the remarkably dignified Ryle Memorial building of the Danforth Public Library at Paterson, New Jersey (Brite and Bacon; Henry Bacon, successor). The great Public Library of New York, to which reference was made in the last review (Jannary-March, 1904), is beginning to display something of its size and final form; but the fence and the scaffoldings about it still forbid any final judgment as to its merit compared with the original design. As is well known, an immense amount of study has been bestowed upon the design since the original competition; and it will be interesting to observe whether the resulting refinement of detail will have been obtained at the expense, as some fear, of the loss of some of the vigor and effectiveness of the original design. There is no question, however, that the building will be a stately and beautiful monument, a new and notable adornment to the city; and the only subject of regret is that it lacks the setting which a great square or esplanade in front of it would afford.

Another unfinished public monument in New York, the Hall of Records, is to undergo extensive internal alterations, costing a round half million dollars. This piece of municipal mismanagement and extravagance — the alteration at great expense of a still unfinished building, whose erection has been so leisurely that there is no possible excuse for late and costly after-thoughts — illustrates the irresponsible way in which our borough authorities are permitted to manage important public enterprises.

In pleasing contrast to the helter-skelter inefficiency of the usual municipal methods in architectural matters stands the administration of the Federal Supervising Architect's office. Not many years ago, our federal architectural enterprises were conducted in a way to excite either ridicule or disgust, according to one's temperament; while under conditions now existing, as administered by the present incumbent, Mr. James Knox Taylor,[1] they are models of efficient management and usually also of excellent design. The new Custom House in New York, by Mr. Cass Gilbert, is rapidly approaching completion, and adds greatly to the architectural dignity of the lower end of New York, not by rivalling its crowded skyscrapers in height, but by its breadth and mass and the large scale of its parts. It bids fair to look better than the original drawings led us to expect.

A competition is announced for a new court house for Chicago, to cost four or five millions. Chicago has not been altogether fortunate in its public official buildings. It is to be hoped that this competition may produce satisfactory results; but the advertisement hardly affords all the guarantees that one could ask for as to its conduct and award. The post-office, by Mr. H. I. Cobb, is now nearing completion.

Among other important governmental buildings now under way are the new buildings for the Naval Academy at Annapolis (Ernest Flagg); the two very important and stately office-buildings for the Senate and for the House of Representatives at Washington, by Carrère and Hastings; and a number of custom-houses and post-offices in various cities, by the supervising architect, Mr. James Knox Taylor. All these are meritorious and praiseworthy edifices, and though all are not equal in merit, yet each, at least, is a conscientious and dignified design, solidly built and not unworthy of the State or nation which is erecting it. The competition for the Wisconsin State capitol, won by Mr. Cass Gilbert with a most excellent design, has been repudiated by the State authorities; a most disgraceful and unhappy performance, the outcome of which it is not easy to foresee, but which can hardly fail to bring grave dis-

---

[1] Mr. Taylor is himself among those who most warmly acknowledge the reforms instituted by his predecessor, Mr. William Martin Aiken.

credit on the State.   Such performances are happily becoming increasingly rare.

Turning from official to commercial architecture, the most conspicuous and important enterprises now on foot, judged both by their cost
and by their relation to the problem of municipal improvement, are the
three great railway terminals for which the excavations are now in
progress — the new Pennsylvania terminal and the reconstruction on a
vastly enlarged scale of the Grand Central Station, both in New York,
and the new Union Passenger Station in Washington.   The first-named
undertaking, which brings the Pennsylvania into Manhattan and abol-
ishes the annoyance of ferrying across the North River, will cost, with
its approaches and tunnels, fifty millions of dollars.   The vast excavations between Thirtieth and Thirty-second Streets and Eighth and
Ninth Avenues look like the work of some city-destroying cataclysm,
and give no suggestion as yet of the impressive and monumental structure which is to be erected from the plans of McKim, Mead, & White.

The works for the Central terminal at Forty-second Street have not
yet disturbed the "old" station erected in 1871, and partially rebuilt a
few years ago; but the preparatory excavations are on a scale second
only to that of the Pennsylvania terminal, and far more difficult because
of the necessity for maintaining uninterrupted the present train service.
The drawings for this terminal, exhibited a year ago, are somewhat disappointing in their handling of scale; but the architects, Messrs. Warren and Wetmore, have nevertheless produced a most interesting and a
broadly monumental design.

The station at Washington will be another conspicuous civic monument; a noble edifice of white marble, to cost, with its approaches,
eight millions of dollars.   It will constitute the first direct step toward
the realization of the plan of the Improvement Commission for the embellishment of the national capital and the correction of its plan.   New
Orleans is also to have a new and greatly improved railway terminal.

Another important, though less extensive, architectural enterprise undertaken by the railways is the new Lackawanna and Hoboken Ferry
terminal in Hoboken, erected jointly by the ferry and the railway company, from designs by Kenneth Murchison.   The problem of ferryhouse
architecture is one of the most difficult that can be imagined, and Mr.
Murchison's elegant structure of steel and copper, with its central clock
tower, is a very interesting and meritorious effort to solve it.   The municipalization of the Staten Island Ferry brought out a pair of admirable
designs by Messrs. Carrère & Hastings and Snelling & Potter for new

ferry and railway terminals on Staten Island; and it is a pity that the present city administration deemed it necessary to cut the appropriation to such an extent as to injure seriously the completeness as well as the elegance of the plans as finally adopted.

In other parts of the field of commercial architecture there is nothing very noteworthy to chronicle. New York and Chicago continue to build skyscrapers, and Mr. Burnham's Railway Exchange Building in Chicago is a rational if not beautiful embodiment — to most eyes it is an ugly one — of the practical, downright, uncompromisingly utilitarian treatment of the office-building, which so widely prevails in Chicago. It is meanwhile interesting to note that, in New York at least, a halt is being called on the skyscraping rivalry, and banks and trust companies are now with increasing frequency erecting buildings of but one or two apparent stories in height, with main cornices not over forty or fifty feet from the pavement. The buildings erected by Speyer & Co. and the National Park Bank in New York are among recent examples.

One of the most significant and interesting movements affecting American architecture to-day is one not by any means wholly architectural, but which leans so heavily upon the arm of architecture as to deserve prominent mention in a review of architectural progress. It is the movement for municipal improvement, and especially for the artistic improvement of our cities, which has taken so strong a hold upon the public-spirited citizens of Washington, New York, Baltimore, Boston, and many other cities. While this movement is primarily civic in character, and wins its support and success largely, and perhaps chiefly, from men and women who have no professional connection with the arts, it is in every case sure to become sooner or later a movement for better architecture and for a more monumental and artistic treatment of buildings, thoroughfares, and municipal utilities.

In Washington, the plans of the Improvement Commission, appointed two or three years ago by Congress, have become an active issue; and the first fight with the governmental Philistines, who proposed to destroy at the outset the lines laid down by the commission for the Mall, by projecting the front of the new Agricultural Department building sixty feet into the Mall, has resulted in a victory for good sense and for the Commission. Cleveland is making progress with the new group of public buildings, following the plans of the commission (consisting of Messrs. A. W. Brunner, J. M. Carrère, and D. H. Burnham) whose report attracted so much attention a couple of years ago. Much of the ground has been cleared, and good progress has been made with the erection of the new post-office and custom-house, the first of the new buildings proposed, a stately design by Mr. Brunner. St. Louis also, a city conspicuously lacking in anything like a civic centre, is now considering the report of a semi-official improvement committee, of which Mr. Manran and Mr. W. S. Eames, among others, are members. Two alternative plans have been submitted, both taking the present City Hall as the starting-point and balancing it by a court house, while adjacent to these are to be grouped a historical museum, a hall of records, a public library, an art gallery, and other public buildings. The two schemes differ chiefly in the extent of parking and in other details of the arrangement of the proposed civic group.

Denver and Los Angeles are two other Western cities which have taken up the question of civic improvement and appointed commissions to report to the municipal authorities. The movement for the embellishment of American cities is confined to no one region, but promises to transform the aspect of American cities in all parts of the Union within the next twenty years.

In New York, where the vastness of the city and of its varied and often conflicting commercial and real-estate interests make the problem of municipal improvement one of peculiar difficulty, the first step toward architectural regeneration lies in the reformation of the channels of transportation. This fact, clearly brought out in the conferences initiated by the Municipal Art Society three years ago, which were among the contributing factors toward the organization of Mayor McClellan's Improvement Commission, dominates the preliminary report of that commission, made public some months since. This interesting document, a monument of patient, broad-minded, and intelligent study of a vast and complex subject, presents only minor features of a directly architectural character, such as the suggested remodelling of the Battery Park, so as to make it a monumental entrance to the city from the bay. The report, however, in its suggestions of new avenues, plazas, circles, bridge approaches, and the like, pictures a New York fitted to receive whatever architectural embellishments the enterprise and skill of citizens and architects may provide — a New York intelligently planned for the worthy display of its monuments, as well as for convenience in travel.

My last architectural review in THE FORUM was written while the Louisiana Purchase Exposition was still in the future, though the buildings were nearly completed. It is now a thing of the past and has already nearly faded from our thoughts. This rapid passing out of thought and almost out of memory of the greatest of all international exhibitions stands in marked contrast to the persistence with which the White City at Chicago lingered in the popular recollection, and was talked of and written about and recalled at every opportunity for several years after the last of its temporary palaces of staff had vanished from sight. The Columbian Exhibition took a powerful hold upon the popular imagination; the St. Louis Fair did not, although it celebrated a historic event of the most momentous national significance, and emphasized this significance by every resource and expedient of symbolism in the nomenclature, sculpture, and decoration of the fair. The war in the East no doubt to some extent accounts for this eclipse of a really stupendous subject of interest; but it explains it only in part. The chief reason for the failure of the St. Louis Fair to touch the imagination and hold the interest of the American people commensurably with the Columbian Fair is to be found in its architecture. Not that the individual buildings of the later enterprise were greatly inferior to those of the earlier ones, though few would venture to claim that they were their equals; but the effect of *ensemble* at St. Louis was not to be compared with that at Chicago.

Above all, it lacked the advantage of novelty. It was a third or fourth edition of the story first told with consummate skill and prodigious success at Chicago, and repeated with variations more or less fundamental at Omaha and Buffalo. Most of those who visited the Chicago Fair had never before seen, had never dreamed of, the splendor of stately colonnades and monumental courts surrounded by palaces and adorned with statues and formal gardens, canals, and monumental bridges. Those who visited St. Louis had many of them seen the Columbian Fair, or the Omaha or Pan-American exhibitions, or the Place de la Concorde and the Louvre, or were at least familiar with pictures of these. The difference in the resulting impression of the two fairs upon their visitors was great, and the later fair suffered by the contrast. Moreover, it was too big, too scattered, and poorly maintained; it began to look shabby before it was half through, and was very ragged around the edges — all which tended to blunt the charm of its best portions.

Now the Lewis and Clark Exhibition has opened in distant Oregon, treading close on the heels of the Missouri enterprise. Is the fair idea being overworked? Time will show. The Portland fair is wisely made regional rather than universal in character; and its architecture — chiefly in variations upon Spanish-American models — has not been exploited as its chief attraction. Probably no future fair, national or international, can ever have the same influence on American architecture as did the

Columbian at Chicago; and whatever is done in this line in the future must be treated predominantly and primarily as an amusement park of transcendent beauty, if it is to make any deep impression upon the popular imagination. And to do this it must keep well within the bounds of moderation as to size.

Architecture in Europe to-day presents no such spectacle of widespread and free activity as in the United States; but it offers many points of interest, particularly in the struggle between the classic and romantic schools, as exemplified by tradition and the Art Nouveau. The comparison of what is going on in France, Germany, and Austria with what our own architects are doing is by no means always, if at all, to the advantage of the older countries. We may well thank our stars that there has been no occasion here for such a reaction against tradition as has resulted in the perpetration of the atrocities of architectural design which the more rabid partisans of "New Art" are inflicting upon Vienna, Berlin, Stuttgart, and other cities. Restless, formless, and without principle, such works can be pardoned only as being possibly the feverish creations of a stage of transition to something which will be more reasonable and conscientious, though still emancipated from the fetters of a rigid official tradition.

The recent suburban houses, or "villas," of Germany, though touched by this new influence, are less eccentric than the more ambitious city buildings, and are often picturesque and even pleasing, at least in general mass. In France there appears to be nothing new of special interest in the field of architecture. Competitions are announced at frequent intervals for town halls, hospitals, abattoirs, markets, etc.; and French architects have been particularly fortunate in winning foreign competitions — a cathedral for Patras, Greece; a great club-house for Madrid; a group of state legislative and administrative buildings for Peru, at Lima, etc. In the modern French work the elegance of plan is the chief merit, and is far more praiseworthy generally than the exterior treatment, which, though usually well proportioned and well studied in detail, too often lacks originality and interest.

A. D. F. HAMLIN.

THE EDUCATIONAL OUTLOOK.

THE people of New York have declared themselves emphatically in favor of the so-called "fads and frills" in the elementary school curriculum. This is probably the first time that parents have been given an opportunity, on a large scale, to record their wishes as to what their children shall be taught in the common schools. It marks the beginning of a return to the principle that the parents are primarily and finally responsible for the education of their children. The referendum in common-school affairs is a most sensible innovation. For its inauguration we are indebted to the political dilettanteism of Superintendent Maxwell's opponents. This is not the first time that tactical blundering has served as the instrument for ushering in an important reform.

The original contention in New York was for a shorter work-day in the first school years. The only tenable consideration, the welfare of the children, was not the point of departure. As explained in this department six months ago, the real purpose of the seemingly humanitarian move was to redeem Mayor McClellan's promise of a full school day for every pupil in the system by officially declaring the time allotted to half-day classes to constitute a full day. The issue was silver-plated with protestations that five hours of scholastic work is too much for children in the earlier years of the course. The thinness of the plating, however, became apparent when Superintendent Maxwell retorted that it would be unwise to deprive the children of a portion of the beneficial supervision of the school and turn them into the streets. He also contended that the work laid out for the first school years could not be accomplished in less time.

This gave the "agin'-the-administration" forces a new clew. They readjusted their halos of humanitarianism and declared that their chief anxiety was to rescue the poor children from under the cruel burden of "fads and frills" with which the superintendent had overloaded the school programme. They declared that the mental strain of the present elementary curriculum was too great for the tender minds, and that a curtailment of the school day was demanded by humane considerations.

As long as they confined their remarks to generalities they were fairly safe. But when they began to point out what they considered useless teaching, their championship of the little children's cause began to assume a quixotic appearance. Mr. Tompkins completed the desolation by rushing to their support with a picturesque attack on Mr. Maxwell, upon the floor of the New York State Assembly. The trend of the discussion came more and more under the sway of personal animosity. The only point seemed to be to discredit Superintendent Maxwell. He was held up to scorn as the originator of all the best things to be found in the elementary school curriculum; some even went so far as to charge him with being the author of a poetical stanza written, or supposed to be written, by Oliver Wendell Holmes. The *opera-bouffe* stage has never exhibited a more amusing performance.

Once the issue of "essentials" versus "fads and frills" was raised, the field was won for the superintendent. The tables were turned. It was shown that the actual waste of time is in pushing instruction in rote work beyond the fatigue point, and that the three R's are the real fads in most schools. The orating demagogues were put on the defensive by being compelled to demonstrate that their antiquarian notions of elementary education supplied the needs of the times. When hard pressed they fell back on the old plea that the children's health could not endure the pressure of the many subjects which the modern educational curriculum had gathered in. Here again they met their Waterloo. For the very studies attacked as useless were shown to afford relief from the ordinary drudgery of the class-room and to give healthful movement and relaxation, besides being useful and making for culture. So sure felt the opponents of Mr. Maxwell of the plaudits of the gallery that they paid no heed to these explanations. At this point the "Globe" undertook an extensive inquiry among the parents throughout the city, and proved by thousands of votes returned that the people did not want a return to the meagre school programmes of the past, but wished their children to have the best that modern education could supply. Never before have constructive manual work, singing, art instruction, and physical culture received so emphatic an indorsement by the lay people. Only about twelve per cent could be induced to give encouragement to the anti-faddists.

It was to be foreseen that the three-hours-and-a-half school-day would not find favor with the people of the city. Social and economic conditions are such that the children as a rule are best off at school. But now that the clouds of agitation have rolled away something should be done to reduce the strain which the sustaining of attention imposes upon the pupils. The strain actually exists and the health of the children is affected by it. In the early years of school, three hours a day are ample for systematic instruction. Moreover, the children must have their share of freedom from schoolmasterly restraint and relief from the feeling of scholastic responsibility. At the same time, the children need at least five hours of educational care and social activity of a thoroughly moral nature. A wise reorganization of the course of study and the tact of the teacher can do much to meet the hygienic demands of the child mind. Where the course is too exacting, there can be no satisfactory solution.

The New York "Evening Post," in its issue of May 26, published an editorial article showing that the difficulties will never be satisfactorily mastered until the various points involved are thoroughly investigated and trustworthy statistics secured and analyzed. It is to be regretted that the writer of the article in question failed to give due credit for his suggestions, which are mainly the revamping of a contribution to the educational columns of the same paper. The discovery of an important scientific clew to the solution of a subtle technical problem ought to be treated with as much consideration as is accorded to new ideas in other departments of research. "The Post" writes:

On both topics, the enrichment of the course by all manner of recreative subjects and the proper length of the school-day, there is abundant confusion of counsel and a paucity of trustworthy data. For example, it does not follow that because basketry, or singing, or lathe work, or sewing are desirable in themselves and a delightful occupation for children, these subjects can be added safely to a course already reasonably full. And it follows just as little that, because poorer children should be off the street, a school-day of two sessions is, for other reasons also, better than a school-day of one. In fine, the whole matter is greatly confused by the injection of humanitarian and alleged sociological considerations into a problem essentially educational. Not that these considerations would not have weight if the case were made out. But, instead of statistics of promotion, truancy, and discipline under whole-time and part-time conditions, we have merely individual expressions of opinion.

For practical guidance, then, we are reduced to the experience of other States or countries, and to the study of results in our own schools. The former we have in abundance; the latter fails us almost entirely. . . .

Only comprehensive statistics are of any value. . . . In this matter we are neglecting a most instructive opportunity for experimental demonstration. Necessity has forced upon the city a system under which many thousand children attend school only for a single session. A statistical study of promotion, truancy, and discipline among this exceptional class — and the materials for such an investigation must be abundant — could hardly fail to settle a problem now merely touched at the rim.

How Mr. Maxwell believes that the problem of rationalizing the course of instruction can be solved, may be gathered from an address he delivered before the New York University School of Pedagogy on June 2. He declared that the trained teacher must be able to make a proper selection of topics for study. The difficulty of managing the course of study can be considerably reduced, he believes, by improved methods of teaching. Furthermore, he advised the elimination of unimportant and unessential details. These, no doubt, are suggestions well worth heeding. They imply at the same time a willingness on the superintendent's part to allow efficient teachers a greater measure of freedom in the choice and arrangement of lesson topics than they have had heretofore. If the supervising officers share these views of Mr. Maxwell and will encourage trained and experienced teachers to weed out whatever they may regard as wasteful in the prescribed studies, the school programme will soon lose its formidable aspect and the worry of children and teachers will be much reduced.

But the removal of rubbish alone will not solve the whole difficulty. One great trouble with the present curriculum is its lack of organization. There is no generally accepted standard for determining relative values in studies and lesson topics. Accordingly, each subject in the course stands out as a separate something. Correlation under such conditions is very unsatisfactory. One tangible central idea, or two or three leading principles precisely stated for the guidance of teachers in the choice, arrangement, and teaching of the numerous topics in the programme, would bring order into the present chaos. Here pedagogical ingenuity may well apply itself and transform the curriculum into a living organism. This is not the whole solution, but it is a most important matter to settle.

What sensible correlation of the scholastic work around a vital, healthy, and practical central interest will do for a school is well illustrated at Hyannis, Massachusetts. The State Normal School located there has connected with it a training-school which is really the local common school. It is the work of the latter school which is here particularly referred to. The course covers the ordinary eight years of the elementary school, and the programme is much the same as elsewhere. The distinguishing feature is the method of correlating all work around garden activities as the central interest. Principal Baldwin's experiment has been very successful. I had heard much of the way in which the practical questions of every-day life were considered in the classroom, and visited the school recently to get a closer view of the scheme and to understand more fully the rationale of the departure.

Hyannis stands for a new thought in education. Social efficiency is the dominant aim. The working principle is an economic one. Industrial considerations are frankly kept to the fore. The home is the central subject in everything — not the home of "me and my wife, my son John and his wife, we four and no more," but Hyannis, the Cape, Massachusetts, the United States. Hyannis is first. What will make Hyannis a better place to live in? What will add to her prosperity? What is her relation to the rest of the world? How does she serve mankind? — these are the questions around which the instruction turns.

The school garden, with its mind-stirring, body-strengthening, spirit-nourishing activities, is the starting-point and correlating centre. From this basis instruction starts out, and to this it returns whenever it can do so without resort to pedagogic artifice. Practical activities — and what more healthful, useful, and educative activities can there be than gardening? — these are the correlating forces. Here we have an objective something to start from. The children are on home-ground and are kept busy from the very beginning. The thought that they are enrolled in the list of producers is before them from the first day in school. The work they are doing impels thought of the product, of the relation of their task to the world in the future, and so on.

"Before the child enters school and after he leaves it, in all times and in all places, the activities of life furnish the real basis or centre, and the three R's are only accessories. If the school is to be a natural preparation for life through living, common sense seems to demand that the methods in school shall correspond with the methods outside of school." This is the logic which Principal Baldwin applies to the organization and work of his school. There is nothing forced in his correlation scheme. As the architect, or the financier, or the farmer makes his work the centre of his thought and activity, and arranges his life accordingly, without permitting himself to be wholly absorbed by his business, so the child gardener at school is occupied with garden work as his chief practical interest around which his activities and studies turn, but without limiting him wholly to the one thing. The garden interest simply serves to give point and cohesion to otherwise disconnected lesson topics, and reduces the curriculum to some sort of order. The child learns to understand the need and the practical use of the three R's, and is constantly called upon to apply in a practical way whatever he has learned. How arithmetic, language, and the lessons out of the manual-training class are drawn into service may be appreciated from these few brief extracts from the diary of a child in the third school-year:

April 6, 1903.—We went out into the garden to-day and measured it. It was 128 feet long and sixty feet wide. We used the surveyor's chain. Each link is a foot long. . . . Our chain is fifty feet long.

Friday, April 10, 1903.—Yesterday afternoon we went out into our garden, and we measured and marked off the long paths in our garden. We measured with the surveyor's chain, and drove stakes at the corners and stretched the twine. We finished the long paths and began to stretch the twine around the short paths.

Tuesday, April 14, 1903.—Last Friday we used the surveyor's chain to measure each plot; we drove stakes at each corner.

Yesterday we took the surveyor's chain and tested everything that we did last Friday.

Wednesday, May 27, 1903.—Yesterday some of the children thinned their lettuce because it was so thick. Some pulled up the worm-eaten radishes. Mary, Harold, Barzillai, and I went over to the manual training-room, and cut laths and placed stakes to hold up the peas.

The eighth-year pupils assume the responsibility of looking after the accounts of the school-garden community. In this way they learn bookkeeping, business forms, and the practical side of advanced arithmetic. Orders sent out for seeds and garden tools are recorded, entries are made of material received, bills are booked and the originals filed, statements of vegetables sold are sent out, outstanding debts are collected, and the cash and checks are deposited at the bank in regular form, and so on. The activities cover all the forms needed by the average citizen in every-day business life, and a practical knowledge of them is acquired in a perfectly natural way as part of the garden work of the pupils. A few selections from the diary kept by an eighth-year scholar may illustrate the scope of the outdoor work :

April 13, 1904.—To-day we went out into the garden to see it ploughed. The garden is about 180 feet long and fifty feet wide, in the form of a rectangle.

The garden was ploughed on the sides first, because it was higher in the middle.

The plough had two cutting blades. One of them was a knife which cut the weeds, and behind this came the share, which threw the soil on only one side.

The other parts of the plough are the wheel in front of the plough and the handles to steer the plough.

The plough ploughed the ground about eight inches deep, and the furrows were about eighteen inches apart.

April 15, 1904.—The boys went out into the garden and hoed the earth level. The boys were placed about two yards apart.

April 18, 1904.—The boys finished hoeing and began raking the garden in order to get it more level.

April 20, 1904.—The boys finished raking and commenced lining off.

April 21, 1904.—The boys and girls finished lining of plots.

April 22, 1904.—The boys and girls drew lots for the plots that they were to have.

April 25, 1904.—The boys and girls raked the stones from their plots and lined off for planting.

May 13, 1904.—The boys and girls went into the garden and planted. I planted one row of beans about one inch deep and two rows of beets about one-half inch deep.

May 16, 1904.—The boys and girls went into the garden.

May 24, 1904.—We went into the garden and planted flower seeds. First we raked the soil, and then we smoothed it off with a piece of a lath. Then we lined off and underneath the line we dug the earth up and then smoothed it off. We then made a drill about one-half inch deep, and then we planted our seeds in the drill. After we had covered the seeds over with the soil we patted it down hard, so that the rain would not wash the seeds out of the ground.

May 25, 1904.—We went into the garden. The boys lined off one plot and made six circles with a thirty-six-inch diameter and about one and a half feet deep. After that the boys got some dressing and mixed it with the soil. We then planted about ten cucumber seeds in the hole, about two inches deep. Then we covered the seeds with the soil, and put four sticks there to show where the cucumbers had been planted. After that we watered the cucumbers.

May 31, 1904.—I went into the garden and planted cucumbers. I measured one yard from the corner line and one yard in. Then I made a circle with a thirty-six-inch diameter, and dug down into the ground about one foot and a half. Then I got some dressing and mixed it with the soil that I had dug up. I then filled the hole nearly full with soil mixed with the dressing. After that I planted about ten seeds in the hole, and put about one inch and a half of soil over them and patted it down with the hoe.

June 6, 1904.—We went into the garden and cultivated our beets. I cultivated my beets and beans by hoeing the ground up around them and taking care not to hit the roots.

From gardening to household activities and interest in village improvement the transition is perfectly simple and natural. There is nothing forced in any of the correlations. The spices and other treasures of the kitchen cupboard relate the home to far-away countries. The geography lessons derive increasing interest from that fact, and remove the study of peoples of other lands from the list of things apart. The literature and songs of the great out-of-doors and of simple personal relationships have their place in the scheme. To the children on the Cape, history is a home atmosphere. Village improvement and the beautifying of the schoolrooms and the homes open the doors to the fine arts. The best feature of it all is the ease with which the different subjects of study are interrelated. The child is not made to pass through so many separate subjects with so many minutes allowed for each, but all the various things come to him as one interest — home gardening — radiating in many directions. Mr. Baldwin describes the significance of his working plans in these words:

Our work is, in a way, a reaction against the extreme organization of the modern city school. It has seemed to us as though the very marked modern tendency toward combination, organization, and systemization — the so-called factory system — has been getting a firmer and firmer grip upon our graded schools. All the in-

dividuality and life is being systematized out of our children, and they are becoming mere automatons, sitting, for the most part, quietly at their desks, and moving,
when they do move, together at the tap of the bell. Now we desire to change all
this. Our motto is, "A live boy in a live school." We are attempting to provide
for some physical activity, such as the normal child demands, and then to base the
other lines of work upon this.

The Hyannis school has no special periods set aside for formal lessons in morals and manners. The garden activities are continually
giving rise to ethical problems which require consideration. By attending to these matters when the need of them is felt most keenly, the
correlation of ethic lessons with the rest of the curriculum becomes easy
and natural. Principal Baldwin cites these examples as illustrative of
the proceeding:

One boy raked the débris from his plot over into the plot of his neighbor. One
boy was not willing to do his share of work on the class plot. One little girl was
sick, and several boys and girls vied with each other in taking care of her little garden during her absence. All of the above furnished opportunities for live discussions, the conclusion of which crystallized into actions. The toad was found to be
a helper in ridding the garden of insect enemies, and the whole attitude of the children toward toads was changed. One day two of the neighbor's hens escaped from
their yard and scratched out some fine pansy plants which had just been transplanted.
The children were very much disturbed. Their teacher quietly discussed the whole
matter with them, allowed them to appoint a committee to wait upon the neighbor,
and proceeded to lay a good foundation for the consideration of a similar question
when in the future these same children might be the trespassers and the neighbor
the aggrieved party. On one occasion, some melons which the children had been
raising with great care were stolen, and they were very glad to discuss the rights of
property and felt keenly the desirability of laws which protect the rights of the
owners of property.

Whether the Hyannis idea will appeal strongly enough to the larger
cities to be adopted as a suggestion for transforming existing courses of
study from articulated skeletons into living and wholesome organisms
remains to be seen. Something must be done to bring order into the
present chaos. Garden work may be out of the question in the crowded
population centres, although Miss Rector has demonstrated in her school
on Rivington Street that a school garden may be a reality and a thing
of joy and beauty even in the most densely populated quarter of the
New York City ghetto. There is no reason, however, why other constructive work closely related to practical life should not be made the
starting-point, centre, and instrument of the correlation of scholastic
activities. Dr. James Parton Haney, the director of manual training in
the New York City schools, mapped out such a plan before the convention of school superintendents in March. The complaints of overcrowded

school programmes will never cease until a proper adjustment of what ought to be done and what can be done is followed by a wise organic unification of the curriculum.

The problems in their logical order would appear to be these: (1) What ought to be done? (2) What can be done? (3) How can we attain what it is possible to attain? Educational philosophy, modified by reasonable deference to the wishes of parents, and with due regard for prevailing conditions, must formulate the guiding principles and specify from time to time what ought to be done. Statistical research and the analysis of results will determine what can be done. Pedagogical technique and common-sense in indissoluble union will settle the best methods of procedure. A model course of study must satisfy the just demands from these various directions. Ultimately everything depends upon the personality, expertness, and tact of the teacher.

The educational importance of the teacher's efficiency is slowly gaining popular recognition. In every school system of any importance there is now a technical examination of those who desire to teach. Most of the larger cities have, in addition to this wise precaution, established graded salary lists with special encouragement to teachers who perfect themselves professionally by a continued study of the history, science, and art of their work. Competitive examinations, almost exclusively theoretical and in writing, are the chief instruments by which the authorities expect to determine the relative superiority of merit. The inadequacy of the tests has subjected them to more or less opposition on the part of teachers who insist that length of service and the practical results of their instruction should be the determining factors.

There is no doubt that an inquiry into the professional reading and attendance at lectures on pedagogy and allied subjects may be supposed to supply important evidence of the teacher's interest in his work and also show something of the development of his professional judgment. But the fact is that it very frequently does no such thing. To begin with, it is very difficult at the present time to find examiners enough to go around who can distinguish between memoriter acquisition and the results of circumspect pedagogic judgment. Next, the literature and lectures provided for the special benefit of teachers range from the veriest rubbish to the most careful expert treatment of technical questions. Neither teachers nor examiners can be uniformly trusted to choose the best. It is a sad fact that an educational paper may be utterly divested of professional standards and supply almost nothing but chaff, with occasionally a grain of wisdom mixed in by accident, and still be as likely to be chosen by teachers as a guide as the most ably conducted periodical with exalted educational ideals and expert discernment back of it. The same applies to lectures. This condition is slowly changing for the better. But meanwhile examinations are being held which not infrequently work an injustice to teachers. The question as to how to measure the value and efficiency of a teacher's work must be settled in some more rational way before merit lists can be entitled to universal respect.

Pedagogy has been, and still is, too exclusively devoted to speculation, and the more direct investigation of realities is neglected. Hypotheses are made to take the place of facts, prophecy is called proof, pseudo-psychological assertion is substituted for tangible results. Education has been treated as if it were something to argue about rather than something to do. Instead of analyzing actualities, educators have spent their strength on the devising, discussing, and disposing of theories. The humble problems of the daily school routine have not infrequently been looked upon with an air of disdain. Such a question as how to teach long division has been considered a shockingly improper one to ask of a professor of pedagogy; but topics like "Hypnotic suggestion as a factor in school government" or "Apperceptive functioning and sensory-motor reaction" have served as eminently respectable excuses for whiling away an ambitious teacher's leisure time.

Teachers cannot thrive on moonshine. To be sure, neither shall men live by bread alone; but they must have bread. Much of the work of the teacher is necessarily of a mechanical nature. A teacher's success depends in no small measure on the skill with which this mechanical part is handled. Much time may be wasted here. Precious material may be spoiled. Hence it is important that the mechanics of teaching should be considered in detail and the various processes thoroughly analyzed in order to make instruction effective and to reduce waste to a minimum. Time-saving devices for calling up and dismissing classes, for fixing word forms in the mind, for correcting composition exercises, and for other time-consuming activities are no less helpful to the teacher than are devices for mixing colors, for applying the brush, and for retouching pictures to a painter. A teacher who has mastered the little things of the school routine can give more time and strength to the big things. That is a simple fact worth remembering with all its logical consequences. Mechanical perfection in the minor activities is, as a rule, underrated in examining a teacher's work.

There are, of course, many ways of estimating value, but there is only one way of determining efficiency. Value is something relative. It depends on the appraiser. Think how much the arbutus means to the lover of nature in New England, and the primrose to the lover of nature in old England. Then compare this valuation with that of him of whom we know that

> A primrose by a river's brim
> A yellow primrose was to him,
> And it was nothing more.

However, pedagogically considered, there are certain fixed standards for rating the values of teachers' working plans and teaching processes. Valuable to whom? is the question here, too; but "to whom" refers no longer to Messrs. Thomas, Richard, and Henry, and their feminine counterparts, but to the present and future social relationships of the pupil. These relations may be classed as follows: (1) To those with whom the pupil lives, the family and friends; (2) to economic society; (3) to the state; (4) to religious society; (5) to mankind in general.

The value which the parents and personal friends of the pupil place upon the teacher's work is of prime importance. The school represents, or should represent, a centre maintained for the purpose of meeting the educational responsibilities rightly belonging to the parents, but whose conscientious fulfilment is of vital importance to economic society and to the state. This means, of course, the value which parents would ideally place upon the teacher's work, the value they would place upon it if they but knew. It is well to remember that parents are ever ready to give good gifts unto their children. They look upon their children as their ideal selves, for whom they covet the best things of life. It is the business of educators to make them see what is best. The value of a teacher's work to the parents and friends of the pupils may be thus in no small degree determined by the opinion those parents and friends have of it. If a teacher has failed to convince parents that what he has done has been best for their children, he has failed in an essential point.

In the past the teacher's work has been too far removed from the world's activities to reveal much bearing upon industrial progress. Some teachers have seemed to take pride in keeping the education of children as little related to the practical affairs of every-day life as they possibly could. The school has been too often turned into a cloister for the pursuit of unrelated branches of knowledge. Reading has been taught for the sake of reading, writing for the sake of writing, 'rithmetic for the sake of 'rithmetic, geography for the sake of lists of useless names.   Is it any wonder that the world could not see the use of all this, and concluded that if teachers liked to do that sort of thing they were well paid in being permitted to do it?   But the change has come.   Economic society has begun to realize how much it ought to be interested in the work of teachers.   In fact, there is a growing belief in education as a wise economic investment.   Through the boy or girl receiving the education the country is enriched.

This new thought is working mighty changes in the attitude of the people toward the schools.   The frequently recurring discussions about the overcrowding of the curriculum, about "fads and frills," about waste in the elementary school course, and similarly irritating topics, show the trend.   People are no longer afraid to suggest that the teacher must heed the demands of practical life.   In sooth, leading teachers themselves are heard advocating a remodelling of the course of study on the basis of practical economic considerations.   The cry of "commercialism" has lost its withering effect.   The people have awakened to the fact that schools which give no heed to the needs of a workaday world are withholding from their pupils a most precious equipment for the battle of life.   When the first beginning was made in applying this new standard of appraising the teacher's work, the examiner's findings were minimized by cunningly devised fables about "character formation," "mental development," "harmonious cultivation of powers, and so on."   Whatever to common-sense appeared as a dissipation of time and energy was cloaked in pedagogical terms and paraded as a means of fashioning the mind.   But this pretence no longer awes any one outside of educational circles.   The mind may be developed just as effectively with useful activities as with artificial devices that are of no earthly service to anybody.

There is, of course, a legitimate and important place for the economically useless in the general plan of education; but this also serves definite purposes.   Anyway, it does not influence the fact that the value of a teacher's work depends to a considerable extent upon the degree in which it meets the needs of economic society.   Adapting a dictum by President Eliot of Harvard University, the demands resulting from these needs may, perhaps, be summarized as follows: (1) The child must be supplied with the elementary knowledge which practical life expects every normally endowed adult to possess; (2) he must be taught to think clearly; (3) he must be given the power to express himself with precision; (4) his intelligence and manual skill should be developed as liberally as time and conditions permit. Still more briefly stated, the duty of every teacher is to do his best that his pupils may become self-supporting participators in the world's work.

The state, too, takes a hand in rating the value of a teacher. The results it particularly expects of the school are that the children acquire respect for law and order and right views of personal liberty, and that some day they may share intelligently, and in a patriotic spirit, in the duties and privileges of citizenship. A teacher who cannot establish respect for justice and order in his school is not fit to hold his office. Religious society as represented by the churches also has some claims to consideration in the common schools. The demands from this direction are at present almost exclusively negative, but the outlook is that some positive demands will evolve before long.

There are yet other definite lines along which the rating of a teacher may proceed. Society, as mankind in general, has a right to insist that the school shall cultivate the morals and manners of pupils. Morality, politeness, and helpfulness are three major virtues which the teacher must instil with all legitimate means at his command.

Lastly, the value of a teacher's work depends on the estimate the children now at school will place upon it when once they have attained to the age of maturity. This is really the supreme test. Nor is it beyond human ingenuity to make the test available for immediate application. The future man will certainly want to be healthy and strong. He has a right to expect his interests to open out in many directions. Pleasure in all that is beautiful, joy in intellectual pursuits, an open mind, and a contented heart — by the measure of his approach to these ideals will he judge his educators. The teacher, then, who cultivates these resources in his pupils is to that degree enhancing the value of his work.

The teacher spoken of thus far is, of course, the superintendent, special supervisor, principal, and class teacher combined in one person. He outlines the course of study and carries out its provisions. He consults the interests of the home, of economic society, of the state, of religious society, of mankind in general, and the future citizen represented in the boy now at his school desk. He tries his best to do justice to all these, and teaches accordingly. However, the modern school system has relieved the working teacher in an undue measure of the responsibility for the value of the course of study. This course is usually determined by an outside power supposed to be expert in deciding what is best. The class teacher is given prescriptions to fill. Under such a condition of things, justice would seem to demand that the teacher should be officially

6

rated wholly on the basis of the greater or lesser ability displayed in carrying out the programme outlined for him.

At the first glance, it certainly does seem as if the value of a teacher's work reflected wholly upon the superintendent, principal, and board of education, and that the teacher should be rated only by the ratio of the results obtained to the requirements established by authority. But this is inadequate reasoning. If the teacher were a mere day laborer performing purely mechanical work, the conclusion might be justifiable. But, however narrowly the teacher may be limited in the choice of studies, his duty is under all circumstances to make the most of the educational possibilities at his command. While doing the required things, he must attend also to the necessary things, and he ought to take care, as far as his opportunities and strength permit, of the desirable things. The measure of the value and efficiency of a teacher's work, accordingly, is not to be looked for in the degree in which the bare requirements of the course of study have been met. That was the test in the dark places of the past. The means consisted usually in questions devised to coax from the memory whatever had become lodged there as a result of the teachers' instruction. The attitude was that of Zophar the Naamathite, who comforted Job with the suggestion that "He hath swallowed down riches, and he shall vomit them up again." These so-called examination questions acted as a sort of emetic, inducing the pupil to bring up whatever had been fed to him in as nearly the erstwhile shape as the laws of psychological operation would permit after the lapse of time.

In those good old days, the weak teacher was as likely to make a good showing as the strong teacher; aye, not infrequently he made the better showing in examinations. The injustice of it became so glaringly evident that all examinations fell for a time into disrepute. The opinion went abroad that the value and efficiency of a teacher cannot possibly be judged by the results of his work. The pupil was entirely eliminated from consideration. With the last prop of common sense removed, educational authorities jumped from one absurdity to another in trying to fix percentages of merit upon the teachers. Books the teacher had read, lectures he had attended, papers he had subscribed for, his age, his church affiliation, his size, his looks, his voice, his father's business, his readiness to adopt or refrain from adopting popular fads — these and even more trivial considerations were given the precedence over the only one method of establishing real efficiency.

A trainer of animals is judged by what his pupils can do. It has never occurred to any one to suggest that a better way would be to rate his merit on his knowledge of zoology, geography, animal psychology, and the history of circuses. These subjects are no doubt very helpful to him, but he is judged by the result of his labors, and not by what he knows about the theory of his profession. Of course, there is an important difference between a lion tamer and a school teacher. The former, if he does not study the nature of his animals, is speedily eliminated from his profession by his watchful pupils. The teacher may live to a ripe old age even if he shrugs his shoulders at child studies. Here is one reason why the preparation of teachers should be thoroughly scrutinized before permitting them to have their names enrolled on the eligible list. But after the teacher is once set to work in the schoolroom, he can and should be measured almost wholly by the results of his practical experience. · Instead of inquiring into the teacher's power to see straight and clear, to remember important facts, to draw intelligent inferences, to express himself with precision, and to take an interest in the higher things of life, the test should rather be applied to the children: Have the children gained power in the directions here suggested? That is the chief question. The next is: How much power? The former reveals the value, the latter the efficiency of the teacher's work. The proof of the pudding is in the eating of it, and not in the chewing of the string. Conscientiousness, refinement, worthy habits, sympathy, and interest in the work are qualities that are presupposed in every dignified calling. Ability to teach is the real test. It is this which is to distinguish the teacher from the rest of the world, and the greater or less degree marks his relative merit among his colleagues.

How shall we determine what children ought to be able to do at different periods of their scholastic career? Certainly not by *a priori* agreements among educators. Dr. Rice has settled this much for all time to come. A surer way of going at the problem is by extensive investigations into the work that is actually being done. Tests must be devised which really determine degrees of power. A number of such tests have already been elaborated, and the Society of Educational Research has imposed upon itself the task of increasing their number as well as their effectiveness. By means of such tests applied on an extensive scale, it has been established beyond all reasonable doubt, for instance, that ten or fifteen minutes a day devoted for a number of years to instruction in spelling will accomplish practically as much as a considerably larger expenditure of time. The conclusion here is that a teacher consuming more than the maximum of fifteen minutes in the daily spelling period is to that degree lacking in teaching efficiency.

Or, to take another example, the investigations of the subject of arithmetic have shown that there is no appreciable gain in giving more than forty minutes a day to that branch. Other tests appear to indicate that fifty minutes a day spent in language work should represent the maximum investment of time. Frittering away of precious minutes is a serious matter in education. Hence we may feel justified in rigidly applying the time tests when measuring the efficiency of a teacher's work.

The children's power to think and express themselves, their ability to apply the knowledge acquired in the lesson period when placed in novel situations — these reveal what a teacher is worth to his pupils as an instructor. Let the official programme be what it will, this power, this ability, can be cultivated everywhere, and the degree to which it is done is the most important item in the rating of a teacher whose character is above reproach, who takes an intelligent and sympathetic interest in the welfare of his pupils, and can manage his class in an American spirit.

It were better, of course, if the teacher could be allowed a greater share than is usual at present in building up the course of study. The principal, at any rate, should have a voice in this important matter. The larger the responsibility placed upon him, the better for the school community over which he presides. He could then be held to account for the value and efficiency of the work in his school. To accomplish this he must be the supreme local educational authority, accountable only to the superintendent, whom he represents in his district. No supervisor should disturb that authority. If the principal understands that he is held responsible for the results in his school, he may be left free to exercise his own judgment in professional matters. The farmyard plan, with a pugnacious rooster jealously protecting his prerogative of autocracy, is not the best model for school organization. Yet there are superintendents who are irritated if a self-assertive voice is raised in any part of their scratching grounds, much as is a rooster on hearing a crow or the semblance of a crow. It may be safely taken for granted that the average teacher is desirous of doing his level best for the children committed to him. What is needed is a strong, level-headed, sympathetic, open-minded, intelligent leader of training and experience in educational investigation to point out the way.

OSSIAN H. LANG.

APPLIED SCIENCE.

MORE than fifty years ago Lord Macaulay wrote, in that famous chapter describing the state of England in 1685, the following words :

> Of all inventions, the alphabet and the printing-press alone excepted, those inventions which abridge distance have done most for the civilization of our species. Every improvement of the means of locomotion benefits mankind morally and intellectually as well as materially, and not only facilitates the interchange of the various productions of nature and art, but tends to remove national and provincial antipathies, and to bind together all the branches of the great human family."

The tremendous progress which has been made since these lines were written is well shown in the work of the Seventh International Railway Congress, held in Washington in the early part of May last. When nearly a thousand specialists gather from all parts of the world to discuss matters connected solely with details of railway transport, it is evident that engineering and civilization are connected quite as closely as Macaulay affirmed.

The discussions of the Railway Congress covered far too wide a scope to be reviewed in detail within the space here available. Broadly, they covered the several departments of permanent way and construction, of locomotives and rolling stock, and of general methods of operation. Prominent among the special subjects were the questions of the value of balanced compound locomotives, of improved valve motions, of concrete construction, and of methods of efficient operation.

An interesting department of the work of the congress referred to the relation of light local railways, electric and otherwise, to the main trunk lines. In some quarters there has been a tendency to look upon such lines as rivals to legitimate railroading, to be opposed at all cost. The discussion showed, however, that such lines could be made efficient feeders to the larger systems, bringing them business from districts not easily reached otherwise, so that harmonious coöperation would be both desirable and profitable.

Another modifying element in modern railroading is interesting as showing a combination of methods of dissimilar origin. The internal-combustion motor, as applied to transportation, has been developed almost entirely in the interests of motor vehicles for use on streets and ordinary highways. The convenience and general advantages of these machines, however, have rendered them an object of interest on the part of the railway engineer; and he soon perceived that a motor which could propel a heavy automobile over a rough road might be equally effective in driving a car upon a smooth track, and thus aid in the solution of the difficult problem of light and rapid transport. The independent motor car, both for service and inspection, as well as for brief local passenger service, is finding welcome acceptance and bids fair to develop into a valuable railway auxiliary.

It is becoming evident to the observant student that a transformation in methods of transportation is now impending. The demands of commerce upon trains drawn by steam locomotives are continually increasing, and efforts to respond to these demands are evident on all sides. Higher speeds for passenger trains, greater capacities for freight cars, greater convenience for local service — all these points must be met either by existing appliances or by new methods. At the present time there are regular trains making more than seventy miles an hour for portions of the regular schedules, and long-distance trains maintaining speeds of more than fifty miles an hour for runs of several hundred miles in length. Freight cars of fifty tons capacity are numerous and are found profitable in service, and the whole transportation question is one which is being pushed to the extreme to meet the demands of commerce and industry.

So far as local traffic is concerned, there is little doubt that electric traction, using some form of multiple-unit control, is best capable of meeting the situation. Competent railroad men have committed themselves to the position that, without a proportional volume of freight traffic, a steam railroad cannot compete successfully with the electric system for local and suburban passenger service. Probably the immediate solution of the question will be the introduction of electricity for much of the local traffic, on the main lines as well as on the rural feeder systems, leaving the steam locomotives to deal with the through passenger trains and the heavy freight business. The experience thus gained will go far to determine the further solution of the problem, and the extent to which the prejudice of the railroad man to the invading power of electricity is overcome will form an important feature in further progress.

Apart from the efforts which are being made to maintain increased speeds in railway service, it is beginning to be realized that the real object to be attained in passenger service is not the attainment of excessive running speeds along the route, but the completion of the journey within the shortest possible time. The two things are by no means the same, and it is not uncommon to find enough time wasted at the terminals, through delays in the yard or at the station, or in waiting for ferry-boats, or other similar causes, to neutralize much of the gain which is made by high running speeds. Anything which requires the passenger to start for his train earlier than is required for the actual covering of the ground between his home and the station, or delays him in getting from the train, through the terminal, and away to his destination, must be considered an impediment to the service and a defect to be removed or minimized. In some cases it is evident that efforts are being made to save time by improvements and conveniences at terminals; but these are weak points in the chain of communication in nearly every instance, and it is here where far greater gain in time might be made than now appears practicable upon the road.

An important link in the line of communication gradually being constructed from the Cape to Cairo is the great bridge just completed over the gorge of the Zambesi, a little below the Victoria Falls. Although the steel arch of 500 feet span is exceeded in dimensions by several other structures, the difficulties due to the location render the work of special interest. The gorge is 400 feet in depth below the line of the rails of the bridge, and the water beneath is estimated at several hundred feet deep. The arch was built out from both sides of the gorge, on the cantilever principle, a steel cableway having first been carried across to establish communication and convey men and materials. The two halves of the arch met in April last, and work has been actively pushed since. One of the serious impediments to the work of the men was the spray and mist from the falls; and, in order to prevent fatal accidents, a net, similar to that employed by acrobats in their public performances, was stretched beneath the structure as the work progressed — a device which was the means of saving several lives.

There has been more or less public misconception concerning the so-called Cape-to-Cairo railway, some conceiving it to mean the building of an uninterrupted railway line from the Cape of Good Hope to the capital of Egypt and the Mediterranean. As a matter of fact, the plan has always meant the connection of various methods of communication, enabling the opening up of the interior of the continent of Africa, to be effected in a general line from north to south, including the use of existing railways, as well as of river and lake navigation, and the construction of as much new line as might be necessary.

The entire distance to be covered is given as 5,611 miles. Of this, 1,800 miles will be by steamer; 400 miles being on Lake Tanganyika, and the remainder on other lakes and the Nile. Of the 3,811 miles remaining, there have been constructed 2,770 miles. Beyond the Zambesi there will be built immediately 350 miles, to reach the copper mines, leaving less than 700 miles to complete the system.

It has been maintained that such a system is not the best for the purpose, and that the opening up of the interior of Africa would be better effected by the construction of shorter lines reaching in from various points on the coast, leaving the through traffic to be carried by sea. There is no doubt that the ocean navigation will remain the most economical for through transport, and there are already numerous lateral railways extending from coast ports inward. At the same time, there is no question that the completion of a trunk system extending the entire length of the continent will be of the greatest value in the development of the country, especially under the cohesive administration of a single Power. Already portions of the system are in connection with the coast, notably at Beira and at Mombasa. The latter port is the coast terminal of the Uganda Railway, connecting directly with the Victoria Nyanza, already assuring British domination of the upper Nile valley; and when the railroad is extended from Khartoum to the lake, this connection will provide an all-British communication between India and the Mediterranean, independently of the Suez Canal. All these points show the vital connection between the work of the engineer, with railway construction, bridges, lake and river navigation, harbors, etc., and the world politics which are partitioning continents, developing colonies, and controlling communications.

There has been but little to record during the past few months in the development of space telegraphy. This has partly been due to the fact that the incubus of patent litigation and of official regulation has been resting upon the art. At the same time investigators have not been idle, and practical applications of existing methods have demonstrated their usefulness. Thus the course of the international yacht race across the Atlantic was frequently reported to Europe and America by the varions steamers possessing wireless apparatus. Again, the liner "Campania" confirmed the practicability of maintaining constant communication with the shore during the crossing of the Atlantic. On the westward trip ending on May 27, communication was maintained with Poldhu, Cornwall, until the vessel was 2,100 miles out, while connection was made with Nantucket when the "Campania" was 1,800 miles east of Sandy Hook. There appeared to be no practical reason why the vessel might not have maintained the connection with Poldhu until the crossing was completed, and there is little doubt that such continuous communication with both shores will become a matter of routine before long.

Some recent developments in another field of space communication, namely, by magnetic waves, have been made in France by M. Edouard Branly, to whom the original invention of the coherer is due. These experiments show the practicability of using wireless communication for other purposes than the sending of messages, and with the crude apparatus already employed it has been found possible to control a number of operations at a distance. The apparatus used by M. Branly has shown itself capable of permitting the distant operator to start and stop an electric motor, to turn on and off a system of incandescent lamps, and to touch off an explosive mine, these operations being selected and controlled at will. These effects are produced by a special piece of apparatus called a distributor, consisting of an insulated spindle carrying metallic discs in contact with brushes and springs for maintaining the passage of an electric current from a local source. Each disc is in the circuit for only a portion of the revolution of the spindle, and each disc also forms a part of the circuit for some one of the special functions to be effected. Magnetic waves sent out at the time any one of the discs is in circuit cause the corresponding connection to be completed, and the lights are turned on, or the motor started, etc., as the case may be. The positions of the discs are continually indicated to the operator at the distant station, so that he can select the proper instant to send the magnetic wave to produce the desired connection.

Although the apparatus has as yet been tested in the laboratory only, there is no reason why it should not be capable of operation over any distance to which wireless messages have been sent. It would therefore be practicable to leave an apparatus in a deserted fort or an abandoned ship, and yet retain distant control of the magazines, of the sea valves, or of any other element of action desired. The promptness with which the Japanese availed themselves of the use of space telegraphy in naval manœuvres renders it more than probable that the further extensions of the scope of wireless control will find applications in military and naval service.

In the domain of what has been called "statical" engineering, there has been much interest awakened of late in the question of the strength and stability of masonry dams. The modern gravity dam is usually made of a section nearly triangular in shape, except that the top is cut off somewhat below the point, usually leaving sufficient width for a roadway across the valley, while the face is slightly curved out toward the toe, the water pressure being upon the other side, against the nearly vertical back. Much attention has been given by noted engineers to the proportions of these structures, the serious nature of any failure being such as to demand the greatest possible assurance of safety. Until recently it has been considered that such a dam might fail in one or the other of two ways, either by sliding bodily from its foundation or by overturning about the toe; and the computations for strength and stability of the most important existing structures of this kind have been made in this manner. It now appears, however, that there is another way in which such dams may fail, namely, by the formation of a vertical break some distance back of the toe, the dam overturning, but this action taking place about some point part way up the face.

From a recent investigation of the theory by Professor Atcherly, of University College, London, it appears that the resistance to rupture in this direction is much less than in either of the other ways, and that dams now in use, holding back large volumes of water, have really only one-half to two-thirds the margin of safety which they were designed to possess. The especial interest which attaches to this theoretical question lies in its application to the great barrage across the Nile at Assouan. This important structure was originally designed to permit the addition of six metres, or about twenty feet, of masonry to the top, allowing a corresponding increase to be made in the depth of the water behind it. After a recent visit of inspection, Sir Benjamin Baker is reported to have expressed an opinion adverse to this increase in the height of the dam, one of his reasons being the realization that the new theoretical investigations of Professor Atcherley had shown the margin of safety to be less than had been intended, in view of the increased stresses which the heavier water pressure would produce.

The question is one not altogether settled even yet, and some very competent authorities appear to be reluctant about accepting the new theory entirely. However this may be, there is apparently very good reason for providing a large factor of safety in any structure of such vital importance as a great dam; and when the factor of safety must provide, as in such a case, for any future discovery in the theory of the structure, it may well be considered a "factor of ignorance."

I have referred more than once in these pages to the important details of engineering work developed in connection with the boring of the Simplon tunnel, and in the last issue of this review the fact that the headings from the Swiss and Italian sides had met was briefly chronicled. Further information concerning the work is now at hand, and some of the points will be of interest. The alignment of the tunnel was found to be practically perfect. So far as the lateral direction is concerned, there was no appreciable deviation from the straight line, the side walls of the two headings meeting with such perfection that no jog or irregularity appeared. The vertical alignment was purposely kept out of exact junction, in order to facilitate the drainage of the accumulated water from the Swiss side through the Italian heading; and the final perforation of the rock barrier connected the upper part of the Italian heading with the lower part of the Swiss heading, so that the impounded water could be fully drawn off before further openings were made. The closeness of agreement between the two headings of this tunnel, the longest yet made, is excellent testimony to the accuracy and precision of the work of both instruments and engineers.

Some information as to the quantities of material handled in the boring of the tunnel will be found interesting. Thus, in boring the $12\frac{1}{4}$ miles there were removed 1,400,000 cubic yards of stone. More than 350,000 machine-drilled holes were made, with an aggregate depth of 1,500,000 feet, or more than 280 miles. In addition to these, there were more than 3,500,000 hand-drilled holes. Nearly three million pounds of dynamite were used to break down the rock. The flow of water from the south side of the tunnel after the great outbreak of September 30, 1901, averaged 3,000,000 cubic feet per day; and for the period of 1,242 days this gives the enormous total of 3,726,000,000 cubic feet of water drawn from the heart of the mountain. A better idea of this quantity will be obtained when it is stated that it would fill a river 30 feet deep, 300 feet wide, and 78 miles long. The flow of water from the north heading was about one-half that from the south side, so that the total quantity drawn off from the two headings would have filled a channel 30 feet deep, 300 feet wide, and 117 miles long.

The subject of alcohol fuel as a substitute for gasoline or petrol for motors has been already discussed in these reviews, but quantitative data concerning its real value have not been plentiful. The results of the tests made last year at the exposition in Vienna are now available. From these trials it appears that a horse-power was secured by the consumption of from 750 to 1,000 grammes per hour, corresponding to about 25 to 35 avoirdupois ounces, or, say, 1.5 to 2 pounds. Since a variety of methods are available for denaturizing the alcohol, so as to render it unfit for drinking, it is entirely practicable to relieve it from the excessive taxation which alone prevents it from being applied to useful purposes; and it is to be hoped that before long suitable legislation will be enacted in all industrial countries.

The numerous discussions which have been held over the possible injury to Niagara Falls, by reason of the diversion of a portion of the water of the cataract to industrial purposes, have until recently ignored the fact that there is ample hydraulic power to be had by utilizing the rapids below the falls, and this without impairing in the least the scenic effect of the great waterfall. From the base of the falls to the foot of the escarpment, about five miles below, there is a descent of one hundred feet, and with the immense volume of water passing down the gorge there is ample power awaiting development. Various plans have been suggested for deriving power from the rapids, most of these involving the driving of tunnels through the cliffs at suitable differences in level. Some of these schemes are made practicable by the bend in the gorge, a tunnel 10,000 feet long tapping the river at the cantilever bridge, and cutting across the point about a mile and a quarter below the whirlpool would give a head of eighty feet, the power depending wholly upon the size of the tunnel and the consequent amount of water passed.

Shorter tunnels on either the Canadian or the New York side might be made, giving heads of twenty to fifty feet, and there appears to be but little doubt that more than a million horse-power might be thus derived from the Niagara River without affecting the falls in the slightest. At present there is small probability of any of these plans being put into execution, since the hydraulic power now developed at Niagara appears to be in excess of any immediate requirements. At the same time it is of interest to realize that there is ample power available when needed at points where no harm can be done to the great cataract, so that the falls need not be imperilled for any commercial reason.

For a number of years the question of the probable duration of the available coal supplies in Great Britain has been seriously discussed, and the matter has been referred to a royal commission of eminent engineers and specialists for investigation and report. The final report of this distinguished body is a matter of much interest to engineering and commercial bodies in all parts of the world, giving, as it does, some definite and authoritative data.

Taking 4,000 feet as the practical working depth limit, the investigators find that the proved coal fields of Great Britain still contain about 100,000,000,000 tons of coal, of which about 80 per cent is in seams of two feet thick and upward. The average annual output at the present time is about 230,000,000 tons, while the annual increase is about 2.5 per cent. Under these conditions there is coal available for three to four hundred years to come, even if no improvements in methods of winning and using are developed.

There has been a continual improvement in steam-engine economy, while the introduction of gas-engines and central power stations of high efficiency will go far to reduce the wastes of earlier methods. It is believed that the substitution of the best modern methods of obtaining energy from fuel would result in a possible saving of about one-fourth the present annual consumption, and this alone would materially prolong the period above mentioned. While it may not be pleasant to realize that the actual stock of fuel is being used up at such a rate as has thus been determined, it is altogether possible that long before the pinch is felt other sources of energy will have been discovered, and possibly it may require some such incentive as a waning coal supply to aid in the development of new sources of light, heat, and power. So far as other parts of the world are concerned, the coal supplies are too vast to be estimated. Leaving aside the great fields in the United States, the beds in China have barely been touched, and there is no possible way of ascertaining the amount of coal awaiting the uses of future generations.

After many years of undisturbed occupation of the field, the carbon filament appears to be about to encounter severe competition in the construction of incandescent electric lamps. As soon as the development of the modern dynamo-electric machine made the current commercially available, numerous inventors devoted themselves to the design of incandescent lamps, and many of the early experiments were made with filaments of metallic wires. Mr. Edison made numerous exhaustive experiments with platinum-wire filaments, but the results were not encouraging as to durability, and the success attained with carbonized cellulose filaments caused other experimental forms to be superseded and abandoned. During the past few years, however, experiments have been made with materials not formerly available, and the once extremely rare metals, vanadium, niobium, tantalum, and osmium, have developed interesting possibilities. The earlier difficulties with metals are now shown to have been due to the presence of minute quantities of impurities, and it is only since methods of obtaining strictly pure materials have been found that success appears near.

The best results have been secured with wires of tantalum and of osmium. The very high melting points of these metals enables them to stand temperatures giving excellent illumination with moderate current consumption. Thus the improved tantalum lamp, due to the combined researches of Dr. Von Bolton and Dr. Feuerlein, has a life of 3,000 hours, at 25 candle-power, with a consumption of electrical energy of only 2 watts per candle. The osmium lamp is reported as doing even better, the life being about 5,000 hours and the energy consumption being as low as 1.5 watts per candle. The consumption for the present carbon-filament lamp is 3 watts per candle, so that, all other things being equal, a gain of 30 to 50 per cent appears. These new lamps are not greatly different in appearance from the present forms, the filaments being enclosed in exhausted glass bulbs similar in size and shape to the common incandescent lamp; and unless some serious defects appear in the course of practical experience with them, they will doubtless come into general use.

Notwithstanding the fact that it has to compete with existing methods of a simple and highly efficient character, the application of the electric current to the smelting of iron and steel continues. There is no reason to believe that there can be any gain in economy; but, on the contrary, it has been demonstrated that the electric process is more costly than the direct combustion of the fuel in the melting furnace. At the same time, the question of cost is not the only element to be considered, and for the refinement of steel and the production of grades of especial purity and high quality the electrical processes continue to find application. With increased experience it has also been found possible to reduce the working costs, so that the electrical methods will probably take their place as valuable auxiliaries to the older processes.

Among the electric refining systems, one of the most interesting is the Kjellin process, now in regular operation at Gysinge, in Sweden. This has the peculiarity of working without electrodes, being what is termed an induction furnace. The principle is similar to that of an ordinary induction coil, a familiar example of which is the common medical battery coil. The same principle is applied in the transformer used in electrical distribution systems for the conversion of an alternating current into one of a different pressure. If a coil of fine insulated wire is wound about an iron core, and around this is wound a second insulated coil of heavier wire, an induced current is produced in the outer coil when the inner one is traversed by an alternating current. The Kjellin furnace consists of an annular ring channel or gutter, formed in refractory material, and in a central space within is placed the iron core with its coil, the fused metal in the gutter taking the place of the outer coil of the transformer. Within this closed short-circuit the current produced appears as heat, and any desired charge of melted metal may be maintained at a high temperature without contact with any external material, a set of lids or covers excluding the air. The melted charge of cast iron is poured in, and the proper addition of scrap is made to give the steel the required carbon content. Since there is no opportunity for contact with any foreign matter during the operation, the purity of the product is governed entirely by the purity of the materials, and steel of the highest grade may thus be made. At Gysinge the electric current is generated by water power, and records show that a ton of steel can be produced for 770 kilowatt-hours of electric energy, the efficiency of the furnace being about 60 per cent.

Experimental work in aeronautics continues, and although the progress has not been great, it has been along lines which should lead to further developments. The use of the spindle-shaped gas bag, with suspended car and motor, appears to have accomplished all that could be expected of it; but while it has proved an interesting subject for attracting popular attention, its possibilities and opportunities are very limited. It is possible, however, that the balloon may prove a useful auxiliary in the development of the aeroplane. Some time ago I made the suggestion in these pages that valuable experience might be gained by suspending an aeroplane from a balloon, thus determining the conditions of balancing and manœuvring, after which the sustaining assistance of the gas bag might be removed, and the aeroplane launched in midair to support itself. This method has now been tried in California by Prof. J. J. Montgomery, and the results have been very encouraging. The aeroplane, managed by Prof. Montgomery, was carried to a height of about 4,000 feet by the aid of a hot-air balloon, after which the connecting cable was cut and the machine allowed to descend. The result showed that the apparatus was entirely capable of controlled gliding flight, the action being similar to that of a large bird, and the landing being effected with safety.

These experiments have demonstrated that one of the elements of successful flight has been secured — the maintenance of guided and controlled equilibrium in the air. There are, however, two still more important elements to be settled; namely, the ability to rise from the surface and the capacity to remain in continued flight. The use of an auxiliary balloon as a preliminary and experimental aid is all right. However, this cannot be expected to be anything but a beginning, and a satisfactory working machine must be capable of lifting itself into the air and staying there. This undoubtedly means that some sort of a motor must be carried upon the machine, and the problem comes back to the development of an extremely light and very powerful motor. At the same time, valuable experimental information is being gained upon the question of equilibrium, and thus substantial progress is being made in one line at least of this important and complex problem.

I have already referred in these reviews to the pressing importance of the derivation of some commercial method for the artificial production of nitrates for fertilizing purposes. The natural supply of alkaline nitrates is being rapidly consumed, and some method of fixing atmospheric nitrogen has been sought. The method of Bradley and Lovejoy, using the Siemens process of oxidizing atmospheric nitrogen by electrical discharges, has been found to produce artificial nitrates successfully from a scientific point of view, but it has not yet been demonstrated to be commercially practicable.

In the mean time another method has been proposed and put into practical execution in England, from the plans of Prof. Eschweiler, of Hanover. This process is entirely a chemical one, and consists in passing a stream of air mixed with steam over a mass of peat in a state of slow combustion. The steam is decomposed, and the released hydrogen combines with the nitrogen of the air and of the peat to form ammonia, which is then taken up by sulphuric acid, forming sulphate of ammonia. It is claimed that the process will produce the sulphate of ammonia at a price which will enable it to enter the market at present prices to advantage, in which case the supply should readily be maintained.

There has recently been constructed in England an important engineering work in connection with the exploitation of certain mining operations.   The low-phosphorus hematite iron ore beds at Hodbarrow, near Barrow, on the east coast of England, extend out into the sea; and in order to continue the excavation of the beds, there has been built a great sea wall, enclosing an area of 170 acres, the wall itself being a mile and a third in length.   This wall is 210 feet wide at the base and 83 feet wide at the top, and is constructed of two parallel banks of rough limestone, with a protection of concrete blocks on the sea side. By puddling with clay and by piling the wall has been made water-tight, and thus the entire area within can be worked as effectively as if it had been on dry land.   The value of the ore deposits may be realized from the fact that the wall cost $2,500,000, and its construction was accepted as an item in the expenses of operation.

The application of the methods of pure science in practice is much more frequent than was formerly the case, and to such harmonious work-ing of theory and practice much of modern progress may be attributed. Thus it has generally been understood that the properties of iron and steel were materially affected by low temperatures, but no definite infor-mation was available upon the subject.   At the recent meeting of the Iron and Steel Institute, Mr. R. A. Hadfield, the eminent metallurgist, of Sheffield, himself the discoverer of the important alloy manganese steel, described some interesting investigations upon the effects of cold. A number of test bars of various iron and steel alloys were prepared, these having properties already well determined at ordinary tempera-tures.   These test pieces were then sent to Prof. Dewar, at the Royal Institution, and tested at the temperature of liquid air ($-180°$ C.). The result showed that in the case of iron and most of its alloys the ductility disappeared, while the tensile strength was more than doubled. The one marked exception to this rule appeared in the case of nickel steels.   A special alloy, containing iron, carbon, nickel, and manganese, showed an increase in ductility at the temperature of liquid air, while, at the same time, the tensile strength was increased from 109,760 pounds per square inch to 178,000 pounds.   It may thus be possible to prepare metal to be exposed to extremely low temperatures and yet be assured that its strength will be increased without any increase in brittleness or danger of breakage.

The reports of the great naval battle of the Sea of Japan have not yet reached us in sufficient detail to enable any definite conclusions to be drawn as to the technical and scientific questions involved.   Probably there is no other department of applied science in which so much important work is done without opportunity of subsequently determining the results as in the case of naval and military engineering. At the same time it seems that the most severe injury inflicted upon the Russian battleships was due to the attacks of torpedoes. Many of these were launched from torpedo-boats, but whether or not submarine boats were responsible for the sinking of any of the vessels remains to be ascertained. In any case it seems to be certain that many of the engineering appliances of warfare will have to be revised by those nations which must depend upon sea power for their existence; and so far as present information is to be used as a guide, the attention of engineers may well be directed to the torpedo-boat and the submarine as the fighting machines of the future.

HENRY HARRISON SUPLEE.

LITERATURE: RECENT FICTION.

In common speech, literature has almost come to be narrowed down to a synonym for fiction. If reference is made to the most distinguished writers of the day, our minds naturally turn to the most distinguished novelists. It is they that can boast of the largest sales and the most dazzling financial returns, and it is of them that popular literary gossip most assiduously prattles. The question, "What new books have you been reading lately?" means, in nine cases out of ten, "What new novels?" It is generally accepted that, if a contemporary writer has any ideas to express, he will express them most effectively in this form. In the twentieth century no other type of literature, unless the daily paper can be included in this classification, can be expected to reach the ear and heart of the democracy. In the course of all the ages there has at last been evolved this supreme literary medium, for lack of which our rude forefathers had to be content with poetry, the drama, philosophy, and the like. To us has come the privilege of achieving wisdom through the study of "truth embodied in a tale." Why should reading be any longer a drudgery when we can take our lessons in the kindergarten of literature?

Yet, although fiction claims so disproportionate a share of the total output of printed matter and by its rewards in money and fame can make it worth while for the ablest writers to enter this field, it may be asserted, with good reason, that there is no other kind of literary work, at least in prose, in which the level of performance is so low. In many respects, the work of modern writers will bear comparison with that of their predecessors of fifty years ago. There has been no falling off in the quality of the best biographies, letters, essays, and scientific and philosophical treatises; for these latter — strange as it may seem to the writer of personal paragraphs about authors — count for something in literary history, to say nothing of contributions to critical scholarship. But to set the most highly praised modern fiction by the side of Thackeray, Dickens, or George Eliot would make even the most pronounced optimist on contemporary affairs hesitate.

Or another test might be employed. Let any one, without bias,
make a list of the books of the last three months or six months or
twelve months, and strike out those which are likely to be still alive
twenty-five years hence. He will find a remarkably small proportion of novels in the list of survivors. According to all the standards
— artistic construction, imagination, knowledge of life, breadth of sympathies, and skill and propriety in the use of the English language — the
best novels of our day are inferior in literary rank even to the best published sermons, although homiletical literature is conventionally supposed to be weaker and more insipid than any other.

For an example of the unsatisfying quality of present-day fiction, one
need not go further than to a book of which no novel-reader just now
could afford to confess ignorance. "THE MARRIAGE OF WILLIAM ASHE"[1]
is the latest work of Mrs. Humphry Ward, admittedly the foremost woman novelist in the English-speaking world. Her preceding novel is
advertised as having reached a sale of over 165,000 copies; and the admiration of the public is supported by the authority of the reviewers,
many of whom have already praised her new production in terms which
would have been thought unduly generous if applied to "Adam Bede"
or "Jane Eyre." The writing of Mrs. Ward, as illustrated here, possesses merits which make it conspicuous in contemporary fiction. She
allows no careless work to be published under her name. She commits,
it is true, occasional oversights, as when Lady Parham, on page 139,
"a small old woman," is described on page 148 as possessing an "ample
figure"; or as when Geoffrey Cliffe, the idol of "the Tory extremists"
and a Tory candidate for Parliament, is represented as throwing up his
prospects at home to fight the friends of his party in Bosnia.

On the whole, however, carelessness is not an offence with which
Mrs. Ward can justly be reproached. It would need a pedant to find
fault with her English, for her style is free from all irritating manner-
isms and is admirably moulded to harmonize with the gravity or gayety
of the occasion. While her account of the fancy ball at Yorkshire
House is an excellent specimen of brisk description, the closing scene in
the book shows that she has mastered the very different problem of depicting a death-bed scene with dignity and pathos. Further, there is a
fascination in the working-out of the plot which holds the interest of the
reader to the end and keeps unimpaired his curiosity as to the dénoue-
ment.

Where, then, is the trouble? The first and most obvious complaint

[1] New York: Harper. London: Smith, Elder.

is against the strange and confusing method with which Mrs. Ward uses the motive of her story. In her preface she warns the reader that he will be greeted in this tale by "ghosts of men and women well known to an earlier England," and that "some few of their long past sayings and doings may be dimly recalled" by the sayings and doings of persons to be met in these pages. The literary historians have discovered without difficulty that the story is based on the marriage in 1805 of the Hon. William Lamb, afterward Lord Melbourne, the first of Queen Victoria's Prime Ministers, to Caroline, daughter of the Earl of Bessborough, and the subsequent infatuation of the latter with Lord Byron. But the book is not an historical novel. It resembles the actual course of events in its outlines and certain peculiar details; but so far from attempting to reproduce these events and to reconstruct their circumstances in the manner of historical fiction, Mrs. Ward transfers her characters, of course with a change of names, to a period sixty or seventy years later. In several places we find references to Lord Melbourne as a statesman of an earlier day, and there are other more exact indications of time. It is two generations after Catholic Emancipation and the Reform Bill; "Macaulayese" has become an accepted term in discussions of style; Renan's best-known book has already been published; M rris, Burne-Jones, and Alma-Tadema are rising artists; Sarah Bernhardt, a "young and astonishing actress," is "the reigning idol of the Comédie Française"; and a journalist can speak of having interviewed Bismarck after Sadowa.

Further, while the acknowledged basis of the book is an incident of the beginning of the nineteenth century, and the story as here recounted is ostensibly one of about thirty-five years ago, the whole movement of the book is an anachronism unless it be placed within the last decade. The entire atmosphere of this novel, particularly in its delineation of London society, is unmistakably modern. It is alleged on good authority that the account of the ball before mentioned would pass very well as descriptive of an actual entertainment given by a society leader a few years since. And this impression of contemporaneity is increased by the fact, to which I shall return presently, that the leading figures bear a strong likeness to well-known living persons. Such a *mélange* of generations is a blunder of the most inartistic kind. Sir Boyle Roche's bird, which could be in two places at once, is outstripped in versatility by Mrs. Ward's characters, who can thus enjoy the privilege of living simultaneously in three different periods.

A more serious objection remains to be made. Long before we

reach the main current of the story, there comes upon us the conviction that we have met the heroine, Lady Kitty, somewhere before; and the identification quickly flashes upon us. She is none other than "Dodo" under a new name. Only very young readers need to be told of the sensation produced in London society when Mr. E. F. Benson gave to the world what was everywhere interpreted as a portrait, though an exaggerated one, of one of the most charming and unconventional women of the day. Now, the original of Dodo, according to common talk, had many wooers, prominent among whom were two rising politicians. It will suffice to indicate them here by the mathematical symbols A and B. She married the suitor whom we shall denote as A. The amazing feature of Mrs. Ward's book is that it portrays the career of a woman with the most prominent characteristics of Dodo married to a man with the most prominent characteristics of the rejected lover, B. The correspondence is so close that Lady Kitty is represented even as belonging to a group, "the Archangels," differing in nothing but the name from the famous "Souls."

There is good reason, therefore, for expecting that "The Marriage of William Ashe" will be one of the notable successes of the season; that, indeed, it will be read as eagerly as was Lady Kitty's own novel, in which the characters were drawn from the society in which she was a prominent figure. After all, the average reader will trouble little about the historical connection with Lord Melbourne. There will be sufficient piquancy in the imagination, with Mrs. Ward's assistance, of what might have happened if Dodo had married B. It is hardly likely that the author deliberately intended any such result; but, whether she meant it or not, the predominant appeal made by the book is not so much to the love of literature as to the appetite for society scandal. For a writer of the antecedents and reputation of Mrs. Humphry Ward, a success of this kind is really a humiliating failure.

A few words may be added respecting the character-drawing, a phase of the novelist's art in which Mrs. Ward has often shown herself especially skilful. In many situations Lady Kitty is credited with behavior which is wildly improbable. The writer, however, is already prepared with an answer to the charge that no woman with so many excellent qualities could be at the same time so stupid and foolish as her heroine. The suggestion is made early in the book that Lady Kitty inherited a touch of insanity, and she is appropriately made to say at the end, in explanation of her aberrations: "I haven't had a brain like other people." Now this is not "playing the game." A novelist is not justified in describing a career lived outside of the asylum, not only in the full light of day, but even in the brilliant glare of rank and public affairs, and then in excusing manifest improbabilities by the plea that the character in question was more or less mad.

William Ashe is an attractive personality, but the development of the story does not bring out the high qualities attributed to him in the author's descriptions.   We are told again and again that he is a great man — masterly in Parliament and powerful in the country — but this information comes to us from the outside, and not from the self-revelation of his character.   Geoffrey Cliffe steps straight out of melodrama. The appalling treachery of Mary Lyster is scarcely credible, in spite of the manifestations of jealousy which precede it.   It is especially hard to believe that a woman with such possibilities should not have been found out long before, during her close intimacy with Lady Tranmore — by far the most engaging figure in the whole circle.   Amid all the intriguing and self-seeking of the crowd that throngs the London drawing-rooms and the country houses, the dignified yet kindly Lady Tranmore stands out in her very unobtrusiveness as a worthy representative of the old-fashioned type of English gentlewoman.

The leading character in "A DARK LANTERN," [1] by Elizabeth Robins (C. E. Raimond), allows one of his patients, who is taking a rest cure, to read "trash," which he explains as meaning "novels without any ' problems' in them."   It is not quite clear whether the book itself is intended to be a problem novel or not.   There are indications here and there that the author is trying to expound some kind of a philosophy of life; but the end of the story leaves the reader with the conviction that the title applied by Miss Robins to her hero exactly describes her book, and that the shutter still conceals whatever illumination might have been afforded.

There is no doubt as to the period covered by the action of this novel. The scenes are set in England and on the continent of Europe in quite recent years.   But if the time had not been plainly marked, one would have been at a loss to say at what stage in the recorded history of the world the existence of the characters would have been probable.   As early as the fourteenth page we are introduced to a whimsical old peer of amazing erudition and remarkable power of hiding it.   "You would know him for years, and never hear him hint at numismatic knowledge; but, the moment come when authorities differed, he would speak the

illuminating word.   You would never have heard him mention Persian
literature, till one night at dinner a discussion would arise between two
Omarites about some Fitz-Gerald rendering, and Lord Peterborough would
write the original line in character on the tablecloth to prove the case of
the sounder disputant." It turns out that he' is equally an expert in
heraldry and in the history of the early Italian manuscripts.

But the unique phenomenon is "the Dark Lantern," a fashionable
London doctor, as much above the level of his profession in skill as below it in manners and morals.   When one of his patients, having no
appetite for the prescribed slice of mutton, throws it up the chimney in
the absence of her nurse, this charming person fishes it out and compels
her to eat it, soot and all.   The nurses whom he supplies to tend deli-
cately nurtured women are dirty and incompetent.   And this treatment
is part of a brilliantly successful "rest cure," by means of which Dr.
Garth Vincent gains a fortune, a knighthood, and the love of Katharine
Dereham, a girl of unusual beauty, poetic temperament, and high ideals
of chivalry.

The episode of the rest cure, which in Katharine's case occupies
seventy-three pages, is at first welcomed by the reader as a humorous
interlude pleasantly relieving the stretches of tediousness which precede
it.   It is a depressing surprise to find that it is not meant as farcical,
but is solemnly detailed as an essential part of the development of the
story.   The brutal antics of the hero and the neurotic vagaries of the
heroine lead up to an ending of idyllic happiness, which, if it had been
found as the conclusion of an old-fashioned story-book about sane people, would have been sneered at as sentimental and untrue to life.   It
is enough to make one despair of the future of English fiction when a
production of this kind, so grotesque in its violation of the elementary
principles of art and literature, can receive eulogistic comment in influential publications.

It is to be expected that the Civil War and the Reconstruction period will long furnish a background for the work of ambitious American
novelists.   There have been striking instances of late of the use of fiction as an instrument in the education of public opinion respecting
political questions with which the war was concerned, but which it did
not solve.   As argument such disguised pamphlets are worthless, for no
serious student could be influenced by them unless they were corrobo-
rated by historical evidence, which, if it exists at all, is already available
independently of the novel.   But this type of fiction may be really in-

fluential in creating or removing prejudices on the part of readers who are controlled by their emotions; and it is in itself of some service to students as an evidence of the feeling of the writer and of the public sentiment, whether national or sectional, by which he is prompted and supported. This period, however, will be found of increasing inspiration to the novelist apart from all implications with present politics. It not only offers scope for the portrayal of those qualities of heroism and self-sacrifice which cast the one gleam of light across the darkness of the battlefield, but it affords material for the study of those conflicts of duty and affection, those intricate questionings of the lover of home and lover of country, which distinguished that great conflict from any war against a foreign enemy.

Dr. Weir Mitchell has selected as the scene of "CONSTANCE TRESCOT"[1] a small town in Missouri, impoverished by the war and still embittered by its disasters. Into this environment is sent, with his bride, a young New England lawyer, in the capacity of agent for his wife's uncle, a wealthy Bostonian. His employer owns in this Southern town considerable property, which is involved in harassing lawsuits. He is a quite impracticable man, and by his constant interference with his previous agent, who understands, as he does not, the local situation, has acquired the hatred of the people and aroused in them a strong desire that the approaching judicial decision may be against him. George Trescot, all unaware of the exceptional difficulty of his task, comes thus to St. Ann, and by his manliness and good sense conciliates little by little the public opinion of the place, except for a few irreconcilables. Dr. Mitchell displays admirable skill in describing the impact of this former major in the Sixth Massachusetts Volunteers upon a community steeped in passionate Southern sentiment and displaying in almost every household some pathetic relic of the struggle.

Up to the determination of the case in the law courts, the progress of the negotiations about the disputed lands, a subject which one would have supposed it hardly possible to make readable, steadily increases in interest through the representation of the human elements implicated in it. A sensational trial in which unexpected witnesses are produced, whose testimony astonishes the court and turns the tables upon a too confident lawyer, is a hackneyed subject in fiction, but old acquaintance with this familiar expedient does not take the edge off the reader's delight in the *peripeteia*. It is all the greater proof of the writer's ability that this freshness of impression should be produced in spite of the fact

[1] New York: The Century Company.

that we have already received more than a hint of the nature of the testimony which is to be sprung upon the court. Immediately after the judgment in favor of the Boston landlord comes the central tragedy of the book — the wanton murder of George Trescot by the disappointed counsel for the other side.

At this point Dr. Weir Mitchell, the novelist, lays down the pen, and it is taken up by Dr. Weir Mitchell the specialist in nervous diseases. The publishers announce that "the main fact is based upon a woman's vendetta that actually came under Dr. Mitchell's observation." No doubt; but the incident should not have been allowed to escape from the pages of his case-book, unless perhaps to find place in some technical treatise on morbid mental conditions. The rest of the story is distressing without being pathetic; it provokes repulsion instead of "purging the emotions by pity and fear." In the first place, whatever the similarity of this narrative to an actual event, it is out of harmony with the truth of real life that the bereaved woman, crazed though she was by her passion of grief, should have overlooked the fact that the fitting object of her vengeance was not her husband's slayer alone, but the community of St. Ann, which, by allowing him to go scathless, had made itself partner in his crime. Yet Constance Trescot is represented as pouring out her benefactions upon the town which had not only treated the murder as naught after it had been committed, but had nourished the barbarous code that stimulated it and made its commission easy. And the author himself describes her vengeance in such a way as to remove it from our interest. The verdict of the doctor in Milan that she has suffered a change in the nervous system is followed by repeated suggestions that she has become a monomaniac. She is as much under an obsession as the poor creature in an asylum who is sane in everything else, but insists that he is Alexander the Great. The second section of the book is, in fact, open to this dilemma. If Constance is in her right mind, the story of her revenge is inexplicable and impossible. If she is not, her madness removes it out of the range of subjects capable of being made to appeal to the imagination of the reader by means of the art of the novelist.

After following the career of three abnormal women, each of them afflicted, to say the least, with some kind of nervous disorder, it is a relief to get into the company of sound, healthy criminals. They are enemies to society, it is true, but the disagreeable taint of the sanitarium is, at any rate, absent from their records. It is now more than a decade since a physician practising in an English seaside town made a sudden success by writing a number of detective stories suggested by the methods of an Edinburgh professor, Dr. Bell, whose classes he had attended when a medical student. Neither the literary critics nor the author himself regarded these tales as reaching anything near the level of "Micah Clarke," "The White Company," and other fiction from the same pen, in which there was no appeal to the detective interest.

It is not difficult to explain the popularity of the Sherlock Holmes series. In the first place, such modern fiction as is not vulgarly sensational and melodramatic has tended more and more to overlook the natural craving of readers for a story with a plot, and the recognition of this demand suited the taste of a public wearied by studies of character and sociological tracts. Again, to English readers at any rate, there was a fascination in the suggestion of romantic possibilities concealed in the dullest routine and most commonplace occupations of London life. Most effective of all was the stimulus to observation in the record of the startling inferences which the leading figure, like the real Dr. Bell, could draw from a shabby hat or a badly cleaned shoe. The reader had an encouraging sense of being educated while he was being amused; he could henceforth use both his eyes and his brains more skilfully, and every railway carriage would give him an opportunity of practising his newly acquired gift. And, whatever may be said in disparagement of these tales as literature, it cannot be denied that Dr. Conan Doyle created in Sherlock Holmes one of the few distinct and memorable characters of recent fiction. How many other novels are there, published within the last twenty years, in which any personality has left so vivid an impression? The name of Sherlock Holmes has, indeed, taken a permanent place in the vocabulary. Its position as a "household word" is no less assured than that of Mark Tapley or Mr. Pecksniff.

But while the appetite of the public was eager for still further revelations of Holmes's genius, Dr. Doyle himself had become tired of his own handiwork and annoyed at finding that his reputation was in danger of resting on the books by which he himself set the least store. Accordingly he made Sherlock Holmes disappear over a precipice in Switzerland, and congratulated himself that the whole affair was now ended. The author, however, had not taken sufficiently into account the persistence of the public or of his publishers. After a long interval, broken only by the appearance of "The Hound of the Baskervilles," he

has now supplemented the earlier stories by a new collection, entitled
"THE RETURN OF SHERLOCK HOLMES." [1]

It turns out that when Sherlock Holmes disappeared at the Reichen-
bach Fall he did not actually go over the cliff.   He thought it prudent,
however, not to make his escape immediately known.   After a while he
went back to London, and some of the consequences of his return are
described in the present volume.   It is evidently the same Holmes.
He has lost none of his marvellous keenness of observation, none of his
swiftness in recognizing the significance of apparent trivialities, and
none of his resourcefulness in hastening the development of a situation
by setting a hidden trap for the criminal and thus making him contribute to his own undoing.   His inferences from the strong smell of powder in "The Dancing Men" and from the three wine-glasses in "The
Abbey Grange" are equal to anything in the earlier volumes, nor did
these record any schemes more adroit than the contrivances which result
in bringing the Norwood builder, the harpooner, and the owner of the
golden pince-nez into the hands of the police.

In spite of this, most admirers of Sherlock Holmes will lay down
this book with a feeling of disappointment.   If one may make a distinction which sounds paradoxical, the defect is not in the detective,
but in the novelist.   The novelist has not shown anything like as much
ingenuity in the construction of fresh problems as the detective shows
in solving them.   If we have gained any familiarity with Holmes's
methods through reading the earlier books, we find ourselves able to a
considerable extent to anticipate what he is going to do, or at least to
understand the purpose of his successive steps.   For instance, in six of
the thirteen narratives collected here we are fairly sure, from our acquaintance with those previously published, that the persons on whom suspicion naturally falls will turn out to be innocent.

In some particular examples the resemblance is especially close.
The hiding of a jewel in one of a set of plaster busts distributed among
various purchasers is strongly reminiscent of a similar situation in "The
Blue Carbuncle," where a hunt for stolen treasure led to the following
up of a consignment of geese similarly scattered.   The story of "The
Dancing Men" has much that reminds us of "The Five Orange Pips."
A coincidence of initials leads the official detectives astray in "Black
Peter" as in "The Noble Bachelor."   A receipted bill suggests the clew
in "The Missing Three-quarter," as in "Silver Blaze."   In "The Second
Stain," as in "The Naval Treaty," a valuable document on which serious

[1] New York: McClure, Phillips.   London: Newnes.

international affairs depend is purloined and is hidden in the flooring. The writer's difficulty in inventing entirely new sets of circumstances is illustrated by the fact that two of the stories in this one book hinge upon the same central motive, namely, the anxiety of a lady of title to recover from a blackmailer indiscreet letters written in early youth.

Consequently the impression of originality left by the former volumes is not revived by this continuation, and the resulting lack of freshness suggests that the writer's hesitation in resuming the adventures of his hero was justified by the limitations of his own creative faculty. At the same time there are scattered here and there such tempting hints of revelations still possible that one would not too hastily discourage the faithful Watson from pursuing his labor of love. We should certainly like to learn "how the dreadful business of the Abernetty family was brought to my notice by the depth which the parsley had sunk into the butter upon a hot day," as well as to hear the stories of the peculiar per- secution to which John Vincent Harden, the tobacco millionaire, was subjected; of the arrest of the notorious canary trainer; of "the shocking affair of the Dutch steamship 'Friesland,' which so nearly cost us both our lives;" and of the surprising results of Holmes's researches in early English charters in one of the university libraries. If Sir Conan Doyle turns his attention to any of these attractive subjects, it will be well worth his while to take the precaution of re-reading his old volumes in order to avoid the duplications which detract so much from the interest of that just issued.

A glance through the window of the cottage was enough to convince Enoch Arden that his reappearance would not promote the happiness of the woman he loved; and when once he had decided to guide his con- duct by that motive there could accordingly be no hesitation as to his self-effacement. But what would happen if the question so easily and quickly determined by Enoch could only be answered by long and diffi- cult observation — an observation involving a dangerous disguise? This intricate problem has been faced by Agnes and Egerton Castle in "ROSE OF THE WORLD,"[1] a book which is conspicuous among recent fiction for the fascination alike of its story and of its characters. So skilful is the construction of the plot that it is not until we have read more than three-quarters of the book that we realize that it contains an Enoch Arden situation at all. On looking back we find one or two faint sug- gestions of the mystery, but so subtle that their full significance is im-

[1] New York: Stokes. London: Smith, Elder.

perceptible except in the light of the subsequent revelation.   The emergence of this hitherto latent interest at so late a period adds a startling and dramatic power to a story which even without it has awakened and retained the unflagging attention of the reader.

At the very beginning, Mr. and Mrs. Castle show an exceptional mastery of their craft in their picture of the household of Sir Arthur Gerardine, an Indian lieutenant-governor, and the intrusion of Major Bethune, who seeks from Lady Gerardine material for a biography of her first husband, Captain English.   Sir Arthur, the "seraphic old ass," as his subordinates call him, is a diverting and almost pathetic specimen of the man, not without ability or good intentions, whose prosperity has given him a ludicrous sense of infallibility.   The effect is heightened by the *naïveté* of his niece, Aspasia, who does not herself see as clearly as outsiders do how ruthlessly she is puncturing her "Runkle's" pomposity. Lady Gerardine inspires our curiosity from the first.   Why should she be so reluctant to help the preparation of the biography?   When the scene shifts a little later to the old house on an English countryside, and Lady Gerardine sets herself to collaborate with Bethune in the work to which Sir Arthur has induced her to consent, the interest becomes more tense.   The most enthralling chapter, with the exception of that which records the reappearance of the first husband, is that in which Rosamond — once Mrs. English and now Lady Gerardine — reads for the first time the packet of letters and diaries written by English during the siege in which he is believed to have fallen, brought to her by his dearest friend Bethune, and left unread until this moment by the woman, in whom they now awaken a passionate affection unknown to her before.

The plot itself is of such a nature as to prompt to a re-reading of the book when one's desire to know the conclusion of the story has been satisfied.   In this second and more critical reading the careful workmanship of the writers is everywhere apparent.   Their exactness in fitting each detail into the place where it will most assist the elaboration of the story might well be taken as an object-lesson by young novelists. The consummate skill with which these details are treated is evident most of all in the fact that their importance is not suspected until, the story told, the book offers itself as a subject for a less superficial analysis.   There is seldom found among novels now issuing from the press a book which, while free from all appeal to appetites for the morbid and unpleasant, nevertheless probes so surely the deep things of the human spirit, or which so powerfully stirs the emotions without degenerating into sentimentalism.

Mr. A. T. Quiller-Couch has not yet succeeded in writing a long novel equal in merit to his short stories. "SHINING FERRY"[1] works out to an unsatisfying conclusion. Apart from other tests, when a novelist unites two of his characters who in the judgment of the reader should have been otherwise mated, he cannot be pronounced convincing in the development of his plot. Somehow the author has failed to realize how charming a creation is Hester Marvin, and has thus been content to give her a husband inferior to her own quality. As in some others of his longer books, Mr. Quiller-Couch seems to start with much enthusiasm for his characters, but presently to become tired of them and to bring their story to an end with the first expedient that offers. This defect, strange to say, does not prevent the book from being well worth reading. There is a savor in it — a distinction not only of style, but of thought and temper — which will enable it to outlive much fiction that is more strongly wrought. It does not shirk the dark side of life, but its prevailing spirit of cheerfulness and restfulness entitles it to a welcome as a delightful addition to the literature of refreshment. It is the kind of volume that one would be glad to take down from the shelf and dip into again and again in an hour of dulness or depression. Some of the Cornish characters, with their quaintness racily brought out yet never exaggerated to the point of caricature, are worthy of a place in "Q.'s" wonderful portrait-gallery of natives of the Delectable Duchy. Nicky Vro, the ferryman, Mrs. Purchase, the skipper's wife, and Mr. Benny, the poetical clerk, are an unfailing source of quiet entertainment.

Of lighter texture is "THE PRINCESS PASSES,"[2] by C. N. and A. M. Williamson. It seems almost too slender to be gravely criticised in matters of plot, character-drawing, and the like. Its staple is sheer, wholesome fun, brisk and bubbling, but not loud or crude. There is a daintiness about it to the end, though without any sacrifice of naturalness. It is of the same type as "The Lightning Conductor," of which it is in some sort a sequel. The new story, like the old, centres around a European journey, and the automobile once more figures prominently. In both books, also, the climax is reached by the penetration of a disguise and the consequent smoothing of the course of true love.

The "Tales of the Youth of the World," which Mr. Maurice Hewlett has collected under the title of "FOND ADVENTURES,"[3] relate not to the antediluvian period, but to mediæval times. The first has its scene at Toulouse, when John was King of England; the second is practically an

[1] New York: Scribner.　[2] New York: Holt.
[3] New York and London: Macmillan.

addition to the "New Canterbury Tales" by the same writer; the third tells of the rivalries of the great families of Florence before the time of Dante; and the hero of the fourth and last is a humanist of Mantua and friend of Politian.   Not one of these stories is lacking in intrinsic interest, yet one's dominant impression in closing the book is not of any of the characters or events, but of the cleverness of Mr. Hewlett.   He has, in effect, cultivated the kind of talent which a generation or two ago would have been spent in writing Latin verses.   Latin verses written by a modern always seem to be a literary exercise rather than a literary achievement; and, though they may appear flawless to a twentieth-century critic, one cannot avoid the feeling that Horace or Virgil might not have admitted their perfect Latinity.   In the same way, there is room for the suspicion that what seems to us the authentic mediæval air of Mr. Hewlett's romances might have seemed to the mediæval writers themselves something not altogether unlike a parody.   .

A trail drover in Texas is responsible for delivering on a certain date at Fort Buford, on the borders of North Dakota and Montana, five million pounds of beef on foot, that is to say, ten thousand cattle.   His task is complicated by an oversight in drawing up the papers for his contract, by which he is exposed to the risk of serious loss through the sharp practice of a supply company.   This does not sound a promising subject for the novelist, but Mr. Andy Adams has turned it to good account in "THE OUTLET."[1]   It is not quite clear to what extent this narrative is an account of an actual "drive" in which the author himself took part; but even if the proportion of history to fiction in its composition should be found to be considerable, no less credit would be due to him for the graphic power he displays in the telling of his story. Not the least effective part of the book consists of the dialogue, and it cannot be supposed that Mr. Adams took shorthand notes of the various conversations at the time.   Some of his descriptions, as of the flooded river and of the discovery of a herd poisoned by alkaline water, make a deep impression.   Certain passages are likely to be skipped by readers not directly concerned in the management of cattle.   But the main action is sufficiently non-technical to interest an inveterate city dweller.

Nothing so absorbs the attention as the last seven chapters.   There is an appeal both to our love of excitement in general and to the sporting instinct in particular as the time draws near for the fulfilment of the contract, and the rival contractors are using all their wits and spare cash for each other's discomfiture.   Our sympathies from the beginning are

[1] Boston: Houghton, Mifflin.

with Don Lovell, the employer of Tom Quirk, the narrator of the story; but in the last few days our hopes and fears are successively aroused as first one and then the other of the combatants appears to be gaining the upper hand. The tension is extreme at the moment of the decision made by the commander of the post and at the subsequent inquiry by the special commissioner from the War Department. The success of this book is the more notable from the entire absence of anything resembling a love story. It should be added that, although Mr. Adams's descriptions do not need drawings to make them intelligible, the admirable illustrations by Mr. E. Boyd Smith add much to their effectiveness.

Mr. Andy Adams reconstructs for us a phase of the fresh and unsophisticated life of the West of twenty years ago. For a striking contrast we may turn to "THE TYRANNY OF THE DARK,"[1] in which Mr. Hamlin Garland deals with that fondness for pseudo-philosophizing — some would say, that tendency to accept the crank as a sage — which is a later outgrowth in a society free from the steadying as well as the cramping influence of tradition. "A friend told me," remarks one of the characters, speaking of a neighborhood which is obviously somewhere in Colorado, "that these towns were filled with seers and prophets. The occult flourishes in the high, dry atmosphere, those of the faith say." A novel occupied with the fortunes of a "psychic" tempts its writer to disquisitions even more remote from the interests of the general reader than are the methods of handling live stock. With all his exposition, Mr. Garland does not make clear his own view of spiritualism, and, by closing the story where he does, he evades the most difficult of the problems which he raises. He represents Dr. Serviss as dispelling by a powerful exercise of "suggestion" the mysterious influences from which Viola has hitherto striven to free herself, but the curtain falls before we have an opportunity of knowing whether her liberation by this means will be permanent. In his discussions of scientific matters, Mr. Garland makes an odd blunder by three times confusing the Royal Society with the Royal Academy. His style is disfigured by some painful examples of fine writing, as: "It was a pity to see one so young and so comely confronting with sad and sullen brow such aërial majesty as the evening presented"; and "The golden eagle of cloud flew home over the illimitable seas of saffron."

If it is the new West that provides a starting-point for Mr. Garland, it is the new South that is described by Marie van Vorst in "AMANDA

[1] New York and London: Harper.

OF THE MILL."[1] So different is this book from the normal type of Southern fiction that one might read it from beginning to end without becoming aware that there was such a thing as a negro problem. But that there exists another urgent problem — that of the relation of capital to labor, and especially to child-labor — it was the deliberate purpose of the writer to bring home to the most cursory reader. What was said above of the ineffectiveness of political novels applies to such a work as Miss van Vorst has undertaken here. Her graphic accounts of the condition of the mill-hands add little if anything to what she has already said with the directness of first-hand experience in "The Woman Who Toils"; and the complication of a somewhat squalid love story weakens the impression they would have produced without such a division of interest. It is strange that the author does not see how little there is to choose between a mill-owner who sacrifices the work-people for his personal gain and a labor leader who is equally ready to sacrifice them at the time of their greatest need to gratify his own lawless passion.

HERBERT W. HORWILL.

[1] New York: Dodd, Mead. London: Heinemann.

WOMEN IN TURKEY.

THE phrase, *Cherchez la femme,* has often been lightly used in regard to woman's influence on affairs. It must now be *seriously* used, because of its bearing upon the literary and educational progress of all civilized lands. This applies also in a far greater degree than is usually supposed to the general development of intellectual life in the Orient. One sometimes forgets to seek the reality in the picturesque and dreamy environment of the East. As the boatmen in the caiques drift down the shining blue waters of the Bosporus in the evening light, with no apparent thought of the coming morning, so the dweller in the Orient often drifts along regardless of the changes and improvements around him which are preparing the way for greater things.

The conditions of life among our sisters behind the lattices are so different from our own that the outward seeming is often considered the reality; and as custom demands seclusion in social life, the careless onlooker does not realize the progress that is being made. In Turkey, the fashions in street costume and the outward relations of Mohammedan women are regulated by law, and the laws of the land are not easily changed. To the superficial thinker, therefore, the condition of Turkish women has not materially altered for many centuries. It is not yet their custom to walk alone in the streets, or to appear in public with their husbands, or to arrange their own marriages. They are obliged to veil their faces carefully, except when at home, and are seldom found in the foreign schools which are established in the country. These things remain much as they have always been, and make it impossible, at a casual glance, to understand the real thought-life that is going on behind thousands of latticed windows. Who would guess, in passing in the streets a woman whose face is thickly covered by the regulation veil and whose black attendant walks carefully behind her, that she may be at that moment planning an article for a daily paper on some subject in modern science, or possibly considering on which side justice lies in the war between Russia and Japan? An intimate acquaintance with the inner life of the Turkish women shows, however, that they have, many of them, a high degree of literary culture and a thoughtful attitude of mind, and that their thoughts range over a very broad field.

It is true that Turkish proverbs and stories present the opposite picture — for instance, "*Sache ouzoun, abul kussa*" (Long hair, little wit), and "Whatever your wife advises, do the opposite." The latter proverb is well illustrated by the story of the man who was invited by a pasha to visit him. "What shall I take him as a present," he asked his wife, "quinces or figs?" "Oh, take quinces," said the wife, "they are so much larger and handsomer than figs." The man accordingly took figs, and when he was told by the pasha to stand at the other end of the room while his host threw them one by one at his head, he murmured to himself: "What a good thing that I did not follow the advice of my wife." Yet women are not without power in the Turkish world; for, side by side with the seclusion which surrounds them, they have developed a firm influence on society, which is very marked, which dates back to the earliest periods of Mohammedan history for its origin, and which rests upon a foundation of some phases of law and ancient customs.

The object of the study which I have made of this subject, is to show something of what is really being done among the women of Turkey along educational and social lines, and briefly to trace the historical reasons therefor.

It is interesting to know that the beginning of all real progress in modern times in education both for boys and girls in the Turkish Empire was associated with two Mohammedan women. The first of these was the nurse of Mahmoud II, Djevri Kalfa, who lived in the latter part of the eighteenth century. She was a very brave, interesting woman who saved Sultan Mahmoud from assassination, when he was a boy, by throwing hot ashes in the faces of the would-be assassins. She founded a school opposite the Byzantine Hippodrome, which is now a large secondary school. The second woman to whom modern Turkish education owes much, belonged to the harem of Sultan Mahmoud, and was the mother of Sultan Mejid, who reigned from 1839 to 1861. The reforming tendency that developed during the reign of Mahmoud II began to express itself in education under Abdul-Mejid; and the Valide Sultana, Bezim Alem, was very much interested in promoting it. The community schools both for boys and girls had been established long before that time. They had originated in the old custom of having a training school connected with the mosques, to prepare readers for the religious services. Girls were allowed to attend these private schools until they were ten or eleven years old. All the training consisted in chanting in chorus from the Koran, which is still a popular method of education in the primary schools and is somewhat used in the secondary schools.

The Valide Sultana, to whom I have referred, introduced more effective methods of teaching into the public schools in general, and she founded the scientific section of the Imperial University, which was the only superior civil school of her time. On public occasions in this school she used to preside in person, and the throne-chair in which she sat is still preserved as a relic. This Valide Sultana began schools for girls by gathering together all the slave girls in the palace and providing teachers for them.

Education for the little slaves in the palace of the King was soon followed by schools for girls in other places. The first public primary school for Mohammedan girls was established about fifty years ago in Boyadjikeui, a village on the Bosporus; and the first secondary school was opened in Stamboul in 1872, under Sultan Aziz. Dating from that period, there are also in Stamboul two schools of fine arts for girls. These were established by a special irade of Sultan Aziz. They were at first independent of the Department of Public Instruction, but at present they are included in the general system. To-day there are schools of three regular grades for Mussulman girls, high, secondary, and primary, besides some others which have arisen in imitation of the two for fine arts founded by Sultan Aziz. These last are called Sinæ, of which there are three in Constantinople, and others in different parts of Turkey. The time of the students in the Sinæ schools is largely given to handwork, music, and drawing.

As all schools supported by the Government are for Mohammedan children and are free, we see that free education of practical value is furnished to Turkish women, and each year shows some improvement in the system. At the present time, the report of the Department of Public Instruction gives a complete plan of primary and secondary schools for girls throughout the Turkish Empire, with the exception of Kurdistan, Arabia, Hejaz, and Yemen. These include 1,500 primary schools containing 200,000 girls, besides 150,000 girls enrolled in the mixed primary schools, and 3,000 pupils in forty secondary schools. Investigation of this report shows, however, that it is based, to a certain extent, upon a definite plan. In reality, primary schools for boys and girls together exist in general all over the Turkish Empire, one near every mosque. Practically, in most cases, the primary education of boys and girls is carried on together, and girls in cities, who do not wish to attend the mixed schools, go to the secondary schools for girls, which also receive young children and provide primary teaching.

The fundamental teaching in the primary schools is the Koran. The school is opened in the morning by repeating one *sura*, often the last. The children learn to read from the Koran, although they cannot understand it, as it is written in Arabic and not in Turkish. This is according to the principle that if they learn to read that which is most difficult, they will be in time able to read that which is easier. The Koran is, however, written with syllabic signs, which make it less difficult to read than it would be otherwise. Fragments of the Koran are also committed to memory. Other things taught in the primary schools are reading and writing, geography, elementary science, and a little arithmetic, that is, addition and subtraction. Multiplication and division belong to the intricacies of the science to be studied later on. It is said that in the primary schools the girls show more aptitude than the boys and a greater desire to study.

Let us visit together one of the secondary schools for girls, of which there are sixteen in Constantinople. These schools are called Rushdie. A Rushdie school is one just above the primary grade, corresponding practically to a secondary school. Yet Rushdie schools for girls are still very elementary and differ also from the secondary schools of other countries by having more handwork. I am sure that there is no other city in the world in which education for girls has advanced to the stage of nominal secondary schools where visitors are received with such leisurely and deferential politeness as in Constantinople. All work is laid aside in order to entertain us, and the four teachers attend us in a body, with their hair adorned with flowers for the occasion. Coffee must be served first in an anteroom, on the walls of which we see quaint interesting pictures of Mecca and Medina. We then enter two large rooms with latticed windows, opening into each other, where over one hundred girls are assembled, the oldest being about fifteen. Each girl has spread her finest piece of embroidery on her desk for our inspection, some of the pieces being very elaborate and well finished.

The girls follow us with their bright eyes as we pass from one desk to another, and finally we are seated before the blackboard, with the help of which the accomplishments of the pupils are freely displayed. They can multiply small numbers; they can read and write; and they can chant well from the Koran, which is the most picturesque thing that is taught in these schools. All the girls in the school have Korans printed in gilt letters, and a pretty young girl with a sweet voice steps forward at our request to chant one of the *suras*. But while formerly the Koran was the only reading book in the schools, we notice that there are now readers quite modern in character, containing harmless stories that young children can understand, and from one of these a chapter, called "The Good Neighbor," is also read. Further investigation shows that the course of study includes not only careful teaching of the Koran, Arabic and Persian, and some arithmetic, but also practical lessons in composition, geography, history, and elementary science. Girls of the middle and lower classes go to the Rushdie schools, and the latter are sometimes patronized even by the higher classes.

In all the schools, boys and girls have the opportunity of committing to memory the whole of the Koran, although this accomplishment is not so frequent as it was formerly. A boy or a girl who has done this is called a Hafiz, and a boy Hafiz is often invited to chant in the mosques. Although it is not the general custom for girls to chant in public, they sometimes do it under the age of thirteen. Thus, for instance a young Hafiz might be told to appear at St. Sophia at a certain hour every day during Ramazan to chant the Koran, for which she would be paid perhaps 300 piasters (about thirteen dollars) for the month. It may happen that a boy or a girl becomes a Hafiz before the age of twelve. The Rushdie school that I have described has one educated Hafiz.

In Constantinople and in some of the other cities of the empire, there has been of late years a new development in education, in the founding of private schools, mostly for boys, of a higher grade than the Rushdie schools. There are twelve such schools in Constantinople, and three or four of them have now established a section for girls. Private schools are often preferred to the Government Rushdie schools, being more select, the pupils paying their way. They are sometimes established by rich men who wish to help their nation, and the Government encourages them, even financially. These schools keep carriages which are sent around in the morning to collect the scholars. They have some apparatus for teaching science, and are in fact little rudimentary colleges. In private schools for girls the industrial side is very strongly emphasized, and music also is taught.

There is as yet only one high school for girls in the Turkish Empire. It is called the Dar-ul-moualimat, or College of the Lady Teachers, and is in Akserai, in Stamboul. It is a normal school and its aim is to furnish teachers for all the other schools, especially for the secondary ones. Therefore many of the girls who attend this school belong to the poorer classes and have to support themselves. There has been a great improvement in the Dar-ul-moualimat during the past ten years. The sleepy atmosphere of former times, and the apparent dread of too much cerebral excitement for young women, have wholly disappeared; and there is now an attempt at regular training, the methods having been improved until the normal school is by far the best school for girls among the Turks. It contains at present 550 students, of whom 150 are in the three higher classes, which constitute the high school. There are forty-eight in the graduating class, apparently from sixteen to twenty years of age. Twenty-three teachers are employed, of whom seventeen are women, and graduates of the institution. The course of study includes arithmetic, geography, history, ethics, pedagogy, Arabic and Persian, composition, and domestic science. All the older girls in the normal school wear the outer garment in the class-room, which conceals the figure and is also brought up over the head, but their faces are not covered. No foreign language is as yet taught in the Dar-ul-Moualimat.

The existence of all these schools for girls creates a profession for women: the profession of teaching. The demand for teachers is supplied by the normal school, and it is an exception for any woman not possessing a diploma to be accepted as a teacher. Furthermore, the Government is obliged to find positions for all graduates of the normal school, if they demand them. There are very few men teachers in the girls' schools. Marriage does not influence the relations of teachers, but is considered a personal matter. Of the four teachers in the Rushdie school before referred to, one was married and three were unmarried. Turkish women may be married even before they finish the course of study in the normal school; and I know of one instance of a married Turkish woman teaching in a Rushdie school, while her husband takes care of the children and looks after the housekeeping at home. The salaries paid to women teachers vary from two to ten Turkish pounds a month (nine to forty-four dollars). The graduates of the normal school are sent into the interior to teach, accompanied by their parents or husbands, and if they are sent to a great distance a larger salary is paid to them.

It is interesting to note that composition, including the teaching of different kinds of style, is one of the subjects that are taught in the schools; and it is in literary work that the advanced Turkish women have most distinguished themselves. In all this progress there is an inheritance of the past, especially in literary lines. The relation of Mohammedan women to letters appears at intervals throughout all

Mohammedan history. Among the Arabs and Moors there were women preachers in the mosques and bazaars; and women professors were employed in at least one university in Spain during the period of the rule of the Moors. In the early centuries of the Ottoman Empire, the art of letters was not entirely neglected by Mussulman women, for there was usually a literary circle in which women were often found. Of the thirty-four sultans who have been girt with the sword of Osman, twenty-one at least have written poetry. The conquest of Constantinople by the Turks did not plunge the city into absolute illiteracy. Indeed, Mahomet the Conqueror, the "Sire of good works," as he was called by his people, was a man of letters, himself a writer, and a patron of poets and other literary men. Several of his viziers were writers. In fact, literary men were preferred for office, and many poets who did not care to serve their country in that way were pensioned.

It was Mahomet the Conqueror who first organized the Ulema, and colleges were established all over the country for their education. In the court of the mosque built by him there were eight of these colleges, four on each side — "the court of the eight," as they were called — and they furnished one of the intellectual centres of the empire. In this atmosphere literature flourished, and there were women in the literary circle of the court, though but one name has come down to us, that of Mihri. This was not the poetess Mihri usually referred to, whose poems we possess. The latter belonged to the court of Prince Ahmed in Amasia, under Bayazid II, and probably wrote during the latter part of the fifteenth century. The former Mihri was the daughter of a cadi. She never married, but devoted her life to her art; and contemporary writers speak of her character with admiration. She herself writes a half apology for being a woman poet as follows:

> Since they say that woman lacketh wit alway,
> Needs must they excuse whatever word she say.
> Better far one woman, if she worthy be,
> Than a thousand men, if all unworthy they.

Mihri was the author of a volume of poetry which compares well with the works of many of her contemporaries. There were presumably other women writers of distinction of the period. We know of one other called Zehneb. She is said to have been the daughter of a learned man who had her carefully educated. She produced a collection of poems, and was also skilled in the music belonging to her age. She and Mihri were companions and often interchanged verses. Zehneb's career was brought to an untimely end by marriage, for her husband commanded her to refrain from further communication with men, and to stop writing poetry.   I shall quote two fragments written by her:

> Throw off thy veil, and heaven and earth illume with dazzling ray.
> Turn thou this elemental world to Paradise straightway.

And again,

> Leave, Zehneb, lust of show unto the world, the woman-like,
> Walk manful, single-hearted be, abandon gewgaws gay.

It was indeed a wonderful thing that a woman of that age should write Ottoman poetry, as it called for an especial technical education and considerable acquaintance with the Persian masters.   Culture made great strides in the Ottoman Empire during the reigns of the Conqueror, of Bayazid II, and of Selim; for the older sultans were friends and patrons of letters, and their courts were centres of attraction for those who loved to study.   Symposia were held in the literary circles, not only in the capital, but in the large cities of the provinces, in which poets recited their compositions; but education did not flourish to the same extent during the succeeding centuries.   The reforming tendency before referred to, however, which arose during the reign of Mahmoud II in the early part of the nineteenth century, had its influence on literature, and from that period also the names of two women writers have come down to us, Fitvet and Leyla.   They wrote in the transition epoch of Turkish literature, and the old Persian manner is still supreme in their poems.

The best woman writer at the present time is Nighiar Hanum.   She writes both poetry and prose, and her last book of poems has been said by Turkish critics to form an epoch in modern Turkish lyric poetry.   Next to her stands Fatima Alihe Hanum, the daughter of Jevdet Pasha, the Turkish statesman and historian, and she seems to have inherited much of her father's talent.   Her father was the president of the Turkish Academy that existed for about twenty years.   It was composed of forty members, who were selected on account of literary worth.   The Academy was short-lived, but Jevdet Pasha did not confine his efforts to that enterprise.   In addition to his historical works, he wrote the first Turkish grammar and prepared books for the Rushdie schools.   Fatima Alihe Hanum is his eldest daughter.

Both father and daughter have done much for the Turkish language. Fatima Alihe Hanum has written largely on serious subjects, and at one time was said to be preparing a commentary on the Koran, which, however, has never been published.   She has a younger sister, Emine Semie Hanum, in Salonica, who also shares the family talent and writes constantly for the journals. We find in the literary circle a sister of Abdul Hak — a man who is considered by some to be the best poet at the present time among the Turks. The sister writes poetry, and her poems show the same quality of talent that is found in the works of her brother. However, she writes very little, and has, in fact, written in all not more than four or five poems, which have appeared here and there in the journals. If she gave her attention wholly to writing, she might stand first among Turkish women writers. There are also a number of women in the literary circle, who are not now publishing original works on account of the strict censorship of the press. Several years ago the "Hanumlar Gazettassi," or "Woman's Journal," edited by women alone, was started in Constantinople. At present it is edited by a man, but many of the contributors are women. The literature in this journal, however, is rather light in character, and has not especially stimulated literary progress.

There are always a few Turkish girls to be found in the foreign schools. The American College for Girls has had two graduates, one before it became a college, and the other in 1901. The latter, Halide Hanum, the only Mohammedan woman in the Turkish Empire who has received an academic degree, has had a rather remarkable career. When she was fifteen years old she translated into Turkish an English book, "The Mother in the Home," by Jacob Abbott, which so pleased her father that he presented a thousand copies to the wives of the soldiers, and His Majesty decorated Hâlide in token of his approbation. Halide Hanum has often written for the local papers, and she has at present three books ready for publication. One of these may soon be brought out in America. The manuscript of one of the novels has been read by Halid Ziâ, the best living Turkish novelist, and he has considered it favorably. Halide Hanum is now Madame Salih Zeky Bey, being married to one of the professors in the Imperial University. Besides those I have mentioned, there are many other women now belonging to the Mohammedan literary circle, especially writers of romances in Turkish and French.

Turkish women have a great aptitude for foreign languages, and not infrequently women of the educated classes speak French, German, and, perhaps, English with characteristic fluency and a good accent. There is also in existence a kind of a Turkish *salon* for women, the representatives of which may be met in prominent Turkish houses. Members of the diplomatic circle and others who visit in these Turkish homes are very much impressed with the degree of culture they find. In the drawing-rooms of the leading literary women, the general subjects of conversation are new books, pictures, music, and other topics of a similar nature.   In music there is no one who has greatly excelled as yet; but there are several. Turkish women who have studied both music and art seriously, and one of them has exhibited in the Paris *salon*.   In fact, the young women of the better class are now ready to undertake anything that conditions make possible.

Another profession, which may be called the leading one among Turkish women, has existed from the earliest period of Mohammedan history, being a natural development of the habits of seclusion in Turkish society, namely, the profession of nursing in various forms.   In olden times Turkish women were never allowed to see physicians of the other sex, and even at present we hear of instances where the husband says openly that if his wife should be seen with another man her life would no longer be of value to him, and it were better that she should die.   In Constantinople alone there are at present over three hundred professional Mohammedan nurses, or half doctors, as they might, perhaps, be called. Formerly these women received no professional education, but the office was hereditary from mother to daughter.   About forty-five years ago a medical class for women was established, in connection with the Turkish Medical School, in which regular lectures were given by professors of the school, both native and foreign.   These classes are now held in the large new medical school in Haidar Pasha, and they are attended by women of different nationalities.   The lectures are given by competent professors, and increasing attention is paid to them by the authorities of the medical school, the classes for women being announced in the published programme.   There are four women graduates of the school who hold the office of assistants.   They are called *repetiteurs*, and they help in the teaching.   No Mohammedan nurse is expected to practise unless she possesses a diploma from this school, although there are some exceptions among the older women.

A good Mohammedan nurse earns from twenty to twenty-five Turkish liras a month, giving her an annual income of perhaps 250 liras. This is by far the best-established and most lucrative profession for Turkish women, and forms a good basis for a well-developed medical profession among them.   Turkish women have always interested themselves in the poor and the suffering.   Bezim Alim founded a large hospital for the poor in Constantinople.   A hospital in Scutari, founded by an Egyptian princess, is very well endowed, and equipped with modern appliances; and other hospitals have been established by women.

The influence of Turkish women in general affairs is greater than it is usually supposed to be. The person with the money in his pocket is the one who usually rules in the family; and the principal cause of the social power of Mohammedan women lies in the fact that Turkish women have complete control over their own property. In Western countries there is a very erroneous idea that Moslem law has overlooked the civil rights of women. This is not the case in regard to property rights, as any impartial student of Moslem law will agree. Far from sacrificing the rights of women to those of men, the Mohammedan law has, from the beginning, very justly recognized woman's full civil capacity. The origin of Turkish law is the Koran. Yet, after the death of Mohammed, problems arose which were not met by the Koran, and the Tesdour of Bagdad, developed about the end of the seventh century, was founded largely on the laws of Justinian. These laws were friendly to women, as they protected individual liberty without regard to sex. The influence of Christianity, in emphasizing the family, narrowed the liberty that Justinian gave to the individual, resulting in the varied limitations of the civil rights of women which appear in the different codes of Christian lands.

The civil rights given to women by the Justinian code met the demands of the state of society produced by Mohammedanism, in which the relations of a woman to her husband were not necessarily permanent. The laws framed in Bagdad were religious, and consequently not subject to change. But more than twelve hundred years ago Moslem law established some privileges for women that the legislatures of many other lands have until recently denied them. According to the Mohammedan law, any woman may sue or be sued, buy or sell, alienate or bequeath, without marital authorization — not being obliged even to inform her husband of what she is doing. Mohammedan law makes no distinction between married and unmarried women, that is, marriage does not incapacitate in any legal sense. Woman's evidence is also admitted in the courts of law. But here Mohammedan law begins to lapse from the path of rectitude, as two female witnesses are required to oppose one male witness. In the matter of inheritance, also, we cannot hold up Mohammedan law as an example, although it is more just than some laws. The daughter of the defunct receives one share, whereas his son receives two, while widows receive one-eighth of the property of the deceased husband, and one-fourth when there are no children.

Turkish women have an aptitude for legal details. No places in Constantinople are more interesting to the student of sociology than the Turkish courts of law. I attempted on one occasion to visit these courts, but was not permitted to enter the Criminal Court, as, nominally, no woman may step across the threshold. The Mercantile Court I was also requested not to enter. However, I saw Turkish women standing in the halls, apparently having some business at the courts, and on inquiry I found that in three different ways it is possible for a Turkish woman to enter the courts: as a prisoner, as a witness, or even to plead her own cause. Therefore an anomalous state of things comes about, namely, that it is not uncommon for Turkish women to plead their own cases— and they often do this with great eloquence—in a court that women are not ordinarily allowed to enter.

The power of divorce is usually supposed among the Mohammedans to belong to men alone; but a woman may have the same power if that condition is put into the marriage contract. However, under these circumstances, she would probably not receive the divorce fee that the husband is usually obliged to pay. The custom of divorce fees is a curious commentary on human nature. The husband promises in the marriage contract to pay a sum of money to his wife if he divorces her; but this sum is ridiculously small, being among the poorer classes sometimes not more than fifty piasters. It is, furthermore, often expressed in a fraction or an uneven number, as 59.5 piasters, or 199 piasters, in the hope that, owing to the difficulty of making change in Turkey, the husband may stop to think and take back the fiat of repudiation while he is looking for small change.

Turkish women make good business managers, and some of them control their own investments, perhaps with the advice of their financial agents, but largely through their own practical judgment; and there are some cases where they have managed the property of their husbands. Owing to the fact that women control their own property, they are obliged to have some business knowledge. It is a very common occurrence to see Turkish women enter the banks of Constantinople alone to transact their business. It is a well-known fact, furthermore, that many Turkish women are engaged in trade, some even carrying on an extensive business involving frequent journeys to Egypt and other places, which presupposes an ability to read and write, as well as some knowledge of arithmetic. Women peddlers among the Turks are also very common.

In the palace of the Sultan the chief treasurer of the women is always a woman, and she has under her control a regular bureau of trained scribes who are all women. These scribes do all their work in the old-fashioned way, never having learned stenography or typewriting. But herein they are not behind the men of their nation, as, in the Mercantile Court, the documents to be referred to are written by hand, tied up in a handkerchief, and kept in white cotton bags. If any one of them is needed, all the papers in the bag must be poured out on the floor. This is very probably the case also with all the documents of the women scribes. The customs regarding financial control in the palace date back to ancient times, as the laws of the palace government do not change. Consequently, there must always have been women in the palace who knew how to write, read, and keep accounts.

In prison regulations the police are usually more lenient to women than to men, and there are separate prisons for the former. I once knew of a woman who was condemned to prison for a few weeks for having been involved in a street quarrel. The police came to take her to prison. "No," she said, "I cannot go now. I have a young baby that needs my care. It is impossible for me to be away from home." "Very well," the policeman said, "I shall come another day." He waited about a year and came back to take the woman to prison. "No," she said, "it is again impossible. I have another young child. Why did you not come before?" "Very well," he said. "Let me know when it is convenient for you." The woman waited until a short time before one of the public feast days upon which it is the custom to give freedom to those who are imprisoned for slight offences. She then put her house in order and sent word to the police that she was willing to go to prison if she could bring her youngest child with her and satisfactory arrangements could be made.

Women as well as men among the Turks are taught to pray. Yet young women are not generally expected to attend the mosques, although as children they are taught to do so. The hereditary function of praying together is reserved for the men. But women may stand and pray in the corners or behind screens, in the larger mosques; and some of the mosques, generally those with one minaret, are largely reserved for women. Any woman desirous of praying in a mosque is always able to do so; but the women seen publicly in the mosques are not young.

From what has been said it is evident that Turkish women form an interesting part of the population of Turkey; and it is to be hoped that in the future the nation may offer satisfactory opportunities for that higher development of which they have shown themselves capable.

MARY MILLS PATRICK.

THE BRITISH INVASION OF TIBET.

In Defence of the Dalai Lama.

THE fall of Lhassa on August 4, 1904, and the entry of the British troops into that holy city of the Buddhistic world, for centuries inviolable and unviolated by any foreign intrusion, has opened a new chapter, of great importance and interest in the history of Central Asia. Although the British Cabinet in London has, as a last refuge, thrown all responsibility for the expedition upon the shoulders of the Government in Calcutta and the blame of exceeding the prescribed limits upon Colonel Younghusband — of course at the same time conferring knighthood upon him, together with a promotion in rank — yet the practice of the Indian Government, contrary to its profession in dealing with Tibet, and the apparent determination of China to enforce her suzerain rights in that vassal state of hers, with evident encouragement from the European Powers, have placed a serious deadlock in the way of the completion of this tragic comedy, and placed the whole question within the scope of international politics, promising to develop before long certain issues of far-reaching consequence. It is, therefore, worth while to review the entire situation from the beginning, and examine the possibilities that may assume great proportions in the near future.

The reason why, according to official declarations, the British Government sent this expedition into Tibet was twofold:

(1) That the Tibetan authorities did not faithfully carry out the terms of a commercial convention made in 1890 and 1893 between China on behalf of Tibet and the Government of India. But this reason could hardly justify the action of the Indian Government in invading the neighboring kingdom. The only proper thing for the British Government to do under those circumstances was to remonstrate against Tibet's failure to comply with the terms of the convention that had been made with China, its suzerain.

(2) That the Dalai Lama, the Hermit King of Tibet, refused to receive a letter from the Viceroy of India, which act constituted an insult to the King of England, whom the Viceroy of India represents in the East.

But it must be remembered that this letter was delivered by an armed force which had entered the Tibetan territory and occupied the military station thirty miles within the Tibetan frontier. The Dalai Lama, whose territory was invaded for no valid reason, simply asked the intruders to withdraw from his dominions before he could hold communication with them. To impute to the Lama the idea of insulting the King of England is nothing short of adding insult to injury.

Lord Curzon, the Viceroy of India, has added two more reasons to the above. Last July, in his speech at Guildhall, when the freedom of the City of London was conferred upon him, his lordship said:

We felt that we could not afford any longer, with due regard to our interests and prestige on that section of the frontier (Tibet), to acquiesce in a policy of unprovoked insults, endured with almost unexampled patience, at the hands of the Tibetan Government ever since they, and not we — please remember this — ever since they, and not we — assumed the aggressive, and first invaded British territory eighteen years ago. And still less did we think that we could acquiesce in this treatment at a time when the young and perverse ruler of Tibet, who, it seems to me, has shown himself to be the evil genius of his people, was refusing to hold any communication with us, even to receive letters from the representative of the British sovereign, at the same time that he was conducting negotiations with another great Power (Russia), situated, not at his doors, but at a great distance away, and was courting its protection.

Herein, in justification of his forward policy in Tibet, Lord Curzon puts forth two additional reasons, namely, the Tibetan attack on British territory eighteen years ago, and the Dalai Lama's friendly relations with the Czar of Russia while refusing to hold communication with the Indian Government. This argument of the Indian Viceroy is like that of the wolf in the story against the lamb at the stream. Sikkim, on the eastern frontier of India, was formerly a province of Tibet; but it has been long since brought under British control, and the Grand Lama has never been able to reclaim it. In this case, the British, rather than the Tibetans, have been the aggressive party. During the last eighteen years there have been three Viceroys in India besides Lord Curzon, some of them men of great ability; but it was left to his lordship to reestablish British prestige in the East, which had suffered so much damage in the time of his predecessors. If the British prestige suffered at all, it was through the recent defeats in South Africa rather than from the Tibetan attack on British territory eighteen years ago; and the conquest of Tibet would not be a bad way to restore it, for it would demonstrate to the Oriental mind the vigor and energy of the English people.

There are three great Lamas — two in Tibet and one in Urga, or Kuren, the sacred city of Mongolia. The Dalai Lama, the Supreme

9

Pontiff of the Buddhistic world, resides in Lhassa, while the Tashi Lama's seat is at Shigatse, in southern Tibet.   The Lama of Urga, who is called the Living Buddha, and ranks next to the Dalai Lama, is the spiritual ruler of the Mongols and Buriats.   Many of the latter are subjects of the Czar of Russia.   So, if the Czar, out of regard for his Buddhist subjects, sent a few presents to the Pontifex Maximus of Buddhism, it could hardly be said that the Dalai Lama was courting His Majesty's protection.   Nor should Russia be suspected of a design on Tibet.   "For a century," says a correspondent of the London "Daily News," "Russia looked at Tibet and drew up, not daring to touch a place so helpless in material strength, so strong in spiritual force."   Had Lord Curzon only taken a leaf out of the Czar's book and sent the vestment of an Anglican bishop to the Lama, there is little doubt that friendly relations between India and Tibet, if desired, would have been established without recourse to bloodshed.

The real reason for England's advance on Tibet is the influence of high finance on the colonial policy of Great Britain.   Travellers and explorers, in spite of the strict vigilance on the part of the Tibetan authorities, have succeeded during the last decade in discovering the mineral wealth on "the roof of the world."   Sarthol and Thok-jalung in southwestern Tibet possess rich gold deposits in considerable quantities. These places lie, roughly speaking, some three hundred miles east of Simla in British India.   The yellow metal is found in the hill ranges lying between the thirty-second and thirty-third parallels of latitude, on either side of the eighty-second degree of east longitude.   Thokjalung is only some sixty-three hundred feet above sea-level, and not far from the sources of the river Indus, which cleaves the Himalayas in its course through Ladakh and Cashmere into the plains of western India.

Some two hundred miles to the eastward of Thok-jalung, in the lake region in the chain of hills just north of the thirty-second parallel, there are also several gold-fields.   These are the Thok Amar, Thok Marshara, and Thok Daurakpa deposits.   About a hundred miles still farther to the eastward are the Sarka Shyar gold-fields, lying right across an explored tract from the northwest that joins a route running nearly due south from Lob-nor to Lhassa, across ranges of mountains, a pass over one of which is 19,600 feet above sea-level.   Again, to the north of this region, among the northern spurs of the Kuen-Lun range, which forms the dividing line between Tibet proper and Chinese Turkestan, there are several important gold-fields.   Chief among these are those of Akka-Togh, at the head of the Giukerma River, one of the tributaries of the

Cherchen that flows into Lob-nor; the Kapa gold-field, between the Mist and Moldja rivers, which lose themselves in the Tarim basin; and the Sorgak mines on the Nia River, which also ends in the Tarim basin. The last two of these lie in the neighborhood of a route from Kashgar, near the Russian frontier, through Yarkand and Khotan to Lob-nor, at an average altitude of less than five thousand feet, where it meets the route south to Lhassa, and others into western China.

When expedition after expedition, which had explored some region of the Hermit Kingdom, returned to India with exciting stories of fresh discoveries of gold-fields, the imagination of men of high finance — the natural collaborators of the British Foreign Office — was wrought to the highest pitch. There was, therefore, at the return of every exploring expedition, an outburst of agitation, "On to Lhassa," in the Anglo-Indian press. In order to justify the British forward policy in the eyes of the civilized world, there were invented, and widely circulated, wild stories of broken treaties, of Tibetan incursions and outrages, of British subjects captured and tortured, of Nepalese yaks carried off, of studied insults devised by Russian emissaries in Lhassa and directed at the Indian Government through the witless person of the Dalai Lama, etc. In 1898 the agitation for the conquest of Tibet had already attained sufficient importance; but the British Government was at the time occupied in the conquest of the Egyptian Soudan, and, consequently, could not well take up a fresh enterprise. Nor did the agitation of 1900 lead to any practical results, owing to the South African war.

In 1903, however, the long-sought opportunity arrived. Russia, the only Power in Asia whose diplomatic protest in reference to the integrity of the Chinese Empire could be effective, was herself embroiled with Japan over the question of Corea and Manchuria. And China, whose territory both in the east and in the west was the object of ambition of two great European Powers, was powerless to protect her outlying provinces. Lord Curzon took time by the forelock, and despatched a commission, headed by Colonel Younghusband and escorted by 300 soldiers, with two guns, into the interior of Tibet, with the ostensible purpose of discussing a commercial treaty with the Tibetan Government. The latter pointed to China as the proper authority to deal with, and asked the British troops to withdraw from the soil of Tibet. Thereupon the British troops occupied Khumba Jong, thirty miles within the Tibetan frontier, and fortified it. They waited there from July until October, 1903, for the arrival of a regular army, on a war-footing, from India. When General Macdonald, with a few thousand more troops, equipped with all necessary requirements for a Tibetan winter, joined the force at Khumba Jong, the whole army marched into the Chumba Valley, 100 miles nearer to Lhassa.

Thus far Russia had failed to evacuate Manchuria as she had promised to do. England, the ally of Japan, being well posted in regard to the disposition of the latter as to war or peace with Russia, regulated her operations in Tibet accordingly. The progress of the British expedition was therefore slow during the winter months, not only because of the unfavorable climatic conditions, but also in expectation of the outbreak of war in the Far East. As soon as the Russo-Japanese war was declared, the British march on Lhassa commenced in downright earnest, and in the beginning of last August the British army made its triumphant entry into the sacred metropolis of the Hermit Kingdom.

Ancient civilization, which had its genesis in the East and which still has its hold there, has ever inculcated the superiority of moral principle over that of utility, and taught the maxim, "It is better to be an object of injustice than to be its perpetrator"; while the modern civilization of the West has been largely utilitarian and greatly influenced by the doctrine of "the struggle for existence and the survival of the fittest," even as applied to the members of the same species. The latest application of these two opposing doctrines has occurred in the dealing of England with Tibet. The former resorted to every possible excuse, or created a plausible one, to invade the latter country; while Tibet, believing that justice was on her side, remained supine for the period of a full year after the inroad of the British into Tibetan territory and before their entrance into Lhassa, and made no adequate preparation to defend the country against the invasion of a powerful enemy. Nay, the Dalai Lama, as a true exponent of the gospel of peace preached by Gautama Buddha, even went so far as to forbid his subjects from making any hostile demonstration against the British by issuing the following proclamation:

If war arises, men and animals will suffer, so we consulted carefully and withdrew our soldiers for the sake of peaceful negotiations. We will, however, act as fate demands, having regard to our Buddhistic faith.

It is inexplicable, and probably it will ever remain so, why a few thousand Tibetans were shot down by the British troops at the beginning of the spring of 1904; for by that time the British army had been on Tibetan soil for about ten months, and had traversed almost two-thirds of the distance from the frontier to Lhassa, while the Tibetans were not once reported to have shown a warlike disposition.

True to his proclamation, the Dalai Lama sent his envoys with peace proposals to meet Colonel Younghusband the moment the British force crossed the Sanpu River.   The intelligence of the arrival of these envoys at the British headquarters caused the Indian press to agitate in favor of stopping the British soldiers from entering Lhassa.   Even the Secretary of State for India announced at that time in the House of Commons that there would be no need for the British troops to advance on Lhassa.   But at the last moment a different council prevailed, and the British expedition, defying the traditions of ages, marched into the holy city, built on "the roof of the world," and hitherto hidden from the vulgar gaze of foreigners.

It is a cruel irony of fate that, when the Indian Government decided to despatch armed men into Tibet, it pooh-poohed the suzerainty of the Celestial Empire over the land of the Lamas; and Lord Curzon himself called it a "constitutional fiction."   But when Colonel Younghusband arrived in Lhassa, he found no authority there but that of the Chinese Government.   On the approach of the British army, the Lama had quit the capital and left the government of the country in the hands of the Chinese Amban, who permanently resides in Lhassa.   Even the entry of the British troops into the sacred city was deprived of its spectacular grandeur.   No soldiers were lining the principal streets of the town to pay homage to the conquerors, nor were there any crowds of spectators curiously looking at the unwelcome intruders.   Men, women, and children were occupied as usual, as if nothing out of the way had occurred. There was no anarchy, no sign of a disturbance of the peace, no danger to life and property from the let-loose populace, although the constitutional government authority was in abeyance for the time being.   The Supreme Pontiff of 400,000,000 souls was himself a fugitive in some unknown place; and yet his unique Tse Potala palace, which in extent and splendor may put even the palace of the Vatican itself into the shade, though tenantless, was in no danger of being looted by a lawless Tibetan mob.

The British commissioner was greatly perplexed at finding no responsible Tibetan authority to negotiate with.   Even the question of supplies for the British troops presented difficulties; and the problem was not solved until General Macdonald trained a battery on the Daipung monastery and deployed the infantry, seriously threatening to bombard the sacred edifice.   Colonel Younghusband had, therefore, to fall back upon the Chinese Amban, who readily paid a visit of courtesy as a representative of the Celestial Government, which visit the colonel returned with great ceremony.   The Chinese Amban tried to accommodate the

British guests in every possible manner and displayed consummate diplomatic tact while dealing with them on matters political.

The days were spent in an aimless marching of redcoats, with military music, through the streets of Lhassa, and weeks elapsed in paying visits of inspection to Buddhist cathedrals and temples; but the object of the expedition was not yet in sight. The British commissioner at last raised the Tashi Lama, whose seat is in Shigatse, to the supreme authority in Tibet, and declared the Dalai Lama, who had fled from the capital, as deposed. A document, so comprehensive in its scope as to bring the entire dominion of the Hermit Kingdom under British control, and to leave no shred of independence to the Tibetan Government, was then presented to the Tashi Lama, who had no alternative but to sign it. The Lama who signed this unusual kind of a document is said to have smiled as he affixed his signature, while the Lama who speeded the parting guests is said to have wept briny tears. But the Chinese Amban, who watched the proceedings with expressionless solemnity, when requested to affix his signature to the document, simply shrugged his shoulders and pleaded want of authority from his august master, the Son of Heaven. As the winter season was not far off in those high regions, and as it was deemed inexpedient that the British troops should remain bottled up among the mountains in the almost blood-freezing cold of Tibet, and cut off from their base of supplies for about six months, the British commissioner was content with any kind of a document he could procure to hang a British claim upon; for any stick is good enough to beat a dog with.

The so-called treaty, thus signed at the point of the bayonet, binds the Tibetan authorities to establish markets for British traders at Yatung, Gyangtse, and Gartok, and to pay an indemnity of seventy-five lakhs of rupees in three yearly instalments, permitting British troops to occupy the Chumba Valley until the indemnity is paid. It also stipulates that without the consent of Great Britain no Tibetan territory is to be held by or leased to any foreign Power; and it debars all foreign Powers from interfering in the affairs of Tibet, from constructing roads, railways, or telegraphs, and from working the mines.

The treaty, which is invalid in the eyes of international law, fully discloses by its terms the real motives which were at the bottom of the British invasion of Tibet. The mineral wealth of the forbidden land, just like that of the Transvaal, has been the dominant factor, as pointed out before, in all the dealings of Great Britain with Tibet. What wonder is it, then, that no fewer than nine mining companies were formed in

London to work and exploit the gold-fields of northwestern Tibet, even before the British army had made its entry into the Lama's capital? The extraordinary monetary demand, which far exceeds the capacity of the Tibetan Government to pay, clearly indicates that Great Britain had originally intended to retain possession of the Chumba Valley for an indefinite period as a vantage-ground in the process of absorbing the dominion of the Grand Lama. We are even now hearing the Tibetans complain that the monetary demand is excessive; declaring that it is beyond the capacity of the Tibetan treasury to pay twenty-five lakhs of rupees annually. The British Government seemed at first to favor the idea of an annual payment of a lakh of rupees, which would extend the British possession of the Chumba Valley to seventy-five years.

When the text of the Lhassa treaty reached Peking, the Chinese Government refused to ratify it, and, through the Chinese press, made known this fact to the civilized world. The Chinese contention is that Tibet is a province of the Celestial Empire, being a vassal state of China, and that the British action in Tibet has been tantamount to an infringement of the sovereign rights of the suzerain power. The Chinese statesmen know full well that the occupation of Tibet by England would ultimately lead the latter country to the acquisition of the Chinese western provinces, and that it is England's aim to reach the Yangtse Valley — assigned to her by an agreement of the European Powers — from the west, through Tibet.

The British activity for some time past in constructing railway lines through upper Burmah toward the southwestern frontier of China has been viewed in the same light by many a far-seeing Chinese statesman. But, owing to the hopeless weakness of the centre of government in the past, the patriotic Chinese could not adequately provide safeguards against these impending dangers. China has now awakened to her dangers and seems determined to ward them off. Fortunately for her, she has been assured by Russia and Japan, as well as by Germany, of the approval of her stand against the British encroachment upon her sovereign rights in the Tibetan kingdom. The Chinese Government, without loss of time, not only repudiated the Lhassa treaty, but also sent to Lhassa as an inspector a graduate of Yale University, "who has the confidence of Yuan-shi-kai, who was a disciple of Li Hung Chang, who was a colleague of old Commissioner Li of the time of the British opium wars, who heartily detested England," to report to the home Government on this Tibetan incident and take charge of affairs at the Tibetan capital.

As soon as this firm attitude of China became known, it did not fail
to impress itself upon the British Cabinet, and consequently the India
Office in London, without delay, issued the following communication:

> With reference to the statements which have been telegraphed from India as to
> the general scope of the agreement signed at Lhassa between the British Commis-
> sioners and the Tibetan authorities, we are informed that the convention still awaits
> ratification by the Viceroy of India, and that the terms are not yet finally settled.

The British army, on returning from Lhassa to India, became snow-
bound on the Phari plains, and scores of men were rendered totally blind
for life. Fortunately, succor arrived in time, otherwise the whole expedition might have been lost. The Dalai Lama, it is stated, has gone to
Urga, where he has been enthusiastically received. He declined the
hospitality offered him by the Russian Government to go into Russian
territory as Russia's guest.

The invasion of Tibet by the British army, the violation of the sanctity of isolation of the Buddhistic capital, and laying bare the secrets of
the holy of holies of the Grand Cathedral (jo-kang) to the vulgar gaze
are events not only significant from a political point of view, but also
fraught with an element of danger from the religious standpoint. For
Lhassa is to China, Japan, and Corea what Mecca is to Turkey, Persia,
and Afghanistan. The desecration of the Holy Land of northern
Buddhism has spread consternation among millions of people in Asia
and created a commotion in the Far East. China is alarmed, Japan is
cut to the quick, and India is filled with gloom and suppressed indignation. The progress of the British soldiers on the sacred soil was not
confined to the killing of a few thousand Tibetans, but was accompanied by rapine and the plunder of the treasure-houses of monas-
teries. A correspondent of the London "Daily Chronicle" says:

> The expedition has looted the monasteries, and for weeks past bales of plunder
> have been coming over the passes into India. Their contents have brought joy to
> the officers' wives and friends, whose houses in the hill stations begin to look as
> some of them looked after the sack of Peking four years ago.

An Indian vernacular paper depicts the deeds more graphically, and,
by the way, gives vent to the feelings of the Hindus on the subject:

> The Dalai Lama has made himself scarce from Lhassa, and there are no early
> prospects of a settlement. In the mean time, syndicates are being formed in Eng-
> land to plunder the wealth of Tibet. Before this systematic spoliation has had an
> opportunity to begin, informal loot has been going on, and Tibetan curios are
> already being displayed in Darjeeling drawing-rooms. The English have such a
> special knack of looting, and they do it in such an adroit manner, that no one can
> venture to call it by its true name.

No flight of imagination would be necessary to conceive the extent of righteous indignation felt by the Buddhistic community at the humiliating events which have recently taken place in Lhassa. But we are indebted to the correspondent of the London "Daily News" for describing the scenes witnessed at Urga, the capital of Mongolia, and the seat of the second Lama, called the Living Buddha, on the occasion of an annual gathering of priests and pilgrims from far-off lands. He says:

For centuries great numbers of priests had met in the same month in Urga to pray for the peace of the world. The Living Buddha and the Buddhas before him had led the prayer. Generations have come and gone; dynasties have risen and fallen; great rivers have changed their courses; but the yearly prayer for peace has never failed to ring out on the clear crisp air of the mountain capital. But in the year of our Lord 1904 the scene changed. . . . There was no talk of peace in the temples of Urga. The traditions of ages were set aside. . . . I went among the five and twenty thousand priests assembled at Urga, and this is the thing I learned. Into every hole and corner of India and Asia where the Buddhistic faith has root, a message is to be sent, and by this time has been sent, condemning Britain's action in Tibet. Pilgrims and priests, packmen and traders — all will carry it as birds carry seeds, to be dropped by the wayside. Under that crusade British trade and influence will shrink as it would never shrink from the blast of a great war.

Religion is still a tender question in the East, and those who violate the sanctity of religion doubtless tread upon thin ice. Cartridges greased in the fat of cow and pig produced a revolution in India in 1857 and brought the British Empire in Asia almost to the verge of destruction. The people of Tibet are of one religion and greatly attached to it. To set the adherents of one religion against those of another, as was done in India with marked success, does not seem to be practicable in the land of the Lamas. Anglo-Saxon ingenuity seems to have been mindful of this element of danger, and has tried to palliate England's offence by means of stories concocted to play upon the Tibetan superstition. When the British troops were marching upon Lhassa itself, the following story was circulated in Tibet and also telegraphed to India, to produce the desired effect:

A Tibetan prophecy predicted that the country would be invaded and conquered by Europeans, when all of the true religion would go for a change to Shambala, and Buddhism would become extinct in Tibet. The Lamas believe that the prophecy will be fulfilled by our (British) entry into Lhassa, and their religion will decay before foreign influence.

Another story, even more striking than the first, was invented when one day last August some members of the expedition at Lhassa paid a visit of inspection to the Grand Cathedral of the holy city, known as Jo-kang, for centuries shielded from the vulgar gaze of ordinary mortals and which now yielded only to brute force. In the holy of holies of that great temple, where the spiritual life of Tibet and of the countless millions of northern Buddhism is wholly centred, were seen two magnificent idols. The more imposing of the two was the statue of Gautama himself, made by no man's hand, but by Visvakarma (the constructive force of the universe) itself, as its legendary history relates. The other one was the statue of the guardian goddess, Palden Lhamo, beset with gold and precious stones from head to foot, and universally worshipped by the Tibetans. The sight of that female statue inspired the Anglo-Saxon mind, and then and there this beautiful story was invented for circulation in Tibet and abroad:

This guardian deity, whose image this statue is, as every Tibetan knows from the Dalai Lama to the peasant in the field, was reincarnated in the last century as Queen Victoria.

The dull-witted Tibetans, however, proved to be impervious to the charm of these stories, and, contrary to all expectation, held the Tashi Lama, whom the British had set up as supreme authority, in supreme contempt. They remained, moreover, loyal to the Dalai Lama, whom the British declared to be deposed; and when the British troops left Lhassa there was no love lost between the unwelcome guests and the unwilling hosts.

There was never a time in history when international affairs were more intricate than they are to-day, nor was there ever a time when a diplomatic move on the part of a nation encountered so many counter moves on the chess-board of world politics; for at no other time in history were there so many great empires and republics striving simultaneously for the acquisition of world supremacy, or competing, so to speak, to secure "a place in the sun." When the British Government decided two years ago to start upon the policy of extending the British Empire in Asia to trans-Himalayan regions, it had calculated only upon the possible opposition of Russia, and with great circumspection made provision to nullify that opposition.

The Russo-Japanese war, in the course of its development, has, strange to say, upset a good many of the Government's plans. China, which has been considered a negligible quantity, has suddenly become, through Japan's victories, conscious of her latent power, and has acquired confidence in herself. She took advantage of the celebrated doctrine laid down at the outbreak of the present war by Secretary Hay and approved by all neutral Powers, namely, the integrity of the administrative entity of the Chinese Empire; and she lodged an unequivocal protest against the British invasion of Tibet, which she claimed to be a part and parcel of the dominions of the Son of Heaven.   She contended that commercial relations between India and Tibet must be arranged between a British plenipotentiary and the Chinese imperial resident in Tibet; that the so-called British Tibetan treaty must be changed into a British-Chinese treaty and dated according to the Chinese calendar; that the terms of the treaty should avoid all offence to Russia; and that the treaty should not be signed until it should be sanctioned by imperial edict.   She was, strange to say, not a little encouraged in this action by the approval of Germany as well as that of both Russia and Japan.

This unexpected development of the situation, to be sure, placed the British Government on the horns of a dilemma, and it tried to extricate itself from the uncomfortable position by simply putting the blame upon the shoulders of Colonel Younghusband, who, it declared, in the Blue-Book recently published, really transgressed the limits prescribed by the Government.   This change of tactics on the part of the Balfour Ministry afforded a good opportunity to the opposition in the House of Commons, and the radical press outside, to ridicule the present Cabinet. "Replying to Lord Spencer," says a London paper, "Lord Lansdowne covered Sir F. Younghusband with eulogies, which shows how insincere and hypocritical was the public censure visited upon him.   If the Government had meant business, they would have cashiered him.   But they are all in the same boat, and they therefore cannot with safety go very far in denouncing each other."   The criticism of the radical press is, doubtless, not extravagant, because this so-called "peaceful mission," involving sixteen engagements, had a total list of casualties on the British side of 202, including 23 officers, of whom 5 were killed; and, apart from the war casualties, the force had 411 deaths and 671 men invalided, in addition to the loss of thousands of transport animals and the slaughter of thousands of Tibetans.   Then, again, the saddling of the already poverty-stricken taxpayers of India with the entire cost of the expedition is not a measure which will tend to make the British rule beloved in that country.

The present Tibetan situation is anomalous in the extreme.   England expresses to the civilized world, through the official declarations in the Blue-Book, her regret for the excesses committed by Colonel Younghusband, and says that she is not in the least inclined to interfere with the integrity of the Celestial Empire, while the Indian Government is playing its old game of absorbing the country by keeping a tight grip upon the Chumba Valley and by constructing a short route to Lhassa east of Bhootan from the province of Assam.   The bellicose tone of the London

"Times," which often echoes the official sentiments, "should China refuse to sign" (the treaty concluded at Lhassa), "her signature, we imagine, might be dispensed with," has inadvertently let the cat out of the
bag in regard to the real British policy in Tibet.

Of course, in a great measure, the solution of the problem rests with
China, and the whole situation lies in the hollow of her hand.   If she
has the will and power to enforce her suzerain rights in Tibet, the independence of the latter country is secure.   There is no lack of evidence
that China means business in this case.   The Chinese High Commissioner for Tibetan affairs passed through Calcutta last March on his
way to Lhassa to make inquiries into the circumstances connected with
the British expedition and the negotiations of the treaty.

Moreover, China has of late inaugurated a new era of internal reforms.   The Chinese Government has already taken steps to put on a
sound basis the fiscal and military organizations of the empire.   A plan
has recently been elaborated by which the land tax of China, amounting
to 400,000,000 taels, or $240,000,000, would be applied to the estab-
lishment of a regular civil service, the construction of a powerful navy, and
the formation of an army of 500,000 men to begin with.   The Empress-
Dowager of China, who only a short time ago was accustomed to behead
all Chinese reformers who fell into her grasp, has become herself an
ardent reformer and a zealous champion of the modern sciences and of
Western institutions.   Her Majesty has even learned the French language, and can now read some of the foreign telegrams which formerly
had to be translated to her.   Surely these are signs of the times which
one may read as he runs.   And surely this unprovoked invasion of Tibet
by England is to a large extent responsible for arousing China from her
slumber of centuries, either for good or for evil, as time alone can disclose.

                                        MOHAMMAD BARAKATULLAH.

THE RUPTURE BETWEEN NORWAY AND SWEDEN.

By its action of June 7 the Norwegian Storthing, with the unanimous consent of the country, severed the last tie that for more than ninety years had bound Norway to Sweden. As far as the Norwegians are concerned, the dual kingdom ceased to exist the moment the Council of State notified Oscar II that it had been empowered by the Storthing to assume the reins of government, and that His Swedish Majesty no longer held control. The Storthing, it is true, in its address to King Oscar, asserted feelingly that Norway entertained no ill-will against him, his dynasty, or the Swedish people, and asked him, besides, to coöperate with the independent Norwegian nation in the selection of a young prince of the house of Bernadotte to become King of Norway. However, the answer of the dethroned Oscar was a decided protest against the action of the Norwegian Government. And, inasmuch as Norway took upon herself every responsibility as regards the severance of intimate relations with her sister nation, it is likely that Sweden will furnish a countermove as vigorous and prompt as that by which Norway declared its absolute independence.

Undoubtedly King Oscar's veto of the separate consular law, at the sitting of the Council of Ministers a week previous to the action of the Storthing, precipitated events which, after all, were inevitable. The ministers tendered their resignations immediately, but the King refused to accept them. They individually pleaded with King Oscar to sanction the law which all Norway demanded as absolutely essential to her welfare; but when all had spoken, Oscar II read his reply, which stated in ringing terms that he fully indorsed the declaration made by the Crown Prince on April 3, to the effect that the question could be decided only by mutual negotiations. The ministers, headed by Premier Michelsen, again asked the King to reconsider his action until it could be discussed in full council at Christiania. Oscar, however, stood resolute, declaring that he must protect the rights of his Swedish subjects as well as those of Norway. As the ministers all refused to countersign the protocol affirming the royal veto of the Consular Law, the veto was constitutionally non-existent.

It is largely problematical whether Sweden will resort to arms for the purpose of bringing Norway once more into the dual fold, or whether she will acquiesce in the independence the sister nation has declared. Whatever the final outcome, the Scandinavian situation looms large in the eyes of the world. The significance of this northern incident may affect Europe to an extent not heretofore suspected. It is of interest to inquire into the causes which have led to an open rupture in a community where peace has heretofore outwardly prevailed. The Scandinavian peninsula has long been free from those disturbing influences which not infrequently mark the progress of a people toward independence.

The union between Norway and Sweden was based on such equity that it gave to each country self-government in its highest form; and the Swedish Riksdag and the Storthing of the Norwegians are the respective parliamentary bodies, than which none more liberal exists in any European nation. The reign of Oscar II has been so impartial that his recent retirement, owing to ill health, was a matter of regret to all his subjects, whether in Sweden or on the other side of the mountain chain which divides the dual kingdom. Nevertheless, while internal peace has characterized the political advance of both Sweden and Norway, certain features of the bond uniting them have for years been objectionable to the people of the latter country. It is claimed by the Norwegians that the Constitution entitles them to privileges that have been withheld purposely in order that Norway may be made to appear the lesser nation of the two. Agitations of a more or less violent nature have on several occasions brought the dispute near to the breaking point. Yet the personality of King Oscar, it must be noted, twice proved instrumental in preventing open hostilities between the twin nations. Due to his conciliatory offices, Sweden conceded the flag question; and the banner of Norway is now free from the "union" mark which, in the eyes of the Norwegians, informed the world that the latter were to be looked upon as the inferior of the two peoples.

With the entrance of the Crown Prince Gustaf as the Regent of Sweden-Norway, during the temporary retirement of his royal parent, the disputes between the Swedes and the Norwegians assumed a form far more serious than when Oscar II held, so to speak, the balance of power. The consular question became the all-pervading problem confronting the Storthing, and several Norwegian cabinets foundered on the rocks that are piled high around the point at issue. The Swedes stood fast, with the assertion that now had come the time to call a halt. Equally persistent were the Norwegians with their claim that they were entitled to separate consulates, and that nothing would stop them from attaining them.

The fact that Russia is so fully occupied in the East has had its bearing as regards the contention between Norway and Sweden. The consular demand is not by any means of recent date; but there can be little doubt that the fear of Russian aggression has heretofore been the check on the insistent Norwegians and the no less unyielding Swedes. Since no danger is to be looked for from the land of the Czar, the Scandinavian hostilities have become aggravated to a considerable extent. Crown Prince Gustaf is known to be absolutely against conceding the point in dispute. His military predilection does not warrant the peaceful solution that might have been expected from his father, who literally regards the pen as far mightier than the sword. Arbitration, whether between nations or individuals, has ever been the watchword of King Oscar. His international decisions have been rendered in a spirit of fairness that has earned him the gratitude of more than one nation in Europe and America.

It may not have escaped the reader of current European events that on each of the several occasions when ill health forced the King to hand over the reins of state to Crown Prince Gustaf, a crisis arrived in the ever-present grievance of the Norwegians regarding the separate consulates. So, too, in the present instance, high words have passed between the leaders of each country. The resignation of Professor Hagerup, the Prime Minister of the Norwegian Cabinet, came as a great surprise to the moderate element, which had hoped that this clear-minded statesman would succeed in bringing about some amicable arrangement. The negotiations had been carried on for months, and then came the final failure, when Mr. Hagerup, during the meeting of the Storthing, informed his colleagues that nothing had been accomplished. He concluded his speech with the words that the crisis had arrived; that while the people were possessed of the ardent wish to preserve the good relations heretofore existing between the kindred nations, the situation had reached the danger stage; and that since he could be no longer of any service to his country, he would resign his office, in order that others might try to effect a settlement of the dispute.

In many respects Norway had justice on her side when she insisted on separate consulates as for her best interests abroad. As at present constituted, the Swedish-Norwegian consulates are open to citizens of either country; but since the posts fall under the jurisdiction of the

Swedish Foreign Office, Norwegians feel that they are hampered in the discharge of their duties as consuls. More often than not, Swedes occupy the posts abroad. Nor are the Norwegians especially anxious to enter this branch of the diplomatic service under the prevailing conditions. Besides, since the merchant marine of Norway is one of the largest in the world, it seems a reasonable desire for the Norwegians to have their own commercial representatives in foreign ports, where the ships of the nation are such frequent visitors. Furthermore, Norway is a free-trade country, while Sweden exacts a tariff.

From the standpoint of Sweden, her objection to the granting of the separate consulates has its merit. It is argued by those who have viewed the situation in all its intricate bearings that, if Norway should gain her point, the entering wedge would be made for that absolute independence which unquestionably is the dream of every patriotic Norseman; for it is but a step from the separate consulate to separate embassies; so that a Norwegian Minister for Foreign Affairs will then become a necessity, and the ties that have bound the two peoples will disappear. In fact, Norway's aim, as Sweden saw it, was for the complete control of her foreign policy. Ever since the arbitration negotiations between the Storthing and the United States, in 1890, it has been a thorn in the side of the Norwegians that, without consulting them, the Swedish Minister for Foreign Affairs refused the offer of the great republic in face of the fact that the Norse parliament had asked King Oscar to sign the treaty to the above effect.

There is another phase in the Norse agitation of the present which is significant because of the intense nationalism it carries in its wake. A revival of the old Norwegian tongue has for some time occupied the minds of the ultra-patriotic sons of the Viking land. To see the language of the "Eddas" and the "Heimskringla" the every-day speech of Norway has been their dream and their desire. Centuries ago the old Norse tongue prevailed in entire Scandinavia; but gradually it changed its ponderous form into what are now the Swedish and Danish languages. Except for certain differences of minor importance, the Norwegians and the Danes now speak an identical language. To revive the ancient speech and make it the true expression of an independent nation is the ambition of those who aim at obliterating every tie that recalls the former Danish vassalage and the present bond with Sweden.

Should Norway succeed in maintaining her independence, whether through peaceful efforts or by armed force, her future relations to both Sweden and Denmark will prove a matter of great concern, not only to the three Scandinavian countries, but to Europe as a whole. As for Denmark, the press of that country is already giving voice as to what is likely to happen in the north when Norway becomes free. The Danes look upon such a change as one making rather for that greater Scandinavia, the thought of which every now and then rises to the surface in the Northlands. On the dissolution of the union with Sweden, Norway's indomitable spirit will blast the way for another union, an alliance, defensive or offensive, as the interests of Scandinavia might crave. Dreams of the olden times, when the Vikings held sway through all Northern Europe, have their revival in the minds of many of Scandinavia's warlike sons. The fighting spirit of the Northmen is but lying dormant, ready to spring to the fore should conditions call it forth. The glorious contests of the past show what the people of Denmark, Norway, and Sweden are capable of doing when put upon their mettle.

But there are other, and perhaps greater, compensations in store for a united Scandinavia. Those more moderate in their estimate of the future feel assured that a commercial union between the three countries is about to be consummated. The possibilities of such a pact give assurance that the industrial and agricultural conditions in the north would attain to proportions decidedly advantageous to each partner in the scheme. In their relations to the rest of Europe, the Scandinavians would then be as united as if one ruler held the sceptre.

Reverting to the possibility of Norway attaining her end and holding the independence recently declared, it is hardly to be inferred that a republic would be established. Under conditions as free and unhampered as in the case of Denmark and Sweden-Norway, the monarchical institution has at no time been distasteful to the Norsemen. Indeed, it has been said, in some of the most radical circles, that to prove their good-will toward the Swedish royal house, the Norwegians would be willing to accept as their king one of the younger princes of the present dynasty. While it is true that Norway some time ago abolished titles indicating an aristocracy, the separate kingly office would in no wise interfere with the Constitution, which makes for self-government as democratic as that of the Constitution of England. The old Norse kings sprang from the people — there are among the peasants of Norway to-day many direct descendants of those Viking fighters — and the ancestry of the Bernadottes agrees sufficiently with this tradition to make a prince of the Swedish house prove an acceptable ruler. On the part of the Norwegians, it would be a graceful acknowledgment that Oscar II had fulfilled his mission as a people's leader, and his remaining days

. 10

would pass amid conditions equally satisfying to the people of the two brother nations.

In an hour when the dispute, unfortunately, is as yet far from settled, it may be pertinent to inquire into the status of Norway when, as a province of Denmark, the country chafed under a tutelage the most distasteful it had ever experienced. Between the years 1537 and 1814 the history of independent Norway is as a closed book. In nearly every activity Danish supremacy held sway. Many wars marked that period, and, instead of gaining by the conflicts in which she was made to participate, Norway suffered losses that sapped her strength.

It was Napoleon's defeat at Leipsic and Bernadotte's invasion of the Danish territory of Holstein which effected the Peace of Kiel, January 14, 1814, when Norway was ceded to Sweden. Thenceforth the spirit of the people asserted itself continually. From a province the country rose to the dignity of a state. As part of the dual kingdom, the Norwegians have prospered materially, although the vision of absolute liberty has been constantly before their eyes as vouchsafing even greater honors in the family of nations. In the spheres of art and culture Norway has already attained a stage of supreme importance.

As distinguished from that other glorious epoch, when the kings of Norway stood as the embodiment of martial valor and the spirit of conquest, the period that began with the union of the Swedes and the Norwegians proved an era of intellectual achievement hardly matched by any other European nation. The patriotic literature of the Wergelands and the Welhavens was the forerunner of the work of that master-spirit among the Norsemen, Björnstjerne Björnson. The labors of this great Norwegian poet and dramatist are bearing fruit throughout the entire land. The school system of the country has been productive of a general culture, which includes the peasant of the mountain district and the laborer in the city. Together with Henrik Ibsen, yet in a manner diametrically the reverse of that characterizing the great sceptic, Björnson has spread the fame of Norway throughout the world. As an exponent of human nature in all its intricacies, Ibsen is to-day proclaimed the foremost of psychological anatomists. With Björnson the superior forces at work in mankind constitute the all-important factor. This proved the inspiration which led him to write the national song of Norway, which even the Swedes admire, since it is emblematic of entire Scandinavia. So, too, in the domain of music, Edvard Grieg strikes the true note of Northern patriotism, which tells the world that here is a people free of fancy and brooking no restraint.

It was the German Emperor, with that prescience which the nations have learned to respect, who first appreciated what a united Scandinavia would stand for in the affairs of Europe.   From the moment when Bismarck was dismissed from office, the policy of the Iron Chancellor toward Scandinavia was reversed by his imperial master.   William II began that *rapprochement* toward the northern countries which not only earned him the good-will of the Scandinavians, but insured international peace throughout Europe.   It is a fact, not easily disguised, that, but for Bismarck, the Danes would not have suffered the loss of Schleswig-Holstein in the manner which caused the Prussians to ask the aid of Austria at the very outset.   Not that Emperor William is better disposed to return to Denmark the conquered territory than to return Alsace-Lorraine gratuitously to the French, yet his desire for the friendship of his neighbors is in evidence through all that he does and says.   His astuteness in this particular has never been more apparent than during his several visits to Scandinavia within recent years.

There is trustworthy information to the effect that, from the political standpoint of the German Emperor, the future Scandinavia must be reckoned with as an entity.   That is, with absolute independence assured to Norway, Denmark and Sweden would be her true allies in everything affecting the three countries, individually or collectively.   Through all the various disputes between the Swedes and the Norwegians, Kaiser William has remained an interested spectator.   In some respects his attitude has been anomalous in Scandinavian eyes; for, while he is the professed friend of Crown Prince Gustaf of Sweden, he nevertheless, when in the north, spends his time among the democratic sons of Norway.   It is still fresh in the minds of the Northmen how William II came to their aid when the disastrous fire at Aalesund laid that town in ashes.   His liberality toward the inhabitants continued during the many months that elapsed before they had recovered from the awful visitation.

The fate of Finland and the ruthlessness of Russia in the governing of what is now a province of the empire may, after all, prove to the Swedes the necessity of acknowledging Norway's independence for the sake of Scandinavian unity.   Sooner or later the Russian bear will cease warring in Manchuria, whether as victor or vanquished.   Whatever the outcome may be, the Muscovite will not forget the anti-Russian sentiment displayed by the Swedes quite openly and unreservedly.   Political agitators have found Swedish soil their haven when escape from their native land has been their only alternative.   Revolutionary literature has come from the printing presses of the country on the Baltic. Of all this Russia has been aware; yet in her present predicament she has been unable to prevent it.   Should Finland be able to make common cause with the Russian patriots in a successful attempt to gain greater freedom, Russian aggression of Sweden may be avoided.   If not, the day of reckoning will find the soldiers of the Czar massing on the Swedish frontier; and only the efforts of Scandinavian armed resistance, backed by the army and navy of either England or Germany, could prevent a catastrophe which would mean irretrievable defeat.   Knowing what Russian supremacy over the Scandinavian peninsula would mean to Germany, it is not difficult to understand why the friendship of the latter country for Russia is but half-hearted and in danger of disappearing entirely.

A reassociation of the three Scandinavian countries, and their alliance with a power like Germany, would augment the navy of the Kaiser to a much greater extent than is generally supposed would be the case. Sweden to-day possesses nine battleships, while Norway has four ships of this construction, and Denmark seven.   About fifteen protected cruisers are in service, and the more than one hundred torpedo-boats would prove invaluable in the waters where the Russian men-of-war would be at the mercy of the Scandinavian seamen, who know every inch of the ground.   The equipment of the Scandinavian navies is of the very best; and as for personnel to man the ships, no nations have better material for that purpose than have Denmark, Sweden, and Norway.   The tonnage of the merchant marine of Norway, Sweden, and Denmark reaches the enormous figure of almost 3,000,000, the tonnage of Norway alone exceeding that of France.   As the tonnage of the German mercantile marine is only a little more than 3,000,000, it may be readily seen how much Germany would have to gain by a union that would make the Kaiser the supreme arbiter in the Baltic and the North Sea, with only England as a rival for that honor.

The feelings of the Scandinavians for the British are of the most friendly nature, and have been augmented recently by the betrothal of an English princess to a prince of the house of Bernadotte; and their desire to retain this friendship completely would be their only reason for not meeting the wishes of William II as readily as might be supposed. Still, the recent greetings between the royal kinsmen have been of a nature to suggest that King Edward himself might wish to enter into a scheme that would include Great Britain, Germany, and the new Scandinavia.   Such a combination would be the best possible check to Russia;

aggression westward, and make inviolate the territory embracing Denmark, Norway, and Sweden.

Europe has had greater diplomatic surprises within men's memories, and a consolidated Scandinavia might bring about a second Union of Calmar, when, for more than a century, the King of Denmark was recognized as the power of the Northern seas. Then Finland was part of the political entity, and the Finns of to-day would ask for no better fate than to be joined again to the people with whom they have so much in common. Russia has not been blind as to what the future may bring to bear against her. Her evident desire to please both England and Germany, while tied body and soul in Manchuria, is probably due to her recognition of a future contingency. Scandinavia, then, is the key to the international situation which will follow upon the struggle between the sons of Nippon and the Muscovites.

Viewing the northern situation in the light of a world-episode of far-reaching consequences, the career of Oscar II must come in for a considerable share of attention. No matter whether an independent Norway results from the present contention, or whether the consular question will once more be relegated to the rear, the King of Sweden-Norway has done his whole duty to the nations he has ruled so ably. As he retires from the active participation in the affairs of the Government, his distinguishing traits are his strength of character, a mind singularly free from prejudices, and an intellectual grasp which makes him equally well at home in the world of letters and that of science. As an enthusiastic student, an investigator, or a critic, his labors entitle him to recognition as one whose sphere of activity has shown him equal to his self-imposed tasks. To the biographer of the future he must appeal most forcefully. Like that other grand monarch, Christian IX of Denmark, both the political and the family life of Oscar II reveals an unblemished record — the reward of faithful guardianship. Should Crown Prince Gustaf succeed in gaining and retaining the respect of his Scandinavian subjects to an equal degree, it would prove one of the strongest factors toward unifying the interests of the Swedes and the Norwegians.

Oscar II came to the throne in 1872, succeeding his brother, Charles XV, who had no sons. His literary and artistic talents he inherited from his father. Oscar I was a monarch of liberal tendencies and his reign was marked by a steady advancement of the two peoples. Many internal improvements were introduced, and the Norwegian Storthing, which up to 1869 had met in triennial sessions, from that year on convened annually.

Oscar, on ascending the throne, displayed the same democratic interest in the people as did his brother and his father before him.   He mingled freely with his Swedish and Norwegian subjects, the law governing the union prescribing that the King of Norway should take up his residence periodically in the latter country.   His visits among the Norsemen were always looked upon as events strengthening the ties that have bound the monarch to his subjects.   Political differences aside, the Norwegians have been a unit in admitting that no other ruler could have done better by them, in view of the fact that he was obliged to maintain the equipoise between them and their Swedish brethren. For thirty-three years Oscar has succeeded in keeping the two nations at peace with each other, in spite of the difficulties engendered through the restiveness of the ultra-national element among the Norwegians.

Had fate decreed otherwise than that the King of Sweden-Norway should assume the royal purple, his high mentality must have brought him into great prominence, no matter what had been his sphere of activity among men.   Oscar II is possessed of that rare individuality which William of Germany displays in his own characteristic fashion.   Yet the difference in their years is no more marked than are the differences in the idiosyncrasies of these rulers.   While both evince the keenest interest in all that concerns the betterment of their people — their intellectual progress, and their endeavors to surpass in the arena of art and literature — in the case of Oscar of Sweden the war-lord spirit does not touch a sympathetic chord.   In this respect his son is much more in harmony with the German Emperor.   Should Crown Prince Gustaf fail to curb his military predilection, he might precipitate at any moment what his father during his entire reign has been assiduous in preventing.

As the patron of scientific investigations, Oscar of Sweden has earned the gratitude of the world.   So, too, the various explorations and expeditions which have made Scandinavia a household word among the nations were made possible largely through his munificence.   Among the achievements due to his patronage of those who did the actual work, those of Nordenskjöld, Nansen, Hedin, and many others stand forth conspicuous.   The fate of Andrée has ever proved a personal loss to the King, who, until the last, clung to the hope that the daring navigator of the air would yet be heard from.   The Nobel prizes and their international distribution are to-day among his most cherished enterprises, and hold his attention with each recurring session of the committee which confers the awards.

Probably the renown of King Oscar as a man of culture rests on

what he has accomplished in the domain of pure literature.   Besides
the Scandinavian languages, his linguistic range includes English, German, French, Russian, Spanish, and Italian.   Among the King's translations which have placed his countrymen in touch with foreign masters,
are " Le Cid " and Goethe's best produtions — to-day standard literature
in Sweden.   The national poetry of the country has been enriched by
many songs, the music of which the King has likewise composed.   The
splendid Easter hymn, now sung in all the Swedish churches, Oscar
wrote and dedicated to his countrymen years ago.   Among his many
other notable contributions may be mentioned " Songs of Nature and the
Sea "; " Tasso "; the drama, " Castle Kronberg "; and the translation of
Voltaire's " Memoirs of Charles XII of Sweden."   As a climax to a literary life unexampled among European royalty, Oscar is now engaged
in writing his memoirs.

The retiring King of Sweden, the fourth sovereign of the house of
Ponte Corvo, is the grandson of Marshal Bernadotte.   This favorite of
Napoleon was elected heir apparent to the Crown of Sweden in 1810.
Eight years later he ascended the throne under the name of Charles
XIV, and at his death, March 8, 1844, his only son, Oscar, became his
successor.   Oscar died on July 8, 1859, and was succeeded by his eldest son, Charles XV.   Oscar II became King of Sweden-Norway in
1872, when his brother died, leaving no male issue.

Oscar II is married to the daughter of the late Duke William of
Nassau.   Queen Sophia has proved herself in every way a worthy helpmate to her royal spouse.   The couple has four children, all sons:
Crown Prince Gustaf, Prince Oscar Bernadotte, Prince Charles, and
Prince Eugene.   It was Prince Oscar Bernadotte, it will be remembered,
who, some years ago, renounced his succession to the throne, in order to
marry Ebba Munck, a lady-in-waiting to his mother.   Of the other
children of the King and Queen of Sweden, Gustaf is married to Princess
Victoria, a daughter of the Grand Duke of Baden.   Charles went to
Denmark for his bride, the charming Princess Ingeborg, daughter of the
Danish Crown Prince Frederik.   Prince Eugene is as yet unmarried,
rumors every now and then linking his name with one or another European beauty.   Indeed, a short time ago it was whispered that a fair
daughter of the United States had been chosen by this artist-prince.
There is considerable doubt, however, that Eugene will search outside
the circle of royal blood when the proper moment arrives.

Many grandchildren bless the home life of the King and Queen of
Sweden.   In direct succession to the throne is Prince Gustaf Adolf,

the eldest son of the Crown Prince.   The close relations with Denmark and the German principalities bring about frequent exchanges of courtesies and royal visits; the reunions of the entire family at Stockholm being most delightful occasions.   As in the case of Louise, the lamented Queen of Denmark, the Queen of Sweden is a mother to all who seek her cherished counsel.   The poor people of the dual kingdom know her charities.   Her ready assistance where struggling genius tries to make its way, has earned her many blessings and repaid itself a hundredfold.   As a champion of the rights of woman, the daughters of Scandinavia look upon the Swedish Queen as their leader in thought and action.

If Norway, as has been intimated, should take to herself a son of this royal lineage, she would gain much in European prestige, while retaining every democratic principle inherent in a free and enlightened government.   As separate entities, the nations may be made strong enough to warrant Scandinavia in taking her place in line with Powers greatly superior in numbers.   Moreover, should the new triple alliance of the north enter intimately into the company of Germany or England, or both, the Scandinavian sphere of influence must once again extend from the Baltic to the North Sea.

JULIUS MORITZEN.

THE FORUM.

VOL. XXXVII, NO. 2.

OCTOBER—DECEMBER, 1905.

NEW YORK:

THE FORUM PUBLISHING COMPANY.

PRESS OF
THE PUBLISHERS' PRINTING COMPANY
82, 84 LAFAYETTE PLACE
NEW YORK

The Forum

OCTOBER, 1905.

AMERICAN POLITICS.

WHEN Congress assembles on the first Monday in December — the proposed extraordinary session having been abandoned — it will find much of importance to engage its attention. Nothing will be accomplished, however, until after the holiday recess. Representative Cannon, who will be re-elected Speaker of the House, will require two or three weeks to frame his committees, and then adjournment will be in order. It is not until the Senators and Representatives return from participation in Christmas festivities that there will be any definite steps toward legislation.

The question may well be asked, whether, even after Congress apparently settles down to its labor, anything of real value will be accomplished. Will there be legislation affecting railroad rates? Will the tariff be revised? These are the two important queries of the hour. There is a very strong possibility that both questions will be eventually answered in the negative. The investigation of the railroad question by the Senate Committee on Interstate Commerce, during the summer, made it clear that while some remedial legislation may be offered, the Senate is not prepared to follow the President to the point advocated by him in his message sent to Congress at the beginning of the last session. As for the suggested revision of the tariff, the fact that the extra session has been abandoned is generally accepted by the opponents of revision as a fact in their favor. It will be remembered that in the last number of THE FORUM the writer predicted that tariff revision had entered upon a rough and rocky road. The grounds upon which that prediction was based are more pronounced than ever.   The Senate Committee on Finance, for instance, was authorized to sit during the summer recess and consider questions pertaining to revision.   Senator Aldrich, the chairman of the committee, and Senator Allison, the ranking member, have been in Europe during the summer, and the doors of the committee-room have not been opened.   Speaker Cannon, who is a power in the House, is outspoken in his opposition to revision; and, as pointed out in THE FORUM, the friends of tariff changes are neither numerous nor influential.

The most serious obstacle to revision, however, is the very general prosperity which is at the present time being experienced throughout the country.   It does not require a sage to know that reforms are not successfully undertaken when everybody is in a contented mood.   The conditions at present are more than satisfactory.   The wheat and corn crop will be immense.   The Western banks have plenty of money.   Railroads in every section are hampered for lack of rolling stock to handle their largely increased business.   The iron and steel mills are being pushed to their full capacity.   Railroad and other securities have maintained their high figures during the dulness of the summer.   These are the conditions which will be cited when the tariff revisionists undertake to present their arguments for new schedules.   Meanwhile, the American Protective Tariff League is doing an immense amount of practical work for the stand-pat element of the party, taking nothing for granted, sending out circulars to the first voters, appealing to business men everywhere to bring their influence against revision to bear upon Senators and Representatives, and urging the leaders in Congress to let well enough alone.

There is, of course, a possibility that the President, undismayed by the untoward fate of the reciprocity treaties which have been pigeon-holed in the Senate, may negotiate a reciprocity treaty with Germany in the hope of offsetting the tariff barrier which that nation will erect against the United States on March 1, 1906.   Already Germany has concluded reciprocal commercial treaties with Russia, Italy, Roumania, Switzerland, Servia, and Austria-Hungary.   These treaties give the manufacturers and producers of the respective countries advantageous rates; and unless the United States enters into a similar arrangement, American products will be forced, in many cases, to pay a duty twice as heavy as is exacted from similar products from the treaty-favored countries.   Since 1870 this country has enjoyed tariff privileges in Germany under what is known as "the most favored nation" clause; but when the new German tariff goes into effect this clause will become a dead letter. Nor is Germany alone in this forbidding attitude. Practically all the continental powers are arrayed against the United States with hostile tariffs.

It is no wonder, therefore, that farmers and manufacturers, who are anxiously viewing the possible curtailment of the foreign market, are advocating reciprocity. They will knock loudly at the door of Congress; they will cite the declarations of the platforms of the Republican party; and they will quote the last public utterance of the martyred McKinley, that commercial wars are unprofitable, and that a policy of good-will and friendly trade relations will prevent reprisals. The probability is, however, that they will knock in vain and that their earnest citations will fall upon deaf ears. This ought not to be the case. The Republican party must realize before long that we cannot have our cake and eat it, too, and that the tariff barrier now erected in this country to keep out foreign competition will find its counterpart in tariff walls built up in other countries to keep out American products.

Every effort will be made by the opponents of tariff revision to present a multiplicity of subjects for Congressional consideration, in order that the tariff question may be crowded to the wall. In the Senate, topics of minor importance will be debated with a thoroughness and persistency far beyond their merits. The House will find numerous matters to engage its daily attention. The earnest and emphatic address of the Chicago reciprocity conference and the appeal of the Merchants' Association of New York for relief from the antagonistic action of European countries will, if the present programme can be successfully executed, be ignored. Meanwhile, Secretary Shaw, who is to leave the Cabinet early next year, and who is a leading candidate for the Presidential nomination, boldly proclaims that the development of our industries is due solely to the protection afforded them from competition with other countries, preaches the doctrine that cheap products of labor mean cheap wages for labor, and insists that tinkering with the tariff is only another name for widespread stagnation and panic.

While the outlook as to tariff and railroad legislation is uncertain, with the likelihood of negative action, there are some things upon which Congress will take a decided stand. First of all, it will favor economy in the matter of appropriations. The deficit of $24,000,000 reported by the Treasury Department at the end of the fiscal year will be a powerful argument for reducing to the utmost the various budgets. The expenditures of the Government, excluding the abnormal conditions created by the war with Spain, have grown largely in excess of the natural development of the country; and, unless they are curtailed, some new method of providing revenue, such as a re-enactment of the Stamp Act, or the imposition of a tax upon tea and coffee, will have to be enforced. In view of the fact that a Congressional election will be held next year, the leaders of the dominant party do not regard the levying of additional taxes with much favor.

Congress will also be asked to enact legislation which will assure punishment of the men who, like certain subordinates of the Department of Agriculture, have proved recreant to the trust reposed in them. They have been indicted for conspiracy against the Government of the United States; but the federal law officers admit that there ought to be a statute more adequately covering the offence. Incidentally, we may expect to hear many speeches in Congress condemnatory of the graft which has been discovered in the federal departments; but it is very much to be doubted whether these outbursts, delivered for campaign consumption, will be effective. There has been graft, of course, but there has also been prompt detection, dismissal of the offenders, and, wherever possible, prosecution. Despite all that may be said to the contrary, graft in the government service is not universal. Indeed, the federal departments are filled with men who protect the interests of the Government to the last degree. The proportion of officials who are dishonest is very small, and experience has shown that neither honesty nor dishonesty is determined by a man's political faith.

Considerable impetus has recently been given to the question of the election of United States Senators by the direct vote of the people. In a stirring campaign, just concluded in Virginia, the principal issue was the United States Senatorship. Under a resolution adopted by the Democratic State Convention, the voters of that party were called upon to decide, at a primary election, between the senatorial candidates. Senator Martin, who had been twice elected by the legislature and who desired to succeed himself, was opposed by Gov. Andrew J. Montague. Both candidates canvassed the entire State, appealing directly to the people, with the result that the men named for the legislature by Mr. Martin were elected by a majority of over 15,000. When the legislature meets, the election of the Senator will be a mere formality. The members will simply register the verdict of the people. The provision of the federal Constitution regarding the election of Senators will be strictly observed, and yet, as a matter of fact, Mr. Martin will take his seat as the choice of a popular majority.

This system of beating the devil around the bush, to use a homely but expressive phrase, seems to be growing in popularity in this country, especially as it becomes more and more apparent that an amendment to the Constitution is practically unobtainable. Virginia is not the only State which affords its voters the opportunity to select the Senator. In South Carolina there is a primary election law which provides that if none of the candidates receives a majority of the total number of votes upon the first election, the two aspirants receiving the largest number of votes shall be voted upon directly. Quite frequently, owing to the fact that four or five prominent and popular men have sought the senatorial office, the second election has been necessary. Senator Burkett, of Nebraska, who took his seat on the fourth of last March, was chosen by the direct vote of the people, the verdict being ratified, of course, by the legislature. In Illinos a similar system is to be inaugurated this year. Senator Foster, of Louisiana, was recently returned as the choice of the majority of the people of his State. "When the Democratic party of Louisiana," says his biography in the Congressional Directory, "adopted the plan of selecting nominees for State offices by a general primary election, he requested, inasmuch as the members of the General Assembly to be so elected would select his successor, that the United States Senatorship be included in the primary, and announced his candidacy to succeed himself. He received 42,990 votes, as against 26,122 cast for ex-United States Senator B. F. Jonas, insuring his return to the Senate as his own successor at the expiration of the present term of service, which will be March 3, 1907." In Alabama, Senator Morgan went before his people in the same fashion; while the election of Senator Simmons, of North Carolina, was also the expression of popular will. In other words, it would seem that the people of the United States were gradually accomplishing indirectly the result for which they have been striving for so many years.

The full extent of the movement in behalf of popular election of Senators is probably not appreciated. It has appeared sporadically ever since the beginning of the Government, but during the last fifteen years has gained remarkable impetus. An examination of the records of the United States Senate shows that the legislatures of no less than twenty-three States have gone upon record as advocating a change in the method of electing Senators prescribed by the Constitution. These States are as follows: Montana, Iowa, Nevada, Wisconsin, Oregon, Colorado, Michigan, Idaho, Nebraska, Tennessee, Pennsylvania, Kansas, Washington, Minnesota, South Dakota, Utah, Florida, North Carolina, North Dakota, Ohio, Wyoming, Kentucky, Indiana.

When these States first brought their resolutions to the attention of Congress, the language was temperate and appealing; Congress being requested to submit a Constitutional amendment to the several States, and the Senators and Representatives being asked to use their best endeavors to bring about this result. Of late years, however, the tenor of the legislative declaration has undergone a change, unquestionably due to the fact that the House of Representatives has four times passed the desired amendment while the Senate has failed to act. The movement at the present time is, therefore, in the direction of securing the calling of a convention of the States. The resolution of the legislature of Montana is a fair sample of the more recent utterances:

Resolved, That the legislature of Montana favors the adoption of an amendment to the Constitution which shall provide for the election of United States Senators by popular vote, and joins with other States of the Union in respectfully requesting that a convention be called for the purpose of proposing an amendment to the Constitution of the United States, as provided for in Article V of said Constitution, which amendment shall provide for a change in the present method of electing United States Senators so that they can be chosen in each State by the direct vote of the people.

Inasmuch as many of the States which originally transmitted simple requests for the adoption of the desired amendment have since adopted resolutions calling for the convention, it may very properly be inferred that the same action will be taken by them all. Consequently, twenty-three States may be regarded as having gone upon record in favor of the convention. Under the provision of the Constitution already quoted, this convention must be called when application is made by the legislatures of two-thirds of the several States. Legislative action by seven more States, therefore, will render Congressional action obligatory. It is safe to say that very few persons realize how close the nation is to a constitutional convention. In the last Congress resolutions were received from four States; in the Fifty-seventh Congress the legislatures of six States were heard from. Many States in which the system of popular choice of Senator is practised, such as Virginia, Louisiana, Illinois, and Alabama, have made no legislative expression. It would take but a slight degree of missionary work among these legislatures to secure the two-thirds action required by the Constitution as precedent to a convention.

The reasons advanced by the legislatures for the proposed change are numerous and emphatic. They are, in the main, that it would always insure the full senatorial representation of each State; that it would prevent protracted and disturbing contests; that it would curb all attempts to influence improperly or corruptly the election of members of the national Senate; and that it would give to the legislature more time for the transaction of legislative business. The legislature of the State of Washington denounced the present method of electing Senators as "expensive, unsatisfactory, and ruinous to the best interests of the people"; while the members of the Utah legislature expressed themselves as favoring a change because "the world is advancing to a higher plane of civilization, and what was found to meet the needs of the Union a century ago is now demonstrated to be inadequate to the needs of a great republic."

During the past ten years, the question of electing Senators by the direct vote of the people has been exhaustively debated in both branches of Congress. In the House the preponderance of the speeches was in favor of the change, while in the Senate the affirmative and negative were equally divided. Mr. Bryan, when a member of the House, was an ardent advocate of popular choice, and has since secured the endorsement of the proposed change in the Democratic national platforms. Several reports have been made upon the subject, the most important being the favorable document submitted by Senator Mitchell, of Oregon, with the opposing side succinctly stated by Senator Chandler, of New Hampshire. These reports deal, however, with the radical change proposed by the Constitutional amendment, which would take the election of the Senators out of the jurisdiction of the legislatures. In none of them is to be found any suggestion of the system now coming into vogue, wherein the voters of a party register their personal preference, leaving it to the legislature to execute the will of the majority. This is the system which is practically accomplishing all that the advocates of the popular election of Senators have attempted to obtain. Much is to be said in its favor. So far as Virginia is concerned, it brought Senator Martin into closer touch with his people, and they have been brought nearer to him. He must, of necessity, feel that the gauntlet of popular approval which he has successfully run is a severer test of critical judgment than if he were the recipient of the votes of the comparatively few members of the legislature. Above all, there can now be no question of his victory. It was achieved in the broad expanse of the State and not in the narrow lobby of the State capitol.

It is not necessary to enter upon an extended discussion of the merits of the question, although the field is wide and attractive. The point to be emphasized is that the people, apparently despairing of securing a Constitutional amendment, are taking the matter into their own hands. From present indications, the much-desired amendment will soon be unnecessary.

Another sign of the times was visible in the Virginia campaign. One of the principal allegations against Senator Martin was that he was neither a brilliant orator nor prominent in national councils, but that, on the contrary, he was merely "the messenger-boy of his State," to quote the phrase used by one of his opponents, spending his time in looking after minor details in the various federal departments. Mr. Martin willingly accepted the accusation. He went into nearly every county in the State, presenting his cause in a direct and convincing manner, not claiming to be more than a plain, practical business man, but pointing proudly to the results he had achieved. The fact that he was overwhelmingly successful carries with it the lesson that in these practical days the people look more to accomplishment than they do to words. Mr. Martin's record was one of continuous industry, of constant consideration for his constituents, of labor in season and out of season for the material advancement of his State. It was this record which the people of Virginia approved; and a study of political conditions in recent years indicates that the same feeling is almost universal. There was a time when the highest claim for elevation to the position of a Senator of the United States was forensic ability. Nowadays the Senate is not an aggregation of great orators; it is an assembly of business men, selected because they are trained in the great art of accomplishing results.

The recognized leader of the Senate, Mr. Aldrich, of Rhode Island, is not an orator. He is a man of affairs, who is largely interested in such prosaic but profitable concerns as street railways. Senator Allison, of Iowa, who stands shoulder to shoulder with him in leadership, makes no pretence to the mastery of rhetoric. His speeches are confined to the explanation of the details of the vast budgets which are prepared by the Committee on Appropriations, of which he is the efficient chairman. Senator Gorman, of Maryland, the chosen leader of the minority, is not eloquent. He contents himself with the use of clear and forcible language, rarely indulging in simile or imagination. His value to his party lies in the fact that he is a wise counsellor and a resourceful manager. Among the recent accessions to the Senate there is none who stands pre-eminent in oratory. In fact, a man who enters the Senate nowadays must have more claim to consideration than the fact that he can deliver an eloquent speech.   He must possess a practical business mind, with a capacity for detail, and, above all, a regard for the material interests of his State.   A public building or a valuable river or harbor improvement is much more highly appreciated than a pyrotechnical address which produces no results.

In the House of Representatives, too, oratory is on the decline.   The day when the galleries were thronged with auditors eager to listen to the outbursts of inspired eloquence has passed.   A speech which electrifies the House by its brilliance is now the exception, rather than the rule.   The work of framing and enacting important legislation is done by men who approach their task with minds accustomed to business affairs and who have never looked between the covers of a treatise on rhetoric.   In the last Congress the two principal positions in the House were occupied by Mr. Payne, of New York, as chairman of the Committee on Ways and Means, and Mr. Hemenway, of Indiana, as the chairman of the Committee on Appropriations.   Neither of these men made any claim to the gift of oratory.   Indeed, if the present temper of the public mind continues, the time will come when a speech other than commonplace in either branch of Congress will be a notable event.   An examination of the broad volumes of the Congressional Record shows that nearly every word which is reported pertains to discussion and debate — merely questions and answers elucidating the measure under consideration.   In the entire session, Representative Bourke Cockran's speech was the only one that really reached the high-water mark of brilliant oratory.

The revelations of political dishonesty in Pennsylvania have been astounding.   Examination of the voting lists in the city of Philadelphia shows that nearly 100,000 names were fraudulently placed thereon. Conditions have been exposed which have led to caustic comment.   Says one forceful writer:

The dominant political machine in Philadelphia is the most shamelessly corrupt ring in control of any American community.   It has for years defied public opinion. It has manipulated finances of the city for the private ends of a few grafters and their henchmen.   It has prostituted the election machinery to its own base ends. There has not been an honest election in the city of Philadelphia for many years. Ballot boxes have been stuffed, gangs of repeaters have marched the rounds, primaries have been reduced to a farce, nominations have been sold to the highest bidders.

This is strong language; but it is not exaggeration.   It is an indictment which will be sustained before the great bar of public opinion. No wonder, therefore, that President Roosevelt, who stands as the great exemplar of purity in administration, should have taken occasion personally to express to Mayor Weaver his congratulations upon the progress of the work of reform.   If Pennsylvania were not so overwhelmingly Republican, one might almost certainly predict that the State would swing into the Democratic column, even as Missouri cast off from her old moorings when dishonesty was shown to be riot in the Democratic party, for the revolt against the machine is spreading into the counties. There is a feeling in the air which bodes ill for the leaders who were once so thoroughly intrenched.   The great mass of the people, the rank and file of the voters, are shocked at the outrages which have been perpetrated, and the work of overthrowing the "bosses" has already begun. Every lover of good government hopes to see the effort carried to a most successful conclusion.

Considerable curiosity has been naturally expressed concerning the reason for fraudulently increasing the list of voters in Philadelphia.   In a city where the Republican majority was so great, an additional 100,000 votes would seem a mere superfluity.   The explanation, however, is quite simple.   In the first place, representation in the Common Council is based upon the number of voters as shown in the assessor's list, one for each 4,000, and the swollen lists of voters gave to the machine managers increased membership in the municipal legislature.   The representation thus secured could, of course, be relied upon to vote for such measures as were desired to be enacted.   In the second place, a rule of the Republican party in Pennsylvania based the representation in the State convention upon the vote polled in the preceding Presidential election, so that the local "machine," by swelling the city vote, secured an undue proportion of strength in the determination of State politics.   Beyond all this, however, the enormous aggregate of votes recorded for the candidates of the "machine" absolutely prevented the organization of an independent movement.   It seemed such a hopeless task to undertake to overthrow a majority of from 70,000 to 100,000 that no one had the temerity to attempt it.   The "ring" was, therefore, secure behind its barrier of fraudulent votes, although no one knew, until the recent investigation disclosed the fact, upon what a flimsy and shadowy foundation that barrier was built.

Ordinarily, as has already been intimated, these disclosures would result in a complete overturning of the party in political power.   It is hardly reasonable, however, to expect this result.   The outlook now is that the Republicans in the State will themselves correct the evils under which they have suffered and will maintain their Republican control, even while sacrificing the leaders who have proved so dishonest. Nor is it likely that the disclosures in Philadelphia will have any adverse effect upon the party from a national point of view. The people throughout the United States will regard the Pennsylvania situation as a local condition, requiring a drastic house-cleaning; but they will rely upon the better element in the party in the State to accomplish this result. Meanwhile, there is a disposition to nominate Mayor Weaver for Governor, if the machine can be ousted from control, and some enthusiasts are already predicting that he will eventually reach the White House as the legitimate successor of President Roosevelt. This fact is mentioned merely to indicate that in the field of politics there is no limit to interesting speculation.

While Pennsylvania is struggling with its corrupt ring, the little State of Delaware comes into view with the proud record of having eliminated J. Edward Addicks from its politics. It is unnecessary to review the peculiar career of Mr. Addicks. It is enough to say that he harbored the idea that the possession of money was the sole desideratum for election to the United States Senate. Delaware is a small State, so that the size of the legislature sought to be controlled is not large; but to the credit of the State it deserves to be recorded that not only did Mr. Addicks fail in his ambition, but that he is no longer a factor in the commonwealth. It might not be necessary to refer to Mr. Addicks at all were it not for the fact that his passing carries with it a gratifying moral.

Political conditions in other States do not lack interest. In Connecticut a law has been passed which is described "as the most drastic act against bribery and corruption at elections that has been adopted in any American State." This law applies to primaries and United States senatorial contests, as well as to Presidential, Congressional, State, and municipal elections. Candidates are prohibited from using money except through committees and political agents whose scope is strictly defined and who must file sworn and itemized statements of election costs within fifteen days after the election. Any voter may within thirty days bring a charge of corrupt practices before a Superior Court judge, who, on finding sufficient cause, must try the case assisted by another judge appointed by the chief justice of the State. Conviction, in addition to other severe penalties, carries with it disqualification for holding office for four years, and the act gives State and local prosecuting attorneys prompt initiative power in bringing cases of this kind to trial. It remains to be seen whether public sentiment of the State, without which no law can be successfully executed, will be virile enough to sustain this legislation. If not, Connecticut will pass through the experience which befell Ohio, when a similar law, after being flagrantly disregarded for many years, was finally repealed.

In Georgia the skirmish of the gubernatorial campaign is being fought upon anti-corporation lines, while in Alabama there is an echo of the national agitation of the railroad rebate question, the principal issue being the State control of railroads through the operation of a commission. In Tennessee, United States Senator Carmack is laying the groundwork of a campaign for his return to the Senate, his opponent being ex-Governor Taylor, who has fiddled and sung himself into popular favor. From Virginia and North Carolina come reports of the efforts of the Republicans to achieve victory. In Virginia a full State Republican ticket has been placed in the field, headed by Judge L. L. Lewis, who resigned his position upon the federal bench in order personally to conduct his campaign. In North Carolina, where the gubernatorial contest does not occur until next year, the Republicans, under the leadership of Representative Blackburn, have entertained Vice-President Fairbanks and Secretary Shaw, and have infused considerable enthusiasm into their organization. It is difficult, however, to share in the optimism which predicts that in these two States the Republicans will win any substantial victories. The Democratic majority in the last gubernatorial election in North Carolina was 40,000, and while the Virginia Republicans expect to profit by the bitterness in the Democratic ranks engendered by the recent primary contest, it is not likely that they can succeed in defeating the Democratic candidates. There will come some time in the future a break in the solid South; but at present it would seem as if, when all other issues fail, the question of negro equality can be successfully invoked.

This is illustrated by Maryland, where the fight is being waged upon the so-called Poe amendment to the State constitution. This amendment creates two classes of voters, following the method which had already been established in Mississippi, South Carolina, and other Southern States. Those whose grandfathers were voters are made a privileged class. The remaining portion of the population must offer to an examining board a satisfactory explanation of clauses of the Constitution submitted to them. The whole purpose of the amendment is to disqualify the negro as a voter. It brings what is known as "the grandfather clause" to a point farther north than heretofore reached, and, if it shall be adopted, insures the dominance of the white voters. The Democrats are confident of success, basing their hopes largely upon the remembrance that the turning point in their favor in the campaign which returned Mr. Gorman to the United States Senate was the fact that President Roosevelt entertained Mr. Booker Washington at lunch. It may be said in passing that the proportion of negro population in Maryland is a little less than twenty per cent.

Up to the present time the gubernatorial campaign in Ohio has attracted little national attention. This is doubtless due to the fact that the State has been so overwhelmingly Republican in recent years that a Democratic victory seems impossible. At the same time, the conditions now existing in Ohio are peculiar. The outlook is that Governor Herrick will be re-elected, but by a narrow majority, and it is possible that before the election is held the result will be involved in uncertainty.

There are many local issues; but, after all, the principal factor affecting Republican success is the protest, now almost universal throughout the United States, against "ring" rule. Senator Hanna, during his lifetime, was able, through the exercise of sheer forcefulness, to hold this sentiment in check, but with his death it has manifested itself with renewed vigor. The dominant Republican organization, which included United States Senator Dick, Governor Herrick, and George B. Cox, of Cincinnati, has hitherto been able to control the State. There is now an open revolt upon the part of the rank and file, especially against Mr. Cox, whose methods and career are alike condemned. In addition to this feeling of dissatisfaction within the party, Governor Herrick has alienated the prohibition strength, which, in Ohio, is considerable, through his antagonism to the bill prohibiting the establishment of saloons in the residence districts of cities and allowing the holding of special elections in business districts upon the signing of petitions by a majority of the voters. The bill passed the legislature, but not until Governor Herrick had forced the addition of amendments which practically destroyed its purpose, on the ground that these amendments were necessary to preserve its constitutionality. The measure was framed by the Anti-Saloon League and opposed by the State Liquor Dealers' Association.

In the campaign now in progress, the temperance element is against Governor Herrick, a defection which, it is estimated, will cost the Republicans many thousand votes. The liquor dealers are endorsing Governor Herrick, their action tending to increase the bitterness of the fight, while the Democrats, in nominating John M. Pattison, a Cincinnati business man, have intensified the situation, their candidate being an avowed advocate of temperance.   Still another disturbing element is the fact that Governor Herrick vetoed the bill allowing pool-selling at all the race meetings held in Ohio.   It is alleged that his approval of the bill was obtained before it was enacted, and his subsequent action has arrayed against him the large interests connected with horse-racing. These interests are non-partisan; and many of the Governor's present opponents are men of wealth and influence who have hitherto been prominently identified with the Republican party.   It is said that the defection of the racing interests will cost Governor Herrick not less than 20,000 votes.

Under all these circumstances, it would have seemed the part of wisdom for the Democrats, in their State convention assembled, to have confined their utterances to State affairs.   On the contrary, the address of Mr. M. A. Daugherty was devoted to national topics.   It was notable because it took direct issue with Mr. Bryan's ideas of government ownership and because it declared for the absolute destruction of the principle of protection.   Upon the latter subject Mr. Daugherty said:

The Democracy believes that the hated trusts and the intolerable monopoly will not be exterminated until the economic policy of protection, which is their refuge and nourishment, shall be buried beyond all hope of resurrection.   The Democracy believes that the overthrow of the protective system and the administration of the government along the Democratic lines of equal rights to all men and special privileges to no man will be the panacea for all evils that now afflict the body-politic.

It may be that the Ohio voters will realize that the election of a governor cannot affect tariff legislation.   Otherwise, in a State where protection is regarded as a cardinal virtue, this outspoken declaration of hostility would overshadow all local issues and seriously jeopardize the Democratic chances of success.

The mayoralty campaign in New York City, although it has not yet fairly opened, promises to be of national interest.   At this writing, it appears that Mayor McClellan, who has given the city an excellent administration, will be nominated by the Democrats to succeed himself. The Republican leaders realize the uphill task before them and are already seeking a fusion of all the organizations opposed to Tammany. The request for fusion also announced that municipal ownership would be the Republican campaign issue, the language being as follows:

The administration of Mayor McClellan has squarely placed before the citizens of New York City the question, Shall the great public utility corporations continue to control and misuse the government of this city against the interests of all our people and for the sole gain of these corporations and the leaders of Tammany Hall?

This question is of such supreme importance to all the citizens of New York as to justify the most earnest effort for a fusion of all elements opposed to the continuance of such a government by Tammany Hall. It is the purpose of the Republican party to effect such a fusion and to give its full power in the coming election to the support of candidates pledged to an administration of the affairs of this city under which the public utility corporations will not be the masters of the people of this city.

Many strange things have happened in New York politics, but the strangest is this slogan of the Republican fusion. It is difficult to regard it seriously. It was natural enough for the Democrats in Chicago to go off at a tangent and adopt municipal ownership as an issue, as the Democratic party accepts with avidity all the new ideas which float through the political atmosphere. The fact that Chicago, after having voted for municipal ownership, seems to be still as distant as ever from the goal of its desires, is, apparently, not a matter for consideration in New York. In addition to this, one is inclined to give Representative "Tim" Sullivan credit for keen, practical sense, when he remarked, upon his return from Europe, that if municipal ownership was adopted in New York, Tammany would be in power for 150 years. Perhaps the Republican managers have the same thought, excepting, of course, that municipal ownership comes under a Republican administration. It does not seem probable, however, that municipal ownership can be made an issue in the near election. The subject is too vast and complicated to be settled without some study and consideration on the part of the voters, unless the latter proposed to rush blindfold into new conditions. A municipal ownership campaign in New York City, ably contested, would excite the attention of the entire country.

In the broader fields of national politics conditions are unchanged. Mr. Bryan continues to be the incarnation of activity in the Democratic ranks. He holds conferences with his friends in various cities, and he addresses his large number of followers through the columns of his newspaper. He still preaches radical Democracy, making it apparent that he is preparing for the great battle of 1908, when the conservatives and the extremists in the Democratic party will engage in a struggle similar to that which disrupted the party in 1896. Unless all signs fail, the outcome of that internecine contest can be anticipated. The radicals will be victorious, even as the advocates of the free coinage of silver were triumphant in 1896, and they will look to Mr. Bryan as their leader. They will nominate him upon a platform crying aloud for municipal and government ownership, denouncing all corporate aggrandizement, and urg-

12

ing the utmost limit of free-trade. In vain will men like Mr. Thomas F. Ryan advise their party that "Democratic success can only come by the Democrats in the Southern States organizing and forcing the party to take a stand for conservatism and by appealing to the sober-minded and thoughtful in the country." In vain will independent and thoughtful newspapers like the Washington "Post" appeal to the Democrats to become the conservative party of the country. In vain will Judge Parker utter sentiments like this:

> Because greed, left to run riot, has produced some bad conditions in cities and in great corporations, we are advised to run headlong into municipal or government ownership and operation. This policy is advocated in spite of the fact that, in other countries and in surroundings far more favorable for these experiments than our own, they have uniformly interfered with development and curbed initiative. In other words, the only alternative thus presented for the curbing of greed is that of rushing wildly into all the perils of over-government.

It may be that in the course of the next three years the present situation will so change as to relegate into the background the men who are now planning to out-Herod Herod in the policies to which they would commit the Democratic party, but at present there is no indication of such an outcome. The campaign of 1908 will, in all probability, be an intensified repetition of the famous contest of 1896.

Believing that this battle for supremacy between radicalism and conservatism is approaching, and believing also that it will result in the downfall of Mr. Bryan and his theories, the Republican candidates for the Presidency are inclined to regard a nomination as equivalent to an election. For this reason there is already much activity in the ranks of the distinguished gentlemen who aspire to the nation's highest office. Experience demonstrates that the work of organization cannot begin too soon. Mr. Cleveland owed his renomination in 1892 to the fact that his friends had been industriously at work during his four years of temporary exile from the White House, while Mr. McKinley's nomination was made certain by the magnificent organization built up by the late Senator Hanna during the two years that preceded the St. Louis convention. The candidate who allows the precious moments to slip by without laying the foundation upon which to erect his column of delegates will experience a sad awakening. Only upon rare occasions is a convention stampeded to a candidate; and still more infrequent are the events which suddenly bring into prominence an available man.

Abnormal conditions are not likely to prevail in the next three years. During that interim Taft and Root and Fairbanks and Shaw and the other aspirants will have ample opportunity to present themselves for public consideration.   At the same time victory is more likely to perch upon the banners of the astute candidate who sends his managers into every State, interviewing the men who control the Congressional districts, selecting men as delegates to State and district conventions, and, in brief, creating an organization which will stand intact and triumphant in the National Assembly.   Organization is the prime factor in political success.   Hanna organized; Reed relied largely upon sentiment. The ballots at St. Louis were the natural sequence.   It only needs close observation during the next three years to be able to predict the Presidential nominee.   The candidate who has the organization behind him will poll the requisite majority of delegates.

This assertion is subject to one exception.   If President Roosevelt continues to make such an ideal Chief Executive — if he scores a few more remarkable achievements such as the Russian-Japanese treaty of peace — it will be difficult to prevent his renomination by acclamation, notwithstanding his honest declaration that he would not accept another term.   HENRY LITCHFIELD WEST.

FOREIGN AFFAIRS.

PEACE again reigns. During the last eighteen months the world has lived through a great drama — one of the mightiest dramas the world has known; a drama in which the actors attained the stature of heroes of mythology; a drama in which with the irresistible force of a Greek tragedy cause produced effect in its logical and sequential order. The history of the world tells us of no more dramatic war than that which began with the midnight torpedo attack at Port Arthur on February 7, 1904, and ended so abruptly in the quiet navy-yard on the New Hampshire coast of the United States on August 29, 1905. There have been few wars which have been so momentous in their effect on the future current of history, the progress of civilization, the advancement of the race.

The rise of civilization, the advancement of man in the steadily ascending scale of progress, can be easily measured by the philosophical student of history who does not read history as merely "the Newgate calendar of nations," but whose perspective is wide enough to enable him to see that there have been a few, and only a few, great epochs that have marked the end of one stage of progress and the beginning of a newer and better.

The world has never retrograded, although at times it has seemed as if it were to revert from a higher to a lower plane of progress. But the waves that have at periods engulfed the world in despair are merely as the ebb and flow of the ever-advancing tide. The derelicts of progress have been dashed on the rocks and stranded; but the eternal sea has majestically swept forward, engulfing the wrecks that have for a brief space impeded fair progress, and encouraged man to renewed ambitions. It is as impossible for mankind to revert to a lower order after he has been raised to a higher order as it is for the individual to rest content with the discomforts of the past after he has once enjoyed the luxuries of the present. It is this heaven-born discontent, this striving after the thing that is just beyond the grasp, this reaching for the unattainable, as men not gifted with imagination view it until it becomes the common heritage of all men — a desire born both of the spiritual and the material — that has lifted the world, that has saved man from himself. This explains why the world has steadily pressed forward and must continue to press forward until it reaches, ages hence, moral perfection.

Japan has given an enormous impetus to the cause of morality. There has never been a war in which calculations were set at such utter defiance as in this war. There has never been a war in which the ending was so unexpected. There has never been a war that has so quickly brought the good that follows in the train of wars. There has never been a war by which the vanquished has profited as greatly as the victor.

When Japan declared war on Russia the world trembled. The friends of Japan feared that she was going to her doom, heroically as the Japanese from time immemorial have known how to die, but as men who volunteer on a forlorn hope and who know that only death can be their portion. It seemed impossible that Japan, small in population and area, with limited resources and a handful of ships, a country that had never fought a white race, and whose sole claim to military greatness rested on her easy victory over China, could stand before the might of Russia. The friends of Japan feared that once again a little nation would die in a glorious struggle for liberty. It was pathetic. It was the heroism of despair. And the world hung in suspense, waiting and dreading what it feared to hear.

The enemies of Japan waited with serene confidence. Racial antipathies are the strongest of all antipathies. Out of the mystery of the Far East there had sprung suddenly into life a race of men with no strain of Caucasian blood — a race that the Caucasian assumed to regard as a menace to his own and to his civilization. Japan, yesterday a curiosity, so wholly steeped in barbarism that she devoted herself to the gentle pursuits of peace and brought joy to the world with her art, her profound sense of color and beauty, suddenly became so highly civilized that she emulated the civilization of the Western world with her engines of destruction and her proficiency in the arts of war. Verily the nation that could so rapidly become so highly civilized was a menace to older civilizations.

The Yellow Peril has been the bogie to affright a timid world. More than one quarrelling nation has ceased its quarrels when that spectre was raised. With the presumption of insolence, Japan, ten years before, had drawn the sword on China. Now at last the Yellow Peril was to show that it was no mere phantasmagoria, that it was no mere figment of imagination. China would submerge Japan with her countless millions; China would strike down Japan as a tiger crushes with a single blow a helpless calf; and China would suck the blood of her vic-

tim, and with the reek of blood still in her nostrils hunger for further
sacrifices. But China, and not Japan, was the victim. The Yellow
Peril collapsed as suddenly as a child's ghost becomes human when
another child with more courage than his fellows tears the sheet from
that most harmless of all domestic instruments, the housemaid's broom.
China with her millions was to be despised, but not to be feared.
Japan was entitled to the world's gratitude. She had laid the ghost
of a Mongolian invasion of the world.

Laid it, yes, only to raise a more terrible spectre. From the mainland of Asia the seekers of the habitat of yellow ghosts wandered across
the sea in their search for the unknown and the dreadful, and in that
little patch of islands that has given birth to a new morality discovered
that here was the real Yellow Peril. China, it was now admitted, was
a scarecrow, and it was foolish for the world, like a covey of timid birds,
to stand in awe of a fleshless thing; but in the blood of Japan was the
iron of the white man's civilization, which constituted the real peril to
the world. Japan cherished ambitious dreams of conquest. Japan
aspired to rule China. Japan was to set her seal upon Asia. Japan
was still a lusty infant. It was easier to kill the infant than to allow
him to reach man's estate.

Of the military history of the last eighteen months I do not propose
to write. It does not properly belong to my province, and it is a history still vividly fresh in the mind of the reader. The victories of the
Japanese were no more amazing to the world than were the defeats of
the Russians. That Japan should have sent her torpedo boats into Port
Arthur, caught her adversary at a disadvantage and disabled three of his
battleships as the signal to the world that the temple of Janus stood
open, was not surprising. That Japan should have destroyed Russian
cruisers in the harbor of Chemulpo was not surprising. That Japan
should have forced the Yalu and beaten back the Russians was not surprising. That Japan was to score the first successes was expected. But
the surprising thing was that from beginning to end the success of Japan
was unbroken. This was the thing that made the world pause.

There must be reason for it. The reason was not to be found in
Japan's overwhelming superiority, because there were times when the
advantage of numbers and position was on the side of Russia; when
the ships of Russia outnumbered those of Japan. No, there was a deeper,
a more subtle explanation. The skill, the persistence, the courage, all
the noblest qualities of heroism and patriotism that came to the front,
convinced the world that more potent even than skill and courage and

persistence when a nation is engaged in a death grapple are the moral qualities that animate that nation. The success of Japan may be ascribed to her religion. It is immaterial what we call it, because religion to the truly religious is only another name for the highest moral code, the attempt to live up to a certain standard of ethics; although geography may influence the concept of ethics.

Bearing these things in mind, the terms on which Japan consented to make peace may be looked upon as simply the logical development of that all-embracing spirit of morality that is immanent in the Japanese character. Japan came to Portsmouth resolved to force Russia to pay her an indemnity equivalent to the expenses of the war, and to retain the territory of Russia, the island of Sakhalin, that she had won by force of arms. In laying down these conditions as the price of peace, Japan did simply what the usages of civilized warfare have sanctioned. The defeated nation has always been compelled to pay tribute to the victor, money being the modern equivalent of the hostages that barbaric warfare exacted. But Russia refused to pay an indemnity, maintaining that while she was defeated she was not vanquished, and that it was only a vanquished nation, a nation physically incapable of further resistance, that paid an indemnity and thereby made confession of its inability to continue the struggle.

It is not worth while to discuss a "principle" so academic as this. When nations discuss principles and they are unable to agree as to their interpretation, there is only one court of last resort — the appeal to the sword. Russia and Japan were then at war in an attempt to settle principles; a further discussion of principles involved a continuance of the war unless there was a recession on one side. Russia, with an air of *"j'y suis, et j'y reste,"* was not to be moved. Japan, in the interest of the world, to promote the cause of civilization, yielded.

It was a magnificent victory, one of the few victories in which both contestants emerge victorious. And the victory fairly typifies the character, the temperament, the moral training, the psychology of the two nations. It was Russia that won the diplomatic victory, Japan that came from the conference-room the moral victor. By sheer force, by grim determination, by what may be termed, but not offensively, a brutal disregard of consequences, Russia compelled her foe to come to terms. It is not possible that Russia accepted President Roosevelt's invitation to the peace conference with her determination irrevocably set not to pay Japan any money to terminate the war. It is quite true that Russia did not officially know the terms that Japan would demand; but certain things are known although they may not be made a matter of official record. It must have been known to Russia, as it was known to all the rest of the world, that Japan would lay claim to an indemnity, and there is every reason to believe that Russia was prepared to make this payment at the outset. But when she found Japan ready to meet her in a generous spirit, to accept very little instead of demanding very much, the Slav character asserted itself. That character is noted for its dogged obstinacy, for the remorseless pressure it puts upon its adversary when the latter shows the faintest sign of yielding.

Russia was perfectly right in all that she did. When two men enter into a "trade," exactly as when two nations meet across the conference-table, it is the right of either to obtain the best terms possible, to pretend indifference, to bluster, to threaten, in a word to pay the lowest price for that which is the subject of the negotiations. Russia manœuvred with admirable adroitness. She conceded to Japan everything that Japan demanded except the indemnity. That she resisted. This placed Japan before the world in the position of threatening to continue the war to collect money. It was not true. Japan was not willing to fight merely for money; but the tactical advantage was with Russia, and had the conference proved abortive, had both sides adhered to their position and declined to yield, the world would have believed that Japan was in the wrong. The responsibility, I think, would have been Russia's and not Japan's; history, I am sure, would have vindicated Japan, but it would have been the vindication of posterity. Japan would have alienated the sympathy of the present generation; and although we may cynically try to assure ourselves that big battalions are more potent than sympathy, we have had very convincing proof during the past year and a half that no nation has battalions big enough or numerous enough to be able to dispense with the sympathy of other nations.

Sergius Witte comes from the conference-room not only the man of the hour, but one of the world's great diplomatists. His is a remarkable triumph. We know who and what the man is. We know that for the last ten years he has been the virtual ruler of Russia, this man who has gained his power solely through the dominating force of intellect, who has had courage enough and strength enough to withstand the temptations of the present, and imagination enough to look into the future. Such a man would make enemies in any country; in Russia, of all countries, it is only natural that his enemies should be legion and that their chief aim should be to destroy him.

We have been told that Witte was not sent to Portsmouth to make peace with honor. We are quite prepared to believe it. We have been told that his enemies hoped either that he would not make peace, in which case the responsibility for defeat would be thrown upon him, or he would make a peace that would be declared "shameful," when his enemies could brand him as a traitor. We may well believe all that we have heard. But Witte has made a peace so unexpectedly favorable to Russia that even his enemies have been compelled grudgingly to accept it and to recognize his diplomacy. Witte goes back to Russia stronger, greater, more powerful than when he left. He is now the hope of Russia.

Russia, I verily believe, has taken the first step in the right direction; but a long and difficult way lies before her. It is Witte who must lead her along this way — Witte, the man with the inflexible will; Witte, the man with a heart as well as a brain; Witte, the man of practical affairs as well as the man with imagination; Witte, the man who combines qualities the lack of which in her rulers has brought Russia to the verge of despair.

Great as was the victory of Russia, greater still is that of Japan. Two lessons Japan has taught the world. The first and most important is the impetus she has given to what I may term the morality of war and the responsibility that war imposes upon the victor. The example set by Japan is one of the turning-points of history.

When the world began to emerge from barbarism and saw the first faint glimpse of the approaching dawn of civilization, the conqueror no longer put his captives to the sword, but with a perverted sense of humanity — influenced by material considerations — made of his captives his slaves. Slavery was a fate often ten times more horrible than violent death; but it was the recognition by society in its rudest form of the sanctity of human life. Civilization made another mighty leap forward when prisoners of war, and especially non-combatants, no longer became the property of the victor, but were to be regarded simply as pledges to be redeemed in money. The right of the victor to exact a money indemnity from his defeated adversary has been engrafted on the code of nations. Every civilized nation has laid tribute upon its prostrate rival. Japan for the first time foregoes this right. With this example of Japan, the world will not assume as a matter of course that a war can only be ended by the payment of a great indemnity. What Japan has done, other nations not only can do but must do. Japan cannot have the monopoly of magnanimity. Japan has taught the world generosity, and the world cannot for very shame forget the lesson.

Another great truth Japan has forced upon the attention of the world.

When Japan accepted the President's invitation to the peace conference, it was taken for granted that she must exact indemnity, and there were cogent reasons advanced for this imperative course. The mental processes of the East are not those of the West. The Asiatic is impressed by power; power is symbolic of force; force is the visible display of strength. To the Asiatic mind Russia was the incarnation of force — that force that every Asiatic could see and feel, that had, at times, been ruthlessly exerted as proof that it was always ready to fall with crushing weight when opposed by puny resistance. Japan with the folly of recklessness threw herself across the path of Russia, and instead of being crushed, as every other Asiatic people heretofore had been crushed, not only stood her ground but turned back Russia, humbled her and ground her face in the dust.

The Asiatic saw in this the transfer of power from Russia to Japan; but one thing more was necessary to carry that complete conviction to the Asiatic mind that Russia was no longer to be feared and Japan was to be respected. The power of Russia was tottering; the armies of Russia had been defeated; the ships of Russia had been destroyed; the strong places of Russia were in the hands of her enemy; now Japan must levy the customary tribute upon her conquered foe. That were proof positive that Russia had been stripped of her power. If Japan could not exact an indemnity she would suffer in prestige; throughout the length and breadth of Asia she would be sneered at; her boasted victories would mean nothing. In a word, all that Japan had won would be swept away because she could show no gold to prove that she had really won everything; all that Russia had lost was as nothing, because she had paid nothing.

We should be as foolish now as we have been many times foolish in the past if we arrogated to ourselves a knowledge of the Asiatic character superior to that of the Asiatics themselves. We may safely assume that Japan knows her Asia a great deal more intimately than we of the West. In those thrilling days when the statesmen of Tokio were conferring and the world waited with breathless interest their decision, whether it should be war to collect the indemnity or peace without the indemnity, we may feel certain that the effect of the decision on the Asiatic mind, the result it would have on the prestige of Japan and its influence upon the known ambitions of Japan, was weighed with that minute care and balanced with all that exact regard to detail that is so characteristic of the Japanese.

Japan could afford to throw away a few hundred millions, much as she would like to have the money to repair the financial sacrifices that have been forced upon her; but she could not afford to take any step that would put her in a false light before the peoples of the Far East. Here then was the great problem confronting her. It was not the mere question of money. It went deeper than that. It involved the whole social and political fabric of the East. It was a revolution as startling as that when the ten tables were given to mankind. Its effects were to be as far-reaching. Asia had taken unto herself a new code of ethics. Asia had suddenly reversed the traditions of centuries.

Japan decided. Japan knew what she could afford to do with safety. The effect of that momentous decision can mean only one thing. It means that the East has kept pace with the West in its advancing civilization; that the East has not stood still, although its advance has been so gradual that it has been almost imperceptible to the vision of the West. It must be obvious that Asia is beginning — perhaps she has made more than the mere beginning that we imagine — to take the same moral view of strength that we of the West take, that strength does not necessarily mean to the Asiatic mind brute force. Hereafter the relation between the West and the East must be more ethical and less material. For this we have to thank Japan.

The war is over. What of the future? What effect has the war on the two countries, now that they can turn their energies to peace? The effect of the war is seen most strikingly in Russia, and it is the Russian people who ought to be the most thankful to Japan for what she has done for them. The war has made Russia realize her strength and her weakness; it has shown her how impossible it is for a nation to hold her position when she clings to an archaic civilization and refuses to keep peace with progress and the great onward march of liberty and individual personal freedom. In the future of Russia I have always believed, because Russia is a country of immense area, with vast but undeveloped natural resources, with a people capable of great accomplishments if permitted the same freedom of action, the same latitude of initiative, that the people of other countries assume as theirs by right of birth.

A beginning has been made in Russia, the direct effect of the war with Japan. Against his will the Czar has granted his people a small voice in the management of their own affairs. The long-heralded and ardently prayed for Douma is not, as many newspapers ordinarily careful in the use of words term it, "a national representative assembly." It is not representative in the same sense that the mother of parliaments is or that her most favored daughter is. There is no such power lodged

in the Douma as there is in the hands of the Commons or the House of
Representatives.   Not only does it not control the purse — and it is the
power to vote or withhold supplies that makes the people through their
duly elected representatives so all-powerful in England and America —
but it has no real legislative functions.   It cannot initiate legislation;
its veto power is circumscribed; it is dissolvable at the will of the Emperor; in case of disagreement between the Douma and the council of the
empire, the latter can disregard the Douma; and the procedure is purposely hedged in with restrictions to deprive the individual member of
that power of obstructive opposition that has more than once proved the
safeguard of the liberties of a people granted the right of free speech in
a real representative assembly.

The student of parliamentary government will find little in the
Douma to approve and much to disapprove if he studies the Douma
simply as the latest development of parliamentary government; but it
would be unfair to weigh it in English or American scales.   Its importance — the influence that it will have in Russia, and through that
influence bring about a change in the relations between Russia and all
the rest of the world — is the encouragement it gives to the men who
have with such rare devotion and with such resolute courage fought to
break down the power of autocracy.   Its effect will be to strengthen the
moral fibre of the nation.

The Czar and his advisers may have thought that the Douma would
put a stop to all further agitation for real representative government.
They may have given it to the people as a foolish mother gives a cake
to a child to quiet its crying.   But the taste of the cake only encourages
the child to cry for more; and once the Russian people have been given
a taste of governmental control, they will not be content until they are
allowed to satisfy themselves with a full meal.   It is the first step that
counts, in virtue as in vice, in liberty as in repression.   A people that
permits its liberties to be taken from it, that submits to the taskmaster,
must make up its mind to give up everything.   Given a people who are
hungering for liberty of action, to whom after a long and bitter struggle
comes the first promise of hope, and they will be satisfied with nothing
short of all that they know rightfully belongs to them.   The Douma is
merely a beginning, "the unification of the seed of the people," as Mr.
Witte so felicitously expressed it in an interview, from which shall
spring a tree life-giving and rejuvenating to the parched souls of the
Russian people, whose development has been stifled by an ignorant and
incompetent bureaucracy.

The future of Japan is to be found in the history of her past. The war has brought to Japan not only the respect and admiration of the world, but to her people a confidence in themselves and an abiding faith in their destiny. Japan has great problems to meet and wisely to solve. A small country with limited resources, she will now feel the effects of the war, because it is not during war but only when peace comes that all that war has cost is realized. It will take Japan some years to make up for the money spent in unproductive enterprise and to fill up the economic vacuum caused by the loss of life on the battlefield. If the Japanese do not get national megalomania, if victory does not encourage luxury and the enervation that comes from success, the future of Japan is assured.

Japan becomes the predominant force in Eastern Asia, a force so great that her influence will be felt throughout the Continent. What the effects of that influence will be on China — China, the most fascinating mystery the world knows, China with all its possibilities but with more cause for disappointment than hope — no one is rash enough to predict; but obviously that influence will be very great. We have seen recently that China is adaptive enough to be able to retaliate by the use of Western methods. The use of the boycott to compel the United States to make a treaty more in consonance with Chinese self-respect is extremely suggestive. Whether the scheme was suggested to the Chinese by the Japanese, as some people are inclined to think, or whether it originated in the fertile brain of former Minister Wu Ting Fang, who did not spend several years in the United States with his eyes closed, is really not of much consequence. The important thing is that the Chinese have shown that they are able to fight the West with the West's own weapons, that they are conscious of their own strength and are no longer afraid to use it. Japan is so close to China, there is so much in common between them, China has been so vividly impressed with all that Japan has done and her victory over the feared, and often hated, white race, that it follows as a matter of course if there is to be an awakening in China, and if China like Japan is suddenly to astound the world by taking all that is best of the civilization of the West and rejecting that which will do her no good, it will be because Japan has set the example.

The Western nations have tried it and failed. England, the United States, France, Germany — not one of these has made the least impression upon China. China has disdainfully rejected the civilization of the outer barbarian, because she has considered her civilization superior to that which the world has had to offer her. With Japan it is different.

Japan and China lie side by side; and although the Chinese and the Japanese may not be ethnologically akin, there is so much in common between them — there is the bond of color, if nothing else — that if China is to be pried from the inertia of tradition in which she has sunk it will be the lever in the hands of Japan that will work the miracle.

A few days before the Portsmouth treaty of peace was signed, the news came from London that a new treaty of alliance between Great Britain and Japan had been signed in London on the twelfth of August. It is evident that the news was not allowed to leak out, but was published with a purpose, probably as a hint to Russia that whether Japan fought or made peace she could still rely upon the support of Great Britain.

The new treaty supplants the treaty made by Lord Lansdowne in 1902, which was to expire by limitation in 1907 unless the contracting parties were engaged in war, when, *ipso facto*, it remained in full force until the conclusion of hostilities. The renewal of the treaty some eighteen months before its expiration proves conclusively that both sides are satisfied with the obligations it imposes and the protection it assures; and it confirms the opinion advanced in the last number of this review that the present British Government would not relinquish power until peace was once more restored in the Far East.

Of the terms of the new treaty we know nothing as yet officially, but the broad outline published by the European press is in keeping with the terms suggested in these pages three months ago. The old treaty was strictly defensive, and no doubt owed its origin in the first place as a set-off to the Franco-Russian treaty, and was also intended as a warning to Germany not to become the active ally of Russia in her policy of adventure in the Far East. By that treaty the contracting powers bound themselves to come to the assistance of each other in case either was attacked by more than one power, the ultimate purpose being to prevent the dismemberment of China, and Corea from becoming an appanage of Russia. There is now no longer any danger of that. The military strength shown by Japan protects China from the rapacity of the Western powers; and Russia having recognized the predominant military and political rights of Japan in Corea, the rest of the world will acquiesce in that recognition.

It will undoubtedly be seen when the terms are made known, that the new treaty is offensive as well as defensive; that Japan and Great Britain are allies in the fullest sense of the word; that neither has to wait for the other to be attacked by two enemies before coming to her ally's assistance. It will be interesting to know if England recognizes in exact words the danger of an attack on India by Russia; that is, if there is an article in the treaty binding Japan to supply England with an army — the expense, of course, to be borne by England — in the event of Russia and England being at war. If Russia and England were at war, Asia and not Europe would be the battleground, and it would be in Asia that Japan would be of incomparable assistance to her ally.

The new treaty is said to insure the peace of the world, at any rate so far as the extreme East is concerned. This is probably not exaggerating the importance of the new treaty and the rank which Japan now takes in the family of nations. Russia having been foiled in her Far Eastern policy, having met defeat at the hands of Japan because England stood behind Japan, what more natural than that Russia would look for her revenge by attempting the long-threatened invasion of India? That is the fear of English statesmen; it is one of the things a British cabinet always recognizes as a possibility; and yet I think it has now been put some years in the background. Russia must recover from the present war before she is in a position to fight single-handed any first-class power, and she will not fight until she has reorganized her army and begun the reconstruction of a navy. Even the bureaucracy of Russia, perhaps the stupidest bureaucracy in the world, cannot be so utterly devoid of all intelligence as not to understand that until Russia reorganizes her system of government and changes her methods, it is hopeless for her to attempt to make war on any first-class power.

Yet, apparently, England does not propose to be caught napping. After the costly experience of the Boer War, she will take nothing for granted, and least of all hold too lightly the strength of a possible foe. The resignation of Lord Curzon as Viceroy of India is the culmination of a marked divergence of views between the civil and military administrations; and as Lord Kitchener is a man as positive in his views and equally as determined as Lord Curzon, when a disagreement so serious as this arose it was obvious that one man would have to go. It is significant that the home government stands by the commander-in-chief and will carry out the military policy that Lord Curzon attempted to thwart.

The cause of contention can be stated in a few words. In India, as in England, the military power has been subordinate to the civil: the viceroy has not only been supreme in civil affairs, but he has been able to control the military policy of the empire over which he rules. The commander-in-chief of the Anglo-Indian army is a British officer appointed by the home government; but the governor-general has a cabinet, or a council, as it is officially termed, one of its members being an army officer who is the viceroy's military adviser. The anomalous sit- uation therefore exists of the viceroy's military adviser being subordinate in rank, and presumably in experience and ability, to the commander- in-chief, and yet being able to advise the viceroy to reject the plans of the commander-in-chief and to veto his policy.

Lord Kitchener is not a man to submit to divided responsibility. He has proved his capacity as an administrator of the highest rank; he has shown that he possesses genius for taking raw material and hammer- ing it into the finished product; and such a man knows that he can do nothing when he is hampered by divided responsibility. What Kitch- ener did in Egypt, taking the Egyptian fellah, than whom there was nothing more impossible in the eyes of military men, and with the as- sistance of a handful of English sergeants making of him a soldier able to withstand the rushes of fanatical dervishes and mow them down with the coolness of veterans, proves his mastery over men and his power to get the very best out of them. The Egyptian campaign was the tri- umph of organization, and organization is Kitchener's great forte. This was again demonstrated when he went to South Africa. It was natural that he should be sent to India as commander-in-chief.

Lord Kitchener has been at work for some time reorganizing the military system of India. No doubt he discovered that sweeping changes in administration were necessary. But here he ran foul of the governor- general and his military adviser, and certain changes proposed by the commander-in-chief were disapproved by the viceroy. The issue was thus squarely joined. Both Curzon and Kitchener appealed to the home government, which sustained Kitchener while attempting to mollify Cur- zon. But Curzon refused to be shorn of his powers. He threatened to resign unless like his predecessors the commander-in-chief was made his subordinate; and when the home government refused to give him the power that he demanded there was nothing left for Lord Curzon except to resign. Kitchener is now given a free hand, and will carry out the reforms he considers essential properly to safeguard the Indian Empire. This again is another great guarantee of peace. If India were easy of attack, it would be a temptation to Russia to retrieve the past by a bold *coup;* but she will not attempt it so long as the chances of success are doubtful, to say the least.

With the conclusion of peace, the role that Germany is to play in the future becomes of absorbing interest. Has Germany been strengthened or weakened by the blood-letting to which Russia has been subjected? Will the Kaiser recognize that facts are stronger than theories, and reconcile himself to facts, or still cling to his theories? The German Emperor has been a theoretical believer in the Yellow Peril, and gave encouragement to Russia in her war against Japan. The Kaiser could afford to look on with cynical indifference to whatever happened, for whatever happened brought grist to his mill. Every day that Russia continued the war a greater strain was put on the resources of Russia, and her credit was weakened. Every soldier sent to the front, every rouble spent for military purposes, every gun that fell into the hands of the Japanese, every ship destroyed, made Russia to that extent weaker; and as she became weaker she was less to be feared by Germany and less to be relied upon by France in case France once again clashed with Germany.

We have had a striking illustration of this. If Russia had not been engaged elsewhere, the Emperor would probably have been more diplomatic and less insistent over Morocco; but he had a free hand and he used it. If, on the other hand, Russia should win and Japan should lose, there were still compensations. Russia would become the mistress of the Far East, Germany would enlarge her Asiatic possessions, because Russia leans on Germany, and Russia would be willing to be complaisant for the sake of enjoying the favors of Germany. The German Emperor stood to win, no matter what cards turned up.

But the *rapprochement* between France and England has disturbed fine calculations. The European situation at the present time is one of the most curious that history has known. Between England and Germany there is open and undisguised hostility. Sovereigns and responsible ministers may attempt thinly to veil it, but the people of the two countries take pride in proclaiming the cordial detestation they have for each other. I do not believe that war between the two countries in the next few years is inevitable; but the Englishman or German who attempts to stem the current finds himself in a hopeless minority and is placed in the uncomfortable position of opposing a wave of national frenzy.

France took out an insurance policy with Russia, and paid heavily for it. She has now reinsured with England, and in case of a war between England and Germany, France could not hope to remain merely a passive spectator of events. What could either Germany or England hope to gain by war? It was the question I asked of a well-informed German not many days ago. His answer was startling. He said:

Germany cannot invade England; England cannot invade Germany. If England knows her business she will make war upon us now, at once, because England can destroy our navy. We quite admit that; but it will not be a Tsushima;

13

the British navy will have fewer battle-ships and cruisers after the naval engagement than she had at the opening of hostilities. Very good; we have no navy, and
England has a smaller but still a powerful navy, what then? We shall make France
pay for it; understand me, we shall make France pay for it — we shall make France
pay three dollars for every dollar England destroys. We shall make war on France.
We shall find the pretext; it is easy enough. We shall go again to the gates of
Paris. What can France do? What can England do? We shall make France pay
all our bills. It will cost us nothing.

Germany becomes the master of Europe. France is crushed. Italy and Austria will not dare to move. England cannot lend military assistance to her ally.
There is Russia, but Russia will do nothing, because Russia has more to make by
remaining on good terms with Germany than by quarrelling with her. You see,
then, what we make by a war with England. You understand why we do not
fear war.

What I quote may sound like the bombastic utterances of an irresponsible Anglophobe. If that were the case it would not be given
space here. The words are not those of a man who speaks without
knowledge or thought. It voices a belief largely existing in Germany
to-day, a belief openly expressed by Prince Donnersmarke, the German
confidential envoy to France, not long ago. In this calm manner the
prince discussed the future with a reporter for the Paris "Gaulois":

Be sure we shall not wait for a menace to take shape. The Emperor does not
want war; he wants only to develop German commerce. In this respect the Emperor is naturally in rivalry with Great Britain, which devotes her attention to destroying the navies of neighbors, or, better still, to preventing them from existing
at all. It behooves you to decide whether it suits you to serve England's interests
and to confront the perils you are exposing yourself to by the verbal understanding
which you are prepared to transform into a British alliance.

The Emperor respects your army; he knows its merits and its failings. In the
event of war you may be victorious; but if you are vanquished, the peace will be
signed in Paris. Do you expect England to make common cause with you and
attempt a diversion which you might profit from on the German coast?

That may be. Let us suppose things are as favorable as possible for you.
She bombards our ports, destroys our fleet, and ruins our colonies. With your milliards we repair damage of every kind that she has done to us. She may think herself invulnerable at home; but if we occupy your territory, she will be powerless to
dislodge us thence.

Verily, when statesmen as well as the people give voice to the same
thought, it cannot be laughed at as fantastic. Nations are moved to
deeds, great for good or evil, when a single thought takes possession of
high and low.

It is necessary once more to refer to the relations between Russia and
Germany, because both countries will for some time continue to bulk
large in the calculations of all European statesmen. What was the
meaning of that mysterious interview that took place between Czar and

Kaiser on the latter's yacht off Bjoerkoe in July, and what influence did it have on the subsequent proceedings at Portsmouth? No one is as yet in a position to answer those two vital questions. We know that it was an interview of the Kaiser's seeking; that it was veiled in the deepest secrecy; and that until the two sovereigns met no one knew of their intentions. The interview took place in private — in the cabin of a yacht, the place of all others where men can talk without the risk of being overheard — with no minister or other person present. Evidently what the Kaiser had to say to his cousin of Russia was intended for his ears alone. Obviously it was a frank talk between the two rulers; and knowing what we do of the temperament of the two men, it is perhaps not unsafe to say that the stronger man — the man who is a great politician as well as a great ruler, the man who has boundless ambition and who knows how to turn a situation to his own profit, the German Emperor — used all his powers to induce the weaker man to commit himself to a policy that should be for the advantage of Germany.

The indiscretions of great men are proverbial. The freedom with which men in high stations blurt out things that should never be told is always the marvel of the public, and especially to men who are trained to keep secrets. Thanks to this inability to preserve silence, the purpose of this yachting trip is known, that is, if reliance can be placed on the statement attributed to a member of the Czar's suite; and it has all the intrinsic earmarks of truth.

Admiral Birileff, the Russian minister of marine, accompanied the Czar on his yacht. The admiral after his return talked to a friend, who straightway published what he had been told in the "Echo de Paris." It is not much, but it affords a clew to what took place.

There were two interviews. First, the Czar went to the German Emperor's yacht, the "Hohenzollern," and remained with him for three hours. Later the Emperor returned this visit, and in the cabin of the "Polar Star" was closeted with the Czar for two hours and a half. At the end of that time Admiral Birileff was summoned. After a few minutes spent in conventional platitudes, the Czar pointed to a paper lying on the table and requested the admiral to sign it. The paper was so folded that it was impossible for the admiral to know its contents. He might have been signing his own death-warrant for all that he knew to the contrary, but the word of his imperial master was law. The paper was lying on a new sheet of blotting-paper, and as the admiral signed he noticed that on this blotting-pad were the reversed signatures of the Czar and the Kaiser. Clearly those signatures had only a few minutes before been affixed to the paper, and the signature of the admiral was as a witness to the signatures, although legally such an attestation would be worthless, as the witness had not been present when the signatures were executed.

If the testimony of the injudicious Birileff is to be relied upon, and I have seen no repudiation of the publication in the "Echo de Paris," clearly a formal and binding contract of some kind was executed in the cabin of the "Polar Star." It must have been a personal agreement — that is, an agreement between the two sovereigns rather than between their two countries; otherwise the signatures would have been witnessed by the ministers of foreign affairs of the respective countries. It would be unusual for a secret treaty to be negotiated directly by sovereigns. For this, the intermediary of the responsible minister of state would be employed. Speculation as to the object covered by the paper is useless, but we shall probably hear of it again.

In August, Francis Joseph, the Emperor of Austria and King of Hungary, celebrated his seventy-fifth birthday. Fifty-seven years ago this fine old man, whose life has been one long grim tragedy, came to the throne in a time of storm and stress, with Hungary in open revolt and endeavoring to divorce the bond that held her to Austria. And now his life is again embittered by the ceaseless feud between the Magyar and German elements of the heterogeneous population over which he rules.

The bitterness between Hungary and Austria increases. Efforts to bring about a reconcilation and effect a *modus vivendi* have failed; and Hungary still remains firm in her determination to make Austria concede the reforms to which she considers herself entitled. So intense is this feeling that in Hungary the Emperor is warned to remember the fate of Oscar of Sweden and not to drive the Hungarians to imitate the example of Norway and imperil his dual throne as King Oscar did. With this thought in mind, Francis Kossuth, the son of the revolutionary leader, whom the Emperor a few months ago requested to form a ministry, thus pointedly addresses his sovereign:

King and nation have stiffened themselves in mutual opposition, and it is to be feared that the constitution may be sacrificed in the struggle, in which the King of Hungary seems to forget that kings are made for nations and not nations for kings; for there are no kings without a kingdom, but plenty of kingdoms without kings.

But it would be a hasty and unwarranted assumption to consider that a complete parallel exists between Austria-Hungary and Sweden and Norway. The latter confederation is outside the great swirl of

European politics, and because it is small and weak can, in a measure, rely on the protection of the great Powers. With Austria-Hungary it is different. Those two countries are wedged in the very thick of the politics of Europe, with neighbors ready to crush them at the first sign of weakness. Neither Hungary nor Austria can exist alone, that is as separate and independent states; and if either wishes to retain its individuality, is proud of its race and birth, and does not want to be submerged in a greater and more powerful state, it is necessary for the confederation not to be dissolved. Despite the bitterness that exists, both nations know this, and would, I think, prefer to remain united rather than surrender their national existence; for it can be accepted as a fact that with the break-up of the Austro-Hungarian empire would follow a remodelling of the map of Europe.

Hungary has had a historical mission in Europe. She stands for much that is fine. Her people are liberty-loving, resolute, and intelligent. The Hungarians constitute the real strength of the empire. Nearly sixty years ago they attempted to sever the union, and Austria in her extremity was forced to call for assistance upon Russia, which sent 200,000 troops into Hungary. If Hungary were again to rise it would not be a repetition of the bloodless Scandinavian revolution. Austria would fight to the death to preserve the integrity of the empire, and in her distress she might again appeal to Russia or implore Germany for succor. That suggests possibilities that one does not wish lightly to contemplate.

The progress of disestablishment in France proceeds smoothly, and the passage of the bill by the Chamber of Deputies by a majority of 108 has been accepted without emotion. If the expressions of politicians and publicists are to be accepted, the evils that were feared when the project was first brought forward to divorce the Church and State will not materialize, principally because even the most ardent supporters of a State Church now realize that religion is not an exotic plant that must be nourished by the State. The cause of real religion has been injured rather than helped by the supervisory control exercised by the French Government. That was seen many years ago by men who had the best interests of the Church at heart and who know the dangers that were almost inevitable when the Church entered into politics and politicians were able to use the Church as an ally. Much of the mutability of French politics may be directly traced to this alliance, which was as bad for the Church as it was for the State.

It is curious that Frenchmen were unable to understand this. They looked across the Channel and pointed to England, with its State-endowed Established Church, and asked why the same union that existed in England should not work equally well in their own country. They forgot, however, the temperamental differences between Englishmen and Frenchmen and the difference between their institutions; and they did not sufficiently take into account the difference between the two religions, the one whose spiritual head was an alien residing in a foreign country.

The effect of disestablishment in France will be, to quote an admirable expression from the London "British Weekly," that "whatever is true and real in the religion of the country will survive and flourish. In so far as religion is dead, the mimicry of life will be at an end, and well that it should be at an end." But religion, real religion, will survive, because religion is as essential to the civilization of to-day as pure air and uncontaminated water. Without it civilization would lapse into a lower stage. The churches will be put to great temporary inconvenience, but they will emerge from their trial stronger, better, more self-reliant than ever.

It has been said by many close observers that France seemingly religious is at heart atheistic. We shall now be able to determine this. In France the people will support their churches as they do in the United States, out of their own means, voluntarily, as they support hospitals and other agencies for good, because they believe in them, because they know that the Church is a great instrument in modern civilization. "The mimicry of life will be at an end," and in its place will be life that is serious and real. The influence of the clericals in French politics will be at an end, which will make the politics of France more nearly represent the true feelings of the French people. France will not be any the less religious because it has no State-supported Church. Rather it will be more genuinely religious, more tolerant, more liberal, with a view more enlightened than it has ever known before.

A. MAURICE LOW.

FINANCE.

It will be remembered that the dominant facts in the financial outlook, when THE FORUM went to press three months ago, were the collapse of an insecure Stock Exchange speculation for the rise, the uncertainties of the approaching harvest, the unsettlement arising from such banking scandals as those of the First National of Milwaukee and the Equitable Life of New York, doubt as to the ouctome of the Eastern war, and, not least of all, a distinct reaction in the iron trade, whose vicissitudes have habitually been accepted as a measure of trade conditions generally. Before undertaking to sum up the present situation, it will be worth while to inquire what has happened during the three past months in each of these directions.

First, as regards the stock market collapse of the later spring, it became evident very quickly that this was a wholesome incident. By cutting down the loans advanced for purposes of venturesome speculation, opportunity was given to finance without awkward strain such large undertakings as the fourth Japanese loan, of which this market subscribed for $50,000,000. More than this, the chance of another such discovery as the Bigelow affair of April — a manifest sequel to the rampant speculation which preceded it — at once became less disturbing. It does not follow that renewal of stock-jobbing speculation, on the scale of last autumn or last spring, may not bring back the same awkward possibilities; but the past season has at least been free from them.

With the money market position thus reasonably guarded, the grain crops have reached the harvest season with exceptionally high promise. Favoring weather has prevailed, almost without interruption, throughout the wheat and corn belts. The high grain prices, maintained throughout the period of the last crop's marketing, had the quite logical result of inducing farmers to increase their acreage. The Government's midsummer crop report figured out a planted area, for early-sown wheat, larger by 2,800,000 acres, or 10 per cent, than that of 1904; an increase in spring-sown wheat of 400,000 acres; and in corn a gain of 1,700,000. For wheat, this planted acreage has never been exceeded, outside of 1901 and 1903; in corn, no parallel exists in the records of the Department of Agriculture, except for 1902, when the area under the growing crop was estimated almost exactly at the present year's figures. The crop of wheat foreshadowed by this active planting work, and by the favorable weather, is commonly reckoned as the second largest in our history; the indicated corn crop, as the largest without exception. The following table gives some notion as to what the produce markets look for from the wheat crop. For 1905 the figures are those of the September estimate; for previous years, they are the Government's final summary:

Year.	Bushels.	Year.	Bushels.
1905	704,400,000	1899	547,303,870
1904	552,399,517	1898	675,148,705
1903	637,821,835	1897	630,149,168
1902	670,063,008	1896	427,684,846
1901	748,460,218	1895	467,102,947
1900	522,229,505	1894	460,267,416

It must be added that the above calculation as to this year's yield has been disputed, some grain trade experts insisting that the Department has been unduly optimistic, and that the actual results may not exceed the yield of 1902 or 1898. This is possible enough, though it should be observed that the winter-wheat crop, where the great part of the estimated increase has been made, has pretty much confirmed the Government figures by its showing at harvest time and in the early marketing. Even if liberal deduction should be made from the Department estimates for 1905, the case of wheat brings up some interesting considerations. These bear primarily on the question, as much discussed since the crop of 1904 as it was after the cotton crop of 1903, whether this country's capacity for production and export of these agricultural staples can or cannot be maintained. Experts answered in the negative at the time, as regards both crops. Nature responded, in the case of cotton, by the "bumper crop" of 1904, which reached 13,693,279 bales — nearly a million in excess of the highest previous record. Now comes this season's answer as to wheat — in some ways more important than the outcome in the cotton trade. For while predictions of a decrease in our future cotton yield were based on theories of partially exhausted soil and insect pests, ignoring the question of available acreage remaining, the adverse view of future American wheat production was based upon the absorption of available wheat lands into town and village sites, along with the spread of population, or their conversion into acreage for the garden crops more profitable in the neighborhood of cities. Nevertheless, the record of the crop of 1905 to date shows that a high bid on the market has the capacity of bringing new wheat area into cultivation, exactly as the 17-cent price for cotton, after the deficient crop of 1903, engaged all the energies of planters in extending capacity for production.

The bearing which the large crop of grain will have this coming year on the country's general prosperity is plain enough. It will give to the railways the business which they need, and, with the good prices commanded by wheat and corn, even in the face of abundant supplies, will insure another year of good times to the farm communities. What it will accomplish, in the case of the export trade, is more interesting, because it will throw light on a disputed problem. I have hitherto spoken of the collapse in our export of what was once our greatest reliance in foreign trade. The exact figures for the fiscal year ending with June are worth reprinting, to show how astonishing this shrinkage has been. This is the comparison for three decades, the figures of quantity including both wheat shipped in grain and the quantity of wheat converted into flour and exported in that form:

The following table shows our total export of wheat in grain and flour during a series of fiscal years:

Year Ended June 30.	Wheat.	Flour.	Total Wheat and Flour.	Year Ended June 30.	Wheat.	Flour.	Total Wheat and Flour.
	Bushels.	Barrels.	Bushels.		Bushels.	Barrels.	Bushels.
1905 .	4,391,061	8,756,915	43,797,178	1883.	106,385,828	9,205,664	147,811,316
1904 .	44,158,744	16,729,550	120,241,719	1882.	95,271,802	5,915,686	121,892,389
1903 .	113,454,452	19,442,780	200,946,962	1881.	150,565,477	7,945,786	186,321,514
1902 .	154,856,102	17,759,206	234,702,515	1880.	153,252,795	6,011,419	180,304,180
1901 .	132,000,667	18,650,979	215,990,073	1879.	122,353,936	5,629,714	147,687,649
1900 .	101,950,389	18,699,194	186,090,564	1878.	72,404,961	3,947,333	90,167,959
1899 .	139,432,815	18,485,690	222,618,420	1877.	40,325,611	3,343,665	55,372,104
1898 .	148,231,261	15,349,943	217,306,004	1876.	55,073,122	3,935,512	72,782,926
1897 .	79,562,020	14,569,545	145,088,972	1875.	53,047,177	3,973,128	70,926,253
1896 .	60,650,080	14,620,864	126,443,968	1874.	71,039,928	4,094,094	80,463,351
1895 .	76,102,704	15,268,892	144,714,146	1873.	39,204,285	2,562,086	50,733,671
1894 .	88,415,230	16,859,533	164,283,119	1872.	26,423,080	2,514,525	37,738,487
1893 .	117,121,109	16,020,339	191,912,634	1871.	34,310,906	3,653,841	50,453,190
1892 .	157,280,351	15,196,769	225,665,810	1870.	36,584,115	3,463,333	52,169,113
1891 .	55,131,948	11,344,304	106,181,316	1869.	17,557,836	2,431,873	28,501,664
1890 .	54,387,767	12,231,711	109,430,466	1868.	15,940,899	2,076,423	25,284,802
1889 .	46,414,129	9,374,803	88,600,743	1867.	6,146,411	1,300,106	11,996,888
1888 .	65,789,261	11,963,574	119,625,344	1866.	5,579,103	2,183,050	15,442,828
1887 .	101,971,949	11,518,449	153,804,969	1865.	9,937,876	2,641,298	21,823,717
1886 .	57,759,209	8,179,241	94,565,793	1864.	23,681,712	3,557,347	39,689,772
1885 .	84,653,714	10,648,145	132,570,366	1863.	36,160,414	4,390,055	55,915,660
1884 .	70,349,012	9,152,260	111,534,182				

It will be seen that the exports of the period were much the smallest since 1872, and were actually much exceeded as long ago as the early days of the Civil War. Now, assuming a wheat harvest this season of 700,000,000 bushels, and the same home consumption as that of the past season, there would be left for export 192,000,000 bushels. The problem will not of course work out with such exactness: the yield may turn out considerably below the figure named, and home consumption will probably be greater with the larger supply, the lower price, and the absence of corner operations. But even with these allowances, the United States will have to spare, for the outside consuming world, as much wheat as it was used to reckoning on a decade ago, when the foreign bread-eater expected to get, from this country, three or four times as much wheat and flour as he obtained last year. The case is all the more fortunate from the fact that the outcome of the foreign harvest promises to create such a void in outside production as will absorb this American surplus. The reason why Europe was able to do with so little American wheat from last year's crop was that, while our yield of 1904 decreased 196,000,000 bushels from that of 1901, Russia's production increased 244,000,000. The result was that, despite our shortage of last year, the world's entire crop of wheat was actually larger than it had been four years before. As I showed in the last number of THE FORUM, Russia has taken our place in the grain-export trade this twelvemonth past, while the United States, once the chief among all exporting nations, dropped to fifth place, ranking not only under Russia, but under India, Australia, and Argentina.

What has happened in the new crop, however, is that while our own crop promises increase of 196,000,000 bushels over 1904, a decrease of 140,000,000 has been currently estimated, in the trade, for the Russian yield. With wheat at the prices which it recently has commanded, this loss by Russia is unfortunate to the consuming world. It is undoubtedly a windfall of luck, however, to our own grain-producers. It will also be observed, as among its wholesome consequences, that the season's results will have added largely to the American export trade — thus strengthening our position on the foreign exchanges — and, on the other hand, must tend to restore a disturbed equilibrium in the world's grain trade. It is at least two years since it could be said that the price of wheat was fixed, as it had been for generations, in Liverpool. Since 1902 it has been largely fixed by the Chicago speculators. With a normally large exportable surplus to dispose of, the price bid by the foreign consumer becomes a more practical question than it was with only 44,000,000 bushels to send out. Of one thing there is no doubt: the discovery of our country's capacity still to meet a good part of the outside world's consuming demands is reassuring from every point of view.

The case is not so clear in regard to the cotton crop; but the situation in that direction is so puzzling that the season gives little clew to what may be looked for in the future. Our 10,000,000-bale crop of cotton, picked in 1903, was so far inadequate, and was greeted by such extravagant bids from the market, that every consideration urged the planter to enlarge his yield next season. The result was the thirteen-and-a-half million bale crop of 1904, and a fall in the price of cotton from the $17\frac{3}{8}$-cents figure of February in that year to $6\frac{1}{8}$ cents in December. With that decline, and the rather general expectation of return to "five-cent cotton," came the movement to organize cotton-planters into a mutually protective union, through which the area planted should be subject to some sort of supervision, and should be kept in such relation to what the spinners' demands were presumed to be that prices could be arbitrarily maintained.

This scheme of organization met with some success. The leaders of last January's New Orleans convention advised a uniform reduction of 25 per cent from the area planted in cotton in 1904. They doubtless did not expect that much reduction, and they did not get it, so far as the cut was voluntarily arranged by individual planters. But while the average farmer was making some moderate reduction in his planting, Nature took a hand in the game. The estimate of the Government's Agricultural Department at the opening of the season was that the planted acreage was smaller by $11\frac{3}{4}$ per cent than that of a year before. The reduction had fallen considerably short of what the Cotton Planters' Association had advised. But the estimate as to condition and promise of the crop, compared with the same time in 1904, showed deterioration of 11 per cent. This was the work of Nature, performed through the medium of a late and unpropitious season. The estimates started the cotton trade into what it called "mathematical forecasts" of the crop. If acreage was $11\frac{3}{4}$ per cent short of 1904, if condition was lower by 11 per cent, and if last year's yield was 13,600,000 bales, then the prospect for 1905, at the opening of the season, was for a cotton harvest $22\frac{3}{4}$ per cent below last year's, or 10,600,000 bales.

Such a yield would be only an average crop, in the light of that of recent years, in which cotton crops have been estimated as follows, at the season's end, by the New Orleans Cotton Exchange:

Year.	Bales.	Year.	Bales.
1903	10,011,374	1899	9,436,416
1902	10,727,559	1898	11,274,840
1901	10,680,680	1897	11,199,994
1900	10,383,422	1896	8,757,964

But these crops have not always been actually sufficient for the needs of the spinning trade. Estimates of the English expert Ellison as to the amount of American cotton consumed by the spinners of the world during those years have been as follows:

Year.	Bales.	Year.	Bales.
1903	10,273,000	1899	10,949,000
1902	10,880,000	1898	10,658,000
1901	10,679,000	1897	10,042,000
1900	10,310,000	1896	8,945,000

Comparison of these two tables will show that in all these eight years, except 1897 and 1898, the consuming world has either used up closely the season's American cotton output, or else has actually much exceeded it and drawn on the stored-up reserves of other years. It also shows that, taken by itself, the 10,600,000-bale crop indicated by the early estimates of 1905 would hardly more than exceed the world's requirements. Later developments of the season made the prospect considerably worse. This happened in two ways. First, the weather continued unpropitious. As against a June "condition estimate" of 77.2 per cent, the August figure was placed at 74.9, and this compared with 91.6 in August, 1904. More important, because more confusing and disturbing to the trade's calculations, the conviction began to grow that the Agricultural Department's early estimates, especially of acreage, were deliberately placed too high. Suspicion was first excited by the discovery that responsible officers in the Department had been secretly giving out to speculators, in advance of official publication, the estimates prepared from data in the Department's hands. A "leak" of this sort was naturally valuable to gambling operators intent on forestalling the movement of a market governed by these estimates, and it was through the confession of some of them that the breach of trust was traced home to the official in question.

So far, the revelations, though extremely discreditable, had no bearing on the accuracy of the percentage estimates. But the accomplices on the cotton exchanges went further in their confession, and broadly intimated that the acreage estimate had been deliberately marked up by the Department official to a higher figure than the returns to the Department warranted. The Cotton Planters' Association, whose officers from the first contended that the Department had not made its estimate of acreage reduction large enough, pressed the matter urgently. Cotton, which sold at the opening of July at $9\frac{1}{2}$ cents a pound, rose to $11\frac{3}{4}$ three weeks later. Reorganization of the Agricultural Department followed immediately; and the new statistical officers were instructed to overhaul the data from which the earlier acreage estimate was compiled. They did so, and announced that the figures of that estimate were inaccurate; that instead of a reduction of $11\frac{3}{8}$ per cent from 1904, the decrease should have been placed at $14\frac{7}{8}$. But $14\frac{7}{8}$ per cent shrinkage in planted area, and a condition — according to the August estimate — lower by 16¾ per cent, would leave the crop indication at only 9,500,000 bales. Reference to the list of annual yields above given will show that such a crop would be practically the smallest in nine years; that it would fall half a million bales below even the crop of 1903, which made possible the extravagant corner operations in the next season's cotton market; and that it would fail, by half a million to a million and a half of bales, to provide the quantity of American cotton needed by the spinners of the world.

There was some reflection of this estimate in midsummer cotton markets, when the price of cotton went to 11¼ cents. But the August calculation was not generally accepted, and the government's own September figures hardly bore it out. The trade has hesitated to accept the Department's revision of its early estimates, and it is warranted in such hesitation. No one knows what was the basis on which the earlier acreage estimates were altered; the element of guess-work enters into the later as into the earlier calculation; and the one certainty remains that pressure to make the figures of reduction larger in the revision was exceptionally strong. How much latitude personal judgment has in such a calculation may be inferred from the chief statistician's testimony of last December to the Congressional Committee as to the basis for his estimate on the crop of 1904. Mr. Hyde then said:

If the individual planters' figures had been used exclusively, the estimate would have been 13,376,741 bales; those of the ginners would have given 12,433,728 bales; those of the State statistical agents, 12,116,108 bales; those of the township correspondents, 11,943,827 bales; those of the bankers and merchants, 11,857,000 bales; and those of the county correspondents, 10,903,196 bales.

Using his judgment as to the relative weight to be given to one or the other of these "field reports," the Department in that month drew up its forecast for a crop of 12,162,000 bales. As we have seen, the yield since ascertained, and stated by the Government itself, was 13,693,279 — not only a million and a half bales more than the December estimate, but much larger than the highest figure named by the most optimistic group of field reports described by Mr. Hyde. Along with the possible inferences from this fact came further inferences based on the great crop of 1904. Since the marketing of that crop began a year ago, the export trade and the takings of domestic spinners have absorbed more than 13,000,000 bales. This is 30 per cent more than was similarly taken from the crop of 1903, and 20 per cent more than has ever been thus used in any single twelvemonth of our history. No such increase within a year in the actual use of cotton for manufacture is conceivable, and, indeed, the best authorities in the trade figured out, in September, a surplus of 2,200,000 bales carried over from last year's crop, into the new cotton season.   In other words, if not enough cotton has been raised during 1905 in the United States to equal the probable needs of the next season's manufacture, spinners are perfectly able to draw on the surplus left over from last season.   If they have raised only 10,000,000 bales this year, they will nevertheless possess, with the surplus from last year's crop, an available supply for the coming season never but once exceeded.   They are not, as they were at the end of 1903, left with depleted stocks, and at the mercy of any group of speculators who might choose to create fictitious values by cornering the cotton market. This gives ground for reassurance to the trade; and, as a matter of fact, the price of cotton, despite some urgent efforts by the gamblers in cotton contracts, has not gone to any such extravagant figures as those of 1904. Just how the cotton producer himself will be affected is another question.   He has the general tendency toward high prices in his favor; but if his crop, in the later vicissitudes of the season, falls to a figure nearer 9,000,000 than 10,000,000 bales, he has himself very largely to blame for it.   The organized effort to interfere with Nature's remedy for one cotton famine, and to restrain the planter from doing what his experience and instinct encourage him in doing, would simply have recoiled upon himself.   The reassuring fact is that after this year's experiences arbitrary action of the sort will be less easy than it has been in 1905.

It cannot be said that the possible shortage in the cotton yield has caused any serious apprehension in the financial community.   This may be because of the large surplus left over from the crop of last year and the generally high prices obtained for it — both of which considerations have gone far toward increasing the wealth and prosperity of the South. It may be said, indeed, that the agricultural outlook as a whole is a favorable influence in the situation.   Nor can it be alleged that the misgivings aroused by the various bank scandals of the year's earlier months have continued to exert the bad influence which they exerted in the preceding quarter.   The settlement of the Equitable entanglement, whether temporary or not, has had the best effect in stopping a feeling of uncertainty and perplexity which for a time seemed ominous.   The intimation, which has been rather plainly given out, that Mr. Ryan, who bought out the Hyde controlling interest in the property, would allow the policyholders to purchase the property from him at the price which he paid, has at all events opened a possible door out of the confusing situation.
However, it has not put an end to the discussion of the evils which

must follow private ownership of a great life-insurance company. Neither has it prevented a continuance of the plans for a rigid investigation of other life companies, to determine whether they have or have not indulged in such methods of employing their policy-holders' funds as demoralized the Equitable and caused last season's scandal. It is quite possible that legislation may be introduced with a view to controlling the use of such moneys. If the Equitable affair has accomplished nothing else, it has at least convinced the community at large that in certain instances these funds have been grossly misused, and that the employment of them in speculative promoting enterprises, on the lavish scale of 1901, ought never again to be permitted. But, in the meantime, the fact that so grave a dilemma has been passed through without either disaster or impairment of credit has had in a certain sense a reassuring and favorable effect on the business community.

The quieting-down of the Equitable's own affairs has not stopped the plans of the New York legislature for investigating the other insurance companies. A searching public examination by the committee of the legislature has been in progress in New York during September. It has elicited much important information as to methods and practices, but in particular it has drawn weighty testimony from the witnesses as to the manner in which the enormous accumulations of these companies have been utilized in stock-promotion schemes. To people conversant with the Wall Street history of the past half-dozen years this was no discovery; to the general public it probably was, and it is likely enough to lead to a serious overhauling of our insurance laws. How far this expedient would be any real safeguard to the policy-holder, so long as the practice admitted on the witness-stand continues, namely, of buying up trust companies, depositing insurance funds with them, and allowing those funds to be used for enterprises in which the parent company itself would not embark, is, however, a serious consideration.

As for the question of the iron trade, concerning which, regarded as a barometer, I had something to say in the last number of THE FORUM, it must be said that this phase of the situation remains perplexing. I explained at the time that sudden reduction in the consumption of iron has for many years been regarded as an almost unfailing sign of a halt in the country's industrial movement. There have been many explanations of the decrease in consumption which began last spring. Perhaps the most plausible was that it simply showed a disposition to await the outcome of the harvests; in other words, people with enterprises in hand involving the use of iron did not care to place too many orders until they were sure of the country's consuming capacity. This explanation may be correct; but it remains to be said that up to August the output of iron from the country's foundries continued to decrease from the maximum of last May, while the stock of unsold iron on hand continued to increase. Such a movement has been an almost unfailing sign, in previous years, that a check of some sort had been experienced by industry. Up to this time of writing, however, it has to be admitted that no other of the familiar financial weather-signs points in the same direction.

The stock markets in particular have at no time during the quarter past shown any real sign of doubt or apprehension. There has been a rather striking absence of reckless speculation, such as prevailed in the early part of the present year and during the closing month of 1904. But the underlying strength of the market has manifested itself in some very remarkable ways. In particular, there has been repeated evidence of the absorption of good investment stock by powerful interests. How far this was done with borrowed money, and how far with the purpose of selling again quickly at a profit, are questions not easy to answer offhand. Perhaps the most remarkable phase of the whole investment movement has been the manner in which it has accepted the successive developments of the Russo-Japanese struggle during the past three months. It is of this exceedingly interesting episode, on whose successive chapters financial affairs have had as important a bearing as the war itself has had upon finance, that I now propose to speak.

I have already indicated in THE FORUM that the movement of Russian and Japanese securities — especially of Russian bonds — during the later stages of the war has at times been difficult to explain. Certainly it could not be said that these national securities have reflected the fortunes of war as did British consols, for instance, during the Transvaal struggle, or, for the matter of that, our own Government bonds in 1898. This seeming lack of response to developments of the first importance has been notably perplexing since the movement for peace became so strong that both belligerents had to submit to it. For instance, Japanese bonds have been comparatively weak at times when peace seemed certain and the payment of a heavy indemnity by Russia equally sure; yet the same combination of circumstances failed to cause any renewed depression in Russian securities.

The two considerations in connection with the peace discussion which most concerned financial markets were, first, the hope of so arranging a treaty that no complications with foreign states should result from it, and, second, the question of an indemnity. As regards the first consideration, the trend of events has been altogether favorable. No opportunity for malign interference by an outside power has at any time during these negotiations presented itself. The conference between the Czar and the German Emperor in the Baltic Sea — an occurrence which at one time caused a flutter of indecision in the markets — was almost forgotten before the disputes involved in the treaty had really come to a head. The question of an indemnity, however, was as vitally interesting to the financial markets as to the plenipotentiaries, and for this reason: If, as was at one time generally believed, Japan had imposed a war indemnity of one billion dollars as the price of suspending hostilities, some of the great European markets would have had to provide the necessary funds. To bring together such a sum, or even half of it, during any other than a most extended period, would tax severely the resources of the most powerful market or combination of markets. If payment had been exacted within a comparatively short time, it is possible that very serious financial disturbance would have ensued. The financial world was not without precedent for such results. When Prussia in 1871 imposed its billion-dollar indemnity on conquered France, the bonds which the French Government sold for the purpose were taken mainly by the thrifty French investors. To that extent it might be said that the problem of raising the requisite funds in 1871 was less serious than it would have been in 1905. Yet these enormous subscriptions of the French people to the loans issued for such purposes were made possible through the sale by the same body of capitalists, in almost unprecedented quantities, of other foreign securities where their money was already invested. The necessary consequence of this double movement was that whenever a large issue of rentes was made to pay an instalment of the Prussian indemnity, it was preceded and accompanied by such an outpour of securities, like British consols and other high-grade government bonds, as completely to demoralize the market for such securities. It is not at all impossible that the enormous displacement of capital, in connection with this famous operation of 1871 and the following year, had more than a little to do with the panic of 1873. What is equally noteworthy is the fact that in that panic the worse sufferer, as between the two recent belligerents, was not France but Prussia.

This historical reminiscence will give some notion of why the indemnity question was considered in most discussions of the day as a stumbling-block in the way of international finance. It was not the less

14

so from the fact that Paris was expected to finance any such indemnity loan for Russia, and that if it did, and on the scale proposed, it could hardly be imagined that the incident would not be followed, as the somewhat similar incident was in 1871, by enormous sales of foreign securities held in France.   To England such an outcome would have been particularly unpleasant, for London has not yet been able wholly to shake itself free from its indebtedness to Paris, incurred during the Boer War.   Nevertheless, the indemnity question did not appear to play any such part in the actual operations of the markets as might have been supposed.   Why this was so is by no means easy to determine. There was at one time current in all the European markets a well-defined report that the indemnity loan to Russia would be assisted not only by the financiers of Paris, but also by those of London and New York.   This was a little hard to believe, unless Russia was supposed to borrow on terms of the most exacting character.   Yet at the same time the word given out, from every good source of information in Paris, was to the effect that while Russia could not obtain another sou from French investors while she continued fighting, unlimited amounts would be provided if she would conclude a peace.

If these views of the matter are to be taken as authoritative, it would be reasonable to suppose that financial markets all over the world ought to have displayed extreme exhilaration when the news rather suddenly came in, at the close of August, that the Mikado had intervened and that the Portsmouth plenipotentiaries had waived the indemnity.   It is to my mind more reasonable to assume that powerful financial interests were opposed from the start to the exaction of a large indemnity, and that they believed themselves able, indirectly, to defeat the proposition. This, I am aware, is pure conjecture; but it harmonizes in many ways with the facts of the episode.   From the beginning of the war Japan has maintained an attitude of deference and self-distrust toward one, and one only, of the interests with which she has had to deal.   This interest, it hardly need be said, was the body of great financial houses. It is now a matter practically beyond dispute that the Japanese Government placed its loans, at the opening of the war, on terms which it need not have accepted, and that its continued proffer, up to the time of the recent $150,000,000 loan floated in New York, London, and Berlin, of a first or second lien on certain branches of its revenue was not only humiliating, but at the last absolutely unnecessary.   There is sufficient reason for believing that many of the Japanese statesmen were themselves originally filled with misgiving as to the financial power of their government and its ability to sustain a prolonged war. The upshot of this peculiar phase of the situation would very naturally have been to render the home government at Tokio peculiarly sensitive to advice or pressure from financial quarters.

Be this as it may, there can be no doubt that the waiving of the indemnity demand has a distinctly favorable bearing on the financial situation as a whole. The financial outcome of the war, as regards the two belligerent states, is a somewhat different question. There is no doubt that both Russia and Japan must presently reappear in the markets as borrowers. Their loans, however, will be chiefly for purposes of refunding — in Russia's case to take up short loans which will soon mature; in Japan's, to retire as soon as possible either the domestic loans floated on very unfavorable terms, or some of the foreign loans with their obnoxious provisions regarding special liens upon the revenue. Whether any more positive after-effect of the war than renewed applications by the two states for loans will follow the conclusion of hostilities depends somewhat on circumstances. Japan has undoubtedly gone through the war with a most amazing show of financial strength. This was partly a consequence of very favorable crops — rice in particular — and partly of the methodical way in which the Japanese financiers, when war broke out, met and agreed to postpone so far as feasible all other enterprises involving extensive use of capital, so long as the government's war expenditure had to be provided for. It may also very well be that Japan in this instance has enjoyed the peculiar benefits accruing at the present time to agricultural states in general. This does not prove, of course, that severe financial reaction will not follow the return of peace. Such reaction probably will come, but it is doubtful if it will recoil to any great extent upon outside markets.

In a measure the same comment may be made in the case of Russia. The war must in many ways have exerted a ruinous influence on Russian affairs; and it is not unlikely that the drain of men to the army, combined with the bitter social discontent at home, has had something to do with the reported bad results in this season's Russian harvests. Yet there is this much to be said, that industrial matters could not be very much worse in Russia than they have repeatedly been in the past under the obsolete system of government which throttles enterprise. They may be vastly better after peace, because of the concessions which have been wrung from the feeble Czar, and which will almost certainly be maintained by the people hereafter. I have had occasion heretofore to say that in these days, when the agricultural state has the advantage over the rest of the world, there is no reason, except its uneconomical system of government, why agricultural Russia should not be a foremost beneficiary. When one reflects that Russia last year led every other nation in its export of wheat to outside markets, some conception may be gained as to the part which it ought to play in the world's finance.

From a financial point of view, it may, therefore, be safely said that the Eastern war has not had altogether unfavorable results. It is possible, and for the longer future extremely probable, that its financial and industrial results will be of the best; and such belief may have had its part in the immunity of most financial markets from seriously disturbing effects of the present war.

A disposition has become rather prevalent in the markets to ascribe the continued forward surge of financial prosperity to yet another influence than that of good harvests, active industrial enterprise, or returning peace. With some array of convincing argument, incidents such as the corn crop failure of 1901 are referred to, and the insufficient cotton yield of 1903, each of them followed by unchecked prosperity. The set-back of 1903, pretty much throughout the world, and largely an industrial matter, is called into reckoning, and the absence of any permanent ill-effect is emphasized. It is admitted by all believers in the influence of a large gold output on values and prosperity, except by the extremists, that experienced financial watchers continue to keep their eyes apprehensively on the growing crops. Business plans are conditioned on a successful harvest. Orders at first hand are cancelled or postponed if the agricultural season takes an unfavorable turn. The Stock Exchange, the most sensitive barometer to tendencies in a financial situation, registers a fall in values with the first hint of a decline in condition and promise of the crops. Nor is this all. The mere fact that the season is near at hand when the question of what the earth will yield this year must be determined results in an expectant pause in financial undertakings. Where values, in an excited speculation based upon easy credit, have been raised by leaps and bounds, approach of such a time of test in the growing crops will usually bring the whole speculative structure down to earth — as it did with emphasis last spring. Nevertheless, the theory is heard — not least at the present time, when the gold output in South Africa has once more reached and passed the monthly maximum of the summer before President Krüger's ultimatum — that the world's increasing annual yield of the precious metal is superseding all other considerations. What is to be said of this theory?

The question, though newly applied in the present circumstances, is in reality very old. It developed years ago a school of political economy quite its own. It stood behind the entire campaign for remonetization of silver in this country and elsewhere. The philosophers carried their inference as to the bearing on the world's prosperity of the output of the precious metals to a point which upset half the accepted ideas of ancient and modern history. The decline and fall of the Roman Empire, it has been seriously argued, was a consequence not of social corruption, official incapacity, military despotism, or popular degeneration, but of the failure of the Spanish mines. The Dark Ages marked, primarily, not political chaos, isolation of learning, oppression of industry, but abandonment of organized search for new supplies of the precious metals. When Columbus spread his sails for America, so contends one author of this school, "he bore mankind and its fortunes in his bark" — not because a fresh outlet for the enterprise, trade, and productive activity of Europe was about to be established, but because the treasures of Mexico and Peru, diverted to the channels of circulation of the Old World, were to rescue it from the decay to which it was otherwise doomed by the steady decrease in its metallic money. It is easy to pursue this line of reasoning through the succeeding centuries. The immense expansion of trade and industry during the past half-century, generally ascribed to the unprecedented achievements of mechanical invention, is credited, in accordance with this logic, mainly to the outpour of gold and silver from the newly discovered mines of California and Australia. The bimetallic campaign of the past two decades had its basis partly no doubt in a determined effort to enhance the value of this country's silver product, but chiefly in a belief that the fall in commercial prices resulted from slackening in the world's gold output, and that admission of the enormous silver product to free coinage, on a valuation where most of it would be carried to the Mint, would advance these prices and stimulate the movement of prosperity. If this general argument is accepted, the corollary would be reasonable that a doubling since 1895 in the world's annual gold output, and an increase this year to a hitherto unattained maximum, must at least be a dominant influence in the prosperity of the period.

In its broader aspects, a controversy of this sort belongs to politico-economic theory. It is because, however, of its highly practical bearing on the present situation, asserted in many quarters, that it becomes necessary to examine it in its practical present aspects. For if it were to be conceded that continued increase in the world's gold output must inevitably bring about still larger prosperity, greater trade activity, and higher prices for investment securities and commodities, then it would follow that an exceedingly useful clew to the business future would be in the hands of every observant man.   Exactly how should an increase in the annual gold output of the world — from $202,251,600 in 1896 to $358,000,000 in 1904, and probably to $370,000,000 in 1905 — have the effect described on prices and on prosperity?   For our present purpose the familiar answer, that the price of commodities depends on the proportion between the quantity of commodities in existence and the quantity of money, is not sufficient.   Even if this were granted, why is it so and how does it come about?   If the production of $10,000,000 more gold this year than last year is supposed to raise prices and increase prosperity, how does it do so?

There are two conceivable ways.   First, the purchasing power of the new gold may create such a new demand for commodities which its owners desire to purchase as to raise the price of such goods and increase activity in the trades connected with them.   It has been argued by one well-known economic writer regarding the case of the Australian gold discoveries of half a century ago, first, that the successful mining communities brought such quantities of merchandise from European markets that prices were forcibly advanced; and second, that the high demand and high price for labor in such communities tended to divert workers from other fields and so raise the labor cost in production.   However well this explanation may have answered in the case of 1850, it is obviously an unsatisfactory explanation to-day.   The world's greater gold-mines — notably in the Transvaal, where the increase in output has been the most rapid — are owned by highly capitalized companies, which pay dividends to scattered shareholders, which are located in poor communities, and which, in the case of the Transvaal, pay to their workers wages which are not attractive, and which could not possibly affect the wage scale elsewhere.   Furthermore, even if the demand for food, machinery, and luxuries in these new communities were tenfold what it is, it would still fall short of the similar demand created, say, by a farming community which has raised and sold this year $40,000,000 worth more of grain or cotton than it raised a year ago.

The result of a greatly increased gold output becomes, however, more obvious when we trace the course of the new gold.   The wheat or cotton raised in a "bumper year" is in the main consumed during the succeeding season; the gold, so far as it is not needed for new coin in hand-to-hand circulation, or for purpose of manufacture, goes into the reserves of the world's great banks.   It is not difficult to see what office it there performs. Loans made by these banks become in turn deposit liabilities. The amount of such liabilities which a prudent bank will keep outstanding depends on the amount of gold or other authorized money lying in its vaults. The more of such gold that is deposited in these banks, the larger the credit fund which they can safely place at the disposal of borrowers. This has unquestionably happened, as a result of the suddenly increased gold production of the past ten years, both in the European banks and in our own. That credit should have expanded immensely along with this doubling of the annual gold output; that borrowing should have become easy, and that projectors of new enterprises should therefore have embarked on plans which not long ago would have been deemed preposterous, are logical results of the phenomenon of the mines. All of this we have seen throughout the world during the decade past. One result which might naturally be expected from such a combination of circumstances is the use of bank credits, on a stupendous scale, by speculators of all classes — including combinations of millionaires who, without at all disturbing the securities, land, or commodities in which their capital has already been invested, can continuously increase their holdings by utilizing the abundant credits offered them by the banks. No phenomenon has been more familiar than this in recent finance.

While this abundant credit fund gives opportunity for an unprecedented number of new industrial enterprises, these enterprises call for equally unprecedented amounts of new material — notably products such as iron and copper. The larger employment of labor increases among the laboring classes as a whole the demand for necessaries of life such as bread and clothing; and a very little increase in the average amount of either, purchased each year by the individual, will enlarge enormously the world's demands on the annual crops of grain and cotton. This also is a matter of statistical fact; and it explains why agricultural crops which a very few years ago were considered exceptionally large would to-day be described as inadequate. It is easy enough to follow this process through all its manifestations, and to see why an upward movement of prices should have penetrated into every domain of industry.

But when all this is said, some exceedingly practical questions intrude, which compel a different view of the matter. Why was this movement not foreseen? Where will it end? And what will end it? Is it an unmixed blessing or not? The last question is likely to find its answer in the answer to the others. The movement was foreseen, but not in its present scope — the reason for that being that nobody could have predicted the daring use which capitalists, speculators, and banking institutions would make of the new gold resources. As to when the process will end, only a reference to what has happened under other more or less parallel conditions can give a clew.

The world witnessed a similar and proportionately much greater expansion of its gold output, within a brief term of years, in the middle of the last century. There occurred then, as now, a prolonged expansion of industrial activity, an era of unprecedentedly abundant credit, a worldwide speculation of very excited character, and eventually a world-wide over-extension of credit to speculators which ended in the famous crash of 1857. Fiat money episodes have had a similar history; for while it is true that inflation of prices through issue of money current for face value only in the country of issue involves other problems than does inflation of prices through increased gold production, nevertheless the factor of expanded credit plays the same part in each. To come much nearer to the present day, we have the incidents of 1903, which are by this time pretty thoroughly understood. The reckoning which then had to be met in the financial and industrial markets was directly a consequence of overreaching through speculation. Vast as it was, the new credit fund was drained. Nothing more was left for enterprises based on expected heavy borrowings, to the completion of which the underwriting capitalists had already pledged their personal credit. A wellremembered period of general liquidation ensued. Recovery came quickly, as it did after the similar collapse of 1884, and, in this country, after that of 1866. But the warning is not to be overlooked. All the episodes referred to are proof of the tendencies which inevitably characterize a period of such speculative expansion. That these tendencies operate under a law of their own, independent of questions of gold production, may be safely inferred by the regular recurrence of financial reactions, where fluctuation in gold output is not regular at all. The industrial "boom" of the fifties came along with enormous increase in such output; that of the early seventies occurred in a stationary period, so far as gold production was concerned; that of the later eighties, at a time when the annual gold output was actually decreasing. Yet the interval separating one "boom" from another was substantially the same in every case, and the "twenty-year reaction" came to a head in 1837, in 1857, in 1873, and in 1893, seemingly without regard to any peculiar conditions underlying the preceding business "boom."

Granting some influence, on credit expansion, of the large gold pro-

duction of the present period, the practical question arises at what stage
of the movement does the financial and industrial community stand to-
day? The strength of the situation lies in the fact that both here and
abroad a period of normal liquidation is comparatively recent. In Europe
during 1901, and in America during 1903, over-extended credits were
heavily reduced. Values, especially in the investment field, were brought
down to the plane of absolute conservatism. At the same time relaxation
in trade activity released such sums of cash, previously held by inland banks
or in channels of retail circulation, that the larger credit institutions gained
an exceptionally strong position. It is the fresh start thus obtained which
has made possible the remarkable movements of last year and this.

No such movement continues long without creating a somewhat
altered credit position. Wall Street has been accustomed to look on the
surplus reserves of the New York Associated Banks as the proper index
to that part of the situation. The statement of these banks certainly
does not show the position of a year ago. At the close of August —
the date when the city bank fund must be prepared to meet the demands
of the harvest districts for capital and cash reserves — the New York
banks held in their vaults, in specie and legal tenders, exactly the sum
reported by them in the first fortnight of the year; but in the meantime
their outstanding loan account had increased some $80,000,000. On the
eve of the autumn season, the deposit liabilities resulting from new loans
had reached such proportions that the surplus over the 25 per cent of cash
required to be kept against deposits fell to the lowest figure reached at that
season in a dozen years. The following comparison of the surplus reserve,
total cash holdings, and outstanding loans of these banks in the closing week
of August for a series of years gives some idea of the relative position:

	Surplus Reserve.	Total Reserve.	Loans.
1905	$8,978,175	$304,279,300	$1,144,607,900
1904	57,375,400	359,201,100	1,099,057,200
1903	20,677,925	250,709,900	923,111,500
1902	9,743,350	246,810,800	918,687,600
1901	18,148,100	260,185,500	887,837,400
1900	23,888,925	249,228,000	817,402,300
1899	12,378,525	226,912,300	756,789,900
1898	21,343,300	211,401,900	672,091,800
1897	39,517,700	198,766,700	560,874,500
1896	9,272,650	123,847,300	458,933,500
1895	37,566,675	180,950,300	513,532,700
1894	66,718,650	213,165,100	488,763,700
1893	*6,737,675	85,882,300	407,607,400
1892	9,887,875	139,158,200	490,667,700
1891	12,767,825	113,618,800	397,347,300

* Deficit.

On its face, this is certainly not a strong showing. Yet the money market reflected no such uneasiness over the seemingly narrow margin as was shown at the somewhat similar juncture in 1902. Where rates for Wall Street demand loans were steadily tightening at that time, and time money was lending at 5 per cent or higher, August closed this year with an almost nominal rate on call, and with sixty-day loans at 3 per cent, a lower figure even than that of a year ago, when the cash in the New York banks was nearly 20 per cent above this year's figure, and the surplus reserves were nearly sevenfold greater. The comparison is singular; and it probably finds its explanation in the state of the European money markets, notably London and Paris, where money rates are not only substantially lower than in the autumn of 1902, but are sufficiently far below current New York quotations to give grounds for expecting aid from foreign capital when the drain on our own banks grows urgent. In fact, gold has already been engaged in London for New York, at this time of writing. The very good outlook for our harvests, and hence for our export trade in grain, provides a further basis for expecting such relief when needed. It will be seen, however, that the financial outlook for the coming season depends very largely on the demands which will be made on capital. If such demands are restricted to the normal requirements of a world-wide industrial activity, the future has nothing in it to disturb equanimity. If, on the other hand, use were made of the strong underlying factors in the situation to provide a basis for a stock speculation such as that of 1901, or a stock-jobbing craze like that of 1902, resources would have to be scanned more distrustfully. The markets will make some interesting discoveries as to the actual tendencies in such directions before the winter is over.

ALEXANDER D. NOYES.

THE DRAMATIC OUTLOOK, 1905–6.

THE dramatic season of 1905–6 opens with large and varied promise. All theatrical years, indeed, look bright at the outset, in October, only too often to end in disappointment and disaster before the ensuing May. But the present has good assurance in its heritage from the one immediately preceding, as well as extraordinary interest through the development of novel, if not unprecedented, conditions. The evolution now in progress in the world of the stage is so bewilderingly rapid that in a twelvemonth the whole aspect and significance of things changes. Old landmarks disappear overnight, and new enterprises loom vast and portentous along the horizon in the morning. For example, within a single month, last spring, occurred the deaths of three active, enterprising and independent American producing managers — Messrs. F. R. Hamlin, Kirke La Shelle, and Samuel S. Shubert. Almost simultaneously was announced the coalition of Messrs. David Belasco, Harrison Grey Fiske, and the surviving Shubert brothers, forming what is practically a second "syndicate," in competition with the original and heretofore monopolistic Theatrical Trust, organized some ten years ago by Messrs. Charles Frohman and Al. Hayman, Klaw and Erlanger, and Nixon and Zimmerman of Philadelphia.

Again, as an odd instance of reversals, during the past year a number of the so-called vaudeville theatres in New York and elsewhere have taken on and maintained permanent stock companies of capable players, offering such legitimate pieces as "London Assurance," "The Henrietta," "Forget-Me-Not," and the like; while no less serious a managerial potentate than Mr. Charles Frohman himself presented at one of his Broadway establishments a frothy melange called "The Rollicking Girl," consisting wholly of disconnected specialties, show-girl exhibits, and interpolated songs from a dozen different sources — in short, a "variety" entertainment pure and simple, good enough in its kind, but differing in little else than name from that so prosperously run all the year round by the unassuming Mr. Hammerstein. On the other hand, in the line of straight comic opera of the Gilbert-and-Sullivan grade, we find Col. Henry W. Savage placing contracts, half-a-dozen at a time, with reputable American librettists and musicians, for new works whose pretensions and merits, it is to be hoped, may justify stage production as elaborate and artistic as that which is habitually lavished upon those imported second-hand from Europe.

New York has to-day in operation not only more, but finer playhouses — speaking with regard to architectural elegance, capacity, comfort, and general mechanical equipment — than any other city in the world.   When all these houses shall be occupied by real actors and managers, and command an adequate supply of plays from native authors, then this will be the artistic, as it is already the commercial, centre of the theatrical world.   We see the car of Thespis rushing down the ringing grooves of change.   Westward the star of dramatic empire is rapidly and surely taking its way.   Here in America's metropolis we are witnessing the dawn-twilight of the New World's Theatre.

As has been remarked, the successes of one season's end dovetail in closely with the beginnings of the next season.   Let us, therefore, as preparatory to the outlook for 1906, first cast a brief glance backward over the more notable things which have transpired since January, when the last preceding series of these notes in THE FORUM was published.

In the fifty-odd theatres of New York, during the nine months from September to May, inclusive, an aggregate of over two hundred "events" is recorded.   Of these, twenty-five per cent were comic operas or music-farces, for the most part entirely devoid of dramatic value.   The number of new and original plays proper, including those manufactured from popular novels, did not exceed eighty.   The majority of these were disappointments to the public, and disasters to the managers.   Only a few rose above the level of crass mediocrity.   To not more than half-a-dozen can be ascribed unqualified success, and even this pitiful list might be conscientiously queried or altered, according to the viewpoints of different compilers.   However, it is safe enough to accord first-class honors to the following six plays — all written, as it chances, by native authors, and all interpreted by American players: "Leah Kleschna," by C. M. S. McLellan, with Minnie Maddern Fiske in the title rôle; "Adrea," by David Belasco and John Luther Long, with Mrs. Leslie Carter; "The Music Master," by Charles Klein, with David Warfield; "Mrs. Leffingwell's Boots," by Augustus Thomas; "The College Widow," by George Ade; and "Mrs. Wiggs of the Cabbage-Patch," by Alice Hegan Rice and Anne Crawford Flexner.   These pieces, now familiar to the playgoing public, are first among the "hold-overs," reopening their respective theatres here or employing their players in other cities at the commencement of the present season.

Possibly a dozen more plays, either quite new and original or at least novelties in this capital, enjoyed a moderate degree of prosperity, and may survive for another year or two.   Conspicuous in this category is Clyde Fitch's yellow-journalistic melodrama of modern city life, "The Woman in the Case " — a work not without a certain crude virility, which Miss Blanche Walsh is able at points to raise to real dramatic force.   "The Education of Mr. Pipp," deftly constructed by Augustus Thomas upon the well-known series of social cartoons by Charles Dana Gibson, was more happy in the superficial stage incarnation of these types than in their combination, for theatrical purposes, with some quite impossible representatives of British and French titled nobility. "Strongheart," by William C. DeMille, has an original hero in a college-football Indian — capitally impersonated by Robert Edeson — but who unfortunately fails to live up to his name when it comes to the crucial climax of a love affair.   "The Prince Consort," a French comedy of court life and etiquette, Englished by W. Boosey and Cosmo Gordon Lennox, was in itself an odd sort of hybrid, yet served very excellently as a vehicle for the introduction of Miss Ellis Jeffreys, one of the most refined and accomplished of English comediennes.   Mr. Lennox also adapted from the French "The Freedom of Suzanne," a rather audacious farce in which his wife, Marie Tempest, found scope for her unfailing vivacity and animal spirits in the part of a wilful, spoiled young married woman.

"Mrs. Temple's Telegram," a home-made farce comedy which was offered without much ostentation at the Madison Square Theatre, proved mildly entertaining and a good deal more decent than the Palais-Royal importations which in other years have held forth there.   A spurious antique, entitled "The School for Husbands," imitated by Stanislaus Stange from the eighteenth-century English comedies, gave Alice Fischer opportunity to win some well-earned plaudits by her spirited portrayal of a slighted wife in the old familiar pursuit of making her errant spouse jealous.   Francis Wilson, having won fame and fortune as a comic-opera star, made a new departure, to the extent of appearing in a "straight" and songless version of "Le Voyage de M. Perrichon," called "Cousin Billy," prepared by the versatile Mr. Fitch.

Three débuts, or first successful hearings, of American playwrights were those of Paul Armstrong, with "The Heir to the Hoorah," a Bret-Harte-like play of Western life; Kellett Chalmers, with a bit of senti-mentalized Bohemia, "Abigail," and an ephemeral skit on "Frenzied Finance "; and Julie Herne, one of the talented actress-daughters of the late James A. Herne, with an oddly interesting piece of reflected Ibsenism, entitled "Richter's Wife." Three elaborate and picturesque failures, which may or may not have deserved a better fate, were: a version of Elinor Macartney Lane's sensational Bobby Burns novel, "Nancy Stair," with Mary Mannering as the heroine; a revamped "Jane Shore," with Virginia Harned as the harrowing courtesan of English history; and Israel Zangwill's provincial idyl of "Jinny, the Carrier," fitted to the pleasingly quaint and elusive personality of Annie Russell.

Mr. Zangwill, who has a saving sense of humor — and, in "Merely Mary Ann," at least one substantial success to his credit — paid his second visit to America during the past season. Since his recent return to England, he has given good-natured expression to certain disillusionments; and some of his remarks have a general bearing. "You cannot," says he, "get actors to combine for art's sake. The tendency of each is to shoot off in his own way." And he continues with the sad reflection that most people nowadays regard the drama as a money-making, and not as an artistic, medium. "Scarcely one will believe that you write a play for the love of it, for artistic expression, and realization in a form that you have chosen because it appealed to you."

"Has your husband given up literature?" they kept asking Mrs. Zangwill, when they learned that he was busy with his plays.

The most important dramatic doings of the past season consisted not so much in the production of new plays as in the revival of old and classic ones, and the experimental presentation of poetic or literary works by authors hitherto rarely or never seen on the stage. Shakespeare was played in New York and other principal cities by such distinguished artists as E. H. Sothern and Julia Marlowe, Ada Rehan, Forbes Robertson, Richard Mansfield, Viola Allen, and Robert Mantell. Mr. Mansfield, in addition to his customary repertoire, played a new version, in English prose, of Molière's famous comedy, "The Misanthrope." His individual success, in the central rôle of Alceste, was indisputable. Miss Wormley's translation of this masterpiece of French comedy, however, was less fortunate, being stilted and literary rather than dramatically terse and epigrammatic, and dropping incongruously into rhymed couplets at the ends of acts only.

Performances of Ibsen's dramas were more numerous, and of wider range, than ever before. Mrs. Fiske played "Hedda Gabler" brilliantly, and Nance O'Neil tried at it, but missed. Ethel Barrymore found sympathetic employment for her growing talents, as Nora Helmer, in "A Doll's House." Maurice Campbell presented "When We Dead Awaken," and the Progressive Stage Society gave us a brief glimpse of "An Enemy of the People." "The Master-Builder," also, was seen at a special matinée. Lastly, though not least in significance, "A Doll's House" occupied the boards for a whole week at one of the popular vaudeville houses on Broadway!

George Bernard Shaw was pushed into further prominence, on this side of the Atlantic, during the past season, by his indefatigable fellow-countryman, Arnold Daly. Not only was a run of over a hundred performances achieved for "You Never Can Tell," but the avalanche was precipitated which this year may bring down upon us the whole Shaw repertoire, including the unmentionable "Mrs. Warren's Profession," "Man and Superman," "John Bull's Other Island," and the rest of the plays pleasant and unpleasant. Even "Cashel Byron" has been dramatized as a vehicle for Mr. Corbett, the ex-champion pugilist. This surfeit of Shaw is undoubtedly in response to some sort of public demand, curiosity or fad, which, being satisfied *ad nauseam*, will probably result in the relegation of the entire mass to the innocuous desuetude where already repose "Arms and the Man" and "The Devil's Disciple."

Mrs. Fiske's presentation of three poignant one-act plays — "A Light from St. Agnes," "The Rose," and "The Eyes of the Heart" — from her own pen, and played with rare distinction by the stock company under her direction at the Manhattan Theatre, helped to bring into vogue again this too much neglected species of composition. Frank Keenan, an American actor of forceful individuality and already marked achievement (in "The Hon. John Griggsby") had already set a convincing example in the same direction, by inaugurating a brief season of playlets or condensed dramas at the Berkeley Lyceum — after the manner of the Théâtre Antoine and the Grand Guignol of Paris. Margaret Wycherly, a young actress with exceptional gifts of temperament and personality, ventured a somewhat similar experiment with the symbolistic masques and moralities of Mr. Yeats, the Irish poet. Neither Miss Wycherly, Mrs. Fiske, nor Mr. Keenan found any reason to regret the valiant attempts they made, putting art first, and profit only as a secondary consideration. The concurrence of three such aspiring ventures would alone suffice to make a season noteworthy; and, whatever the eventual outcome may be, the essay illustrates the eager spirit of innovation in the air.

The costly but spiritless revivals of "She Stoops to Conquer" and "London Assurance" made no decisive popular appeal; while the galvanization of "Trilby," with the original cast, revealed the curious fact that Du Maurier has become deader in ten years than Dion Boucicault in fifty, or Goldsmith in more than a century.

New York's German stock company, in Irving Place, under the energetic direction of Mr. Conried, has kept well abreast of the leading theatres of continental Europe, and given first American production to many world-famous pieces — such as, for recent examples, Maeterlinck's "Monna Vanna" and Maxim Gorky's "Night Refuge." The last-named, a powerful and fearfully realistic work, had also two or three representations by a company of Russian players, during the past winter. In the Bowery, and the lower East Side district of this cosmopolitan city, Manhattan, a Yiddish or Hebraic population of more than a quarter of a million maintains several flourishing theatrical companies, who put on plays of the most ambitious order, and who have given to the English-speaking stage at least two artists of recognized genius — Jacob Adler and Bertha Kalich.

Mme. Kalich's appearance in Sardou's "Fedora," at the American Theatre last May, was something of a revelation. She then played in English for the first time, and it was her début before those greater audiences which her talent and acquirements so well qualify her to reach. This success opened a new and broader field for her ambition. Her name is now added to the list of legitimate American stars, and she is to be seen in such notable modern pieces as "Monna Vanna," "Magda," and Ibsen's "Rosmersholm."

On such a basis of preparation and material, then, the theatrical season of 1905–6 opens with great expectations, and some measure of immediate fulfilment. When the October-December number of THE FORUM shall be before its readers, all the half-hundred theatres of Greater New York, with the exception of the Metropolitan Opera, will have thrown open their doors, the majority of them upon new and ambitious productions, some of which will already have received their verdict of "success" or "failure" ere this commentary appears in print.

Let it be remarked here, *en passant*, that dramatic criticism in America, while not yet raised to the dignity of an academic department of literature as in France, shows nevertheless an elevation and amelioration quite commensurate with that of theatrical art itself. Its main drawback has been, and is still, the haste, superficiality, and "snap" judgment necessitated by the requirements of the morning newspaper — forty minutes in the midnight rush for the analysis of perhaps an epoch-making play, and an appreciation of the best efforts of an actor, which may be the culmination of a lifetime of study. Moreover, the dramatic critic's desk is a favorite and traditional berth for the callow college graduate newly embarked on his journalistic career — the studious youth from up-State who has a wide class-room acquaintance with Elizabethan dramatic literature, but had seldom or never before visited a modern theatre on Broadway. These men may be our Hazlitts and Sarceys of the future — only that seas of sophomoric essay-writing have to be waded through before that wished-for consummation can be reached. However, the spirit of criticism to-day is more frank and liberal than it was yesterday. It is gaining in breadth, in honesty, in impersonality. As the dean of the guild has admirably said:

"The most important part of the critic's function is the perception and proclamation of excellence. . . . He accomplishes all that should be expected of him when he arouses, pleases, and benefits the reader, clarifying his views, and helping him to look with a sympathetic and serene vision upon the pleasures and pains, the joys and sorrows, the ennobling splendors and the solemn admonitions of the realm of art."

A prospectus of the season's novelties may be more conveniently grouped about the names of players and playwrights most conspicuously in the public eye at the present moment, than fixed upon the individual theatres, their managers, and dates of opening.

Among the first of the offerings, chronologically as well as in importance and interest, are the new comedies of George Ade. These include: "The Bad Samaritan," with a quaint character rôle for Richard Golden; and "Just Out of College," another gentle satire on the "jay" educational institutions which Mr. Rockefeller delights to endow. In both these instances Mr. Ade has adhered to his recent and wisely chosen course of writing only straight character-comedy, of familiar every-day life. Edward E. Kidder has provided a somewhat similar piece, though with two or three songs interspersed, for that droll and original comedian, Raymond Hitchcock, under the title of "Easy Dawson." William T. Hodge, who was the delectable Mr. Stubbins in "Mrs. Wiggs of the Cabbage Patch," last season, has made himself a characteristic play out of one of his own stories, called "Eighteen Miles from Home." Annie Russell plays "The Little Gray Lady," by Channing Pollock. Ezra Kendall enacts "The Barnstormer." This first-hand quarrying from the wealth of untouched material lying about us in all sections of the country is work whose significance can hardly be over-estimated in laying the foundations of a real National Theatre.

Clyde Fitch's latest comedy of manners, "Her Great Match," on the attractive theme of an American girl's matrimonial alliance with European titled nobility, was written, like "Her Own Way," for Miss **Maxine** Elliott, and makes the reopening of the Criterion Theatre, this year, a brilliant semi-social function. Also from the busy and versatile pen of Mr. Fitch are promised: "The Comedy Mask," a George IV costume play for Viola Allen; "His Grace de Grammont," rewritten for that sterling legitimate-romantic actor, Otis Skinner; "The Toast of the Town," an opera-libretto to be set to music by Puccini, for Emma Eames; and a modern play, as yet unnamed, for Eleanor Robson.

Augustus Thomas is to be congratulated upon his achievement in fitting John Drew, our most finished society actor, with a new and congenial rôle in the Empire Theatre's initial presentation, "De Lancey," a three-act comedy of American life. For Lawrence d'Orsay, the ineffable "Earl of Pawtucket," Mr. Thomas has devised another exuberant and gentlemanly Englishman, to be the central figure in a polite farcical affair entitled " The Embassy Ball," the scenes of which are laid in the high diplomatic circles of Washington, D. C. The light, crisp, and sparkling touch which this author has mastered, as exemplified particularly in "Mrs. Leffingwell's Boots," gives an especial piquancy to his successive announcements.

Maude Adams, the Empire's other bright particular star, and whose personal following is probably more numerous and devoted than that of any other American actress, will assuredly enjoy new conquests as "Peter Pan, the Boy Who Wouldn't Grow Up " — a dramatization, by J. M. Barrie, of his own fantastic juvenile story, "The Great White Bird." This is in no way like Miss Adams's other well-remembered boy-part, "L'Aiglon," nor does it bear the remotest resemblance to Lady Babbie in "The Little Minister "; yet it gives opportunity for the unusual character denotement of the one, the arch and exquisite tenderness of the other; and besides, as a production, it develops a vast deal of picturesqueness in the scenic and spectacular line. Another Barrie play is "Alice-Sit-by-the-Fire " — the playwrights are hard put to it for titles nowadays! — which will occupy the attention of the intelligent, vivacious, and altogether interesting Ethel Barrymore.

James K. Hackett and his wife, Mary Mannering, have one of the few unequivocal successes of the past London season, in "The Walls of Jericho," a modern society drama by Alfred Sutro. This author, who has emerged into sudden vogue abroad, also wrote "Mollentrave on Women " and "The Way of a Fool," both of which Charles Frohman intends to present here later on. "A Maker of Men," an unimportant one-act trifle of Mr. Sutro's, has served as a curtain-raiser at the Lyceum.

Finally, the newest forthcoming Sutro play will be the vehicle of Miss Ellis Jeffreys's New York reappearance in January.

Minnie Maddern Fiske, who has surrounded herself at the Manhattan Theatre with the finest stock company in New York, will appear in a comedy of contemporaneous metropolitan life, written by Rupert Hughes, entitled "What Will People Say?" In addition to this, Mrs. Fiske may carry out her long-contemplated plan of playing Rebecca in "Rosmersholm" — unfamiliar on the stage, because it is one of the most intensely emotional and poetic, as well as the most disheartening, sinister, and questionable of all Ibsen's dramas. This project will not be realized, if at all, until late in the season. Meanwhile, the theatre opens with Edith Ellis Baker's homely play of "Mary and John," followed (according to schedule as arranged at present writing) by Bertha Kalich's "Monna Vanna." This latter phenomenal Maeterlinck piece is typical of the genius of decadence. It marks the extreme limit, up to date, of the cold-blooded, deliberate, unmoral effrontery of the twentieth-century sophist. At the same time, it has a last act that is theatrically stupendous. This, undoubtedly, is what attracts Mme. Kalich to the part, as it has attracted other great actresses before her. And can we blame them? Their art, as they understand it, has little or no concern with ethics and morality. Theirs is the genius of expression, not of philosophy or reason — which is the affair of the author and of the audience.

David Belasco's plans for the growing list of star players under his direction are usually kept secret until the eleventh hour, then sprung with an effect bordering upon the sensational. All that is positively known at this writing is that he has a play of "the Golden West," with the potentialities of another "Leah Kleschna," for Blanche Bates and a distinguished supporting company of actors, including Frank Keenan and Robert Hilliard. There is a vague though plausible rumor that Mrs. Leslie Carter may be seen as Domini Enfilden, the heroine of Robert Hichens's fascinating novel of the Sahara Desert, "The Garden of Allah." A foreshadowed event which links Mr. Belasco's name for the first time with a lyrical production is the New York hearing of Puccini's new opera, "Madame Butterfly," based upon the Japanese playlet of that title, by Messrs. Belasco and John Luther Long.

Charles M. S. McLellan, the American dramatist who has leaped into international celebrity as the author of "Leah Kleschna," is prepared to follow up this success with at least two fresh offerings — one a serious work, described as a modern morality play, entitled "The Jury of Fate"; the other, "On the Love Path," in the comedy vein. Mr. McLellan has also written an opera, called "The Butterfly of Fashion." William Gillette has framed himself a new part, in "Clarice." Henry Blossom, who wrote "Checkers" and "The Yankee Consul," now comes forward with "A Fair Exchange," equally smacking of the soil. Henry Miller and Margaret Anglin start with an original production, "Zira." George Broadhurst and Charles T. Dazey are to stand sponsors, this season, for the veteran character comedian, William H. Crane, in his venture as "An American Lord." Ella Wheeler Wilcox, in collaboration with an exotic playwright, has completed a four-act poetical drama called "Mizpah," which is underlined for early presentation. William Faversham, in "The Squaw Man," has something positively aboriginal. Richard Harding Davis's latest work, in a congenial line, is "The War Correspondent " — to be first done by William Collier in London. Eugene Presbrey is the author of "Mary, Mary, Quite Contrary," the forthcoming comedy which will engage the blithe talents of Henrietta Crosman, latterly identified with "Sweet Kitty Bellairs."

The above specified works of American authorship include only the more important early announcements, and by no means represent all the present activity of our native playwrights, and the opportunities opening for them. They are also busying themselves to an unprecedented extent with musical pieces and melodrama.

The English and French writers, at the same time, are getting more and more of their work before the American public, since the development of Charles Frohman's plan whereby whole companies and outfits can be interchanged between New York, London, and Paris. Mr. Pinero's latest play, for example, is likely to have its original *première* on this side of the Atlantic. Henry Arthur Jones's new play for Virginia Harned will have its first representation on any stage at the Hudson Theatre, New York City. "The Duel," which Louis N. Parker has adapted for the English-speaking stage, comes direct from the Comédie Française. "La Belle Marseillaise," a recent sensation of Paris, and "La Petite Bohême," a Mürgeresque musical piece, also figure among the latest importations.

Kyrle Bellew, whose polished art can give distinction even to a "Raffles," is expected to impersonate another of E. W. Hornung's conceptions — this time a sort of Australian Claude Duval, who is the leading character in the English author's drama, "Stingaree." Nathaniel C. Goodwin is a low comedian once more, in one of W. W. Jacobs's happy idyls of the Thames, called "The Beauty and the Barge."

Of dramatized novels, in addition to those already named, a score or so are impending, some of which are awaited with keen interest and favorable anticipation.   Mrs. Humphry Ward's "Marriage of William Asche" and Hall Caine's "Prodigal Son" come near the head of the list, which also includes: Lorimer's "Letters of a Self-Made Merchant to His Son," the late Gen. Lew Wallace's "Prince of India," Egerton Castle's "Secret Orchard," Winston Churchill's "The Crossing," Thomas Dixon's "Clansman," Edward Peple's "Prince Chap," Marion Crawford's "Zoroaster," Jesse Lynch Williams's "Stolen Story,' Cyrus T. Brady's "Corner in Coffee," Sir Gilbert Parker's "Pierre and His People," Mrs. E. T. Thurston's "The Masquerader," Harold McGrath's "The Man on the Box," Miriam Michelson's "The Bishop's Carriage"; also "The Redemption of David Corson," "The Dragon Fly," and Alfred Henry Lewis's "Wolfville Stories."   To this list should be added new stage versions of Victor Hugo's "Les Misérables" and Dickens's "Oliver Twist," in each of which the principal rôle will be assumed by Wilton Lackaye.   Generally speaking, the "scissors and paste-pot drama" has long since fallen into deserved disrepute, as a result either of the inherent undramatic nature of most of the stories thus experimented upon, or else because as a rule in such cases genuine technical dramatization is not accomplished.   Wherever there is real character there is legitimate material for the stage. Many of the world's most effective acting dramas, from Shakespeare's "Merchant of Venice" and "As You Like It" down to "Uncle Tom's Cabin," have been in their original form popular novels, not to say, in all likelihood, "best sellers."

Chief among the legitimate and classic revivals looked forward to are those of the Sothern-Marlowe combination.   These splendidly equipped artists will add to their "Hamlet," "Romeo and Juliet," and "Much Ado About Nothing," of last season, three more of the favorite plays in the Shakespearian repertoire — namely, "Twelfth Night," "The Merchant of Venice," and "The Taming of the Shrew."   Richard Mansfield, besides reappearing in his old familiar round of parts, threatens to do Schiller's much-bepraised but turgid and antiquated drama of "Don Carlos."   There is a possibility, too, that Helena Modjeska may give a few farewell performances of "Macbeth" and "Mary Stuart."

Sarah Bernhardt is the most eminent of the few foreign stars who will visit us this season.   The great French tragedienne has perhaps no new creation of first magnitude to show us, beyond what she revealed five years ago — unless we accept Sardou's "Sorcière" at its face value. But to the famous rôles in which Mme. Bernhardt has won her triumphs of the past, at least two notable additions will be made.   She will give

Victor Hugo's "Angelo" for the first time in New York, and will appear in her own version of "Adrienne Lecouvreur," which aroused lively interest in London last spring.

Sir Charles Wyndham will be with us again, and probably with one or two additions to his repertoire of last season, the principal feature in which was Robertson's "David Garrick." In any case, the visit of this actor will be an important event of the dramatic year. Wyndham's popularity in America is second only to that of Irving — whose proposed farewell tour does not appear to be an immediate certainty. The early years of Sir Charles's stage apprenticeship were passed in the United States, and this will be his third visit since arriving at artistic maturity and his present proud position at the head of England's light comedians and actor-managers. His precept and example are at once conservative and progressive. He says frankly:

"The commercialism of the drama, with its irrational star system, has wrought great damage in the American theatre. In England we still have the stock company as well as the actor-manager, as an established and permanent institution. The British press and public hesitate to accept a new 'star' until his or her ability has been proven by merited successes in some recognized company. All the European countries, France and Germany in particular, are loyal to the idea that dramatic art can be fostered only through organizations of players trained together under a continuous managerial direction, with conservatory methods and on a basis of accumulated, vital tradition."

Yet it is a stubborn fact, and eloquent of the changeful tendency of our time, that Sir Charles Wyndham himself, cherishing these fine old ideals as he does, finds it expedient nevertheless to return again as a star under this same commercial system of management which prevails in America to a greater extent than abroad, chiefly because here is the more vast, the richer and freer field.

Forbes Robertson is another welcome visitor who comes more or less under the classification just outlined. Olga Nethersole, a tropically endowed emotional actress who has found in the Saphos and Carmens of modern dramatic fiction congenial exercise for her tempestuous powers, will make a *risqué*, though interesting, contribution in presenting Hervieu's typical French divorce drama, "Le Dédale." The optimistic E. S. Willard, also, will try his fortune once again in New York.

Twenty-five per cent, at the very least, of our theatrical enterprise and resources go to the production of musical burlesque and comic opera. In fact, nearly half of our theatres at the present moment are given over to entertainments which either fall under one of these two categories, or else are vaudeville shows pure and simple. "The Pearl and the Pump-

kin," "Babes in the Wood," "Beauty and the Beast," "The White Cat,"
"The Catch of the Season," "Moonshine," "The Maid and the Million-
aire," "The Earl and the Girl," "The Ham Tree," "Miss Dolly Dollars,"
"Mlle. Modiste," "Happyland," "It Happened in Nordland," "Higgledy-
Piggledy," and the Rogers Brothers, head the interminable list, as the
season buoyantly starts.   This means augmented demand for the work of
American musical composers, in response to which we see light and bright
lyrical talents springing up on all sides.   Especially has a helpful impetus been given to the budding genius of the Afro-American school.
Messrs. Williams and Walker, Cole and Johnson, Will Marion Cook,
and Ernest Hogan — to name only a few conspicuous individual examples — have successfully conquered for the genuine negro minstrel, with
his jovial "coon songs " and wistful, dreamy melodies of sentiment, his
legitimate place on the American stage, so long usurped by the clownish
white impersonator with blackened-up face.

Why do burlesque, music-farce, and vaudeville bulk so large in our
theatre?   Because they are sure attractions for the multitude, easily
adaptable to the passing fancies of the moment, and involving no responsibility to art or ethics on the part of the producing managers.   The
producing managers, especially those who indulge in the luxury of high
artistic ideals, frequently "need the money."   To cover their risks on
the classic and legitimate drama, they are compelled to compromise with
the illegitimate.   It is a well-known fact that the late Augustin Daly
paid for his brief revivals of Shakespeare, Sheridan, Farquhar and Van-
brugh with six-months' runs of "The Runaway Girl," and other "Girls " of
that ilk.   Messrs. Klaw and Erlanger emptied their lovely New Amsterdam Theatre with "A Midsummer Night's Dream," but filled it again
by lavish exploitations of "Mother Goose " and "Humpty Dumpty."   The
Shuberts lost money on Edward Terry's engagement, and on other laudable high-class ventures, but fairly minted it with an unbroken year of
" Fantana."   Charles Frohman recoups himself for losses, on nobody
knows how many splendid failures, by presenting "The Rollicking Girl "
and Edna May.   Thus is the balance kept even, and all is to the good
in the long run, as the building of new theatres goes on, and public interest in them is kept increasingly alive.

In England, as in France, the lines are more sharply drawn.   Each
first-class house is identified with a certain line of productions — farce,
melodrama, emotional comedy, pantomime spectacle or comic opera —
and does not vary.   We cannot, for example, imagine George Edwardes
"plunging" on a poetic drama by Stephen Phillips, or Beerbohm Tree

or George Alexander building up a Gaiety production around a Floro-dora sextet.   These latter gentlemen, like Irving, Wyndham, Bourchier, Hare and the rest, are actor-managers — a type in our country unfor-tunately quite extinct.

All the American actors who might and ought to be actor-managers in New York or elsewhere are erratic wandering stars, and rarely have the authority even to select the plays in which they appear.   The man-ager-magnate, who has been chiefly instrumental in making them what they are, declares that there are practical reasons why.   He says:

> There are no actor-managers in New York simply because no one actor can play there for more than four months in any one year.   We must remember that in Amer-ica it is not "London first, and the rest nowhere."   There are a dozen New Yorks throughout the Union.   Even New York is not big enough alone to support several "seasons" in the year by one actor-manager.   And there are great cities with beau-tiful theatres in the various States, awaiting the popular stars, and eager to pour money into their treasuries.   These centres would not submit to being put off with the touring substitutes, as is the case in England.

This is true enough, so far as it goes.   But while undoubtedly there are few if any individual players sufficiently well equipped to be able to profitably put in the whole theatrical year as metropolitan fixed stars, they might readily do so as heads of producing stock companies.   That is the way the great actors and actresses of the European capitals man-age themselves.   It was Lester Wallack's method in New York a gen-eration ago.   Mrs. Fiske has done what practically amounts to the same thing for two or three years past, at the Manhattan Theatre, personally directing her company in the presentation of a number of plays in which she herself did not appear.   Her triumph of last season, "Leah Kleschna," is emphatically a non-star piece, in which at least four other players share the full equivalent of stellar honors with the great and liberal artiste who has created the title rôle.

Scarcely second to the actor-manager, as an informing power in the theatre, is the author-manager — who is almost always incidentally a consummate stage-manager as well.   In this class David Belasco stands prominent and alone.   He is, first of all, a diviner and creator; and then, what he has divined and given substance and form, he realizes in working perfection on the stage of his theatre.   This is a rare combina-tion indeed, and it is still rarer to find so many essential attributes of the ideal theatrical director absorbed in the destinies of one sole house.   However, of late Mr. Belasco has expanded his enterprise and activities, assumed additional artistic as well as business responsibilities, and formed alliances both defensive and offensive which make him at once a prime factor in the contemporaneous affairs of the American stage. At present Mr. Belasco is in absolute managerial control of at least half-a-dozen of our most important native actors and actresses — Mrs. Leslie Carter, Blanche Bates, David Warfield, Bertha Galland, Brandon Tynan, and Robert Hilliard.   He is allied with Harrison Grey Fiske, manager of Minnie Maddern Fiske and Bertha Kalich; and with the firm of Shubert Brothers, who have many theatres in cities and towns which are strategical points on the war-map of the booking agencies.   In other words, a new theatrical syndicate comes into the field, headed by Messrs. Belasco, Fiske, and the Shuberts — a coalition formidable enough to oppose and compete with, on something like equal terms, the original Trust, of which Messrs. Frohman, Klaw and Erlanger are the head and front.

On the assumption that the average layman and the theatre-going public in general take but a remote interest in such shop-talk, no reference to the Syndicate as such has been made in these notes; and the various plays and players have been passed in review without discrimination or regard to partisan lines and affiliations.   Yet this matter of theatrical dictatorship and monopoly control is really one in which every thoughtful person is more or less directly concerned.   Moreover, it has been and is the subject of so much discussion in the press, since the differences of certain managerial factions have been exposed in court, that in no consideration of the general dramatic outlook can the "syndicate" question be wholly ignored.

Broadly speaking, that close corporation of half-a-dozen influential and wholly mercenary managers known as the Theatrical Trust, has in the past two years suffered disastrous reverses, not only financially, but in loss of professional prestige and of the public confidence and respect. Its operations have made it the target of much severe legitimate criticism, as well as of some intemperate abuse, from one end of the country to the other.   Starting in New York ten years ago at the routine end of the business, as a shrewdly organized booking agency for the touring companies and the hundreds of theatres in principal cities throughout the States that depend upon this centre for their "attractions," the Trust has gradually turned the American stage into one monstrous machine, and now controls the situation with an absolute despotism.

Obviously, the answer to this condition of affairs is — revolution. Where one syndicate is undoubtedly an evil, two or more syndicates may constitute the remedy.   The monopoly once broken, healthy competition and higher enterprise must speedily ensue.   In such competition it will be edifying to observe the contrasted methods of the different managerial leaders, as typified, let us say, by Charles Frohman and David Belasco.

Mr. Frohman is still a dominant figure in the theatrical world. As such, he may be justly characterized as "more Syndicate than sinning." A blunt, unimaginative, impassive, saturnine nature is his, yet big, generous, and quick to respond to any real or supposed demand which appeals to him as a good business proposition. He says with truth and candor that he has no idea of educating the public, but only strives to "give it what it wants." Unfortunately, being neither an actor, an author, nor a student of dramatic literature, and having no partner who can be included in any one of these three classes, he is obliged to judge of what the public wants solely by whether or not enough people can be induced to patronize this or that combination in his various theatres to make them profitable. In this restricted view of the managerial function, Mr. Frohman and his associates must be credited with unexampled enterprise and success, along the by no means despicable commercial line of dealings with the drama.

David Belasco, as we have seen, is a creator and builder of the stage. He writes plays, or has them written, in close accord with the temperaments and qualifications of the players whom he has schooled to interpret his ideas; and then, with the craftsmanship of which he is past master, he stages these creations with an ideal luxury and a perfection of detail which virtually eliminate the chance of failure. These considerations, it appears, overbalance everything else in Mr. Belasco's mind as a producing manager, including the matter of pecuniary returns — which, nevertheless, have been in his case uniformly large.

The great essential fact is, then, that our theatre of the present day, despite some real abuses and many venial faults incidental to a state of transition, rises upon a sound basis of material prosperity and popular esteem. Given the men adequate to the means already at hand, and we may see realized at its best in our own country and time a National Theatre — one of the most potent educational influences of society, the embodiment of all the arts, a power universal as humanity in its possibilities for good, or evil.

The American theatre at the beginning of the twentieth century has magnificent and incalculable prospects for the future, because as a world-wide institution it is the heir of all the ages, while as the expression of a youthful giant nationality it takes utterance precisely at the moment when we are beginning to "find ourselves" in the higher creative arts. Just as in statecraft and diplomacy the unprecedented initiative of the

United States brought about the peace conference of Portsmouth, when the Old-World powers were at a deadlock, so in the realm of the drama this youngest scion of Shakespeare's race and language is planting trees indigenous to the soil, and manifestly destined to mighty growth.

In plainer words, our American dramatists have effectively begun putting on the stage original native types of character, which should become permanent, because their appeal is broad and genuine; while those transplanted from alien lands wither and fade away as soon as their ephemeral vogue of curiosity is exhausted. At the present moment, in the theatres of New York City, we can point to at least four conspicuous examples bearing out this optimistic assertion. Maxine Elliott, in Clyde Fitch's comedy, "Her Great Match," portrays with vivid loveliness, yet sincere and simple charm, an American girl brought face to face with the problem of a European marriage. John Drew, in Augustus Thomas's "Delancey," *is*, rather than assumes, the part of the shrewd, kindly, chivalrous, "sporty," up-to-date Manhattanese gentleman-of-the-world at forty, or what is often erroneously called "middle-age." David Warfield, in Charles Klein's "Music Master," achieves a veritable *chef-d'œuvre* of tender characterization as the German artist in exile amidst the shabby bohemianism of this hurly-burly metropolis. Richard Golden, as Uncle Ike Gridley, the retired hide-and-tallow merchant, in "The Bad Samaritan," is only one of the scores of real folk whom George Ade has gathered into the theatre from the every-day life of the Middle West — real folk realistically treated, yet with just enough of humorous imagination to make them, as *dramatis personæ*, creations of art.   HENRY TYRRELL.

APPLIED SCIENCE.

ONE of the pressing problems which are confronting the engineer at the present time in various parts of the world, and which are growing daily more urgent, is the question of personal transport in great cities. In London, Paris, New York, and Berlin the demand continues for increased transport facilities, and while improvements are continually being made, the congestion increases at such a rate that the capacity of the new works is exceeded almost before they can be put into operation. In New York, as in Paris, the subject of rapid transit has been broadly considered by a special commission; and the works of which the present subway in one city and the *Métropolitain* in the other are the immediate results are but portions of much larger schemes, intended, when completed, to furnish comprehensive systems of conveyance over all parts of the respective cities.

The latest candidate for radical improvements in local traffic is the greatest city of all, London. Notwithstanding the existence of the old underground railway and the modern "tube," the congestion has increased to such an extent as to demand the formulation of a complete scheme, the execution of which may be conducted as rapidly as possible, and be available for service as the work proceeds.

For several years a Royal Commission has been at work studying the question, having in view the special local requirements, and taking into account the work which has been accomplished elsewhere. The report of this commission and the radical recommendations which it contains constitute an excellent indication of the extent to which the engineer is expected to come to the relief of the municipality. Thus, it is seriously proposed to open two new main avenues, one running north and south, connecting Holloway with the Elephant and Castle; the other east and west, extending from Whitechapel to Bayswater Road. These new streets are each to be 140 feet wide and about four and one-half miles long, and are to be provided with four lines of surface tramways and four lines of subway track, providing for both express and local service.

To cut two such avenues through the heart of the metropolis and to construct the railways will involve the expenditure of about £30,000,000 sterling, or say $150,000,000. While much of this money will be needed to meet the value of the property taken, a large portion will be expended in engineering work. Since the control of the transport systems is to remain vested in the municipality, it is reasonable to assume that the income derived from the operation of the surface and underground railways will be sufficient to pay the interest on the cost of the works; and if the results in New York may be taken as a guide, sufficient surplus should accumulate gradually to extinguish the original indebtedness.

In connection with the discussion of municipal transport problems, it is interesting to note that a few independent attempts are being made in New York to realize a plan of improvement which has been suggested more than once in years past. Thus, it is seen that private connections have been made from several large department stores to stations of the elevated railway. Crude and irregular as these bridges are, they show an appreciation of the advantages to the merchants of the provision of a second-deck entrance, so to speak, and confirm the merits of a plan which would provide similar advantages for the entire street. Briefly, then, the plan would be to construct sidewalks upon the second-story levels of important business streets, these structures to be not unlike the so-called "board walks" in vogue at the various seaside resorts, and available solely for foot passengers, all vehicular traffic being relegated to the street level below. Such structures would naturally be much lighter and cheaper than those required for elevated railway trains, and so far from being opposed by property-owners, they would be welcomed as affording double opportunities for entrances and business display. The heavy electric traction would then be transferred to the solid ground or to subways, while all heavy vehicles, delivery wagons, automobiles, etc., would have full sway below, the foot passengers walking in safety and comfort above. Such an arrangement would practically double the capacity of the streets both for traffic and for business; and the efforts now being made in New York by a few establishments to accomplish something of the sort on their own account may be taken as indications of the manner in which it would be received by the property-owners and business men along the streets so equipped.

The development of high-speed transport on railways is bringing out some very interesting problems for study and solution. I have referred more than once in these reviews to the experiments made in Germany upon the military railway between Marienfelde and Zossen. After it was demonstrated that speeds of 125 to 130 miles an hour could readily be made by properly constructed electric cars upon a suitable track, the apparatus and road were turned over to a special research committee to enable detailed studies to be made of the various portions of the problem. Some of the results of the work of this committee have been made public, and they form valuable contributions to the general subject of high-speed traction.

The action of the resistance opposed by the air to the motion of a high-speed train is one of the questions studied by the committee, and this resistance naturally becomes of vastly increasing importance as the speeds are increased. Thus the 100-ton experimental car is found to require about 150 horse-power to drive it at a speed of 50 miles an hour, no especial provision being made as to the shape of the front end to reduce the air resistance. When the speed is doubled, however, it takes six times the amount of power; while, if it is attempted to triple the speed and run the car at 150 miles an hour, it is necessary to use eighteen times as much power as to drive it at a speed of 50 miles.

Another important matter for experimental test was the question of signalling. It soon became evident that human vision could not be depended upon to perceive and interpret stationary signals when passing them at speeds above 100 miles an hour. Even in fair weather, objects closer than 50 feet could not be clearly distinguished from the train, while in dull or rainy days, or at night, the difficulty became even greater. It has, therefore, been decided to place the signals directly in the car, the operation being made by electric contact, the signal being immediately before the driver and perfectly distinct and clear at all speeds. Signals of this sort have also been given trial on some American steam railways, and there seems to be every reason to believe that they will be found wholly successful. The work of the committee is to be continued upon the Marienfelde-Zossen line, working with both steam and electric traction, and much valuable experimental information will doubtless be gained.

The part which is being played by applied science in the exploitation of the world can only be realized by a comparison of modern with older methods of development. An interesting example of the development of modern methods is found in the growth of telegraphic communication in Africa. The most important telegraph project in the once dark continent is the line extending from Cape Town through the entire length of the continent to Cairo and Alexandria, a distance of 11,000 kilometres, or 6,835 miles. This line has been under consideration for fifteen years, and naturally forms a portion of the so-called "Cape-to-Cairo" railway scheme. At the present time there have been constructed 1,400 kilometres (870 miles) north from the cape to Mafeking and 3,500 kilometres southward through Egypt to Fashoda, leaving about 6,000 kilometres (3,728 miles) to be built to connect the southern portion of the Egyptian Soudan with Salisbury, the capital of Rhodesia. Portions of this intermediate work have been already constructed, the stretch between Karonga and the northern end of Lake Nyassa being opened in 1898. The prolongation of the line northward involves construction either upon German territory or upon that of the Congo Free State, and already a line has been run from Ujiji to the northern end of Lake Tanganyika.

The construction of the through telegraph line is not wholly dependent upon the progress of the Cape-to-Cairo railway. There are long stretches of that route made up by connecting links of waterway upon the lakes and rivers, and hence no clearing is made for the telegraph route. Some portions of the route between Ujiji and Fashoda are at present impracticable for line construction, and wireless telegraph communication will have to be employed until the country is more fully opened up. There is little doubt, however, that the whole length of Africa will be traversed by telegraphic communication before many years, and with this and the railroad combined, the development of the natural resources of the continent will proceed at an accelerated rate.

During the past few months some interesting features have been brought out in connection with the application of the steam turbine to marine service. Turbines have been installed in a number of channel steamers, and some valuable comparative results have been secured. Thus, four vessels for the Midland Railway service in connection with the Belfast trade and for the Isle of Man summer passenger traffic have been fitted partly with steam turbines and partly with reciprocating engines. The results of the practical operation have shown that the turbine steamers are operated with a fuel economy of eight to nine per cent better than the reciprocating engines, while the entire elimination of vibration is an added point in favor of the steam turbines. I have already referred in these reviews to the plans which are being made to equip the new express steamers of the Cunard line with steam turbines. The German lines, however, do not yet appear to be convinced of the superiority of the turbine over the reciprocating engine; and the new liner to be built by the Vulkan Works at Stettin for the North German Lloyds is announced to be practically identical with the Kaiser Wilhelm II, with vertical reciprocating engines of about 40,000 horse-power, for a displacement of 26,500 tons and a length of 707 feet. The methods of balancing four-cylinder reciprocating engines by adjusting the crank angles according to the forces acting upon each, known as the Yarrow, Schlick, Tweedy system, has been found so successful in practice as to reduce the vibration to an almost imperceptible minimum. It will be interesting to compare the performances of the new British and German steamers, both as representatives of different types of motive power and as competitors in the contest for national supremacy at sea.

The transatlantic turbine steamers of the Montreal line, the Victorian and the Virginian, appear to have given satisfaction. They stand midway in dimensions between the boats of the English Channel and the Irish Sea and the giant liners of the Cunard and German Lloyd companies, being 540 feet long and of 10,630 tons displacement; and with turbines of 12,000 horse power they have made speeds of 19.5 knots, an excellent showing. Doubtless there is room for both the steam turbine and the reciprocating engine in marine service, and practical experience with both types will enable them to find their respective places.

Since the development of the large internal-combustion motor for stationary service has been attended with marked success, it is to be expected that attempts should be made to apply the same type of motors to marine propulsion. The success with which small motors of the automobile type have been applied to the propulsion of launches and small motor boats lends additional force to the idea of extending the scope of such machines to vessels of larger size. The high efficiency and consequent low fuel consumption of the internal-combustion motor renders it especially desirable for application to marine service, since everything which reduces the quantity of fuel to be carried or increases the steaming radius for a given amount of fuel is to be welcomed. The use of light hydrocarbon fuels, however, such as petrol, gasoline, and the like, is impracticable for large motors, and attempts have recently been made, with some success, to install gas producers of the suction type on shipboard, employing coal as fuel, and drawing the semi-water gas directly from the producer to the engine by the suction strokes of the machine itself. There are numerous details requiring attention in such a combination, but some very successful equipments have been made in Germany by Capitaine, and more recently upon the same principle in England by Thornycroft. In these boats the fuel is partly burned to carbon monoxide, while the admission of the vapor of water into the mass of incandescent fuel causes the dissociation of the oxygen and hydrogen, the latter enriching the gas. The producer thus takes the place of the boiler, while the engine uses the gas directly in the cylinder.

One of the difficulties about the use of internal-combustion motors for marine service lies in the fact that such engines are operated to advantage only when running continuously at normal speed in one direction. They are not easily reversed, nor are they readily controlled as to speed variation. The use of change gears or similar devices, as in automobiles, is impracticable with engines of larger power, and some other means is most desirable. One plan which has been devised for use with the Diesel motor is the so-called Del Proposto system. In this plan the engine is not connected positively to the screw propeller, but drives a dynamo which delivers the current to an electric motor, this latter being on the propeller shaft. The electric motor is regulated as to speed or direction of motion by a suitable controller, so that the Diesel motor may be kept running at full power in one direction while the propeller is run at any desired speed in either direction. The principal objection to the system is the fact that the loss by reason of the conversion of the mechanical into electrical energy and back again is considerable, reaching about fifteen per cent. This, however, is incurred only at the wharf, or at times when much manœuvring is necessary, since the motor can be directly connected to the propeller by throwing a clutch into gear, when the full efficiency of the motor is obtained on the wheel. By use of a storage battery, the electric motor may be held available for use at any moment, so that an extreme flexibility is secured, while the high efficiency of the Diesel motor and its ability to burn crude petroleum directly in the cylinder are fully retained.

I have referred in these pages to the recent developments in connection with the improvement of the incandescent electric lamp. These include the use of filaments of tantalum or of osmium instead of the carbonized cellulose which has been employed for many years; those metal filaments enabling lamps of much longer life and lower consumption of electrical energy to be made. The stimulus of this competition has resulted in the production of an improved carbon filament, this being produced by subjecting the ordinary carbon filament to the intense heat of the electric resistance furnace. At temperatures of between 3,000°

16

and 3,700° C., the filament becomes partially converted into graphite. The specific resistance is reduced and its specific gravity increased, the toughness and flexibility being also greater than before the treatment. There is every probability that carbon-filament incandescent lamps will be made by this process of much higher efficiency than the ordinary lamp, enabling an economy of more than twenty per cent in the consumption of electric energy to be attained.

Although the American Pacific cable has been in operation for some time, connecting with the Philippines by way of Hawaii and Guam, it is now evident that telegraphic communication with Asia by the northern route, following the coast line of Alaska, the Seward Peninsula, the Aleutian Islands, and Kamchatka, is approaching realization. The advantages of this route were forcibly advocated several years ago by Mr. Harrington Emerson; but the United States Government had already committed itself to the longer and much more expensive route, and the great circle line was rejected, notwithstanding the fact of its lower cost, shorter stretches, and valuable connections with Alaska and Japan. Commercial reasons have now compelled the plan to be developed, and already there are 2,300 miles of cable connecting the Pacific coast of the United States with Alaska, and forming an important instalment of the northern telegraph route to the Orient. The value of the line is apparent when it is seen that in this incomplete condition it is already active with business communications; and with the extension of the line to Dutch Harbor and the Aleutian Islands, and the construction by the Japanese of the short section required to unite their northernmost telegraph post with the system, there will be in operation the line which should have been chosen first. It is rather amusing to note that the very officials who were most pronounced in their opposition to the northern, great-circle cable route when it was first projected are now first in claiming the credit for the work. Apart from the commercial advantages of the route, it has the merit of giving connection to the valuable northern naval bases at Dutch Harbor and Kyska Island. The line also gives communication to the important Alaskan coal fields, an abundant source of supply for naval and merchant vessels on the Pacific; and following, as it does, the storm route of the Northern Pacific, it will enable a prompt and efficient weather service to be maintained. A line composed of short stretches has a great advantage over a long submarine cable as regards speed of operation and consequent cost of transmission of messages; and the business superiority of the northern route can readily be demonstrated in this respect when the two lines are in competitive operation.

Work on the Panama Canal has reached a stage of much importance, although the present condition of affairs is not one of display or of great apparent activity. At the isthmus the principal work is that of the important department of sanitation, water-supply, and general preparation of the field, to render it habitable in safety and comfort. The important work is now transferred to Washington, into the hands of the advisory board of engineers, and upon its decisions and opinions the plans for the great undertaking will finally be settled. The last really complete plan for a canal at Panama was that of the French *Comité Technique*, this being for a lock canal with a summit level of 20.75 metres, or about sixty-eight feet, with a dam and lake at Bohio, and a controlling dam for the upper Chagres at Alhajuela. Of late, however, there has arisen a feeling that the sea-level scheme should be adopted, while at the same time doubt has been thrown on the practicability of obtaining a satisfactory foundation for a dam at Bohio. It has also been suggested that the control of the Chagres River might be effected through the construction of tunnel spillways into both the Pacific Ocean and the Caribbean. A number of variant plans have been submitted to the Canal Commission, these coming from many sources and being of varying degrees of merit; and it is upon all these questions that the advisory board of engineers is to pass.

The constitution of the board is such as to warrant broad confidence in its judgments. Among its members are to be found engineers who have had wide experience in similar problems upon great canal works in all parts of the world. Thus the British representative, Mr. W. Henry Hunter, has been engineer of the Manchester Ship Canal, involving in its construction and operation an intimate knowledge of the advantages and disadvantages of locks for great sea-going vessels. M. Quellenec, the French representative, is consulting engineer for the Suez Canal, with experience in its enlargement, and was also chief engineer of the Corinth Ship Canal. The German delegate is Mr. Tincauzer, of the Kiel Canal; while from Holland comes Director Welcker, of the Waterstaad, the dike system of the Netherlands. Among other members of the board we may name Gen. Henry L. Abbot, one of the leading authorities on hydraulic engineering in the United States; Mr. Isham Randolph, chief engineer of the Chicago Main Drainage Commission; and Mr. Joseph Ripley, of the Sault Sainte Marie Canal.

While this board is only advisory, its opinions will doubtless be followed upon such broad questions as the choice of level, if a lock canal is to be built, together with the important matter of the section of canal prism, dimensions of locks, and all the provisions for the future demands in the light of the growing dimensions of cargo-carrying steamships. The merits of the sea-level plan will also come before the board, together with the problems for the control of the Chagres, in case of the adoption of this plan. These broad questions having been settled, the details of execution may well be left to the commission and its engineers; and it is to be hoped that they will then be given freedom to carry on the work as it would be done by any of the great railroad companies of the country, without the petty bureaucratic restrictions usually so evident in work under government control. An undertaking like the Panama Canal is no place for the "Tite Barnacles" of a circumlocution office, and the policy of "how not to do it" should not be added to natural obstructions which are in themselves sufficiently great.

There is a general tendency in applied engineering science at the present time to develop experimental methods of investigation, not for the determination of purely empirical data, but rather for the confirmation and extension of theoretical principles. In such combinations of theory and practice, the work of the investigator is at once made available for use in the workshop and manufactory, and soon accrues to the benefit of the entire world. An example of the value of experimental investigations is seen in the progress made in model experiments on the best lines for the hulls of ships. The use of small paraffine models, drawn along through a tank at various rates of speed, has long been found of much value in determining the relative merits of various forms of hulls. With experience in this mode of research, and with the confirmation of the mathematical laws of similarity, by which the relations between small models and the full-size vessels have been established, the importance of such experiments has increased. By employing larger models — those in the tank at Washington being twenty feet long — and by using electric traction and automatic recording devices, the performance of a hull and many questions relating to its powering may be determined before a stroke of the actual work of construction has been made.

The latest improvement in the study of models for ships is that used by Mr. Froude in the testing tank at Haslar, this being the addition of a wave-making device for imitating the conditions of a rough sea. A vibrating diaphragm at one end of the tank is so driven as to produce waves of a uniform and determinate character; and by drawing the model hull through these waves at various speeds, the behavior of vessels under actual conditions may be closely approached. Experiments already conducted in this manner have yielded valuable information in regard to the power required to propel ships in rough water, and the relation of displacement to speed is also being investigated under actual conditions.

Although the war between Russia and Japan has been happily terminated, the engineer has always to realize that it is only by constant improvement and continual development in the art of constructing fighting machinery that the rights and liberties of nations can be maintained. In the struggle which has just ended, it has been the one nation of Asia which has adopted modern military methods and equipment which has shown itself able to contend against a first-class European power. Had China, or even Corea, been as fully provided with modern weapons, ships, and scientific appliances, it is extremely doubtful if there would have been any war; and it is almost a certainty that one of the results of the war will be a rapid acquisition of modern fighting appliances by other Asiatic nations.

In the progress of scientific warfare there is to be expected a continual advance in the use of electricity, both for methods of defence and for communication. In the United States Army there exists a special school at Fort Totten, New York, this constituting practically a postgraduate school in which selected men from the Military Academy at West Point may be given a special training. At the present time, careful instruction is given in the electrical control and explosion of mines for harbor defence, as well as in the use of electric motors and appliances for the handling of artillery. Special attention is also given to the manipulation of field telephone systems; and the extent to which telephonic communication replaced individual messengers in the Japanese campaign in Manchuria is evidence of the growing importance of this department of applied electricity in warfare.

There is little doubt that the use of special forms of wireless telegraphic apparatus will become of increasing value in the warfare of the future. As an ordinary means of communication in naval operations, it has already demonstrated its value in the Japanese navy; but it will doubtless find still wider uses in the operation of distant motors, mines, lights, and other apparatus, either according to the method of Branly, to which I have already referred in these pages, or by some distinct advance on that system by which both the impelling and the controlling forces shall be transmitted across space by magnetic waves.

Much interest has been aroused of late in the influence which the application of modern engineering methods may have upon questions of finance and economy in connection with the rapid increase of the gold supply of the world.

Formerly the industry of gold-mining was rather supposed to be somewhat of the nature of a gambling venture, and the old saying was held to be true: "He who digs for iron will grow rich; he who digs for silver may grow rich; but he who digs for gold will never grow rich." At the present time, however, two applications of scientific methods are changing all this, and in consequence the industry of extracting gold from the earth is becoming much the same as any other manufacturing business. The two methods which are working this transformation are the application of the cyanide process to the working of gold-bearing quartz, and the introduction of the dredge for the exploitation of gold placers. Leaving aside the cyanide process for the present, it will be of interest to consider the action and possible influence of the gold dredge.

In working a gold placer by hand, only the richer portions of the deposit can be handled to advantage; the labor element forming too large a portion of the expense to permit of the extraction of the gold without loss. The result is the working of many known placers containing millions in gold which it has been hitherto unprofitable to work. By the use of the gold dredge the bulk of the work is performed mechanically, thus rendering it possible to exploit to advantage placers containing less than ten cents' worth of gold to the cubic yard of gravel, placers such as exist in abundance in many parts of the world, but from which it would hitherto have been as impossible to extract the gold as it now is to draw the metal from the water of the ocean.

The gold dredge is similar in construction to the so-called "ladder" dredge in common use for removing the mud from harbors and channels. Strong buckets, carried on an endless chain, driven by a powerful engine, scoop up the gold-bearing gravel and deliver it to the deck of the scow on which all the machinery is carried. The gravel is here passed through riffles and amalgamators, by which the gold is completely separated, and the barren gravel stacked up behind the machine by a mechanical conveyor. If the gold-bearing gravel is at the bottom of a river, the whole equipment floats upon the surface; otherwise the dredge is floated in a small pond of its own excavating, the water of this pond flowing into the space dug out by the dredge in front, while the discharged tailings fill up the space behind. No supply of running water is needed for the treatment of the gravel, since the water of the travelling pond is used over and over again. Such a dredge will travel steadily through the entire length of a placer, leaving in its trail nothing but barren and exhausted gravel, having extracted all the gold in its passage.

It has been estimated that the introduction of these machines will raise the present gold product of about one million dollars per day to double that amount inside of ten years, and with the vast extent of lean placers available for their action in the United States, in Central and South America, and especially in Australia and Siberia, this prediction appears to be moderate. Yet this great increase in gold production, with all the important industrial and economic changes which must follow, is a simple application of principles and appliances long since known to the engineer and used by him for similar work for half a century.

There have been some interesting investigations of late into a branch of applied science which, when freed from the quackery which has sometimes become associated with it, demands serious consideration. This is the use of scientific methods of protecting buildings from the effects of lightning. Both in England and in Germany there have been established scientific societies for the critical investigation of the effects of lightning discharges; and these bodies, by keeping accurate and systematic records of all such occurrences coming to their notice, have enabled some reliable information to be obtained. Among other things, it has been shown that the material of which a lightning conductor is composed has an important influence upon its action. Thus it appears possible for a lightning-rod to be too good a conductor, and when made, for instance, of copper, the disruptive discharge passes so quickly as to produce a shock of much violence.

An iron rod is much better, since it offers more impedance to the current, and produces a damping effect upon the oscillations. In arranging a lightning-rod system, according to the experience of the latest investigators, care should be taken to provide numerous and complete earth connections, and to make sure that metal portions of the building, such as the roof, gutters, water-pipes, etc., are in electrical connection with the conductors. The air terminals need not project far above the building; but horizontal conductors should be run along ridge-poles, and these connected to salient points in the iron-work of the roofs, all being fully and carefully grounded.   Such a system will prevent the occurrence of dangerous side discharges, and if iron conductors are used the effects will be so dampened as to be freed from serious results.

I have referred in these reviews to the problems connected with high-speed service on railways, and there has developed in this connection an interesting problem bearing upon the stability of locomotives and cars.   It is well known that the movement of the reciprocating parts of a steam locomotive, for example, acts to produce vibration, both in vertical and in horizontal planes.   Numerous attempts have been made to prevent these actions, the most successful being by the employment of four cylinders, with separate cranks, and connections, arranging the crank angles so as to cause the opposing forces to neutralize each other. Apart from the successive vibrations, however, it is realized that the whole machine itself has a period of oscillation, and that if the number of vibrations of the moving parts forms a complete multiple of this period of oscillation, the swaying will continue to increase in amplitude until it becomes dangerous.   The action is similar to that of a pendulum to which a slight push is given at the extreme end of each swing, thus giving it oscillations of increasing extent, while the same number of pushes given at other points during the swing would serve only to check its motion.   In like manner, any very small periodical oscillations in a railway car become of importance when they coincide with the period of the whole vehicle, since they then have a cumulative effect which may become very serious at high speeds.

A remedy for this difficulty appears in the damping effect of friction, existing in various places in the machine, as between the plates of the springs, in the pivot of the bogie truck, and between the tires of the wheels and the rails of the track.   Extreme rigidity in the construction of a locomotive is found to be undesirable, and with a moderate degree of elasticity, combined with a sufficient degree of friction between the yielding parts, the most serious effects of cumulative oscillations may be avoided.   It is also very desirable that the period of oscillation of an engine should be observed, and that such rotative speeds be maintained as will avoid synchronism with this period.

In the preceding review I called attention to the criticisms which have been made of the stability of the Assouan dam and of the postponement in the raising of this important structure.   It is not yet admitted that this postponement is due to the revelations of the new theory of stresses in dams, as propounded by Professors Atcherley and Pearson; on the contrary, it is distinctly stated that the feature in the work demanding attention is the scour caused by the discharge of the water through the sluices and upon the apron of the foundation.

It is now reported that the strengthening works are making rapid progress, and the dam will soon be beyond criticism as to strength. At the same time, it is practically admitted that the dam is not realizing all the results which were hoped for, so far as the extension of the agricultural resources of Egypt are concerned. It is understood that a dam is also to be constructed at Esneh, and, what is more important, that extensive irrigation works are to be undertaken in the Fayoum. While the exact nature of these latter works has not yet been announced, there is little doubt that they include the conversion of the Wady Rayan into a storage reservoir, upon the plans proposed in detail by Mr. Cope Whitehouse more than twenty years ago. The extent of the new works may be grasped when it is understood that a total storage capacity of four milliards of cubic metres of water is required for the proper irrigation of Egypt, and that the Assouan dam provides for but one milliard of cubic metres, leaving three milliards to be provided for.

Probably one of the most extensive engineering works, as regards area covered, now under consideration, is that of the United States Reclamation Service. The eight projects already under construction cover irrigable land, nearly eight million acres in extent, in Arizona, Colorado, Idaho, Nebraska, Wyoming, Nevada, New Mexico, and South Dakota; the cost exceeding $17,000,000. In addition to these there are projects for areas totalling more than a million acres in California, Oregon, Montana, and North Dakota.

Aside from the agricultural and economic importance of these immense undertakings, the engineering features involved are of much interest. Reinforced concrete is being freely used in the construction of the dams and diverting weirs, and the discussions as to the influence of tension and temperature stresses in masonry structures have no bearing upon these works. In this great work, the influence of engineering upon civilization is well seen; and while diplomats and soldiers are disputing about indemnities and cessions of barren islands, the engineer is adding to the permanent wealth of the world at a continually accelerating rate.   HENRY HARRISON SUPLEE.

LITERATURE : POETRY AND ESSAYS.

It is a commonplace of the publishing business that poetry has fallen upon evil days. In the lists of the best-selling books of the month it is absolutely ignored. In the stacks of books on store-counters it rarely appears except in the form of reprints of the classics, with which everyone is supposed to be already familiar. When a publisher discovers in his morning's mail a bundle of manuscript verses he receives the boon without exhilaration, and the sender may seldom expect to get in return any more generous offer than the invitation to print at his own risk. Indeed, to say that poetry is a drug in the market is a reckless exaggeration of its vogue at a time when the fortunes made by selling medicines, compared with those made by selling poetry, are as a thousand to one. And if poetry is no longer bought and sold, it is fair to presume that it is no longer read.

Yet this condition of disfavor would seem to be a startling exception to the general literary tendency of the present age. In everything else the movement is away from a narrower to a wider field. It is the great boast of the eulogists of modern civilization that literature is no longer the privilege of the few, but the enjoyment of the many. The appeal of history, science, and especially fiction is now made to the millions; is it not then a strange anomaly that poetry should affect only a few superior atoms, dotted here and there over the reading world? Actually, the apparent decline in the popularity of poetry is largely offset, when quantitative estimates are concerned, by the use that is now being made of a new medium of circulation. Poetry, like almost every other form of literature, has taken advantage of the most characteristically modern method of transmitting ideas. That is to say, the writing of verse, like the writing of philosophical reflections, historical and scientific articles, and novels, has had a journalistic development. Now it is notorious that the demands of journalism have made a powerful impression upon the style of contemporary prose writers. Authors who have themselves never published a line in a newspaper are nevertheless affected by the requirements of a public taste which has been largely influenced for good and evil by the daily press, which has been trained to expect a lucidity, a directness, and, if one may so say, an "interestingness," not demanded by a previous generation, and which, at the same time, has reconciled itself to the defects which too often accompany these qualities. If any considerable proportion of the poetry of the future is to reach its destination through the agency of the news company, it is worth while to consider how far the character of the product is likely to be benefited or injured by this important change in the method of its distribution. Will it be possible for poetry to be printed on the same sheet with stock exchange quotations and reports of baseball games, without absorbing some new and alien element from its environment?

For the purpose of such a speculation not much help is to be gained from a study of such occasional contributions as those by which Mr. Alfred Austin and Mr. Rudyard Kipling attempt to stimulate the nationalist feeling of readers of the London "Times." These are obviously nothing more nor less than political editorials versified. Indeed, they might almost be called stump speeches versified, for the same end might be attained by their recitation in Hyde Park, if only the population of the British Isles could be collected there within earshot. The competition of these writers with the party journalist is too incidental to warrant any generalizations. The only fair basis for a judgment must be the work of someone who uses the newspaper press not as a megaphone for the delivery of a casual exhortation, but as the normal voice of his muse.

Perhaps the best living instance of the poet-journalist or journalist-poet is Mr. Wilbur D. Nesbit, whose verses in the Chicago "Tribune" appear with no less steady a regularity than any other ingredient of that journal. While a wide circulation does not by any means prove the possession of high merits by an author, it is a presumptive claim to critical attention; and this challenge is the more insistent when what was first published for the multitude in a daily paper is collected between boards and tempts fortune in the shape of a book. In "THE TRAIL TO BOYLAND AND OTHER POEMS," * Mr. Nesbit supplies material for an estimate of the literary significance of writing which, in the conditions of its composition and publication, differs widely from the poetry of tradition. The point with which we are most concerned is to discover whether in this alliance between poetry and journalism, the poetry or the journalism is the predominant partner.

The verses collected in this volume are advertised as having first appeared "in their original form" in the Chicago "Tribune" and the Baltimore "American." It may therefore be inferred that they have been

* Indianapolis: The Bobbs-Merrill Co.

touched up here and there since their first publication.   With every allowance for later editorial revision, they give remarkable evidence of the
author's readiness of resource and of his skill in rapidly contriving verses
that flow with an easy melody.   It is not possible to read many pages,
however, without coming to the conclusion that the journalist has been
too much for the poet.   The unsatisfying quality of these verses, when
they are considered as candidates for permanence, is due not merely to
the lack of time for elaboration, but also to the necessity imposed upon
the writer by the nature of his audience.   Whether conscious of it or
not, he has succumbed to the temptation to play excessively upon superficial emotion.   It is natural and not unwholesome for the grown man
to reflect at times upon the scenes and events of his boyhood.   He may
be forgiven if now and then his meditations upon the past, particularly
upon its unfulfilled promise, verge upon the sentimental.   But when this
resurrection of early feelings and associations spreads itself, as it does
here, over scores of pages the net result is not merely sentimentalism,
but slush.   The difference that is made to legitimate emotion by being
watered down will be seen at once by anyone who turns from this thin
and interminable effusiveness about the old home to the simple pathos
of Hood's "I remember."

The obligation which rests upon the journalist, whether he works in
prose or in verse, to find access to the sympathies of his readers by the
quickest route, accounts in great measure for the sentimentalism which
is the distinctive note of Mr. Nesbit's verses even when he takes other
subjects than the wistful longing for a vanished youth.   At times the
strain into which he falls is flagrantly inconsistent with the actual truth
of life, as when, for instance, he tells us that

> Grief has a wondrous softening:
> It betters every soul it sears.

This is the kind of reflection that appears impressive to a reader who
is hurrying over his breakfast and has no time to think, but it will not
bear the test of comparison with human nature as it exhibits itself in
the world in which we live.   Mr. Nesbit is particularly rash in taking
the case of Hezekiah as a text for this generalization, for he could
scarcely have happened upon a more obvious instance of a man upon
whose character grief left only the most transitory impression.   This
sentimentalism, again, is obtruded with a zeal for commonplace moralizing that approaches dangerously near the ludicrous.   A boy trudging the
street and swinging a bell to announce an auction recurs to the memory
of the adult and sets him moralizing on "the glory of the sunset on the

boy that used to be," and regretting his own folly in auctioning off "the happiness we did not know was gold." Mere existence must surely be a painful thing to anyone whose remorse is stirred by so remote a provocation.

Yet there are indications that Mr. Nesbit might leave behind him verses capable not only of being read, but of being re-read, if he would chasten his desire to be prolific and would be content to write, say, once a week instead of once a day. In the lines entitled "His First Day at School," "Where He Got It," and "A Song for Flag Day," the poetry does not surrender to the journalism without a struggle. In these verses we catch a glimpse of something that counts for more than facile talent, and suggests the level which the author might reach if he could be released from the fetters of the journalistic habit. It is tantalizing to meet hidden here and there in a mass of commonplace sentiment a poem so nearly approaching the qualities which would make it an abiding treasure, and yet missing the goal through haste in thought or execution.

Both in discussing the general question of the mutual relations of poetry and journalism and in attempting to assess the merits of this individual writer, it must be remembered that the verses contained in this book are only a selection, and, as far as one can see, a selection made according to topics. Probably many readers who receive great pleasure from Mr. Nesbit's poems day by day in the newspaper will be vaguely disappointed with this volume, and will feel, without knowing why, that it does not fairly represent the most pleasing characteristics of the author. My own deliberate opinion is that Mr. Nesbit's reputation would have been better served if he had rejected almost everything that appears here, and had brought together instead an equal number of specimens of those verses which he has regarded as unworthy the distinction of reprinting. He has made the mistake of supposing that his most satisfactory verses must necessarily be those whose topics are of the most general and abiding interest. On the other hand, it is precisely in dealing with ephemeral — that is to say, journalistic rather than literary — subjects that his journalistic methods are most successful. In the rereading, greater pleasure would really be given by Mr. Nesbit's brisk comments on some topic of an hour that is past than by his experiments with themes for which so light and airy a treatment is inadequate. In the present volume, the most "readable" set of verses is an account of the troubles of a lecturer perplexed by the number of towns in the West whose names are full of K's. There is no temptation here to philosophizing, and, the end and the means being suited to each other, the reader's entertainment is without irritation.   A book composed of such pieces would have put Mr. Nesbit in the front rank of writers of topical verse; as it is, by attempting to rival more deliberate writers on their own ground, he has entered himself in a competition in which he is hopelessly outclassed.   The conclusion of the whole matter seems to be that while there is lawful scope in journalism for the use of verse in comment upon the news of the day, it is out of the question to expect from the daily press more than very rare contributions to the body of classical poetry.

In taking up the "LATER POEMS" * of John White Chadwick, we turn from the professional to the amateur; from the writer whose verse is the main expression of his talent to one who cultivates the poetic art in the leisure left to him from the strenuous exercise of another vocation. The contrast between these two books shows the difference that is made by practice.   Mr. Nesbit's verses run with as great ease and lucidity as the sentences turned out by an expert editorial writer, while Mr. Chadwick's frequently show signs of his unfamiliarity with the medium in which he is working.   His awkward inversions especially reveal a certain clumsiness in the handling of his tools.   Such a passage as

> With ceaseless toil
> He wrought, until at length, half-blind with tears,
> Some secret flaw his whole creation spoil
> He saw too late,

is reminiscent of Tate and Brady.   In confirmation of the belief that such defects are mainly due to want of practice, it may be noted that the latest verses in this volume, which is arranged in chronological order, show a much greater smoothness of execution and mastery of the writer's instrument.   A more radical disqualification lies in the fact that Mr. Chadwick's leading interests were not so much poetical or even literary as philosophical, and controversial-philosophical at that.   He was consequently too much inclined to attempt to use verse as the vehicle of ideas better suited to prose.   The ratiocinative and argumentative instinct was more fully developed in him than the poetic, with the result that his verses breathe the atmosphere of discussion rather than imagination.   Perhaps the best instance of the undue preponderance of non-poetical interests is to be found in the sonnet which hails the appearance of a new Father Abraham in — Kuenen!   A similar violation of artistic proportion is seen in the extravagant sonnet entitled "In Extremity," in which the writer calmly assures us that even though science should

* Boston and New York: Houghton, Mifflin & Co.

"pluck the warrant out" from Scripture and destroy "every hope that harbors in the breast," he would still retain the conviction of immortality as long as Shakespeare was left him.

It is some compensation for the over-polemical character of Mr. Chadwick's verses that their serious thoughtfulness leaves an impression of sobriety and dignity. In the first poem in the volume, "A Common Weed," the author is reminded by a casual flower of the days of his boyhood, but his recollections are not vulgarized by mawkish sentiment. So, too, the lines on "My Father's Quadrant" link the reminiscences of youth with thoughts of high ideals while avoiding the temptation to overstrain and unnatural homily. And if at times Mr. Chadwick erred in making verses the expression of his views on controverted subjects, his very earnestness gave these verses a glow of emotion which would have been absent if he had written about topics on which he felt less intensely. This ardor of passionate conviction gives exceptional vigor — with a corresponding nearness of approach to the traditional *abandon* of the poet — to several of the concluding sonnets, whose burden is an indignant attack upon false conceptions of patriotism. "Doest thou well to be angry?" is a question that the poet may readily answer in the affirmative, as long as he stops short of the hysterical stage. The sonnet of national protest is a form of poetry which lends itself admirably to the concentration — one might almost say the condensation — of powerful emotion; and the models set by Milton and Wordsworth will never be overlooked in periods when the public mind is confronted by new and strange crises. Of recent years, Mr. William Watson has been easily supreme in this field. Mr. Chadwick's sonnets do not reach so high a level either of inspiration or of artistic texture, but it will be surprising if some of them do not win a place in anthologies of American literature.

It is a curious evidence of the variety of type capable of an inevitable poetic impulse that the three writers whose verses we are particularly considering in this article should be respectively a journalist, a preacher, and a schoolmaster. There can be little doubt that, of the three, the schoolmaster exhibits least of the didactic and most of the poetic spirit. Perhaps it is by reaction from an occupation commonly held to be monotonous that the thoughts of Mr. Arthur Christopher Benson have turned to the meditations upon life which have found expression in "PEACE AND OTHER POEMS," * while he owes to the training for his profession his refinement of taste and delicate appreciation of the exact

* London and New York: John Lane.

value of individual words.   The scholarly flavor of his verse reminds one of the work of another poet who, if not actually a schoolmaster, found the main task of his life in the no more exhilarating labor of school inspection.   Mr. Benson's verse resembles Matthew Arnold's not only in its culture but in its gentle brooding over the dark and mysterious facts of life, and in the calm and strong resolution which confronts the mischances of human experience.   Yet Mr. Benson's melancholy is not as cold as Arnold's: there is in it a warmth of sympathy redeeming it from austerity and even imparting to it a tone of friendliness and geniality.   The motto on the title-page is, "Thou shalt make me to understand wisdom secretly," and the key-note of the book is the discipline of the spirit apart from high public affairs through quiet activity in an obscure corner.   Early ambitions are laid aside without any tinge of bitterness, but with a cheerful assurance that his lot is happily cast whose daily duty can be fulfilled without stress or storm.

Most of the poems in this volume record Mr. Benson's own reflections upon nature and life.   Occasionally he attempts, with unequal success, to express the emotion of others.   "The Charcoal Burner," for instance, contains a finely wrought description of the sights and sounds of the forest; but the personality depicted is not really that of any charcoal burner whom one might hope to meet, but of the author himself, projected into unfamiliar surroundings.   Mr. Benson's imagination takes a bolder flight in the poem which immediately follows.   Here Icarus soliloquizes when on the point of making his fatal venture.   The conflict between the passion for discovery and love of "the dear world" he is leaving is powerfully portrayed, leading up to the fine concluding stanza :

> Soon, soon I may be lying, racked and torn,
>   On yon sharp ledge, to hang and moulder there;
> Or I may learn His secret, strongly borne
>   Through viewless wastes of air!

With these few exceptions, Mr. Benson contents himself with gathering up the chastened experience of the twentieth-century cultivated man who in middle age counts up his assets and reckons himself rich in the things that are ignored by the merchant's ledger.   The poem whose haunting melody and wistful spirit will give it a longer life than that of any other in this volume is the one beginning

> Twenty long years ago,
>   And it seems like yesterday!
> And what have I got to show,
>   What have I gained by the way?

and containing such other memorable verses as

> Thirsting for love and joy,
> Eager to mould and plan,
> These were the dreams of a boy,
> These are the dreams of a man.

It is interesting to compare these specimens of contemporary verse-writing with such examples of the practice of the art during a period of several generations as have lately been published in "SOUTHERN WRITERS: SELECTIONS IN PROSE AND VERSE," * edited by Professor W. P. Trent. It will be observed that poems of sentimental reflection on the days of youth have always had a vogue, which is no more than to say that human nature is much the same at all times and places. The motive of "Resignation," by St. George Tucker, who died in 1828, is quite in harmony with the favorite theme of Mr. Nesbit, and further illustrations of it might be given, coming down to "The Grapevine Swing" and "Aunt Jemima's Quilt" of Dr. Samuel Minturn Peck. The last fifty pages of this volume, devoted to "Latter-day Poets," show that the types of poetry represented by Mr. Nesbit, Mr. Chadwick, and Mr. Benson, respectively, have no local limitations. Least frequent is the wistful melancholy characteristic of the last of these three writers. The South has had reason enough to learn the vanity of human wishes, but it expresses alike its sadness and its contentment in a somewhat more robust fashion.

The old tradition of "the poet's eye in a fine frenzy rolling" is upheld in this collection to an extent that would be impossible in any volume of contemporary verse written by an American. When the whole personality of a man of strong feeling was shaken by the earthquake of the Civil War, it was little wonder that his emotion should find an outlet in verse which, whatever its other merits or defects, was intensely passionate. The Southern poetry of this period is a part not only of the literature but of the history of America in its revelation of the mind and heart of the followers of the lost cause. Read to-day in cold blood, these verses appear extravagant and hysterical, but it must be remembered that a war-poet never envisages the situation with the impartiality of a member of The Hague Tribunal. Such lines as "Stamp upon the accursed alliance!" "The despot's heel is on thy shore," and "Fling down thy gauntlet to the Huns" appear forty years later rather theatrical than dramatic; but we may be sure that there was no tinge of insincerity about them when they were written.

* New York and London: Macmillan.

17

It is in a collection of "MISCELLANEOUS ESSAYS AND ADDRESSES " *
such as those of the late Professor Henry Sidgwick that a writer who has
reached the front rank as a student of some particular subject shows
whether or not he conceives the world to be bounded by the limits of
his own parish.   A life spent mainly in the investigation of problems
of ethics and political economy might be supposed to offer little opportunity for other interests.   Many years ago, however, Walter Bagehot
showed that zealous devotion to the dullest of the sciences was not incompatible with a keen appreciation of art and literature.   Sidgwick's
outlook is here shown to have been as wide as Bagehot's, though, as
might have been expected, he had not at his command so brilliant a literary style.   It is difficult to say whether he is happiest in discussing
matters falling within his special province, such as "Bentham and Ben-
thamism," or in dealing with the use of the hexameter in English
poetry, and comparing Shakespeare's tragedy with his comedy.   Of
the essays in this volume, written at different times during nearly forty
years, one of the earliest chronologically is an admirable analysis of
"The Theory of Classical Education."   Its criticism is largely directed
against methods of teaching now abandoned by most intelligent schoolmasters — as when the composition of Latin and Greek verses is referred to as, in the opinion of the scholastic world, "an essential part"
of classical instruction — but it gives an earnest of the freedom from
bias and the soundness of judgment which were afterward to distinguish the writer's work in his chosen pursuits.

Perhaps the most delightful essay in this volume is that in which
Sidgwick turns the tables on "The Prophet of Culture."   Even Matthew Arnold himself, accustomed as he was to a variety of attacks from
many quarters, must surely have enjoyed the novel experience of being
accused of Philistinism.   The arrow again hits the mark when Sidgwick
goes on to point out that "when he [Arnold] commences his last lecture
before a great university by referring to his petty literary squabbles, he
seems to me guilty of what he calls ' provincialism.' "   Most wholesome, too, is this protest against the narrowness shown by culture in the
attitude it often assumes toward enthusiasm:

The fostering care of culture, and a soft application of sweetness and light, might
do so much for enthusiasm — enthusiasm does so much want it.   Enthusiasm is often
a turbid issue of smoke and sparks.   Culture might refine this to a steady glow.   It is
melancholy when, instead, it takes to pouring cold water on it.   The worst result is not
the natural hissing and sputtering that ensues, though that cannot be pleasing to culture or to anything else, but the waste of power that is the inevitable consequence.

* London and New York: Macmillan.

Through overlooking its opportunity in this direction, says Sidgwick, culture is frequently in danger of degenerating into dilettantism. Its educational or missionary function would be much more successful if it would condescend to love common people and common things. Culture turns up its nose at Macaulay, but Macaulay has done more than the avowed propagandists of culture in opening the heart of the average man to literature. An equally telling criticism is to the effect that present-day culture shows a disappointing want of appreciation of the "sap of progress," the creative and active element of things. Culture disparages the work of the system-maker, and complains of the unsightliness of his scaffolding and the noise of his hammers. But when the house is built it is seen to be serviceable, "and culture is soon found benevolently diffusing sweetness and light through the apartments."

It would be easy to illustrate the value of Sidgwick's clear and shrewd comment on other topics connected with literature and education, but it is time to turn to those essays which are occupied with questions arising in his own special field. In "Political Prophecy and Sociology," his penetrating good sense makes short work of George Eliot's much-quoted epigram that "of all the mistakes that men commit, prophecy is the most gratuitous." This epigram is often flung at the heads of writers and speakers who forecast the probable results of such and such political measures; but Sidgwick does not exaggerate in calling it "an audacious inversion of the truth." He points out that when we make positive statements as to unimportant details of past history — e.g., as to the place at which, or the manner in which, the Battle of Hastings was fought — we incur a risk of error which may fairly be called gratuitons. But all rational action is based on belief of what is going to happen; and all experts in all practical callings are always prophesying. "The physician who orders a dose, the engineer who determines the structure of a bridge, no less than the statesman who proposes a tax, can only justify what they do by predicting the effects of their respective measures." Further, the importance of prophecy has increased for the present generation through the increasing prevalence of the historical method of dealing with political and social questions. It has therefore become easy to represent any desired result with plausibility as the last inevitable outcome of the operation of the laws of social development. In this paper the writer attempts not to stop such prophesying, however dangerous it may be, but to make clear the limitations within which the guidance offered by such forecasts may reasonably be accepted.

The claim of sociology to supersede political economy is met several

times in the course of this volume. Sidgwick boldly denies its authority, and justifies his denial by two tests of the real establishment of a
science recognized by Comte in his discussion of this very subject —
namely, (1) consensus or continuity, and (2) prevision. Comparing
the three most elaborate treatises on sociology — Comte's, Spencer's, and
Schäffle's — he finds that they exhibit a complete and conspicuous absence of agreement or continuity in their treatment of the fundamental
questions of social evolution. Not only do they adopt diametrically
opposite conclusions, but each of them adopts his conclusion with the
most serene and complete indifference to the line of historical reasoning on which his brother sociologist relies. When every writer on the
subject starts *de novo* and builds on his own foundation, it is idle to
speak of such a thing as a positive science of sociology. Elsewhere
Sidgwick examines in detail the sociological conception of "the social
organism," and challenges the Spencerian parallel between sociology and
biology. This discussion leads up to an illuminating account of the
mutual influence of ethics and sociology. It is a type of several similar
discussions which give this volume both a practical and a speculative
importance. The form of an essay or address is especially suitable to
topics of this kind, which belong to the border land between the sciences
rather than to the content of any one of them.

The second series of Mr. Paul Elmer More's "SHELBURNE ESSAYS" *
is likely to win the favor of book-lovers in no less degree than its predecessor. Mr. More exhibits the virtue of courage, at any rate, in venturing
upon subjects which have already been discussed almost to the point of
tedium. At this time of day one takes up essays on such topics as
Shakespeare's sonnets, Hazlitt, Lamb, Hawthorne, and Fitzgerald, to
say nothing of Delphi, with little hope of anything beyond a rearrange-
ment of what has been said over and over again. But the interest of
an exposition depends less upon the text than upon the personality of
the man in the pulpit. The most familiar theme recovers its freshness
when handled by an expositor of an independent type of mind, especially when his own originality is seconded by so wide a knowledge of
literature that he is able to place old truths in new settings. It would
be hard to say which of these two qualifications does Mr. More the
greater service in these studies. His independence, never degenerating
into the freakishness of the mere eccentric, would be in itself an adequate justification for taking the risks involved in the issue of a book of

* New York and London: Putnam.

this kind. But the value of his insight would be greatly lessened if this were not accompanied by what one might call "outsight," if his catholic acquaintance with other writers did not equip him with the material for making illuminating comparisons with the writer whom he happens to be considering at the moment.

Mr. More's freedom from provincialism is manifest even in his style. It is rare to come across a writer in the English language who does not reveal by his vocabulary or phraseology whether he is of British or American origin. In the two hundred and fifty pages of this volume, there are only two passages where the author's use of words indicates even faintly that his portion is with the Western development of the English tongue. The one American topic included in these essays, namely Nathaniel Hawthorne, is treated with a detachment befitting a subject which is not of America only but of the world. It is characteristic of Mr. More's method — of his fondness for considering individual writers in their relation to great issues and long processes — that he contemplates Hawthorne as a connecting link between Cotton Mather and Mrs. Mary Wilkins Freeman. His presentation of what he calls "the tragedy of New England" is such as, once brought to our notice, can never be forgotten:

> From the religious intolerance of Cotton Mather to the imaginative isolation of Hawthorne, and from that to the nervous impotence of Mrs. Wilkins' men and women, is a regular progress. The great preacher sought to suppress all worldly emotions; the artist made of the solitude which follows this suppression one of the tragic symbols of human destiny; the living novelist portrays a people in whom some native spring of action has been dried up, and who suffer in a dumb, unreasoning inability to express any outreaching passion of the heart or to surrender to any common impulse of the body.

Not less suggestive is Mr. More's concluding query as to whether, in the future development of New England, a blind materialism will succeed the morbid spirituality of the past.

In estimating the work of contemporary writers, Mr. More reaches out and up to generalizations of real value both to the student of letters and to the practitioner. Meredith prompts the notable comment that "it is not profundity of reflection on human life which causes obscurity so much as the refraction of this into innumerable burning points." Herein, continues the essayist, lies much of the difference between real depth and mere cleverness; and the contrast is illustrated by a comparison of "Henry Esmond," where the thought is presented in broad masses which rest the mind while stimulating it, with "The Egoist," which confuses with its endless clashing epigrams. A still more acute observation is made in criticism of the false realism of Mr. Meredith's dialogue — an observation which is obviously appropriate to the dialogue of some other recent novelists. Mr. More reminds us that in actual conversation "there are, besides words, a hundred ways of conveying our meaning which the printed page cannot employ. To produce the same impression, the novelist's language must necessarily be fuller and more explicit than is needed in life, and true realism should realize this difference." Mr. More probes even deeper when, calling attention to the continual evidence in Mr. Meredith's books of the intellectual machinery by which his characters are created, he maintains that it is the part of the scientist rather than of the artist to evoke a character from conscious analysis of motives.

The chapter on "Kipling and Fitzgerald" is packed with stimulating suggestion. The explanation offered of the deficiencies of Kipling should be read in conjunction with the analysis of the same author by Mr. Chesterton in the book to be noticed presently. In showing how Kipling, while exalting "the will to act," ignores "the will to refrain," Mr. More incidentally points out that much of the confusion of mind in regard to genius and degeneracy spread abroad by Lombroso and Max Nordau is due to the same oversight. Out of "the deliquescence of character and loosening of the grip on things actual" comes "a flaccid dream state which the ordinary observer associates with mysticism," but which is really quite different from "the mysticism of an Emerson or a Juan de la Cruz or a Plato, where in a strong character the higher will to refrain holds the lower will as a slave subservient to its purpose."

As already mentioned, the value of Mr. More's contributions to criticism is largely enhanced by his resources as a student of many literatures. Especially is he profited by his classical scholarship. In a volume of essays on literary subjects, the late Frank Norris warned his fellow-countrymen against troubling themselves about "the sodden lees of an ancient crushing." No more glaring exposure of the short-sightedness of this depreciation of classical learning could be made than by simply placing side by side the critical work of Norris himself and that of Mr. More. All through this volume the appreciation of writers of whatever period gains immeasurably from the existence of a background.

Most of all does Mr. More's classical training serve him in his essay on "Delphi and Greek Literature." In the very outset of it he is bold enough to declare his opinion that "in our own land no important revival, or shall we say creation? of literature is likely to arise except from a renascence of interest in Greek"; and further, that "such a study may throw a curious light on the religious and moral confusion now troubling our minds." The body of the essay expounds and illustrates the eternal significance of the two inscriptions, "Know thyself" and "Nothing too much," over the temple of Apollo at Delphi. In this discussion Mr. More deals with profounder questions than any that present themselves in the other essays, and it is precisely here that he achieves his greatest success. The concluding pages of this inquiry, in which scrutiny is made into the causes of the rise and fall of nations, show that his critical powers are exercised with greater effectiveness in proportion to the magnitude of the subject with which they are concerned. If he is disposed to continue his analyses of the work of individual writers, they will deserve and gain a hearty welcome; but it is even more to be desired that he may address himself to the more difficult and more fruitful labors of which we have an example in this penetrating investigation of the Greek spirit.

When Stevenson died, the pessimists assured us that the last of the real essayists — the writers whose frankness and disregard for popular idolatries made them akin to Lamb and Hazlitt — had departed. Only a few years have passed and there has appeared in Mr. Gilbert K. Chesterton a writer whose influence is likely to be as wholesome and permanent. Those whose admiration for Stevenson was wholly on account of his style will find little to their taste in Mr. Chesterton, for his literary manner has in it scarcely anything of the *curiosa felicitas* of R. L. S. But in their philosophy these two are brethren. It is perhaps a good omen of this new author's ultimate victory that as yet the real character of his work is only beginning to be dimly apprehended. It is the fashion to write of his "mental agility," his "daring flights of fancy," his "intellectual gambols," his "scintillating epigram," and the like. He is regarded by many critics as a literary acrobat who contributes to the gayety of his readers by standing on his head and recording his outlook on life as it appears from that attitude. The general comment on Mr. Chesterton is that he is extremely ingenious, but so inordinately whimsical that it would be absurd to take him seriously. The true account of him is that he is not ingenious at all, but exceptionally straightforward and matter-of-fact. If he has at any time hesitated about the printing of his essays, it must have been the fear not of their eccentricity, but of their obviousness, that made him pause.

In "HERETICS,"* Mr. Chesterton has shown us once more that if you

* London and New York: John Lane.

want to startle the world you need do nothing more than call things by their right names. When anyone adopts this simple method of winning distinction he is, of course, met at once, as Mr. Chesterton is, by the charge that he is calling black white and white black. Say instead that a good deal of what has been conventionally called black he is calling white, and *vice versa*, and he must plead guilty. As this essayist himself points out in defending a contemporary, people never ask whether the current color-language is always correct:

> Ordinary sensible phraseology sometimes calls black white: it certainly calls yellow white and green white and reddish-brown white. We call wine "white wine" which is as yellow as a blue-coat boy's legs. We call grapes "white grapes" which are manifestly pale green. We give to the European, whose complexion is a sort of pink drab, the horrible title of a "white man" — a picture more blood-curdling than any spectre in Poe. Now, it is undoubtedly true that if a man asked a waiter in a restaurant for a bottle of yellow wine and some greenish-yellow grapes, the waiter would think him mad. It is undoubtedly true that if a government official, reporting on the Europeans in Burmah, said, "There are only two thousand pinkish men here," he would be accused of cracking jokes, and kicked out of his post. But it is equally obvious that both men would have come to grief through telling the strict truth.

From a practical point of view, it does not perhaps matter very much whether or not we are strictly accurate in the color-names we give to wine and grapes. But it is of supreme importance whether or not we use our color-names correctly in questions of ethics and politics. There is nothing more perilous to right thinking, and consequently to right conduct, than the tendency in common speech whereby the denotation of a term changes, while its connotation remains unaltered, or, more exactly, the tendency for a word to be applied to a new class of things while carrying over with it the associations of praise or blame which were appropriate in its earlier use, and in its earlier use only. The main service that Mr. Chesterton is now rendering alike to speech, thought, and practice — such a service as Ruskin rendered before him — is his reiterated demand that words shall be used consistently; that they shall not be employed in such a loose fashion as to confuse our notions of light and dark, of wise and foolish, of right and wrong. It is not Mr. Chesterton that performs the conjurer's tricks: it is we who are convicted of the offence of habitual juggling.

A leading article in Mr. Chesterton's creed is the absurdity of expecting any fruitful result from discussions which ignore fundamentals. This is most certainly a truism, but its very obviousness has caused it to be generally overlooked. He makes great play with the various modern phrases which are employed as "dodges" in order to shirk the problem of what is good. For example, one man says: "Away with your old moral formulæ; I am for progress." This, logically stated, means: "Let us not settle what is good; but let us settle whether we are getting more of it." Another says: "Neither in religion nor morality lie the hopes of the race, but in education." This, clearly expressed, means: "We cannot decide what is good, but let us give it to our children." And Mr. Chesterton can appeal to the justification of history in reminding us that since general ideals have been driven out in literature by the cry of "art for art's sake," and out of politics by the cry of "efficiency" or "politics for politics' sake," both literature and politics have dwindled. It is only when a nation is growing weak and ineffective that it begins to talk about inefficiency, as it is only when a man's body is a wreck that he begins to talk about health. "The time of big theories was the time of big results. The sentimentalists conquered Napoleon. The cynics could not catch De Wet."

The self-deception of which we become the victims by our loose use of words is well illustrated in Mr. Chesterton's exposure of the fallacy underlying most modern eulogies of "the simple life." The very talk about one's simplicity in itself makes one less simple. "It does not so very much matter whether a man eats a grilled tomato or a plain tomato; it does very much matter whether he eats a plain tomato with a grilled mind." And the trouble with the enthusiastic advocates of simplicity so-called is that they would make us simple in the unimportant things but complex in the things that matter. The only kind of simplicity worth possessing is destroyed when it is reduced to a system. "There is more simplicity in the man who eats caviar on impulse than in the man who eats cereals on principle." A good instance of the same clear-sighted method as applied to politics may be found in Mr. Chesterton's stripping away of the false sentimentalism which makes futile so much talk about union. Union, we are reminded, is no more a good thing in itself than separation is a good thing in itself:

Union is strength; union is also weakness. It is a good thing to harness two horses to a car; but it is not a good thing to try and turn two hansom cabs into one four-wheeler. Turning ten nations into one empire may happen to be as feasible as turning ten shillings into one half-sovereign. Also it may happen to be as preposterous as turning ten terriers into one mastiff. The question in all cases is not a question of union or absence of union, but of identity or absence of identity.

This is surely as obvious as any truth can be. An object-lesson of it stands out for the world to read in the relations of England to Scotland and Ireland respectively. Whereas England and Scotland do not clash, "England and Ireland are so united that the Irish can sometimes rule England but can never rule Ireland."

I must refer readers to the volume itself to learn how Mr. Chesterton proves that the great tragedy of the artistic temperament is that it cannot produce any art; that it is materialistic business men to whom idealism is most dangerous; that most of the talk about "young nations" is based on a fallacy; that it is absurd to speak of the Irish as Celts; that the fault of the yellow press, in England at any rate, is that it is not sufficiently sensational; that across the fierce old literature of the sturdy fighting English in early days is everywhere written "the policy of Majuba"; that Mr. Chamberlain is neither, as his friends depict him, a strenuous man of action nor, as his opponents depict him, a coarse man of business, but an admirable romantic orator and romantic actor; and that the great gap in Mr. Kipling's mind is his lack of patriotism. It is such conclusions as these that lead many of his critics to declare that, although Mr. Chesterton may be very entertaining to read, his paradoxes make him a negligible quantity in any serious calculation of contemporary influences. They would scarcely say that if they recalled the use made of paradox by some of the greatest teachers in the history of the world, or even if they took the trouble to look out the word "paradox" in the dictionary.

HERBERT W. HORWILL.

THE EDUCATIONAL OUTLOOK.

THERE has not been a saner, more significant, or more all-around satisfactory convention of the National Educational Association in twenty years than the one lately held at Asbury Park and Ocean Grove. Boston had larger numbers, enrolling almost twice as many tourist members. The 1905 meeting had an unparalleled accession of active members, raising the permanent membership to above five thousand. Besides, it was honored by the presence of President Roosevelt. The educational duty of the United States has never been more comprehensively or more clearly presented. There was but little desultory talking, and few attempts were indulged in to make the welkin ring. Seriousness and purpose characterized the programme from beginning to end. Minor topics were crowded to the rear, even in the department meetings. Largeness of view prevailed. That pettiness, which according to tradition is inseparable from the composite character of teachers, was less in evidence than ever before — less than one meets with ordinarily in conventions of journalists, physicians, and clergymen. There were few really great papers, though as many as at any previous meeting.

Mr. Maxwell was a superb presiding officer. His presentation of Mr. Roosevelt is especially commended to future generations of chairmen. Without flourish or fulsomeness, he said: "Ladies and gentlemen of the National Educational Association, the President of the United States." A lesser man would have said more.

The preparations were perfect. Everything went off without a hitch. The decorations of the convention hall were simple and thoroughly appropriate in their patriotic character and quiet beauty. The music, under the direction of Tali Esen Morgan, was in itself a feast of rich things. Mozart, Handel, Berlioz, Mendelssohn, Wagner, Gounod, and Schumann, together with inspiring patriotic music rendered by a chorus of several hundred voices, good soloists, a fine orchestra, with von Nardroff at the organ, contributed materially to the success of the meetings.

A sermon by Dr. Hillis opened the convention. It was essentially a heart-to-heart talk with teachers, full of comfort, of encouragement, of inspiration to go ahead and make the world a brighter and more beautiful place for future generations to dwell in.   In glowing words the work done in the thousands of school-rooms throughout the land was illumined.   Never was the teacher's reward more eloquently pictured.   Dr. Hillis's text was: "One soweth and another reapeth. Other men labored, and ye are entered into their labors."   Civilization, he argued, would perish were it not for the fact that we have educators who gather up the achievements of society, and give them over to the plastic minds of the children and youth of the land.   It is this, he said, that makes the educator immortal in his influence.

Mayor McClellan, of New York City, made a sincere but obsolete plea for a narrow elementary curriculum.   It had a certain value in that it summed up in convenient form the stock arguments of the opponents to a generous educational programme for primary schools.   He was respectfully listened to from beginning to end.   Later on the convention embodied this resolution in its "declaration of principles":

The N. E. A. regrets the revival in some quarters of the idea that the common school is a place for teaching nothing but reading, spelling, writing, and ciphering, and takes this occasion to declare that the ultimate object of popular education is to teach the children how to live righteously, healthily, and happily, and that to accomplish this object it is essential that every school inculcate the love of truth, justice, purity, and beauty through the study of biography, history, ethics, natural history, music, drawing, and manual arts.

Dr. Lyte, chairman of the committee on resolutions, was careful to state in parenthesis that this particular paragraph was written several weeks before the convention.   The remark only served to emphasize the application to Mayor McClellan's arguments.   Superintendent Harvey, of Menomonee, made the point that the trouble is not that there are too many subjects in the curriculum, but that in these subjects too many things are taught which are not worth teaching.   There is where he locates the waste of time and effort, with correspondingly poor results.

President Roosevelt, "the best loved man in the whole round world," as Miss Blake called him in a burst of enthusiasm, was plainly delighted to appear before the N. E. A.   He spoke as one who realized the important bearings of the occasion upon the welfare of generations of citizens to come.   He regarded the teachers as young America's true priests and priestesses, who are shaping the ideals of the nation to be. He talked about fundamentals in a straightforward way and in a spirit of humane charity.   His predominant purpose seemed to be to impress upon his audience the supreme duty of heading the young in the right direction. He warned especially against the false notions of "success" which a narrow commercial spirit has fostered into wide acceptance and which the newspapers have magnified into popular idols. There was no extreme statement. His phrases were carefully chosen. It was the voice of wisdom that seeks not after plaudits, but for the spreading abroad of truth.

The addresses by Dr. Hillis and President Roosevelt supplemented each other admirably. The President's words were the more serious and profound; Dr. Hillis pictured the common topic in more vivid colors. The latter sought to reach the heart of the teacher as a human individual hungering for divine comfort; the President knocked at the door of the teacher's conscience. If there had been no more than these two addresses, the convention would have been amply worth while. They gave a glorious setting to the thoughts that should be uppermost in the minds of educators at the present time.

Mr. Frank Vanderlip described the economic importance of trade schools. Germany has taught the world how to train youths into efficient industrial units. Her trade schools have been so designed that they supplement the cultural training of the elementary schools. They are the direct auxiliaries of the shops and the offices and have been powerfully influential in training to high efficiency the rank and file of Germany's industrial army. Mr. Vanderlip advised that a similar auxiliary system of trade schools be provided for the youth after he has left the direct influence of the present school system.

The address by United States Commissioner W. T. Harris deserved better attention than it received at the time of its delivery. But the opinion is abroad that Dr. Harris reads better than he listens. Statistics are not calculated to hold an audience indoors on a warm summer night, no matter how weighty they may be.

The newspapers generally gave extensive reports of each day's proceedings. The New York City papers were especially generous in the amount of space accorded. But, true to their straining after sensational elements, they printed as much fiction as fact. On the whole, the news was as reliable as convention news usually is — no better, no worse. It was to be foreseen that the reporters would describe the teachers after their own fashion, drawing for coloring chiefly upon their prejudices. However, there is no need to worry about it. The people generally care little for the real facts. Newspapers are read for entertainment rather than for instruction.

The election of State Superintendent Nathan C. Schaeffer, of Pennsylvania, as president of the Association for the coming year, met with hearty approval on all sides. He has served the organization faithfully for twenty-five years, and there is no more popular man in the whole Association, unless it be Superintendent James M. Greenwood, of Kansas City, Missouri, who has been president. Dr. Schaeffer's name was brought forward by his friends without his knowledge. He is a whole-souled, big-hearted, generous Pennsylvanian, a man of unsuspected intellectual resources, an able administrator, a fine scholar, and an educator whose whole life is consecrated to his calling.

In its declaration of principles, the N. E. A. adheres to the traditional policy of conservatism. It reiterates its endorsement of the National Bureau of Education, and urges upon Congress the need of enlarging the powers and widening the usefulness of the Bureau. The establishment of rural high schools is approved. Industrial education is commended to all schools. The increasing utilization of school buildings is advised. There is a cautious word of praise for the humane regulation of child labor and the proper enforcement of compulsory education laws. The attention of the Federal Government is directed to the need of adequate legislation to provide schools for the children of citizens of the United States living on naval reservations. The secondary schools and colleges are congratulated on the efforts made to remove the taint of professionalism from student sports: "Interscholastic games should be played for sportsmanship and not merely for victory." The tendency to replace large school committees on boards exercising executive functions by small boards which determine general policies, but assign all executive functions to salaried experts, is "observed with satisfaction." Intelligent, judicious supervision is emphatically declared to be necessary for all grades of schools. The attitude toward people who would reduce elementary school programmes to the three R's has already been explained. Here are two paragraphs which impress us as particularly virile and timely:

Local taxation, supplemented by State taxation, presents the best means for the support of the public schools, and for securing that deep interest in them which is necessary to their greatest efficiency. State aid should be granted only as supplementary to local taxation, and not as a substitute for it.

The National Educational Association wishes to record its approval of the in creasing appreciation among educators of the fact that the building of character is the real aim of the schools and the ultimate reason for the expenditure of millions for their maintenance. There is in the minds of the children and youth of to-day a tendency toward a disregard of constituted authority; a lack of respect for age and superior wisdom; a weak appreciation of the demands of duty; a disposition to follow pleasure and interest rather than obligation and order. This condition demands the earnest thought and action of our leaders of opinion, and places important obligations upon school authorities.

Even more remarkable, considering the former policy of the N. E. A., is the endorsement of the widespread movement to increase the compensation of teachers in the public service. Less than five years ago the Association would have scorned the idea as beneath its dignity to consider. Now it puts itself on record with this declaration:

> The National Educational Association notes with approval that the qualifications demanded of teachers in the public schools, and especially in city public schools, are increasing annually, and particularly that in many localities special preparation is demanded of teachers. The idea that any one with a fair education can teach school is gradually giving way to the correct notion that teachers must make special preparation for the vocation of teaching. The higher standard demanded of teachers must lead logically to higher salaries for teachers, and constant efforts should be made by all persons interested in education to secure for teachers adequate compensation for their work.

It would seem only reasonable to suppose that with the increase of the demands made upon teachers as regards preparation, professional efficiency, and social position, there should have come a corresponding increase of remuneration. As a matter of fact, the people are taking a more enlightened view of this matter, and have in several praiseworthy instances raised the pay of teachers to something like a respectable basis. But, generally speaking, the teachers in the United States still continue to be the most poorly paid public servants. Relatively high salaries are provided by some of the larger cities and in a few other places where equitable views of educational work have won a victory over parsimony and over intellectual and spiritual callousness. If it were not for these exceptions, a look at the statistics of the yearly salaries in the various States would bring the blush of shame to the cheeks of every fair-minded citizen. The average pay of teachers in this country — the average, not the lowest — is less than $350 a year. The teachers of New York City,· by careful organization, strong and persistent argument, and wise management, induced the State legislature a few years ago to pass the Davis-Ahearn bill assuring to them something like just compensation. Superintendent Maxwell, then as now firmly believing in good pay for teachers, placed the whole weight of his influence in support of the measure, although his board of education was arrayed against it. Mr. Roosevelt was Governor of the State at the time, and when he signed the bill he said: "Teachers do so important a work for the State that they should be encouraged by adequate pay." That as President of the United States he still adheres to this opinion was evident from his address at Asbury Park, in which he exclaimed:

> You teachers make the whole world your debtor. If you did not do your work well, this Republic would not endure beyond the span of the generation. You substitute for the ideal of accumulating money the infinitely loftier ideal of devotion to work worth doing, simply for that work's sake. There are few movements in which I more thoroughly believe than in the movement to secure better remuneration for our teachers.

President Butler, of Columbia University, and President Harper, of Chicago University, have also publicly aided the movement. And so the N. E. A. has at last permitted itself to go on record in support of a better compensation for teachers. Its interest in the matter was kindled at the Boston meeting chiefly through Principal McAndrew of the Girls' Technical High School of Manhattan, to whom the teachers of the country are greatly indebted for ever fresh and effective campaign material. A committee was appointed with Mr. Carroll D. Wright, former Commissioner of Labor, as chairman, to investigate the whole subject of teachers' salaries, tenure of office, and pensions. The other members of the committee were: Miss Anna Tolman Smith, of the United States Bureau of Education; Superintendent E. G. Cooley and Miss Catharine Goggin, of Chicago; Prof. Franklin H. Giddings, of Columbia University; Principal R. H. Halsey, of the State Normal School at Oshkosh, Wisconsin; and Principal William McAndrew, of the Girls' Technical High School of Manhattan. This committee organized and appointed a subcommittee to draft a schedule of inquiries relative to salaries. Mr. Charles H. Verrill, an expert statistician, was appointed to collect data and classify and present them in a serviceable and effective manner.

The result of the committee's labors is a volume of 458 printed pages, which was submitted to the National Council of Education at the Asbury Park convention. This report is a noteworthy contribution and constitutes one of the most valuable documents ever issued by the N. E. A. Its distinguishing characteristics are careful elimination of doctrinarianism, and painstaking investigation and tabulation of data representing actual facts. As a work of reference it occupies a field all its own. So comprehensive a study of the questions it seeks to illuminate has never been attempted before. There will now be something approaching definiteness to refer to when the compensation of teachers is under discussion. Here is a paragraph from the introduction:

> One of the most striking developments of recent years in connection with city schools is in the exacting nature of the requirements for teachers. Such require-

ments are becoming more and more severe. The idea that any high-school graduate can teach school has quite generally been succeeded by the conviction that no person, however well educated generally, can properly teach without special preparation for that duty. The higher standards which are being insisted upon for the teachers must lead logically to better compensation. The inadequacy of the salaries in some of the cities, as shown by this report, after the training that is necessary to secure the positions, has been used successfully as an argument for their increase, and in some cities it has been admitted where financial reasons have stood in the way of granting an advance.

The facts collected by the committee with reference to teachers' salaries represent 85 per cent of the cities and towns of 8,000 or more inhabitants, and a vast amount of information " from typical towns of less than 8,000, and from representative rural districts." The following lines of inquiry were selected as best calculated to yield the desired information :

1. Actual salaries paid in cities and towns of 8,000 or more inhabitants. These are 547 in number, with a total population of nearly 25,000,000, or 33.1 per cent of the total population of the United States.
2. Fixed salary schedules in cities and towns of 8,000 or more inhabitants, wherever such schedules have been adopted. These schedules should, of course, be studied in comparison with actual salaries — the salary roll.
3. Salaries in typical towns of less than 8,000 inhabitants.
4. Salaries in typical ungraded rural schools.
5. The nature of the fund or appropriation from which teachers' salaries are paid (*i.e.*, whether a special salary fund, not subject to diminution from the fluctuation of other expenditures, or drawn from a general educational fund).
6. Important incidental facts relating to teachers' salaries.
7. The purchasing power of teachers' salaries in different localities.
8. Tenure of office of teachers.
9. Pensions of teachers.

The committee did well in publishing the names of the towns of which no report could be obtained. And, when we read, for example, that of all the cities and towns of 8,000 population or over in New York State, only two failed to respond to the call for information, we have pretty eloquent testimony of the universal interest taken in the investigation and also of the thoroughness with which the work was done. Massachusetts has the distinction among the States of upward of 2,000,000 population of having in every instance supplied all the data asked for. Many interesting items are scattered through the report. We learn that in Boston 10.5 per cent of the total number of teachers employed by the city are engaged in high-school work; in St. Louis and Baltimore, cities of almost exactly the same size, the percentages of teachers in high schools are 6 and 6.1 respectively. In Pittsburg there is but one principal to sixty-four teachers, while in Milwaukee sixty-one teachers are supervised by four principals. The women

18

teachers in elementary schools constitute 74 per cent of the entire number of persons employed either as teachers or in supervisory positions. Only 2.1 per cent of those engaged as teachers in elementary schools are men. White day laborers employed on municipal work, such as sewers and street cleaning are, on the whole, better paid than teachers. Chicago appears to be the only exception to the rule.

Among the cities of 200,000 to 1,000,000 population, the highest average salaries are to be found in Boston, the lowest in Washington and New Orleans. Buffalo teachers seem to be the most poorly paid of any in the larger cities of the North. Montgomery, Alabama, holds the record of $120 as the lowest individual salary. Annapolis, Maryland, is at the foot of the line in averages for high-school principals and teachers. Frederick, Maryland, stands in the rear with an average of $244 a year for elementary teachers. Leaving out the four great cities Boston, New York, Chicago, and Philadelphia, where the pay is more nearly what it should be, California leads in salaries for every grade of principals and teachers. The averages in that State, with eleven cities, are for elementary teachers $814; for elementary-school principals $1,443; for high-school teachers $1,254; and for high-school principals $2,364. Montana stands second in average salaries for elementary teachers, with $792; New Jersey second for elementary-school principals, with $1,443; Colorado second for high-school teachers, with $1,150; Massachusetts (not including Boston) second for high-school principals, with $2,261. When the great cities are counted in with the rest, the State of New York becomes the leader in every division, with Massachusetts as second in the matter of the highest average salary for high-school principals.

The teachers in the small rural schools naturally receive the poorest pay. Few people can have any conception of how poorly the labors of these workers are compensated. In Missouri one teacher receives an annual stipend of $100; Illinois can produce a town where a man does his work for $120 a year; in Maine there is a place called Orneville, where the remuneration is fixed at $118. This is in the North. It is worse in the South. South Carolina can show an average in one county of $107 for white teachers and $56 for colored teachers, and two counties in the State give the negro teachers only $39. What the people expect the teacher to be and to do for the money it is difficult to tell. But here is what Baltimore has established as a standard of requirement for entry on the salary roll as teacher in the elementary schools: The candidates before being permitted to take the competitive examinations must have completed the course in one of the Baltimore training schools for teachers, or a course in some other training school whose standard of admission and whose requirements are equivalent to those of the Baltimore training schools; or they must have taught acceptably for two years, and must have passed an examination in the following subjects: English, including grammar, composition, and literature; history and civics, arithmetic, algebra, plane geometry, physics or botany or zoology, geography, physiology, and hygiene.

The reward of the successful contestant for a place in the schools is $300 a year, with three annual advances of $48 and one of $60.

It does seem to be high time to tell from the housetops the story of the estimate placed upon the work of the teachers as shown by financial recompense. The colleges and universities do no better. This fact was brought out into the open when Mr. Carnegie contributed $10,000,000 toward a pension fund for college teachers. President Thwing, of Western Reserve University, presented in "Harper's Weekly" some startling figures. "It is nothing unusual," he writes, "for an instructor to receive, at the start, $750, sometimes less; after three years he may be increased to $1,000, and probably six years will elapse before he reaches $1,300." With the facts to back up his statements, Dr. Thwing is charitably mild in concluding that "to a man of thirty who has spent all his life in preparation up to this time, and who hopes to have a home, $1,300 is certainly an insignificant sum." How can fathers expect their sons to obtain practical views concerning business life in institutions where the teachers are reduced to the barest living expenses? There is not likely to be any appreciable change of conditions until the donors who supply the colleges with funds begin to divest themselves of thoughts of self and other weaknesses of frail humanity and permit themselves to be governed wholly by philanthropic motives. Dr. Thwing only states what must be patent to every reasonable observer when he says:

There seems to be a greater desire to put more money into beautiful buildings and equipment than into teachers' salaries. It is much easier for people to give money to colleges to erect halls, libraries, and chapels. These beautiful buildings can be seen, and tablets may tell the passer-by of the generosity of the donor. It would not be right to put such a motive upon the generosity of college benefactors. But now that Mr. Carnegie has set the example, perhaps others will follow, in giving their money for the invisible and less conspicuous service of teaching.

It is the warning which Professor Thompson, of Cambridge University, uttered at the commencement of Columbia University in 1903, when he pointed to the danger in the higher institutions of learning in America of spending too much money proportionately on buildings and equipment and too little upon men. President Nicholas Murray Butler reiterated the admonition in a recent letter to the trustees of Columbia University.   For its laboratories and lecture-rooms, he wrote:

A university must attract men of the first order of ability, who will not permit themselves to be diverted from teaching and from research, and these men should be rewarded, not lavishly, but becomingly.   So long as participation in the work of higher education requires a large material sacrifice which many men cannot, and many others will not, make, a great proportion of the best intellect of the nation will not enlist in the service of education. . . . A compensation that will enable a university professor to live decently, to educate his children without undergoing privation, and to take a becoming part in the public life and service of the community in which he lives, is a standard at which we should aim, and below which we cannot afford to fall.

The Salary Committee of the National Educational Association expresses the thought in this form with reference to the common schools:

Ambitious schemes to erect fine buildings may result in poorer education, because there is not money enough left to employ good teachers, or to enable good teachers to do proper work.

Mr. Carnegie's generous gift, aside from the direct benefits it will bestow, may be the beginning of a new order of things.   It certainly marks an important forward step in our civilization.   The work of the teachers may gradually become rated at something like its financial worth to the world.   The demands upon the teachers' efficiency will, no doubt, increase in proportion.   This is in itself a consummation devoutly to be wished in some quarters where the light of to-day has not yet penetrated.   What is done for the teachers is done for the youth of the country.

The meeting at which the report on salaries, tenure, and pensions was presented failed to attract the attendance its importance merited. There was but little opposition to the conclusions of the committee, which were admirably presented by Mr. Verrill.   Dr. Draper, State Commissioner of Education in New York, appeared to be the only one feeling altogether out of sympathy with the movement to which the report owes its origin.   He said that he had never been able to get himself to consider the discussion of salaries and pensions of primary worth.   He was not in favor of legislation on the subject.   In his opinion, the salaries reported as lowest may represent more than the recipients could earn in any other occupation.   Among other *ex cathedra* assertions he made was this: that the product of the country school is good, and that the best teachers are needed in the city school, because the most difficult conditions are found there.   He was right in declaring that efforts should be directed toward preventing incapacity from competing with capacity in appointments, by the formulation of equitable standards of qualification. The sort of competition least assuring to educational progress is found especially in the smaller cities, where politics is rife and the governmental system lacks healthy resistiveness.   With regard to the pensioning of superannuated teachers he was most radically out of harmony with the common sentiment.   He expressed a deep-seated repugnance for any form of pensions except for occupations which are exceptionally hazardous to life and health.   He strongly disapproved legislation which levies a tax upon the salaries for the creation of a pension fund.   This sort of thing means a reduction of the pay due to the teachers.

In conclusion, Dr. Draper recommended moderation and dignity in agitating the salary question.   He urged that methods be devised for limiting the number of candidates for teachers' positions, thereby preventing unfair competition.   The rest he would leave to the free evolution of public educational sentiment.   In a recent article, Mr. McAndrew has turned very neatly the point of Commissioner Draper's chief argument.   If the assertion be true, he replies, that the poorly paid teacher earns no more than she gets, then the whole argument is reduced to a business proposition, viz., the bulk of education in this country is in the hands of poor workers, poorly paid.   Now the people may decide for themselves whether they want their children taught by those who are not bright enough to occupy other positions and by those who are getting ready for better things.

Associate Superintendent Albert G. Lane, of Chicago, pointed out that the larger cities are now paying fair salaries.   The organization of teachers and the consequent enlightenment of public sentiment have produced a salutary effect.   The problem to occupy the N. E. A. would seem to be how to secure better conditions in the country districts.   In the earlier days of the country, rural life was controlled more largely by native Americans than it is at present.   The newer immigrants are turning more and more to the farming districts.   The problem of properly looking after the interests of teachers in rural communities is considerably more complicated by the change.   The beginners in teaching, Mr. Lane explained, usually gain their first experiences in poorly paid rural positions, and then by dint of constant self-improvement pass into the better-salaried village and city systems.   Tenure of office is practically a settled matter in the larger cities.   Here the difficulty is rather how to eliminate the inefficient in a humane way.   Voluntary effort to provide annuities for the superannuated is good.   Legislation for the provision of pensions is in harmony with humanitarian ideas.   Mr. Lane questioned the comparison in the report of the salaries of men and women.   The conelusions, he averred, were misleading.   He felt firmly persuaded that an examination of all conditions would show that there is a greater equality than appears on the surface.   Salaries, he held, should be dealt with by legislation.   Minimum standards fixed by law are desirable and worth working for.

Superintendent Maxwell laid down two considerations as fundamental: (1) Salaries should be good living salaries to attract and hold the best and most efficient workers; (2) every teacher should do the best work of which he or she is capable, wherever placed and whatever remuneration accorded.   He argued that good service must be paid for. He would take away from local authorities the power of fixing the amount to be expended for teachers' salaries and would place it in the hands of the State.   He urged that we must get rid everywhere of the miserable system of annual appointment.   Permanent tenure is the desideratum.   As to pensions, there is everything in their favor. New York City has a pension roll of nearly half a million dollars.   No superannuated teacher receives less than $600.   One important argument in favor of pensions is that they free the minds of teachers of wasteful anxiety regarding old age.   The State, he holds, has virtually a monopoly of education in America, and can and ought to establish annuities by law.

Miss Anna Tolman Smith pointed out some of the hopeful features of the report.   She commended the stand taken by Commissioner Draper regarding the most effectual means of improving the condition of teachers, namely, by maintaining high standards for admission to the service and thus cutting down the competition of mere numbers.   How much has been done in this direction may be gathered from the report of the United States Commissioner of Education for 1903.   In this valuable document are to be found significant summaries of requirements for teachers' certificates in the several States of the Union.   Miss Smith had searched the pages of the report for hopeful signs, and had found that quite a large number of women receive salaries above $2,000 a year, and more than half of all the elementary school teachers in the cities have $600 or more — a striking contrast to conditions that prevailed formerly.   Nearly 5,000 women teachers in elementary schools get $1,000 or more a year.

The small attendance at the discussion of the salary problem may have been due to the prevalent feeling that the council is an exclusive body which prefers to keep its own sources of wisdom untainted from tributes by the *hoi polloi* of the pedagogic fraternity and sorosis.   There are people who will not go to any place where they do not feel free to talk whenever they choose to do so. The being in a gathering where some are privileged to talk and others are merely tolerated to listen is too much of a trial to them. Otherwise the feeling of being excluded from the roll ought not to be so irritative. Although the material of which the council is made up is excellent on the whole, there is enough of mediocrity in it so that the mere onlooker need not feel himself neglected. Those who are very anxious to get into the council usually have no difficulty in getting in. The committee on nominations has no easy task. Some must be chosen because of friends and positions, others must be kept in year after year because their names look so well in print. This may explain why there is so little room for those who ought to be in. However, that should not have kept anyone away. An educational meeting may sometimes be profitable even to a listener.

OSSIAN H. LANG.

AN UNSATISFACTORY APOSTLE OF PEACE.

WHO that has a spark of human feeling in him would not wish to prevent the horrors of war wherever it can be done? Who would not assent to a peaceable arbitration, if consistent with national honor and future security? But there are affairs in which there is nothing to arbitrate, affairs to which that procedure could no more be applied than it could to the burglar who breaks into our house, and, in case of need, is bent upon murdering us.

The Baroness Bertha von Suttner is one of those preachers against each and every war, who take no heed of ingrained human nature or of the stern necessities of a given situation from which there is no issue but by the arbitrament of the sword, regrettable as that solution may be. "Down with weapons!" is her invariable and absolute cry. She might as well say: "Down with all jealousy! There shall be only love!"

Unfortunately, whatever good motives are to be attributed to her in her propaganda, she too often omits laying proper blame upon certain real or would-be disturbers of peace, who, through an autocratic lust of conquest, are impelled to seek further extension of an overgrown empire, or who are hankering after "revenge" for having been foiled in a campaign of annexationistic aggression. There have been clamorers for "arbitration," I remember but too well, who have endeavored to make things easy for both these dangerous tendencies. Having myself been active for years in the cause of arbitration and peace, I can speak from full and sad experience on that point.

Unfortunately, also, Bertha von Suttner, who is a novel-writer, has repeatedly mixed up with her propaganda fictitious stories which have done a great deal of harm to the very cause of peace. Thus, some years ago, she gave an account of the hanging of a French priest by a German court-martial in 1870. It bore all the traces of invention, but it was calculated to arouse universal indignation, and to feed the sentiments of revenge and of hatred against the German nation. The story was copied eagerly in the French press, and found its way into English and other journals. No name, no date, and no locality had been given in the account!

It was only said that the writer had received it from the very officer who had taken part in the gruesome execution.   Having myself narrowly escaped, during the Revolution of 1848, from being stretched on the sand-heap by court-martial bullets, I felt at once, being acquainted also with the rules of martial law in international war, that the story could not be true.   The inquiries instituted showed this to the fullest extent by documentary evidence.   The Bavarian Minister of War, Freiherr von Asch, proved the falsity of the narrative in the most irrefutable manner; seeing that, from some indication, the alleged deed would have had to be done by Bavarian troops.   A Bavarian ex-captain, a friend of mine, and a man of humane and liberal views, who had been through the whole campaign, attached to the staff, gave witness in the same effective way.

As I sincerely wished to clear the lady-writer of the charge of invention, I entered into correspondence with her.   She then informed me that the German ex-officer from whom she said she had heard the story, lived out of his country.   Consequently, he was in no danger of being subjected to any unpleasantness, assuming even that the statement of a plain historical fact could be charged upon him as a crime.   I suggested that the simplest principles of chivalry ought to impel him to come forward, in view of the official declarations that he had given a fictitious and impossible story.   But this appeal was made in vain.   Neither did he give his own name, nor was the slightest information vouchsafed either as to the name of the priest who was said to have been hanged, or as to the locality where, or the time when, the event was alleged to have happened.   Nor was any hint offered as to the appearance of a report in the contemporary journals of France.   In fact, the whole story was proved to have been a calumny.

I truly regretted that after this no retraction took place.   Some may, under these circumstances, have been inclined to question the shadowy existence of the alleged source of information; but for my part I never uttered such a doubt.   I may say, moreover, that I would gladly have refrained from mentioning this matter — though, years ago, it gave rise to bitter foreign attacks upon Germany — were it not that, at a recent Peace Congress, the Baroness Suttner told another story about the Polish Revolution of 1863, which I can equally prove to be quite baseless.   This time it is even against women that her story is told.   But of that, more anon.

Lest I should be misunderstood in what follows now, I shall say at once that nothing could be further from me than to contend in any way that women did not have as much right as men to urge their views in matters concerning the national welfare. During a whole lifetime I have always maintained that women ought to be made to understand these affairs; and personally I have always done my best to act on that principle at home and in society. I hold, however, that the final decision in matters of government properly belongs to men. Without entering into the various reasons therefor, it is a fact that the defence of the state, including its women, necessarily rests with the men. The horrors of war come most closely upon them. They have to bleed and to die in it.

Now, if ever a majority of women were to resolve upon a war which men, being in a minority against the tenderer sex, should disapprove, how could it be expected that men would fight out, at the risk of their lives, what they looked upon as a wrong cause? And if men held a war to be necessary, in opposition to the views of a majority of women, how could the women prevent the men from carrying their point? From a beleaguered town, women and children are generally allowed to leave before the final assault. It may be doubted whether this chivalrous custom would be maintained if a hostile army knew that the female sex of the country in which the war was carried on had participated actively and decisively, by their votes, in the government of the state. Surely, a warless time might be desirable; but before that golden age arrives, the very character of mankind has to be changed in a manner scarcely imaginable now.

There are two kinds of war — those between different nations and civil wars. Now, Bertha von Suttner says:

> Not because they are daughters, wives, and mothers, will modern women oppose the institution of war, but they do it because they are the reasonable half of a mankind which is to become all reasonable, and because they see that war is a hindrance to civilization; that it is pernicious and damnable from every point of view — from the moral as from the economic, from the religious as from the philosophic view.

In such generalities, according to the Latin saying, deception lurks. The truth is, there have been good wars and bad wars between nations, good civil wars, or revolutions, and bad ones. In the latter case they are called *coups d'état*, or reactions. War has sometimes been a hindrance to civilization. Such, for instance, was the Thirty Years' War for Germany, when foreign armies sucked the very life-blood out of that nation. A highly prosperous land was then utterly devastated. In numbers, Germany dwindled to nearly one-third of its normal population by the end of that horrible war! Its consequences are, as regards prosperity, felt even now. But war founded Swiss freedom. War rendered possible the restoration of the unity of the United States in its struggle with the slaveholders' rebellion. War destroyed the Jesuit Separatist League (Sonderbund) which aimed at the dissolution of the Swiss Confederation. Through war, slavery has been abolished in the great American Republic. The Sonderbund and the Slaveholders' League were dangerous impediments to the development of civilization. By raising their weapons, not by laying them down, did the champions of liberty in Switerzland, and the Republicans of America, promote the cause of culture.

Again, Baroness von Suttner asks:

Was the theory that slavery is an insult to human dignity perhaps less just, and the antislavery movement less promising and reasonable, at a time when the traffic in human beings was still a domineering fact? And in the days when — another fact! — justice was dealt out by torture, and heretics and witches were still burned at the stake, was the proof perchance given then that thumb-screws are, and must remain, the rightful means of justice?

Certainly not! Such things as these are as unreasonable and as abominable as can well be imagined. But the antislavery movement became "promising" only when the North of the United States fought the matter out against the South with arms in hand. Had the war not been carried on and "fought out on that line," the United States would no longer exist. Similar things may be said about the Mexican Republic as against the "Latin Empire" planned by Napoleon III. What else could or should have been done in those cases than to raise weapons in the name of freedom and civilization? "Down with arms!" — which is Bertha von Suttner's cry — would have meant to leave the course free for barbarism and tyranny, and to leave that wholesome work of civilization undone.

By what means was Italian unity founded? Did Garibaldi do wrong in the expedition of the Thousand? Ought Italians to have left the government of the States of the Church to a papacy which claims universal dominion in matters temporal and spiritual? Are they to be blamed for making a breach in the walls of Rome, and allowing their troops to enter the city?

In a speech addressed to a deputation, the late Pope, Leo XIII, declared that Giordano Bruno, one of the world's deepest thinkers, had been rightly burned alive. When Luther began his agitation, adherents of the Reformer's views were still tortured and murdered on the flaming pile at Köln, at Munich, at Passau. Was the forcible armed rising against such inhuman misdeeds not justified? Where would we be if obscurantists — among whom Louis Veuillot, not so long ago, still declared that "it was only to be regretted that Huss was burned so late, and Luther not at all " — had gained the conviction that there were no longer fearless men, ready to meet death, who would oppose such infamies by force of arms? Shall we allow the champions of popular and national right, who rose in France, in Germany, in Hungary, in Italy, in 1848–9 — men on whose deeds, even though princely reaction once more obtained the upper hand for awhile, present liberties still mainly repose — to be reviled, because they had to fight for their cause? Should the watchword then still be: "Down with arms!" if to-morrow a criminal hand were to try to undo what has been gained and regained?

Speaking of the horrors of the recent war between Japan and Russia, the Baroness von Suttner points to the "permanent Tribunal at The Hague" as to the sign of a better time which has begun. But what about the readiness shown by Japan to submit to that Tribunal, and the refusal of the Czar's Government? She says not a word of it! One might have expected, too, that she would use this occasion for duly castigating that despotic ruler who with one hand apparently erected the so-called house of peace in the wood, and with the other immediately signed decrees for further preparations on land and sea; who broke the constitutional oath he had sworn to the Finns; and tried to cut the very life-nerve of progressive Japan. But there is not a word of blame about all that in her harangue. Well, ought Japan to have quietly bowed her head for slaughtering?

Suppose that, in the wake of lasting war troubles, a forceful movement for freedom were to occur in Russia, and blood were shed for its attainment; would not that be useful for the development of culture? "Even the Japanese possess a representation of the people," Russians might say; "and yet we are to be denied it forever!" Again, suppose the Young Turkish party should rise in arms, in order to compel the Sultan to reconstitute the Ottoman Parliament, which was solemnly promised by him when he prorogued it in 1878, and suppose such uprisings were to succeed; would not that be useful for the "deliverance of the people from enslavement" (*Entknechtung des Volkes*), of which Frau Bertha von Suttner speaks?

Fine words about arbitration and peace are not always effective. Bold deeds often must decide. But for deeds, strength and force are required; and these are essentially man's qualities. At all times there have been also heroic girls and women; and to them full honor is due.   But what true man would like to throw the tenderer sex into the terrible combats which, seeing the character of mankind, may possibly be diminished, but can never be prevented altogether?   Who can believe that there will not always be domineering natures, bent on oppression, filled with ambition, and aiming .at conquest, who, with the aid of venal and violent men, will try to attain their pernicious aims?   Against such dangers the word must be: "Raise the weapons!"

Frau von Suttner is not happy in her quotations from ancient or most modern history.   She says:

> The poetic episode of old Roman history, the deed of the Sabine women, may have been a good omen.   In those days women prevented a war by their courageous intervention.   Now, their work of prevention is directed, not against a single war, but against all war.

Then she speaks, in curiously Frenchified language, of "*rasant* and *brisant* powerful arms (*rasant- und brisant-mächtigen Waffen*), in consequence of the use of which there is no longer, in battle, a hand-to-hand fight, such kind of struggle being at present impossible."   She is mistaken on that point, too.   The war between France and Germany proved the contrary.   In the recent war between Japanese and Russians, there have been repeatedly bayonet charges, and the most terrible hand-to-hand fights.   In speaking of such things, Baroness von Suttner treats of subjects she does not and cannot know.

Are we to forget, moreover, that, after all, there have been wars between Romans and Sabines, and that it was only after repeated wars that the Sabine women, fully reconciled to their lot, threw themselves with dishevelled hair between their Roman husbands and their kinsmen by race?   Evidently, history is as little the *forte* of that lady-writer as knowledge of the possibilities of modern war.

Then Bertha von Suttner states: "Somebody told me the following episode.   It occurred before the Polish insurrection of 1863."   This "somebody" (again, as usual, no name!) asserted that in the house of an aristocratic lady at Warsaw, in the year mentioned, the chief notabilities of society had been invited to dinner.

> Among those present were the leaders of the subsequent insurrection.   After dinner, in the smoking-room, the gentlemen agreed among themselves that a rising could only lead to a useless massacre; but the ladies were not to be informed of this resolution, as this would only lead to the men being subjected to reproach for it. However, one of the gentlemen did not keep to the understanding made in regard to the preservation of silence.   He talked about the resolution of non-action to the ladies.   "How?   What?   Is that possible?" the chorus of ladies broke forth; "that

can only be a joke. Of such cowardice no Pole is capable!" "Of course," the other men said, "it was merely a joke!" as the contempt of the ladies would have been unbearable to them. And on the following day the revolution was begun by the very same men who had decided among themselves not to make a revolution.

By this story the writer means to give a lesson to her own sex. But the incident, which might read well in a novel, is again a manifest fabrication. Frau von Suttner has once more been deceived, even as in the case I have mentioned in the beginning. No worse shot could have been made than by this impossible tale. Polish women are, no doubt, very patriotically minded. But the idea that an armed rising is plotted, or the countermanding of it resolved upon, in such an off-hand way, after dinner with ladies, does not strike as credible anyone who has had experience in conspiracies. I can say that with a degree of certainty.

Again, the rising of 1863–64 did not originate at all in aristocratic Polish circles. It was, on the contrary, of democratic origin. Whoever knows anything about that insurrection should know so simple a fact. Add to this that the statement about a resolution of non-action having first been passed after an aristocratic dinner party, and yet a rising effected "the day after," can be proved palpably false from other evidence. On this point I can once more speak from full personal knowledge.

The way in which the revolutionary movement of 1863 was planned in Russian Poland, many months before it actually took place, was unknown to the public at large as well as to foreign diplomats. Its outbreak came like a thunder-clap from the blue. Yet a small circle of men who, after the stormy events of 1848–49, had found refuge on English soil, had been kept well-informed of what was coming. Above all, this was the case with Mazzini, with whom I was associated by intimate friendship. At first he had expressed an opinion, by letter, to the secret committee at Warsaw, that he "held an armed rising to be premature, and could not recommend it at present." But the well-known decree of the Czar's Government to take all the able-bodied young men out of the country by recruitment did not leave the Polish democrats any choice.

Besides Mazzini, Ledru-Rollin and I had early information. In the early days of January, 1863, the envoy of the "Secret Warsaw Committee" (of the later "National Government"), Mr. Czwierczakiewitsch, made to me in my house this confidential, most definite communication: "*Between the 21st and 22d of this month the armed rising will take place in Russian Poland.*" So, literally, it happened. I stated this, after the overthrow of the movement, with more details — especially also in reference to the participation of General Langiewicz, with whom I had become connected by friendship.

In blaming Polish women — wrongly, in a double sense — Bertha von Suttner again carefully omits branding the Czar's tyranny. That, too, is rather significant of the spirit of her propaganda.

In advocating the principles of the "new woman," the lady writer in question expresses regret that the female sex, by the admiration it shows toward heroes in war, and by the pleasure it takes in looking upon uniforms, has hitherto tacitly, but often also loudly by encouraging hostile conflicts, committed great wrong. All this, she thinks, is henceforth to be changed. Well, when just struggles for country and freedom have to be fought out, why should not woman highly esteem man's courage?

That too many of the sex delight in looking upon the "different sorts of cloth" in uniforms (*zweierlei Tuch*, as the German popular saying is) cannot be denied. The color sense, which in women is more highly developed than in men (painters exeopted), is partly answerable for this. Such natural characteristics have their advantages, but also develop their disadvantages; and they are not easily expelled either by the pitchfork or by soft preaching. However, in actual warfare, at least, the uniforms of soldiers are gradually becoming colorless. If, in times of peace, the brilliant red in English uniforms is still retained, recruiting sergeants could easily supply the reasons for that custom.

By mere words like "feminism" and "pacificism," which Frau von Suttner uses, and which in German look as odd as "rasant" and "brisant," certain female dispositions and tastes are not to be overcome. But that women should honor and admire heroic deeds, is right and fair. Men do the same. Feeling her own comparative bodily weakness, woman knows that she needs protection against enemies, even as against wild beasts. That is in the very nature of things. And a true man holds with Körner's famous war song, "Männer und Buben." That song was a fiery appeal to manly courage in the struggle against Napoleon I, and gives a terrible scourging to laggards and cowards, despised by all true women:

> Das Volk steht auf, der Sturm bricht los!
> Wer legt noch die Hände jetzt feig in den Schoos?
> Pfui über dich Buben hinter dem Ofen,
> Unter den Schranzen, unter den Zofen!

Bist doch ein ehrlos erbärmlicher Wicht!
Ein deutsches Mädchen küsst Dich nicht,
Und deutscher Wein erquick' Dich nicht!
Stosst mit an, Mann für Mann,
Wer den Flamberg schwingen kann!

As one who, many years ago, long before there was a woman's movement in England or in Germany, argued in favor of the promotion of the higher intellectual culture of the female sex, the abolition of oppressive laws, and the opening up of vocations for women, I should not like to be misunderstood.   The remarks I make are only directed against what I hold to be exaggerations, which inevitably issue in impossibilities. Those who denounce all war as "murder," and would take every weapon out of the hands of men, simply work for the furtherance of highly dangerous political schemes, menacing to country and freedom; for never will the whole world be put under one peace hat.   Such restriction would be the worst prospect for woman herself.   KARL BLIND.

LIFE-INSURANCE METHODS.

IN the seventeenth century when a trader carried merchandise for some distance across the seas, his creditors induced him to insure ship and cargo against loss for their benefit. This engendered the thought that he was himself of importance to his family, as well as were the goods to his creditors, and he obtained a policy on his life for the benefit of his kin. The first policies so written terminated with the venture. The premiums varied with the physical condition of the applicant, and the risk and extent of each journey. The skipper soon found that it would be more advantageous for him to take, in place of frequent renewals, a life policy, which would protect his people whenever he might be called away. The ready reimbursement of losses, for which Lloyd's underwriters were then already distinguished, led to an extension of life insurance among persons engaged in other perilous occupations.

By the fundamental principles of modern life insurance, the terms depend on the probable duration of life, according to established mortality tables. Prompt payment of the premium when due, under penalty of forfeiture, is required; and as soon as the insured fails to pay the premium the policy is cancelled. The value becomes greatly impaired when the insured is obliged to surrender the contract because he cannot pay. These self-imposed conditions lead to an accumulation of savings which might otherwise be encroached upon. To save his policy, a man whose life is insured will make sacrifices, when his income is decreased, which he would be loth to make to increase voluntary savings. Notwithstanding, many forfeitures occur because sanguine persons, persuaded by overzealous agents, are unable to pay even the second premium. Twice as much insurance lapses and is surrendered as is paid for at maturity. The insured who keeps up his policy in hard times is compensated for his self-denials when good times come around again.

There is no country where sudden changes of prosperity are more likely to reduce incomes, none where life is in greater daily peril, than here. It is, therefore, quite natural that life insurance should have flourished in the United States more than in any other country. Over fifty years ago this was recognized, and foundations were then already

19

laid for a business that commands the world's attention. The number of persons insured in ninety American companies is estimated at ten millions, who pay five hundred million dollars annually for the insurance of twelve billion dollars. These companies are carefully conducted; money intrusted to them is judiciously administered; and the policies of almost all may be considered safe. But contracts with them are made for a lifetime, on terms that involve serious loss if inability to pay or suspicion of insolvency should impel the insured not to comply with those terms. A person who contemplates taking a policy should not only investigate for himself the solvency and management of the company to which he desires to intrust his present and future savings, but should also carefully consider whether he is able to bear the burdens that the fulfilment of the contract will impose on him.

The most successful system in this country has been the "mutual," so called because policy-holders are supposed to participate in the management of the companies, and to share with the administrators they elect the profits of the business. These profits are made by investing premiums, raised or "loaded" one-third above their cost, to provide for expenses and contingencies to the best possible advantage. A large part of this money goes to the agents, who receive from 50 to 75 per cent commission on the first year's premium, and thereafter an average of 5 per cent per annum during the life of every policy they procure; other expenses, salaries, fees, rent, and so on, are larger than they need be. They aggregate 22 per cent of the premium receipts of the American companies, against 14 per cent of the English, and 10 per cent of the German, life insurance companies.

Contingencies comprise: First, an increase of mortality. While in cases of epidemics this occurs once in a while, the tendency is in the other direction. Longevity has increased over six per cent during the last fifty years; with better sanitary conditions, and a more rational hygiene in other ways, it will probably continue to increase. The second contingency is the interest obtainable on investments. With a greater supply, the usage of money has been cheapened, and the companies seldom derive as much profit by their investments as they had calculated upon. It will probably continue to diminish.

When the profits of a business exceed the estimates, the surplus of a stock company belongs properly to the stockholders, while in a mutual company it ought to be divided among the policy-holders, who created it. A proper division of the profits of a stock company leads to complications when it issues "mutual" policies. It is probable that the acrimonious controversy that has arisen in one of our largest companies over this question will finally be adjusted in the equitable spirit that secured the success and led to the prestige which this company has so long enjoyed. There can be no reasonable doubt of the solvency of this company, nor of its ability to meet every obligation, unless vituperation ruins its reputation and litigation absorbs its substance. It has become difficult to find lawyers enough for its prosecution. The quarrel among officers, stockholders, and policy-holders has called attention to the incautious selection of investments and the unjustified extravagance which prevail in this business.

Almost all companies who have succeeded in swelling to enormous proportions a surplus made from profits on high-priced policies, and all who try to emulate their example, are guilty of such extravagance. It was engendered by the custom of retaining for improbable eventualities a larger surplus than is necessary or judicious. Instead of dividing among policy-holders from the accumulation of assets all they can spare, managers direct their actuaries to credit what dividends they please, not explaining to their policy-holders how they were earned or apportioned. The example of wanton expenditure by large and wealthy companies is followed by their small, less fortunate competitors. An assessment company with a premium income of four millions paid $40,000 salary to its president in 1904. Such needless prodigality, the suspicious concealment of the details of the business, together with a few doubted investments, were reasons for the exclusion from Germany of two large American life insurance companies. The latter fact, indicating that our authorities guard the interests of their citizens with less care than is customary abroad, together with the more recent developments, have combined to create a distrust against our companies, not alone among present policy-holders, whose confidence has been rudely shaken, but also among those who would otherwise have become policy-holders. Savings diverted from life insurance companies begin to flow into banks and real estate.

Some methods of certain stock companies also deserve censure. During the hard times that followed our commercial crisis of 1873, their managers conceived the idea of establishing "industrial" insurance on a plan that had become successful in English centres of industry. Canvassers were sent into our tenement-house districts to solicit from laborers insurance for a few hundred dollars, and accept weekly instalments of from five to fifty cents each in payment of the premiums. The first response came from Irish Catholics, who thus found means to provide for a decent burial of their kindred when they were suddenly called away. Gradually it grew in extent and popularity among a large number of the poor in all industrial centres. Canvassers are obliged to collect in their territories a certain amount before they are entitled to the fifteen per cent commission allotted on weekly collections; and, in order to keep their places, they are often obliged to add from their own savings enough to fill unavoidable gaps.

While premiums paid for "industrial" insurance are far in excess of the ordinary life-insurance premiums, the terms are not made as easy as they ought to be; and the same, or almost the same, inexorable rules of cancellation, in case of non-payment of the premium, apply. By lapses as well as by premiums more than fifty per cent above the average, these rich companies have grown richer, and their poor clients poorer. While they have done good by imbuing the minds of our common people with a sense of duty toward their families, they often become encumbrances on their scanty means.

The premium income of two companies of this class exceeds ninety million dollars annually, more than one-third of which is used up for expenses. Each of these two companies began in a modest way. Their stock capital has gradually been increased by the issue of new stock not paid for in cash, but representing earnings chiefly contributed by poor working people. On this capital, now amounting to millions, both companies pay annually from seven to ten per cent in dividends. They could afford to be more lenient than they are to the industrious classes who have laid the foundation of their fortunes, and who continue to be their best customers, without injury to their opulent stockholders. Some of our great railroad companies and other corporations insure their employees against disability through disease and old age, and their families against death, on more favorable terms. If this system were to become more general, it would increase the loyalty of employees to employers, and reduce the enormous rates of "industrial" insurance.

When these industrial companies began to flourish, other corporations were obliged to liquidate. Their failure created a widespread anxiety; and insurance which had been in force shrank from two billions in 1870 to one and a half billion in 1880. A shrinkage of this proportion from the amount insured before the recent troubles began would be disastrous; it would mean a decrease in the amount of valid life insurance of four billion dollars. This may be expected unless managers take some such timely measures as the following to restore confidence and to attract new business:

1. Sell stocks and securities the values of which fluctuate, investing proceeds in first mortgages on improved city realty for two-thirds of its marketable value. Savings of the thrifty should not be exposed to the risk of speculation.

2. Dispose of superfluous buildings acquired in all parts of the world to advertise business, and invest likewise. Policy-holders care for absolute safety more than for marble halls.

3. Cut down salaries and other expenses. The measures taken by the Equitable do not go far enough; retrenchment should be instituted by every other company which does not want to become the target of criticism.

Owners of mutual policies are entitled to a yearly statement of the details and results of the business in which they are interested, just as much as holders of stock in banks, railroads, and industrials. Managers who find a disclosure of these details distasteful should quit the business.

Mutuality has been abandoned by insurers against fire losses, and is almost extinct among marine underwriters. Why should underwriters of life risks, which can be more accurately gauged, continue to adhere almost exclusively to this system? There is one good stock company which does a large and successful business by the issue of non-participating life policies at reasonable rates. Before confidence in them is shaken and their surplus impaired, other independent companies would do well to follow this example. They could all do a larger and safer business if they were to return to the first principles of life insurance, selling, for the smallest premiums consistent with safety, old-line non-participating life policies. By larger and easier sales, agents would find compensation for smaller commissions; to persuade the public, they would not need to misrepresent values of accumulation, endowment, and deferred dividend policies.

For the extensive sale of these expensive policies the public is largely to blame. The most audacious canvassers could not have succeeded by their most insinuating manners to place the large number they did, if the expectation of the insured, that during their lives they would participate in the profits, had not induced them to take them. With the money for premiums, they have left proxies for indefinite periods, empowering the managers to administer the business without restraint. Their credulity has created the vast power of the huge companies which they now ask the Federal Government to control.

Louis Windmüller.

THE NEW MUNICIPAL CODE OF INDIANA.

UNIFORM government in all the cities and towns of Indiana is the end which the new municipal code enacted by the General Assembly this year seeks to achieve. It marks a distinct step forward in city government, and is intended to work a number of important reforms in the general conduct of municipal affairs, placing them on more of a business basis.

The code repeals all so-called individual city charters and separate incorporation acts, with special grants, under which the different municipalities of Indiana have been organized heretofore, and extends the same broad principles of local self-government to all. Owing to the varied systems of management that these cities and towns have had in the past, the experience of one contributed but little to the well-being of its neighbor, each being compelled to learn the same lesson for itself. This fact inspired the code, and it was drafted for the express purpose of meeting the wants of all similar communities within the confines of a State. Indiana's municipal code is constructed after the pattern of the city charter that prescribed the government of Indianapolis, the State's capital city, from early in 1891 until the middle of April, 1905, when the new law went into effect. Thoroughly tried and tested during the fourteen years that it was in force, the Indianapolis charter came to be regarded as one of the best to be found in our country.

In some quarters, what is known as the "city-made charter" is the most approved form of municipal law at the present time. This means a body of law that has been made and adopted by the people themselves for whom it is intended, after which it has been ratified by the legislature of the State, as distinguished from a code of laws originating in the General Assembly, as most city charters do. Constitutional provisions in Missouri and California authorize "city-made charters" for cities having more than 100,000 population. Kansas City, Missouri, is the latest municipality to make its own government. Fourteen years ago Indianapolis, through a committee of public-spirited citizens, built for local needs the body of law which the Indiana legislature approved at the time; and so satisfactory has been its operation in the interim that this year's assembly saw fit to apply the provisions of this organic law, "city-made" according to the latest meaning of the term, to all the cities of the State.   For the larger cities the same machinery of government employed in Indianapolis for fourteen years has been adopted, though minor modifications have been made to adjust it to the varying needs of the smaller ones.   Where a sort of governmental chaos has existed in the local affairs of municipalities within the State, this act is expected to bring about systematic regularity.

The municipal code embodies the federal plan of government.   In adapting it to city needs there have necessarily been some departures, but the fundamental principles have been preserved, and the functions have been separated into three divisions — the executive, legislative, and judicial — very much after the manner outlined in the national Constitution.   The scheme is comprehensive, and its strength lies in its simplicity.   The code is written in direct language, and is stripped of technicalities and legal phrases as far as it is possible for such a document to be.   Complexity has been avoided, and so far no conflict of powers has been encountered.   At the head of the executive department stands the mayor, who is elected by the people for a term of four years. He is not eligible to succeed himself.   Heretofore, all municipal officers in Indiana have been chosen for two years, with no limit to the number of terms.   As experienced in other places, there was a constant temptation to play politics, to the end of securing re-election.   This did not always protect the interests of the people.   Moreover, the two-year term was too short for a mayor to learn how to do things and to get them done.

The position of the mayor in Indiana municipalities under the new order resembles that of the President in relation to the Federal Government.   He is not only responsible for the enforcement of the law, but also exercises a general supervision over all subordinate officers, and is accountable for good order and the efficient government of the city.   He sends an annual message to the Common Council giving a financial statement, and makes such recommendations in writing from time to time as he deems expedient.   All bonds issued and deeds and contracts executed must be signed by the mayor for the city.   He is authorized to appoint competent persons, when required, to examine the accounts of any department.   Power is conferred on the mayor to suspend or revoke any license issued by the city when after a hearing it is proved that any of the stipulated conditions have been violated.

In the enforcement of the laws of the State and the city ordinances, the mayor, as chief executive officer, is assisted by six administrative divisions, known as the departments of public works, public safety, public health and charities, law, finance, and collection and assessment. Excepting for the last department, the mayor appoints all the heads and has the power of their removal within certain limitations. They are directly accountable to him. This organization is like a big machine composed of six interdependent cog-wheels. If it is possible to consider one administrative cog more important than another, since the smooth operation of the entire mechanism depends on the faithful working of all the parts together, it might be said that the department of public works is charged with the greatest responsibilities. As the name implies, it directs all public improvements, besides attending to various other lines of municipal business. Three commissioners, named by the mayor, not more than two of whom may be of the same political party, make up the board of public works.

The services of a city civil engineer appointed by the mayor are at the disposal of the board, and through him it executes the greater part of all public improvements. All street work is done under the direction of this department. Property owners may petition for street improvements, or the board may originate a resolution to improve. But the character and ultimate disposition of a proposed improvement is controlled entirely by the will of the majority of abutting property owners residing on land subject to assessment for the improvement. Property owners cannot defeat a sewer resolution by remonstrance, even though a majority of those affected may be opposed, if in the opinion of the board it is deemed a public necessity. The board cannot order a street improvement the cost of which exceeds one-half the aggregate tax valuation of the property, exclusive of permanent improvements on it, subject to assessment. This limit is determined by a bureau attached to the board, which derives its figures from the assessor's books. Improvement assessments may be paid in a lump or divided into ten payments, each a year apart, the only additional cost being six per cent interest on the unpaid principal.

Land required for city purposes can be condemned by the department of public works. It also has charge of all real and personal property belonging to the city. The board must approve all city plats, as well as those four miles outside of its limits, and has exclusive power to open and vacate streets and alleys; to repair, clean, light, and sprinkle any street, wharf, or public place; to construct and operate public gas works, water works, electric-light works, heating and power plants; to authorize public-service corporations to occupy the streets and alleys; to straighten and deepen watercourses and to control their banks in the city and four miles beyond its limits. These, as well as a number of other powers, are specified.

Three commissioners similar to those in the department of public works make up the board of public safety. This branch of the city government is charged with the exclusive control of all matters and property relating to or connected with the fire and police forces, including the inspection of boilers, of market-places and the foods sold therein, as well as of the pounds and prisons. A civil-service code, or, more properly speaking, a sort of merit system, is provided to govern the fire and police forces. Not more than half of either force may be chosen from one political party. Appointees may be removed for any cause other than politics after a hearing. Safety commissioners and their employees are prohibited from participating directly or indirectly in politics on pain of a heavy penalty.

Salaries for department commissioners are prescribed by the municipal code according to the size of the city which they serve, while the pay of their subordinates is regulated by local ordinance. The code authorizes police and firemen's pension funds under municipal direction, supported by the city and members of the respective forces. Attached to the safety department is the building inspections bureau, which is charged with the enforcement of building regulations adopted by the city council. Humane officers, police matrons, and an inspector of weights and measures are other auxiliary attachés of the board of public safety.

The board of public health and charities consists of three doctors chosen by the mayor under the same restrictions as the other boards. These members appoint a sanitarian, who also acts as secretary to the board. He is the executive officer of the board, charged with the enforcement of all the laws and ordinances pertaining to health, and toward this end he directs the sanitary police and inspectors. This department has supervision over the city hospital and free dispensary, naming superintendents for each. It issues regulations concerning contagious diseases, and establishes quarantines whenever necessary. Inspectors of meat, milk, and other food, are attached to the board, and it is their duty to keep a close watch on matters intimately connected with the health of the community. The health office keeps a complete register of the city's vital statistics.

Park affairs in cities having more than 45,000 inhabitants are administered by an auxiliary department of public parks, composed of four members appointed by the mayor, not more than two of whom may be of the same political party. This board is regarded as non-political because of the division which is supposed to be equal between the two leading parties. It is so constituted as to be continuous. The term of one member expires every year. Each commissioner is appointed for a term of four years. In the case of all other boards, the terms of the commissioners end with the administration that appointed them.

It requires a majority vote of all members of the park board to take action. In case of a tie, the mayor, as *ex-officio* member, has the deciding vote to prevent deadlocks. Park commissioners get no pay for their services, but allowances can be made to them for expenses incurred while performing their duties. This department has full authority over all parks, parkways, boulevards, and public playgrounds; controlling, improving, and maintaining them subject to the laws and ordinances in force. The board is assisted by a superintendent of parks and such engineers, surveyors, clerks, and other employees as it may appoint. The board disburses all money allotted to it for parks by the city council. It has authority to make rules prohibiting objectionable business or amusement, such as saloons and dance-halls, within 500 feet of land under its jurisdiction.

The management of municipal finance is divided between two administrative divisions of the city government according to the code. The city controller, appointed by the mayor, presides over what is called the finance department. He acts in the capacity of auditor and must approve all allowances made by the other branches of the city management. Each claim for $25 or more must be accompanied by an affidavit that it is fair and just. The controller must guard against the drawing of warrants for the expenditure of money for purposes for which there is no specific appropriation available. He is required to keep a complete set of books, independently of the other departments, in order to have a check on them at all times. It is a part of his duty to keep a record of the city's bonded indebtedness and to make preparations to pay off the obligations as they fall due, or to keep up the interest payments. Under a constitutional provision of the State, the municipal borrowing power is limited to two per cent of the taxable valuation of a city or town. The controller makes up the annual budget of expense each year in advance and recommends to the city council the appropriations needed, consisting of specific items for all departments, as well as the tax levy required to raise the money. The council may decrease the controller's recommendations, but it cannot increase them. No appropriation can be made without the controller's approval, and a two-thirds vote of the council is necessary for favorable action.

The city treasurer has actual custody of the funds. He is the head of the department of assessment and collection. Municipalities that are county seats can call upon the county treasurer to act as city treasurer. This arrangement is a part of the State's general tax machinery, and as the duties are very much alike, they have been combined to simplify matters and in the interests of economy. Where an arrangement of this kind cannot be made, the people elect a city treasurer. The treasurer collects the taxes, license fees, and public improvement assessments, and he disburses the city's money on orders from the controller. Assessments for taxation and their equalization are made by the State and county boards of review. In cities of 100,000 population and over, the council may assess not to exceed 90 cents on each $100 of taxable property for city purposes. Smaller municipalities are permitted to levy $1.25 on the same basis.

The head of the city's law department is the city attorney, appointed by the mayor. He has charge of all the city's legal affairs. As corporation counsel, he advises the different departments when consulted, draws up ordinances at request, and prepares all of the city's legal documents and contracts. When the city is involved in any litigation, he represents it. The city attorney is prohibited from appearing for any person or corporation in any controversy or negotiation in which the city has any interest.

The municipal code vests the judicial power of Indiana communities in a city court which is presided over by a police judge, assisted by the city clerk and a bailiff. Judge and clerk are elected by the people for a term of four years, and, like the mayor, they are not eligible to succeed themselves. The court appoints the bailiff. It has jurisdiction in cases of crimes and misdemeanors within certain limitations, while exclusive original jurisdiction is given over all violations of city ordinances. Infractions of statutes are prosecuted by the prosecutor for the judicial circuit, a county official. The city attorney prosecutes all violations of city ordinances. Both prosecutors may have special deputies at the court to represent them. The city court can assess fines up to $500, and can also impose a jail or workhouse sentence of six months. Appeals from the findings of this court may be taken to the circuit or criminal courts of the district. All records of the court are kept by the city clerk, who also collects the fines and costs assessed by the court, making a monthly report of them to the controller, and turning over the money received to the treasurer. The clerk is custodian of the city seal. In addition to these and similar other duties, the clerk is required to attend all meetings of the city council, acting as its secretary and keeping a full minute of its proceedings.

The municipal legislative authority is vested in one body — a common council elected by the people. Each city ward is represented in this body by one member, and the whole city elects one-half as many members at large as there are wards. In the larger cities the council designates one of its number to preside, and the presiding officer names the standing committees. The mayor presides over council deliberations in the smaller ones. The council has the power, by a two-thirds vote, to expel any member for violation of his official duty. One regular meeting must be held each month, and special meetings may be called as often as necessary.

Fifty-three paragraphs in the code define the powers conferred on the city council in regard to purposes for which ordinances may be enacted. They are explicit and include almost everything in which municipal government is concerned. Besides the usual powers possessed by city councils, those in Indiana have new ones which are regarded as important. By ordinance, cities may decide to collect and destroy their garbage or to put the city waste to beneficial use. Municipal ownership of all public-service utilities may be authorized by ordinance. Power is given to limit the height of buildings in any locality to insure beauty and symmetry. The right to license, tax, and regulate vehicles is made general instead of being limited to those used for freight or hire, as heretofore. The council can regulate, license, tax, and even prohibit shows and entertainments by ordinance. This authority extends even to those that do not demand and receive money. Saloons may be excluded from residence districts which the council can define, and railroad companies can be compelled to light their track crossings with lamps such as are in use in other parts of the city.

A veto power is vested in the mayor. All ordinances passed by the council must be signed by him within ten days after receiving them. If he fails to approve, the measure must be passed again by a two-thirds vote of all members before becoming effective. All ordinances passed must be published for two consecutive weeks in a newspaper of general circulation. The council can authorize a sinking fund for the gradual extinguishment of the bonded indebtedness, a special levy being permitted for this purpose. Sinking-fund commissioners, three in number, are appointed by the mayor. They have charge of the fund and must lend it to the highest bidder. The controller acts as secretary to this commission.

For the purposes of this general law, all cities in Indiana are divided into five classes according to population based on the United States census: First class, cities of 100,000 and more (Indianapolis is the only city in this class); second class, cities between 45,000 and 100,000; third class, cities between 20,000 and 45,000; fourth class, cities between 10,000 and 20,000; fifth class, cities of less than 10,000. The various sections of the act explain fully how the different powers are assigned to the cities of different sizes. As the municipalities become smaller, there is a telescoping of powers, because the demands are not so extended as to require a form of government so highly developed. Cities of the third class may provide by ordinance that the department of public works shall discharge the duties of the board of public safety; and in cities of the fourth and fifth classes, they are to be so discharged without the passage of an ordinance. In the last two classifications, the mayor appoints the marshal, fire chief, and street superintendent, while the council exercises the power of the main departments which are curtailed. All but cities of the fifth class have a police court and special judge. In the last class the mayor acts as judge.

The mayor's power of appointment concerning the members of the different boards and other city officials, as already indicated, is broad, and he is permitted to remove any appointee at will, only being required to file his reasons in writing for the removal with the city clerk. The code permits the boards to name their clerks and subordinate employees and to adopt regulations to govern them. To eliminate corporation influence from municipal government, no officer, agent, employee, or servant of any corporation, firm company, or persons holding or operating under a franchise granted by any city, or having any contract with the city, shall be eligible to any city office. Neither can a city enter a contract with an employee. Violation of these provisions renders the offender liable to a fine of $1,000 and from one to ten years in the State prison. Different city attorneys have given conflicting opinions as to the validity of these prohibitions, and thus far there has been no appeal to the courts for a construction. There is much fear, however, that, taken literally, the section may deprive many Indiana cities and towns of the valuable services of experienced men who would not let their business connections influence them in the discharge of their civic duties.

After the fashion of the Federal Government, the municipal code provides that the heads of the administrative departments shall constitute the mayor's cabinet. These advisers are to meet each month with the chief executive to consult on the affairs of the city and to exchange ideas, keeping minutes of the cabinet meetings. A similar requirement was contained in the Indianapolis charter, though it has never been carefully observed. The new code makes it obligatory upon officials to heed it because of the benefits to be derived from mutual consultation. The fullest amount of publicity possible for all public business transacted is encouraged by the municipal code.

Public contracts are to be let at all times to the "lowest and best" bidders after advertisement in the daily papers soliciting representative competition. Bidders to qualify must make affidavit that they have not entered any "combine" and that they are not parties to any collusion. By prescribing uniform methods of making public improvements and letting contracts throughout the entire State, it is believed that the law will be the means of obtaining more extended competition. Until now the different municipalities in Indiana have been proceeding under varying laws. As a result of this condition, contractors with limited means were afraid to branch out and bid on work where they were uncertain of their rights, and they could not afford to hire counsel for each job to look up the law. Under such conditions, a few big contracting firms got the major part of the public-improvement work at their own figures, with little or no competition, and it has been the experience that small contractors bring the prices down.

The code places no limit on the time for which public franchises may be granted. Under former laws the limitation ranged from ten to thirty-four years, according to the nature of the franchise. The new law permits cities and towns to contract for water, light, heat, and motive power for a period of twenty-four years. Formerly the limit was ten. All franchises and contracts coming under these regulations are entered by the board of public works on behalf of the city, and after having been approved by the mayor, they must be ratified by ordinance passed by the city council.

Henceforth, all municipal elections in the State will be held at the same time, coming once every four years. The first city elections under the code will be held next November, and the officials chosen at that time will take office January 1, 1906. As a result of this change, the terms of some persons now holding city offices will be shortened, while those of others will be slightly increased. The law provides that city elections shall fall in odd years, to remove any possible influence that national, State, or county campaigns coming at the same time might exert to prejudice the result of local contests. It has been demonstrated in the larger cities of Indiana that municipal elections fought out purely on local issues, away from the distractions of general elections, are usually carried on their merits, the voters casting their ballots independently of party affiliations. Property qualifications are not necessary to hold municipal office in Indiana, and all persons are entitled to vote at city elections who can qualify at general elections under the State constitution.

Communities having less than 2,500 inhabitants are regarded as towns, and the municipal code (called the cities and towns act) provides a separate form of government for them. To organize a town, one-third of the voters living in the district to be incorporated must file a petition with the board of county commissioners, and, if they approve, a majority of voters must ratify the incorporation at a special election.

Towns are governed by a board of trustees, one member being chosen from each ward. A clerk and treasurer — one person attending to both duties if desired — is also elected. As clerk, he has charge of the records of the board of trustees, issues all licenses authorized by law, and keeps the town seal. As treasurer, he receives and disburses all town funds. The board selects one of its number to preside. It names the marshal, who may also be required to act as street commissioner and fire chief.

The town board has executive and legislative powers. As a law-making body, it can pass ordinances on almost all subjects over which the municipal code gives city councils similar power, and in turn it directs the enforcement of these ordinances. The board can buy, hold, and dispose of real estate for the town. It must provide fire protection and prescribe police regulations; supervise the public health; open and vacate streets and alleys, as well as order their improvement; regulate railroads and interurban cars in the town; contract for light, water, and heat or build plants for them; these besides many other powers. The board can borrow money and issue bonds. It is authorized to levy the town taxes for general purposes and schools. The code gives the town trustees charge of the public schools, while in cities the school community is independent of the rest of the city government. Prosecutions for law violations in towns are brought before the circuit court of the county or a justice of the peace.

After a town reaches 2,500 population, it can incorporate as a city. A petition signed by one-third of the qualified voters must be filed with the trustees, whereupon they can order a special election, and if on that occasion a majority of the voters favor the change, the town becomes a city and is governed by the provisions of the code relating to municipalities of its size. The law also provides a method whereby cities may become towns again, and towns dissolve their incorporation as individual communities.

These are the principal features contained in Indiana's new municipal code. There are many other details not mentioned in this outline which will be of more than passing interest to the student of city government. To treat of them all would require a volume of liberal size, as the law itself consists of 272 sections and covers 191 printed pages. The code marks the first serious effort on the part of an American State to give to all its cities and towns a uniform system of local government. A code of municipal laws was adopted in Ohio some years ago as an expedient, because it had been held by the courts that the individual acts under which the different cities were operating, which created separate classes for special purposes, were unconstitutional. It became necessary, therefore, to take a radical step to correct this condition; and a body of law was hastily drawn up and enacted, which, according to reports, has proved to be anything but satisfactory.

The Indiana code is the result of a sincere desire of the cities and towns of the State to get on a firmer and sounder business basis. In response to this desire, the General Assembly of 1903 appointed a commission to frame a suitable bill. After working on it for two years, the bill reported to the legislature in 1905 by the commission did not conform entirely to the requirements of the people, although its contents showed a tendency in the right direction. The citizens of Indianapolis were loath to give up the charter which had been in force for fourteen years, and upon their approval it was taken bodily and inserted into the municipal code, with such slight changes as were necessary for the smaller towns. Several modifications were also made in the light of fourteen years of experience in Indianapolis, though the major part of the law retains the same phrasing that was adopted in 1891.

Just how the new law will affect the various communities of the State remains to be seen. However, most of the important points in the law subject to question have already been raised during the fourteen years of operation of the Indianapolis charter, and the Supreme Court of Indiana has passed on many of them. Thus the cities and towns of the State have the benefit of a code of laws the fundamental principles of which have been construed and firmly established. This was one of the strongest arguments put forward in its behalf, and the one that was largely responsible for its ultimate adoption.   H. O. STECHHAN.

THE FORUM.

VOL. XXXVII, NO. 3.

JANUARY—MARCH, 1906.

NEW YORK:

THE FORUM PUBLISHING COMPANY.

PRESS OF
THE PUBLISHERS' PRINTING COMPANY
82, 84 LAFAYETTE PLACE
NEW YORK

The Forum

JANUARY, 1906.

AMERICAN POLITICS.

THE first session of the Fifty-ninth Congress opened on the fourth of December and recalled the Republican landslide of 1904. Of the 386 members who answered the roll call, only 137 were Democrats, giving to the dominant party a majority of 112, a much larger total than any political organization has enjoyed in recent years.

The two parties, so far as the House is concerned, entered upon the work of the session with well-defined purposes. Under the lead of Speaker Cannon, who has been a consistent "stand-patter" on the tariff question, a majority of the Republican contingent was aligned against any revision of the schedules. In order to make it certain that the ways and means committee would not introduce any measure relating to the tariff, the personnel of that committee was radically changed, and none but the most avowed opponents of tariff reform were assigned to it. This policy was so openly followed as to lead to the transfer of Representative Mc-Cleary, of Minnesota, an ardent protectionist, from the appropriations committee, where he held the ranking place and was the logical choice for chairman, to the ways and means committee, while Representative Tawney, of the same State, who believes in revision, was taken from the ways and means committee and given the chairmanship of the committee on appropriations. Speaker Cannon, by this action, killed two birds with one stone. He made it practically certain that any suggestion in regard to a revision of the tariff would meet with disfavor in the room of the committee on ways and means, and he also placed in commanding position an able and forceful exponent of his ideas with respect to federal economy.

It has long been emphasized in these contributions to THE FORUM that revision of the tariff, if not absolutely declined by Congress, would be undertaken with grudging assent. The progress of events has abundantly demonstrated the accuracy of these predictions. The President, realizing that the sentiment of the national legislature is not in sympathy with his own views, contented himself with referring to the subject in his annual message only in the slightest possible degree. It may be that he will later discuss tariff reform more fully in a special message; but none the less will he still find determined and persistent opposition. Under these circumstances it may be taken for granted, therefore, that the question of tariff revision will not figure to any large extent during the present session of Congress.

Very different, however, is the situation in regard to the proposed railroad rebate legislation. The question of railroad rates belongs, primarily, to the consideration of the financial department of this magazine, so that no discussion of the commercial aspect of the matter will be here attempted. Politically, however, railroad rebates and other alleged discriminations are certain to have a potent effect in approaching campaigns, and the first skirmish of future battles will be fought in the Capitol at Washington this winter. Thus we find Representative John Sharp Williams, of Mississippi, the minority leader, asserting, in his speech to the Democratic caucus, that the Democrats will stand solidly behind the President in the latter's efforts to secure reasonable railroad rates and in applying the most stringent legislation against the trusts. He claimed, at the same time, that the President's position regarding the railroads was more Democratic than Republican.

As a political issue, the regulation of the railroad rates through governmental supervision will undoubtedly be a popular one. Senator Burkett, of Nebraska, did not exaggerate the sentiment in the West when he asserted that in his State the railroad problem overshadowed every other issue. In a country so thoroughly dependent upon transportation as the United States, every question relating to the railroads touches an innumerable throng of people in all classes of society. The tariff, with its multitudinous schedules, is the only subject comparable with it. Not only the manufacturing centres of the East, but the great agricultural regions of the West as well, are vitally affected. "The farmers," said Secretary Wilson, upon his return from a Western trip, "have never been so interested in anything as they are in the railroad rate question. They are not particularly against the railroads," he added, "but they are anxious to get a square deal and prevent further discrimination." The great mass of the people who must, wittingly or unwittingly, pay tribute to the railroads are, therefore, with the President. They want federal interference and supervision to the extent of freeing them from real or fancied imposition, and they believe that the President is the Moses who will deliver them from their bondage.

As with all great questions, however, there is a divergence of views as to the wisdom of federal legislation concerning railroads, and this difference is not marked by party hnes. It will be found, when the proposed legislation reaches the voting stage, that both parties will be divided. Senators and Representatives will be influenced not by party dictates, but by their environments. The split in the Republican organization is already more than a mere rift. Senator Elkins, of West Virginia, whose railroad interests are very extensive, and who has lived all his life in a railroad atmosphere, so to speak, is outspoken in his hostility to the more advanced ideas of the head of his party; while Senator Foraker, of Ohio, is also in avowed antagonism. Senator Elkins occupies the important and influential position of chairman of the committee on interstate commerce, which has the railroad rate question under its jurisdiction, and it is certain that any bill which he will support will be of the most innocuous character.

Nor does Senator Elkins stand alone. The list which is presented as purporting to give the President's opponents includes Senators Platt and Depew, of New York; Kean and Dryden, of New Jersey; Penrose, of Pennsylvania; Alger, of Michigan; Scott, of West Virginia; Hopkins, of Illinois; Perkins and Flint, of California; and Heyburn, of Idaho. It is impossible to vouch for this list at the present time, but none the less is it certain that many Republican Senators who are inclined to support the President upon every other issue will come to the parting of the ways with him when railroad legislation is placed before them. On the other hand, some twenty Democratic Senators, including Bacon and Clay, of Georgia; Bailey and Culberson, of Texas; Overman, of North Carolina; Stone, of Missouri; and, in fact nearly the entire Southern and Western representation, will earnestly support the President. We find, then, in this question of governmental supervision of railroad rates, an issue large enough to rend party lines in Congress; and any issue which produces this result among the people's representatives is certain to have the same effect among the people themselves.

Congress is, therefore, entering upon an important political struggle. It may be that the opponents of railroad-rate legislation in the Senate can successfully exert their influence and prevent the enactment of the proposed measure. This, however, will only prolong the contest. As in the case of the contest for the free coinage of silver, the halls of Congress will be the great forum wherein the issue will be formulated in order that it may be presented intelligently to the people. The chances are almost entirely with the ultimate success of the President's views. In the first place, it is a plausible appeal to the country to ask for the abolition of all discriminations made by the railroad corporations in favor of the large shippers. The latter are comparatively few; the small shippers are legion. There is in the air, also, a spirit of revolt against corporations, and any suggestion to restrain their power by federal legislation meets with a responsive sentiment. There is a growing feeling that the public is not strong enough to cope with the great combinations of capital, and governmental aid is welcomed. In addition to this, the personality of President Roosevelt has attracted to him a following of enormous proportions, made up of persons who believe that everything he does is right. These people will stand by him in the railroad issue, satisfied that he is upholding their interests. Eventually, therefore, some legislation along the line of the President's suggestion will be enacted; and the railroads would be wise if, foreseeing this certain result, they would compromise now upon legislation which, under the circumstances, would be most favorable to them. It is easy to believe that the time is not far distant when their position in the matter may receive but scant consideration, and when the undesirable Government ownership of railroads may be a political issue forced upon the people.

The outlook in Congress, therefore, is that there will be no legislation upon the tariff, despite the appeals of the reformers, and that railroad-rate legislation will be the absorbing issue, with the probability of some action. These two questions do not include, by any manner of means, all the important matters which ought to receive attention. Congress has been too prone in late years to avoid legislating upon subjects which ought to receive earnest attention. It has been the proud boast of more than one leader in the past that Congress has met, debated, and adjourned without doing anything more than passing the various appropriation bills. It is true that too little legislation is better than too much legislation; and yet Congress can devote much time to excellent advantage if it will take up and settle those questions which have been allowed to drift over from session to session without final decision.

Important legislation is demanded for the Philippines, while conditions in Porto Rico require the most careful consideration. Some attention ought also to be given to the wants of the people of Hawaii, while the situation in Alaska is one that should be remedied at the earliest possible moment. Alaska, like Topsy, has "jest growed." It has reached its age of maturity a neglected child. Its government is a makeshift and an apology. Notwithstanding the fact that for years it has poured its wealth into the parent country, its appeals to Congress have gone almost unheeded, until now the feeling is prevalent in the Territory that Congress has little or no concern in its welfare. The Philippines, Hawaii, Porto Rico, Alaska — all these are our possessions and must be regarded with paternal care. We cannot, as seems to be the case, accept the position of guardian to all these peoples, and then shirk the enormous responsibilities which that guardianship entails upon us.

There is work for Congress also in the matter of the admission of new States. Indian Territory, Oklahoma, Arizona, and New Mexico have knocked at the door of Congress without avail. Political considerations of the most selfish character have, in the main, been interposed successfully against these appeals. In the cases of Arizona and New Mexico, the delay may not have been unwise: Oklahoma and Indian Territory, however, are flourishing communities and might well be admitted as one State. There ought to be legislation, also, to develop the merchant marine, to punish severely the adulteration of food, to throw additional safeguards around our immigration, and to prevent the people from being defrauded of the public lands. The question of dealing fairly with the Chinese without letting down the bars is one that might well command the thoughtful attention of our legislators. This does not by any means exhaust the list of subjects upon which Congressional action is demanded. It is to be hoped, therefore, that the Republican leaders, who have behind them a majority of such proportions that the Democrats can hardly muster sufficient force to demand a roll call, will, in the very beginning of the session, formulate a programme which will embrace all of the important topics, and then see to it that the legislation is enacted. In his address to the Republican caucus, prior to the opening of the session, Speaker Cannon expressed the hope that all business would be transacted promptly, in order that an early adjournment might be reached. The prompt disposition of business is, certainly, much to be desired, but an early adjournment is not equally commendable if it is accomplished at the expense of many omissions.

One of the first acts of the Republican caucus was the adoption of a resolution continuing the rules of the last Congress. There was no objection. The protest against the rules which has been spasmodically made during the past few years was not even heard. The one-man power which, since the days of Thomas B. Reed, has been dominant in the House of Representatives was continued without a murmur.

This unanimous action on the part of the Republican representatives indicates their complete and perfect satisfaction with the rules under which they are governed. If the majority of the House is, therefore, content, it may not be in the province of an outsider to interpose any objection. At the same time, it is worth while to call attention again to the manner in which the members of the House abdicate their positions and allow supreme control of all business to be vested in the Speaker. The *modus operandi* is easily explained. Thousands upon thousands of bills are introduced in the House at each session and referred to committees. Such of these measures as are reported are placed upon the calendar. It is easy to see, however, that this docket is soon so overcrowded as to make it impossible to secure consideration for even a small number of the various measures, especially as each committee is restricted to a certain day upon which it can bring its measures before the House. In order to extricate favored legislation from this accumulated mass upon the calendar, a committee on rules is appointed, which committee has the power to report an order for the consideration of a certain measure, and it fixes the day and hour upon which the final vote shall be taken. It is, of course, within the power of the House to vote adversely upon this rule; but, as a matter of fact, the Speaker and the committee on rules can confidently rely upon the requisite support, because few of the majority members are willing to run the risk of opposing the desire of the men who dominate the House.

This committee on rules is merely a pleasant fiction. It is composed of the Speaker and four members, the latter representing equally the majority and minority parties. The two members of the majority, appointed by the Speaker, are really reflections of his will. They vote with him, as otherwise they would be displaced for more willing colleagues; and so, in the last analysis, the committee on rules is the Speaker. Practically, therefore, he controls the entire legislation of the House. If he is against the measure, it will die upon the calendar; if he is for it, consideration is certain to be obtained. Nor is his power thus limited. He appoints the committees in the very beginning of the session; and these committees, in their personnel, are exponents of his own views. If he is opposed to revising the tariff, the ways and means committee is composed of ultra-protectionists; if he desires a change in the schedules, he places men upon the committee who will frame and report the necessary statute. He still further has his hand upon the legislative throttle in that he can recognize or not, at his pleasure, any member who desires to bring a subject to the attention of the House. Any member who rises to address the House is at once questioned by the Speaker as to his purpose, and if that purpose be not agreeable to the occupant of the Speaker's chair the desired privilege is immediately denied.

It can be easily seen that this enormous power, when lodged in the hands of an unscrupulous man, can be improperly exercised. Fortunately, this charge does not lie against the present Speaker, whose rugged honesty and intense patriotism insure a wise dispatch of Congressional business. Any one familiar with the records of the House, however, knows that the beginning of the isthmian canal would not have been postponed until President Roosevelt's administration if an effort to secure the necessary authorization by Congress had not been refused by an occupant of the Speaker's chair in the face of an appeal signed by a large majority of his own party on the floor. As long as he denied consideration for the canal measure, it was impossible to bring it before the House. What happened in this instance may be repeated at any time.

The system has been accurately described as un-Republican, un-Democratic, and un-American. It may be asked, therefore, Why is it continued? The answer is, first, that the large membership of the House makes autocratic direction and control a necessity. It has been realized that unless the final word of authority was lodged somewhere, either the House would drift along, frittering away its time in the consideration of innumerable minor bills, or else it would become inextricably tangled in the meshes of endless debate and possible filibustering. The plan by which this undesirable situation is now avoided may not be perfect, but it is the best that has been devised. Substitutes which have been suggested do not seem to be acceptable, and in the lack of a more desirable method the present system obtains. The fact that it is endured does not, however, prove that it is either right or just. On the contrary, it is responsible, among other things, for the constant change in the personnel of the House. Members are being retired session after session because of their apparent inability to accomplish anything for their constituents, when the fault is not with them, but with the system that renders them utterly powerless. The House, in the olden days, developed great debaters and great leaders. Men with force and ability carved their way to the front because they had ample opportunity to display their masterful qualities. To-day, no man can propose and advocate any measure with any hope of success unless his ideas are in harmony with those of the coterie that controls the business of the House. Few men have the courage to run counter to this all-powerful domination. The path to success lies in acquiescence, not in antagonism. Under these circumstances, it is not remarkable that individual brilliance and ability are repressed.

This system of governing the House has undoubtedly worked to the detriment of that body in the prominence which it has forced upon the Senate. The session of Congress began, as usual, with the attention of the country riveted upon the upper body. With each succeeding year the lower branch of Congress has become less and less important. It may pass a railroad-rate bill, as was the case during the last session; but, in

20

the confident knowledge that the Senate will not sanction such legislation, the action of the House is allowed to pass without comment. Even if the House should, during the present session, decide that tariff reform was desirable — a result not likely to be reached — the Senate would still be considered the paramount factor. It has come to be admitted nowadays that the House has lost its former hold upon public attention. The focus of concern is the Senate.

One reason for this state of affairs is that there is no longer any House, speaking in the broad sense. In former times, in order accurately to forecast the outcome of proposed legislation, it was necessary to make a canvass of that body, or, at least, to learn the position of some twenty or thirty leading exponents of its sentiment. To-day it is only necessary to know accurately whether the Speaker is for or against any proposition, in order to predict confidently whether or not the measure will be considered and acted upon. It is, in other words, the Speaker who must be consulted, not the House. Another potent consideration is that, while the House has expanded in numbers until it has become a large and almost unwieldy body, the Senate has remained small, compact, and well-disciplined. In the first Congress there were twenty-six Senators and less than fifty Representatives. In more than one hundred years the membership of the Senate has only increased to ninety, while the total of the House has reached nearly four hundred.

As has already been shown, the immense size of the House compels the direction of all legislation by the Speaker and a coterie of his personally selected advisers, every member of the House being largely dependent upon the favor of the Speaker for opportunity to demonstrate and develop his legislative talent. In the Senate, however, each Senator is a law unto himself. He is the one-ninetieth part of an organization composed of individual factors. His right to bring to the attention of his colleagues any matter which he may deem important is not abridged. He commands recognition from the chair, without regard to the purpose which he may have in mind when he arises. He is not beholden to the favor of any one man for his committee assignments; for appointments to committees are determined by a committee of seven or nine representatives of each party, and individual preferences are consulted and regarded in the largest possible degree. In the Senate a man is, in the fullest sense of the word, a Senator of the United States, with all the participation in legislation that the name implies, and is not, like a member of the House, subjected to rules and limitations which repress ambition, neutralize intellectual vigor, and discourage even the most optimistic soul.

The second point of vantage possessed by the Senate is the term of six years enjoyed by its personnel. The member of the House, elected for two years, is scarcely in his seat before he is on the eve of another campaign. He must bow to every wind that blows, unless, indeed, he values his independence more than his position. The Senator, on the other hand, is not disturbed by the fear of an immediate verdict upon his action. Long before the Legislature of his State has occasion to pass upon his name again, his position, if for a time at variance with public sentiment, fades away into forgetfulness, and later and more engrossing questions absorb the public mind. In addition to this, each Senator stands in a closer relation to the President than a member of the House. He is a part of the treaty-making power, and it is by his vote that the appointees selected by the President are confirmed. The President naturally treats every Representative with courteous consideration; but, after all, his chief reliance for support must be upon those who are closest to the Speaker. In the Senate, however, the good will of each Senator is almost essential to the unobstructed accomplishment of his plans. In the scheme of legislation, each Senator is an important individual factor, occupying a position vastly different from that maintained by a member of the House.

The power possessed by a Senator is greatly enhanced by the fact that he can, at any time, interpose himself as a substantial obstacle in the pathway of desired legislation. The rules of the Senate do not recognize the limitation of debate. Any Senator may, therefore, discuss any measure as long as his vocabulary is not exhausted; and if he can bring to his opposition even a small minority of his colleagues, he can seriously menace, if not actually prevent, the passage of any bill. It should be added, however, that this power of blocking legislation is not often exercised, unless a vital principle is at issue or unless the minority is so nearly a majority that a straw would turn the scale. In other words, a strong, determined majority of the Senate, backed by public sentiment, has never been successfully thwarted. In two notable instances, the so-called force bill and the bill for the repeal of the Sherman silver purchasing law, the former was defeated because a majority of the Senate voted to displace its position of privileged consideration, and the latter was passed, despite the three months' struggle of its opponents, because it was supported by a majority of the Senate and desired by a large proportion of the people of the United States. The point which it is desired to emphasize here, however, is that each Senator has the opportunity and the power to make his individual impress upon legislation if he so desires; and until the position of practically every Senator is clearly defined, the fate of a measure may be in doubt. It is this uncertainty which makes the Senate an object of interest, an uncertainty which is all the more perplexing because votes may be changed in the closing hours of a debate.

The opening of Congress, therefore, impresses upon the public mind these two important facts: that the Speaker is the controlling factor in the House and that the dominance of the Senate is becoming more and more apparent.

It is unfortunate that there exists between the Senate and the House a jealousy which ought not to have any foundation, and which, in fact, frequently interferes with the accomplishment of definite results. This feeling may be, during the present session, again manifested to the detriment of desirable legislation. Upon one question, however, both branches of Congress will be united. The appropriation bills will be held down by the respective committees in the House to the lowest possible figure consistent with the proper operation of the Government, and the Senate will consider wisely and well any proposed additions. It is now quite evident that Congress must not only avoid extravagance, but must reduce to a minimum the amounts needed for current departmental expenses. This condition of affairs is fully appreciated by Speaker Cannon, and his influence toward a healthy economy will permeate the House. The necessities arising from the war with Spain led to a freedom of expenditure which it has been difficult to curb; but the time has come when the greatest amount of care and self-denial must be exercised, as otherwise the deficit will reach an aggregate which will command the adverse attention of the country. Above all things, Speaker Cannon desires to go before the country with an even balance sheet; and, to accomplish this result, he must lay a restraining hand upon every unnecessary item proposed for the federal budgets.

Inasmuch as a Congressional campaign will occur next fall, we can expect to find, during the session, a political trend in all the debates. The Democrats, as usual, will attack the trusts and insist upon a revision of the tariff. The Republicans will emphasize the present prosperity, attributing it to their administration of national affairs, and will defend their non-action upon the tariff question by asserting that it is wise to let well enough alone. Incidentally, there will be some discussion of municipal ownership and possibly of the advantages of governmental possession of the railroads. We may also expect to hear an echo of the testimony elicited during the life-insurance investigation regarding contributions to the campaign fund of the Republican party.

When the fact was disclosed that the New York Life Insurance Company had given $150,000 in aid of the election of Republican candidates in three Presidential campaigns, Judge Parker, erstwhile Democratic candidate for President, emerged from his seclusion long enough to denounce the action. He asserted that practically all the large corporations had contributed to the treasury of the Republican party. "The officers responsible for these raids upon the treasuries of corporations," said Judge

Parker, "have received their reward in unfettered management of different insurance corporations; in unembarrassed raids upon the public through trusts, condemned by both common and statute law; in refusal to punish criminally the officers of railroad and other corporations violating the laws; and in statutory permission to manufacturing corporations to levy tribute on the people." And, according to Judge Parker, not only was this immunity thus purchased, but worse results were attained "in the gradual demoralization of voters and the dulling of the public conscience caused by the efforts to make these vast sums of money procure the ballots they were intended to procure, corruptly or otherwise."

All this is undoubtedly true; but, unfortunately, the Democratic party, of which Judge Parker is the chief spokesman, does not come into court with clean hands. Everybody who is at all familiar with the operations of a campaign knows that the Democratic managers have always been as anxious to secure and as willing to accept the contributions of the great corporations as have been their political opponents. Neither party can plead not guilty to the charge of accepting monetary considerations from questionable sources. Any effort to still further probe into this matter will therefore be looked upon askance by the practical politicians in both parties. This will not, however, deter many honest and well-intentioned souls from attempting to free political organizations in this country from being under obligations to great corporations.

The present programme is to seek the enactment of a law which will compel the national campaign committees to make a public record of the names of their contributors. The first step in the direction of curbing corporation contributions was taken in February, 1901, when Senator Chandler, of New Hampshire, introduced a bill in the Senate to prohibit corporations from making money contributions in connection with political elections. The bill provided that it should be unlawful for any national bank, or any corporation engaged in interstate or foreign commerce, or any corporation organized by authority of the laws of Congress to make a money contribution in connection with any election to any political office. The bill also provided that it should be unlawful for any corporation whatever to make a contribution in connection with any election at which a Senator or a Representative was to be voted for. The penalty for making such contribution was fixed at a fine of $5,000 against the corporation, with an additional fine of $1,000 against each officer, stockholder, director, or employee who consented to the contribution.

The measure was reported from the committee on privileges and elections, of which Senator Chandler was chairman; but inasmuch as only a few days of the session remained, it expired with the Congress. It is hardly likely that it would have been passed, even with ample time; but it would have given rise to much discussion, which was possibly the main object of its introduction. During the last session ex-Representative Belmont, of New York, suggested a bill compelling the publication of the names of all contributors to national campaign funds, and a measure of this character is likely to be presented during this year. It will receive Democratic support; for, in late years at least, the money of the corporations has not been finding its way very generously into the Democratic treasury.

The amount of money received and disbursed in a national campaign is always a subject of popular interest, although necessarily involved in much secrecy. An interesting contribution to the literature of this subject was recently printed in the Washington "Post," wherein facts and figures were presented with a confidence that indicated more than the usual degree of knowledge. From my own acquaintance with the conduct of national campaigns, the figures are near enough to the truth to be worthy of reproduction here. They are as follows:

Fund of the Republican National Committee in 1904.........$1,900,000
Fund of the Republican National Committee in 1900.......... 2,800,000
Fund of the Republican National Committee in 1896.......... 3,800,000
Fund of the Democratic National Committee in 1896......... 4,100,000

According to the same authority, the Republican fund last year was disbursed as follows:

Remittances to State committees...........................$700,000
For literature... 550,000
Maintaining Speakers' bureau............................... 175,000
For lithographs, advertising, etc.......................... 150,000
Salaries and expenses at headquarters...................... 150,000
Miscellaneous expenses..................................... 75,000
Balance at close of campaign............................... 100,000

These sums are much smaller than are popularly accredited to the total of campaign contributions. It has always been supposed, for instance, that the fund at the command of Senator Hanna during the campaign of 1896 was between $5,000,000 and $6,000,000. At any rate, it is likely that the subject of corporation support of Presidential candidates will receive more attention at the Capitol this session than it has received in the past. It will be remembered that when Senator Stone, of Missouri, touched upon the subject, in a speech delivered during the last session, he addressed an inattentive audience; but since that time there has been an awakening of public sentiment in the matter. The direct evidence as to the disposition of the funds of the policy-holders in the various insurance companies — for Senator Platt's testimony as to the contributions from the Mutual and the Equitable companies only supplemented the previous disclosures concerning the amounts paid by the New York Life — affords a basis for interesting comment. It is doubtful, however, whether the politicians in Congress will consent to a further probing, no matter how much the public may desire enlightenment. The fact is that, except in the Bryan campaigns, the large corporations have been impartial in their contributions. Mr. John G. Havemeyer, it will be remembered, openly testified without hesitation that the sugar trust had contributed to both sides. In addition to this, political managers in both parties simply assert that money is necessary for the conduct of a campaign, and that if it can be obtained its source ought not to be regarded. Whether the public agrees with this position is quite another matter.

President Roosevelt's position upon this subject is clear. In his message to Congress a year ago he recommended publicity in the matter of contributions, and at the opening of the present session he repeated his previous suggestion. Personally he would have been gratified if the last campaign could have been entirely free from corporation contributions, and he would have returned their donations if such action had been possible. He could, and did, insist that no money should be received which had attached to its offer any condition whatever. His determination in this regard was so emphatic that many sums were rejected because of their attached stipulations; and Chairman Cortelyou was able to declare, at the close of the campaign, that every part of the campaign fund

has come from voluntary contributions made without demand, importunity, or pressure, and without any agreement, pledge, promise, assurance, or understanding, express or implied, regarding the action or policy of the administration, or looking to any benefit or advantage to any contributor, except the benefits which will come to all business and to all our people from the continuance of Republican policies and Republican administration.

As stated in the last number of THE FORUM, the legislature of Connecticut has enacted what is known as the corrupt practices law, which absolutely prevents the use of money in political campaigns for improper purposes. A national statute of this character would undoubtedly clear the political atmosphere. It ought to be passed if the political managers are sincere in their professions that all the money contributed in a campaign is expended for legitimate purposes.

If the handwriting upon the wall means anything, it indicates that the present temper of the American people is in favor of purity in political and official life. The elections last November were a triumph for clean government everywhere. The corrupt ring in Philadelphia was overthrown with signal emphasis, while in Cincinnati "Boss" Cox went down to defeat and carried with him the entire State Republican administration. In New York, William Travers Jerome, District Attorney, without a party, without an organization except such as was volunteered by his friends, and without money except such as was spontaneously offered him, was re-elected, simply because he had been an honest and efficient public servant. Only the fact that George B. McClellan had also been a good official saved him from defeat, for thousands of Republicans supported him and enabled him to win by a narrow majority. His opponent, William Randolph Hearst, nominated upon the Municipal Ownership ticket, embodied in himself all the sentiment of revolt which the revelations of lavish use of money for corrupt purposes and of official "grafting" had aroused in the community. Everywhere the people exhibited a spirit of independence which bodes ill for those who openly and flagrantly violate every legal and moral obligation.

For three years the wave of reform has been rampant in the United States. It began by permeating cities wherein rascality was apparently firmly intrenched, and succeeded in overthrowing dishonesty and corruption. Out of the upheaval there have emerged many men to whom the title of reformer can be applied without reproach — Folk, Weaver, Jerome, and others less publicly known, but all equally sincere and praiseworthy. President Roosevelt's firm stand for clean government stimulated, if it did not originate, this great popular movement, the result being that there is a wholesome house-cleaning in many municipalities. It is too much to hope that the people will always be as alert and responsive as they are at present to every appeal for honesty in administration. Experience in the past has shown that these eras of reform are followed by periods of indifference, during which the wicked sit in high places. Every American citizen ought to be thankful, however, that when the time comes to clean out the faithless and unworthy, the work is done in no uncertain fashion. The lesson of the recent election is that civic virtue is not an atrophied characteristic of the American people.

HENRY LITCHFIELD WEST.

FOREIGN AFFAIRS.

WITH the issue of this number of THE FORUM ends the first lustrum of the twentieth century. To the student of international politics, those five years are years that well repay study. The beginning of the twentieth century has marked the beginning of a world-wide movement the significance of which no man can mistake.

If it were possible to weigh each century by itself, the historian would be almost tempted to say that the nineteenth is to the world what Shakespeare and the Bible are to literature — all else might perish, but so long as these remained literature would be left. If it were possible to sweep away the past and still leave the nineteenth century the world's progress would be not much less than it is to-day. The beginning of that century saw the beginning of the two great forces that have made for modern progress — genuine democracy and empire building. And the one is the complement of the other, although at first it may appear as if they were antagonistic instead of being complementary. But the fact remains, and history is our warrant, that an empire to endure must be an empire of the people, one in which the people govern and direct the energies of their governing class.

With the close of the Napoleonic wars began that great industrial and commercial movement that turned men's activities into new channels. The wars of Napoleon were wars for the acquisition of territory and the aggrandizement of his power, without a clear idea of the use to be made of that power, or the conception by which power, or its equivalent force, could be converted into wealth. The wars of England were wars to retain and extend commerce. Napoleon with all his genius was not genius enough to see that the very thing he sneered at, his taunt at the English as a nation of shopkeepers, was not only the reason for their success, but the only reason that could justify success. To fight for the mere glory of fighting, to pull down a throne and set up another, to crush a dynasty and out of clay raise up a new race of kings, all this was magnificent, but it led nowhere. It was the commerce of the world that England strove for. It was that commerce England wanted, to attain which or to defend

21

which she was willing to fight; for commerce is wealth, and the foundation of empire is wealth.

The beginning of individual liberty, and, what is greater, the
humanitarian spirit that is so markedly the distinguishing note of
present day civilization, even though at times greed seems more insatiate than it ever was, and force rides triumphant, were coincident
with the beginning of the last century. It was not until men stood
side by side in the factory, and began to feel the moral effect that
comes from numbers and their own strength, that they began to assert
their political rights. The great body of humanitarian and sociological
laws, those laws that prescribe the conditions and terms of employment, that guard the health and welfare of men and women working in
shops, factories, mines, that stand between the weakness of labor and
the greed of capital, and which to-day constitute more than half the
statutes in America and England, first began to appear on the statute
books, roughly speaking, half a century ago. So accustomed have
we become to such laws, so much a matter of course does it seem that
men shall be protected in their rights, that we forget that it was only
yesterday that these rights were ignored and legislatures were blind
to them. The recognition of these rights is the great dower that the
nineteenth century has bequeathed to posterity.

Since the beginning of the twentieth century empire building
has continued to spread; but, in recent years, the strength of democracy
and of the new play of world forces has been spreading in proportion.
The student of international affairs must perforce follow not only
effects, but causes. A revolution means much, but the causes that
produce it mean more. We close the year with the glare of revolution
over Western Europe, and the light of progress burning steadily and
brightly in the East. There were mutterings and rumblings in Central
Europe. In that witches' caldron, the Balkans, by the light of the
moon, men in peasant's dress, but with weapons in their hands, passion-
ately talk of liberty and independence. In the north of Europe there
has been a bloodless revolution and a dual kingdom has been cleft in
twain. There is a spirit of unrest. Blind obedience to the divine
right of kings no longer exists.

In the last number of this Review it was pointed out that one,
and perhaps the leading, result of the war with Japan was to make
Russia realize that if she would hold her position in the family of
nations, it would be necessary for her to keep pace with progress
and the great onward march of liberty and personal freedom. The
Douma, it was said, while not in the true sense of the word a national

representative assembly, was, nevertheless, the beginning of a grant to the people of a voice in the direction of their affairs; and that is a step so radical in Russia that it betokens the dawn of a new era.

What the Czar has conceded was not granted freely, but was wrested from him. He was foolish enough to believe that the people would be satisfied with the shadow instead of the substance; but once having been given a glimpse of freedom, nothing less than its full measure will satisfy them. The war ended, it was no longer unpatriotic for the Russian people to make war against their rulers, in order to attempt to regain the political rights that the world now recognizes as belonging to men by the right of birth. The Douma was a sop to Cerberus. The Czar was compelled to issue a manisfesto which for the first time in the history of Russia confers on the people the right of suffrage, grants civil liberty, and ends the rule of absolutism. By this manifesto, Russia is given a constitution and a cabinet form of government, with Count Witte as the first premier of the Empire. The bombastic tile of "Autocrat of all the Russias" is now an anachronism. The Czar reigns but does not govern. In all constitutional monarchies power centres in the people, and the sovereign becomes an executive with limited functions.

It is impossible to exaggerate the importance of this ukase. For years the Russian people had vainly prayed for a small measure of that liberty which has been enjoyed by the people of all other civilized nations, and to which a deaf ear was turned by the Czar and the men who had him under their influence and control. Had a tithe of the liberty which has now been granted to the Russian people been theirs a few years ago, it is more than probable that Russia would not have made such an inglorious showing on land and sea in the recent war with Japan. The Russian soldiers and sailors, inspired by feelings of patriotism, would have felt that they were fighting for something that was worth preserving; and the corruption and jobbery that made Russia so helpless, and that were almost as fatal to her success as was the military skill shown by the Japanese, would have been impossible. All that Russia has suffered in the past she owes to herself.

What the Czar has done is historically as momentous as was the signing by King John of the Magna Charta at Runnymede; and the Magna Charta, like the Russian constitution, was not an act of grace, but was won by coercion. Had John of England yielded to the barons his head would have paid the forfeit. Had the Czar attempted to stand in the way of the demands of the Russian people, in all probability the Romanoff dynasty would have been brought to an end. The historical parallel between the signing of the Magna Charta, the constitution of England, and the granting of the constitution of Russia is still further complete in that both were gained without the dethronment of the king or a civil war. Seven hundred years ago an English sovereign saw that he must yield to the demands of the people or resist and loose his head. Seven hundred years later a Russian Emperor was confronted with the same alternative. Like a wise man he yielded.

Broadly, the manifesto by which the constitution is granted to Russia confers on the people real legislative power instead of the sham power which the Douma possessed. The people now are the controlling factors in the affairs of government; for the first time they are to be permitted freedom of speech and full civic liberty; they meet and discuss their affairs without being subject to arbitrary arrest; and they can only be punished after trial, and by due process of the law. When we compare the present with the past, the new order of things with that which existed only a few months ago, it will be seen what an enormous advance Russia has made, and why she is now fairly entitled to take her place among the great civilized nations.

The world would have more confidence in the future and would believe that the Russian people were capable of self-government had those same people shown greater restraint in their hour of victory and a more profound appreciation of what they had won. It is disquieting to note that the men who were foremost in the fight for freedom, and who always looked to Witte as the man to lead them, once they had gained that for which they had striven treated lightly what was offered to them, and turned against the man who, more than any other, had forced the change. Count Witte found himself in danger of being deserted by both sides. His insistence that the Czar should grant a real constitution to his people, instead of trying to delude them with a sham, had made him hated by the grand ducal oligarchy and its satellites; and now he found the Liberals and the Intellectuals unjustly and illogically denouncing him as the tool of the aristocrats.

For a time it looked as if Witte would in despair abandon the task on which he had embarked, and as if once again the folly of the people would restore the autocracy to power. There was, however, enough sense left among the members of the reigning family to see that that would be the signal for their doom. However much the Liberals might denounce Witte, they would never consent to see the autocracy re-established. While there has been almost chaos in Russia, and while the moral sensibilities of the civilized world have been shocked by the massacres for which the Government must in a measure be held responsible, there is reason to hope that the Russian people will not abuse the rights that have been conferred on them, and that liberty will not be struck down by folly and passion.

It will, of course, be many years before the Russian people will be able to make proper use of the power that has been lodged in their hands. The weakness of Russia at the present time is the low standard of civilization of the masses. As a rule, the peasants are industrious, good-natured, and in a large degree law-abiding; but they are illiterate, sunk to the depths in superstition, and easily incited to anger when they think they have been wronged and their passion is stirred. In such cases, their ferocity is terrible and uncontrollable. It is not to be wondered at that the moujik should so frequently show his hatred of those in authority over him. Church and State have combined to crush him and to reduce him to the level of the serf. Nominally a free man, actually he is in the hands of his masters, from whom escape is impossible. He knows little of life except its toil; and life holds nothing for him except exhausting labor, frequently under the burning sun or while exposed to cold so intense as to sap his vitality. He suffers much from hunger. If, therefore, in the *vodka* bottle and the stupor of drunkenness he finds his only solace, it is not surprising.

With a proper system of government may be expected a vast improvement in the material condition of the masses of the people; for it will now be the real interest of the real rulers of Russia to raise the general scale of civilization and develop the intellect of the people. In the past, it was in the interest of the autocracy to keep the peasants as illiterate as possible; and the more nearly they resembled the beasts of the field, the less able they were to ameliorate their condition. Education and despotism cannot exist side by side. Whenever the people are able to act and think for themselves, the rule of the despot is threatened. To make Russia as powerful as she ought to be, and to enable her to take her place among the great industrial and commercial powers, it will be necessary for the people of Russia to reach the level of those of England or America. Free schools and a free press are the two agencies that Russia needs more than any other.

Since the preceding issue, the text of the new Anglo-Japanese treaty has been made public, and it fully confirms all that was said on that subject in the last number of THE FORUM. The primary purpose of the treaty is clearly defensive; but this does not restrain the allies from assuming the offensive, if that course shall be necessary for the protection of their interests. The frank purpose of the alliance is to protect the possessions of the contractors in the regions of Eastern Asia and India. Should the interests of either ally be threatened in those regions by one or more Powers, then the alliance, *ipso facto*, is operative. In other words, any attempt on the part of Russia, with or without allies, to menace Japan or to attack India would find her confronted with the combined military and naval strength of England and Japan. It is the general opinion of statesmen that this overpowering force insures the peace of both the Far and the Near East for many years.

In a notable speech made by the Marquis of Lansdowne, the Secretary of State for Foreign Affairs, in November, he explained, at some length, the reason why the British Government concluded the treaty and its purposes. In the course of his speech he remarked:

What are the objects of the alliance? They are set forth in the document itself. The first is the maintenance of peace — the greatest of all British interests. Now I will ask who will take exception to the promotion of the interests of peace? The memory of our own war with South Africa is still present to our minds, and in Manchuria the grass is not yet green upon the graves of the brave men who fell there fighting for their country. I believe that our alliance will make not for war but for the maintenance of peace, and I think that we may venture to say that if Great Britain and Japan desire that peace shall be maintained in the Far East peace will not be broken.

Now for the second object of the Anglo-Japanese alliance. It is the maintenance of the integrity and independence of China and the preservation of what we usually speak of as "the open door," equal opportunity for the commerce of all nations in that great populous part of the world. Does any one suppose for a moment that that is a policy which we are imposing on reluctant Powers? Nothing is further from the truth.

Lord Lansdowne quoted from the circular letter sent by Mr. Hay to the great Powers in 1899 inviting them to subscribe to a declaration in favor of a policy of the open door and equal opportunity in China, to which all the Powers assented. After referring to the Anglo-German agreement respecting China, as well as the Boxer outbreak and the events which followed as a result of that uprising, he said:

Finally, in the present year, the United States again came forward, and taking the lead in emphasizing the necessity of a policy of disinterestedness on the part of the Powers issued a circular in which they affirmed their desire to maintain the integrity of China and the open door, and inviting the Powers to disclaim any intention of seeking reserved territorial rights or control of the Chinese Empire. That circular, like the other, was unanimously subscribed to by all the Powers.

Lord Lansdowne then proceeded to the consideration of the third object of the Anglo-Japanese alliance:

What is that object? Mutual defense against unprovoked attack. I ask, is there any nation which does not claim for itself the right to resist unprovoked attack, and will any nation blame either ourselves or our allies because we have joined hands to enforce that salutary principle? Pray remember that this is not entirely a new obligation, because by the original agreement of 1902 we had already bound ourselves to act together, and to meet any attack on the part of a coalition of other Powers. Surely it was reasonable that we desired to assist Japan, and that Japan should desire to assist us, in the case of an attack of a hostile coalition. I have heard this alliance described as of a provocative character. All that I can say is that it would be just as reasonable to say that by taking out an insurance against fire this club had provoked a conflagration in Piccadilly. I believe that these considerations are thoroughly realized by our own people, who regard this alliance certainly without misgiving, and I believe that they are well understood abroad, where that alliance is regarded with increasing good will.

Lord Lansdowne is guilty of no mere rhetorical flight of fancy when he pronounces the new treaty as guaranteeing the peace of the Far East; and by guaranteeing that peace it tends in a large measure to preserve the peace of the world in quarters other than those covered by the scope of the arrangement. Great Britian has little or nothing to fear from an attack by Russia on her Indian Empire so long as she can rely not only on her own means of defense, but can summon to her assistance those veterans of Oyama whose fighting has commanded the admiration of the world. Not even a mad Czar would be mad enough to risk his all in a chance so desperate as that. And Japan, able to rely on the assistance to be furnished by the British fleet, can feel secure that her supremacy in the waters of the Far East cannot be challenged. Neither from Russia nor from Germany is there anything to be feared for at least a decade, and morally and politically Great Britain and Japan stand together as the guardians of the maintenance of the integrity of the Chinese Empire. The dismemberment of the Middle Kingdom, which seemed so imminent only a few years ago, will be impossible so long as Great Britain and Japan shall deem it to their advantage to preserve the *status quo*.

The question has been asked, naturally enough, whether the treaty would become operative in case any Power should attempt to challenge the Monroe Doctrine that England has virtually set up in the Persian Gulf. If Russia, for instance, relinquishing for the time being her policy of expansion in the Far East, should attempt to find compensation in the Near East, and should secure the active or moral support of Germany in an attempt to obtain a naval station in the Persian Gulf, which England would be compelled to resist, would the latter be able to regard that as a menace to her "special interests" in India and invoke the assistance of Japan? It must be obvious that the acquisition by Russia or Germany, Russia especially, of a *point d'appui* in the Persian Gulf would be a menace to Great Britain as threatening her line of communications, and would therefore justly entitle her to request Japan to observe the obligations imposed upon her by the treaty. And I am fully prepared to believe that if that contingency should arise, and if at that time the mood of Japan should be its present mood, there would be no hesitation on the part of the Government of Japan in placing its military and naval forces at the disposal of Great Britain. The fact that these forces are available will perhaps do more than anything else to prevent any act of wanton aggression on the part of Russia.

Germany, only second to Russia, must appreciate how vitally the treaty affects her ambitious plans in the Far East; and the ambition of Germany has been almost as great as that of Russia, although it has been less ostentatious, and its cost but a trifle of the ruinous price which Russia has been made to pay. In Kiaochau, Germany has secured a foothold on the Chinese mainland, which it is well understood was intended by Germany to be merely the beginning of her territorial possessions in the Far East. But so long as Great Britain and Japan stand side by side in maintaining the integrity of China, it will be impossible for Germany to secure an additional foot of territory beyond that which she now holds, and her long-cherished dream of the acquisition of the rich and populous province of Shantung must be abandoned. Any move in that direction would be regarded by Japan as detrimental to her own "special interests" and compel Great Britain and Japan by force of arms to resist the encroachment. Without coaling stations or a fortified base in the Eastern Hemisphere, Germany would be impotent to meet Japan, to say nothing of having to meet Japan and Great Britain combined. Germany now knows the difficulties of carrying on a colonial war several thousand miles from her base. Her campaign in German East Africa has taught her military lessons that before she was ignorant of, and has made her take a more just view of the Transvaal War. Germany would proceed very cautiously before she would risk her position by inviting a conflict with the greatest military power of the Far East, re-enforced by the greatest naval power of the world.

Germany is content to sit tight, but her position may be forced by China. I am in possession of information that enables me to state that China is determined that Germany shall evacuate Kiaochau; and among all the Powers that have taken a hand in the spoliation of China, Germany has more than any other Power aroused the resentment of the Chinese — more so even than Russia, curious as that may sound to persons who are unfamiliar with the Chinese character and German Colonial methods. China is looking forward to the day when she shall have a modern navy; and when that day comes, if it ever does, China will then bluntly say to Germany that the territory that she seized without any shadow of justification must be restored to its rightful owners.   China, to show that she is not discriminating against any of the European Powers, will request England to evacuate Wei-hai-wei, which England would no doubt be willing enough to do, as Wei-hai-wei has lost its strategic value now that Port Arthur is in the possession of her Japanese ally, instead of in the hands of Russia, an always potent menace.   England has done practically nothing to fortify Wei-hai-wei, and without fortifications the place is useless, while to fortify it would involve an expenditure which, in the opinion of the military authorities, would be out of proportion to its importance.   Wei-hai-wei, however, would be of great value to China as an advanced naval base in the Gulf of Pechili, and enable the Chinese navy, if it were a navy worthy of the name, to make a sudden and bold dash on Kiaochau that it would be difficult for Germany to withstand.

Will China obtain the navy on which her future so largely depends? It is impossible for any man to make satisfactory answer to that question at the present time; but it must be frankly admitted there is little in the past history of China to justify much hope that the idea slowly crystallizing will assume concrete form.   Yet it has been pointed out more than once in this Review that there has recently been a great awakening in China; and it becomes evident to the close observer that the Chinese are beginning to emerge from the spell under which they have lain by a too profound and slavish belief in the virtues of the past and their refusal to attach some value to the virtues of the present. But when men of great importance in the affairs of China frankly admit that the dignity of China demands that Germany shall be made to restore stolen property, and that the only means whereby this recovery can be effected is by the possession by China of a navy, it becomes self-evident that China no longer is content to be satisfied with the methods of the past, but has at last begun to readjust her point of view.

In this connection, it is not without significance to note that, for the first time in her history, only a few months ago, the Chinese army engaged in a series of military manœuvres that had more the semblance of actual military operations than a comic opera stage, of which Chinese military movements have heretofore been suggestive.   The foreign military observers were impressed by the marked progress shown by the troops in executing military commands and by their general manner and appearance.   If China follows in the footsteps of Japan and shows that she appreciates the virtues of civilization by adopting the weapons of civilization with which to fight civilization, no longer in the sisterhood of nations will China be the Cinderella to be kicked and cuffed because she is poor and weak. Cinderella met her prince, and her wooing and wedding were the envy of her sisters. The time may yet come when a great and powerful nation may seek the hand of China in alliance and thus bring about another international relation between the East and the West. Still, one is bound to say, that the day for the wedding bells to ring does not appear to be very close at hand. But while it may not be easy to hustle the East, even in the East events move with dramatic swiftness when once the great force of public opinion is behind them.

While in other parts of the Far East events may move with a deliberation that takes no account of time, Japan at least has shown that she can act with the same quick decision that is the dominant characteristic of the western world. While her troops are still in occupatiou of Manchuria and the great internal problems arising out of the war are still to receive the consideration of her statesmen, the affairs of Korea have been taken in hand; and Korea, as an independent kingdom, exercising the full rights of sovereignty, no longer exists. After the recognition of the predominant interests of Japan in Korea, which Russia accorded to Japan by the treaty of Portsmouth, it was inevitable that the Government of the Mikado should at the earliest opportunity readjust the relations between the two countries. So long as Korea remained an independent kingdom in charge of her own foreign relations, there was always the possibility that by the inherent right of sovereignty capable of making alliances and negotiating treaties, Korea might fall under the influence of a power hostile to Japan, which would prove to be the weak point in the Japanese armor. Self-preservation demanded that Japan should without delay fortify herself against danger.

Persons whose ethical sense is theoretically so finely developed as to obscure practical considerations may see in this act of Japan a proof that she was not governed solely by unselfish considerations when she made war on Russia, and that in effect, if not in form, she has broken her word after declaring that she was not inspired by territorial greed. If, however, one realizes that statesmanship is practical business, one must admit that there was no alternative open to Japan.

The sympathy of the world has always been given to the small nation whose national existence has been crushed out by a dominant power. Rightly that pity has been extended when a powerful nation, influenced solely by greed and unrestrained by morality, has seized its neighbor's vineyard, as Ahab did that of Naboth the Jezreelite. But with nations, as with species, the immutable law of the survival of the fittest prevails. Great nations have become great because they have been the fittest to survive, because by surviving they have spread civilization, which little nations frequently encumber. The relation that Korea occupies to Japan is on all fours with that existing between England and Egypt, which existed between the Transvaal and England, and might still be in force had it not been for the foolishness of bigots who sought to stay the never to be stayed march of civilization, and who were encouraged in their folly by the envious rivals of England. Egypt, nominally acknowledging the Sultan of Turkey as her suzerain, governed in name by the Khedive, is ruled actually by her English agent; and it is only since Egypt has come under English rule that she has been prosperous, that justice has been dealt with an even hand, and property has been secure. Assuredly, it will not be denied that Egypt and the world at large are the gainers by the transfer of authority and real power.

Japan now proposes to be to Korea what Engand is to Egypt, and I believe that the same beneficial results will follow. The Emperor of Korea still remains emperor in name, but he is shorn of all his real power and authority, which was more frequently used for the injury of his subjects than for their benefit; and the real ruler of Korea henceforth will be a Japanese administrator, who will govern Korea under the Emperor, exactly as Lord Cromer, the British agent, governs Egypt under the Khedive. It is natural that the Japanese should follow the example set by England. The Japanese have the faculty of absorbing the best wherever it may be found. In military matters they took Germany for their model; in naval matters, as in diplomacy, they patterned after England. To deprive Korea of the power of contracting alliances or entering into diplomatic negotiations that might be injurious to Japan; the conduct of Korean diplomatic affairs has been taken over by Japan, and these affairs are now carried on from Tokio, Korea being prohibited from making arrangements with other Powers without the consent of Japan. The Korean diplomatic corps has been virtually abolished, and the United States and other Powers have recognized the suzerainty of Japan by agreeing henceforth to negotiate with Japan in any matter affecting Korea.

Prior to the South African War, the foreign relations of the Transvaal were lodged in the hands of England, and the Republic was not permitted to enter into negotiations with a foreign Power except with the consent of England. This was one of the things the Boers resented, and which they attempted to recover, and by their failure lost all. It is my belief that the rather interesting parallel between the Transvaal and England, on the one hand, and Korea and Japan, on the other, will manifest itself here also; but fortunately for Japan she will not have to pay the price that England did, as the Koreans are a weak and feeble people, and mere puny children in the military grasp of Japan. Before very long, it will be quite on the cards for anarchy, disorder, and revolution to arise in Korea, whereupon Japan will step in, that imperial puppet, the Emperor, will be deposed, and Korea will be annexed to Japan. It will make little difference whether Korea is under the protection of Japan or under her own flag. The regeneration of that country is in the hands of Japan, and Japan alone can bring the Hermit Kingdom in touch with the rest of the world.

The long expected fall of the Balfour Government has at last happened. In the second week of December, Sir Henry Campbell-Bannerman kissed hands on his appointment, and his colleagues took over the seals of office from their predecessors. Thus, after ten long, weary years of wandering in the wilderness, the Liberals are once again in the promised land. However, it is a land in which they are likely to find little milk and honey, but many scorpions and much gall. It is a thorny path on which the new Moses has set his feet. He comes into power not by the mandate of the people, but because the Conservatives have grown stale, because even they have recognized that they have outlived their usefulness.

It is always a dangerous thing to predict the life of a British cabinet, and especially a cabinet that exists on sufferance, as this does. It is a curious turn in the wheel that brings Campbell-Bannerman back to power. Ten years ago Lord Rosebery went down because of an adverse vote in the Commons arising out of the dissatisfaction with the management of the war office, and the then secretary of state for war was Sir Henry Campbell-Bannerman. At that time few persons would have predicted that Sir Henry would be the next Liberal premier. He was overshadowed by more commanding figures. But the men who were great then have passed away or have fallen into the background. Lord Rosebery, the most brilliant member of his party, holds aloof, and the succession falls to Campbell-Bannerman.

Parliament, in the normal course of events, should meet within the next few weeks; but it is much more probable that, instead of the present Parliament reassembling, the premier will exercise his prerogative and dissolve Parliament, so as to obtain the verdict of the country. That verdict, it is believed, will be favorable, and Sir Henry will face the Commons with a working majority. But after then, what? The Irish are again determined to make home rule for Ireland the great issue, and the Liberals will find themselves between two fires. If they give Ireland the concessions that the Irish demand, that is, a sweeping measure of home rule, Campbell-Bannerman will as inevitably go to destruction on that rock as Gladstone did. If, on the other hand, the premier attempts to satisfy the Irish members with vague promises and legislation that does not go to the heart of the question, the Irish will join hands with the opposition, thus putting the Government in the minority, and forcing the resignation of the cabinet. The Irish have nothing to lose by these tactics and everything to gain; because, while they have no more hope of securing home rule from the Conservatives than they have from the Liberals, this demonstration of their power will make them listened to with more respect at Westminster. Another shuffling of the cards within a year, with the Conservatives holding the trumps, would not be surprising.

Sir Henry Campbell-Bannerman's premiership is noteworthy in that for the first time in the history of England the premier is given recognition in the table of precedence. Heretofore the prime-minister of England has had no official standing. The British cabinet, like the American cabinet, is an extra-constitutional creation. It is in theory simply one of the committees of the privy council; but the cabinet, as the Government of England, was non-existent. Certain great officers of state were accorded their place in the table of precedence; but the premier, as such, had no place. The anomaly was therefore presented of the real ruler of the British empire, if he were a commoner, on occasions of state having to give the *pas* to peers of his own creation and the nobodies of noble birth. The King has now corrected this, and by proclamation ordered that the premier shall take precedence immediately after the Archbishops of Canterbury and York and the Lord High Chancellor, although logically the premier should outrank the chancellor, as the latter owes his office to the premier by being a member of his cabinet.

The new cabinet is not brilliant, but it is composed of all-around strong men. It is not a cabinet of all the talents, but it is a cabinet of many shades of opinion. There are strong imperialists and equally strong " Little Englanders," and only a few years ago that was anathema to the majority of Englishmen. Aristocracy is represented by the Marquis of Ripon and the Earl of Crewe; radicalism by that brilliant Welshman, Lloyd-George; labor by John Burns, who only a few years ago was a mechanic; the great middle class by the premier himself; and letters by Morley, Bryce, Haldane, and Birrell. The four most interesting figures are Sir Edward Grey, the new foreign secretary; Henry Asquith, Lord Rosebery's secretary of state for home affairs and now

chancellor of the exchequer; Lloyd-George, president of the board of
trade; and John Burns, president of the local government board.

The Balfour government is a magnificent illustration of the truth
of the statement that "the secret of all successful government is
personality." It is a nebulous, indefinable thing, this so-called personality, and subtle and as intangible of analysis as the aroma of a flower,
but as all-pervading. Consider for a moment what the Balfour cabinet
has done, and how a man of commanding personality, a Beaconsfield,
for instance, with the luxuriance of an Oriental imagination, who knew
how to appeal to the imagination of the phlegmatic Englishman, would
have used those achievements to make himself the idol of the mob.
Having brought about the Japanese alliance, an event as momentous
as Beaconsfield's purchase of the Suez Canal shares or the bringing
of Indian troops to the Mediterranean when war with Turkey was
threatened, and having restored friendly relations with France, than
which there has been nothing more popular, except, perhaps, the
open defiance of Germany, when she sent her minatory communication
to France over the Morocco dispute, the Balfour administration has
done things that has placed it far above the commonplace. Indeed,
its foreign minister, Lord Lansdowne, has shown himself to be a man
of extraordinary ability, who takes rank as the greatest foreign minister
of his day; and yet, because Mr. Balfour is without that peculiar
quality of personality, he has made little impression upon his time,
and will pass into history as a colorless and somewhat weak, but
amiable man, whose heart was in his music and his golf and his polemi-
cal discussions, rather than in that Titan's task, the governing of the
British Empire.

At the end of November, the condition of the Sick Man of Europe
was so alarming that it became necessary to call a consultation of
international physicians, who, after a careful diagnosis, determined
to administer iron and steel in heroic doses. It was not a tractable
patient the physicians had to deal with; but they knew his vagaries
of old, and that, after declaring he never would take their horrid mess,
he would turn his back, swallow the dose as gracefully as possible in
the circumstances, and console himself with the reflection that he would
not pay the doctor's bill.

What at one time seemed like a contest between the Christian Powers
of Europe and Turkey was settled as those disputes always have been
settled when Abdul Hamid has convinced himself that the Powers
are really agreed, and he cannot play one against the other. An
amazingly shrewd and cunning man is this Caliph with the henna-

dyed beard, who sees in every face a possible assassin, who trusts no one and fears everybody. Abdul Hamid has matched his cunning against the jealousies and intrigues of the Powers, which he has turned to his own profit. He has played Russia against England and England against Germany; and he has even used the United States as a pawn in the game. On one occasion, he told the Washington Government that he was willing to pay its claim; but he cynically observed, at the same time, that it would be setting such a bad example to Europe. The American claim was a bagatelle; it could be paid without any trouble; but it was the principle involved, and the principle was a dangerous one. If he paid the United States, the European Powers would be encouraged to press their demands for payment, and it would be necessary to disappoint them. Rather than be accused of discriminating in favor of one Government as against another, he felt that he must decline to pay the United States.

For all the misrule, the nameless atrocities, and the long series of horrors that have made Turkey an abomination in the eyes of Christendom, the great Powers of Europe are solely to blame. They have it in their power at any time to bring Turkey to terms, to force her, as they have forced her occasionally in minor matters, to behave herself and make trivial reforms. The Sultan is no fool. He knows well enough that it is impossible for him to resist Europe or even successfully oppose two of the Powers; although he might not be averse to fighting a single Power, trusting to the jealousies of the rest to save him in a desperate extremity, just as England called the Congress of Berlin after Russia had made the Sultan sign the treaty of San Stefano. The one thing that the Sultan fears, the only thing, in fact, that he fears, is the European concert; and when the voice of Europe speaks in concert, it is a very meek and yielding Caliph who bows his head in submission to the hated giaour.

That the Sultan knows that he is merely a puppet in the hands of Europe has been proved again and again by the fact that his latest attempt to defy Europe was promptly abandoned when Europe showed that it was united and in earnest. The Powers having determined that the Ottoman Government must make certain financial and administrative reforms in Armenia, the Sultan was told to put his house in order without delay. He resorted to his favorite method of playing one Power against the other. He appealed in turn to Austria, Russia, and Germany not to join the coalition, feeling certain that if only one Power came to his assistance the others would hesitate before applying the final remedy. These appeals, however, were fruitless, and the Sultan was warned that unless he yielded the allied Powers would make a naval demonstration against a Turkish port. But it was not until the allied fleet had sailed and covered Mytilene with its guns that the Sultan acceded to the demands of the Powers. Germany took no part in the demonstration, although Germany, according to official statements, had advised the Sultan to make the reforms demanded.

Southeastern Europe is always a powder mine with the fuse ready to be lighted at a moment's notice. An Englishman who has for years studied German and Austrian politics, and whose sources of information are excellent, writes me:

"I have recently returned to London from an interesting tour abroad, visiting Austria and Servia, and some of the Balkan States. We shall hear, if I mistake not, a good deal of this neglected corner of the world during the next few years. Certainly the Germans, whatever may be their trans-oceanic dreams, have their eyes primarily fixed on two bits of water: to wit, the Rhine and the Mediterranean. They have to prepare for two events that may come any day — the breakup of Austria, and next the outburst in the Balkans. As to the former, I had a good deal of talk with influential people in Vienna and Budapest; and I concluded that the Hungarians, in their pride and self-sufficiency, are prepared to take the greatest risks. And as to the latter, Bulgaria has been preparing for the next war with Turkey with an almost Japanese thoroughness, and is quite determined to become the dominant Power in those regions. If there is another rising in Macedonia, or a revolution in Servia — and one is as probable as the other, as you know that Macedonia is always in a state of ferment — the Bulgars might seize their opportunity. That might bring Austria and perhaps Germany upon the scene. All this enters much more into German calculations than, I think, is commonly supposed in this country, where the prevalent idea is that Germany is animated by a frantic, apparently purposeless, animosity against England.

"Apropos of Germany. The Germans have one reason for not allowing the French to collar Morocco, which is not unimportant, but which few persons outside of the highest German military circles understand. There is a pretty large fighting population away in the back of Morocco — not Moors, but Berbers and Fuzzy-Wuzzies — who if drilled and disciplined by French officers might come in handy in the next Franco-German war. It is true that the Turcos were not of much use in '70; but these are a different breed, and there are more of them. If the French have an iron organizer like Kitchener, a fighting brigadier like Hector MacDonald, and a few Sergeants "Whatshisname" to manhandle this raw material and hammer it into shape, this would be an army that even the best-trained German troops might not find it easy to rout. But have the French a Kitchener? I doubt it."

Whatever may be the denials of diplomatists, it is certain that only a few months ago, last June to be exact, Germany, Great Britain, and France were so perilously close to the verge of war that, for a few days peace hung balanced at the end of a hair. The resignation of M. Delcassé, the French Minister of Foreign Affairs, was forced because he advocated a policy of resistance to Germany over Morocco, relying on the support of England in case Germany deemed it advisable to make Morocco a *casus belli*. When Germany notified France that she did not recognize the Anglo-French agreement respecting Morocco, and demanded to be given a vote in the settlement, France sounded England and received assurances that she could rely on her support. There is every reason to believe that this was a verbal statement made by the Marquis of Lansdowne to M. Paul Cambon, the French Ambassador in London, and that had the necessity arisen the precise position of England would have been formally stated in writing.

England was not anxious to go to war or to see Germany and France at war. In the effort to avert war, the decision reached by the British Government to support France was communicated to the German Emperor through his ambassador in London. The German Emperor was then confronted with the alternative of losing prestige by withdrawing his objection to the Anglo-French Moroccan agreement or challenging France and risking the danger of France accepting the challenge backed by England. To have sent an ultimatum to France would have left no way open for retreat; to send an indirect ultimatum was as effective, but did not close the door to peace. Accordingly, the Italian Government was notified by the Emperor that he regarded the Anglo-French understanding regarding military assistance as a *casus belli*. This information was immediately communicated by the Italian Government to the French ambassador at Rome, and by him transmitted to Paris. There is reason to believe that when the Italian Government made this communication to M. Barrère, the French ambassador, it was accompanied by a pointed intimation that it would be a very simple matter for the French Government to show whether it wanted peace or war. If it wanted peace, M. Rouvier, the prime-minister, could show his sincerity by dismissing M. Delcassé from the cabinet, as it was known that M. Delcassé was in favor of the British alliance and openly defying Germany. If, on the other hand, M. Delcassé retained his portfolio and was permitted to conduct the foreign relations of France, Germany would consider that France was anxious for war.

On receipt of this information the French cabinet at once met. There was a stormy scene. M. Delcassé urged his colleagues to make no surrender to Germany, and he gave an assurance that the military support of England could be relied on. But he was immediately interrupted by M. Rouvier, who said that he had a despatch from M. Barrère, which made it clear that there would be war unless the Declassé policy was abandoned. Then he turned to the ministers and asked them if they preferred war to an honorable retreat. The opinion of

22

the cabinet was unanimous in favor of "an honorable retreat," which left no alternative to M. Delcassé except to resign. His resignation was immediately accepted; the German Emperor was satisfied with having forced his most dangerous opponent out of the cabinet; and the crisis was safely tided over.

Although this happened in June, it was not until late in October that the world knew the facts concerning this most important chapter in the history of Anglo-German-French relations. It was the Paris "Matin" that first gave them publicity, and there is extrinsic evidence to show that the "Matin" received its information from one of the important characters in that historical scene — in fact, no less a personage than M. Delcassé himself, who was only too willing to have it known why he was forced out of the cabinet. The revelations were, as always happens in such cases, diplomatically denied; but a diplomatic *dementi* may always be accepted with reservation. The salient facts have been correctly stated. There would have been no retreat possible for Germany had France believed it advisable to take up the German challenge, and it is difficult to see how England could have escaped being drawn into the war. Reluctant as the English people are again to engage in war, war with Germany would be extremely popular, and many Englishmen regret that an opportunity so favorable was missed. Englishmen who believe that war with Germany is inevitable would rather have it now than a few years hence, because to-day the preponderance of naval strength is all on the side of Great Britain, and the French alliance would place in the field an army that Germany might vanquish, it is true, but not without taxing her resources to the utmost.

There was a minor cabinet crisis in France in November, when M. Berteaux, the minister of war, retired after an acrimonious debate in the Chamber of Deputies. For a time the fate of the Rouvier Government hung in the balance; but again the Chamber showed that it was not inclined to displace men of tested power merely for the wanton satisfaction of causing trouble and rearranging the cards. M. Rouvier stood ready to resign; but the Chamber would not force him out, and the present cabinet remains in office.

There will be a presidential election in France in the month of January. A presidential election in France is no such long drawn-out affair as it is in this country. In France the President is not elected by the people or through the archaic machinery of the electoral college, but by the chambers, which meet in joint session for this purpose in Versailles, and not in Paris, where the regular sessions of the chambers are held. The French President is elected for a term of seven years, and the French constitution, like that of the United States, is silent as to his eligibility for re-election. President Grévy was re-elected. President Loubet, whose presidency has given general satisfaction, has announced that he will not seek re-election; but some of his opponents affect to treat this declaration in the same way that American politicians do the disclaimer of an ambitious politician who is suspected of designs on the White House.

M. Loubet's announcement that he is not a candidate is questioned; and the preparations that he is making to return to private life, one of them being the rental of an apartment, are characterized by the opposition as obviously transparent devices to lull his opponents into a false sense of security. If M. Loubet should be a candidate, it is believed that he would be re-elected, which is the reason why the field is anxious to get him out of the way. M. Loubet's decision not to be a candidate will be influenced, it is generally believed, by the strength shown by his opponents. If it appears probable that an extreme Radical is to be elected, M. Loubet, to prevent what he regards as a danger to the Republic, may take the only means to avert it by himself becoming a candidate; but if a Conservative is shown to command a majority of the Assembly, M. Loubet will in all probability make no effort to secure re-election. A new Chamber of Deputies will be elected in June, and it would then be possible, if the majority should be Conservative, for M. Loubet, in case he should be re-elected, to resign and permit a man in harmony with his own views to be elected his successor.

The election of Prince Charles of Denmark to the throne of Norway under the title of King Haakon is another of those small pieces of luck for which the entire history of England is famous. Prince Charles is the son-in-law of King Edward of England, which puts Norway under the protection of England and guarantees the independence of Norway. King Haakon married Princess Maud, King Edward's youngest daughter, against the wishes of his mother, who had formed other matrimonial plans for him. The position of Princess Maud was made so unpleasant in Copenhagen that it was seriously proposed at one time that she and her husband should take up their residence in England, and that Prince Charles should become a naturalized Englishman and enter the royal navy, following the precedent set by Prince Louis of Battenberg and other Germans of princely blood. Prince Charles has always been popular in England, and his popularity would have been increased by entering the navy; but the King of

Denmark vetoed the suggestion, and the Prince's mother having become reconciled to the marriage, Princess Maud has in recent years enjoyed her life in Copenhagen. As the consort of a reigning sovereign, even if her throne is somewhat diminutive, she ranks higher among the great than as the wife of the son of a crown prince; and if she becomes as popular in Norway as she has always been in England and in Denmark, she will do much to make her husband beloved by the people who have selected him as their King.

Norway and Sweden having amicably dissolved the union, there is no reason to fear that their relations in the future will not be harmonious, or that any opportunity will be presented for the interference of either Germany or Russia in the affairs of the two kingdoms. It was thought at one time that on some pretext or other either Russia or Germany would find it necessary to "preserve order," which would have been the end of Scandinavian independence. That danger is now removed. The old King of Sweden, with his pride sorely bruised, is more than ever the idol of his people. The Norwegians are proud of their young, vigorous King and want to be allowed to live in peace. With England interested in seeing the throne of Norway preserved for the children of Princess Maud, the Norwegians can feel secure against aggression.

A. MAURICE LOW.

FINANCE.

In concluding the review of the financial situation in THE FORUM, three months ago, after pointing out the many highly favorable elements in the situation, I suggested that if the demands on capital should be restricted to the normal requirements of a world-wide industrial activity, the future would have nothing in it to disturb equanimity. If, on the other hand, use were made of the strong underlying factors in the situation to provide a basis for a promoting speculation such as that of 1901, or a stock-jobbing craze like that of 1902, resources would have to be scanned more distrustfully. This forecast of the situation has since been verified.

The circumstances under which the world's markets entered upon the concluding quarter of the year were encouraging in an unusual degree. To sum up briefly the ruling conditions of the time: (1) peace had just been concluded between the two belligerent powers in the Far East, and Europe was, therefore, looking forward to relaxation from the strain on her investment markets; (2) money rates throughout the world were at low figures, discounts commanding only three per cent in New York, two and a half at London, and one and a half at Paris; (3) the Bank of England's reserve stood at 45 per cent, or well above the traditional minimum; (4) within a comparatively short period the Bank of France and the Bank of Germany had reported the largest cash reserves in their history; and (5) so far as concerned the United States, a wheat crop never but once exceeded in our history was assured, and with that assurance came news of a Russian crop shortage such as should apparently guarantee to the United States the entire restoration of its grain export trade and the entire command of the foreign exchanges.

These various factors were sufficient ground for the feeling of high optimism with which the season opened. That feeling, it is now entirely clear, induced some very large capitalists, in the United States and abroad, to embark on extensive speculation for the rise. Their belief was that the tangible wealth certain to accrue to the American people during the season would provide a market for investment stocks at a level of prices far higher than those which then prevailed. A similar conviction, as applied to its own financial outlook, appeared to exist in Germany, where it resulted not only in great activity by the Stock Exchange operators, but in a rush of the German public into an excited speculation not wholly unlike that in which our market engaged at the close of 1900.

Readers of these articles are familiar with the principle that the test of a situation, through which facts are often disclosed which had previously been concealed, comes at a time when active general trade, especially in the spring or autumn, brings large demands to bear on the resources of the money markets. If those resources turn out to be sufficient, as was the case a year ago, the large demands are met with little or no difficulty. If, on the other hand, the speculator, the promoter, the negotiator of great loans, and the investor who borrows money for his purchases, have already quietly absorbed in days of easy money the surplus resources of the money markets, then it will sometimes be discovered that there is not enough left to provide on comfortable terms for the needs of ordinary trade. Such a situation was unexpectedly disclosed in the early autumn of 1902, and a precisely similar situation has developed in the present season. It may be said, in fact, that the course of events three years ago was much less striking and sensational than it has been this autumn. In 1902, the full force of the strain fell on the American market. European markets were then in a comfortable situation. The money rates were low and the bank reserves large, chiefly because there was no extensive boom in Europe's trade. Europe, in fact, at that time still labored under the depressing influence of the "Boer War panic" of 1899 and 1900, and its resultant industrial reaction.

The peculiarity of this season's situation, on the contrary, is that the money strain developed, in a form exceedingly acute, at practically every great money market of the world, and that it developed simultaneously as soon as the autumn "harvest demands" arose. At London, for example, a very rapid fall in the reserve of the Bank of England, taking $20,000,000 out of that fund during two weeks around the opening of October, brought the ratio of reserve to liabilities suddenly down to the forty-per-cent level, traditionally accepted as the ordinary minimum of safety. A year before it had stood at 53 per cent. The bank had already, in the first week of September, advanced its official discount rate from two and a half to three per cent; on September 27, the rate was raised to four per cent, in spite of which the reserve percentage fell to 38⅝ in the following week. Raised for a time above that level, it sank back at the opening of November to 38½, a figure remarkable for the fact that no ratio so low as this had been reached by the Bank's reserve at that time of year since the famous Baring panic of November, 1890.

While this was happening, events at Berlin were taking a still more striking course. On October 3, 1905, the Imperial German Bank advanced its discount rate from four to five per cent. This advance itself was striking enough, in that it fixed the highest rate reached by that bank's official rate since the industrial panic of 1900. The remarks of the president of the bank, however, at the time of announcing its advance in rate, were more startling even than the showing of the bank. That part of the outstanding note circulation, he announced, uncovered by specie and therefore regarded as an emergency device, had reached the highest mark ever known in the history of the institution. Its loans, discounts, and advances had similarly surpassed all records. Along with the consequent expansion of liabilities, the cash reserve was shrinking rapidly, through withdrawals for the general circulation, to an entirely insufficient figure.

Concluding this remarkable diagnosis, the president plainly stated that the acute phase of the situation must be ascribed to speculation on the Stock Exchange, and that the raising of the Imperial Bank's discount rate was designed expressly to put a brake on such dangerous speculation. The effort met with indifferent success; speculation, checked for a moment, was resumed as soon as it was seen that the bank was not yet out of the money market. The situation grew from bad to worse; on November 4 — a Saturday, and hence an unusual day for altering the rate — the bank marked up its discounts to five and a half per cent, the highest in seven years, announcing at the time that the bank's reserve had not been so low since 1898, before the German financial "boom" began which culminated in the industrial crash and the seven per cent Imperial Bank rate at the beginning of 1900. On December 11, with further weakening of the Imperial Bank's position, the rate was again raised to 6 per cent — usually deemed a "panic figure."

These movements of the money market at London and Berlin met with quick response at Brussels, Vienna, Genoa, Geneva, Copenhagen, and Stockholm, at all of which points the banks moved up their official minimum. At Paris, events pursued a somewhat different course. In the middle of October, despite some loss of gold from its reserve, the Bank of France was able to report a gold reserve $65,000,-000 larger than what it had held at that date a year before. A more or less similar showing was made by the Imperial Bank of Russia. But it soon appeared that these two institutions, though apparently well provided for their own immediate needs, had no intention of helping out other markets. While the Bank of France made no change in its official discount rate, money moved up on the Paris open

market, and the most urgent efforts of American and English bankers
to get gold in Paris came to nothing.

It was plainly stated on the Bourse that the bank's position was
being purposely maintained at its existing status because of a feeling
that the Russian situation was sufficiently disquieting for the markets
most vitally concerned to need a powerful anchor to windward.   Foremost among such markets, necessarily, stood Paris, where the banking
community had to keep its eye on the $2,000,000,000 worth of Russian
Government securities held by the French investors.   The French
financial community was indeed confronted by two considerations —
one, the understood fact that the Russian Government was about to
apply to the market for a $250,000,000 loan which France alone might
have to care for; the other, that the state of affairs in Russia, socially
and politically, was of such a nature as to create a highly precarious
situation.   I shall have more to say of these considerations later on.
For the present, it is enough to point out that the only two great
banks in Europe whose position seemed to be relatively strong were, for
reasons of their own, holding jealously to their resources.

There remains to be described the position at New York, where,
indeed, events moved more sensationally even than at Berlin.   I
noticed, in concluding my article of three months ago, that the New
York surplus bank reserve at the close of August was too low to be
regarded as sufficient provision for the strain of harvesting time
demands.   This was admitted; indeed, no banker could have failed
to see the force of that assertion, when the surplus, at the opening of
September, was at much the lowest figure reached at that date since
1893.   But the common answer to such warnings was that our command over foreign trade would enable New York to draw freely on
capital of foreign markets.   There were those, even then, who had
their doubts about this consummation.   Despite the large wheat
harvest, grain moved out slowly at the export points, and cotton
still more slowly.   The reason then assigned was that active speculation at Chicago and New Orleans, sustained by the holding back of
their merchandise for higher prices by the wheat-farmers and the
cotton planters, made it impossible for foreign buyers and American
sellers to meet on mutually acceptable terms.   However this may
have been, and I shall have something more to say of it hereafter,
it was a fact that, in September and October, cotton exports fell
short of 1904 by $27,000,000, while the increase in all kinds of cereals,
over the same period last year, footed up only $12,000,000.

Wall Street, however, did not readily relinquish its belief that gold could be obtained in Europe. Early in September, when exchange in London moved in our favor with the first outward movement of our produce, agents of New York bankers began to make urgent efforts to secure a portion of London's gold supply. During that month and the next they were able to obtain no less than $8,000,000, consisting mostly of new gold that had arrived at London from the Transvaal mines. It was alleged in Europe that this gold was obtained on terms which were not warranted as a normal commercial operation. Whether this was true or not, the New York bankers undoubtedly expected that a still larger sum could be obtained. With the growing stringency in Europe's markets, however, during the last days of October, foreign exchange turned so decidedly against New York that further gold imports were impracticable, and the attempt to draw on Europe was abandoned.

Thrown back in this way on their own resources, the New York banks were confronted by a somewhat awkward situation. As in 1902, one obvious recourse to relieve the situation was that the very large loans, already made by banks to Wall Street speculators, for the purpose of sustaining stocks at their high existing prices, should be cancelled and the banks' liabilities thus reduced. In the end, this was exactly what took place in 1902; but it soon developed, as events unfolded during the present season, that the people involved in the heavy stock speculation were of a different class from the reckless adventurers whose schemes collapsed in the November market of 1902. There were plain indications that the promoters of this season's speculation had such affiliations with important banks that they were able to insist on retaining their extensive lines of credit, which would hardly be taken from them except in extreme emergency. This belief was confirmed by the action of some of the largest New York banks, which allowed their position, later on, to grow so weak that, under the bank law, they were subject to the severest penalties, and yet whose officers declared that they proposed to violate that law, if necessary, to oblige their customers.

The same situation was abundantly defined by the movement on the Stock Exchange itself. Certain stocks with large outstanding capital seemed virtually to be cornered. Their prices were pushed up, in the face of the weakening bank position, by such leaps and bounds that the only possible conclusion left was that a speculative clique and its friends held virtual control of all the stock outstanding. This was the case even with the $70,000,000 Reading stock, which rose twenty per cent in two weeks during the money strain. Loans to these capitalists were not called in; and they remained a burden on an already much-strained money market when the full force of the interior demand for cash set in. This demand, as had been expected from the extreme activity of internal trade, was quite unprecedented. Usually the outflow of currency for the purpose of harvest payments lasts until November, when it ceases and a moderate return movement supervenes. This year, the heaviest currency movement of the season from New York occurred in the first and second weeks of November, in one of which weeks the New York banks lost $10,000,000 cash, practically all through remittances to the interior.

The reason for this abnormal drain unquestionably was that the interior banks, confronted with large demands from their own communities, and with a six to eight per cent rate for money, added so largely to their own loans and liabilities that New York balances had to be drawn upon to fortify home reserves of cash. For a time, to disguise the real position, the banks made use of the other banking institutions of New York which do not publish weekly statements. There is no doubt that the trust companies were utilized, as they have never been before, to take up loans which the banks transferred to them. Proof of this fact was found in the November 9th reports of both banks and trust companies to the Government authorities. The National banks have, during many years, reported a steady increase in the fund held to the credit of trust companies and savings banks. Last November's figures for all the National banks of the country showed a decrease of $65,000,000 in such credits, as compared with a year before. The trust companies of New York, reporting the same day, showed a decrease of $68,000,000, as compared with 1904, in cash deposited by them in banks. They had withdrawn it to invest in loans. But this cash deposit is a part of a trust company's reserve, held for protection of its own deposit liabilities; and the same statement showed that, during the year, such liabilities had increased $109,000,000. It was therefore plain that not only banks, but trust companies as well, were deliberately weakening their position.

Whether or not these institutions went too far, in the light of the ordinary rules, it cannot be positively said. Their reports to the bank department, under the call of November 9, showed a much impaired reserve; and of the weekly bank report which was helped by this device, the president of one of the most conservative institutions, in a speech to the associated bankers, said:

"The present statement is a farce so far as it conveys any general idea of banking conditions. It is partial, it is half the truth, and unworthy of quotation as an indication of the trend of business in our line."

What Mr. Nash meant was that the real existing credit situation was much weaker than the reports of the banks alone, on Saturdays, disclosed. And even with this relief by the trust companies, the status of the banks themselves, as the money drain and the stock speculation both continued, went from bad to worse. The surplus bank reserve, which had been falling rapidly during the two preceding weeks, at length, on November 11, entirely disappeared, and was replaced by a deficit below the twenty-five-per-cent requirement, for the first time since September 20, 1902. Call money quickly rose to 25 per cent, and even sixty-day loans rose in Wall Street to a rate equivalent to seven per cent. During the three ensuing weeks, these high rates attracted so much outside capital that the surplus was restored; but the heavy Stock Exchange speculation continued, and, on December 9, the New York bank statement again reported a deficiency.

This fall in New York reserves below the ratio of twenty-five per cent to deposits was a matter of some considerable significance. With the clause of the National Bank Act dealing with this question, most people are familiar. In brief, that Act provides that when a National Bank in one of the larger cities finds that cash holdings have fallen below the twenty-five-per-cent ratio, it must make no more loans until that ratio is restored; the one exception being that such banks may lend on foreign exchange bills, that operation being a means of drawing on foreign markets to relieve the local situation. Penalties for continued deficiency in reserve are severe, though optional with the Government. If a bank is warned by the public officers to make good its reserve, and if it fails for thirty days thereafter to obey, the Comptroller of the Currency, with the concurrence of the Secretary of the Treasury, may, in his discretion, appoint a receiver and throw the offending institution out of business.

This option has never been exercised, chiefly because banks, as a rule, are quick to make good a deficit. Nor can such deficits in reserves be described as wholly abnormal. They are unusual, however, and have occurred only four times in the past fifteen years. It is the circumstance and the sequel to those episodes which give most significance to this season's incident. The four deficits referred to were those of September, 1902; of November, 1899; of July and August, 1893; and of August, September, October, and November, 1890. Not all of these deficit periods had the same cause. In 1890, the approach of the Baring disaster on the London money market caused such hasty and wholesale withdrawal of English capital from New York as instantly to cripple the position of our banks, which had to take the place of the English lenders. In 1893, it was the panicky withdrawal of cash for hoarding purposes, by American depositors, which drained the bank reserve fund, and made it, for a time, flatly impossible for banks to keep up their proper ratio to deposits. In 1899, it was the outbreak of the so-called "Boer War panic" which caused England to call home capital as it did in 1890. Such demands caught our market wholly off its guard, and sent the New York banks to a deficit within three weeks.

In 1902, the case was different from all the three instances just described. On that occasion, mischief was distinctly caused by a rash and ill-timed stock speculation, which loaded the New York banks with excessive loans and liabilities at the very moment when demands for the interior and for the uses of ordinary trade were particularly urgent. It will be seen that in its immediate cause the deficit episode of 1902 was the nearest parallel to that of the present season. Having thus noticed the cause of these former deficits, let us see what the sequel was. In the case of every such deficit in the early autumn — which would embrace those of 1890, 1899, and 1900 — the result was, first, a period of hesitation; next, some measure of emergency relief, either increase of cash through gold imports or Government deposits, or else decrease of liabilities through extensive loan reduction; then easing-off of money rates when reserves had been made good; finally, in the last weeks of the year, a convulsion in the market, in the course of which money rates went to a higher figure even than in the period of deficit.

It is these precedents which have caused such misgiving as was aroused by the New York deficit of last November. The banks dealt with the question rather singularly. They had no means of quickly increasing cash reserves, and they apparently were not willing to cut down loans incurred to sustain the Stock Exchange speculation. What they did was to draw heavily on London, placing in that market, during the twenty-five-per-cent money rate in New York, such large blocks of loans as to relieve the local bank liabilities and restore to the New York Associated Banks as a whole, within a week, the twenty-five-per-cent reserve. Yet, in spite of this expedient, banks which appeared to have been most closely identified with the stock speculation failed for many weeks to make good their required reserve. One of the largest banks of the New York clearing house remained for four successive weeks below its twenty-five per cent reserve; another showed three successive shortages. Even after the general reserve fund of the New York banks as a whole was again above that limit, thirty banks in one week, and twenty-three in the next, continued to report deficiencies.

Furthermore, the consideration arose in many minds as to

whether the maintenance of such a situation — borrowing abroad to sustain domestic speculation — was prudent pending such world-wide tightness in money as I have already pointed out. It is this foreign stringency, quite as much as the stringency in New York itself, which still confuses the situation and makes it difficult to draw a plain inference as to how the financial markets will respond to the great prosperity of the country. This question as to the real status of financial Europe cannot be answered wholly by the argument of increased trade demands. One influence which, though obscure, is possibly paramount, is the not unfamiliar financial reaction after a costly war. The world learned something of this influence during 1902. England had spent in the Transvaal struggle nearly one billion dollars. In June, 1902, the contest ended, and the more hasty optimists at once predicted rapid recovery in the world's finance. The sequel, as readers of these pages know, was something very different. We are able now to say that the actual situation, at the peace of 1902, was that markets which had contributed capital to that war were financially exhausted. London particularly had before it nearly two years of liquidation and depression; but Paris and New York did not escape. The Eastern War has probably cost each of the two belligerents $500,-000,000; but, whereas, in the Transvaal War, the fighting state raised the bulk of its loans at home, and was therefore the principal sufferer from the post-bellum reaction, the Russo-Japanese War was paid for in the main through money contributed by London, Paris, Berlin, and New York.

Borrowings for productive enterprise are no such burdens on the world's supply of capital as loans raised purely for purposes of destruction. In the one case, increase in the supply of capital goes on rapidly as a result of consumption of capital. In the other case, capital procured is for all intents and purposes thrown away. How far the exhaustion from the Eastern War will go, and how long it will continue, is no easier to answer now than was the similar question after the peace of 1902. The more hopeful view of this phase of the situation is clearly stated in the following remark of M. Paul Leroy-Beaulieu, of Paris. Calling attention to the fact that the Transvaal War had caused suspension of an important part of the world's gold output, whereas nothing of the sort had occurred in the Eastern War — during which contest, indeed, the Transvaal gold production once more broke all records — M. Leroy-Beaulieu thus puts the case:

"With this colossal gold production, it would be astonishing if the extreme money tension which has lasted, with almost daily tightening, during the past two months, could continue very much longer. This tension had for its causes, on the one hand, the movement of precious metals incidental to the end of the Eastern war, and the huge international loans in contemplation; on the other, the heaping up of gold, virtually as a war treasure, by the banks and treasuries of the great Powers. It seems as if this tension ought gradually to relax when the direct effects of the Eastern war no longer weigh on the money market."

The simple question of war exhaustion does not, in fact, make up all the peculiar conditions bearing on the present situation. There remained, even after the peace agreement of last August, practical certainty that Japan and Russia would, for various purposes, presently be in the market again for loans of $250,000,000 each. This was not a prospect wholly agreeable to the straitened European money markets. Russia, if not Japan, would obviously be compelled to place the bulk of her loan at Paris; and Paris, foreseeing this probability, held jealously to its gold supply and its credit fund. It did this all the more because of the extraordinary outbreak of Russian anarchy and rebellion in October. Delegates sent in October by the world's great banking houses to St. Petersburg, to conclude the Russian loan, found themselves in the midst of a revolution. They instantly withdrew from negotiation and escaped by sea. Russia's old bonds, which had risen to 93 after the peace, dropped at this time to 86½, the lowest figure reached during the whole Eastern War; in a stock exchange convulsion, on December 4, at Paris and Berlin, they fell to 72½. As the movement of anarchy spread over Russia, trade necessarily was in the main suspended, as a result of which German bankers who had advanced money for the use of Russian merchants found themselves virtually unable to collect. This was the situation as the autumn season drew to a close. It was relieved unquestionably by the Czar's concession to the demand for an honest suffrage and for a genuinely representative popular assembly.

But the Russian outbreak did not end with this. Until it has reached a definite termination, it will be quite impossible to say what Russia's influence will be on the great markets of Paris and Berlin, and, indirectly, on all the other money markets of the world. It will, in fact, be impossible, until a stable government is restored, to say what will happen to the Russian government's credit. The "Bourse crash" of December 4 was distinctly based on predictions that interest on Russia's external debt would be defaulted. Panic was then checked by the French premier's declaration that Russia had on deposit, in the markets of other nations, money enough to pay her external coupons for two years to come. This was unquestionably true; but the awkward question was nevertheless left unanswered as to how Russia could provide for her home expenditure, with industry, railway traffic, and taxation all at a standstill, unless she were to draw on these very credits.

Such is the more or less confused situation which confronts the financial markets of the world, our own not less than others. With us, the extremely favorable agricultural and industrial situation offsets in part, if not entirely, these money complications. The hopes of the early autumn regarding this country's staple crops have been verified; and though as yet the export movement of both grain and cotton has been disappointing, nevertheless the feeling still persists that if the produce speculators can only be persuaded to desist from reckless forestalling operations, by which wheat and cotton have repeatedly been forced to prices at which the foreigner would not buy, we shall see our export trade again at a high level. As it is, excess of merchandise exports over imports, since the opening of September, has been less by $39,000,000 than in 1904; and is, in fact, the smallest for the period since 1895. On the other hand, it is now assured that the United States has raised the second largest wheat crop in its history, and the largest crop of corn. Iron production and consumption have surpassed all precedents; and exchange of bank checks at American clearing houses has similarly broken all records. As to the cotton crop, the confusion of the Government estimates makes it impossible, even at this date, to say with assurance what the country has actually produced. Apparently, the yield will slightly exceed 10,500,000 bales — a sufficient crop if Europe's requirements are very light. That they will be light is rendered somewhat probable not only through the fact of the wholly abnormal foreign purchases from the great crop of a year ago, but from the fact that England has thus far taken from our present crop barely one-half as much as she bought in the similar period of 1904. This light buying in the early autumn was not the English spinner's policy in 1903, when he knew that our 10,000,000-bale cotton crop would not provide for the season's needs.

There has been one other important influence overhanging the past three months' American finance, but its practical effect has been hard to trace. No review of the financial events during the past three months would be in any sense complete without taking account of the life insurance investigation which has been busily in progress during that time. I mentioned, in the last number of THE FORUM, that the arrangement by which control of the Equitable Life was transferred from Mr. Hyde to Mr. Ryan, and the subsequent announcement of partial "mutualization," had largely cleared up the situation for that company. This was true for the reason that serious misgivings had been entertained as to the status on the market of the institutions surrounding the Equitable Life, if the situation remained what it was six months ago, when the winding up of the whole concern was openly discussed. When this apprehension was removed, acute fear of financial complication to results from the insurance scandals largely disappeared; in Europe it seemed to disappear entirely. It was even said, when the Armstrong Committee of the State Legislature began its investigations last September, that the public itself would soon lose interest in the question.

This was a very mistaken idea, however. People who held it underrated the possibilities of exposure which surrounded the past misconduct of these companies and their officers. From that time up to the present date, the investigation has developed almost daily such shocking evidence of irregular finance, extravagance in management, and false ideals generally regarding the life insurance business, that public interest in the disclosures has not for an instant flagged. It has, if anything, been growing to a climax. That the life insurance scandals played an important part in the outbreak of popular sentiment shown in the November elections, there is, in my judgment, no doubt whatever.

To attempt a detailed summary of the facts established and the evidence produced, up to the present date, would be out of the question in an article limited like this; and I can do no more here than describe very briefly certain salient facts, bearing on financial policy or practice, which have been established without question in the course of this examination. First, perhaps, in interest, in the eyes of those who have followed Wall Street history during the four or five past years, were the disclosures regarding syndicate operations. What was brought out was not wholly new, for much on this point had been elicited by the Frick Committee in its examination of the Equitable Life. It was then discovered not only that the company had been engaged as guarantor and underwriter along with its own trustees and officers in syndicates to float securities, but that, in some cases, trustees of the institutions, operating in such syndicates by themselves, had sold such securities to their own company, acting, therefore, both as seller and buyer. In the case of the Equitable, the officers who had done this made restitution of their profits. The Legislative Committee, in its examination of the other companies, found considerably less of the practice of security sales by trustees to their own companies, but considerably more of participation by the companies in underwriting projects in which trustees appeared as participating with their companies.

The purpose of the underwriting syndicate is simply to guarantee that a market for a new security issue shall be found. If outside interests buy the securities on the public offer, the underwriter merely takes up his profits on the underwriting. If, on the other hand, the offer to the public fails, the underwriter then becomes liable to pay for such securities with his own money, and to become in fact the purchaser. Much controversy developed, during the early stages of the examination by the Armstrong Legislative Committee, as to whether joint participation of this sort, by a life insurance company and its own trustees, was right. The theory was set up, by numerous well-known financiers affiliated with the companies, that sales directly by railway and other security-issuing corporations to the life insurance companies were impracticable, and that the life insurance companies could not obtain desirable investments for their funds except by sharing in the underwriting. This theory was taken by the financial world with a considerable grain of salt. One of these life insurance officers testified that the bankers or corporations offering such securities required the companies to "underwrite"; that they would not sell to the companies except on that condition; and that the securities could easily be disposed of on the foreign markets, if the bankers chose to shut out the life insurance buyers. The experience which these very same bankers and corporations had with the investment market during 1903 — when home investors would not buy, and when Europe thereupon refused to take even first-class railway bonds and insisted on obtaining short term, high-rate notes — was sufficient commentary on the new idea, and turned it promptly into ridicule.

The question whether trustees of a life insurance corporation had the moral right to take for their personal account a share in an underwriting to which they had committed their company was also hotly canvassed. Defenders of the system argued that such participation was the surest guarantee that a safe investment had been found for the funds of policyholders. To this it was rejoined that a trustee thus committed to a scheme of personal profit for himself could insure himself from loss by bringing the vast resources of his own company into play, and that the temptation thus to involve the company where it ought not to be engaged was so great that the operation ought to be condemned. This, it may fairly be said, became the general view as time went on.

These more or less ethical considerations were, however, far superseded by two disclosures which had an intensely practical bearing on the financial situation. The first was brought to light by the Frick

23

report in its remarks on the purchase of subsidiary banking institutions by the Equitable. In August, 1903, during the "rich men's panic," the opportunity for investment of life insurance funds in sound securities and at inviting prices was greater than has existed at any other time in the past half a dozen years. On the thirteenth of that month, President Alexander of the. Equitable, referring to such investment opportunities, wrote to an officer of his company: "We would be buying a good many such things were it not that we are so strapped for money by engagements already made"; adding, "all this is very annoying, because if we had $5,000,000 or $10,000,000 to invest now, we would make a great deal of money." The Frick Committee pointed out that on that very day of August, 1903, the Equitable had on deposit, with its affiliated banks and subsidiary institutions, no less than $36,399,788. What the Frick report had to say regarding this affair was that "these funds, through alliance with other concerns, were so tied up that the opportunity was lost."

In what were they tied up? This is the question which up to the present has had no answer. Some light was thrown upon it by the admission before the Armstrong Committee, in November, that the New York Life, being unwilling to enter directly into participation in the famous Steel Trust underwriting of 1901, but having on deposit upward of $2,325,000 with a trust company under its control, directed that company to engage to that extent in the Steel Trust underwriting, and received three-quarters of the profits, leaving the balance for the obliging subsidiary institution.

The disclosures of extravagance in the management of the life insurance companies, which were numerous, do not bear so directly on the general financial situation. However, in so far as concerns the impression made on the public mind, it is probable that the annual salary of $150,000 granted to the president of one of the great insurance companies, who on the stand gave few signs of anything but ignorance of his company's affairs, had very great effect. So did the very extraordinary fact that, on the very day when the evidence had shown this president's relatives to have taken $2,000,000 in salaries and commissions from the company within ten years, the president himself gave testimony that in his view a life insurance company was a benevolent institution. Confronted with the facts as to shrinking dividends paid to policyholders, this gentleman replied that the company was not organized for dividend purposes, which might involve the granting to a policyholder, at the end of the fiscal year, of "seven dollars, which he would spend for billiards and cigars." This sort of evidence was calculated to inflame the popular indignation to a white heat. It was also unfortunately well adapted to drive away from the life insurance field the American insurer.

Indignation reached a focus at another point, when the officers of the three greatest life insurance companies in the United States confessed, one after another, that they had paid, in sums ranging from $25,000 to $50,000, yearly contributions to one of the two political parties for its presidential campaign fund. It was alleged by the officers, when confronted by this evidence, that they gave these sums to the sound-money party during 1896, 1900, and 1904, when they believed they were serving their policyholders' interests by such contributions. This argument was met and shattered instantly by the indignant protests of a number of Southern and Western policyholders of the companies, who replied that, as citizens, they, in 1896 and 1900, had both opposed and voted against the party to whom their companies had made such contributions. The gist of the matter, then, as it seemed to them, was that their own money had been used illegally against what they regarded as their own political interests. It soon became evident, moreover, that the apology that such political contributions insured the safety of the life insurance policyholder was a sham and an evasion. Senator Platt, of New York, taking the stand in the last half of November, testified specifically that the life insurance companies had been in the habit of making contributions to the Republican campaign fund for its New York State campaign alone, while maintaining an extravagant lobby at Albany.

It was only slowly that one principal root of the trouble in this matter came to light. The committee's counsel repeatedly returned to the question of deferred dividend policies—meaning by that a policy which, instead of insuring its holder for his life, gave him insurance for a period of twenty years, paid to him no dividends during that period, and paid none to his heirs if he died before that period's expiration, but which undertook to insure participants during the twenty years, and to divide between the survivors of the "pool" all of the dividends which had accrued from payments made during the twenty-year period. Unbiased writers on insurance have been from the start practically unanimous in opposition to this form of policy, which has never appealed to such critics as legitimate insurance. This objection, and the further and very serious objection brought to light by the recent disclosures, are summed up in the following statement made by Insurance Commissioner McGivney to the Insurance Commissioners' Convention last September:

The purpose of a mutual life insurance company is not to have its members gambling on the misfortunes of its other members. The deferred dividend plan is the medium for building up large surplus funds, which are not required by law to earn any interest; it furnishes a ready means to make up losses from extravagance and waste; and is a temptation to the management for hazardous and risky speculation in the policyholders' funds.

This may be supplemented by the following language from the Frick report:

The annual dividend company is held to accountability each year. The deferred dividend company is never held to accountability by the whole body of its policyholders, and is so held by its individual policyholders only when their opportunity for action has passed. This absence of accountability makes possible the pursuit of rapidity of growth at undue cost, because the effect of that cost is not felt by the policyholder until it is too late for his availing protest.

As to the logical force of these arguments, there seems to me no doubt whatever. Policies of this sort are defended energetically, however, by the companies. President McCall of the New York Life went so far, when testifying in October, as to declare that he did not believe in straight-life annual dividend policies. His point of view was that to increase the business of the companies, good solicitors must be obtained; that to obtain good solicitors, large commissions must be paid; and that the largest commissions in the field are those obtained on twenty-year, deferred-dividend policies. After this, in testifying later on, Vice-President Tarbell, of the Equitable Life, defended such policies on the ground that they add to the safety of insurance by a large surplus fund accruing in the interim; that they provide for the family when the policy matures; that they attract "good lives"; that they induce people to insure who would not insure on the simple ground that the policy would be payable at their death; and that they do not lapse as the ordinary policy often does. It is hardly necessary to reply in detail to these arguments. It will be seen at once that all of them are derived from the point of view of the insurance business, and that the primary purpose of the latter is to obtain an enormous surplus. This is, however, the very root of the evil out of which all the existing scandal has arisen.

It has been impossible, within the limits of a paper such as this, to do more than summarize briefly and inadequately the disclosures of this three-months' inquiry. Enough has been called to mind, however, to confirm the conclusion already reached by daily readers of the testimony. These conclusions are: (1) that the stupendous assets — $1,247,000,000 last January for the three companies, the Mutual, the Equitable, and the New York Life, and increasing, for the three, at the rate of $90,000,000 annually — have provided temptation for loose practices, extravagance, and waste, such as the managements were unable to resist; (2) that the rapid growth of these huge surpluses was largely due to a species of insurance whereby excessive premiums were collected while the normal return was withheld from policyholders during twenty years; (3) that the existence of such piles of capital has made the great companies a ready mark for Wall Street promoters; (4) that such promoters have made it their purpose to commit insurance trustees to such use of life insurance funds by entangling them personally in those operations; (5) that money has been flung about by these managers as if the property were their own; (6) that when embarking the companies' funds in schemes improper for life insurance surpluses, the device has been employed of depositing huge sums of money with certain trust companies, and seeing that those companies used the money in the forbidden ways; (7) that the ratio of expense in management is abnormally great, and the percentage of income on the investment abnormally small; (8) that men of high character and broad experience in finance, placed on the boards of trustees to ensure sound financial management, have remained habitually in ignorance of what was going on, and, when confronted publicly with their neglect of duty, have fallen back on the apology that they were too busy to attend to it. No one, I think, will deny these eight conclusions.

What is to be done about it? Little has been said as yet of this; but it will occupy, before very long, a first place in discussions of the subject. Let us first dismiss the idea of "State insurance" managed by public officers; because, whatever may be said for or against that project, it will not in the least help to reform the existing half-billion-dollar corporations, which will necessarily continue to do business.

There are, I think, several definite reforms toward which all thinking citizens ought to bend their energies. The size of the insurance company should be limited by law. Its scope of investment should be prudently restricted. Its ownership of subsidiary companies should be wholly prohibited. Its issuance of deferred dividend or "semi-tontine" policies should, if possible, be suppressed. Its officers and trustees should be forbidden by law to engage in any syndicate operation in which they have engaged their company. Fees of soliciting agents should be rigidly limited. Finally, whether by law or by the public's absolute demand, the "dummy director" should be excluded from every life insurance board.

This is not an easy programme; but it is perfectly possible, and, in my judgment, indispensable to the recovery of public confidence in life insurance. The size of a company can be limited by forbidding it to solicit new business after existing contracts or assets have reached a given figure. This is no academic suggestion, but has been seriously made by at least one president of a very great life insurance company. Without some such regulation, it has been affirmed by the officers of one of these companies, which typifies them all, that in a dozen more years the assets of this single company may arrive at the stupendous figure of one billion dollars.

The restriction of investments should be undertaken with the utmost care. To prescribe the "savings bank list" would be unwise in the extreme; because, although careless management has made the average yield on present life insurance investments little above what the savings banks actually pay to depositors, and in some instances less, still such limitation of the field would deprive the companies of many wholly legitimate opportunities, and would bring an unwholesome competition into the field of savings banks. But engagement in purely speculative ventures — such as the Steel and Shipping Trust promotions — ought to be positively prohibited. "Syndicate participations" as a class should be forbidden, save under the most scrupulous restrictions. If the companies were prohibited from "underwriting" as preliminary to getting a chance at the investment, we should soon test this new-fangled notion that these great investment companies cannot obtain investments except by deferring to all the arbitrary wishes of the issuing banker.

To my mind, the problem of the "dummy director" is the least troublesome of all. We were told, at the outset of the pending inquiry, that it was indispensable to get men of great experience and prestige to direct these undertakings. Next, when the "syndicate participation" matter came into the case, the public was informed that men of the calibre required could not be obtained unless they were allowed to embark in financial ventures with their companies. Hardly was the ink dry on reports of this last testimony, when the very directors under discussion testified that they had no time to give to the company's affairs, that they were not consulted on its important operations, and that they were, as one of the most eminent of them put the matter, a "negligible quantity." This was *reductio ad absurdum* of the two earlier arguments.

Direction of a life insurance company is not so intricate a business as to require a whit more prestige or experience than direction of a savings bank. The Equitable, which lost last spring, by resignation, most of its old trustees from high finance, is trying the experiment of taking directors from the more ordinary walks of life. With proper exercise of choice, the success of such an experiment is to my mind unquestionable. The Equitable also tentatively brought forward an expedient which may be the solution of the problem—that of asking public policyholders to vote for their own trustees. All mutual policyholders have the right already, though they do not exercise it. The obvious trouble is a lack of organization, and this is also the defect of the Equitable plan, so far as yet developed. Some of the company's Southern policyholders, who met in a State convention, and in that assemblage fixed on their candidates for the new trustees, have hit more nearly to the logical expedient than has anywhere else been done.

It cannot be said that the life insurance scandals at New York have visibly shaken the confidence of the investing community. Uneasiness on that score has undoubtedly existed; and there has been talk in banking circles, from time to time, of a disposition, in the inland communities, to argue that practices which have honeycombed with rottenness our great insurance companies must exist in other financial institutions. But to venture this as a general conjecture, and to sell investment holdings because of it, are two very different things. That such selling has not existed is sufficiently proved by the fact that investors have clung to their stocks in the face of the season's extravagant prices. The assertion of Mr. Thomas F. Ryan to the Armstrong committee, that he bought Mr. Hyde's Equitable stock, in June, "to avert the most tremendous panic that this country has ever seen," has not been taken altogether seriously. Yet it is true that, at ordinary times, the insurance episode would almost certainly have overclouded the financial horizon.

Why has it not done so during these past three months? The familiar answer is that the country's financial, commercial, and industrial outlook is so extraordinarily strong. The much more perplexing question is why the speculative markets have to all intents ignored the signs of a heavy strain on capital; why they have snapped their fingers at the threatened collapse of Russia, with its $2,500,000,000 foreign debt; at the admitted weakness of the great foreign banks; at the excessively high rates for money in New York; and at the repeated impairment of the reserve required by law from our banking institutions. The remarkable thing is not that our markets have escaped disastrous declines as a natural consequence, but that speculation for the rise has grown increasingly wild with the tightening of the money strain. As I write, a week of a deficit in bank reserves, of 27 per cent money at New York, and of a temporary panic at Paris and Berlin, has been accompanied by a violent rise in prices on the New York Stock Exchange, and followed by a day of new advances, with transactions approaching the portentous two-million-share days of April, 1901.

Reasoning on one line, it will be and is contended that such a spectacle means a financial position utterly impregnable. Reasoning on another, it will be and is insisted that the spirit of speculation has so turned the heads of enormously wealthy financiers that they are taking risks from which men in their sober senses would shrink. We shall know before very long which line of reasoning is right. Of one fact there seems, however, to be no doubt whatever. Our great banking institutions have not played the part of conservatism, even to the extent which they did in 1901. They have, with some honorable exceptions, gone with the stream, placed their resources at the disposal of the millionaire speculators, and provided the fuel for the fire. This is a fact in the situation which, in its bearing on the longer future, goes far to counterbalance the great and genuine prosperity of American industry. It is a well-known path of dangers. To those who look only to the immediate future, the prospect is fortunately bright.

ALEXANDER D. NOYES.

THE EDUCATIONAL OUTLOOK.

IT is one of the sad experiences of the present day to discover that men who have been singularly honored by positions of prominence have been guilty of gross dishonesty. Nevertheless, it is not necessary, on that account, to lose one's faith in humanity, for investigations will not cease until the corrupt minority has become the majority; and while the problem of restoring in American life the sturdy principles of simple honesty is great, it is not overwhelmingly so.

Time was — not so very long ago — when the temptations to self-indulgence were less general than they are at the present time. Things which in those days were considered an exceptional treat are now counted among the daily needs. The living expenses have increased accordingly, and the art of mere money-making has been raised in popular estimation beyond the bounds of rationality. The man who knows how to bring in dollars and cents is the commanding figure in public life. How to amass a large amount of money, without incurring the risk of going to prison, has become the predominant consideration. The producer of solid value has become the servant of the trafficker, who uses the products as a basis for financial speculation. The standard of reward is not what a man or a man's work is worth to his country or to the world, but financial shrewdness pure and simple. Men whose dealings have corrupted the Government and social life, and whose influence has brought thousands of young people under the dominion of false gods, have become in not a few instances the masters.

What is to be done about it? The first thing to do would seem to be to establish righteous and just standards of living. The daily press can help on the cause by ceasing to report the doings of the people whose only distinctions are the possession of wealth and lavishness in the selfish uses thereof. This altogether too common practice is a menace in that it fosters immoral notions of human destiny. The palliation of unmistakable infringements of enacted laws is another corrupting force which the newspapers not infrequently foster. The churches, too, may reasonably be expected to render substantial help, though a weakening of their influence is not to be denied. This weakening is due chiefly to a decline in the intellectual and moral fibre and maturity of the men installed as pastors. Authoritativeness and rational breadth of sympathy cannot be expected of a stripling. A moral leader is not produced by doctrinal formulæ and passing through a divinity school. Admission to heaven is not regulated by examinations in theology; nor do attractive presence and soothing sermons stamp the minister as a source of power. Emotional cream-puffs do not develop moral stamina. Sturdiness and vigor are at the present day less often clothed in the clerical garb than they were in the years gone by. But in spite of all this there are splendid opportunities for good inherent in church organizations, aside from the pastors. Association of people for a moral purpose forms the best possible basis for the accomplishment of moral results. Leaders who will utilize the dormant possibilities are needed; and these leaders will arise when the great awakening comes.

The surest foundation on which to build hopes for the future would seem to be supplied in the schools for the young. Here the most effective work may be done. Whether common, parish, or private, the schools are the true temples of the humanity of to-morrow. Great opportunities entail great responsibilities. Are the schools equal to the task? It may seem hard to say it, but it is nevertheless true that the schools of the past are in no small degree responsible for the gross corruption which cries to heaven daily from the columns of the newspapers. The limitation to the three R's and a contemplative life held out as a reward to the ambitious pupils have something to do with the matter. The sturdy American pioneer life which formerly surrounded most of the children in their homes was a powerful antidote. But when that passed away, and the industrial occupations of the home and the farm no longer exercised their educational influence over the young, the bookish school curriculum became a growing menace to society. It bred a desire for comfort; for living by one's wit rather than by honest labor; for getting something for nothing. The softening of teaching methods has had an unfavorable influence. The educational seers pointed out the gravity of the danger, and the gradual development of industrial phases of work in the schools shows that their warning is being heeded.

The girls and boys who are learning to produce something in lines that constitute the actual wealth of the world are getting a valuable education. They are given a chance to develop the conviction that there is joy in making something, and that money obtained in any other manner than by giving actual value in return is not earned. That is worth considerable. Sincere regard for conscientious labor and an honest trade, or at least adaptability for the kind of work best suited to his nature — these form the best equipment a pupil can take with him into the world. Considerations like these must help shape the school programmes of the present day. Let those who will delight in quarrelling over "fads and frills." When the needs of the times change, the duties of the schools change with them.

An atmosphere of honesty is essential to the growth of honesty at school. To the child the school represents society and the State. Here he acquires knowledge of the purposes and doings of the world. He participates in the world's business. His tasks are as serious as those recompensed in dollars and cents. His reward is the pleasure which comes from putting the best that is in him into his work. School, as Colonel Parker used to insist, is "not a preparation for life, it is life." The spirit of the school is of supreme importance. The staunchest kind of honesty ought to rule everything. Does it? Alas! there are dishonest schools. There are schools which reward possession rather than effort. The boy who stands highest in a memory test, the boy who is shrewdest, and the boy who has the best native endowment and the largest amount of help at home — these are the boys who most frequently carry away the prizes. Mr. Hartwell, of the Boys' High School, Brooklyn, N. Y., has devised a practical plan for overcoming this iniquity. His "Lincoln Improvement League" is enlisted for the establishment of honest standards of rewards. The degree of improvement and the effort put forth to rise are to be encouraged by the school, and not mere ability.

Other schools there are whose pretensions and practice run far apart. Their programmes are prepared for the eyes of the outside world; the actual work is something entirely different. They crave for present plaudits more than for the consciousness of honest toiling for the abiding welfare of their pupils. They take pride in medals and diplomas received at exhibitions rather than in the nurture of sturdy principles of Americanism in the consciences of the young. They labor for showy products rather than for persistent progress. An honest school is willing to have its practice speak for its purposes: it looks for its approval to the pupils matured to men and women, to the future manhood and womanhood in the boys and girls now toiling for the development of their natures. Here is where honesty is most needed.

One species of dishonesty is nurtured by examination systems which grade worth by remembered facts. Such examinations still flourish, though their reign is less extensive than in years gone by. One result is that the schools ruled by these systems shape their whole course of teaching by the examination requirements. They may explain their slavery as they choose; but the fact remains that

they are not governed by honest considerations as to what is best
adapted to the actual individual needs of pupils.   Forsooth, one much
lauded school system which prides itself on doing "Individual" work
is chiefly a coaching machine for the Regents' examinations in the
State of New York: the individual needs are explained with reference
to the Procrustean requirements instead of by an understanding of
humanity.   Another town manages to win for itself year after year
the gratification of having all (or nearly all) children who try the
Regents' examinations pass them with fairly high rating.   The children know the dishonesty beneath it, as preliminary examinations are
resorted to in order to weed out pupils who are not likely to win out
in the test.   Honesty cannot thrive where the race is to the swift.
The schools must have a higher standard.

Teachers and school officers may reasonably be expected to be
representatives of noble manhood and womanhood.   Better that
knowledge be lacking — for the world has a surfeit of cyclopædias —
than that conduct reveal the slightest taint.   Integrity is *sine qua non.*
The example of a dishonest superintendent is of fearful consequence
for the system.   School boards that fail to inquire minutely into
the past conduct, character, and moral reputation of a candidate for
an educational position — superintendent, principal, or teacher — are
guilty of criminal neglect.   The choice of a caretaker, too, should be
well considered; for his conduct is before the eyes of the young, and
his personality is a factor in the life of a school.   School regulations
not in harmony with ethical manhood should be speedily abrogated.

What public spirit, honesty, and expert judgment can accomplish
when united in the administration of a city school system has been
strikingly illustrated in Rochester.   Improvements have been inaugurated in the short space of five years that are nothing short of marvellous.   Wise economy has made the many thousands of dollars required
produce the fullest measure of results.   All the expenditures have
been met from the regular annual appropriations from city and State
provided for by law.   The one exception, if it may be called such, is
the bond sale of $260,000 borrowed on the city's credit.   But ultimately
this amount, too, will be paid from the regular funds, as $30,000 are
annually laid aside to meet the obligation.   The sinking-fund already
amounts to $120,000.   The bond issue simply made it possible to
distribute the financial burden over the appropriations of ten years.

Since 1900 there have been erected five large grammar schools at
a total cost of $278,000.   Substantial additions have been made to
four other buildings at a cost of $77,000.   Two fine high schools have

been built and equipped at a cost of $650,000. Assembly halls have been supplied or fitted up in ten schools outside of those provided in the new buildings. The sanitary condition of all the schools have been improved. Land has been purchased to enlarge the grounds of five schools. In some cases this has been done to protect the light of the rooms from encroaching buildings, and in some to provide for a future growth of enrolment. Experts have pronounced the new East Side high school a model of its kind. The heating and ventilating plants are exceptionally good. The furnishing and equipment of the laboratories, gymnasia, lunch room, and library are excellent. The West Side high school is built on substantially the same plan.

The new grammar schools contain from sixteen to nineteen rooms. In each building there is upon the first floor a large hall, lighted from above. These halls are 45 by 58 feet. They are in constant use and have become the centre of the life of their respective schools. They are used as assembly rooms; for classes in music, gymnastics, and free games; for exhibits of the work of pupils; and as gathering places for the patrons of the schools. There is in each building, also, a well-equipped principal's office, a waiting-room and teachers' room, and a library. It has been the policy of the board to supply ample grounds for each school. The buildings have cost, on an average, about $57,000. They are constructed entirely in the interest of the children and of public health. Probably in no other American city can be found grammar-school buildings, two stories in height, with such liberal provisions for halls and other conveniences for pupils and teachers.

The beginnings of school reform in Rochester were not accidental or the result of any sudden or impulsive change of sentiment. Six years before there was any well-defined demand for a reform of the schools, a movement in the interest of good government was started which enlisted the co-operation of many of the best citizens of the community. Two hard-fought municipal campaigns were won squarely by the issue of good government. In the second of these campaigns, the dominant political organization met with an overwhelming defeat as the result of good government opposition; and the leaders of this organization were wise enough and far-sighted enough to completely reverse their policy and nominate men for office who could be heartily endorsed by the good government element. This change of attitude, and this alone, made it possible to throw overboard the existing school administration and so to change the school law as to put the administration in the hands of a board of five elected on a general ticket, and to select candidates for the school board who were unexceptional in character and ability. Thus it was the long period of agitation and education conducted by the good-government ·clubs which raised the ideals of the community to a higher level, and made reform in school administration, as in all other departments of the municipal government, possible.

The leaders of the good-government movement were self-sacrificing men, actuated solely by public spirit, giving of their time and money without stint, and refusing all suggestions of public office or emolument for themselves. Mr. John T. Alling was head and front in the campaign for honesty and business sagacity in municipal administration. Rochester owes an immeasurable debt to his public spirit, his zeal, and his persistence in redeeming the city from the bondage of political corruption. His unselfishness and firmness of purpose, his faith in the civic conscience of his city, his unfaltering courage, and, above all, his never-wearying readiness to sacrifice personal interest and comfort for the good of the cause, were the inspiring forces which rallied the best citizenship around the good-government platform. Mr. Barber was another leader of this stamp. So was Mr. Townson. The latter is most closely identified with the remarkable educational reform that has transformed the common school administration of Rochester into a model for the whole country. With him should be mentioned also Mrs. Montgomery and Professor Forbes, of Rochester University, as foremost in the struggle for better things. There is no need of multiplying names. After the campaign was once under way, civic pride drew many leaders into the ranks eager to make the name of their city stand for all that is best in American citizenship.

The reform of the city began with the reform of the schools. On this ground, as is usually the case, the consciences of parents responded most speedily. The good accomplished here spread to other departments; and to-day the whole city government is under the control of worthy principles. The schools redeem the town.

Under the present school law, enacted in 1900, the school board consists of five members, three of whom are elected at one time and two others two years later for a term of four years. The board is a corporation, authorized to spend money appropriated for its use. The annual appropriation is based upon the number of pupils, $25 being allowed for each pupil enrolled. In the councils of the school board, the one consideration deciding all questions which arise is what is best for the schools.

The superintendent is appointed by the board for four years. He is given the initiative in the appointment of supervisors, principals, and teachers; and he transfers teachers. He is also made responsible for the general management of education. He is assisted by five

supervisors, who direct instruction in primary schools and kindergartens, in manual training, drawing, music, and domestic art. Thirteen assistants are employed in the department of manual training
alone. Carpentry is part of the course of study for the boys of the
seventh and eighth grades, and desk work for the boys of the fifth
and sixth grades. In every primary class instruction is given in basketry, weaving, raffia work, clay modelling, and cardboard cutting.
The girls of the fifth, sixth, seventh, and eighth grades have two hours
in domestic science each week. One assistant is employed in the
department of music and one in the department of drawing.

The grade institutes of Rochester are deserving of special notice.
At least three of them are held each year. The teachers of a given
grade dismiss their schools usually on a Friday, and are organized as
an institute for an entire day. In this way the teachers of every
grade are in session annually for at least three entire days. The
superintendent and supervisors furnish the necessary instruction
and directions. Two or more classes of children are under instruction
at such institutes a part of each day. The superintendent calls a
business meeting of principals the first Wednesday of the month. A
round-table of principals is held on the third Wednesday for the professional study of educational questions.

Connected with nearly every school is an active organization of
mothers or parents. These organizations co-operate with the schools
in beautifying the grounds, decorating the class-room walls with
pictures, or providing reference books. They meet at regular intervals.
A mass meeting is held in June of each year, and a flower-show in
September. The Women's Union is another large body organized for
educational work. It has done much to develop right public sentiment
with reference to public education. At least once a year is held a general exhibit of school work on a large scale in each building. It is
arranged by grades and subjects to show representative work and
to illustrate the courses of study. These exhibitions are usually
planned in connection with meetings of the mothers' clubs and are
visited by throngs of patrons.

Kindergartens existed in many of the schools before 1901. In
that year they were made a part of the system in every building.
The board assumed that the kindergartners could serve as many hours
as teachers in the grade schools, and so required them to handle one
class in the morning and another in the afternoon. The classes are
usually very small, numbering not more than ten or twelve pupils.
This experiment is certainly very significant. It has enabled the board
to offer the advantages of the kindergarten to every neighborhood

and to every child in the city. The health and spirit of the kindergartners have not suffered in the least by the somewhat unusual, but
not at all unreasonable, demands upon their time.

Commercial and manual-training courses are now offered to pupils
in the high schools. This is a new departure for Rochester. The
plan endorsed by the school authorities in New York and Brooklyn
is followed, which provides that a business or industrial high school
course should be four years in length, and should represent in intellectual training the equivalent of any course offered in preparation
for college. The special business features of the commercial course
are supposed to be taken up principally during the last two years in
school. The intention is to begin with the laying of a broad foundation
of general information and culture in the study of English, mathematics,
history, and language, and in addition to emphasize those branches
that help to prepare for commercial or industrial pursuits. A lunch-
room 81 feet by 70 feet is provided in each of the high-school buildings.
These rooms are abundantly fitted with small tables and chairs for the
use of the students. The session of the high school extends from
9.00 until 2.30. Lunch is served at 12.15. A salaried woman manager
superintends this department. It is the purpose of the board that
the food shall be provided at such rates as merely to meet the necessary
expenses, and to provide for repairs and breakage. The average
number of pupils daily served in these restaurants is 1,000. The
lunch-rooms are also patronized by students and instructors from
the training school and from the university.

Not the least of the heroic work of the school board has been the
restoration of the school library funds to their proper use. Two grades
out of eight are already supplied with generous school-room libraries.
Additional supplementary reading matter has been furnished in every
grade, until the equipment of the schools in this respect has become
second to none. For years the Central Library had been maintained
by school funds as a circulating and reference library for the general
public, contrary to law. On discovering the illegality of the custom,
the board determined not to let the warm regard in which the library
was held by the citizens weigh against its plain duty. It discontinued
the general circulating and reference library so long established, and
turned to plans for the founding of school libraries such as may be
legitimately maintained by school funds. Rochester is at the present
time without a public library.

The high schools and the normal training school have received a
large number of valuable reference books on literature, history, education, art, and science from the distribution of books formerly held by

the Central Library. From the remainder, the books best suited to the purpose have been distributed among the grade schools, where they will form the nucleus of a school library. With the fund available from the annual appropriation, the board intends to supply carefully selected libraries to each grade. The plan of supplying these grade libraries has been in successful operation in Buffalo, Pittsburgh, and other cities, and experience has proved the wisdom of it.

Another recent change has been the organization of the truant school. The old truant-school building with its dormitories and barred windows has been given up. In its place a room for truants has been opened in one of the day schools. Here, under the care of a skilful teacher, the truant boys are given individual attention and suitable training. Whenever their improvement warrants, the boys are promoted into the regular school grades. Regularity of attendance is secured, the interests of the boys are aroused, and often astonishingly rapid progress is made. Indeed, the transfer to the truant school is often the turning-point in the boy's school life. Rochester's experience is that the boys are not for the most part vicious, but that in many cases truancy has been occasioned by mortification over poor clothing, or by such backwardness in their studies as to place the boys with children far younger than themselves. Sometimes the inability readily to understand or use English has proved a predisposing cause, and sometimes the mere lack of any firm control in the boy's home.

The night schools have made splendid progress. The law provides that boys or girls under sixteen who are working in factories and have not completed their grammar-school course must attend night school. The number of pupils in the night schools has in consequence increased three-fold during the past four years. The quality of the work accomplished has steadily improved. There are large classes of Russians, Poles, Germans, and Italians learning to read and write English. There are classes in book-keeping, stenography, mechanical drawing, electrical science, arithmetic, history, geography, vocal music, carpentry, sloyd, dressmaking, sewing, millinery, and cooking. Certificates are given on the completion of a subject and to pupils regularly promoted from the grades to the evening high schools.

The physical training in the grades consists of formal instruction and free games. There is a gymnasium for boys and one for girls in each of the high schools. A director is employed for each gymnasium. Gymnastics are required of all pupils in the high schools in the first, second, and third years. Music and drawing are required in the grade schools, but are optional in the high schools. The children of every room have free play, either in their school-room or in the school hall,

24

every day. The old-fashioned and familiar games are most popular. Free construction grows out of manual training and drawing, and has become a useful means of expression in connection with the common-school subjects. The aim is to stimulate the children's interest in this work both at home and at school. The familiar classics are studied intensively in every grade, and this study generally results in a more or less elaborate dramatization of interesting selections. Nearly every building has class gardens, and children are urged to plant seeds at home. Over 40,000 packages of seeds were planted by school children last spring. An extensive flower-show is held in September. Here children exhibit the flowers and vegetables they have raised, and compete for prizes offered by the Women's Union.

A most remarkable piece of educational investigation has recently been accomplished at Springfield, Massachusetts, which goes far toward deciding the question as to whether or not the schools of our fathers and grandfathers, with their narrow curricula, produced better spellers and better cipherers than the present-day schools, with their more elaborate programmes. It came about in this way. Some eight years ago, in cleaning out the garret of the old high school in Springfield, there was found, in a rubbish heap, a bound volume containing spelling tests and examination questions, with answers, of the year 1846. Dr. Balliet, to whose work as superintendent is due the exceptionally good name of the city's schools, placed the volume in his safe, and, on leaving Springfield, brought it to the attention of Mr. Riley, a very efficient and keen-sighted grammar-school principal. Mr. Riley at once recognized the peculiar value of the find, and made it the basis of a series of educational tests which established, beyond reasonable doubt, the superiority of the work of the modern elementary schools over those of sixty years ago. The results of his tests were published in the Springfield "Republican" and reprinted in the "School Journal."

Since the appearance of THE FORUM articles on needed lines of educational research this is probably the most important contribution to tangible pedagogy. For the want of testimony such as this, there has been no end of lamentation over the decline of the efficiency of the schools in the so-called "practical" branches. We have been told in season and out of season that spelling and arithmetic were never more poorly taught than at present, and that the only salvation was to be found in a return to the Three-R fleshpots of old. Now comes the awful disillusionment of the pleaders for the ways of the fathers. There is no getting away from the cold logic of the tests supplied by Mr. Riley. He shows that the pupils attending the present-day grammar schools of Springfield not only do much better in arithmetic, but spell better than their forebears in 1846.

The results of this investigation confirm emphatically the contention of Dr. J. M. Rice to the effect that increase of the time devoted to the three R's does not produce corresponding increase of efficiency. His researches established that spelling and arithmetic may be as successfully taught where a rich curriculum is in force as where the programme confines itself to the narrowest possible limits. In spite of the comprehensiveness of his proofs, some people sought shelter behind assertions going back of present conditions to the past, claiming that, whatever may be said of the schools of to-day, those of the past grounded the children more thoroughly in the so-called "essentials." This prop of comfort must feel rather shaky after the Springfield examination.

The tests were given to 245 ninth-grade pupils, last March. In 1846 they were applied to high school pupils whose average age was about the same as that of the high school sophomores of to-day. If Mr. Riley had wanted to be absolutely fair, he would have given the tests to the second-year pupils or at least the freshmen of the high school. The pupils of 1846 had still other advantages over their successors in 1905. English was spoken in all the homes — the large non-English speaking element of the schools of to-day was entirely lacking. The school year was about one-third longer, covering forty-four weeks, with an aggregate of 1,340 working, hours, as against the present allowance of forty weeks, with an approximate aggregate of 1,000 hours. The child who attended school three years then spent as many hours in school as one who at present attends four years; and as there were fewer studies, more time and attention could be devoted to each than now. Springfield had an expert superintendent at the head of its school system then, as now. The high school was an established and well-managed institution. As to the curriculum of the elementary schools, there is no doubt as to its definiteness and insistence upon thoroughness in the very studies in which the children of 1905 did ever so much better than those of 1846. Reading, writing, arithmetic, geography, and spelling were about all the branches taught below the high school. The following extracts from the course of study of those days and from Principal Ariel Parrish's report, show the emphasis laid upon spelling:

No one shall be advanced to the second class (third year primary) who cannot spell with ease and propriety the words in "My First School Book."

No one shall be advanced to the first class (fourth year primary) who cannot spell words easily in the first fifty pages of the Spelling Book.

Accuracy in spelling and excellence in reading are deemed of the first importance.

Ability to spell correctly is deemed highly important, as lying at the foundation of all requirements, without which no person can be accurate or intelligible as a scholar, or ever safe from exposure to great mortification in after life.

Regular exercises are required in this branch (in the high school), which are rigidly criticised until the pupils make it obvious that they are no longer necessary.

Mr. Riley's tests, therefore, must be considered more than fair to the pupils of 1846. He had the questions in arithmetic reprinted exactly as they appeared in the original papers, and both tests were given under the direction of one examiner. The children of five schools took part. Their papers were sent to the directing principal, and he examined and rated according to a uniform standard the work of 1846 and 1905. The results are summarized as follows:

	1846	1905
Number of pupils.	85	245
Spelling, per cent correct	40.6	51.2
Arithmetic, per cent correct	29.4	65.5

These were the twenty words of the spelling-test with the results of the examination in 1846:

	Times correct	Incorrect.
accidental.	61	24
accessible.	31	54
baptism.	54	31
chirography.	30	55
characteristic.	39	46
deceitfully.	40	45
descendant.	24	61
eccentric.	39	46
evanescent.	17	68
fierceness.	42	43
feignedly.	28	57
ghastliness.	23	62
gnawed.	33	52
heiress.	42	43
hysterics.	40	45
imbecility.	50	35
inconceivable.	20	65
inconvenience.	32	53
inefficient.	33	52
irresistible.	13	72

Only fifteen of the eighty-five pupils passed the seventy per cent mark in this spelling-test. Two pupils did not spell a single word correctly; nine had only nine right; more than one-fourth of the entire class misspelled seventeen or more words. The thirty-one pupils who misspelled the word "baptism" spelled it in fifteen different ways; forty-three pupils discovered twenty-two varieties of "heiress," ranging from "airest" to "aries." Here are some samples of spellings from Mr. Parrish's pupils;

heirress	babtism	Agsta
hurriss	babtisism	Bristic
heirruss	batism	Suffork
heirees	batisim	Midlesex
heirness	baptsim	Esexx
hieress	baptisim	Berkshiere
heress	baptisimn	Eirie
hirress	baptisem	Ontareio
hereis	baptisom	Mane
airress	baptisum	Vamont
airess	baptisemn	Rodiland
airest	baptisim	Connetticut
airresst	baptysm	Cornedicut
airhess	baptisiam	Newjessy
arress	baptiasm	Pencilvany
arris		Louseanna
arriss		Mishegan
aries		Mysurie
airest		Misury
areress		
arerest		
eirress		

These problems were used in the arithmetic test:

1. Add together the following numbers: Three thousand and nine, twenty-nine, one, three hundred and one, sixty-one, sixteen, seven hundred two, nine thousand, nineteen and a half, one and a half.
2. Multiply 10008 by 8009.
3. In a town five miles wide and six miles long, how many acres?
4. How many steps of two and a half feet each will a person take in walking one mile?
5. What is one-third of 175?
6. A boy bought three dozen of oranges for 37 cents and sold them for 1 cent apiece; what would he have gained if he had sold them for 2 cents apiece?
7. There is a certain number, one-third of which exceeds one-fourth of it by two; what is the number?
8. What is the simple interest on $1200 for 12 years, 11 months, and 29 days?

More than one-fourth of the examples were skipped as too difficult. Less than one-half of the class solved the first example; fifty managed to get the second correct; only eleven accomplished the fourth task. Answers to the fifth example varied from 5⅓ to 6312. The eighth problem was correctly answered by only thirteen pupils; the rest having every conceivable answer from $87.58.00 to 1103898000, with the easily explainable 4593600 of the unsophisticated multiplier thrown in. Only seven boys and not one girl mastered the fifth example. Of twenty-nine girls, not one had the right answer to the fourth or the sixth example, and altogether they averaged only nine per cent on the test.

The examination in geography is of little consequence, as it is based on memoriter work, an abomination which is now fortunately dead, at least so far as the large majority of city schools is concerned. But even on memory grounds the grad-grind schools could not hold their own with the modern. That the poor showing did not seriously affect the post-scholastic development of several of the pupils may be gathered from these personal observations supplied by Principal Riley:

Among those who were most successful in the tests were two boys who are still living in Springfield. One has been mayor of the city, the other is a leader in business life. Some of the girls and boys who failed in spelling became leaders as well. One girl, who attempted only four of the eight examples, and had them all wrong, became an honored member of the Springfield school board. A boy who missed 19 of the 20 words, and who solved only three of the eight examples correctly, became president of a bank. His life as a citizen was truly noble, and at his death his city paid unusual honor to his memory. Another boy is to-day at the head of a bank in Albany. Still another boy, who could not do a single example and who could spell but six words correctly, became mayor of a western city.

The chief point is that the Springfield schools are doing better work and accomplishing better results to-day than they did sixty years ago in the very studies which then comprised the whole programme, while to-day they are only a portion of it. What is true of Springfield may safely be accepted as applicable to the whole country. The enriched curricula of the elementary schools have not reduced one iota the possibility of producing as good results in the three R's to-day as have been attained at any time in the past. The spelling of our grandfathers and grandmothers was no less fearfully and wonderfully made, on the average, than that of their descendants. Abstention from thinking when doing arithmetical problems is also no new number in the catalogue of scholastic shortcomings.

OSSIAN H. LANG.

MURAL PAINTING.

THE article on Painting published in the FORUM for January–March, 1903, contains a general examination of the condition of the art in the United States. The names of the men generally accepted as the most powerful are given, and their important works discussed.

It appeared that mural painting had become a decided influence in America. The architects of large buildings, in advising their clients, had insisted upon the adornment of great panels of walls, and even of ceilings, with metaphorical and historical paintings. In like manner, the committees in charge of great public works had seemed ready enough to consent to such decorations, finding the large popular interest which they wished to excite far more powerfully stimulated by paintings of great size and of considerable pretension than by any architectural work whatsoever. The architectural work, indeed, may be thought to pass as the necessary and fitting presentation to the world of such building as is needed for daily use; but the mural painting is evidently something more and something much higher than that. It appeals directly to the spiritual life of man; and even those lookers-on who may not realize the essential importance of such works of art are still impressed, and even excited, by their presence. At least so we are led to believe by the experience of twenty years. And more than twelve years ago, even the temporary buildings of the Chicago Exhibition received paintings by men of rank in their profession.

But all this was considered in the article above referred to; and our business is now to go on with this same inquiry into the state of American art, giving special attention to the matter of the pictures which occupy permanent places in not inaccessible buildings. For the portable picture, though it may, indeed, find place in a museum and be kept there on view, is much more likely to pass into a private collection; and even if happy chance leads it to a place in a public gallery, the community has not yet learned to use its few public galleries with much judgment or much enthusiasm. The pictures, too, are moved about. Even in a museum they are hung here and there, and are in imminent danger of being "restored" at the bidding of irrespon-

sible committee men. For these and other reasons they may disappear once in a while and be lost to sight in the store-rooms. That
"restoration," too, which destroys their essential value, can be done
in secret—is done in secret—when the pictures can be moved; but
it is hard to ruin a wall-picture in that way. A painting once completed on the walls of a public building is felt to be a permanent possession. It is a lesson for its generation, to be handed down to its successors. Few are the instances of great wall-pictures which have suffered the fate of William Hunt's wall-paintings in the Albany capitol.

It has been my intention to follow, naming painters and their
work, the order adopted in the former article; but one can only deal
with the pictures that he knows, and I find that Elihu Vedder does not
appear as the author of any recent mural work. It is well, therefore,
to speak here of works of his, hardly mentioned in the former article,
namely, those lunettes in the Library of Congress at Washington.
These pictures are in the lobby which leads directly to the great
"rotunda," the huge octagonal room which serves as the reading-room;
and each painting fills a lunette under the vaulted ceiling. Good
government and order are represented by a massive female figure
enthroned on a marble seat of much dignity, with her left hand resting
on an originally designed heraldic shield, which bears, as its only charge,
the Scales of Justice on a quartered ground; while her right hand
holds up and ready for use the actual scales themselves. Two figures,
evidently representing Diligence, and Wise Labor and Public Service,
serve as supporters: the one, a female, is apparently squeezing the
juice of grapes into a vase; the other, a young man with books under
his arm, is dropping a fluttering paper into another vase, and we suppose this is The Voter. A spreading fig-tree loaded with fruit forms
the background of the throne and fills the crown of the arched panel.
The inscription "Good Administration" is to be read on the foot-pace
of the throne.

The other picture is Anarchy, and represents the destruction of
a stately building apparently by the direct action of a Fury—a nude
female figure with a torch in one hand and a cup in the other; while
the Genius of Construction and Work—with machinery and leveling-
staves—on the left, and, on the other hand, the actual stone-mason,
as it would seem, are interrupted in their very peaceful toil by the
inrush of savage violence.

Now, there will be occasion enough, in the course of this paper,
to speak of the rather wearying sequence of metaphorical, symbolical,
non-natural subjects in our mural painting. Personification as a theme
for design has been overdone by our painters, and not in the United

States alone. And, therefore, it is worth while saying here, and in connection with those straightforward, manly, but hard and harsh presentations by Vedder, that such set drawing, such firm and decided outline, such a denial of color and of the higher charm of light and shade, go to make up the style which best befits such metaphysical subjects. If you are going to put Anarchy and Civilization and the like upon your canvas, you cannot do better than to give them a treatment far other than that which you would most enjoy if you were painting the real as you see it. The solidity of the figures and the cold, dry light which invests them have, as they certainly should have, a certain relation to early work—to those epochs in which metaphorical painting was first greatly developed: and then it seems altogether well to deny your abstractions those soft gradations of colored light which are the charm and the strength of pictures founded rather closely upon nature herself. The charm of daylight upon colored surfaces, the external and visible beauty of men and women and inanimate things, are not for embodied Truth, Patriotism, Science and Art, Virtue and Vice! Let us make such compositions *purely* architectural—decorative in the architectural sense, and nothing more gentle and kindly than that!

Mr. Frederic Crowninshield, whose admirable painting in the Manhattan Hotel in New York City was our theme three years ago, has painted another series of pictures in a New York City restaurant. Here, on each side of a huge central court for lighting, runs the blank western wall of an enormous room: and each of these wall-surfaces, perhaps sixty feet long, is filled with a painting. Each is divided by pilasters into three panels; and, as the wall is low, relatively, each panel is wider than it is high. A great landscape fills each long wall: it is a garden in the foreground, with fountains and statues, but also with noble oleander trees full of flowers; and young men and young women with pet animals walk and sit and stand in conversing groups; all the figures being a little over life size. But beyond the garden spaces are the belts of hills which nearly fill the picture. At first, and nearer, are low hills, densely grown with olive trees, from amid which emerge the roofs and higher walls of Italian-seeming villas and castles of the South. This belt of grayish-green, broken by warm brown, fills the middle distance. Beyond, and rising high against the sky, are blue and purple mountains like those which rise above Florence.

As this picture now stands, its charm is almost wholly in the landscape, and it is the most perfect instance obtainable of the full value of landscape used as a principal subject for wall decoration. More fully realized, more strongly painted human figures may be incompatible with this plan of decoration, but there is no evidence that this is so. The paintings named, in the Simpson & Crawford building on Sixth Avenue, are worthy of long study by any to whom such questions are of interest.

In connection with Mr. Crowninshield's use of landscape as a powerful means of wall decoration, something was said in the former article already alluded to. And the work in this direction of Puvis de Chavannes, the most eminent of French mural painters of our time, has been alluded to, also, in that connection. But, indeed, more should be thought of this use of landscape; its possibilities should be more frequently, more carefully considered than has been the rule. It is easy to say that the one branch of the painter's art in which nineteenth century men excelled is landscape, but hard, very hard, to apply this truth in all instances, and to set landscape art to all the uses which it might fulfil. Landscape has indeed come to the front. It has been utilized even for splendid and costly windows made with the rich "American glass," of which so much is said in advertisements in France and elsewhere; and the effect of such translucent color decoration has been unmistakable. This use has been more frequent in connection with figure subjects, where the landscape serves as a background; and yet it is known also as a primary subject, where the figures hardly tell in the general composition. If this can be in translucent decoration, then all the more may landscape serve our turn in mural painting; for this is what Crowninshield's work, already examined, is ready to teach us.

The work of Puvis has shown for thirty years past that his sense also of this truth has been strong. The Fountain, exhibited in 1869, where a herdsman stands watching a girl whose beautiful bronze vase is filling from a spouting spring in a little hillside, has no other subject than this and the Sicilian landscape painted as it was imagined, and well imagined, by the modern Frenchman. In the Salon of 1879 was hung his not large easel picture, with three half-draped girls on a seashore. In this picture, the sea itself with the sky above formed the chief background; but a steep, rocky hillock rose on the left, from the surface of which sprang flowering plants in close, solid groups. And these landscape details were as solidly painted as the figures, the whole forming together a decorative pattern of great charm. Other powerful paintings of this character could be named: The Magdalen, who contemplates a skull while she stands erect in a rocky desolation of wild land; the beautiful picture of Sleep, in the Lille Museum, where that primitive family life which Puvis loved to imagine is surrounded by an unchanged, unmodified nature; Autumn, the picture of the Lyons Museum, where undraped and half-draped female figures are gathering grapes in great bunches, and pomegranates as well—because of their nobly rounded form and their hue of sombre red.

Such smaller but still important works marked with this characteristic are numerous, but it is when we approach the greater paintings, the mural decoration proper, that our subject becomes interesting in the highest degree. A step in this direction was taken when Puvis painted the pictures of Peace and War for the Picardy Museum at Antwerp. These are not mural paintings; that is to say, they have not been painted upon or for the piece of wall which they may never leave. But their conception is nearly the same; they are decorative in every sense of the word; and their great size makes them still more important to our inquiry.

Immediately afterward, however, the staircase of this museum was adorned by Puvis with pictures which are mural paintings indeed. These were, first, the paintings called Work (le Travail) and Rest (le Repos); and, indeed, these were painted to form the series with the Peace and the War. Then followed the first of two magnificent, epoch-making works—"Ave Picardia Nutrix," a term which, perhaps, we may translate as Hail to Picardy, the Nourishing Mother. And its subject is the continued fertility of Middle France. It is divided into two panels or sections by a high doorway, and each of the panels is broken into by a lower doorway, so that an irregular shape results, of which, however, the artist has known how to make good use. The simple labors of the field and wine-press, the building of a wooden bridge across a stream, and also the resting and bathing of the moments of leisure, are perfectly rendered by figures of slight relief, incomplete modelling, and calm and restrained action.

So of the painting which was to follow it, Ludus pro Patria, a title which one dares hardly seek to translate, but which expresses the thought that the amusements and slighter occupations of simple and virtuous people tend, as well as their immediately productive labors, to the glory of the Fatherland. This picture is a long parallelogram; and the quiet landscape is filled with groups amusing themselves with throwing a javelin at a mark, and in slighter and less arduous occupations. As to the landscape, 1 have noted an account of its origin, to which I have lost the reference. It is to the effect that when Puvis was asked what landscape he had represented, he said that he had painted what he had seen from the window of his railway carriage as he travelled down to Amiens and returned to Paris. In other words, it was the impression of the still rivers edged with willow trees, the flat and low country, with but small hills, and evidences of fertility everywhere—it was these things which, embodied in a single composition, he had tried to preserve.

It has seemed well to make these allusions to the earlier work of Puvis before speaking of the tremendous painting which fills the wall behind the speakers and the presiding officers in the Hall of the Sorbonne. That was his latest work, and was felt, probably by himself, to be his final achievement. It is probably the largest picture in the world, eighty-five feet long, as far as my computations can be trusted, and follows the surface of a slightly curved wall. Here the landscape is reduced to a very formal arrangement of trees, the trunks of which, with only a little of their lower branches and their lowermost foliage, form a setting for the figure composition. The trees, never more than eight or nine inches in diameter at a man's height above the ground, grow straight up, like pillars carrying an unseen roof.

The grove so characterized fills the middle of the long, low — comparatively low — surface, and beneath its shade sit and stand the personages who are to be taken as embodiments of Literature, Philosophy, Poetry, and Ideal Art. The Pierian Spring rises in the very middle of the composition; and above it is enthroned a presiding influence embodied in that which has been called *une Vierge laïque* — evidently an attempt to realize in a good influence presiding over earthly occupations the same feminine supremacy which the Catholic Church maintains in its representations of the Virgin Mary. We are not to forget that this picture takes shape in a community still in its structure Catholic, as it has been for centuries, and that the enthroned Virgin is a type familiar to all who visit, even on rare occasions, the great churches of France. Outside of the grove are groups which signify Archæology, with research among ruins, and the bringing of artistic treasures to light; and on the other wing are those signifying Modern Science, with Physics, Zoölogy, and the rest.

The now popular idea of a world of personifications has never been carried so far! Forty-five or more personages, one and all representing abstract ideas, figures larger than life, and disposed over a painted surface eighty-five feet long, certainly constitute a formidable work. And, in view of such a composition, the question will inevitably arise as to how far these embodiments are desirable as a chief subject of art. The Amiens pictures are not of this class. In them there is the human element in full action; there are men and women striving, laboring, suffering, resting, running, bathing, or sitting in quiet groups. There is, if you please, a symbolical meaning in the general tendency of a group, or of the whole painting; but there is no symbolical meaning in any single figure.

Human beings, nude or draped, in action or in repose, form the natural and the obvious subjects for the painter's art. Nothing else is so noble. Even landscape — much as the modern success in landscape consoles us for modern feebleness in figure work—is not equal in importance to the human figure as the chief subject of graphic art. But it is easy to tire the mind and confuse the patient observation of the student by leaving him to find out for himself which figure of those half hundred figures is meant for Eloquence and which for Physics, and whether there is any profound significance in the dipping of the water from the Fountain of Knowledge by a youth who hands it to a laurel-wreathed old man. I have said elsewhere, but I cannot help repeating it here, that the reverse of this is the custom in our institutions of learning.

Many persons will think that this general acceptance of impersonation and symbolism is not the best way to use figure subjects. But the distribution of well-modelled figures in a landscape appropriate to the character and seeming action of those figures pleases perhaps every student of painting who is not immediately enlisted in behalf of another doctrine.

Consider, for instance, the Boston picture by Puvis—that one which fills the wall at the head of the great staircase of the Public Library. A dark landscape, generally grayish-green in tone, is so treated that slopes of grass, thinly bedecked with flowering plants and broken by a few slender trees without novel character, serve as the background for the white-draped figures of the Muses which rise — five at the left and facing to the right, four at the right and facing to the left — to greet the Genius of Light, or of Enlightenment, who is rising straight heavenward in the middle — a nude body and broadly spread wings relieved against the sky. There is in their white drapery a marked sense of translucency. It may be assumed that the Muses have been painted thinly over the dark painting of the landscape. At the time when this picture was first on view in Boston, a work nearly as large by a living painter of great ability showed precisely the reverse disposition — dark and opaque figures with a pale and transparent distance behind them, and with nothing in the picture as solid as they.

Now in the realities of fact and nature this is what we are accustomed to — is it not so? Men and women are the solid and positive things, and everything else is of secondary force. It is so that we see the world! But it is curious how the world of decoration differs from the world of fact. It was not easy to avoid feeling a definite superiority in the white and floating beings of more than human rank. Their very superiority is evidenced in their translucent lack of physical weight. To make this more distinct, the artist has put in two foreground figures, close to the eye and seated solidly on square plinths. They are symbolical also, but they are ponderable human beings. It is strange by what magic the floating spiritualities are seen yet to have strength of arm enough to hold solid-looking lyres and to raise on high laurel branches, and a sistrum with its rattling rings.

This paper is not intended to be a plea for the use of landscape in the decoration of our walls; and yet the tendency to use in mural painting that one branch or kind of painting in which the nineteenth century excels is certainly not to be ignored, nor is it to be deprecated. Florentine fresco painters, Venetian oil painters, Byzantine mosaicists, and the British experimenters of the mid-century, with their waterglass and modifications of fresco, were all of them on the right track when they ignored landscape, or else painted it in a very abstract fashion. For who would say: We must have a background! They possessed, and used for their compositions of color and form, such a basis of history or legend as had been for centuries familiar to their predecessors, to their immediate teachers, and to themselves.

The modern man, and especially the American of 1880–1905, has no such traditions of his own; and when he must give figure subjects, he is apt to be at his wits' end to select effective ones. The costume of his own time is impossible; the costume of the time immediately past — of the century before his day — is ugly in its lines and masses and dull in color, however quaint it may appear in book illustration. The finer costume of earlier days is not for American history; and it comes even into recent European painting rather awkwardly, half the time, except in the decorations of some *hôtel-de-ville*. His attempts at personifying the Virtues and the Sciences are tiresome enough. They are probably tiresome even to the modern painter himself, as they would be assuredly to his public, were the members of that public disposed to spend time in studying the paintings. But there is one thing which belongs to his time — we are speaking still of the American painter of the years since 1880 — to his surroundings, to his own inner sense of what is available. Landscape is the one subject which the graphic artist, born since 1825, may feel to be really his own; and this is as true of John Leech, and his suggested landscape backgrounds in Punch, as it is of Puvis de Chavannes, with his vast hemicycles of painting.

John La Farge is a marked instance of this tendency to landscape in mural decoration. His well-known Ascension of Christ in the

Church of the Ascension at Fifth Avenue and Tenth Street, New York, was considered in the article of 1903; but since that time the tendency in his work to employ landscape for important decoration has not become less strong. And it behooves the student to consider in their general bearings the four paintings, each twenty-seven feet long, which fill four corresponding lunettes in the Supreme Court Room of the Minnesota State Capitol. These pictures are, in a marked way, the creation of a scholar who is also a man of singular range and grasp of mind, and insight into the world of men. And they deal with four important events in the slow development of human Law — all as befits the walls of a great court-room. The Giving of the Moral Law is embodied in the picture of the three leaders of Israel amid the rolling smoke and the glowing light around the top of Sinai. The Relation of the Individual to the State is shown as exciting the interest of Socrates and 'his friends as they stand and talk in an exedra with an Athenian landscape around them. The Recording of Precedents gives name to a picture of Confucius with four of his pupils and followers seated in a quiet garden of Oriental taste. The fourth, and the fourth only, contains no landscape and is an indoor scene: The Adjustment of Conflicting Interests explained as going on through the Middle Ages and condensed in the statement of how Count Raymond of Toulouse took oath in the cathedral of his own city.

It seems to me that this fourth picture loses much in losing that landscape background. One must be a great composer in line and mass to make half a dozen life-size figures wholly interesting when they stand up in a somewhat bare room; and splendor of color and wonderful painting of minute details do not give all the interest that is needed. But the surprising success of the Confucius picture, with its seated Oriental figures rather widely scattered in their grouping, while evidently a remarkable achievement in line composition, would not be remarkable in this respect but for the highly wrought landscape of small scale and delicate parts, in which the figures are set.

It is true, of course, that the more excellent the painter-work, the better the landscape picture. With all our interest in the great leading lines of the landscape, the hills and the valleys, the rocks and the meadows, the clouds and the distant mountains, the trees and the undergrowth, we have still to acknowledge that great excellence in painting, and this taking the form of lovely color, is, in landscape art, the chief thing, the one thing, which cannot be imitated or matched in any other fine art known to man. A plate from Liber Studiorum in pure brown and white, with nothing to charm except gradations of monochrome, and these expressing mainly the solidity, the mass,

and the weight of the earth-forms, or the graceful slightness and the
bowing flexibility of young trees — this indeed is of quite immeasurable
value to all of us when we have fitted our minds to enjoy monochrome
and its bold translation of fact into convention. But Turner himself,
the creator of that world of form, is also one of the greatest of modern
colorists and one of the men who sought throughout his life for bril-
liancy and glow in chromatic composition.

Mr. La Farge is a solitary figure among artists, in that he is not
so much a draughtsman and composer — not so much a trained and
accomplished painter — as a man of great intelligence who has also
the gift of *coloring*. Oddly enough, that seems to be the very rarest
of gifts among painters. They will study, conscientiously, the external form of things, and their make and their solidity; they will
compose in line and mass, as if they were busy with bas-relief; and
they will strive less wisely to express in pictured form what words
alone can render. A thousand of them will be busied in these tasks
for one who will make color itself, and colored light upon objects, his
especial study.

Mr. Henry O. Walker has given the world some important pictures
since the day of those lunettes in the Library of Congress which have
been discussed already. There is one, very recent, in the Minnesota
State House, where are also Mr. La Farge's pictures, above described.
It deals with the passing of the Torch of Enlightenment from Yesterday to the hands of To-day, and then to the inevitable Future. Heri,
Cras, Hodie — that triple name may well be the name of the painting
in question. But this picture is known to me only by the photograph,
and it would be better to speak of those semi-historical pictures in the
round room — the "Memorial Hall" — in the Boston State House.

In that room there are two pictures by Mr. Edward Simmons and
two by Mr. Walker, these last not quite as purely historical as the
public had been told to expect these memorial paintings to be. The
strong leaning toward metaphor, toward association, toward symbolism, and all the rest of it, has prevented these from taking the strongly
historical trend which Mr. Simmons has given to his work; and the
crowded deck of the Mayflower on her outward passage is shown in a
highly imaginary way, without much attempt at verifying the situation, while the sky is filled with a group of superhuman beings riding
upon a cloud, in which there floats a vast scroll bearing words of
piety and faith.

There is no mistake about the skill of composition when dealing
with many figures which Mr. Walker's paintings exhibit; but here
in the absence of a reproduction we are compelled to deal the rather

with a significance which can be described in words. And one may well prefer the frankly symbolical picture in the Appellate Court House, New York City, where embodied Wisdom stands among winged genii and human sufferers coming for protection; the whole representing The Wisdom of the Law. These pictures have some of the severity which has been commended in Mr. Vedder's highly metaphysical work.

Mr. Edward Simmons has carried his art onward in the same direction, and certainly no one has ever seen a more fascinating historical picture than his Concord Bridge. It is fixed to the wall of that round room, and opposite to it is the same artist's picture, The Dedication of the Battle Flags in 1865, while the pictures by Henry Oliver Walker, above named, alternate with these. If one were to say that the Concord Bridge was more of a picture than a mural decoration, he would have some obvious reason for his comment, but this merely because the extent of country shown, the conception of the central incident, the artistic vision which made the scene possible, called for a depth and a marked perspective in the picture which is often found to mar the solid and reposeful look which we ask for in a mural painting. The young farmers are running along a raised country road, and some of them stop to fire over a low stone wall; for, two hundred yards away, the road and the bridge are wreathed in smoke lighted up by the blaze of musketry. The charm of the picture, the free movement of the figures, the delicate coloring of spring-time green, the well-understood and well-handled masses of white smoke — all these are quite beyond description; and the most ardent believer in the decorative importance of mural painting might hesitate to order its modification even in the least-important feature.

One picture of epoch-making character was put up in the Boston Public Library two years ago. This is the decoration of the south end of Sargent Hall, by that powerful artist for whom the hall was named. His work at the north end has been described and pictured very frequently. At the south end there is, at present, only the single large painting which may be called the Christian Dispensation. It fills the whole lunette and the broad patch of wall beneath, and is separable into a large composition above and a smaller one, a sort of frieze, below, in this respect closely following the arrangement of the paintings at the north end.

In other respects, however, the difference between these two great compositions is wide, and is of a nature to seem especially important to lovers of mural painting. For in the earlier work the drawing is free and large; the pose and the gestures are emphatic in a way, sug-

25

gesting movement and strong human feeling. At the south end, on the other hand, there is a design composed in the spirit of the strictest ecclesiological tradition, the figures imagined in close observance of what the churches — and more especially the Catholic church of western Europe — have taught; and the design is like one made for a mosaic rather, as one thinks, than for a composition to be wrought out upon canvas by the designer's own hand. Three vast figures fill the lunette, the three being draped as one; and the three heads, in slight relief, were all moulded, we are told, from the same mask. The border of this robe is lettered with the constantly repeated word Sanctus, Sanctus.

Impinging upon this group is the strange panel of generally cruciform shape filled with the figure of the crucified Redeemer accompanied by our first parents; the three figures being combined in a way not easy to describe in a few words, and all modelled in high relief. The frames of this panel, very much broken into curves and cusps, are brilliant with gilding, and the relief sculpture is painted in full color. This cross-shaped member, perhaps ten feet high, forms the very middle of the composition, and, together with the Persons of the Trinity, the principal feature of the design. The drapery and the three suggested figures fill the lunette, the curve of which is marked strongly by six haloed birds flying inward and downward.

It is hardly necessary to insist upon the extreme formality of the abstract and highly decorative conception of the whole; but the reader should also be told that the background is of a noble sombre blue, reminding one of a midnight sky, while the figure subject is, if not rich in color, yet magnificent in sombre strength. All the band below the springing line of the arch — the frieze below the lunette — is filled with a long array of the Angels of the Passion; and here also modelling in relief is used, and here again the color is strong and grand. Nothing more splendid than the red robe of the angels who seem to support the foot of the great cross above has been seen by the light of the twentieth century.

The surprise which awaits him who, knowing the magnificent daring and dash of Mr. Sargent's portrait work, first stands in front of this grave and restrained composition, may indeed count for much in the admiration it is sure to excite. Still, this is mentioned merely that its existence shall not be ignored: it is important in the judgment formed of the picture, for that can only be the result of many visits and of much thought given to this astonishing composition.

Mr. Blashfield has added very much to the already long list of his mural work. There has been always an elegance, a daintiness about it which has attracted people of discretion and of studious habits; while yet there has been very commonly a certain coldness of appeal which would prevent, I should think, any one from becoming greatly interested in these huge compositions. Except for one painting which will be mentioned, I continue to think that the finest thing that I have seen by this artist is the ring of figures around the oculus of the dome in the Congressional Library. And probably the reason for this feeling, which some others share, is that in that ring of figures there is no attempt at record or the presentation of a fact, and because nothing is mingled with the decoration described except that obvious symbolic significance which we have in mind when we say: This figure stands for the Middle Ages, this other for the Renaissance. All the student asks for in such a case is a nobly conceived figure, with perhaps some allusion in the costume or the attributes to the epoch, to the spirit, expressed by the name.

Therefore, when we pass from so absolutely decorative a frieze as that one to the paintings in the Baltimore Court House, where Lord Baltimore is in converse with Civilization and Toleration and Religion and the Aborigines; or to the painting in the Minnesota Capitol (Senate Chamber) in which the Manitou sits at the head of the Father of Waters with his native Indian people, while bodies of explorers and settlers come from the left and from the right to express the passing of one era and the bringing in of another — in such cases the introduction of more immediate significance, more story-telling, more detailed and romantic legend, is felt to be not an unmixed good. I cannot really care for the triple composition in Baltimore, the French officers grouped under their blowing white flag, the Americans under the Stars and Stripes swelling like a balloon above their heads, while in the middle is a seated Columbia, upon the pedestal of whose throne Washington lays his sword. Such a composition requires some splendid artistic quality to give it interest; and splendor is not what we have been accustomed to expect from the careful and complete drawing, the somewhat chilly elegance, of Blashfield's figure subjects.

Even now, as I dictate this, there is in New York, waiting to be put in its place at Des Moines, a picture which promises to give a new Blashfield to the lovers of mural painting. It is very large, sixteen feet by forty or thereabouts, and shows the first settlement of Des Moines — or of any other western city — in a perfectly natural way. The wagon and its double team of oxen are passing slowly along the trail which, already broken by other wagons passed out of sight, sends up a thin cloud of dust. Many persons are present, figures of a little larger than life-size, some of them the travellers of the wagon party, others apparently men who have already occupied and planted the ground, for maize in well-grown shape fills the picture at the right-hand end. A girl stops to fill her arms with prairie flowers; a child is attracted by a butterfly, the whole series of figures passing slowly on from right to left with large and dignified gesture, or quiet pose upon the wagon seat or the slow-moving horse. But the sky is filled with those imaginary beings which seem to have been thought as essential here as in other such public works. At the left, and flying in advance of the immigrants, are the genii who carry the Book of Laws, the winnowing basket, the armorial bearings of the State of Iowa; and in the rear of the column float three figures which embody Invention and Discovery, carrying the obvious signs of their mission — telephones and such-like aids and disturbances of our modern life.

But thus far the description might not promise a new field of thought for Mr. Blashfield's admirers. The power and charm of the work is to be found especially in a new-born beauty of color which is delightful to see. There is the color in strong masses, with shadows full of that beauty which the eye but slowly detects in nature, and which it is the business of the artist to reveal. The foreground is full of fine and interesting color; and yet that which is the most charming is the translucent and pale, the high-light color of the floating draperies above, masses of white which are full of those surprises of colored light which white under sunshine is capable of revealing to the eye which can see aright. The existence of this picture gives me the greatest hope for our future mural painting.

Mr. Charles Yardley Turner has used historical painting for mural decoration and has done it nobly. The two pictures just finished — November, 1905 — for that High School house in New York which is called after Governor Clinton, set forth very peaceful and even commonplace subjects. The opening of the Erie Canal was a great event, no doubt, and De Witt Clinton deserves unlimited credit for his services in that matter; but the closing scenes — the triumph, the procession of canal boats, the pouring of lake water into the ocean — are not thrilling in themselves. The pictures are not exciting. And this is said because the Baltimore picture named below is a thrilling event enough, having every characteristic which might give it special interest; while yet it cannot be said to form a more fitting historical decoration than the peaceful scenes in the New York school house.

To think that twenty-five years ago we were all pooh-poohing historical painting! The dulness of it, the lack of trustworthy record, the general air of pompous inanity—these were the thoughts that arose in the mind of a reformer in the Fine Art world of that day. And now we find that, given the life-size figure, the permanent place on the wall, the not inappropriate surroundings, historical painting in the right hands makes noble decoration.

As for the Baltimore painting named above, it concerns the burning of the "Peggy Stewart," a tea-ship of 1774. And this event is as important historically as the famous tea-party of Boston Harbor — with the added feature that the Annapolis people did not disguise themselves, but braved all the penalties of high treason. And so Mr. Turner has taken the actual conflagration for the centre of his elaborate design, the hot color of flame and lighted smoke forming a background to the principal figures, who are shown in the costume of the time, but engaged in no violent physical action.

A long corridor has its walls divided, on either side, by pilasters, into five great panels, and of these the second and fourth are pierced with doorways having very elaborate architectural features in their frontons. The corridor is narrow in proportion to its length, and therefore there is no point from which you can see all Mr. Turner's work at one moment. It is sequence, therefore, and not a single overpowering impression, which was the inevitable motive of the design. The middle panel between the doorways has been briefly described; and the other panels continue the composition to right and to left. The first and fifth panels are filled with men and women, full-length figures, larger than life; and the panels where the door-heads had to be show, above the stone casing, the heads and shoulders of other members of the crowd. The still water of Annapolis Harbor and ships resting upon it with furled or half-lowered canvas, and one vessel under sail running out, form the greater part of the setting for the figures; but there is an interesting house in the right-hand composition where family life also is suggested.

Here is, then, a great composition full of narrative, carefully based upon ascertained facts, full of well-studied costume, full of such portraiture as was possible; and, in this way, is gained what may be truly called history embodied in art, with such patriotic thoughts as an honorable and self-devoted action in the past may rightly suggest. And such work is a relief, indeed, from the personification of the State, the City, the Fatherland; or Patriotism, with two or three Sciences, two or three Arts, or half a dozen national Virtues.

The death of Robert Frederick Blum, two years ago, left us without the possibility of realization of what was a bright promise. Mr. Blum, an American, a New Yorker, whose work was much admired, was primarily an illustrator of books, and furnished illustrations to the successful and wealthy magazines. His journey to Japan, which was an epoch-making journey for him, came of his vocation; for it appears to have been by the wish of one of these great magazines that he made those admirable water-color drawings which enchanted us all about ten years ago. Now it is true that there are not, in Japan, mural paintings in the sense in which we use that term in this article; but, on the other hand, there are in that country what there is not in the United States nor yet in Europe, namely, monuments, on every side, of a consistent, harmonious, steadily developing, truly national, and single-minded fine art. Mr. Blum recognized this. He saw, with clear eyes, that here there was an art single and direct in its purposes, knowing its own possibilities and its own limitations, going straight to its aim; and enlightened by this experience, as well as strengthened by active work in so inspiring an atmosphere, he came home ready for any class of painting to which he might be allowed to devote his singular ability. So it was that when Mendelssohn Music Hall was to be adorned by painting, Mr. Blum had his one chance to show what his studies of decorative art and his studies of humanity would be as viewed by one who sought to tell a tale — to narrate and to represent, as well as to give impressions.

The reader will understand that our modern glory in art — the one achievement of the second half of the nineteenth century — was to see more clearly than had been seen before for many ages that the chief purpose of the painter was to convey and preserve his impressions of the external beauty of nature. Not to tell any story about the actions of men or even about the presence of certain features in a landscape was his task, but to give upon canvas that side of external nature which the ordinary man's eye does not behold. This it was that made the chief and especial merit of the Barbizon school — this it was that Rousseau and Corot and even that strong and gentle spirit, Millet, offered to the world. This, it is plain, was almost as perfectly given in a small and unpretending study as in a huge painting. When it became necessary to produce wall-paintings, men brought up in that same school of thought — that school which undertook to render and not to represent, to convey impressions, not to tell stories — were still found ready to modify its processes, to adapt them to the new conditions. For, obviously, you cannot well present to the public on a wall of their own building, designed for their own business, a study of the beauty of external nature in man or in hill and valley or in cloudy sky, and stop there. The public has a right to ask for more, and a certain amount of representation has to be given to large mural pictures — as, indeed, the reader will perceive if he looks over the descriptions and the suggestions of this article and its predecessor.

Now, it so happened that Mr. Blum's studies had led him directly to the most delicate refinements of colored light and shade; and his desire to preserve the high, pale key in color and in chiaroscuro was intensified, perhaps, by a certain difficulty in reconciling strong and masterful painting to a quiet, not richly adorned hall of moderate size — one in which, also, the daylight was not quite sufficient, while electric light could not be thought wholly fortunate for the showing of such compositions if rich in coloring. The pictures in Mendelssohn Hall are therefore pale. That one painted first, and called Music, is about fifty feet fong and represents a sort of procession of charming young people clothed in that modification of the Græco-Roman dress which we have taken as an ideal costume — fit for all times and all occasions, so long as they are festal and the subject is pleasant and inspiring. This picture is certainly pale; and if one would see it — and it is well worth the pains and care to see it aright — the time of day must be chosen carefully, and a good opera-glass, neither too strong nor too weak, must be used. Moreover, there must be a loving interest in the work before its full significance can be understood.

The other picture may be called "A Feast of Bacchus"; and the coloring is more forceful, deeper, with more contrast in it. In this, rather than in the light and shade, is the tone of this picture made stronger and more insistent than in the beautiful "Music" of the west wall. The figures, too, are a little more decided in their action, a little less reposeful in their attitude. In spite of these changes wrought by the artist in his second experiment, it may well be thought by some that the "Music" is the more charming composition.

Year by year it grows more plain that mural painting is what we can do best in America. Our attempts at architectural sculpture are very few — so few and so widely separated in time that no sequence, no tendency, can be noted, no definite purpose perceived. Porches of Trinity Church, Boston, in 1897; stairways and doorways of Washington Library, soon after; then, in quick succession, early in 1904, the porches of Saint Bartholomew's and the Stock Exchange pediment, in New York, and the bronze doors of the Boston Public Library. That is nearly all our record in sculpture of architectural character, unless the recent bas-reliefs by Mr. O'Connor in a Fifth Avenue business building may be added to the list. We must exclude the many statues which stand or sit on cornices or on the ramps of entrance doorways, for they arc simply studio pieces out of place.

On the other hand, the record for mural painting is excellent. In 1898, there was prepared a list of what then existed: 101 paintings by 31 artists, and, of all those, only Blum's two pictures have been named in this article, so far. The list would hardly bo doubled if completed in 1905. The rate of production of mural painting has not greatly increased, in mere numbers, since 1898. It has remained fairly steady, however, in mere numbers, while the dignity and the average merit of the paintings have certainly increased. And then, these important, yes, and really painter-like paintings are widely distributed. Think of the four lunettes in a little art building at Bowdoin College, far away down east, in the little town of Brunswick, Maine! They are four in number, "Athens" and her glory, by John La Farge; "Rome," by Elihu Vedder; "Florence," by Abbott Henderson Thayer; and "Venice," by Kenyon Cox. The treatment of these is free — the everlasting symbolism has here taken noble shapes. Thus, Mr. Thayer's picture has a charming view of Florence and a successful use of heraldic bearings, and Mr. La Farge's picture shows his customary novelty of conception, for Pallas Athene is making in her notebook a drawing of the Nymph of the Acropolis.

Mr. Edward Simmons has finished his pictures for the Minnesota State Capitol. They are by this time (mid-December) in place, around the springing of the great cupola. There was but little time to study them as they came through from Paris, bound westward; and although the photographs, at least, are before me, I am hardly prepared to explain their spiritual significance to the full. Landscape has been a less powerful influence here than in the Boston picture described above, but it still controls the disposition. The group over which Athene presides, and which includes a powerful male figure setting up a monument of rude stone, is grandly composed of figures nude and figures lightly draped, and is set in a landscape of wonderful charm.

Mr. W. B. Van Ingen has, in advanced preparation, with three or four of the canvases approaching completion, a series of small lunettes for the State House at Harrisburg. The theme that the painter has chosen is religious toleration, extended by that colony alone to people of all religious beliefs. Accordingly, we have the Moravian enthusiasts; a hermit of one peculiar ascetic movement of early times; the Dunkers engaged in their sacred ceremonies; and Quaker women seated in their tranquil and contemplative meeting. The variety and interest of costume is an evident artistic reason for this choice of subject.

There are, however, pictures which there has not been time to study or which are out of the way. Mr. Van Ingen tells me that in the Harrisburg State House the corridor corresponding to his own is filled by Mr. John W. Alexander, the subject being "Landscape as Modified byHuman Action." There are paintings in preparation by Mr. Childe Hassam which should be exquisite in color harmony, and other pictures by Frank Vincent Du Mond, of all which the writer of a year hence may take cognizance.   RUSSELL STURGIS.

APPLIED SCIENCE.

A CHARACTERISTIC feature of modern engineering is the extent to which means are modified to suit the desired ends. Formerly the materials to be used in a machine or structure were examined and tested, and the quantity and disposition made accordingly. Now, however, the reverse is frequently the case. A piece must be made of given dimensions, or within certain limitations of weight, and yet be able to resist certain stresses; and the engineer must produce a material capable of meeting the requirements.

This reversal of methods is not altogether a modern affair, but it has progressed with an accelerating pace. Thus, the demand for larger and stronger ships led to the replacement of wood by iron, and again, to the supercession of iron by steel; and in each case it was the demand for better material which led to the improvement. A similar demand has led, and is leading, to still greater advances in the production of special materials, resulting in the development of the science of metallurgy, and particularly the metallurgy of the special steels, to a high degree. In some recent discussions of the subject, attention has been directed to the remarkable products among the so-called alloy steels, developed as a result of the application of scientific investigation to the demands of the manufacturer. In the construction of automobiles especially the requirements for materials have become most severe. In some parts great strength is demanded, in others toughness. Some portions must resist extremely high temperatures, while others are to be subjected to rapid vibratory stresses. All pieces are required to be of minimum weight and maximum resistance; and reliability is most essential.

These demands have done much to bring out materials to fill the strenuous requirements of the motor-car builder. Formerly steel was steel, a compound of iron and carbon; its properties varying according to the carbon content, and depending, within certain limits, upon the heat treatment. At the present time there are steels containing iron, carbon, and one or more other elements, giving results in character and variety almost equal to the most severe demands of the constructor. According to the recent researches of M. Léon Guillet, the so-called ternary steels, containing iron, carbon, and one other element, may be made to fulfil nearly every structural requirement, while the quaternary steels, containing iron, carbon, and two other elements, are also impressed into special service. The nickel alloy steels, containing iron, carbon, and nickel, have been much used in various forms, but it is only recently that their constitution has been understood. It is not only the percentage of nickel which affects the properties of the metal, but the relative proportions of nickel and carbon. It is really meaningless to speak of a 5 per cent nickel-steel, for instance, without stating the percentage of carbon; since the properties of the steel depend upon the relative proportions of the nickel and carbon to each other, as well as to the amount of iron present.

Among the useful nickel alloy steels may be mentioned one containing 0.12 per cent of carbon and 7 per cent of nickel. When pieces made of this alloy are subjected to the so-called "cementation" process, by being given prolonged heating in contact with carbon, the exterior becomes extremely hard after a slow cooling, while the interior of the pieces remains tough and resistant. It was sought to accomplish this result formerly by case hardening, but the quenching of case-hardened pieces always caused much trouble from warping and cracking. With the nickel-steel no quenching is required, and the troubles from this source are removed. Another important nickel-steel is the alloy of low carbon and high nickel, containing about 32 per cent of nickel and 0.12 to 0.20 per cent of carbon. This has such a high resistance to shock as to render it particularly adapted for the valves of the high-speed internal-combustion engines used on motor-cars. The quaternary steel containing nickel and chromium, with medium carbon, is both hard and tough, and so especially adapted for crank shafts. Other alloy steels, containing chromium, or silicon, are used for special parts; and at the present time nearly every demand of the constructor for a steel to meet a special stress can be supplied by the metallurgist.

Since the last review in these pages, there has been an interesting gathering of scientific men in connection with the meetings in South Africa of the British Association for the Advancement of Science. I have already noted in these reviews the completion of the great steel arch across the gorge of the Zambesi River below the Victoria Falls, and the work was sufficiently far advanced in September last to permit of the formal opening of the bridge by Prof. Darwin, the President of the Association. The railway is now in operation from Cape Town to the Falls, a distance of 1,631 miles, covered in about three and a half days; and the site can at present be reached from London in twenty-one days.

Among the addresses delivered during the meetings of the Association in South Africa, the paper of Prof. Ayrton upon the electrical distribution of power attracted much attention. Referring to the possibility of utilizing the hydraulic power of the Falls of the Zambesi, he showed that notwithstanding the fact that the height of the Victoria Falls is more than double that of Niagara, the volume of water is so much less that the available power is only about one-fifth that of Niagara.

Prof. Ayrton is inclined to look with favor upon the use of continuous currents of high voltage for long distance transmission lines, as opposed to the alternating current; and the success which has attended the experiments in Switzerland, to which I referred some months ago, sustains this view. The insulation difficulties appear to be minimized with the continuous current, while the absence of resonance effects is an advantage. The principal difficulty appears to be in the dynamo; and in the experiments of Thury in Switzerland this was avoided by running several machines in tandem, although it is believed that improved designs will enable commutator troubles at high pressures to be avoided.

In connection with the subject of the utilization of hydraulic power, attention may be called to the fact that the Welland canal has been suggested as a means of tapping the Niagara supply still further. The real source of hydraulic power at this locality is the difference in level between Lake Ontario and the upper lakes; and the Welland canal forms a cut-off channel around the falls, and renders it possible to tap the waters of Lake Erie and deliver the discharge to a point at the foot of the escarpment at the level of Lake Ontario. This would add the head of the rapids to that of the falls, and give an available head of nearly 300 feet. Already this plan has been used to develop about 25,000 horse-power; and it appears to be capable of almost indefinite enlargement, altogether independently of any further works at Niagara Falls.

The influence which the development of one department of engineering has upon another is shown in the relation between the changes in dynamo-electric machines and the engines by which they are driven; and this interaction is being especially shown at the present time in connection with the introduction of the steam turbine.

When electric lighting came into use, about twenty-five years ago, the dynamos were connected directly to the engine shafts of small, quick-running engines, or else were belted to engines of medium speed. The superior economy of the slower-running engines of the Corliss type, however, led to the design of electric generators of large size to be used in connection with corresponding dynamos, and the development of the high-speed continuous-current dynamo was checked. At the present time, the steam turbine, with its high rotative speeds, calls for redesigned dynamos; and both vertical and horizontal types are now made. If the gas turbine should become a practicable machine, it would probably involve still higher speeds, and again the dynamo would require modification to adapt it to the motor by which it would be driven.

So far as the gas turbine itself is concerned, there is little or no progress to be reported. In a recent address, Mr. Dugald Clerk has shown that a successful gas turbine involves a very efficient rotary compressor, together with a highly efficient expanding nozzle and a correspondingly efficient blade arrangement on the wheel. Even assuming 90 per cent efficiency in the compressor and in the nozzle, and 80 per cent in the wheel, such a cycle as can be employed in a gas turbine would not give a final efficiency of more than about 22 per cent, according to Mr. Clerk. This includes no allowance for heat conduction losses; and these would undoubtedly lower the thermal efficiency to about 16 per cent, which is below that of good reciprocating gas engines.

It has been maintained that even if the gas turbine did not show a better thermal efficiency than the reciprocating gas engine, the advantage of a continuous rotary motion over the irregular action of the four-cycle gas engine would render it acceptable. While this is undoubtedly true, there are operative difficulties which necessarily appear in connection with the gas turbine which at present seem to be insurmountable. The high rotative speed necessary to secure even moderate efficiency involves centrifugal stresses of magnitude, while, at the same time, the high temperatures necessarily reduce the strength of the material employed. It is altogether unsafe to predict the limitations of any department of applied science; but the difficulties in the way of a solution of the gas-turbine problem appear to be insurmountable in the present state of the art of mechanical construction. The only gas-turbine which has been practically operated, that made by MM. Armengaud and Lemale, in Paris, is really a mixed turbine, using both steam and gas in the jet, and hence does not come within all the restrictions involved in the dry-gas turbine.

An interesting feature which has arisen in connection with the operation of the gas engine is the possible field which it may open for the utilization of peat fuel. I have mentioned in these reviews the advantages of the suction gas power system, in which the suction strokes of the gas engine are employed to draw air and the vapor of water through a bed of incandescent coke, thus producing a semi-water gas for direct use in the engine. In such apparatus the fuel generally used is anthracite or coke, the vapor of water being supplied by a boiler or evaporator, heated by the gas itself on its way to the engine. The requirement of anthracite or coke as fuel has materially limited the use of the otherwise advantageous and efficient suction gas-power plant, but its scope will be materially widened with the application of peat fuel. The principal difficulty with peat as an ordinary steam-raising fuel is the large percentage of moisture which it contains, and any of the methods devised for the removal of the moisture add too greatly to the cost of the product to be commercially successful.

The moisture in peat briquettes, however, is not objectionable in the gas producer, since it simply takes the place of a corresponding amount of steam from the vaporizer, being dissociated into hydrogen and oxygen, the latter forming carbonic oxide with the carbon of the peat, and the former enriching the gas. The small amount of ash and solid impurity in peat renders it especially suitable for the gas producer, owing to the small proportion of slag and clinker formed. The vast deposits of peat and lignite in Great Britain and on the Continent may make this method of utilization an important one.

A peculiar situation has arisen in connection with the plans made for the conversion of portions of the main-line service of two important railroads from steam to electric traction. Ever since the disastrous collision in the tunnel approach to the Grand Central station in New York City, the New York Central Railroad has been engaged in the work necessary for the elimination of the steam locomotive in the tunnel, station, and yards; the plans including the use of electric traction for moderate distances from the city, the trains being picked up by steam locomotives at North White Plains or Croton. The plans include also the use of the continuous current with third-rail connections, the whole following out the lines already well tested by experience on a smaller scale in other places. The trials of the type of electric locomotive intended for this service have already been noted in these pages, and the work is now well advanced, both upon road and equipment.

More recently, the New York, New Haven and Hartford Railroad has also determined to introduce electric traction for a portion of its line, extending from New York to Stamford, a distance of about thirty-five miles; but of this distance about twelve miles are over the tracks of the New York Central line, the trains entering the same station. The New Haven road has decided, however, to install the single-phase alternating-current system on its own line, thus necessitating an arrangement which will permit the same locomotives to be operated by the continuous current on the New York Central portion of the route. This arrangement is not impossible, but it may be accompanied with some inconvenience; and it is unfortunate that the two systems are to be given such extensive trial upon lines using joint tracks, since any difficulties which may occur will serve to retard the general introduction of electric traction for main-line service.   At the same time, it must be realized that if electricity is to replace steam for railway service, there must be free interchangeability throughout, so that it may be just as well to have the question brought up at the start, and carried to a conclusion which shall guide subsequent work in this most important service.

A welcome announcement in connection with the subject of electric railway traction is the statement that electric locomotives are to be used from the start for hauling the trains through the Simplon tunnel.   It was originally intended to operate the new route with steam locomotives, as in the case of the older Alpine tunnels; but the employment of electric traction will obviate trouble from smoke and escaping steam from the outset.

The tunnel is now enlarged to the full dimensions for the main passage, and the masonry lining is being rapidly completed.   The auxiliary tunnel is now open throughout; and with the improvement in ventilation, and the gradual drawing off of the water from the hot springs, the temperature has been lowered from 130 degrees to below 80 degrees. It is expected that the line will be opened for business by May 1, and there appears to be nothing to prevent the operation of traffic during the summer.   Active measures are at last being taken to improve the lines of access from France; and the new route from Dijon to Geneva, by way of Lons-le-Saulnier, including the construction of the Faucille tunnel, will enable the full benefit of the Simplon route to be secured.

An interesting example of the manner in which an improved technical process may change the entire current of an important industry is seen in the development of the Louisiana sulphur deposits.   It has long been known that extensive deposits of sulphur existed beneath a layer of difficult quicksand; but the cost of reaching the strata, either by freezing or by sinking metallic-lined shafts, appeared prohibitory.   A new plan, recently put into operation, has been most successful.   This process consists in melting the sulphur in place by forcing superheated water down through pipes, the fused sulphur being brought to the surface in a liquid state.   As sulphur melts at about 240° F., the temperature is easily attained in an ordinary steam boiler; and the hot water is sent down through pipes 10 inches in diameter, to a depth of about 450 feet. By providing a second tube within the main pipe, the liquid sulphur may be drawn up; and as its specific gravity is about double that of water, it is correspondingly balanced by the column of descending water, the balance of the lift being effected by compressed air.

At the present time more than 1,000 tons of sulphur are thus being taken out per day, or about 350,000 tons per year; and the sinking of additional pipes will enable this production to be doubled. The result is the sudden appearance of a formidable competitor to the sulphur industry of Sicily, which has long had a monopoly of the trade and has practically controlled the market. The Louisiana sulphur has entered the European market, besides supplying the home demand; the American market having until recently taken fully one-third of the Sicilian product. The application of a simple scientific process, due to the ingenuity of Mr. Hermann Frasch, has thus resulted in a complete transformation of an old-established industry.

The completion of the first year of active operation of the subway in New York City gives opportunity for the compilation of some instructive figures showing the extent to which that important engineering work has succeeded in meeting the rapid-transit problem in the metropolis. The average number of passengers carried has been 300,000 per day, or 106,-000,000 during the year. The line at present in operation is practically crowded to its limit during the rush hours of the morning and evening, while the elevated railway and the surface electric cars have almost regained the traffic which they lost at the opening of the subway.

There appears to be little doubt that the traffic has almost overtaken the increased facilities in the course of a single year; and it is fully expected that the extensions of the subway to Brooklyn on the south and to the upper portions of the city will cause the capacity of the tunnel to reach its maximum. This is not surprising, and indeed it was predicted in these pages shortly after the opening of the route. The subway has proven an enormous benefit to the community by enabling more people to travel up and down the island of Manhattan, but it has not solved the transport problem, because, like all other travelling facilities, it has created sufficient new traffic to occupy its full capacity.

In another department of transportation, namely, transatlantic steam-ship service, progress continues to be made. The *Amerika*, the recently completed liner of the Hamburg-American Company, marks the attainment of the greatest size which has yet been reached by a steamship. The length is 690 feet, beam 74 feet 6 inches, and depth 53 feet, giving a total displacement of 42,000 tons, with a gross tonnage of 23,000 tons, of which 16,000 tons is cargo. The *Amerika* belongs to a class which is becoming more and more appreciated both by the travelling public and by the owners; the great dimensions giving roomy comfort and steadiness at sea, while the moderate speed permits economical running and a large proportion of paying cargo. While the Cunard Company is supposed to be preparing to regain the speed record with the new turbine steamers now under construction, the German lines appear to be content to rest on their laurels, so far as speed is concerned, and to be devoting themselves to the profitable large ships of medium speed and maximum comfort for the passengers.

The increasing dimensions of the newer vessels is causing renewed attention to be given to the vital question of the improvement of harbor entrances. In a recent discussion of this subject, Mr. Brysson Cunningham, an engineer of wide experience in connection with the docks and port of Liverpool, shows that the principal limitations which surround the further development of shipbuilding are those of the ports which the ships must enter. The draught of the average modern ship now closely approximates 30 feet; and it has been shown that there are but three ports in the world, those of Marseilles, Genoa, and Tacoma, which can receive vessels of such draught at all times. The ports of New York, Quebec, San Francisco, Southampton, and Liverpool are also accessible to such ships with proper attention to channels and tidal restrictions, but so soon as greater draughts are attempted there is difficulty in navigation, and there are risks of delay and injury from grounding. The United States Government is expending four million dollars at the present time in endeavoring to dredge a forty-foot waterway in the Ambrose channel at the entrance to New York harbor, but the results are not very encouraging, and the maintenance of a dredged channel is sometimes a more difficult task than the cutting of the original opening.

Apart from the limitations which the accessibility of the ports impose upon the dimensions of vessels, the delays which are frequently occasioned bear upon the question of transport in a material fashion. It is of small use to drive a great liner across the ocean at top speed if delays of possibly ten per cent of the time of the whole crossing are met at the port of arrival. In this respect, the question of harbor improvement is similar to that of railway terminals; and it is beginning to be realized that there are greater opportunities for gaining time at the ends of a run than exist by forcing the actual running speed *en route*.

An important improvement recently introduced upon the later ocean liners is a modification of the microphone for the detection of submarine signals. Since the rate of transmission of sound is much more rapid through water than air, it has been realized that the sounds given off by a submerged bell would afford an effective warning of a dangerous coast, a lightship, or an approaching vessel, if a satisfactory receiver could be devised. The hull of the vessel itself may be used to form the main receiving instrument; the actual point of reception being a microphone placed within a tank containing liquid and attached to the inner side of the ship's plating. The principal difficulty with this arrangement was found to be the extent to which the local noises on the receiving vessel interfered with the distant bell signals. It has been found, however, that if the tank containing the microphone is filled with a liquid of greater density than water, such as a solution of brine, the internal noises are damped, or dissipated, while the external signals are distinctly audible in a telephone placed in the microphone circuit.

In practical tests it has been found that bell signals from five to eight miles distant are clearly and distinctly heard through the microphone receiver on shipboard; and, in view of this success, a number of the lightships on the North Atlantic coast and at some of the North Sea ports have been fitted with the submerged bells; while the larger vessels of the German, British, and American lines have been equipped with receivers. The introduction of this system of signalling should aid in removing much of the danger which hitherto has attended the approach to coasts in time of fog, and its use may lead to further important developments.

In the course of the development of automobile vehicles, it is encouraging to note that more attention is being paid to the improvement of industrial vehicles than was formerly the case. The interest in road racing appears to be distinctly on the wane, while endurance trials of trucks, delivery wagons, military vehicles, and the like are being conducted in a scientific and instructive manner. The *Automobile Club de France*, the most influential and important organization of the kind in Europe, has recently conducted an extensive series of road trials for omnibuses, light and heavy merchandise wagons, and military vehicles, over a circuitous route extending from Paris to Amiens, Dieppe, Havre, Rouen, and back to Paris, a distance of about 540 miles in all. The speeds made were from 30 to 100 miles per day; and of the 56 machines entered, all but four completed the course. The majority of the vehicles which entered in these trials were propelled by gasoline motors; but some of the machines were so arranged that alcohol could also be used if necessary, thus giving a greater flexibility as to fuel on the road.

Although the full report of these trials has not yet been made public, some interesting features were noted indicating the lines along which improvements are demanded. It was made apparent that pneumatic tires are unsuited for heavy vehicles subjected to continuous traffic condi-

26

tions on highways, while it was also evident that iron tires permitted too much jarring action to reach the driving mechanism. Solid rubber tires, or at least some form of elastic, non-inflated tires, are undoubtedly required; but the combined questions of cost and durability have not yet been satisfactorily solved. As in previous tests, the question of wheel construction showed itself to be of importance. There can be no doubt that a wheel through which the propelling power is transmitted from the hub outwards to the rim is under much heavier strain than a wheel which is rolled along from the perimeter, even though the actual weight carried is the same in both cases. There is no doubt that the motors used in industrial automobiles are far more satisfactory than either the wheels or the tires; and until a marked improvement is made in these latter details the commercial side of the question must remain somewhat uncertain.

Another interesting investigation recently conducted in connection with the operation of automobiles is that recently conducted by the Automobile Club in England in connection with the production of dust by swift motor vehicles upon highways. In localities where there is much travel and the roads are well cared for, the dust evil can be minimized by sprinkling, and in some places excellent results have been secured by treating the surface of the road with oil. It has been found, however, that the design of the automobile has a material influence upon its dust-raising action; and the investigations of the Automobile Club, which were conducted by taking instantaneous photographs of motor cars driven at various speeds over a track covered with flour, showed the effects very clearly.

Naturally, those cars which have low bodies, near the ground, raise more dust than those which are higher; but a greater effect is produced by irregularities under the machine, such as a tool box or other projection. By giving proper care to the shape of the underbody of an automobile, avoiding forward coning, and reducing irregularities in contour to a minimum, it is practicable to reduce very materially the dust-raising action of an automobile; and by giving proper scientific study to this element in design, the skilful builder may benefit by the researches which have been made.

The extended introduction of superheating into steam locomotives is apparently warranted by the good results which are being obtained, and both in the United States and in Europe superheaters are accepted as elements of value in improving steam economy. Two principal types are used. One of these consists of a set of pipes in the smoke box, abstracting heat from the discharge gases and delivering it to the steam on its way from the boiler to the engine; while the other uses superheating tubes introduced into a portion of the fire-tubes of the boiler. Both arrangements appear to work well. With superheating, as with compounding, the advantage gained by improved steam economy is largely that of securing more power from the same boiler capacity. The dimensions of the boiler in the large modern engines have about reached the limits of the space available, the width being governed by the side clearance between trains, and the height regulated by the head room under bridges and in tunnels. The coal-handling capacity of firemen has also about reached its limit on the large freight engines, so that anything which aids in getting more power from the steam is to be welcomed; and this readily explains the interest which is taken by railroad men in the economy effected by superheating.

So far as stationary engines are concerned, some very remarkable results have been obtained by a judicious combination of compounding and superheating. Some recent tests of a semi-portable tandem compound engine, with double superheaters, the steam being passed through one superheater before going to the high-pressure cylinder and through another set of coils between the two cylinders, show a consumption of only 9.55 pounds of steam per horse-power per hour. This is a most excellent performance when it is understood that the engine is of small size, developing a total of only about 60 horse-power. The fuel consumption was only 1.17 pounds per indicated horse-power per hour; and the thermal efficiency works out a little over 19 per cent, or as high as is attained by gas engines in ordinary practice. One element in the attainment of this high economy is doubtless the close proximity of the engine and boiler, the highly superheated steam passing directly from the superheater to the engine without traversing a long line of piping, a condition which also obtains in locomotives. The loss of efficiency in long steam mains is especially marked when superheated steam is transmitted, a point which engineers are just beginning to appreciate.

The completion of the great masonry viaduct at Plauen, in Saxony, demands notice in connection with the revival of masonry after many years of supercession by iron and steel for bridges. Structural steel work will doubtless continue to be employed for many purposes, and its limits for great spans are much greater than can be possible for stone. When freedom from subsequent cost for repairs, as well as general permanency and durability are considered, the use of the masonry arch, one of the very oldest forms of construction, will doubtless persist. The arch at Plauen, over the valley of the Syra, has a span of 90 metres, or a little more than 295 feet, thus exceeding in width its greatest predecessor, the Luxembourg viaduct, by more than 17 feet; and as the rise is but one-fifth of the span in the former case, as against more than one-third at Luxembourg, the pressures are correspondingly greater. The Plauen arch is built of a local phyllit-schist, the ring being made of cut and dressed stone, with the haunches pierced with openings to relieve the distribution of the load; and the total cost of the structure was only 500,000 marks, about $125,000,

An interesting counterpart to the great masonry arch at Plauen is the span of the new cantilever bridge across the St. Lawrence River at Quebec. The central span here is 1,800 feet, making it the largest yet constructed, being nearly 100 feet greater than the spans of the cantilevers of the Forth bridge, or 200 feet greater than the suspension span of the Williamsburg bridge at New York. When it is remembered that the famous Eiffel tower at Paris is only 300 metres, or 984 feet, in height, it will be seen that this cantilever span is practically equal to two Eiffel towers erected not vertically upon solid foundations, but projecting out horizontally, and meeting in mid-stream, while supporting a level roadway — an altogether different proposition.

The engineer necessarily devotes a large portion of his time to the making of accurate measurements; sometimes in the workshop in the determination of magnitudes involving a precision within the ten-thousandth part of an inch, and at other times in the field, in work in which the absolute error may be greater, but the relative error is kept within the one-millionth to the one five-millionth part of the entire distance under consideration. It is a noteworthy fact that no sooner is a territory freed from the disturbances which accompany its conquest, than it is invaded by the peaceful work of the engineer, covering the area with his base lines and triangulations, and determining, with the highest possible degree of precision, the positions of salient points and their relations to other parts of the world. Thus, the island of Madagascar was no sooner conquered by the French than a geodetic and topographical survey was begun, so that now the island has been brought into precise measurement relations with other lands. In like manner, the southern portion of the African continent has been surveyed in great part since the Boer war; and the work, begun as far back as 1840, has been carried well up into Rhodesia.

The real geodetic survey of South Africa began with the work of Sir David Gill in 1879; and the triangulation begun by him, including a base line measured in Natal in 1883, has been carried northward to the Zambesi. A number of base lines have been measured in the course of the survey, a portion of this work having been in charge of M. Tryggve Rubin, who was a member of the Swedish party engaged in the measurement of an arc of the meridian in Spitzbergen several years ago. When the geodetic triangulation of Southern Africa is extended sufficiently far north to be tied in with the surveys on the Nile, the line can be carried across the Mediterranean and united with the Roumanian and Russian surveys to form a complete arc extending from Cape Agulhas to the North Cape, and including an amplitude of 105 degrees, far longer than any which has yet been considered.

At the time of writing this review, the condition of affairs at the Isthmus of Panama, or rather at Washington, is indeterminate. The advisory board of engineers has completed a report in which a sea-level canal is recommended; but this conclusion has the endorsement of but eight of the members of the board, the remaining five members advocating a lock canal, but differing among themselves as to the height of the summit level. The foreign engineers, Messrs. Hunter, Tincauzer, Quellenec, Welcker, and Guerard, all favored the sea-level plan; but it does not follow that this plan will necessarily be accepted. In any case, the work of the advisory board shows that, in the opinion of the ablest specialists of Europe and America, there are several excellent plans available for a ship canal at the Isthmus of Panama; and the adoption of any one of these will assure the commercial world of a satisfactory short cut between the Atlantic and Pacific oceans.

The attempts which are being made to create political capital out of a question which is wholly an engineering one is to be deplored; and, as I have already indicated in these pages, the total cost, even of a sea-level canal, is far below the amounts being expended on works of equal importance in the great cities of the United States and elsewhere. The spectacular nature of the undertaking naturally appeals to the public and may afford occasion to the demagogue, but to the engineer the subject is but one of a number of examples of his art to be accomplished with the minimum of fuss and the maximum of efficiency.

HENRY HARRISON SUPLEE.

NEW EDITIONS OF FRANKLIN.[1]

IT was to be supposed that the approach of the two hundredth anniversary of Franklin's birth would be marked by the appearance of books dealing with his extraordinary life and presenting afresh those unpremeditated writings which for many years have gained him·the position of a true classic. And even if there were no interesting anniversary almost upon us to account for the books here to be noticed, the two smaller would be welcome as convenient reprints, while the larger—the first·volume of Prof. Smyth's notable edition — would justify itself by the new material it announces.

Besides, in these days of active scholars and publishers, and of an ever enlarging public, we have no right to be surprised, and still less to complain, that the great writers of the past are brought to our attention in a large variety of forms. Franklin, modest as he was, never dreamed that future members of his craft would set up edition after edition of his "Autobiography," or that, in less than sixty years, his miscellaneous writings would be thrice collected, each time into ten large volumes. Neither he nor his editors nor his publishers should be held responsible for the fact that the shelves and card catalogues of our libraries are being year by year more and more taxed to accommodate books by and about this most many-sided of all Americans. He could not help being interesting, and for nearly two centuries the world has not been able to help being interested in him.

If there is any resemblance between a review and a repast, Prof. Smyth's volume ought to be sandwiched between the less substantial books of Mr. Cutler and Mr. Macdonald; but it seems easier to speak of the latter before

[1] "The Writings of Benjamin Franklin." Collected and Edited with a Life and Introduction by Albert Henry Smyth. Volume I. New York: The Macmillan Company, 1905.
"Selections from the Writings of Benjamin Franklin." Edited by U. Waldo Cutler. New York: Thomas Y. Crowell & Co., 1905.
"The Autobiography of Benjamin Franklin now First Printed in England from the Full and Authentic Text." Edited with a Bibliographical Preface and an Historical Account of Franklin's Later Life, by William Macdonald. London: J. M. Dent & Co. New York: E. P. Dutton & Co., 1905. [The Temple Autobiographies.]

commenting upon the first instalment of what promises to be the most complete edition of Franklin and one of the most valuable of recent contributions to American historical and literary scholarship. Mr. Cutler's "Selections," which appear in Crowell's well-named "Handy Volume Classics," are intended to furnish that sedulously cared-for individual, the busy reader, with a sufficient amount of Franklin's miscellaneous productions to give him a fair idea of their author's versatility and charm, and also, it may be presumed, to whet his appetite for a larger knowledge of the man and his writings than a single volume can convey. Denying himself the privilege of making excerpts from the "Autobiography," Mr. Cutler has tried to present "the inner character of the great Franklin" by means of his selections, which he has taken from "Poor Richard's Almanac," from "The Busy-Body" essays, from the simpler scientific and political papers, from the effective canards, from the delightful "Bagatelles" written in France, and from the inimitably easy and sensible correspondence.

It would seem that the book ought to answer its purpose, and I am personally glad that the editor saw fit to include in his appendix that memorable document entitled "Examination of Franklin in the British House of Commons Relative to the Repeal of the American Stamp Act, in 1766." It remains only to say that there are a few notes and that the introduction is unpretentious, as befits the volume. Mr. Cutler makes a suggestive comparison of the careers of Franklin, Jonathan Edwards, and Dr. Johnson; but he seems to push his contrasts a little too far when he represents the Cham of Letters as "dying in obscurity" and the greatest of American theologians as dying "comparatively young." Windham, Burke, Langton, and Fanny Burney, to say nothing of the most distinguished physicians and surgeons, were constant in their attendance upon Johnson, and within a few days from his death he was laid, to quote Macaulay, "among the eminent men of whom he had been the historian, — Cowley and Denham, Dryden and Congreve, Gay, Prior, and Addison." Franklin's death was mourned by a larger world — with more of display, apparently, in France than in his native country — but he had no such final resting-place as Johnson, nor were his ministering friends so illustrious. As for Edwards, his "Original Sin" was published about the time of his death in his fifty-fifth year, and although a new sphere of usefulness was opening to him at Princeton, he had surely accomplished a rather full life's work. Mr. Cutler's phrase would apply more fitly to Pascal. But these and other similar trifles detract scarcely, if at all, from the usefulness of this little book. Its carefully chosen selections should be put by the side of the "Autobiography" on the shelves of the many Americans who are interested in the history and literature of their country, but are unable to allow themselves the luxury of owning either of the two best editions of Franklin's works.

Mr. William Macdonald's edition of the "Autobiography" has the distinction, claimed in its title, of being the first authentic version of that famous book published in England. His preface tells in a concise way how it is that Englishmen have read for over a hundred years, and are still reading, a text differing in more than a thousand particulars from that which Franklin, shortly before his death, ceased to compose. This bibliographical romance is familiar to students of Franklin; but as imperfect versions of the "Autobiography" still circulate in this country — a reason for gratitude to Messrs. Dutton & Company for importing this edition — it may be presumed that many persons are unacquainted with the strange fortunes of the book they so thoroughly enjoy, and that a brief recapitulation of the story, thrice told though it be, may not be out of place here.

The manuscripts of at least three important works by colonial Americans underwent curious adventures — Bradford's "History of Plymouth," Winthrop's "History of New England," and Franklin's "Autobiography" — and of the three series of happy accidents it is easy to affirm that the happiest was that which secured us the possession intact of the single American book of the eighteenth century that everybody reads. An even greater book of the eighteenth century that everybody reads, "Robinson Crusoe," saw the light with difficulty and was written when its author was an aging man; but the world came much nearer losing Franklin's masterpiece. It was not until he was sixty-five that it seems to have occurred to him that it might be well for him to write an account of his varied and full career, and then the thought that was uppermost in his mind was that he might in this way give useful instruction to his descendants. The wider public his utilitarian predecessor Defoe certainly had in mind was hardly within Franklin's purview. Mr. Macdonald is surely right in saying that the American's work gained greatly in having originated "as a sort of holiday gayety, a long retrospective chat, a budget of personal and moral memoranda, written for the gratification and the uses of his own folk at home."

In 1771, while he was visiting his friend Bishop Shipley, Franklin addressed his natural son, William, then Governor of New Jersey, what forms a little more than the first third of the "Autobiography." The visit over, he let the matter rest, and, the Revolutionary War coming on, his mind was too much occupied with affairs of public concern to permit him to resume the narrative of his personal doings in a period that must have seemed to him very far away. When he went to France in 1776, he turned over his papers for safe keeping to his friend, the noted Loyalist,

Joseph Galloway. The latter took them to his home in Bucks county and placed them in an out-house. Perhaps he did not set so high a value on documents as Franklin, who, though careless in watching them, saved even the most worthless scraps of paper. Soon the recalcitrant Galloway had to fly from Pennsylvania and his estate was confiscated. His house was raided by troops; the trunk containing Franklin's papers was smashed, and its contents scattered on the floor. Prof. McMaster attributes this act of vandalism to the British; Prof. Smyth declares that no one knows whether it was the rebels or the enemy; Mr. Macdonald, with overabundant caution, it would seem, contents himself with saying that we do not know through what adventures the fragment of the "Autobiography" had passed before it finally reached Franklin in France.

The early pages of the "Autobiography" were not alone among Franklin's documents in experiencing those ravages of war for which he thought that a good and sufficient reason could never be discovered. Although Mr. Bache hurried to the scene of disorder and destruction, he was able to rescue only what Prof. Smyth calls a "poor remnant"; six out of the eight letter-books containing the drafts of Franklin's correspondence during his fifteen years of official service in England having been irrecoverably lost. Whatever the historian may think in the matter, the general reader would not exchange for these letter-books the twenty odd pages of manuscript containing the opening of the "Autobiography," which fell, in some way or other, into the hands of a Quaker friend of Franklin's, Mr. Abel James. Delighted with the narrative, James copied it, sent the copy to Franklin, and begged him to continue the story. This was in 1782. Franklin was old and busy, and hesitated to undertake any new task; but he showed the fragment to French and English friends, who urged him to complete the work. Prof. Smyth quotes Benjamin Vaughan, who wrote in a letter included in the text of the "Autobiography," that it would be "worth all 'Plutarch's Lives' put together."

It is not likely that, even if Franklin had carried his story almost down to his death, it would have been rendered fit to inspire a second Shakespeare to write several great plays; but we may all be glad that in 1784 the old philosopher and statesman did set to work and that he continued adding to the narrative, though with small results, until he sailed for America the next year. His friends kept on beseeching him not to give over the task; but he was ill and busy and did not get at it again until 1788, when he brought the story down to 1757, where it stopped in the old editions. Copies were then sent to English and French friends; but Franklin did not altogether relinquish the hope of covering his later and more important years, and he actually wrote a few additional pages, which carried the work to 1762. These pages were not printed in English until Mr.

John Bigelow gave the world the authentic "Autobiography" in 1868.

Meanwhile the adventures of that masterpiece had increased in interest, if not in danger. Franklin died in 1790 and left his grandson, William Temple Franklin, as his literary executor. The latter seems at once to have endeavored to secure one of the copies that went to France, and probably he took other steps to restrain until such time as should suit himself the publication of what the reading world was eagerly demanding. Then, as Mr. Macdonald says, "a wonderful thing occurred," or, as we may more accurately express it, several mysterious things happened. In the first place, William Temple Franklin got some unknown work to do which brought him in £7,000 in a few months and gave him an excuse for postponing his edition for a while. This postponement soon grew chronic; and it was not until 1817, twenty-seven years after Franklin's death, that the first volume of his grandson's edition appeared. Meanwhile, many discreditable rumors had been circulated to the effect that the British Government had an interest in suppressing the papers of such an important agent in the affairs of the Revolutionary period, and that ways had been easily found to induce William Temple Franklin and his father to make the cause of the Government their own.

The details of the scandal may be read by the curious in the pages of Bigelow, Smyth, and McMaster. Here it is sufficient to remark that, although the light of noonday can scarcely be said to have been thrown upon the matter, it seems clear that the main cause of the delay over which so many people chafed is to be found in the fussiness, laziness, and general literary incompetence of Franklin's grandson. Political reasons connected with ex-Governor Franklin's pension may also have weighed with the procrastinating editor; but the latter's total lack of resemblance to his efficient grandfather seems adequate to account for all the faults that can be charged to him.

In the interim, however, a second set of mysterious events had happened. Early in 1791, Buisson published at Paris a French translation of the "Autobiography" containing the portion dealing with Franklin's life down to the year 1731. The translator has been identified as Dr. Jacques Gibelin, and he seems to have been convinced of his ability to secure the whole of the manuscript for translation and publication. How he got hold of the copy he used has never been ascertained, but all authorities are agreed that he bungled his work. It was popular, however, and in 1792 it was translated into German, and the following year was made the basis of two English versions. One of these, edited by Dr. Price, appears to have been freed from Gibelin's blunders; the other improved upon them.

To quote Prof. Smyth: "Ignorance and pompous pretension burden its pages. The Frenchman had translated Franklin's juvenile ballad, 'The Lighthouse Tragedy,' being an account of the drowning of Captain Worthilake, as 'La Tragédie du Phare.' Parsons's translator converted it into 'The Tragedy of Pharoah.'" After this Bottom-like, if not bottomless, translation, the "Autobiography" appeared in 1794 in a German translation from the better English translation of the bad French translation — the Teutonic version being "on the whole well done" — and four years later a Frenchman, J. Castéra, took the same English translation of the original Gibelin translation and turned it back into French, adding, however, a considerable portion of the remainder of the narrative, which he obtained from French sources. Then, in 1806, followed a London edition of the works in three volumes, and there was a natural fresh outburst of indignation against William Temple Franklin for his procrastination. He defended himself in an obscure Paris newspaper, and went on dawdling over his task and entering into fruitless negotiations with publishers.

At last, after three times the nine years' delay recommended by Horace, the long-heralded edition, put together with the help of a clerk of Colburn the publisher, gave British and American readers what they long fondly believed to be the "Autobiography" as it had been left by its illustrious author.

But the adventures of the book were not yet over. In 1828, Jules Renouard made a fourth translation, which was based on the original Franklin manuscript and contained the portion covering the years 1757 to 1762. This manuscript had come into the hands of the heirs of Franklin's friend M. LeVeillard, who was guillotined during the Terror. Le Veillard had originally possessed a copy only; but this was a fair one, and William Temple Franklin, being lazy and perhaps contemplating numerous corrections of his grandfather's inelegant English, made the astonishing proposition to the Frenchman's heirs that they should take the original manuscript and give him the copy. They closed with the offer, and for nearly forty years after Renouard completed his translation the precious relic remained in France hidden from Anglo-Saxon collectors.

In 1866, Mr. John Bigelow, then Minister to France, at a dinner he was giving, began to talk about Franklin to the publicist M. Édouard Laboulaye, who had been translating some of the philosopher-statesman's writings. Mr. Bigelow, from certain premises that need not be cited, had reached the conclusion that the original manuscript of the "Autobiography" must still lurk concealed in France. M. Laboulaye undertook to search for it, and in about seven months was able to write a letter beginning "Eureka!" The manuscript and other Franklin relics had been traced to MM. de Senarmont, who were willing to part with them for 25,000 francs. Mr. Bigelow paid the price, and in 1868 was able at last to give English readers Franklin's life in Franklin's own words. He found that William Temple Franklin, after the guardian-angel fashion of the older editors, had permitted himself to make about twelve hundred changes in his grandfather's phraseology. For example, Franklin's racy statement that the eccentric printer Samuel Keimer (who, by the way, is another of the many links between Franklin and his prototype Defoe) "stared like a pig poisoned" was changed to the certainly less forcible though possibly more elegant affirmation that Keimer "stared with astonishment." Objurgations upon the offending grandson are needless now; it seems better to hope that the genuine "Autobiography" will supplant the older form in our schools and libraries, and also to call attention to the fact that a good book rightly seems to have as many lives as the traditional cat. The emendations of William Temple Franklin and the blunders of the early translators could not prevent the "Autobiography" from taking its place at or near the very top of such self-revelations; and neither the accidents of war nor those of peace, perhaps more to be dreaded, could rob the world of so valuable a possession as so useful a man's account of his own life.

This recapitulation of the adventures of the "Autobiography" has taken so much space that it precludes any discussion of the book itself — not a matter of much consequence in view of its abounding popularity — or of the "Later Life" of Franklin which Mr. Macdonald has appended. In a little more than a hundred pages, he sketches in an interesting way the main achievements of the cosmopolitan sage and statesman; and surely no American can complain that Franklin is judged from an insular or unfriendly point of view. Mr. Macdonald's treatment of the affair of the Hutchinson letters, and a long footnote on the relations between Franklin and John Adams, almost lay him open to the charge of being a partisan admirer of his hero. Perhaps if he had learned from Franklin to simplify his own style, if he had left a less definite suspicion that one of his chief aims in writing is not merely to avoid the commonplace, but to attain the exceptional, a few old-fashioned readers would enjoy his pages more; yet even these cannot but be grateful for this convenient edition of a delightful classic superintended and augmented by so well qualified and enthusiastic a Franklinian.

Passing now to Prof. Smyth's volume, we find that his preface and introduction carry us back into the region of bibliography. He begins by paying due tribute to his two distinguished forerunners, Jared Sparks and Mr. Bigelow, though it is worth noticing that he is rather harsher in his treatment of Sparks's editorial deficiencies than Mr. Bigelow was. His own labors to add to the materials amassed by his immediate predecessor have evidently been very great and successful. He has utilized the

Franklin papers, obtained in 1903 by the University of Pennsylvania, as well as the famous Stevens collection in the Library of Congress, and the thirteen thousand documents that are the property of the American Philosophical Society. He has also ransacked the archives of Great Britain and of four continental nations, and has made many interesting "finds." Furthermore, he has taken pains to secure accurate transcripts and has corrected more than two thousand errors that had crept into former editions.

According to his figures, Sparks published 1016 of Franklin's manuscripts, of which 407 had not appeared previously. Mr. Bigelow gave 1,357 Franklin manuscripts, of which 380 had not appeared in Sparks. The earlier editor had added 370 letters addressed to Franklin; Mr. Bigelow printed only 210, most of which were identical with those selected by his predecessor. To this enormous mass, Prof. Smyth intends to add — his first volume contains only his own introduction and the "Autobiography" — 385 letters and 40 articles all by Franklin. He has searched American and English newspapers and collected quite a number of Franklin's essays, including the "Dogood Papers." He will reprint many of the prefaces to "Poor Richard's Almanac" and will also publish several important letters to Franklin not to be found elsewhere. Room for the new material will be gained, in part, through the exclusion of tracts and papers formerly attributed to Franklin but now known not to be his — such as "The Principles of Trade," written by George Whatley, and "An Humble Petition presented to Madame Helvétius by her Cats," written by Franklin's friend the Abbé Morellet. Space will also be gained by the omission of " a few slight unmeritable essays " and of compositions marked by " the coarse Rabelaisian humor " exhibited in the letter to the Academy of Brussels; and the editor promises to be "brief and sparing in annotation." He has borne in mind, he tells us, the sarcasm of John Quincy Adams concerning one of his predecessors, that "he had impoverished his edition with his notes."

I do not wish to have Prof. Smyth subject himself to the sarcasm even of less important and less sharp-tongued persons than the younger Adams; yet, as I belong to the perhaps fast vanishing tribe of those that enjoy footnotes, I cannot but hope that, as his future volumes go through the press, he will find it impossible here and there to resist the temptation to annotate even to the point of divagation. On page 272 of the present volume, I should have welcomed a longer note on that interesting writer James Ralph. Should Prof. Smyth answer by referring me to an essay by Leslie Stephen and an excellent article in the "Dictionary of National Biography," I should reply that the true footnote lover wants his information, or whatever else, not in a work of reference, but in close connection with the passage in the text that cries out loudly or gently whispers for annotation. I have confessed, however, that probably Prof. Smyth has consulted the desires of the majority in this age of far from leisurely readers, and I suspect that he has also consulted them with regard to the only other suggestion, or rather query, that I have to make.

I wonder whether the time has not come to include in an edition everything known to be from the pen of Franklin, whether or not it may suit the taste of a more fastidious generation than that of which he was far from being the most fastidious representative. This does not necessarily mean that purchasers of the present edition should be compelled to buy volumes which they would be tempted to keep under lock and key. It merely means that a supplementary volume might be made to include material either worthless from most points of view or objectionable from one, and that this volume might be procurable by librarians and other parties presumably competent to look after their own welfare and that of those dependent upon them. We delight in calling Franklin a classic author; and it is, or should be, one of the prerogatives of a classic that his writings should be accessible, to students at least, in their blushing or unblushing entirety. If experience has demonstrated anything, it has shown that no editor can with safety assume that any scrap of a great writer's work ought to remain forever in manuscript or should be denied the privilege of being reprinted. I am free to confess that I think the world would derive greater profit if Prof. Smyth were forced to add a volume to his edition in order to include belated discoveries — such letters, for example, as those Franklin wrote to Bishop Shipley, Sir Edward Newenham, and Jan Ingenhousz, the confidential physician of Maria Theresa, as well as those he probably wrote to Erasmus Darwin and other no less distinguished men, the loss of which our accomplished editor deplores. But I believe none the less in complete editions of authors worthy of study, having suffered not a little from the eccentricities of editors in this particular, and also, I may add, from the unwillingness of some librarians to put upon their shelves books the value of which they could not personally recognize.

Prof. Smyth's introduction fills about half his volume and seems to me to be excellent. In view of the fact that Franklin tells part of his own story and that an essay in the final volume is to tell the rest, Prof. Smyth decided very wisely to omit the usual formal biographical sketch and to devote himself to the more congenial and needed task of reviewing the history of Franklin's writings and giving a summary and running appreciation of his extraordinary achievements as writer, scientist, sage, publicist, statesman.

The account of the fate of the Franklin manuscripts is particularly interesting. We have already traced briefly the fortunes of the "Autobiography"; but those of some of the other papers are almost as curious. The documents filling the seventy-six folio volumes owned by the American Philosophical Society were left behind in America by William Temple Franklin, because he did not perceive their value, and they came to the Society through the gift of a son of the George Fox to whom the careless editor bequeathed them. The manuscripts taken abroad by William Temple Franklin and made the basis of his edition were deposited, after his volumes had appeared, with his London bankers. When he died in 1823, his widow removed the manuscripts, but exactly what she did with them is not known. She married a Frenchman and went to France to live; and perhaps she had no compunctions, if indeed she heard of the matter, when the papers were discovered in loose bundles on the top shelf of a tailor's shop in London where her first husband had lodged. They were being cut into patterns when they were found; but their rescuer had no great cause to bless his lucky stars, for he could not persuade the British Museum or two American ministers or any patriotic private citizen to buy them. In 1851, however, that devoted bibliophile, the late Henry Stevens, secured them. He put them in order, and finally sold them to the United States Government. They now fill fourteen folio volumes, which are in the main kept in the Manuscript Department of the Library of Congress.

The third of the three chief collections of Franklin manuscripts, that belonging to the University of Pennsylvania, formed originally a part of the bequest made to George Fox by William Temple Franklin. These documents remained for many years in a stable garret, were taken out to be sold to paper mills in order that a new kitchen carpet might be paid for, were rescued after one barrel had thus been destroyed, and, finally, after about forty years, were secured for the University through the agency of Dr. S. Weir Mitchell. *Habent et sua fata libelli* is the only fitting comment, unless one vents maledictions upon Mr. Warburton's cook. The indignant reader must not, however, allow his wrath to keep him from following Prof. Smyth through his interesting description of the minor Franklin collections — that of the Historical Society of Pennsylvania, that of the British Museum, and those of Paris, for example — nor should the still more interesting section devoted to the printed editions be skimmed or left unread.

From bibliographical details Prof. Smyth passes to a cursory discussion of Franklin's works considered as a whole, after which he proceeds to comment upon the philosophical, political, and economic writings, the satires and bagatelles, and the correspondence. There is, of course, little that is new to say about Franklin in his capacity as writer or man of letters; but the obvious things are well put at the beginning of the critical discussion, and then, under the categories named above, the editor, from his large stores of information, gives proofs of Franklin's astonishing acumen, prescience, versatility, practicality, humor, and general range of efficiency which will, I think, surprise by their interest and, in many cases, by their unhackneyed character, even those readers who have thought themselves quite familiar with the attainments of the most variously gifted and thoroughly representative son of the delightful eighteenth century.

The longest and most important section of the introduction is that devoted to the "Philosophical Works." Doubtless many persons have quite a clear conception of Franklin as statesman, sage, creator of "Poor Richard," writer of a classic autobiography, humorist, inventor, and general utility man on a cosmopolitan rather than a parochial scale; but when they come to think of him in his capacity as scientist or natural philosopher, their imaginations get tangled up with his kite, and they can give no very clear account of his scientific acquirements and achievements. Such persons may never find time to read in their entirety Franklin's contributions to "subjects of electricity, seismology, geology, meteorology, physics, chemistry, astronomy, mathematics, hydrography, horology, aeronautics, navigation, agriculture, ethnology, paleontology, medicine, hygiene, and pedagogy"; but they will do well to read what Prof. Smyth has to say about this extraordinary mass of writing done, as it were, all in the day's work, with practically no thought of fame, but with every desire to be useful to the world. Only in connection with an early paper on the causes of earthquakes does the editor, who has evidently taken pains to inform himself on the present state of knowledge in fields of inquiry remote from his own specialties, find himself obliged to characterize Franklin's views as crude and worthless to-day. His anticipation of the wave theory of light, his observation of storms and whirlwinds, his experiments in the production of cold by evaporation, his ingenuity in constructing "magic squares," his interest in nautical matters, in scientific agriculture, and in paleontology, his contributions to the study of medicine and hygiene, would alone suffice to prove him to have been one of the most wide-awake mortals that ever lived; and his pioneer discoveries in electricity afford that solid basis of knowledge and achievement in at least one department of inquiry which seems the necessary foundation of abiding greatness.

It is hard to read Prof. Smyth's pages without coming to the conclusion that the utilitarian printer and citizen of Philadelphia was probably the most many-sided and acute scientist of his remarkable age, and a similar conclusion is forced upon us when we pass to a consideration of what he accomplished in other spheres of usefulness. He does not

stand apart in lofty isolation as does Washington, his personality is not
so overpowering as that of Johnson, or so dazzling as that of Voltaire; but
his nearness to the men of his own day and to us — in a word, the homeli-
ness of his character and his interests, should not be allowed to obscure his
essential greatness.   A broad plateau is no less wonderful a work of nature
than a towering peak.

It would be unfair to Prof. Smyth, upon whom I have already drawn
with great freedom, to extract from his introduction many of his choice
illustrations of Franklin's phenomenal activity of mind and spirit.   I
cannot forbear, however, to call attention to the fact that Franklin did
not altogether escape the tendency of his age to discover providential
purposes in nature, though he fell far short of Bernardin St. Pierre in this
exemplary exercise of the imagination.   Like Lord Bacon he suffered
physical ills from his ardor for making experiments, but fortunately only
to the extent of catching an intermittent fever from bending over stagnant water.   As he seems to have come in contact with almost every
notable figure of his time, we are not surprised to find that Marat and
Robespierre wrote him letters.   The communication of the latter, who
was employed to defend a client who had dared to protect his property
with what many regarded as a dangerous nuisance, to wit, a lightning
rod, is one of the most interesting of Prof. Smyth's discoveries.   Very
interesting also are the pages devoted to Franklin's little known services
to medical science, which, by the way, brought him in contact with another Frenchman of sinister reputation, however little deserved — Joseph
Ignace Guillotin.

Other topics of importance are the indebtedness of Malthus to Franklin, the latter's firm belief in free trade — remember that he was the first
citizen of Philadelphia! — Matthew Arnold's failure to perceive the satiri-
cal purpose underlying the modernization of six verses in the first chapter
of Job, the light thrown on Franklin's comparative inability to write in
French, and upon the history of Turgot's famous epigram, the begging
letters received by Franklin—one of them from a Benedictine who would
pray for the success of the American cause provided his gambling debts
were paid — but there is no use in trying to exhaust the list.

Everywhere we touch him he is the human and therefore the fascinating Franklin.   This statement is, to be sure, an exaggeration — one of the
sort at which he would have smiled with deprecating modesty or else, with
a malicious twinkle of the eye, would have told an unsavory anecdote with
disenchanting results.   There were sides of Franklin's character — well
remembered, it would seem, in Philadelphia — that were not at all attractive.   Prof. Smyth calls attention in a paragraph to the "smudgy trail"
the facetious printer left behind him in the "Pennsylvania Gazette," to
27

the grossness of some of his letters, to the effect of his strong animal instincts upon his conduct.

It is this, combined with his comparative insensibility to poetry and to spiritual religion — which Prof. Smyth does not emphasize — that puts Franklin, in the final analysis, below such men as Johnson and Washington, to whom he was vastly superior in many intellectual respects and who may themselves be justly taxed with æsthetic deficiencies. But when his limitations have been duly considered, it remains true that Franklin, like Defoe, and for much the same reasons, is one of the most fascinating of mortals, at least to students who examine minutely every phase of his character by means of his self-revealing writings. Both men had in its fullest development what may be called the genius for the prose of life. In both this genius is fused with a sort of plebeian spirit, with the result that they do not greatly appeal to over-sensitive souls. Other souls less squeamish, more robust, more catholic, if you will, take a special delight in watching the effects of this combination of democratic and aristocratic elements upon the lives and writings of these two great sons of the people, whose masterpieces will not cease to be read until the precious style affected by numerous moderns becomes an eternal possession of the English-speaking masses. When that delectable day comes, "Robinson Crusoe" and Franklin's "Autobiography" may be banished from whatever substitute the æsthetic world shall have devised for homely bookshelves. Pending this consummation, it is to be hoped that each of the three books here noticed will obtain a broad circulation.[1]

W. P. TRENT.

[1] Since the above was written, Prof. Smyth's second volume has appeared. It contains practically everything written by Franklin between 1722 and 1750. The items are given in chronological order, and information as to where they may be found in manuscript, etc., is appended. "The Dogood Papers," "Journal of a Voyage from London to Philadelphia, July 22–October 11, 1726," and prefaces to "Poor Richard" will probably first attract the attention of readers. The correspondence is, in the main, divided between William Stahan, Cadwallader Colden, and Peter Collinson. An excellent reproduction of the Martin portrait forms the frontispiece, and there are several plates.

FINANCIAL JAPAN AFTER THE WAR.

I do not say that the terms of peace ending our war with Russia were satisfactory. However, I do not wish to say that, because they were not as we wished them to be, the financial circles of our country are about to be plunged into a sea of troubles. Neither do I wish to harbor any such idea. From the very start, we did not take up arms that we might become enriched through an indemnity. From the beginning, we knew very well that it would be difficult indeed to drive our enemy to the foot of his citadel and compel him to see the wisdom of concluding the "peace under the castle." More than once — and this from the very opening of the war — we were in doubt whether, after all, the war would bring us anything like an adequate compensation for the expenditure. It would be out of tune with all things, therefore, for us, at this hour, to be looking upon financial Japan after the war with a sad eye. Nevertheless, as we are well aware of the disturbances which the war has brought to our finances, we must look to the best possible measures for restoring to health and prosperity what the war has disturbed. That is all.

Some of our industries were busier in the very midst of war than in times of peace. Among these may be mentioned the manufactures of arms and ammunition, and of cotton and hemp goods, as well as spinning. Now that the war is over, and many demands having been suddenly brought to a close, such branches of industry find themselves confronted with numerous more or less annoying problems, all calling for immediate solution. In the case of some of these industries, spinning for one, this sudden cessation in the demand from the battle-fields might be looked upon as a healthy appeal to their activity in other directions. It should stimulate them to widen their markets abroad, as it is better to expand than to economize. The export trade, being large in possibilities, is always a tempting field; and in that direction these branches could doubtless be able to make their way. Whether they would find sufficient demand to replace entirely the demands of the Manchurian army and of the navy is another question. How to change their field of activity wisely and well is without doubt the most serious problem with them. But granting that success in other fields of activity is possible, there still remains another difficult problem for solution. It is this, namely, that it will be impossible to effect the change successfully without sufficient capital; and where can our business men find all the capital that is required?

Of course, the industries whose activities were at their height in the very midst of the war, and to which the war proved a source of growth and profit, are comparatively few in number. To other lines of business — much larger in number than those I have mentioned — the war proved to be a bitter winter. To them the conclusion of war means the coming of spring. And, as in nature, so in business, the severer the winter, the more active the awakening to life. At the conclusion of the China-Nippon war of 1894–95, we saw a sudden expansion of our industrial and commercial activities. That the same principle holds true with the conclusion of the recent war there can be no question. It is only that the struggle through which we have just passed surpasses in magnitude that of our little affair with China by many a tenfold; and it is not beyond reason to suppose that its effect upon our industrial and commercial world will be immense in proportion.

We have seen what commercial wrecks, what biting commercial tragedies, trailed in the wake of the expansion movements following the Chinese war. Ten years ago we received over three hundred million yen of indemnity from China. In spite of it all, two years after that war we felt the coming of the storm which has become known as the crisis of 1898. I need not recall here all the ups and downs of our financial world during those trying years; how we, in 1899, thinking we had weathered the storm, and, as people sometimes do, after passing a pretty bitter period of trial, congratulated ourselves in advance upon our success; how we awoke a little later to find that all was not yet over, but that the excess of our convertible notes had another panic in store for us; and how we were called upon, in 1900, to suffer another period of financial trials. From our experiences of those days, it may be wise for us to take a hint as to what may be in store for us in the days now before us.

At the present time we are, I hope, a little wiser than we were then. And, too, to look back upon the hardships of those days cannot fail to give us a certain measure of comfort now. However hard it was for us for a time, we nevertheless cannot be blind to the fact that the trials of old have been transformed into the blessings of to-day. Many disasters we have seen; but, in spite of them, our nation has grown. There are men who contend that the prosperity of Japan after the Chinese war, and whose fruits we are permitted to see to-day, has been due to the three hundred million yen indemnity. I am not saying that the indemnity had nothing to do with the growth of our national wealth. All I contend is that our national growth since that time cannot be explained altogether by the indemnity.

It may be — and I am one of those who expect it — that in 1915 the people will look back upon this year of grace, 1905, with much happier eyes than those with which we look back upon 1895. I do not see why the next generation should not be permitted to chant the epic of the signal growth of the ten years from this day onward, and to indulge in the same pleasant reverie as we do when our eyes turn upon the days following the conclusion of the Chinese war. We were none too happy then at the turn of things. Nevertheless, to-day we take up a bit of statistical literature, famous in every country as the driest of literary work, and find in it more consolation than in the latest romance which recounts the heroic deeds of men and the justice of the gods in saving the virtue of a noble girl. Why? Simply because we find in the statistics the statement that our railways have more than doubled in length within the ten years past, and that our foreign trade has grown many hundred per cent.

However, this work of commercial and industrial expansion demands a good deal of capital, much more than that required in those lines which must find new markets and create new demands. Moreover, the expansion of domestic industries and enterprises in Nippon is not the only field that calls for capital. We must ever be mindful of the enterprises on the Asian continent. This is true especially of our activities in Korea. At the present time these are almost altogether confined to three branches — railways, banking, and shipping. In the future, however, there is ground to suppose that in that country mining also will be very promising. My individual efforts in that direction count, of course, only for little; but I am of the opinion that the people of Nippon ought to take more seriously into consideration the work of developing the natural resources of Korea.

Although I am not at present able to formulate any definite policy in regard to mining enterprises in Korea, or to map out any set scheme for the development of her other resources, nevertheless, of one thing I feel rather strongly convinced, namely, that the improvement in agriculture in Korea should, by all means, be undertaken by the Nippon people. And I wish that the mining work would also be carried on, to a very large extent, by our own people. Rather than leave those activities in the hands of the Koreans, I would have our people take hold of them either individually or through companies. Naturally, it would be a very good thing if we could carry on this work under a single control. But if the gathering together of all these enterprises under a single power cannot be expected, we should at least have as free and healthy an understanding as possible between those who control the separate enterprises, so that they might work together harmoniously. I have already established one company under the name of the Korean Industrial Company. It is impossible, of course, especially in agricultural enterprises, to see the fruits

of one's labors within a few years. Nevertheless, I am pushing the work as much as I can, as I thoroughly believe in it.

As for enterprises in Manchuria, these would naturally have to be on a much larger scale than those in Korea, so that they would call for larger capital. And the capital — the all-important factor — where are we going to find it? Most certainly either at home or abroad. According to his own lights must a man judge of the wisdom or unwisdom of raising it at home or among the foreign capitalists. In deciding this question, however, many things must be taken into consideration.

If our country were to raise another loan at home, it goes without saying that, to make the flotation a success, the Government would have to make the conditions at least as attractive as those of the fourth and fifth domestic loans; and, perhaps, the conditions of the new loan would have to be made still more attractive in order to find a ready and responsive market. I have been given to understand that no less than 130,000,-000 yen of the fourth and fifth issues of our domestic loans have passed into foreign hands. And, for this reason, the Government might not find any serious difficulty in floating successfully another loan, in spite of the national temper of to-day. However, in that case, our people would be very much in the position of the middle-man; for, judging by the ultimate result, we should simply be raising a foreign loan at home. And as the conditions of our domestic loans are not so advantageous as those placed in foreign markets, it would mean that we should be placing a foreign loan through the home market on less advantageous terms than we could place a straight out foreign loan. This is a rather pointed statement as to the place where the capital should be raised. But it shows, if it tells any story at all, that money is cheaper abroad than at home.

But the war and its conclusion have not been altogether unkindly to us. Indeed, the war has brought us one very great and precious gift, namely, it has admitted us into the household of the great economic world. In a word, it has given a wider horizon to the economic circle of Nippon; has brought us into the very heart of the comity and exchange of the economic interests of all human kind; and has linked us, in a sense hitherto unknown to us, to the markets of the world.

In the case of the Hokkaido Colliery and Railway Company, the negotiations for the introduction of foreign capital have been already concluded, being no longer a topic of discussion. While things are not yet quite so far advanced in the matter of the Sanyo Railway Company, this company would have no more difficulty in interesting foreign capital for' the purpose of extending either its lines or its business than the Hokkaido Company, if it should wish to do so. I have, moreover, heard of a certain gentleman engaged in coal-mining work in Hokkaido who is even now concluding arrangements with a foreign capitalist for the introduction of capital to increase the facilities for the further development of his enterprises. Not only those companies and people whose credit is beyond all question, but also many who, from the standpoint of financial rating, cannot be classed with them, have succeeded in interesting foreign capitalists. And these cases seem, to my mind, to point to a better understanding between ourselves and foreign capitalists. Perhaps we owe this golden understanding, as all other good things, to the splendid work of our army and navy, a matter quite independent of our financial world. For present purposes, however, this matters but little. The fact is simply that to us of financial Japan after the war is given an opportunity beyond all price. Like all valuable opportunities, it calls for great wisdom and care in its handling. To-day our commercial world is before a very serious tribunal; and in the manner in which we handle the foreign capital shall we be judged, once for all, as to our wisdom and honesty.

Of the many important works calling for our activity there is nothing in all the financial world of Nippon so important as that of enlarging the scope of our economic enterprises. In almost everything — in banking, in spinning, and in commercial matters generally — consolidation seems to be the order of the day. Those companies which are working for one and the same or a similar end, with the same sort of history, and with similar interests, ought by all means to combine under one management. In our economic world nothing is quite so important as to accomplish great things through the union of many small forces. That it is a difficult piece of work I know from experience. In a number of cases, when one examines into the details of different organizations, into their respective ideas and fields of interest, the difficulty of uniting them becomes very evident. In some instances I have succeeded in bringing about such union, while in a number of cases I have failed. However that may be, and in spite of the evident difficulties in the way, I am nevertheless convinced that the first question that commends itself to the most serious consideration of our economic world after the war is consolidation, i.e., the creation of large forces. And the combination of many into one seems to be the most effective way of bringing about the end most piously prayed for. The days of small things are over; the war has brought them to a close. And, whether we like it or not, we have been brought face to face with many great problems requiring very great forces for their solution.

BARON SHIBUSAWA.

THE NEW CHINA.

Now that all is over between us and Russia, the world is asking the question: What, then, is the greatest significance of the war? My answer is that it means, in particular, the birth of the New China, and, in general, the birth of a new era for the people of the Asian lands. As for the rise of Nippon, it is purely incidental. In 1903 we were pretty nearly as great as we are in 1905.

All the Asiatic people now recognize that the axis of the Asian world has been shifted. They had been resigned to their fate, and had given up all hope of regaining the lost freedom of the state of nature. The Japanese success, first on sea and then on land, struck this enervated world like a cannon ball. The eyes of the nations of Asia are now turned upon Japan; and it is upon her that they base their hopes.

So writes a gentleman who signs himself a French Diplomatist; and many others are of the same opinion. The war made one thing rather plain. In Japan, the victor of the struggle, China, from this time on, will have a champion, and, in a critical hour, a protector who will do something more than talk. As for us of Nippon, we have known for many years that China would find in us a champion. It was only that we were not at all sure whether or not our ability and power were quite up to the mark of our enthusiasm and wishes. In this matter, Nippon is far from being a disinterested champion; and this is the beauty of the situation, as well as the thing that makes our relation with China permanent. In safeguarding the interests of China, in fostering her powers, in maintaining her strength, and in holding her territorial integrity as sacred and inviolable at the gamblers' table called the world's council of diplomatists, Nippon is simply safeguarding the peace of the Far East. And the peace of the Far East is the *sine qua non* of her prosperity, and, to some extent, of her very existence.

Not always did Nippon take this view of the situation. Time was when we were very much afraid of China, and we expressed our anxiety of those days in the war of 1894–95. At that time it was our desire to strike her a blow serious enough to cripple her in the north, where she was nearest to us, to the extent of compelling her to let us severely alone in our own affairs not only at home, but also in Korea, which is closer to us than the outside world seems to think. Since then, years have brought us wisdom. We are very much surprised to-day that we mistook the apparently aggressive measures of Li-Hung Chang in Korea in 1893 and 1894 as an index of the national temper of China. To our thorough satisfaction, we have come to know that the heroic traditions of Genghis Khan were ancient history to the throne at Peking; that, after all, the Chinese love their trade, their quiet at home, and the tilling of their fields much better than the sword and the broken dreams of a red field of battle. China is no prophet's jar which homes a genius; she is after all the greatest country in Asia. As she has no craving for conquest, we no longer are forced to sit up nights to watch her; and the least we can do for ourselves, and quite incidentally for her, is to do all we can to foster her strength, to develop her powers, and to bring about the new birth of that great country.

As to-day there is only the "White Peril" which threatens the peace of the Far East, can we build a wall more secure than the New China with her strength born again? Why should not we, already burdened with toilsome hours, weighty taxes, many ships of war, be permitted to receive help from the greatest power of Asia? The history of Nippon policy toward China since the unhappy years of 1894-5 has stated the above in a much plainer and more eloquent manner.

We have turned completely around in our attitude to our neighbor. But, as I have said, in those days we were far from knowing whether our strength was equal to our wishes. Russia was a great power, the greatest military power in Europe; and she was in Manchuria, and quite in love with her dream of a great Eastern empire. Had she not already created — by what authority we of the Far East did not, of course, quite comprehend — the office of the "Viceroy of the Far East," and, moreover, given that distinction to a decidedly reckless man? In the East we all asked: What mortal has the right to confer such a title, and what mortal has the right to receive such a title? But we spoke low in the East; and the Czar, who listens only to the explosion of a bomb, did not hear us at all.

The war came and made it plain both to us and to China that Nippon can and will shelter China in the critical hours of her rebirth. The year 1905, so eventful to Nippon, is to China a great year indeed. From all indications, China is likely to look back upon this year as we of Nippon look back upon 1868. That was the birth-year of the New Nippon, the first year of the present period of Meiji. Now that she is able to do so, the end and aim of Nippon effort seems to be to bring China to herself, to make her know what she is. On the fine morning when China finds herself—if only we could bring about this simple consummation so devoutly prayed for — the vivisection of the Chinese empire may appeal to the sense of humor of enlightened Europeans, but never to their territorial ambitions. And already many voices, much more eloquent than the voice of a prophet crying in the wilderness, are telling us of the breaking of the dawn of a new day for China. The fact is that the China of yesterday is farther away from the China of to-day than are the days of Washington from the United States of the year of grace 1905.

Not so many years ago, a French fleet went up the Min River and anchored within ten miles of the city of Foochow. A short time prior to that, France had a little trouble with the people of Tonquin. The French wanted to rob them of their native land; and, to their honor, the inhabitants fought for it against the French. France suspected that the Chinese Government might have done something to encourage this outlandish sentiment—which in other countries bears the beautiful name of patriotism. That is to say, France suspected that the Government of China might have done its duty toward the people of Tonquin. Through her Minister in Peking, France had demanded an indemnity; and this Christian power was dumfounded to see that China was not in a hurry to pay an indemnity for being so reckless as to dare to do her duty to the people of Tonquin. And the presence of the French fleet in the Min River was one of the usual arguments which civilized Europe used to employ in those days. To the still greater amazement of both the French Minister at Peking and the country he represented, China declined to apologize with a pretty heap of gold for one of the few right things she had done. The French Minister turned to the French admiral of the fleet, anchored in the Min River; and without the slightest intimation of war, the French fired upon the pitiful Chinese fleet which was trying to defend the city of Foochow. Three thousand Chinese bodies floated out to sea and came back into the river with the return of the tide; and for days the mutilated remains of the dead sailors of China spoke with gruesome eloquence of the humanity and manly justice of civilized France!

On November 1, 1897, in the Province of Shantung, two German missionaries who went into China without an invitation were killed. One might suppose that their Government would have taken a rather philosophical view of this incident, regrettable in the extreme though it was. Such, however, was far from the case; for on the fourteenth of that month, German marines were landed at Kiaochau, and, through the famous treaty signed on March 6, 1898, the world saw how Germany received what she considered a fair price for the misfortune of the two missionaries, namely, the cession of the finest deep harbor on the Chinese littoral; 3,000 taels of indemnity; the dismissal of the Governor of the Province of Shantung; the building of three "expiatory" chapels; concessions for the building of two railways in the province; and the exclusive right of exploiting the mineral resources of the province within twenty kilometers of the railroad on both sides — all of which goes to show that the Kaiser sets a great value upon the lives of the pious men under his flag.

After that, the Chinese officials took the liberty of informing the Germans in the Shantung province of the feverish condition of the people, and of their feelings toward foreigners in general and Germans in particular; and they told them, moreover, with extremely un-Chinese frankness, that the interior of the province was not at all a healthy place for the Germans to take their holiday trips in. A few Germans, three of them, I think, wishing to prove how enterprising they could be when it came to serving their Kaiser in his laudable work of sending the German flag to all sorts of places where it had not the slightest business to be, laughed at the warning of the Chinese officials and wandered into the interior, whence they were barely able to escape with their lives. The German commander at Kiaochau also went into the interior. However, being a wise man, he did not go alone, but took with him many guns. On his trip he burned two villages, and did not even take the trouble to count the number of Chinese he killed. Of course, such a thing as the Germans paying for the Chinese lives a millionth part of the price that the Germans required the Chinese to pay for the fright of their own pious countrymen never entered his head.

Now, the Kaiser, who knows the word of God, and, judging by what I have read, uses it not too rarely, did not even frown very harshly upon the act of the commander at Kiaochau in destroying their homes or killing a large number of villagers who had not the slightest hand in the high-priced luxury of threatening the lives of the three foolish Germans. Perhaps, in his heart, the Kaiser very much regretted the unhappy incident; but this did not cause him to overlook the fact that the affair might be turned to good account. He had been trying for many years to convince his people of the importance of building a formidable navy, while for some reason or another the people, on their part, had failed to be convinced by his eloquence of the necessity of spending so many millions for that purpose. But this incident showed clearly how necessary it was to possess a formidable fleet in order to maintain the dignity of the German flag on a distant sea, and how, without it, it would be impossible to carry out the great policy of trade expansion in the Far East with which he had been baiting the commercial imagination of the Germans. In a word, the Kaiser could well afford to pay a few marks for the lives of the defenceless Chinese villagers, as well as the entire cost of the two villages that had been burned. But, of course, China did not receive a tael from the power to which she had paid the price above mentioned for the loss of only two very rash men.

Next, there was issued at Peking, on March 15, 1899, an imperial decree by means of which there was conferred upon the Roman Catholic bishops an official rank similar to that of the viceroys and the governors of provinces in China. In this, China did not particularly wish to put into practice the injunction of the Master in whose name those French missionary bishops everlastingly raised so much mischief, namely, "Love your enemies." But then there were, back of the French demand, the "battalions and cannons" which the Kaiser worships as the guardian gods of peace, and China knew better than to resist.

Finally, the method by means of which the Czar robbed China of something like 3,000,000 square miles, that is to say, of an area about twenty times as large as Japan, is too well known to require discussion.

Not so many years ago many thoughtful people excused the Peking Government for neglecting to attend to many important governmental functions, because it seemed almost impossible for it to do very much beyond throwing away valuable concessions for railway construction. Russia received the East China Railway concession; Germany, that of Kiaochau (343 miles); England, the Tientsin-Shanghai-Kwan (130 miles); the Shanghai-Kwan and Shinmin-tun (240 miles); the Tientsin and Chinkiang (600 miles); and seven others calling for the construction of over two thousand miles of railroad. The French and the Belgians received the Peking-Hankow and five other concessions, while the Americans received the Canton-Hankow concession. With the single exception of the American concession, China gave these valuable things away, not because she wished to do so, but because she could not help herself.

Such, then, was the China of yesterday. Let us now turn our attention to the China of to-day.

On the authority of Sir Chengtung Liancheng, the able and distinguished Chinese Minister to the United States, we have it that the days of concession-giving in China are over. On August 29, 1905, China purchased back from the Americans the Canton-Hankow railroad concession, at a rather fancy price, it is true, but one which was, nevertheless, very low when one looks upon it as the price of the command by China of her own artery.

To-day there is no Li-Hung-Chang at Peking, neither is there a Count Cassini seated across the table from him. Nothing is more remarkable than the rise of Chang Chihtung of Nan-p'i, that famous viceroy at Hankow, to the supreme power in the council chamber of the Chinese empire. It was this enlightened Viceroy who wrote, in his famous work, "Chuen Hio Pien," which he published shortly after the China-Nippon war:

In order to render China powerful, and at the same time preserve our institutions, it is absolutely necessary that we should utilize Western knowledge. But unless Chinese learning be made the basis of education, and a Chinese direction be given to thought, the strong will become anarchists and the weak slaves. Thus the latter end will be worse than the former.

Happily for China, he looks upon education as the salvation of the Chinese empire. He was the pioneer in sending students to Nippon. And Nippon was delighted to receive with the students from Hupeh a grandson of Chang Chihtung, to whom the Nippon Government extended the courtesy of permitting him to enter the Nobles' College at Tokio. Viceroys Liu K'unyi and Yu-lu, and the governors of Chekiang and Kiangsi, as well as many others, followed the example of Chang Chihtung. To-day over four thousand Chinese students, including both sexes, are to be found in the Nippon colleges and schools.

One day in August, 1904, there was held in Tokio a meeting attended by a majority of the sixty Chinese girls then carrying on their educational work in the girls' schools of that city. To see those young ladies of China mounting a public platform was certainly a novel sight. But what they said upon that occasion was still more amazing. In their modest way, they had just formed an association for the purpose of accomplishing something that would have shocked even the most extravagant immodesty of the most ambitious statesman of China. In a word, they had united in order that they might work for the abolition, once for all, of the evil custom called the "golden lily," which tyrannizes over the women of China with a refinement of cruelty worthy of Nero; which tortures the tender years of their girlhood with an excruciating pain that does not cease even in the hours of sleep; which threatens the freedom of motion in their maturer years; and which totally destroys the grace and form of their feet. But these Chinese girl students did not content themselves with smashing the ancient sense of propriety by thus haranguing a public audience; for the association actually went so far as to print, in pamphlet form, the addresses made by the students, and to send the copies of their speeches home for distribution among the women of China. Such acts as these are certainly a far cry from the action of Chinese women generally, and particularly as the latter are understood by the people of the Western hemisphere.

All over China, schools for girls as well as for boys are springing up to-day; and many Nippon women, graduates of the various normal schools of Japan, have been engaged by the Chinese viceroys to instruct in their schools. For years, Chang Chihtung has looked to popular education as the means of accomplishing the thing of greatest importance to China, namely, the awakening of nationalism in the minds of her people; and education is now beginning to bear the desired fruit. "The Chinaman has no fatherland, he has a native district. He has no nation, he has a family. He has no state, he has a society. He has no sovereign, he has only Government officials." So wrote Alexander Ular not many months ago. He should have written it ten years ago.

Now that the guardianship of the territorial integrity of the Chinese empire has been committed not only to England and America, but to Nippon as well, and to the latter particularly, China may, with peace of mind, work for her own military salvation. In fact, we have already heard of the return to China of Yin-Tchang, the Chinese Minister at Berlin. Yin-Tchang has been appointed to an important post under Gen. Yuan Shi-kai, Viceroy of Pe-chi-li, to create the army of the New China. The empire is to be divided into twenty military districts, and by 1910 is to have 500,000 men thoroughly trained in the art of modern warfare.

China has seen, on her own ground, two great powers conduct a great war; and the bitter days of the Boxer trouble were not without good lessons for the men of her army. But, unquestionably, the greatest lessons in the conduct of war that China has ever learned have come to her through her students living in a number of cities of Nippon while the recent war was in progress. Those young Chinese students were thus placed in a position to see for themselves the fire of patriotism which is the life of our army; the sacrifices our people have been willing to make, both enthusiastically and cheerfully; how they arose as one individual for the defence of the honor of the empire; and with what care our Government conducted even the most trivial of the many thousand details of the campaign. These students are going back to Hupeh, to Szechuen, to Peking, and to the provinces of the south; and they are to become the prophets and apostles of the New China.

Now the powers of the world may turn to China, as Sir Robert Peel once did to the merchants of London, and say: "What favor can we show you?" And the New China can say, without a tremor in her voice, as the London merchants said to Sir Robert: "Let us alone!" And very likely they will.

ADACHI KINNOSUKE.

RUSSIA'S ECONOMIC FUTURE.

Is Russia hurrying toward national bankruptcy, or is she, now that her war with Japan is over and radical reforms in her internal administration have been granted, on the highroad to a degree of prosperity she has never seen before? Will not the Russian people, freed at last from the physical and mental fetters forged by an incompetent, vampire-like bureaucracy, at once seize upon those manifold opportunities hitherto neglected, and begin the energetic exploitation of the great natural resources now lying fallow?

Questions like these are being asked nowadays. Every thinking person has a natural curiosity concerning them, and the more so because Russia has been all along, and is still, the land of riddles, the sphinx among modern nations.

Assuming, for instance, that the immense empire is not only politically but economically in a bad, a very bad, way, is it safe to conclude that, with Russia's internal political conditions changed for the better — and the prospects are that they will be, in the near future — with her destinies entrusted to one or several bodies of electorally chosen representatives, the complete collapse of her credit, in a word, the financial crash of her governmental finance system, will be averted? I fear not.

The deadly parallel columns of history seem to show clearly that the political sanitation of a country mismanaged for many generations by no means implies its economic resurrection. To quote just one instance, known to all, there is France. In 1789 she showed similar economic conditions to those latterly prevailing in Russia. Did the summoning of the National Assembly and the devoted and highly patriotic labors of this body stop the financial evils under which the nation was groaning? Quite the reverse. As the great Revolution proceeded, gathering momentum with its own power, the financial morass grew deeper and more treacherous, and the credit of the country sank lower and lower, both at home and abroad. The assignats, running much the same course as did the American Confederate currency between 1861 and 1865, despite their being made the legal tender, and at last becoming nearly the sole medium for the payment of all internal debts, steadily fell, until in the days of Robespierre it required nearly a cartload of these notes to pay for a pair

of boots. It was only on the reëstablishment of a powerful, though despotic, government, that of Napoleon, that the national credit began to
revive. And the causes which led to this state of things were about the
same as those which we see operative in Russia to-day, and which we shall
probably see much more actively operative as the control of her national
finances passes more and more out of the hands of a Russian minister of
finance into those of a national parliament, be it the douma considered at
this hour or a body of more sweeping powers and more radical makeup.

I am quoting this somewhat analogous case merely to show that the
case of Russia, economically considered, is even harder to cure than her
political disease. Of course, it is not possible to state that case fully
within the compass of a magazine article; but it shall be here my endeavor
to make at least the leading facts — which are few in number — plain to
the reader.

The near economic future of Russia must be based on:

(1) The continuance of her borrowing powers at home and of far
greater moment abroad.

(2) The rehabilitation of her national industries.

(3) The thorough reform of her agriculture.

(4) The capacity to raise by taxation sufficient funds to keep the
administrative wheels going and to pay the interest, in gold, regularly to
her foreign creditors.

These four points are, in the case of Russia, interrelated to a great
extent. Indeed, they can scarcely be considered separately, since much
that is said of one can also be said of another, or of all.

As an industrial and financial factor of importance, the great dominion
of the Czar dates only from the advent of Wyshnegradsky as minister of
finance, whose term was from 1887 to 1893. He was Witte's forerunner,
and really his teacher — only Witte has far outdone him. The distinctive
feature of Wyshnegradsky's financial policy was its commercialism;
Witte enlarged this into state monopolism or fiscalism.

In 1887 Wyshnegradsky found a national debt of four and a half
billion roubles, and an interest charge of 262 millions in gold. Between
1862 and 1887 the balance of trade had consistently gone the wrong way
for Russia. Wyshnegradsky applied the tax screw, and also inaugurated
a rigorous enforcement of the collection of delinquent taxes — always a
distressing feature of Russian national finances. The percentage of the
cereal harvest exported increased under him from fifteen to twenty-two
per cent. The tariff was twice raised by him, and in 1890 it averaged 80
per cent ad valorem. In 1891 he placed prohibitive tariff duties on many
articles manufactured in Russia, the majority of these being still in force
to-day. In this way he increased the cereal export from 312,000,000 pood

(=40 pounds, approximating the bushel) to 442,000,000. The gold reserve rose from 281,000,000 to 782,000,000 roubles. He decreed a uniform tax-collecting date for the whole empire, the first of September, thus compelling the peasant to sell his crop early in the fall to pay his taxes. Those six years of strenuous finance administration made a physical and mental wreck of Wyshnegradsky. He had to resign office, and ended in a sanitarium.

His successor, Witte — incidentally a man of much more powerful physique — first terminated the tariff war with Germany by commercial treaty. Under the terms of this treaty, the imports from Germany have become two-fifths of the total (202,000,000 out of 504,000,000 roubles), and the exports to Germany 203,000,000 out of 825,000,000, or one-fourth. On the other hand, the figures for the United States are 39,000,000 imports and only 4,000,000 exports — about a tenth those of the Russo-German trade.

Witte next made it a part of his policy to increase the gold reserve, with the design of an eventual adoption of the gold standard for Russia. The gold standard was established by him four years later, and is still maintained. His method of accomplishing this measure was, of course, principally to still further increase the balance of trade in Russia's favor. By 1902 he had contrived to bring Russian exports up to the respectable sum of 825,000,000 roubles, and the imports down to 527,000,000, a balance in Russia's favor of almost 300,000,000 roubles. Every year a new foreign loan was contracted; and the alliance with France was financially exploited to the utmost. Altogether, during the past twelve years, French money alone has gone to Russia to the amount of $1,700,000,000. Foreign private capital, too, was invited by Witte. It was his aim to build up a large native industry, or, at least, an industry on Russian soil. France and Belgium alone put 1,650,000,000 francs (over $300,000,000) into Russian iron and steel works, especially locomotive shops and rolling mills.

A certain recklessness in dealing with such enormous sums obtained from foreign capitalists can be distinctly traced in Witte's operations. We need but study his own budget reports to become convinced of this. He declares frankly, again and again, that all this foreign capital is intended, primarily, to increase Russia's productivity, and that he cares but little what ultimately becomes of the rest. There is not a word said as to any plan of his own regarding the probability, or even possibility, of ever repaying these gigantic sums. And why should he not be frank? What palpable risk does Russia run in the matter? Should Russia ever find herself unable to pay the interest and the sinking fund on her sixty thousand verst of railroads, built entirely with foreign capital, it would indeed

28

be a difficult task to enforce payment of the debt.   By January 1, 1900, Witte had contrived, by negotiating at least one new foreign loan every year, to enhance the Russian national debt by an additional 1,579,000,000 roubles.   The internal debt was converted into a 4 per cent irredeemable one.

In 1902, according to an eminent Russian economist, S. Golovine, the nation owed at home and to foreign countries a gross total of 8,500,000,000 roubles.   Deducting from this mammoth sum private liabilities, and retaining only those of the Government, we see them stated by Witte himself for the same year at 6,497,000,000 roubles.   In this sum, however, are not comprised the $220,000,000 worth of railroad bonds sold by him in Berlin alone, and the hundreds of millions of them sold elsewhere, nor the shares of certain Russian banks, such as the Agrarian Bank for Nobles, and others, to the tune of a couple of hundred millions, which he placed on the continent.

Between 1892 and 1902, the sum of 2,252,000,000 roubles was invested by foreign capitalists, at the instigation of Witte, and used in buying up for the Russian Government existing railroads and enlarging their systems.   By 1897 there had been already sunk by foreigners about 4,000,-000,000 roubles in Russian railroads.   Prince Hilkoff, the Russian minister of railroads, declared, in his report of 1902, that the Russian railroads formed an aggregate system of 60,000 verst (about 42,000 miles [1]), of which the Government owned two-thirds.

Nevertheless, the Russian railroads do not pay.   In 1900 they showed a deficit of 31,000,000 roubles (374 against 405); by 1903 the shortage had grown to 73,000,000.   During the first year of the war with Japan, when the Siberian system and its two branches were monopolized by the Government for the army and the navy in Manchuria, the deficit amounted to about 400,000,000 roubles.   For 1905 the figures will be not much lower. During perfectly normal times the Siberian roads will always be — at least for a score of years or more to come — a heavy drain on the budget.   The new road to Tashkend will not be self-sustaining, while a number of other Russian roads do not earn more than a very low rate of interest on the capital invested.

It must be borne in mind that fully half of the Russian railroads run through territory more sparsely settled than our own far Western States.   Then, there is the fearful impoverishment of the masses in Russia.   The " zone " system was introduced on Russian roads for the simple reason that very low passenger rates for long distances could alone bring traffic.   These " zone " rates are lower even than those on the Hun-

[1] As against 221,000 miles in the United States, which covers a territory but three-eighths as large as that of Russia.

garian roads, and they average only about 32 per cent of the passenger rates in the United States. Freight, during certain seasons of the year, is sent below cost on almost all Russian roads, in order to move the cereal exports to the shipping ports, such as Odessa, Riga, Libau, and Reval. On other large trunk lines, notably the Siberian, it is insignificant in bulk.

Among the chief items in Witte's financial programme was the creation of a number of state monopolies, designed to yield large revenues for the Government. Most important of these was the liquor monopoly. The state compelled all the distillers to sell their products to it, the price being fixed by the Government. All "traktirs" and spirit shops were conducted for the sole benefit of the Government, retail prices being raised to nearly treble the cost, so that the revenues from the sale of liquor now amount to 525,000,000 roubles, or over one-fourth of the total national receipts. Curiously enough, too, this sum is precisely the amount of all the imports into the empire. In justification of this spirit monopoly, it was claimed that it would lead to a diminution of drunkenness, a curse from which Russia has suffered for centuries. But, thus far, no decrease in this vice has been observed.

Another Government monopoly introduced by Witte is the production and sale of beet sugar. This also has proved highly profitable to the national exchequer, yielding taxes (internal revenue) amounting to many millions. But among its effects has been the cheapening of this product for the foreign purchasers (Russian sugar abroad, of course, competing with German, Austrian, French, Belgian, and others) and the increase in price for the Russian consumer. The latter often is compelled to pay three or even four times the price which an Englishman or an American pays for precisely the same grade. The beet sugar law has made sweetening of any kind an expensive luxury for the Russian masses. It is droll to observe Russians of the poorer classes drinking tea. The husband will carefully place a small lump of sugar between his teeth, letting the tea run slowly past, then he will as carefully hand what is left of the lump to his wife, that she may repeat the operation.

However, the most important reform which Witte had in mind on assuming his post of finance minister was the creation of national industries of the type of the more advanced Western countries. True, there had been Russian industries before Witte's day; but they were the so-called cottage industries — of which something will be said further on — susceptible neither of taxation nor of rapid expansion. Between 1894 and 1899 some 927 stock companies were organized in Russia, wholly or in part with foreign capital, the amount thus invested being stated at 1,420,000,000 roubles; 151 of these new enterprises — the largest and those working with the most advanced methods — being entirely foreign.

The Government set itself the task of nursing this industrial baby. The construction of new railroads, the extension and improvement of existing ones, the building of naval vessels, the accumulation of army supplies and ordnance, and the financial strengthening of the merchant marine, all furthered immensely the whole iron and steel industry in Russia. With a lavish hand, too, the minister scattered the money of the state to aid in the process of industrial development. At his instance, numerous banks were founded and aided by the Government; and through them money was advanced for new and important enterprises. Technical and commercial schools were established. The same industrial fever which raged throughout adjoining Germany and far-away America now spread over the somnolent Russian steppes.

Then came the great collapse, and its cause was simple. Of the 140,-000,000 population of Russia, only a beggarly two or three millions are to-day financially capable of being consumers of the finer grades of industrial products. The other 92 per cent of the total population, the *moujiks* (peasants), earn only enough to half satisfy their hunger with rye bread, cabbage soup, and corn grits, and their women spin their own linen and cloth. The 30,000,000 of Asiatic Russia have but little demand for the manufactures of European Russia.[1] It was, save for the needs of the few millions of upper-class Russians, the Government which had been the main customer of this new-born Russian industry — for its railroads, its army, and its navy.

There came a time when the huge foreign loans raised by Witte to build railroads showed signs of exhaustion. Government orders became scarce. A panic set in, and during 1899 and 1900 the complete downfall of the new industries ensued. The Government itself had gained another fruitful source of taxation; and during 1898, when industry flourished most, taxes thus collected had amounted to 236,000,000 roubles. But with the almost total extinction of the new industries, a large source of internal revenue ran dry. How complete the crash was is little known outside of Russia. During 1900, no less than 146 of the foreign corpora-·tions, with a capital of 765,000,000 roubles, were wiped out of existence. French and Belgian investors were the largest losers, to the extent of four-fifths; next came the Germans, with 122,000,000, and then England, with almost 100,000,000. Throughout the same year industrial values in Russia fell rapidly, and early in October the bourse in St. Petersburg was wholly demoralized. The best securities declined fearfully: Nobel petroleum shares dropped 70 roubles per share, Agrarian Banks 144, and so on.

[1] The latest statistics show only 28,000,000 roubles of exports to the whole of Asia.

I shall pick out twelve of the leading Russian industrial establishments owing their inception to Witte's industrial boom, and all of them among the soundest and the most wisely managed. These are the great steel works at Alexandrovsk, Bransk, Donetz, Yuriev, and Ssormova, the machine works at Kolomma, Maltzeff, Putiloff, the Russian Locomotive Works, the Baltic Car Works, the St. Petersburg Metal Works, the Gleboff Works, and the Phoenix Car Works. By January 1, 1902, all these establishments, so far as their shares at the bourse are concerned, had depreciated, some of them by 95 per cent, others by 90 and 80 per cent, respectively, and none of them less than 70 per cent. The Gleboff Works were utterly wiped out.

What was Witte's remedy? To obtain new loans abroad; to build more railroads; and to give larger orders to those Russian manufactories which had survived the crash.

That Russian industry, of the Western type, stands on no solid foundation. That it is a mere creation of fiscalism, and can only live as long as the Government stimulates it with paying orders, may thus be understood. Conditions are not yet ripe for the normal rise of such an industry, for these conditions presuppose a nation financially potent and intellectually advanced enough to be a regular and liberal consumer of manufactures; and in Russia this is the case with only a very small minority of the population.

The products of all this hot-house industry can in no wise compete with those of more advanced countries. Here are a couple of glaring instances. The Siberian Railroad, with its two branches, was constructed during Witte's administration, and for the most part with the products of Russian industry. Its cost, roughly computed, was $750,000,000. Subsequent expert opinion is to the effect that this road could be duplicated for $300,000,000, if built with foreign material and foreign labor. For thousands of miles the roadbed had to be relaid, and the light and unserviceable rails replaced by heavier ones. Between 1884 and 1895 Russia bought 113,000,000 pood of home-made rails, for which she paid 92,000,000 roubles more than if they had been bought in England. Since 1895 enough Russian rails have been used in the construction of the Trans-Siberian, the Orenburg-Tashkend, the Moscow-Kazan, the Bogoloye-Sedletz, and the Northern Line to make the sum paid in excess of what would have been the price for first-class foreign rails about 300,-000,000 roubles.

Nevertheless, thanks to the great cereal exports, the new state monopolies, the enormous taxes drawn from new industries, from the telegraph, electric power plants, telephone lines, etc., Witte accumulated every year a larger surplus in the treasury. He was able to realize at least one of his dreams — the establishment of the gold standard for Russia. By January 1, 1897, his gold reserve had attained the fabulous height of 1,247,000,000 roubles. The old paper roubles were redeemed at the ratio of 1½ paper to 1 in gold. All Russia was amazed. The living generation had never seen gold imperials in actual circulation. The benighted peasant thought Witte a pastmaster in the black art.

Mention has been made of the enormous increase in the national, especially the foreign, debt of Russia during the Witte régime, an increase made unavoidable by the creation of the new Russian industries and the purchase by the state of two-thirds of the entire national railway system. How long things might have gone on smoothly in this way it is futile to speculate. However, the true state of Russian finances, although to this day a sealed book even to many otherwise well-informed moneyèd men in Europe and the United States, began to be suspected several years before the outbreak of the recent war with Japan. Distrust of Russia's ultimate ability to repay these enormous loans, distrust of her national finances, and of the reliability of her published budgets and other official reports, began to filter, slowly but irresistibly, through the prudent and potent minds of the world's financiers. This distrust became for the first time palpable in 1901 — three years before the first naval assault by Japan upon Port Arthur. For the first time the devoted ally, France, failed Witte. A loan of but 151,000,000 roubles, which he had vainly attempted to place in Paris, had to go at last to Berlin and Amsterdam; but, in agreeing on the terms, the Russian negotiator was obliged to pledge as special security for this sum the Chinese war indemnity. Again, but a month after the outbreak of the hostilities with Japan, Russia found much difficulty in securing a new loan of 100,000,000 roubles.

The unavoidable conclusion, then, is that the borrowing powers of Russia in foreign money markets are on the wane. For various reasons, Russia is a country poor in capital, though rich in undeveloped natural resources. If she loses the one capacity she has maintained uninterruptedly since the days of the great Catharine, that of borrowing abroad, she must perforce alter radically her whole internal and external policy.

Despite the great industrial crash of 1898–1903, wiping out, as it did, hundreds of enterprises, and teaching foreign capitalists a severe lesson, the output of Russia's industry has considerably increased under Witte. In 1887 this annual output was only 802,000,000 roubles, and now it is 1,800,000,000 roubles. But this is only the twentieth part of the manufacturing output of the United States—an eloquent testimony as to the relative insignificance of the Russian market, due to the extreme poverty and utter lack of material culture on the part of Russia's masses.

How the national revenues of Russia likewise augmented under Witte

we have also seen. They have grown, in fact, at the rate of about 125,-
000,000 roubles per annum. In this, the annual increase of 2,000,000 in the
population of the country counts for something as well. At present we
find these revenues amounting to over two billions of roubles — that is,
over a billion dollars. But the expenditures have increased proportionately. Up to the time of the Boxer rising in China they had kept pace
with the revenues; but that event led to an excess of 300,000,000 roubles
over and above the national income, necessitating a new loan, above
referred to. Of the regular revenue of about 2,000,000,000 roubles,
some 300,000,000 in gold go to pay the interest on the foreign debt. It is
what Russians usually speak of as the "gold tribute," and which they
earnestly deplore. Some 500,000,000 are eaten up — in normal times —
by army and navy, while 70,000,000 or 80,000,000 pay for the railroad
deficit.

During the past eighteen months, however, things have become far
worse. To the $3,000,000,000 of foreign indebtedness, in round numbers,
has been added another burden of $900,000,000 for war expenses. Army
expenditures for a twelvemonth or longer will be much higher, under
present conditions, than in normal times — probably amounting to 800,-
000,000 roubles. The navy, which is to be rebuilt, will swallow up another
600,000,000 at least. The new railroads decided upon involve an outlay
of 170,000,000, and the railway deficit for 1905 will mean another 300,-
000,000. Adding these items together, it becomes evident to any observer
that more foreign loans, and large ones at that, are absolutely required to
enable Russia to tide over her present economic crisis. And in the above
list no mention has been made of the famine in Russia this year, a public
calamity which will probably require both remission of taxes and relief
in money and supplies running up into another 100,000,000 or more.

It is a trite saying that one man's loss is another's gain; but that will
hold good in the present case. Of recent years, American enterprise has
begun to look toward Russia as a field for economic exploitation. Small
wonder, this; for Russia has been practically overlooked so far by our
capitalists, manufacturers, and export merchants, except in the one item
of agricultural machinery, and even in that the peculiar credit customs
and tariff complexities of Russia have acted as a strong deterrent, so that
the annual statistics of Russo-American trade look like an anomaly in
these pushing days of American export. These figures, though, are not to
be relied upon. Our actual trade with Russia is not quite so small as they
would show. Our own official statistics as well as those of Russia apportion
exports according to the first port of destination, and not the ultimate one.
Thus it is that every year millions of dollars' worth of American goods
which go to Russia via Hull or Hamburg, and through German or British

agents, are accredited to England or Germany. On the Russian side it is similar. Probably Russia consumes about twice as much in American commodities as she is given credit for on our Washington tally-sheets; and we, on our part, may use three or four times the amount of Russian goods (only $2,000,000 worth, according to the latest available figures) spoken of in official Russian tables, since the great bulk of them reach us by way of Germany.

However, in any case, there are now unusually promising opportunities for American export to Russia. Her own industry, as we have seen, is dead — if not for all time, at least for years, probably decades, to come. The products of her short-lived industry could scarcely compete even locally in price with many of ours, even under Russian prohibitive tariff charges, and most assuredly not in quality. This is especially true of just the class of manufactures in which we excel, namely, agricultural and industrial machinery of every description, railroad and electrical supplies, machine tools, bicycles — which are still in great demand in Russia — automobiles, hardware, "notions," office furniture, etc.

Several years ago an extra tariff duty was clapped on most American-made goods reaching Russia, the intention being to punish us for having discriminated against Russian beet sugar and its veiled export bounties. Immediately after the successful conclusion of the Peace of Portsmouth, the Czar, out of gratitude for the kindly offices of President Roosevelt and the American people in bringing about that event, voluntarily removed these extra tariff burdens from American goods. Thus, in nearly all those exports in which we can outstrip the world, we shall be on an even footing with Germany — despite her new commercial treaty with Russia — and England, and that is sure to give us a large trade, always provided that we properly bestir ourselves. One of the conditions with which we must reckon in this, however, is the slow rate of payment in vogue in the Czar's empire.

Asiatic Russia is steadily becoming a more and more important field for American commerce. Altogether, the population there is over 30,-000,000; and this increases not only at twice the birth-rate of European Russia, but by a constantly maintained immigration from the older portions of the empire, the annual number now being about 150,000. This huge part of Russia is not so hampered by bureaucratic conditions, and the fruitfulness of the soil, in large districts at least, is considerable. Our own Pacific shore is much nearer to Asiatic Russia than are the European countries, and we thus enjoy a porportional advantage in competition with the latter. Of this, Seattle, Portland, and Tacoma are beginning to make good use, as the rapidly rising figures of our trade with that part of the world show.

Another opportunity of which our capitalists are only just beginning to avail themselves is the investment of American money in Russian enterprises, particularly in Siberia — such as mines and railroads. Some of it has gone into factories in the interior of Russia.

Of course, it may be argued that from the showing above made the inducements held out to American enterprise in this line do not seem enticing. And there is force in such a contention. It will be wise to go slowly; that much is certain. The Russian market will have to be studied very carefully, and on the spot, before investments are made. One factor, however, of great benefit to us is the almost universal liking which Russians have for Americans; and the favor shown recently by the Russian Government for American endeavor in this line is also very encouraging.

A careful study of the situation induces me to the strong belief that modern Russian industry, as created by Witte, is doomed. I have stated already several of my reasons for this belief. Russia has very nearly reached the limit of her borrowing power in foreign countries. She will find it more and more difficult, if not impossible, to continue her system of constructing state railroads on loans. And such loans failing her, she will have no further orders for railroad shops and rolling mills. Again, the Russian artisan and mechanic is half a peasant, retaining his joint ownership in a bit of field and tilling it in the summer, while he toils for the manufacturer during the winter only. He was slowly beginning to be a fair sort of factory hand when the industrial crash of 1898-1902 overtook Russia. There is less demand for him now than there was years ago, and hereafter there will be still less.

I shall speak more in detail of this Russian peasant-mechanic further on. Suffice it to say here that the whole trend of events at present makes it likely that this peculiar product of Russian social and political conditions, the artisan-peasant, will from now on develop along different lines, such as will not bring him into direct competition with the far better trained and immeasurably more efficient industrial toiler of the United States, England, and Germany. His salvation, and the industrial rise of Russia on legitimate and national lines, will come through the medium of the cottage industry, a feature of Russian life which is well worth noting here.

This rural cottage industry arose by slow stages on Russian soil, and smacks of it. Even in the days of serfdom it grew in extent and variety. Owners of estates would send some of their cleverest serfs to Germany, Holland, Belgium, or France, there to learn a trade which afterward they could teach their fellow-serfs, and which could be profitably plied on the estate itself, the product being sold in the vicinity. Such trades introduced in that way into Russia, or else indigenous for centuries past, were the weaving of linens, the spinning of silks and cottons, the making of laces, the carving of wooden utensils, of *icons* (pictures or shrines of the saints), the making of signboards, tools, agricultural implements, nails, horseshoes, sleighs, wagons, carriages, etc. In all these things the Russian peasant-craftsman shows, as everybody must testify who has spent some time in Russia, a natural skill, a sure taste, and a peculiar gift of inventiveness. I myself saw in a village far in the interior, a sleigh fashioned simply out of wood, with nothing better for tools than an axe, a knife, an adze, and a saw, the sleigh being afterward painted, gilded, and varnished. The finished product was decidedly handsome, and thoroughly adapted to the uses of Russian roads.

These rural industries are worked on the coöperative plan, and are called *svietelka*. Often two or three *volosts* (rural communities) join in this way for a common purpose, establish an *artel* (coöperative society), not only for the manufacture of more or less complicated articles — one village doing the first part of the work, then passing it on to the second and third for further elaboration — but also for the sale of the products, and the collection of the money, which afterward is distributed *pro rata*. Under present conditions the average daily earnings of each full member of an *artel* are low, in most cases not exceeding ten cents of our money. But women and children help to swell these earnings. The work is done, as a rule, in rude, cheap buildings, hardly better than a peasant's *izba* (hut), but larger and with more light, and standing in a central spot in the village. The joint earnings of such villages are, however, sufficient to sustain the inhabitants during the long winters, and to help them pay their taxes.

Curiously enough, the Russian Goverment has never perceived that in this village industry the nation has had the nucleus of a real national industry, capable of infinite expansion. Only of late has there been any encouragement given these rural toilers. Even as it is, though, enterprising capitalists in Russia have discovered the industrial possibilities slumbering in this feature of national life. Some of these capitalists, in Moscow, Vladimir, Pensa, Kaluga, Tver, Kremenchug, and even St. Petersburg, have begun to assist with small sums such peasant *svietelka* in the manufacture of commodities of more intricate workmanship and commanding a ready sale, such as cloths — of wool, linen, and silk — earthenware, and articles of tableware, and the results are said to be satisfactory all around. The evolution of such rude types of industry into a more advanced craft is necessarily a matter of slow growth and of much patience, and this peculiar process of manufacture, moreover, does not lend itself readily to purposes of taxation. But the industries of Scotland had a similarly lowly beginning; and, in fact, the same may be said of the national industries of France, Germany, and England. At any rate, it is my fixed belief that the rise of Russia as an industrial nation of the future will be along these lines.

This, if anything, will be in large measure the solution of Russia's gravest economic problem — the agricultural one. Advisedly I say the gravest. For Russia's peasant population forms 92 per cent of her total of 110,000,000 in European Russia, and 85 per cent of the whole of the empire. Of course, it would require more space than is here at my disposal to show in detail the condition of Russia's agriculture and peasantry, and the remedy at hand to cure conditions which, if allowed to go on unchecked, would inevitably end in the nation's complete ruin. I shall confine myself to tracing broad outlines. And to that end it is advisable to select the so-called "black-earth belt" of Russia for purposes of illustration.

This "black-earth belt" comprises the twenty-two governments of Central Russia, the very heart of the empire, having Moscow at its centre; and grouped around it are what were formerly the most fertile regions of Russia, inhabited by the Great Russian race. Here also are the vast Volga provinces, Little Russia, and New Russia. Altogether, this is a territory of 625,000 square miles, with a population of 52,000,000. In every respect this is what we mostly mean when we speak of "Russia" — it is typically Russian, and it furnishes more than two-thirds of the brawn and brain for the remainder of the empire. With its ultimate fate stands or falls Russia as a whole.

Ever since the emancipation of the serfs, or during the past forty-four years, this vast region has been addicted to the one-crop system — wheat, wheat, nothing but wheat. To-day, the traveller, rushing on the wings of steam from St. Petersburg through the vast plains on to Odessa and the shores of the Black Sea, sees nothing but one immense waving wheatfield, stretching endlessly along both sides of the railroad. Back of him the horizon is marked by a dim, trembling line, and before him is another such trembling line, as far as eye can reach. Wheat, wheat, nothing but wheat. We see here on a gigantic scale what we can see in some of our own Prairie States, notably Iowa and Nebraska. And this forty-four years of incessant wheat-raising, with no rotation of crops, with no manuring and re-fertilizing, has had in the "black-earth belt" of Russia — as, in smaller degree, in some of our own Western States — the inevitable result, impoverishment of the soil.

But there is this difference: the Russian peasant has been forced by the tax-gatherer, by Witte and his predecessors in the finance ministry, to raise on his land wheat, to the exclusion of everything else, in order to meet the harsh and excessive demands of the Government for revenue taxes.

The whole financial policy of Russia has been bent to that end. Wheat, being a commodity always in demand outside of Russia, by making September the time to pay taxes, by reducing freight rates to shipping points of wheat, the peasant has been compelled to raise nothing but wheat on his strip of field; and while the peasant population of Russia has been doubling since Emancipation day, the lands allotted to the freedmen have not increased. The average size of a Russian peasant family is seven, and despite famine and pestilence, despite starvation and emigration to Siberia, there are now over one hundred million of Russian peasants tilling the land which, forty-four years ago, produced just about enough to feed the fifty millions of serfs.

In some respects, a striking analogy could be shown between the "black-earth belt" of Russia — so called, of course, because it once consisted of a thick bed of black fruitful loam, the richest agricultural land in Europe, and rivalling our own Mississippi bottoms — and our own South after 1865. In the South the negro was freed, and it took that region so richly favored by nature the better part of forty years to regain the wealth and comfort of ante-bellum days. The liberated 50,000,000 of Russian serfs were as ignorant and helpless as our Southern negroes; but they were made to bear the heavy burdens of taxation, of conscription to army and navy, of living in a country poor in capital, energy, and enterprise. And as their numbers constantly increased, as their small holdings had to be again and again divided and subdivided for the sustenance of the growing generations, they grew poorer and poorer, and their ignorance prevented their bettering these frightful conditions. The Government, instead of aiding them, instead of devising means to pull them out of the mire, sank them deeper and deeper into it.

Some years ago, while in Moscow, I paid a visit to Russia's greatest pathfinder in chemistry, Prof. Mendeleyeff. He had just finished a series of analyses. On his worktable lay tiny heaps of soil, and he was drawing up a report for the Ministry of Agriculture. "Our black-earth belt is doomed," he said, "unless the Government can find both the courage and the money for sweeping reforms and ameliorations. My chemical analysis shows that this soil, once deemed of perennial fertility, is speedily becoming exhausted. Within ten years it has lost twenty-five per cent or more of its nutritive qualities." And he exhibited a long and carefully prepared table of figures. In the large province of Samara — even at this writing the scene of another frightful famine — two decades ago a granary of phenomenal wealth, the productiveness of the soil had decreased: for winter wheat, from 31 pood to 27 pood per dessyatine ($2\frac{1}{2}$ acres); for spring wheat, from 34 to 25; for rye, from 41 to 30; for oats, from 33 to 26; for barley, from 33 to 18; and for potatoes, from

301 to 213. Of course, no action was taken by the Government on this report nor on subsequent ones.

But it is not the Government alone which has helped in the undoing of the peasantry. The Orthodox Church of Russia likewise has been and is at fault. It battens on the poverty of the *moujik*. And there are various strange features in this general condition. Thus, the religion of the peasantry is an odd compound of gross formalism and ancient pagan superstition, thinly overlaid with Christian rites. For the Orthodox priesthood the peasant harbors undisguised animosity and scorn. He calls his parish priest *batyoushka* (little father), but his attitude toward him has nothing of the filial. He believes that meeting the priest in the village street brings ill-luck, and will expectorate to break the anticipated train of evil. According to the standards of Western nations, the Orthodox priest is underpaid—his income (in money and kind) rarely exceeds 600 roubles per annum, and out of that he is expected to maintain his proverbially large family. But to the peasant such an income seems very large and the manner of earning it very easy. For the disdain felt for the priest, the fact that drunkenness is his besetting sin is partly responsible.

For all that, the peasant is controlled by the church. He keeps the 150 holy and fast days in the year enjoined on him by the Holy Synod, and he maintains with his offerings and dues the enormous apparatus of the church. Thus the priests fasten on the half-starved peasantry, depriving them of part of their scant fare. And this is but the economical loss the *moujik* suffers. Far greater is the intellectual and moral injury which in this way is inflicted on him, keeping him in that unreasoning condition which amazes all who first become acquainted with Russia.

The average yield per acre of the whole of the "black-earth belt" has steadily sunk. It is now lower than in any other country of Europe. It is, for instance, just one-third that of the average of Germany, and yet the latter country has, by nature, rather meagre soil. But the Russian peasant is too unprogressive and unintelligent to till his land properly, and too poor to buy manure or fertilizer.

But the greatest drawback, in a certain sense, is that the Russian Government has helped to keep the peasant in his present degraded state. Indolent and improvident as a result of centuries of serfdom, the Government has made him more so: (1) by insisting on his keeping the 150 holidays in the year which the Orthodox Church enjoins; (2) by compelling him to pay his taxes — averaging in some districts between 50 and 60 per cent of the gross crops — as soon as the harvest is done, at a time when prices rule lowest; and (3) by encouraging the consumption of Government monopoly *vodka* (liquor distilled from potatoes, sold by the Government at from two to three dollars per gallon, though costing but fifty cents to make), and thereby promoting his chief vice, drunkenness.

The average annual earnings of a Russian peasant family are given in the latest Government statistics at sixty-three roubles (thirty-four dollars), of which they spent, after paying the taxes, an average of only twenty-two roubles on food.   The latter consists of the coarsest of black bread, cabbage soup (the famous *stchi*), grits, potatoes, an onion now and then, and four times a year only, on "high holidays," a bit of meat or fish; some cucumbers, berries, and mushrooms being added during the short summer season.   The peasant's only recreation is to get drunk, whether he can afford it or not.   His family suffers in proportion.

Thus, his life is dreary and sordid beyond anything we of the West can conceive.   But such are normal times with him.   Famine stalks the land every few years.   Famine is now a recognized, almost a regular, visitation in Russia.   The famine of 1901 affected mostly the Volga provinces.   That of 1891 covered a territory amounting to one-third of European Russia.   In 1901, in the province of Samara, 50,000 human beings are said to have literally starved to death.   Whole groups of villages were graveyards, with no living creature remaining, even the cats and dogs, the rats and mice having perished.   That famine cost the Government in relief moneys alone a matter of a round hundred millions.   Famines will recur in Russia at regular and short intervals as long as present conditions last.   They are occasioned by the great changes in climatic conditions that have come with the deforestation of the whole of the "black-earth belt," and by the impoverishment of the soil, together with the pauperization of the peasant, rendering it impossible for him to save money or husband reserves in grain.   Between 1882 and 1905, six distinct and well-defined famines, covering vast areas, have occurred in Russia, more than one of them extending even to Western Siberia.   How are the peasantry of Russia to prosper with such an endless chain of adversities?

The most striking proof of the utter economic exhaustion of the Russian peasant population is found in the tax delinquencies, a feature of national finance which forms a portentous item in every budget. Despite the fact that the taxes are collected with the utmost rigor, causing thousands of peasant families annually to be driven to the road by the forced sale of their chattels, these delinquencies are growing, and several times have amounted to 30 and even 35 per cent of the total amount imposed upon the starving peasantry.   If no radical changes take place in the condition of Russian agriculture, it is safe to predict the utter economic collapse of the empire.

One far-reaching change has just been promised by Nicholas II.   It comes late, very late, this promise, but if faithfully carried out may avert the doom of the overburdened, almost crushed Russian peasant. The Czar has promised nothing less than to dispose of his Crown domains for the benefit of the peasant population. These domains cover more than one million square miles in European Russia alone, *i.e.*, one-third of the total area of the empire, west of the Caucasus. Much of it is morass or otherwise unsuitable for cultivation; but enough of it is available for tilling to insure to each peasant family more than double its present average holdings, namely, about twelve acres. To carry out this project on any terms should be, for many years to come, the salvation of the peasantry, no matter whether the land be given as a free gift or, as planned at this writing, sold on small instalments running through a period of thirty-five years.

To sum up:

Russia's borrowing powers in foreign markets are on the decline. It will require the internal economic, and, bound up in that, the political, resurrection of Russia to give non-Russian capitalists renewed confidence in the ultimate ability and willingness of Russia to repay further, or, indeed, past loans.

Russia's young industry, fashioned after the Western type, has received such a severe setback that without additional large foreign loans to act as fructifier it will not revive for decades. Should these, however, be forthcoming, then the national cottage industry — to which the financial geniuses of the empire have acted so far in a stepmotherly way because of its necessarily slow, though normal, growth — would develop into something like a really national industry.

Above all, Russian agricultural conditions must be altered radically in order to lay the foundation of a stable and healthy national wealth. The great reform now held out by the Czar will be one highly important step in that direction. Others doubtless will follow; for the Russian peasant is desperate, at the end of his patience, and with weapons in hand demands a life worth living.

Finally, in the absence of foreign loans, the capacity to raise by taxation sufficient sums to keep the administrative wheels going will be regulated very largely, nay, chiefly, by the outcome of the agrarian problem in Russia.

In any event, however, Russia of necessity will cease, for a period of some length at least, to be an aggressive, conquering power, ever bent on expanding her frontiers. What has enabled Russia for two centuries to be an expanding and aggressive nation, and to maintain a huge army and, of late, a strong navy, has been, for one thing, her unchallenged ability to borrow enormous sums abroad, and, secondly, to spend them, under her system of autocracy, on conquest, and on maintaining a "showy front," as one of her own statesmen once termed it, allowing meanwhile internal conditions to remain stagnant and averse to all rational progress. With the breaking down of this autocratic system, and, more important yet, with the failure to raise new gigantic loans, is ushered in the day of representative government, when the needs of the nation itself will become the paramount issue, and when the taxes will be mainly expended to improve the lot of the average man — which in Russia means, above all, the peasant.

The day of political bondage over, Russia will at least be able to direct her mind into the channels of economic reform as well. There is probably many a severe economic crisis ahead for Russia, for such unparalleled misgovernment as hers has been since the days of Peter the Great cannot be cured in a day. But one thing at least seems certain: there will be no more blind tottering along the path that must in the end lead to ruin. What is to be done by the nation in the way of economic sanitation will be done with seeing eyes. And that, surely, is an immense gain over the past.

WOLF VON SCHIERBRAND.

THE FORUM.

VOL. XXXVII., NO. 4.

APRIL—JUNE, 1906.

NEW YORK:

THE FORUM PUBLISHING COMPANY.

PRESS OF
THE PUBLISHERS' PRINTING COMPANY
82, 84 LAFAYETTE PLACE
NEW YORK

The Forum

APRIL, 1906.

AMERICAN POLITICS.

ALTHOUGH the election of Representatives to the Sixtieth Congress will not occur until next November, preparations for the campaign have already been inaugurated. The Republican Congressional Campaign Committee will soon be organized, and in view of the fact that Representative J. W. Babcock, of Wisconsin, who for twelve years has been the active and efficient chairman, has declined reëlection to that position, it will be necessary to name his successor. The choice is understood to lie between Representative James S. Sherman, of New York, and Representative J. A. T. Hull, of Iowa, both of whom are experienced legislators and politicians. The Democratic Congressional Campaign Committee has held its preliminary meeting for the consideration of campaign issues, and has chosen as its chairman Representative James W. Griggs, of Georgia, who has previously acted in a similar capacity. There had, however, been manifested a desire on the part of some Democrats in Congress to bestow the chairmanship upon some Northern or Western man, in view of the fact that the political complexion of Representatives from the South is assured. In many Congressional districts, nominating conventions have been, or are about to be, held, a notable case of prompt action being shown by the Republicans of the eleventh Ohio district, who have nominated Albert Douglass to succeed Charles H. Grosvenor, who is now serving his twentieth year in Congress. General Grosvenor is thus practically retired to private life, although, literally, he has yet another year to serve, his term not expiring until March 4, 1907

In view of the fact that the attention of Representatives in Congress is already being centred upon their chances for renomination, and that an early adjournment of the session is deemed essential in order that the members may go home to mend their fences, as the saying is, it is worth while to note that Representative Bourke Cockran, of New York, has introduced a proposed constitutional amendment providing that the terms of Representatives shall be four years instead of two. The measure does not seem to have attracted very general public attention. This may be due, perhaps, to the fact that there is little or no probability of any amendment to the Constitution ever becoming effective. Every effort in this direction during the past forty years has been futile; and the sentiment against any change seems now to be more definitely fixed in the public mind than ever before. At the same time, the proposed lengthening of the Congressional term has much to commend it to favorable consideration. The elections which are now held midway in a Presidential administration do little more than disturb the peace and tranquillity of the country. It would seem to be much wiser to elect a President and a Congress in sympathy with his views to serve the same length of time. Both could then enter upon a well-defined and settled policy, with a sufficient period in which to develop it to its fullest extent, and all the time conscious that if the course of action did not meet with popular approval a dissatisfied people would relegate the responsible party into retirement at the next election.

As the case now stands, the last two years of a Presidential administration frequently witness a deadlock between the White House and an opposing political majority in the lower branch of Congress. In such case, the President, powerless to carry into effect the policies outlined by him at the beginning of his term, sits with his hands literally tied behind him. All legislation, except of the most perfunctory character, is checked. The President extols the benefits that would bless the nation if his party had full sway, while the antagonistic majority in the newly elected House adopts measures that cannot possibly receive the approval of the Executive. The spectacle is not edifying.

There are other considerations, too, which deserve attention. For instance, it now happens that almost as soon as a Representative is chosen, he is compelled to begin his campaign for renomination. Elected in November, he does not take his seat until a year thereafter, unless an extraordinary session is convened — a contingency which very rarely occurs — and after five or six months of actual service he is again confronted by a nominating convention. If he fails to be returned, which is quite frequently the case in these days of discontent, he comes to Washington to attend the closing three months of the session in a more or less indifferent frame of mind. His political future has been settled.

He no longer feels a keen sense of responsibility to his constituency. If, however, his term were for four years, conditions would be different. He would be relieved, in the first place, of the almost immediate struggle for renomination; and, still more important, he would have an adequate period in which to prove to his constituents his efficiency and fitness for his high office. He would have an incentive to make a record for himself in the management of public affairs. He would enjoy larger opportunity to adjust himself to his new environment. If, after four years of service, he had accomplished nothing, a verdict could very properly be rendered against him.

It may be said, and with some degree of plausibility, that it is a good thing in a republic to hear frequently from the people. This assertion may, in the abstract, be true. In actual operation, however, constant uncertainty and change are more injurious than beneficial. If it were known at the time of a Presidential election that both the Chief Executive and the Congress would remain in power for four years, the people would, in the first place, vote with more sobriety of judgment than may now be the case; and when the choice had been made, the country would adjust itself accordingly. It would settle down to its normal state. Business interests, appreciating the fact that no disturbing question of politics could alter the status of projected enterprises, would proceed confidently to their development. It is a well-known fact that when the political wave surges highest, the commercial world experiences its greatest lethargy and depression.

The only argument that can be advanced in favor of a short term for Representatives in Congress is the fact that a party wantonly abusing its power can be speedily ousted. Anyone familiar with the history of Congress must recall the fact, however, that any legislation considered by the country to be detrimental to the public interest must, perforce, remain upon the statute books for several years, even though the majority in the House be changed, inasmuch as the President still remains in the White House. There can be no question, for instance, which more intimately concerns the great mass of the people than the tariff. The McKinley tariff bill, enacted in the first two years of President Harrison's administration, created a revulsion of sentiment which resulted in the election of a Democratic House of Representatives; but the measure remained a law until 1893, when the Wilson-Gorman tariff bill became a law in President Cleveland's administration. Again there was a political upheaval, but again there was no possibility of providing a substitute until after Mr. Cleveland had been succeeded by Mr. McKinley. In other words, an election in the middle of a Presidential term may be significant as an expression of public feeling, but it cannot be productive of any real result. This being the case, is there any reason why the country should be subjected to the turmoil and expense of a Congressional election every two years? This is the question which is being seriously considered in Washington. The arguments pro and con are being discussed with much force and vigor. It is, perhaps, unfortunate that the only answer to the question depends upon an amendment to the Constitution.

President Roosevelt continues to be the central figure in American politics. Notwithstanding the fact that his determination not to serve again as President of the United States is universally accepted as final, it is no exaggeration to say that Mr. Roosevelt is the dominant factor in party councils and in national affairs. With a man of less forcefulness in the White House, the eyes of the politicians would even now be turned from the descending orb toward some rising sun. As a matter of fact, there is little or no talk of candidates to succeed him. He is still the all-commanding figure. His tremendous activity shows no sign of decrease. At one minute he is impressing his views upon the leaders of the Senate and the House with all the power of his strong mentality; the next instant he is writing to John Mitchell in an effort to avert a coal strike. He finds time amid his multifarious duties to write an essay upon the necessity of preparing for war in time of peace, taking as his text the address of Admiral Togo to the Japanese navy. He is in touch with the minutest details of official life; and, between times, as a squirrel nibbles at a nut, he delves into the latest books and keeps himself posted upon the literature of the day.

Every country knows the meaning of the phrase, "The king is dead! Long live the king!" In the United States, where the people, as a mass, are restless and change-desiring, very few wait until the king is dead. As soon as his end is in sight, he is deserted, except by his chosen friends. Politicians, naturally variable, turn toward his possible successor. It is significant of Mr. Roosevelt's strength that he is still foremost not only in the minds of the people, but in those of the politicians themselves. He still leads, while Congress follows. This is due principally to the fact that with his keen insight he judges intuitively the needs of the people, while his mental and physical energy furnishes him with the power to impress his views upon the national legislators. The fact that he is so thoroughly uppermost in the public mind affords the only reason, it seems to me, for the absolute lack of all speculation as to the next-Republican candidate. In Washington, the centre of political gossip, the subject is rarely mentioned. There is some little talk of Vice-President Fairbanks' conferences with Southern leaders; there is an occasional whisper as to the likelihood of New York declaring for Elihu Root; the fact that the next nomination ought to go to the West gives basis to the consideration of the name of William H. Taft; but, after all, the talk is of the most desultory nature, and nothing like a definite organization seems to be anywhere attempted.

Senator Aldrich, of Rhode Island, accurately expressed the situation when, in answer to a direct question upon the floor of the Senate, he stated that the mind of his party was still in a most uncertain state. There is one man who, if he were a few years younger, might well be considered a formidable aspirant for the Presidency. Only the advanced age of Joseph G. Cannon, of Illinois, prevents the serious consideration of his name. He will be seventy years old next May, and, therefore, seventy-two in 1908, when the nominating convention is held. This fact militates against him. Otherwise, with his rugged and democratic personality, his plain and sterling qualities, his honesty and detestation of shams, he would be popular in the largest sense.

The Democrats, too, are drifting. They have no candidate in sight. They do not even know what faction of the party will control their convention. If the radical wing is uppermost, it would not be surprising if Mr. Bryan were again the nominee, or, if not Mr. Bryan, Mr. William R. Hearst. The latter has his eye upon the Presidential chair; and, what is more to the point, he is working to attain his ambition. He has an organization; and, in the long run, organization is the winning factor in a contest. As for a possible conservative candidate, one might as well put twenty names in a basket and trust to luck in the selection of any one of them as to essay a prediction at the present time. There is not only an entire absence of anything like definite expression of a choice, but almost an absolute lack of suggestion. Misty and nebulous uncertainty envelops the Democratic situation. It is coupled, if the truth must be told, with a feeling that nothing less than a miracle will bring about the election of a Democratic President in 1908.

The attention of Congress has been occupied by three important questions. These are, the Philippine tariff; the admission to statehood of Arizona, New Mexico, Oklahoma, and Indian territories; and the regulation of railroad rates. The latter is the only one likely to be crystallized into law at this session of Congress.

The Philippine tariff bill was in the nature of a helping hand to a people who must necessarily look to us for fostering care. It provided for the free importation into the United States of all articles which were the growth and product of the Philippine Islands, except sugar, tobacco, and rice; and the tariff upon these latter articles was placed at twenty-five per cent of the duty charged upon them when imported from other countries, with the final proviso for absolute free trade with the Islands in and after 1909.

It will be seen that the sugar and tobacco interests of this country were most affected by the proposed legislation; and the report of the Ways and Means Committee was an argument to placate those interests. The report asserted that the reduction of the duty on Philippine sugar did not adversely affect the American growers of beet and cane sugar—first, because of the low grade of the Philippine product, and, second, because of the freight charges. It was asserted that Philippine sugar, refined, laid down in New York, cost 3.8 cents per pound, without adding the duty, as against 3.9 and 3.7 cents per pound for the refined beet sugar at the Michigan and Colorado factories, respectively. "The freight on sugar from New York to the markets of the country," continued the report, "will certainly average as much as the freight from Michigan or Colorado to the markets. Thus it is seen that free sugar from the Philippines would only equalize conditions. The duty of thirty cents per 100 pounds imposed until April, 1909, leaves the Philippine sugar at a great disadvantage." With equal emphasis the report asserted that Philippine sugar would not become a menace to the domestic article when, in 1909, it should be admitted free into the United States.

Very technical and unimportant all this may seem, especially as the enactment of the bill into law is not now imminent. But, as a matter of fact, a question of grave political effect might be presented. The possibility that lower duties on Philippine sugar would affect adversely the beet-sugar industry, now assuming large proportions in Western States, was sufficient to create a revolt among the Representatives from those States; and, when the final vote was taken, no less than fifty-seven of them were recorded in opposition to their party programme. Never was Hancock's famous saying that the tariff is a local issue more emphatically shown than in this action upon the Philippine bill. When it came to choosing between party dictates and home interests, the latter prevailed. As for the future, the Republicans may well hope and pray that the predictions of the report of the Ways and Means Committee will be realized. If the Philippine bill should eventually become a law, and importations should interfere with the manufacture and sale of beet sugar, the resulting dissatisfaction would be sufficient to throw Michigan, Wisconsin, Minnesota, Colorado, California, and possibly one or two other States into the Democratic column. It is no wonder that Secretary Taft made formal addresses in Michigan to allay popular dissatisfaction; for it is quite within the range of possibility that the Philippine tariff bill, regarding which it is safe to say that not half of the country knows anything at all, may be an important factor in deciding a future Presidential election.

The debate upon the bill was anticipated with some anxiety by the party leaders, who feared an explosion on the subject of tariff reform. As a matter of fact, their fears were not well-founded. Mr. Lawrence, of Massachusetts, voicing the sentiment of an increasing faction of the Republican party in his State, expressed his desire for free hides, free coal, free lumber, and free alcohol in the arts; but even Mr. Lawrence was sufficiently alive to party discipline to add that, while he believed the time had arrived for tariff revision, "the Republicans of Massachusetts still hold their allegiance to the principles of protection, and, therefore, do not wish revision through an alliance with the Democratic party." The high-protection Republicans naturally applauded this conservative utterance, while their satisfaction was plainly evidenced when Representative Champ Clark, of Missouri, who long ago asserted his willingness to raze the custom-houses, lifted aloft the banner of absolute free trade. It was noticeable, however, that Mr. Clark's radical ideas were not very generally supported upon his side of the House. Whether the Democrats felt that it was useless merely to fulminate, or whether they did not coincide entirely with Mr. Clark's free-trade position, was not made manifest. The fact that they did not join in a general chorus of free-trade advocacy is interesting, to say the least.

The general debate allowed prior to the vote upon the bill afforded opportunity for the delivery of the usual number of speeches intended for home consumption. The "stand-patter," so-called, emphasized the wisdom of an unchanged tariff; the revisionist pictured the prospective benefits of lower duties; while one and all joined in denouncing the rapacity of the trusts. Whatever might have been other disagreements, this theme of abusing monopolistic corporations brought everybody into harmony. It is true that at least one amendment which would have proved detrimental to the sugar trust was defeated; but none the less did the hall of the House echo with rhetorical attacks upon the combinations which control the prices of human necessaries.

It is now evident that the tariff will be the principal topic in the approaching Congressional campaign. The railroad-rate legislation will doubtless have been enacted ere the session ends, and no other national issue except the tariff has, up to the present time, presented itself. It would not be at all surprising if the President emphasized this topic by a special message to Congress just before the adjournment of the present session. He has thus far refrained from giving utterance to his well-known opinions in favor of adapting the tariff schedules to new conditions, but this reticence has been due to a desire not to divert attention from the railroad-rate legislation, upon which he has centred all his hopes. If he submits a tariff message to Congress, it will be in the nature of a rallying cry to the voters of his party, for he will tread the safe and sane path of necessary tariff revision, avoiding the extremes of high protection and free trade, promising continued security to the legitimate manufacturer, but combating the exorbitant schedules which now tend to create monopolies.

Despite the obstinacy of the stand-patters, the country will eventually come to the President's position. The people, no matter what certain politicians may assert, are not likely to endure what have been happily called the outrageous abuses of protection; but, on the other hand, there is no more danger that this country will swing over to free trade than there is of a profession of allegiance to Great Britain. When the Democrats enacted a tariff bill in President Cleveland's administration, they shot wide of the free-trade mark; and should they again come into power, it is safe to predict that the principle of protection will still be embodied in any tariff law which they may pass.

The Statehood bill, as it passed the House, provided for the admission of Oklahoma and Indian Territory as one State under the name of Oklahoma, and of Arizona and New Mexico as another State to be known as Arizona. The Senate, voting upon the measure on March 9, adopted an amendment offered by Senator Foraker providing that in the case of Arizona and New Mexico the union of the two territories as one State shall be contingent upon the consent of the people therein. The bill has been returned to the House, where, at the present writing, it is very much like Mahomet's coffin, suspended in mid-air.

The absolute defeat of the bill would not be unwelcome to many leading Republicans, notably Speaker Cannon. The latter makes no secret of his opposition to the creation of rotten boroughs, and is especially averse to giving them representation and influence in the Senate equal to New York and other populous States. He is also opposed to a large increase in the electoral college. He is quoted as saying, however, that by admitting the four territories as two States the danger will be reduced one-half, and he fears that if the admission is entirely postponed, the Democrats may recover control of Congress and legislate the four territories into separate States, with eight new Senators and from twelve to eighteen electoral votes. Inasmuch as the Senate is likely to be Republican for many years to come, it is sufficiently evident that this fear is not well founded.

The passage of the bill through the House was made the occasion of an episode which came to be popularly known as an insurgent uprising. It is not necessary now to rehearse all the details of the struggle. Suffice it to say that a certain number of Republicans undertook to rebel against the wish of the dominant leaders of their party, the latter including President Roosevelt and Speaker Cannon, and they were overwhelmingly defeated. There was, it is true, something drastic in the method by which the measure was forced through the House. A rule was reported from the Committee on Rules which proposed that after one day's debate the bill should be voted upon and that no amendments should be allowed to be offered. There was much talk of gag and coercion; but, after all, the administration won.

The moral of the episode is simple. A rebellion in the House of Representatives must be of gigantic proportions if it is to be effective. In my experience in Washington I can recall numerous occasions when for a few brief days the controlling powers were threatened with the defeat of their announced plans. Time and time again, however, I have seen these revolutions, after much sputtering and frothing, fade away into nothingness. It is practically impossible for any member of Congress to organize a force which will stand against the all-powerful influence of the President and the Speaker of the House. It stands to reason that this must be the case. The organizer of the rebellion may gather around him a few who have personal interests at stake, but beyond this little coterie he has no leadership whatever. Even those who might be personally affected more frequently find it easier to assert to their constituents that they stood with the head of their party, the President of the United States, than to explain why they aligned themselves in opposition to him. It will be recalled that the Democrats organized in opposition to President Cleveland when the latter desired to accomplish the repeal of the Sherman silver purchasing law, but in due course of time Mr. Cleveland had won enough of them to enact the desired legislation. In fact, I do not recall a single instance where the insurgents, so-called, were successful. Experience has shown that any administration can, in nine cases out of ten, have its own way with Congress.

It is a curious anomaly of our government that even if the President and the Speaker had been defeated in the issue raised by the Statehood bill, there would have been no change in the political complexion of affairs. The Speaker would have continued in his high office; the committee which reported the repudiated measure would have remained undisturbed. In deciding whether two territories should be admitted as one State, there was not, perhaps, a great vital principle involved; but even if this had been the case, the result would have been the same.

It would seem as if the English manage these things with more regard to the appropriateness of events; for when their government is defeated by an adverse vote upon any measure of importance which it champions, an appeal is immediately taken to the people. Gladstone's Home Rule Parliament, as I remember, lasted little more than six months; and yet, on the other hand, a wise and conservative Ministry may continue undisturbed for many years. We lack the adaptability and the elasticity of the English system. We must have an election every two years, whether or no. There may be no important issues before the country; there may be general satisfaction with the conduct of affairs; and yet, under the inflexible workings of the Constitution, we must turn away from business to listen to the voice of the campaign orator as he appeals to us from the hustings. Of course, our system will not be changed. It is made sacred by the fact that it is the plan prescribed by the founders of our government, and, as I have already stated, an amendment to the Constitution seems a practical impossibility. At the same time, the fact remains that should the popular branch of Congress go upon record against the dominant party, there is no opportunity of appealing to the country until the next election comes according to the calendar, which may be a date quite remote from the time when the revolt occurred.

The engrossing topic in Congress is the proposed legislation affecting railroad rates. The bill reported from the House Committee on Inter-state and Foreign Commerce by its chairman, Representative Hepburn, of Iowa, was passed by the House and later was adopted without amendment by a close vote in the Senate Committee on Inter-state Commerce, and is now before the Senate. Senator Tillman, of South Carolina, a Democrat of radical type, was selected as the agent of the committee to report the bill to the Senate. This action naturally excited widespread comment at the time, and an analysis of the vote which led to the selection indicated that the pique of the opponents of the measure was something of a factor in the matter.

According to the unanimous report of Mr. Hepburn's committee, the railroads themselves are responsible for the legislation which it is proposed to enact. The criticism against the railroads is expressed in direct and vigorous language, as follows:

It is proper here to say to those who complain of this legislation that the necessity for it is the result of the misconduct of carriers. Not necessarily of all, but certainly very many of them have indulged in some form of violation of the law. The law of to-day would be fairly satisfactory to all shippers if the spirit of fairness required by it had controlled the conduct of the carriers, and the necessity for the proposed legislation is the result of and is made necessary by the misconduct of parties who are now most clamorous against additional restraint. If the carriers had in good faith accepted existing statutes and obeyed them, there would have been no necessity for increasing the powers of the Commission or the enactment of new coercive measures.

The law above referred to is known as the Elkins act of 1903, which gave additional strength to previous legislation through its more specific prohibitions relating to rebates, discriminations, and preferences. It is charged, however, that the ingenuity of some of the carriers and shippers has resulted in avoiding the provisions of that act through the use of joint tariffs, involving, in some instances, a railroad and a mere switch owned by a shipper, through arrangements whereby excessive mileage was given to the shipper of products, who owned his own cars; through the use of refrigerator cars; through the permission given to independent corporations to render some service incidental to the shipment, as the furnishing of ice in the bunkers of the car; through what is known as the "midnight tariff," a method involving an arrangement with a shipper to assemble his freights, and have them ready for shipment at a particular date, whereupon the carrier would give the necessary three days' notice of a reduction in the rate.   Competing carriers and shippers would know nothing about this arrangement.   The freight would be shipped at the new, lower rate, and then there would be a restoration of the old rate.

The first section of the bill seeks to remedy these evils, so far as private cars and refrigerating cars and express companies are concerned, by an enlargement of the words "railroads" and "transportation," as used in the inter-state commerce act of 1887, although, during the debate, some doubt was expressed as to whether this result had been actually accomplished.   The one important point of the Hepburn bill is that it gives the Inter-state Commerce Commission the power, when any complaint is made that any rate charged or any regulation or practice followed by any railroad is unjust, unreasonable, unjustly discriminatory, or unduly preferential or prejudicial, "to determine and prescribe what will, in its judgment, be the just and reasonable and fairly remunerative rate or rates," and also to fix and determine a just, fair, and reasonable regulation or practice.   The order embodying the decision of the Commission is to go into effect in thirty days, unless suspended or modified or set aside by the Commission, or suspended or set aside "by a court of competent jurisdiction." A penalty of $5,000 is imposed for disobedience of an order of the Commission, each violation to be regarded as a separate offence, while in case of a continuing violation each day is to be considered a separate offence.

This measure is, unquestionably, one of the most important ever given serious consideration by Congress.   It affects property conservatively estimated as aggregating $15,000,000,000 in value, while hundreds of thousands of persons are directly or indirectly dependent upon railroads for their support.   As might be expected, the struggle over the bill has developed extremists, who, like Senator Foraker, on the one hand, oppose the bill in its entirety, or who, like Senator Dolliver, on the other, believe that the proposed enactment deals in the mildest possible manner with existing evils.   Between these extremes stands Senator Lodge, of Massachusetts, who realizes that "a sudden and ill-considered revolution in our methods of railroad management would bring on a business panic, reduce wages, and probably carry disaster to our trade and commerce in a degree which it is impossible to estimate," and yet who also appreciates the necessity for proper government supervision and regulation.

Senator Lodge, too, is not willing to substitute an executive commission for the courts, and herein is the crux of the whole matter. It is held by the opponents of the bill that the Inter-state Commerce Commission is, in reality, made the final arbiter in the matter of fixing railroad rates, inasmuch as the words of the Hepburn bill, " a court of competent jurisdiction," are too vague and indefinite. They quote the decisions of the United States Supreme Court to the effect that no court has jurisdiction unless definite designation is made in the law. The friends of the bill, on the other hand, regard with suspicion the efforts to throw disputed questions into the courts; believing that an abundance of litigation will destroy the purpose of the legislation. It is possible, however, that some amendment will be adopted providing a judicial review of the Commission's action in terms that cannot be misunderstood.

Senator Foraker, of Ohio, presented the first, and perhaps the ablest, argument against the measure. He laid down, first of all, the principle that the bill is unconstitutional because the power to regulate commerce conferred upon Congress by the Constitution does not include the specific fixing of rates. Even should this be the case, he argued, Congress has no power to delegate its authority to an administrative body like the Inter-state Commerce Commission; and, in support of this contention, he quoted the State laws creating railroad Commissions, which laws specified the maximum rates and then directed the Commission to enforce the law. He pointed out, also, that the proposed legislation is radically different from the Inter-state Commerce act. Under that statute, the Commission is empowered to hear complaints as to unreasonable rates, but in the event that the Commission decided against the railroad, the enforcement of its order was obtainable only through judicial decree. Mr. Foraker also opposed the bill because it eliminates juries, although on this point the President is understood to hold that the Federal bench is better adapted to deciding the intricate questions that may arise. In conclusion, Mr. Foraker expressed the belief that an amendment to the Elkins law would secure all the reforms which are needed and would avoid the doubt of constitutionality to which the Hepburn bill is open. Mr. Foraker's arguments have, of course, been combated by the friends of the bill; but they are presented because, when the measure shall have become law, they will be repeated before the courts.

It is quite evident that there will be a long and bitter struggle in the Senate, however, before the rate bill reaches its final vote; but that it will be eventually enacted, there is little reason to doubt. THE FORUM pointed out some months ago that the outlook was favorable to the adoption of railroad-rate legislation, and this prediction rests now upon still stronger ground. It is not within the province of this article to deal with the question from its legal and economic standpoints, and I have, therefore, only referred to the details of the measure in a most general way. From a political point of view, it is difficult to see how legislation for the railroads can become a serious issue. The proposed bill was passed in the House with only seven dissenting votes. Members of both parties literally tumbled over each other in their desire to be recorded affirmatively.

It would appear, therefore, on the theory that the House reflects popular sentiment, as if the people, irrespective of political affiliation, were thoroughly in sympathy with the proposed reform. If anybody profits by the situation, it is President Roosevelt, upon whose initiative the remedy was undertaken, and whose energy and persistence forced Congress into line. The Republican party, as a whole, can hardly claim credit, inasmuch as the most outspoken opposition has emanated from Republican sources, and the seven negative votes were cast by Republican Representatives. If President Roosevelt were a candidate for renomination, it is easy to see how his advocacy of the rate bill might be a factor in the political situation, because the great influence of the railroads would naturally and inevitably be combined to compass his defeat. He is, however, in a position where he can do his duty without regard to his future. It is an ideal position, for it enables him to strengthen his party with the people without injuring his personal political status. The railroads could, of course, combine in antagonism to the Republican party, but this is unlikely. As a matter of fact, it is not evident that political considerations have influenced the President's attitude in the slightest degree.

The critical disposition of the public mind in regard to the administration of affairs has been thoroughly manifest in Congress. The bill providing an emergency appropriation for the Panama Canal, for instance, was made the occasion for a detailed examination into the financial status of the enterprise, with the result that salaries are in the future to be submitted to Congress as regular estimates, thus giving the legislative body control over them. It has also been settled that the work is to be done by contract, a step most wise when it is appreciated that the prosecution of the work under the direct management of government officials might be provocative of serious criticism, if not scandal. During the consideration of the appropriation bills, also, the tendency toward economy was evident, and all items were subjected to careful scrutiny. Indeed, so committed is the House to a reduction of expenses that it is exceedingly doubtful if the ship-subsidy bill, which passed the Senate by a vote of 38 to 27, will be given consideration. This measure establishes thirteen new contract mail lines, and increases the subvention to the oceanic lines running from the Pacific coast to Australasia, the aggregate compensation being estimated at $3,000,000 annually. Five Republican Senators — Burkett of Nebraska, Dolliver of Iowa, Warner of Missouri, and Spooner and LaFollette of Wisconsin — voted against the measure. The Republicans in the House are by no means a unit in favor of the proposed subsidies.

The issues in the Congressional campaign which will be waged during the approaching summer and fall will grow largely out of legislation or non-legislation at this session of Congress. As already indicated, the one great and overshadowing issue will be the tariff question. The Democrats will contend for a rational revision of the tariff, especially of all schedules that pertain to and shelter the trusts, while the trusts themselves and all illegal combinations of capital in restraint of trade and competition will be attacked. The Democrats will claim that the railroad-rate bill was stolen bodily from the Democratic platform by the Republican administration, but, having been emasculated by the Republican Senate, the people cannot expect any beneficial railroad-rate legislation by the dominant party. The assertion will be made, also, that proper investigation into illegal combinations and into the condition of public affairs cannot be expected unless the Democrats are placed in power.

While the Democratic leaders appreciate the fact that they have a tremendous task in front of them to wipe out and overcome the Republican majority in this House, they claim that the task is more apparent than real. A normal Republican majority in the House is not over twenty, and the present great majority was the result of a Roosevelt landslide in the last campaign, and the refusal of a million and a half of Democrats to vote. In view of the demand for publicity regarding political contributions, it will be difficult to raise money for campaign purposes this year, but this, it is claimed, will be more to the disadvantage of the Republicans than of the Democrats. The latter claim another advantage in the fact that Hon. James W. Griggs, recently elected Chairman of the Democratic Congressional Committee, has had the experience of conducting one campaign, while the Republicans will lose the services of their former managers. The Republican leaders do not concede, for a moment, the likelihood of a Democratic victory.

HENRY LITCHFIELD WEST.

FOREIGN AFFAIRS.

WHEN the last issue of this review appeared, Sir Henry Campbell-Bannerman had formed his government, but he had not yet gone to the country. The general election, which was held in January, resulted in such a crushing defeat for the Unionists that they have not yet recovered, and are still trying to discover why the country so unmistakably showed that it was tired of Mr. Balfour and his policies. The Unionists expected defeat, but not annihilation. They looked to see Sir Henry Campbell-Bannerman come in with a working majority that might at any time be turned into a minority by a coalition of Unionists and Irish, instead of which Sir Henry is swept into power with 378 Liberals behind him, while fronting him are only 156 Unionists and 80 Nationalists, so that the Premier has nothing to fear from a combined opposition. Even if the entire Labor group, estimated at fifty, should "cross the floor," the Liberals would still have the handsome majority of 92 votes. The Liberals, therefore, are safe from assault, and may reasonably count upon retaining office for the average duration of a parliament, between five and six years.

The election will always be memorable for two things. A new party in British politics was born. A new issue was submitted to the judgment of the electorate. For the first time since Peel struck down the protective tariff, the British voter was asked to determine whether he would sanction a change in his fiscal system. His answer was an emphatic No. But this is not the last word; rather it is only the beginning.

For the present, let us leave economics to consider the much more fascinating question of humanity — schedules have always been sordid things. The election of some fifty workingmen — not professional labor leaders, but actual workers at the lathe, the bench, and the loom — to Parliament is a political and social event of the first importance. Some enthusiastic laborites have termed it a revolution. Hardly that, but an evolution it certainly is. Just as the Reform Bills and the extension of the suffrage destroyed the power of the aristocracy and ended their control over Old Sarum and other rotten boroughs and made the great middle class of England the real governing class, so the democratization of England has brought the wage-earner to the front and made him representative of his class. It is not a revolution, but it has been a gradual evolutionary movement that ought not to have escaped the attention of shrewd political observers. But in England there is no such elaborate party machinery as there is in

30

this country. The committee chairman, in the American sense, is unknown. Small as the parliamentary districts are, no attempt is ever made to test the sentiment of voters prior to an election. There are no ways to make a canvass or to make converts.

In the last Parliament there were seven laboring men; in the present Parliament there are about fifty. It is impossible to be more precise, because of the peculiar conditions under which the candidates were nominated. Some of them were directly nominated by the Labor Reform Committee, which, roughly, for the convenience of the American political reader, may be likened to a National Committee in this country. There were labor candidates independently nominated; others, although workingmen, are avowed socialists; and in some constituencies, where the labor vote was important, the Liberals supported the Labor candidate, which led to the candidate being classed as a Liberal. But at heart they are all more concerned in the interests of labor than they are in Liberalism or Conservatism. They have flung to the breeze their own banner, and under this banner they will fight in Parliament. Mr. John Burns sits on the front bench as one of the King's Ministers; but to John Burns, "Right Honourable" although he has become, the cause of labor is dearer than the Liberal party.

The name of the youth who fired the Ephesian dome is lost in the maze of antiquity, and the name of the humble "pointsman," which is the English designation for a railroad switchman, who is really, although unconsciously, responsible for the Labor party, has long been forgotten. It is an impressive illustration of how great movements, like great oaks, spring from tiny acorns, and how often they thrive best where the soil is most sterile.

In 1900 there was a strike on the Taff Vale Railway, a minor Welsh railway system; and this strike, which was merely a skirmish compared to some of the great battles between labor and capital, had results so far-reaching that they are only now being appreciated. The causes that led up to the strike are not important; but the assigned reason was the discharge of a pointsman, a member of the Amalgamated Society of Railway Servants, a powerful labor union. Failing to secure his reinstatement, the other members of the union went on strike and resorted to the usual methods to prevent non-union men taking their places.

The railway company thereupon sought to enjoin Bell and Holmes, officers of the Amalgamated Society, to restrain them from "watching and besetting" the station and adjacent property, which was alleged to be in violation of an Act of Parliament. The injunction was granted. The company next applied for an injunction against the union, naming Bell and Holmes as two of its officers, also to restrain them from watching the property of the company or the residences of its workmen. The Society vigorously opposed the granting of the writ of injunction, on the ground that a trade union, being neither a corporation nor an individual, could not be sued, and that an action in tort would not lie. But the plea was overruled and the injunction granted.

A trade union in England, up to the time of the decision in the Taff Vale case by the House of Lords, occupied a peculiar position in the eyes of the law. It was a legal entity by an Act of Parliament enacted for its own benefit. In many respects it was treated almost as a ward of the state, being granted certain special privileges and immunities. One of these, it was commonly believed, was exemption from suit, although the union had the right to sue for its own benefit. If a trade union was responsible for the action of its members, criminally as well as civilly, trade unionism weakened instead of strengthening the position of labor. Damages could not be recovered from an individual workingman because the workingman is unable to satisfy the judgment, but many of the English unions have full treasuries and cannot escape their obligations.

So important was it to both sides to win their case that it was fought with extreme bitterness and it became a judicial *cause célèbre*. Capital rallied to the support of capital courageous enough to meet the tyranny of trade unionism with a weapon of its own forging. Labor, in encouraging the Amalgamated Society to resist to the last, felt that it was fighting for its very life. The suit was carried through every court to the court of last resort, the House of Lords, which affirmed the trial court and held that a trade union could sue or be sued. The Taff Vale Company then brought suit for £20,000; and the Amalgamated Society, seeing that further litigation would only mean additional expense, admitted itself defeated and paid the amount claimed.

Both in and out of Parliament the decision of the House of Lords gave rise to endless discussion. The unions regarded it as another illustration of the perversion of the intent of Parliament and a scandalous example of "judge-made law," and it is one of their grievances that laws are distorted by judicial interpretation. Mr. Richard Bell, the titular secretary of the Amalgamated Society, but actually its controlling spirit, who had opposed the strike until he was forced into it by his associates, was at that time a member of Parliament. He introduced a bill to exempt trades unions from damages under similar circumstances, and spoke at length in support of his bill; asserting that a new construction had been given to the law, and that without warning a blow had been struck by the courts at the unions. He was answered by the attorney general, who maintained that no new principle had been established, and that a union, like an individual, was responsible for an unlawful act. The Government, however, admitted that, in view of the construction hitherto given by the courts to the menacing of the trades unions acts, their amendment was necessary. But no action was taken.

Up to that time labor as a body had taken little interest in politics. There were a few laboring men in Parliament, the most conspicuous of whom was Mr. John Burns; but the union in England, much like the union in America, looked askance at parliamentary representation and feared that the injection of politics in the union would mean its disintegration. But the Taff Vale decision turned the scale. Workingmen in general were induced to believe that the only way by which they could obtain justice was by cutting loose from the old parties and forming a party of their own. They have been persistently and intelligently agitating ever since. As English members are not paid, it was impossible for a workingman to sit in Parliament; but the unions met this difficulty by levying a small tax on their members and paying their representatives a modest salary, so that they could devote their entire time to their parliamentary duties.

What the Labor party can accomplish is a speculative inquiry of much interest to Englishmen of all classes at the present time. What it can accomplish depends partly on its homogeneity and its moderation; it may go to wreck by trying to accomplish too much. Its programme is ambitious, which may be translated into radical. The labor programme in part includes universal suffrage for both sexes, free meals for school children, old-age pensions, work for the unemployed, the municipality to supply the public with coal, wood, milk, bread, and other necessaries of life, as well as to control street railways, gas and water works, and other public utilities, the enforcement of union wages in all public contracts, picketing to be made legal, their immunities to be restored to trades unions, the reduction of hours of labor for miners, railroad employés, and employés of the state, local control of the drink traffic, taxation of ground values, a graduated tax not only on incomes, but on the sources of incomes, and help to the farmer so as to promote British agriculture. This is not the full programme, but it will suffice. Men steeped in the habit of conservatism will undoubtedly term it socialistic to the last degree, but no English champion of labor will shrink before that blow.

The Labor party put between eighty and ninety candidates in the field; and fifty-three of them, according to Mr. James Keir-Hardie, the chairman of the Labor party in Parliament, are avowed socialists. Of the remainder some are perhaps more Liberal than Labor, and others, like the candidates nominated by the miners' and other unions, are more particularly interested in a single occupation than they are in labor as a whole. But all of them, despite individual differences — and these differences are many and violent — have a common purpose.

The jealousy of labor, the envy of the men in the ranks against the few who rise to the top, has always been the great, if not the greatest, reason why there has been no political solidarity of labor. It took a long time and much persuasive argument on the part of labor leaders to convince their followers that it was for their advantage to pay one of their members two or three pounds a week so that he might give up his trade and sit in Parliament. The moment a man left his trade and went to St. Stephen's, to the proletariat he had ceased to be one of them and had become that most abhorrent of all things to the workingman, a gentleman without gentility. It is true that he was simply paid the wages of his craft, and financially he was no better off as a member of Parliament than he had been in the past. But instead of working eight or nine hours a day in a factory, he lived what was supposed to be a life of ease, and it was believed he soon took on the airs and ideas of the men with whom he associated. Distinctly this is not true, so far as the Labor members of the last Parliament are concerned. John Burns, Richard Bell, Will Crooks, Keir-Hardie, and others have not changed in the slightest from what they were before they entered Westminster.

This jealousy and suspicion were typically shown when Mr. Burns was made President of the Local Government Board in the present Cabinet. The salary of the President of the Local Government Board is £2,000 a year, which is, of course, a fortune for a man in Mr. Burns's position. But his acceptance of office at the hands of a Liberal Premier was savagely denounced by many workingmen as treachery to his party and his cause. They vociferously insisted that the duty of the Labor member was not to sell himself to either of the great parties, but to fight both, as occasion might arise, for the benefit of Labor. Mr. Burns is to-day concededly the foremost representative of labor in the United Kingdom; but it is extremely significant that in a long article by Mr. Keir-Hardie in "The Nineteenth Century," in which he outlines the plans and aspirations of his party, the name of Mr. John Burns is not once mentioned. If the Labor members can hold together and are not torn up by internecine strife, they will undoubtedly be a force in Parliament and make their impress felt upon legislation. But the Unionists, and to some extent the Liberals, although at present there is strong sympathy between the Liberals and the Laborites, are hoping that jealousies will nullify the power of labor.

Turn now to the other thing that made this election so interesting and so memorable. An issue was brought before the electors that three years ago practically no Englishman would have been expected to be called upon to pronounce in this generation. England seemingly was wedded to free trade, and free trade was so impregnably buttressed in the social as well as the political system of England that it could not be overthrown. Yet when Mr. Chamberlain brought forward his scheme of preferential tariffs for the Colonies in their interest as much as in that of the mother country, it found many adherents, and it became evident that it was an issue that would become as important in British politics as the tariff has been in American politics ever since Alexander Hamilton made his illuminating report to Congress.

In a sense, the election was a crushing defeat for protection and a magnificent reaffirmation of free trade; and yet, despite the fact of Sir Henry Campbell-Bannerman's majority, a majority distinctly pledged not to change the present fiscal system, the fact remains that Mr. Chamberlain and his cause are stronger than they were in the last Parliament. The issue can no longer be dodged. Mr. Balfour, who is by education and inheritance a theoretical free-trader, was able to prevent the House from giving an expression of its opinion. But Mr. Balfour was repudiated by his constituency at Manchester, while Birmingham not only triumphantly re-elected Mr. Chamberlain, but sent a solid Unionist delegation to Parliament.

Mr. Balfour's defeat and Mr. Chamberlain's victory naturally made the Unionists turn to Mr. Chamberlain as their new leader, and had he raised his hand he could easily have become the leader of his party in Parliament. Mr. Chamberlain, however, with his accustomed shrewdness, declined the honor and insisted that Mr. Balfour should retain his leadership; but he was forced to pay the price. In February, correspondence that had passed between Mr. Chamberlain and Mr. Balfour was made public. Writing to Mr. Chamberlain, Mr. Balfour said that much misapprehension existed as to the differences between fiscal reformers.

" My own opinion," he said, " which, I believe, is shared by the great majority of the Unionist party, may be briefly summarized as follows:

"I hold that fiscal reform is and muts remain the first constructive work of the Unionist party.

" That the objects of such reform are to secure more equal terms of competition for British trade and closer commercial union with the Colonies.

" That while it is at present unnecessary to prescribe the exact methods by which these objects are to be attained and inexpedient to permit differences of opinion as to these methods to defeat the party, though other means may be possible, the establishment of a moderate general tariff on manufactured goods, not imposed for the purpose of raising prices or giving artificial protection against legitimate competition, and the imposition of a small duty on foreign corn, are not in principle objectionable, and should be adopted if shown as necessary for the attainment of the ends in view or for purposes of revenue."

To which Mr. Chamberlain briefly replied:

"I entirely agree with your description of the object which we both have in view, and gladly accept the policy which you indicate as the wise and desirable one for the Unionist party to adopt."

Mr. Balfour's letter shows how far he has now progressed on the road toward fiscal reform. During the last two years he repeatedly declared that he was opposed to any duty on corn (wheat), no matter what offers might be made by the Colonies in return for this effort on the part of Great Britain to provide a home market for Colonial wheat to the discrimination of the wheat raised in America and other countries. Mr. Balfour also opposed a general tariff, which Mr. Chamberlain regarded as one of the most effective weapons in retaliating against countries that imposed excessive duties on British products; but while he was opposed to the Chamberlain scheme he had no alternative proposal of his own to advance. Now Mr. Balfour agrees with Mr. Chamberlain in favor of "the establishment of a moderate general tariff on manufactured goods" and the "imposition of a small duty on foreign corn," which he declares "are not in principle objectionable, and should be adopted if shown to be necessary for the attainment of the ends in view."

The Unionist party, therefore, through its acknowledged leaders, is committed to tariff reform. Parenthetically it may be mentioned that the phrase "tariff reform" is given a meaning in England the reverse of what it is in this country. In the United States tariff reformers desire to see a reduction of the present high duties so that a freer interchange of commodities may take place between this and other countries. In England the tariff reformer desires to see duties imposed, so that if necessary a restriction may be placed on the market for foreign goods in Great Britain.

There are, of course, free-traders in the Unionist party exactly as there are high protectionists in the Democratic party. One of the most influential of the great territorial magnates is the Duke of Devonshire, who, because of his high rank and great wealth, rather than his intellect, exercises no inconsiderable influence on English public opinion. The Duke of Devonshire has repudiated Mr. Balfour's fiscal policy, and has announced that although he will not forsake his party, he will not acknowledge leadership which compels him to accept the fiscal views of Mr. Balfour and Mr. Chamberlain, and neither will his friends. How great a following the Duke of Devonshire can command has not yet been made clear. In the debate in the Lords on the fiscal question following this announcement, Lord Lansdowne, the Secretary of State for Foreign Affairs in the last Cabinet, defended Mr. Balfour's policy, while Lord Goschen, Mr. Balfour's Chancellor of the Exchequer, ranged himself on the side of the Duke of Devonshire, in repudiating protection. This division of opinion among the members of the last Cabinet shows the extent of the split in the party.

But the success of protection does not depend upon the Duke of Devonshire or Lord Lansdowne or Lord Goschen or men of that stamp. To succeed it must be acceptable to the great mass of the electorate, and that means the workingman and the middle class. Up to the present time, both of these great elements in British politics have opposed protection because they believe that protection will increase the cost of living without bringing a corresponding increase of wages or salaries. So long as that belief exists protection is doomed. No sane man dependent upon his own exertions will vote to change a fiscal system that makes the struggle for life harder.

It has already been said that the Liberals ought to be able to count with reasonable certainty upon smooth sailing for the next five years or so, and yet it will require skillful seamanship if the craft which they command is to go through unbattered to smooth water. The Government is partially pledged to enact some of the advanced social legislation which is part of the Labor programme. The Premier inclines toward old-age pensions, which is a seductive campaign cry, but not so easily carried into effect. Mr. Chamberlain, a few years ago, nibbled at the scheme, but it met with so little response that he saw the wisdom of not pushing it. It is a measure, of course, that commands the enthusiastic support of workingmen generally; but as the great middle class will not profit by it, and will see in it only an increase of taxation, it may be doubted whether they will be so unselfish as to sanction a scheme that entails an extra burden on them and from which they derive no benefit.

It has often been said by students of social conditions in England that the "lower middle class" is really in a more deplorable condition than the class immediately below it — that is, the workingmen. The intelligent, industrious, sober artisan can earn good wages and live in fair comfort and decency. The average city clerk or salesman earns little more, and frequently not so much as the engineer or cotton spinner, but he is compelled to live in a neighborhood where rents are higher and provisions cost more. A married clerk with children frequently finds it more difficult to make both ends meet on his three, four, or five pounds a week than the artisan making his two or three pounds.

These men have even less chance than the workingmen to provide against the proverbial rainy day. Even with the strictest economy they cannot save, and when they are too old for active service there is nothing for them. The workingman, on the other hand, is usually a member of the union, with which is associated a saving fund; and in his old age, or when misfortune overtakes him, the union comes to his relief. The lower middle class should properly be included in the old-age pension scheme; but while workingmen are convinced of the justice of the state making provision for their support when age incapacitates them from earning a living, they have not so far progressed toward altruism as to admit that the state owes the same obligation to any other class.

Ireland also threatens more than one unpleasant quarter of an hour for the Premier. How far the Government intends to go in the direction of home rule for Ireland has not yet been made clear; but that the Irish are to be given a much larger control in the management of their own affairs than heretofore has been granted to them is clearly indicated by the King's speech at the opening of Parliament. While, theoretically, the King's speech is a message from the sovereign to Parliament, in fact it is the King's message merely in name. Unlike the President's message to Congress, it does not originate with the Executive, for which he alone is responsible. The King's speech is prepared and written by the ministry of the day, formally submitted to him for approval, and approved by him as a matter of course. It is in the power of the sovereign to veto any act of his ministers, and the sovereign might refuse to accept the speech to Parliament; but in that case the ministry would resign, and the sovereign would be compelled to entrust the government of the empire to men more in harmony with his own ideas. Therefore, when the King speaks of Ireland, it is the voice of Edward, but it is the hand of Bannerman. That part of the speech devoted to Ireland was as follows:

My ministers have under consideration a plan for improving and effecting economies in the system of government for Ireland and for introducing thereinto means for associating the people with the conduct of Irish affairs. It is my desire that the government of the country, in reliance upon the ordinary law, should be carried on so far as existing circumstances permit in a spirit regardful of the policy and sentiments of the Irish people.

In the debate that followed the address, Mr. Chamberlain said that any measure looking to home rule would meet with strenuous opposition. In the House of Lords, Lord Lansdowne also discussed Irish affairs and asked whether the King's speech meant home rule by instalments. Any change in the present method of governing Ireland, he said, would cause serious alarm and uneasiness to the country. The Premier refused to be drawn by the opposition. He declined to go into details regarding Ireland, but simply confined himself to the statement that Ireland had not sufficient voice in her own affairs. The next day the debate was resumed, and Mr. Bryce, Chief Secretary for Ireland, was more explicit. He said the speech from the throne simply meant that much was necessary to improve the administration of Ireland. Mr. Bryce declared that home rule had no terrors for him, and that he still believed now, as firmly as he had in the past, in the principles of the Liberal party, so far as Ireland was concerned, as laid down by Mr. Gladstone in 1886. While admitting that the Government proposed to carry into effect a plan for the extension of self-government for Ireland, he did not consider it expedient at that time to be more specific.

It is said in parliamentary circles that an understanding exists between John Redmond, the leader of the Irish party in Parliament, and the Premier, and also that the Unionist and the Labor parties have a working agreement and will coöperate for their mutual advantage. No half-way measure of self-government, it is believed, will be satisfactory to Mr. Redmond and his followers. Mr. Redmond, it is said, aims at an Irish parliament, which has always been dreaded by Englishmen as the entering wedge toward separation. But the supporters of home rule say it would mean nothing of the kind, and would simply give Ireland the same control over her domestic affairs as is now exercised by a State legislature in this country, while the power of the Imperial Parliament would remain unimpaired whenever any question arose dealing with Imperial relations.

Since I last wrote the sceptre of power in France has passed from the hand of M. Loubet to that of M. Clément Armand Fallières. Undoubtedly France has many things to learn from the United States, but the United States may well take a lesson from France when it comes to the method of electing a President. In England some of the newspapers have been denouncing the time required for a general election and the annoyance and confusion which it causes, and have suggested that the whole business might just as well be done in a week as in the three which were found necessary. What would they say if they had to go through the five months of turmoil and excitement inseparable from an American election? And what would Americans think if the Presidential campaign was begun and done for in less than a week, as it is in France?

On January 17 the Senate and the Chamber of Deputies met in joint session at Versailles and elected M. Fallières to be President of the French Republic in place of M. Loubet, whose term had expired, and who was not a candidate for reëlection. M. Fallières had only one opponent, M. Doumer, president of the Chamber of Deputies, who was able to command 370 votes to the 449 of the successful candidate. It may be interesting to add for the benefit of American readers who are unfamiliar with the French Constitution that the President of the Republic is not, as in this country, elected by the direct vote of the people, but by the Legislature, as are United States senators. Owing to the numerous groups in the French parliamentary system, it is impossible for a candidate for the presidency to bring about the election of members favorable to his candidacy, as so often happens with a senatorial candidate before a State legislature. The French President more nearly represents the real voice of public sentiment at the moment when it is given expression than does any other man in this or any other country who holds office by election.

The President of France has often been termed a mere figure-head, who does not reign like the King of England and does not govern like the President of the United States. This, however, is not strictly correct. It is true that his powers are limited, but at the same time he is not entirely deprived of all power. No act of the President is valid unless it is countersigned by a minister, but the President selects his ministers and can dismiss them. The President has no veto over legislation, although he can require the Chambers to reconsider a bill if it does not meet with his approval. It is a power, however, that has not been exercised by any French President. The President, with the consent of the Senate, can dissolve the Chamber of Deputies; but that authority has been sparingly exercised. In France, as in America, the President has power to make treaties, although they must be ratified, except in a few isolated instances, by both Chambers. Yet there is a good deal of freedom of discretion lodged in the hands of the President and his Cabinet, a great deal more than is given to the American President.

M. Fallières, although he has had a distinguished and long public career, is a somewhat colorless person, the grandson of a village blacksmith; and despite his partisan training and his Parisian associations, the traditions of his class dominate him. He is a provincial rather than a Parisian, simple, good-natured, honest. He oomes fully equipped for his work so far as intimately knowing the inside workings of public departments and a long training under various ministers can equip him for the task. He began his parliamentary life exactly thirty years ago, and he first held office as an under secretary in 1880. He has been successively Minister of the Interior, Minister of Public Worship, Minister of Foreign Affairs, Minister of Justice, and Minister of Public Instruction, in the cabinets of Ferry, Freycinet, Rouvier, and Tirard. For twenty-two days he was Prime Minister. He was the first man asked by President Carnot to form a cabinet, but failed. Seven times he was successfully elected president of the Senate, and he was elected for the eighth time a week prior to his selection to the presidency.

M. Fallières, like his predecessor, is a man of peace, and will not, one feels justified in predicting, let off fireworks merely for the fun of frightening the public. It was not without ample justification that M. Loubet said to his successor:

Throughout my administration, which is now brought to a close, I have sought to establish peace, union, and concord among all good citizens, that they might labor together in the upbuilding of our institutions and of social progress, and in strengthening the bonds between France and other countries. The future will

tell whether I have realized some of this programme, to which I have consecrated all
my efforts.

The new President will endeavor to keep on terms of peace with his
neighbors.   If the peace is broken it will not be because M. Fallières has
wantonly given cause for quarrel.   A man of tact and of that amiability
which is the priceless heritage of a Gascon who inclines to corpulency, the
new President will promote that "concord among all good citizens" that
was so dear to the heart of M. Loubet.   An advanced republican, but not
a radical, he is also a Catholic, but a Catholic who believes that the Church
should be subordinate to the State and should not interfere in politics.
There is little likelihood that the abrogated Concordat will be revived with
his consent.

That peculiar strain in the character of the French that makes them so
delightful and at the same time so childishly illogical was never more
strikingly shown than when the Chamber of Deputies overturned the
Rouvier ministry at the close of a minor debate on the Church disorders.
Out of pure wantonness, it would seem, the opposition combined to
defeat the Government.   There was nothing to be gained by a change,
as while the opposition was strong enough in combination to defeat the
Government, it was made up of so many discordant factions that it could
not agree on a cabinet of its own making.   Politically, therefore, it was
a senseless play, and circumstances made it almost treason to the Republic.   For just at that time the negotiations at Algeciras were in their
most critical stage, and a change of government threatened to rob France
of all that she had gained by shrewd diplomacy.   Fortunately politics
stopped at the water's edge, and the foreign policy of France remained
unbroken, to the relief of all the world.

This incident emphasizes anew that increasing stability of the French
character that has more than once been commented upon in these pages.
A few years ago the fall of a French cabinet was reflected by a nervous
tremor in the bourses of all European capitals, and had a cabinet been
overthrown while delicate negotiations were pending, Europe would
have been badly frightened.   Nothing of the kind happened now.
Europe felt no more alarmed than when Bannerman succeeded Balfour,
or when an American President goes out of office.   Men might change,
but not a policy.   The enemies of France would profit nothing from a
new Premier, or a new minister of foreign affairs.   Even if the French, as
the result of inherited tendencies, are childish at times, they are no longer
children to set a continent afire for the mere fun of seeing the blaze.

The new cabinet is respectable but not brilliant, and, somewhat like
the new English cabinet, it includes in its make-up elements almost antag-

onistic. The Premier is less known outside of France than the foreign minister, M. Bourgeois, who was Premier eleven years ago, and who is an "intellectual" in politics; or than M. Clémenceau, the minister of the interior, who went into obscurity under the cloud of the Panama scandal. The cabinet is not less radically republican than its predecessor, and no less firmly resolved to carry out the policy of separation of Church and State, while preserving good relations with Germany as well as with England.

When sovereigns and statesmen talk of peace their words often thinly veil a fear of war, but there is no insincerity about military precautions. Nothing better illustrates the changed and friendly relations existing between England and France than the redistribution of the most powerful fighting ships of the British navy. For years the whole naval policy of England centred on her ability to maintain, in the English Channel and the Mediterranean, fleets so powerful and in such a state of efficiency that, instantly following a declaration of war with France, the two fleets would join hands and destroy whatever force France, with or without allies, could oppose to her, and then, having cleared the sea of the foe, blockade and bombard French ports, while England would feel secure from attack. Time and again British admirals have carried out these manœuvres, and the latest and most powerful battleships and cruisers were sent to the Channel and the Mediterranean as soon as they were commissioned, as it was believed that it was there they would be needed if they ever were.

A few weeks hence, after the naval manœuvres are over, England will withdraw four battleships and four armored cruisers from the Mediterranean and send them to reinforce the fleet in the North Sea — to watch Germany. Thenceforth, instead of the Mediterranean being one of the most important stations, with an admiral in command and a couple of vice-admirals in command of divisions, the reduced fleet will be a vice-admiral's command, with a rear admiral as his second in command. The Channel fleet will also be reduced by the withdrawal of four battleships, which will likewise be sent to the North Sea, for German edification. The flower of the British navy will then be in the North Sea and the English Channel — in a word, within easy striking distance of German territory. France is also expected to reduce her naval strength in southern waters and send it north.

The Anglo-French *entente* is met by a Russo-German exchange of compliments that may be as hollow as most compliments are, or something a great deal more sincere. On the anniversary of the German Emperor's birth the Czar, with the German ambassador as his guest, drank this remarkable toast, that has made all Europe ask its meaning: " I drink to the health of the German Emperor and King of Prussia, my brother and very dear friend — brother, which is more than ally." According to the reports, the last words were pronounced with proper emphasis and as if to mark their importance.

History is made rapidly these days. It was only twelve years ago that all France was aflame over the Russian alliance, that was the offset to Germany's alliance with Italy and Austria. To celebrate this alliance, the French President entertained the Russian diplomatic and naval officers, and it was at this banquet that toasts were drunk to the success of Russian and French arms on the field of battle.

The Slav, no less than the Latin, is noted for his emotionalism, although the Slav temperament is a curious blending of emotion and stolidness. The Russian alliance was a thing for the French to rhapsodize over; it titillated their *amour propre*, for France no longer stood isolated, but once more had an ally, and that ally was the Colossus of the North, whom all the world at that particular moment regarded with awe. So while France indulged in copious libations of champagne in honor of the alliance, Russia turned that alliance to practical account. A month after the banquet in which Russians and French pledged themselves as allies and figuratively tightened their sword belts, Paris bankers offered to the French public a Russian loan of 100,000,000 rubles. It was eagerly taken up.

Up to that time Berlin had financed St. Petersburg, but Berlin had reached the limit of her resources. Some $500,000,000 of German money was invested in Russia, and Germany found herself needing money at home rather than being able to send it abroad. Since then it has been Paris that has kept Russia out of the bankruptcy court, but France has at last tired of the hopeless task of the Danaides and has shut down on further Russian loans.

Does the effusive toast of the Czar mean that there is a new politico-financial alignment, and that once more Berlin is to attempt the titanic task of financing Russia? Or is it merely a veiled threat to France that she must for her own safety continue to satisfy Russian demands? The Russian loans have placed France in almost as precarious a position as Russia herself. It is the old story of the creditor and not the debtor walking the floor. Suppose Russia could borrow no more money. Russian credit would go to smash; and there would be a heavy fall of Russian bonds on the French bourse, which would mean a panic in France such as the world has never known. Russia certainly cannot afford to quarrel with France, and France is in no position to pull down the Russian temple of finance that has been built with French gold. In all probability Paris will finance Russia for some time to come, but it will be done grudgingly and as sparingly as possible. The day when a Russian loan was eagerly taken up by the French people has passed.

M. Witte, the one really great constructive statesman that modern Russia has produced, is devoting all his dynamic energies and his great ability to the attempt to restore order out of chaos; but the reactionary forces opposed to him are so powerful that he makes headway slowly, if at all. If Witte were only given a free hand he would accomplish much in a short time. But he is in the position so often described by the late Secretary Hay in his dealings with the United States Senate. He is hampered by a ball and chain. Only a few weeks ago M. Witte asked the Czar to permit him to resign because Durnovo, the Minister of the Interior, nullified all that Witte had done by his repressive and illegal measures. For the time being a truce has been patched up between the titular Prime Minister and one of his subordinates; but it is absurd to suppose that any real progress can be made so long as a man of Witte's advanced liberal views is forced to use, as one of his instruments, a reactionary of the type of Durnovo.

Witte unquestionably favors a complete understanding with England; and the change of government in England makes the time peculiarly opportune, if the British or any government could feel sure that a contract made with Witte would be observed by his successor. To-morrow Russia may again be in the grasp of the grand ducal oligarchy. It was during the Portsmouth conference that M. Witte outlined to me at length his views — which I published with his consent — on the relations that ought to exist between England and Russia. M. Witte said frankly that he favored a complete understanding with England, and he advanced reasons why such an understanding would be not only in the interests of both countries, but also for the world at large. To my question whether a *rapprochement* with England would not rupture the good relations existing between Russia and Germany, M. Witte said it would be possible for England and Russia to be on good terms without Russia being disloyal to her other friends.

The hand of friendship has been held out by England. It is an unheard-of thing for an English member of the Cabinet, the Premier especially, to write to the correspondent of a foreign paper on the foreign policy of his government, but that is what Sir Henry Campbell-Bannerman did only a few days after the election. In a letter to the London correspondent of the "Novoe Vremya," the Prime Minister expressed his cordial friendship for Russia and a wish that closer relations might exist between the two countries.

It is unnecessary to weigh in an exact balance the losses and gains that would follow such an *entente*. Russia perhaps might receive more than she gave, but England certainly would not be an actual loser. With England, France, and Russia working together, neither England, nor France, nor Russia would have anything to fear from Germany; and although the Kaiser may be a much-wronged man, the fact remains that all Europe does fear him and believes that he only abides his time to draw the sword.

With the peace of Europe secured, the peace of Asia would follow. The position of England's Indian dependency has been greatly strengthened since the Russo-Japanese war and the conclusion of the Anglo-Japanese treaty, by the terms of which the military forces of Japan are at the disposal of England in case of an attack on India. But with Russia as a friendly neighbor instead of an armed foe, the danger of attack disappears. Russia would undoubtedly demand as part of the settlement Constantinople, the goal of Russian ambitions, which would not be the menace to England that English statesmen believed it to be half a century ago. And not the least advantage to Russia would be the opening of the English money market, which would also mean its profit to English bankers and manufacturers. Russia can borrow no money from England so long as Englishmen fear they may have to fight her in the near future; but if that fear were removed, they would as willingly invest in Russian securities as they do in those of any other friendly nation. What Russia needs more than anything else, next to a stable and liberal government, is capital for the development of her enormously rich undeveloped natural resources. It is in England and America — and American financiers would coöperate with those of England — that this capital can be found.

It has been remarked that history is made very rapidly these days, and nowhere do events move with more dramatic swiftness than in the Far East. If anyone had predicted even two years ago that Japan would have felt her military position strong enough to advise Great Britain to put her military house in order and bring it up to modern requirements, that prophet would have been scouted as too fantastic to be worthy the respect of serious men. But that is exactly what has happened. In the Japanese House of Representatives, in February, Mr. Oishi, one of the leaders of the progressive party, asked General Terauchi, the Minister of War, in the course of the debate on the military budget, to what extent the Japanese army would have to be increased in view of the obligations imposed upon Japan by the terms of the Anglo-Japanese treaty. The British army, Mr. Oishi added, was not up to the standard of the British navy, and he asked the Minister of War if that fact did not indicate the necessity for improvement in order that there might be no one-sided responsibility. General Terauchi briefly replied that the two governments would confer on the subject, and the matter was then dropped.

This "disregard of the common rules of international courtesy," to quote the London "Daily Mail,"was sharply criticised by the English press, the general feeling being expressed by the "Daily News" that "it is not an agreeable pill for a proud people to swallow." But Japan has too much at stake to let any false delicacy stand between her and disaster. If Japan has to take part in helping to safeguard India she naturally wants to feel that the sole responsibility is not thrown upon her shoulders; and Japanese statesmen have only to read the English newspapers, follow the debates in Parliament, and heed the warnings of such an eminent military authority as Lord Roberts, to become convinced that Great Britain is as militarily deficient now as she was when she plunged with such light heart into the South African war and Pretoria was only a handstretch away.

It is a curious thing that in matters military the English out-Bourbon the Bourbons. They learn nothing and forget everything. War, which has been more costly to them than perhaps to any other nation, conveys no lesson of experience, and the mistakes of the past are turned to no profit. In everything else, especially in trade and commerce, which demand the highest executive abilities and the qualities of specialized organization, the English have few equals. It is when they attempt to create a military machine that they go to pieces. One has only to read the investigation of the Crimean war and compare it with the War Office inquiry into the South African war, to see that the blunders of half a century earlier recurred with almost mathematical exactness. There was much talk in England, after the Transvaal, of a new order of things, but it is to be doubted whether England is in any better shape now to wage an offensive war of large proportions than she was five years ago. It is no wonder that Japan, the very embodiment of preciseness, system, and readiness for action, should want to know whether her ally is equally ready. And yet none the less marvellous is it that Japan should teach England the lesson.

And soon the world will come to realize that Japan is not the only great power in the Far East. If the world does not want to experience a shock as great as that caused by the emergence of Japan from the obscurity of bits of delicate porcelain and quaintly colored paper birds and fishes to the blazoning light revealed by army corps and battleships, it will keep its eye carefully centred on China, for in China the sleeper is awakening. It has more than once been said in this department that a new spirit has been born in China, a spirit that bodes no ill to the world if the world will readjust its point of view. The day is fast closing when China will meekly submit to being treated as the Cinderella among nations; when with sub-

31

missive humility she will permit herself to be kicked and cuffed for the pleasure and profit of aliens; when with a Christian humility more Christian than all the Christian nations she will turn her cheek to the aggressor. The world were blind if it were unable to interpret the signs. The American boycott is only one of many. It is the outward and visible sign of the twentieth-century struggle for liberty in Asia, exactly as "the year of revolution" was the struggle of continental Europe, in the last century, to free herself. The boycott is magnificent. There is something more ennobling than trade statistics and piece goods; case oil and barrels of flour are not the sole reasons to justify civilization. If justice can be secured only by attacking trade, then China has at last discovered the vulnerable joint in the armor of Western civilization.

But China has done more than merely to decline to trade in certain commodities. She has begun to assert her independence. The recent Shanghai riots were a manifestation of this. It has been for so long a matter of course for Europeans to bully China, that the consular officers in that country, in the exercise of extra-territoriality, have transcended even the broadest construction of the treaties, counting on the submissiveness of the Chinese not to make resistance. To be suddenly confronted with resistance, to find Chinese officials standing up for what are clearly their rights, comes as a shock. The remedy, of course, is obvious. There is always a gunboat near at hand, there are always marines ready to be landed, and an army of invasion is never far distant. Before force China quails and yields, but not forever. China is struggling not only against the oppressor from without, but also against the oppressor from within. When the power of the ruling class is struck down and a progressive government rises on the ruins of a slavish adherence to the past, China will deal with the world on level terms, as an equal and not as an inferior.

If the Western nations had the courage of their greed and were not more afraid of each other than they are of China, they would do now what a few years hence it will be impossible for them to do. They would partition China. That could be done with comparative ease, for China is a weakling in the grasp of these military giants. But when the Western nations confront a resolute, determined, armed China they will hesitate long before attempting a task so stupendous.

A resolute, determined, armed China is a world-wide terrifying spectre. But again I venture to advance the opinion that has been before expressed in these pages, that the world has nothing to fear from China, no matter how formidable, if China is civilized in the Western sense and becomes a competitor for the commerce of the world. She may reduce the dividends of our Southern cotton mills, which would be unfortunate for their stockholders, but it would not be the first time that the centre of a manufacturing industry has shifted, to the temporary injury of individuals and the advantage of a people. The laws of trade are as immutable as those of nature, for they are based on nature's most primal and most scientific, albeit most brutal, law, the survival of the fittest, and it is a law which man cannot combat. Commerce and wanton military aggression do not go hand-in-hand, for the commercial nation has no surplus energy to waste in military adventures; they are too costly ever to be profitable. The history of the world is the history of nations striving for trade and only fighting when they are forced to. Why should China prove the solitary exception?

Things go from bad to worse in the conflict between the Emperor of Austria and the Hungarian Nationalists, and an attempt on the part of Hungary to dissolve the union, as she essayed to do forty-six years ago, may not improbably be the outcome. On the nineteenth of February the Hungarian Diet was dissolved by royal rescript; Parliament was literally turned out of doors, just as Cromwell by military force put an end to its sitting in England; and Hungary is now governed by a cabinet that has been out of sympathy for a long time with the representative assembly. The old Emperor has done a shrewd, although possibly a very dangerous, thing in his attempt to deprive the Hungarians of power because of their insistence that words of command in the army shall be given both in Hungarian and German, instead of solely in German, as the Emperor stubbornly decrees. Hungary is merely a geographical expression, as the Hungarians proper, that is the Magyars, form less than one-half of the population, the remainder consisting of Croats, Serbians, Wallachians, and a goodly sprinkling of the forty-odd races that go to make up that modern Babel known as Austria-Hungary. Yet although the Magyars are numerically in the minority, by gerrymandering districts and other political devices they exercise a preponderating influence in the Diet. This power the Magyars are to be deprived of by the grant of what is practically universal suffrage, which would reduce the Magyars to their proper proportionate representation. Very naturally the Magyars have resisted this, and the Diet has been dissolved. The Magyars contend that the proposed extension of the suffrage is unconstitutional, inasmuch as the Emperor of Austria, who is also King of Hungary, and as such rules Hungary by virtue of the Hungarian constitution, has no power to modify the constitution except with the permission of the Diet. As the Diet has refused to sanction a change in the basis of representation, the Emperor has been guilty of an unconstitutional act, which, the Hungarian Nationalists assert, it is their duty to obstruct because it is a curtailment of their rights and is opposed by the Hungarian nation.

In taking this stand the Nationalists have placed themselves in an indefensible position. If their contention is true—that is, if the extension of the suffrage is not desired by Hungary as a nation, and is merely an Austrian trick to deprive them of their rights — it is at least curious that they should fear to have the question submitted to the judgment of the country. The reason, of course, is obvious. The Magyars would be defeated, and the dominating power of the Magyar element in the dual Empire would be destroyed. What the outcome will be it is impossible to predict, but unless Francis Joseph is willing to see the union dissolved he must, if the Magyars are foolish enough to provoke a conflict, meet force with force. There can be no peaceful rupture of the dual kingdom such as there was of Sweden and Norway. The geographical and political position of Austria-Hungary, unlike that of Sweden and Norway, makes it vital for the salvation of Austria — and in a measure no less for that of Hungary — that there be no segregation of the Empire. It is a critical time in Austrian affairs, and unless there shall be more moderation and wiser statesmanship shown than has hitherto been displayed on both sides, a conflict seems inevitable.

At this time of writing the conference at Algeciras, called to devise a settlement of the Moroccan question, is still in session without an agreement having been reached, which has led some of the professional pessimists in the leading European capitals to see a break-up of the conference and war between France and Germany as a consequence, the offensive to be taken by Germany. Reasons why the present writer refuses to believe that the German Emperor is always looking for an opportunity to make war on all the rest of the world, have before been advanced in these pages, and nothing that has happened in the last few months warrants any reversal of that opinion. The German Emperor is an amazingly adroit diplomatist, and he is playing diplomacy with his usual skill; in fact, it would not be unparliamentary, nor would one be guilty of *lèse majesté*, to term it bluff. He bluffed France into calling a conference to discuss Morocco, and when the delegation assembled at Algeciras he bluffed from the beginning to the end. So threatening did he become at times that he bluffed his opponents into believing that he was ready to fight if needs be to carry his point; but I doubt if he had any real intention to fight, for the simple reason that Germany cannot afford to fight unless she is absolutely sure that she will win, and of that outcome she can by no means be certain. Single-handed, Germany might meet France and defeat her; but as a war over Morocco would not be a duel between France and Germany, and would bring in England as the ally of France, with the possibility of other powers becoming involved, the Kaiser would be a madman if he plunged with such desperate odds against him. And the Kaiser is no madman. He may bluff, he may bully, he may bluster, according to circumstance, but that does not indicate madness. The German Emperor will fight, but not until he sees at least an even chance for victory and can feel certain that he will not have to pay too dear a price for victory.

He could gain nothing by war now, unless by war he could bring both France and England to the verge of ruin and exact from them such a heavy indemnity that they would be unable to repair the damages of war, and as military powers cease to exist. But not even the most rabid Anglophobe in Germany believes that to be possible. The best that could happen, from the German standpoint, would be the defeat of France, because England cannot be reached; even the Germans admit that an invasion of England is impossible. But at what cost would Germany purchase her victory? The French army, unless military observers are greatly at fault, is vastly more efficient than the armies Moltke crushed thirty-five years ago, and the march from the Rhine to the Seine, conceding that a German army for the second time battered at the gates of Paris, could only be made at a tremendous sacrifice of men and money. Indemnities, no matter how large, cannot make men or replace in the industrial ranks those who have fallen in battle. Germany wants her sons in her factories; she needs them in trade competition with England, not to be killed by English shells or to be carried down to their death in German battleships sunk in the North Sea; and a war with England would mean the annihilation of the German navy, and leave Germany at the mercy of any power with half-a-dozen battleships.

It is impossible to conceive that the Emperor wants war or that he can be so foolish as to provoke war, when there is so much to lose and so little to gain. And once more it is pertinent to ask, What can he gain? There are no more French provinces that he covets; the colonies of France are not worth the price he would have to pay for them. It is true that a crushed France and a weakened Russia would give Germany nothing to fear for a decade or two, but it would take her at least a decade to recover from the strain of the war, and while she was recovering England and the United States would be vigorously pressing forward to supply the world with commodities that are now furnished by Germany. If Germany went to war, the real gainers would be her two most formidable commercial rivals, the United States and Great Britain. For these reasons I do not believe that Germany meditates war. But we have not heard the last of war talk, and shall not so long as a man of such audacity and ability as Kaiser Wilhelm II. is the ruler of the German Empire.

A. MAURICE LOW.

APPLIED SCIENCE.

TRANSPORTATION problems continue to occupy a large share of the attention of the engineer. Whether it be for merchandise or passengers, over land or over sea, in the transformation of motive power or the reconstruction of old routes and the opening of new ones, the best efforts of the engineering profession in all parts of the world are directed toward the application of scientific methods to the improvement of means of transport. Nearly every method of conveying goods or men from place to place appears to be in a state of transformation, and systems considered wellnigh perfect but a year or two ago are already falling into the second class, or even becoming obsolete.

Thus, in railroading, electric traction is passing from the uncertainty of the experimental stage into the intermediate state in which the question is rather the choice of system than the feasibility of the change. The problems of continuous or alternating currents, of single-phase or polyphase motors, demand attention, while the desirability of replacing steam by electricity has almost passed beyond discussion.

This is not because the steam locomotive is an especially wasteful machine. The recent trials of modern locomotive engines in connection with the testing plant of the Pennsylvania Railroad Company at the St. Louis exposition demonstrated very clearly that the steam locomotive is a much more efficient machine than had been generally supposed. Thus, some of the four-cylinder compound locomotives tested at St. Louis developed a horse-power from as little as 16.60 pounds of steam, and even the simple engines gave performances as low as 23.43 pounds; these records comparing very favorably with the results accomplished by non-condensing stationary engines.

There are other things to be considered besides fuel economy, however, things which in some situations become of controlling importance. The growing tendency to provide underground entrances into the terminals at great cities and the necessity for the use of tunnels in many instances give electricity an incontestable advantage. For the present, electric traction will be used to radiate fan-like from the great centres within whose limits the steam locomotive will soon be forbidden to enter, although the travelling power house will continue yet for a time to serve for the long-distance through traffic; picking up the trains where the electric locomotives drop them, at points from thirty to fifty miles beyond the terminals. This much is conceded, nay, almost accomplished already, and the present feature of interest to the engineer appears in the respective merits of the direct and the alternating currents.

The direct or continuous current has had great advantage in possession of the field, practically without a rival, from the inception of electric traction. It has thus acquired certain claims to consideration, some of which appear stronger than they really are. It is the general opinion, for example, that the continuous-current electric motor is susceptible of a great range of speed control without difficulty; and this opinion is largely confirmed by the manner in which the electric tram-car progresses through crowded city streets, responding to the manipulation of a pair of levers in the hands of a man of about the same order of intelligence as his mate who collects the fares, or his predecessor who handled the reins on the horse-car. As a matter of fact, however, the continuous-current motor is a one-speed machine, the speed depending upon the voltage, and varied by the use of resistances, an operation about as economical as it would be to control the speed of a team of horses by the brake. When, as in most tram-car systems, two motors are used, speed changes may be secured by operating them in series or in parallel; but in general the speed regulation of the continuous-current motor is by no means satisfactory, a fact long since made apparent in connection with the use of electric driving in the machine shop.

With the use of the alternating current the transformer is carried on the car or locomotive; and by tapping the winding of the transformer at successive points, a corresponding series of changes in voltage may be obtained, thus giving the alternating-current motor better opportunity for graduated speed control than any other type. The high voltage used in the line wire with the alternating current offers an especial advantage in the collection of the current by the contact device on the car. With the large consumption of current now demanded for the propulsion of heavy trains, the overhead wire and under-running trolley of the street-railway car must be replaced by something more substantial, in order that sparking and burning of contacts may be avoided. The third rail, now extensively used for elevated and underground electric railways, is by no means satisfactory, both because of danger and by reason of difficulties with insulation, but it appears to be the best that can be done with the direct current. When the higher voltage alternating current is employed, however, a smaller conductor and a light sliding contact may be used. Both systems are soon to be given practical working trials on a large scale: the continuous current by the New York Central and Hudson River Railroad, on its tracks entering New York City, and the alternating-current locomotives on the New York, New Haven, and Hartford system, between New Haven and New York.

Passing from railway traction on main lines, we turn to passenger transport in large cities, and there find similar transformations in progress. In London the automobile omnibus is coming into active service, and replacing the venerable horse-drawn vehicle to great advantage. Paris, the home of the automobile, has, curiously enough, been slower than London to introduce the mechanically propelled omnibus; but this tardiness has been explained by the greater cost of the fuel, the duty, and the octroi taxes, bringing the cost of petroleum essence in Paris to more than double the price in London. In spite of this handicap the motor omnibus is now appearing in the streets of Paris, and its general introduction will depend mainly upon questions of manufacture.

Apart from changes in transport upon the surface, the developments in underground communication continue. The old London underground has now been converted from steam to electric traction, to its manifest improvement. In Paris the extension of the *Métropolitain* goes on, and soon all parts of the city will be rendered easily accessible. In New York the existing subway has been in operation only long enough to show its merits and its defects, and to enable the plans for further structures of a similar nature to be made with certain reasonable and effective improvements. There was never any necessity for providing a bacterial culture-bed about the tracks in front of each station, nor should the ventilation problem have been left to a mere afterthought. Passengers should not have been compelled to pass in opposing currents in leaving and boarding trains; and there is no reason why the flow of people should not be given at least as much attention as the engineer gives to the flow of steam, air, or gas. In the light of these and other similar experiences, there is reason to believe that subways for passenger traffic may be built, in the immediate future, which shall be reasonably comfortable, satisfactory, and hygienic.

Transport by water is another branch of applied science which is in a state of transformation. In transatlantic navigation the question of turbine propulsion is being studied in the only practicable way — by building vessels of various sizes and speeds, and fitting them with turbine engines for use in actual service. Already the *Caronia* and the *Carmania* have been put into active commission, these two vessels being identical in dimensions and displacement, and differing only in their engines, the latter having steam turbines of the Parsons type and the former being fitted with vertical reciprocating engines. These vessels are of the intermediate class, as regards speed, making no pretensions to compete with the record-breakers, but giving steady and satisfactory service at a speed of about seventeen knots. No official reports have yet been given out as to the comparative fuel consumption of the two ships; but the turbines have proven themselves reliable in operation and free from the vibration which, even with the most scientific counterbalancing, cannot be wholly obviated with engines in which large masses are set in rapid motion and brought to rest twice in every revolution of the propeller shaft.

While the motive-power machinery of large vessels is thus in a transition stage, and the completion of the 70,000 horse-power turbines of the new Cunard flyers is impending, there has also been accomplished a transformation in the engines for the smallest type of craft. Until very recently the swiftest small boats were driven by light and powerful steam engines supplied with steam of very high pressure from water-tube boilers of remarkable steaming capacity. The names of the *Norwood*, the *Fei-Seen*, the *Yankee Doodle*, and other similar craft are well known as representing the high-water mark of this department of engineering work. These and other flyers, however, are now almost obsolete through the introduction of the so-called "motor-boat," in which the steam engine and boiler have been replaced by the internal-combustion motor, identical in design, lightness, and power with engines of modern automobiles.

As a pendant to the development of vessels for merchandise transport, a vast amount of engineering work is being planned and executed in connection with the enlargement and improvement of the ports between which the traffic must be maintained. In the last issue of THE FORUM I referred to the review of existing ports and their limitations, by Mr. Brysson Cunningham, and to the necessity, in most instances, for harbor improvements as preceding any great increase in the dimensions of vessels. A notable exception to the contracted entrances of most of the great seaports of the world is found in the harbors situated on the Puget Sound, and an important factor in the development of the Pacific coast appears in the great advantages possessed by this region. Mr. Cunningham spoke of Tacoma as typical of this favored region, but the entire Sound forms a natural deep-water harbor, upon which such ports as Seattle, for instance, can receive vessels like the *Minnesota* or *Dakota*, with a draught of thirty-eight feet, regardless of tide or channel considerations.

Ports which are not so favored by nature, but which, by reason of their commercial situation, have become great trade centres, must compensate by engineering works for what they lack in natural advantages. Probably one of the most ambitious schemes for harbor improvement which have yet been devised is that for the development of the port of Antwerp. Here it is proposed to make a cut-off by constructing an entirely new channel for a portion of the river Scheldt, straightening the route for navigation, besides providing space for a number of new docks, and giving a depth of thirty-seven to forty feet of water at high tide. The old curve of the river is to be kept as a great basin, 1,465 acres in area, with a dam at the lower end to maintain the level independently of the flow of water in the new channel. It is estimated that these new works, to be undertaken solely to enable the port of Antwerp to keep pace with the demands created by the development of marine construction, will cost the Belgian Government the sum of 287,000,000 francs, or about $57,400,000. The result will be to render Antwerp the finest port on the North Sea, and compel improvements of a similar nature in the ports competing with the enterprising city on the Scheldt.

Already there is talk of improving work at other ports. The barrage on the Thames, in connection with the extension of the harbor and dock facilities at London, I have previously referred to in these pages. The idea of duplicating the Suez Canal is being revived, although without any immediate prospect of accomplishment.

At Panama the work should now assume a more active phase, since the President has overruled the majority report of the advisory board of engineers, and decided upon the minority plan for a lock canal with a summit level of 85 feet. There is no doubt whatever that a lock canal will answer satisfactorily at first, and probably for a number of years. It is extremely unsafe, however, to predict the limitations of any department of engineering work, and the dimensions of the locks will necessarily have to be based upon present judgment of future requirements. With due regard for the ability of the eminent American hydraulic engineers who have advocated the lock canal, and whose views have been accepted by the administration, it must not be forgotten that all the European engineers, united in recommending the sea-level plan, have had active experience in the operation as well as the construction of ship canals, and their opinions should not be lightly cast aside.

Probably the most extensive experience to be found in connection with the handling of large sea-going vessels in canal locks exists on the Manchester ship canal; and the engineer of that canal, Mr. W. Henry Hunter, joined with the engineers of the Suez and the Kiel canals in recommending the sea-level plan for the waterway at the Panama isthmus. It is to be regretted that the members of the advisory board could not have agreed upon a unanimous report, relieving the administration from the responsibility of passing upon what is purely an engineering question, and leaving the matter in a position for the free exercise of executive and administrative ability. The questions of cost and time are wholly secondary in a work of this magnitude, for which the world has been waiting for centuries, and which is to serve the world for centuries to come, until transport by water shall be replaced by navigation through the air.

So far as aerial navigation itself is considered, there is nothing new to report, and yet there has been undoubted progress. The Lebaudy dirigible balloon has shown itself of sufficient importance to be under critical examination by the experts of the French army, though there is small prospect of any apparatus of this type proving of much value in active warfare. A more interesting matter is the well-authenticated report that the French Government has acquired an interest in the latest machine of the Wright brothers, of Dayton, Ohio. I have frequently referred in these reviews to the excellent work which these experimenters have done in connection with gliding flight, taking up the experiments of the lamented Lilienthal, and making a number of valuable discoveries concerning the area and form of supporting planes as well as in the all-important problem of balancing. The published accounts of the experiments of the Wright brothers relate wholly to gliding, the impetus being obtained by leaping from a hillock or other point of elevation. But it is credibly reported that they have succeeded in applying a propelling motor to the aeroplane and in accomplishing independent flight, and it is this combination which has appealed to the French Government with sufficient force to warrant the sending of a special commissioner to the United States to secure the control of such a vital element of warfare. In this connection it is interesting to remember that the offer which Fulton made of his steamboat to Napoleon's government, just about a hundred years ago, was rejected by a committee of scientists, *amis des arts*, as they were called, one of whom was Montgolfier himself, the inventor of the balloon.

Several months ago, in noting the progress which had been made in extending the line of railway in South Africa forming a portion of the route ultimately destined to connect the Cape of Good Hope with Cairo and the Mediterranean, I referred to the fact that the opening up of the interior of Africa depends largely upon the construction of lateral lines of railway from internal points to the sea coast. Some such lines have already been constructed and are in successful operation, notably the Uganda railway, extending from Mombassa to the Victoria Nyanza, and the French railway systems in Algeria and in Senegal, reaching out to grasp the Sahara.

The latest railway opened in Africa is the new line inaugurated in January, extending from Port Soudan on the Red Sea to Berber on the Nile, 170 miles below Khartoum. This line, extending 325 miles through the Soudan, opens up a region otherwise accessible only through the intermittent connection by river and rail from the Mediterranean, a distance of more than 1,200 miles, while now the interior of the Soudan is reached in a few hours from the sea. This line is but the beginning of a system reaching the Abyssinian frontier and connecting with Khartoum, and ultimately with the Cape-to-Cairo system, so that the whole of one of the most difficult portions of Africa will be thrown into communication with the rest of the world, and no longer remain isolated.

In the last issue of THE FORUM I referred to the fact that the amount of hydraulic power to be derived from the Victoria Falls on the Zambesi is much less than is generally supposed. Nevertheless, plans have been formed for the development of the hydraulic power of the falls and the electrical transmission of the energy to the Rand, and there has been more or less discussion as to the feasibility of the project.

It has been computed that about 500,000 horse power may be taken from the Victoria Falls, and there is no doubt that this, or any desired portion of it, might be transmitted electrically to the Rand. The question is rather a commercial than a technical one. It has already been shown that the real limit to the commercial distance is that of cost compared with the selling price at the far end of the line. The working district of the Rand is about 750 miles from the falls of the Zambesi, and at the present time there is used in the mining and other operations about 150,000 horse power. The plans contemplate the transmission at first of 20,000 horse power, at a pressure of 100,000 volts. The matter appears to depend upon the relative cost of power developed on the spot from coal and that transmitted from the falls. The initial cost of the transmission plant and line will burden the latter system with heavy interest and depreciation charges, and the question is an open one.

For some time there have been no developments of special interest in connection with space telegraphy, but there has been a continually increasing proficiency in the use of apparatus, and a general improvement in working efficiency. For distances under 150 miles the simple untuned system of Marconi is employed, and for use on ocean steamers for making communications between passing vessels, or with the shore, this is effective and convenient.

When it is desired to produce selective effects, so that a station shall respond only to the messages especially intended for it, some method of tuning or discrimination must be employed. The principle now generally used is that of superposing one set of vibrations upon another. Thus, if at a station there is an oscillator having a certain predetermined rate of an amplitude too small to actuate the receiving mechanism, and a series of oscillations of the same rate are delivered from a distant transmitting station, the combined influence of the two sets of similar oscillations will cause the receiver to be affected, while the appearance of waves of any other rate will produce no effect. Various methods are used to produce the effects thus broadly described, but the principle in all is the same. Some time ago Mr. Marconi discovered that wireless messages were delivered more effectively, and over greater distances, by night than by day, and more recent investigations appear to indicate that there is a distinct periodicity during the twenty-four hours, with two points at which there is a maximum of efficiency in transmission, and two minimum points. The actual causes for these periodic effects have not yet been clearly determined, but it is supposed that they must be produced by the action of the sun upon the electrical properties of the atmosphere.

I have mentioned from time to time the suggestions which have been made in connection with the construction of some sort of a fluid-pressure wheel, similar to the steam turbine, but driven by the gases of combustion, this forming a gas turbine, and enabling continuous rotary motion to be produced instead of the extremely intermittent action of the ordinary gas engine. The idea of a gas turbine is really very old, probably the earliest operative machine of the kind being the mediæval turn-spit, in which a sort of propeller wheel on a vertical axis, placed up the chimney, was caused to revolve by the velocity of the ascending gases, the motion being transmitted by cords and pulleys to the revolving spit on which the roast was placed before the fire. A well-known toy for children consists of a spiral of paper or metal, suspended over a lamp and made to revolve by the rising current of heated air. These things embody the principle of the gas turbine, the improvements necessary to convert it into a practical machine being simply those of construction.

In the machines thus far devised it has been intended to compress air to a moderate pressure, similar to the degree of compression in the cylinder of an ordinary gas engine, and permit this air to flow through a combustion nozzle, supplied with liquid fuel, into a combustion chamber, whence the products of combustion and the air, now greatly increased in volume and temperature, are discharged at a high velocity through a nozzle upon the blades or buckets of the revolving turbine wheel. This operation, theoretically practicable, involves some difficult problems when attempted to be put into execution. The high temperatures and the high rotative speeds cause much trouble, besides which much of the power generated is absorbed in driving the compressor which delivers the air to the combustion chamber. As in the case of the reciprocating gas-engine, a fairly high degree of compression, say 80 to 120 pounds to the square inch, is necessary to secure high efficiency, but no rotary compressor has yet been devised for such pressures, possessing at the same time a high efficiency. A reciprocating compressor introduces into the apparatus most of the objections to the ordinary reciprocating gas engine which the gas turbine is expected to remove, so that these constructive features must be simplified before a commercial machine can be made. In the mean time the sugges-tion has been made that experimental work with the gas turbine may be carried on in connection with the ordinary reciprocating gas engine; the turbine being driven by the discharge gases from the engine. The cylinder of the gas engine thus forms the air compressor and the combustion cham-ber, and incidentally develops more than enough power to drive itself, while the turbine utilizes the energy in the exhaust gases. By combining the exhaust of several cylinders upon a single turbine wheel, a fairly con-tinuous impulse might be maintained and valuable experience with such apparatus gained for future use.

With the rapid exhaustion of the world's supply of natural nitrate fer-tilizer, especially the sodium nitrate beds of Chili, attention is being again strongly directed to the practicability of effecting the fixation of atmos-pheric nitrogen for the manufacture of artificial nitrates. At the present time the natural deposits of Chili saltpetre are being consumed at the rate of about a million and a half tons a year, and it is estimated that the entire deposit will be exhausted by 1950. As nitrate fertilizers are essen-tial to the growth of wheat, some method must be found to meet this demand. I have already noted the method of Lovejoy and Bradley, at Niagara Falls, to fix the nitrogen of the atmosphere by utilizing the com-bining action of the electric arc, but this has unfortunately not proved a commercial success. The apparatus included a revolving drum within a hollow cylinder, the exterior of the drum and the interior of the cylinder carrying numerous platinum points between which the electric discharges took place. The air passing through the annular space had its oxygen and nitrogen partly combined to form nitric oxide, and this was delivered to towers containing water and milk of lime, the final product being calcium nitrate. The principal defects in this system were the amount of power required, and the difficulty of cooling the gases quickly, since the combi-nation is separated by an inverse action if the gases are allowed to remain hot.

Although the Lovejoy and Bradley process has not proved a commer-cial success, the principle has not been abandoned, but is being conducted in a modified manner by Birkeland and Eyde at Svaelgfoss, in Norway. This process utilizes the magnetic deflection of the electric arc as an inter-rupting device. By using alternating currents and water-cooled copper electrodes in a strong magnetic field, a powerful intermittent flaming arc is produced. When the air is passed through this flaming arc about two per cent of it is converted into nitric oxide, and this, by absorption, is used to make calcium nitrate, an available form for a fertilizer. The success which has attended the original plant at Christiania has led to the extension of the works at Svaelgfoss, where 30,000 hydraulic horse power will be applied to the process, and it is confidently expected that a product will be obtained which can compete with the natural nitrate.

The production of liquid air was hailed at first as an achievement of great possibilities, but the very extravagance of the early claims made for its applications rendered its uselessness the more conspicuous. Of late, however, it has been found that liquid air has one very practical application, that of enabling pure oxygen to be produced on a commercial scale. By taking advantage of the difference in the boiling points of liquid oxygen and liquid nitrogen, it has been found possible to separate them from each other by fractional distillation; and by using the reduction in temperature caused by the evaporation of the liquefied gases to cool the incoming charge of air to be compressed, the whole apparatus is operated with a high degree of efficiency. Another method of obtaining pure oxygen is by the electrolytic decomposition of water; but in a recent communication to the French Academy, M. Georges Claude states that he now has in operation a plant of a capacity of 1,000 cubic metres of oxygen, 96 to 98 per cent pure, in twenty-four hours, using the process of the rectification of liquid air, the cost being only one-twentieth of that required for the electrolysis of water.

The possession of an ample supply of pure oxygen, apart from its value in medicine, is an important addition to the resources of the engineer and manufacturer. The oxy-hydrogen blowpipe is no longer a piece of laboratory apparatus only. It has become a workshop tool, and by its use pieces of the most intricate shape in iron or steel may be rapidly and economically welded. The theoretical temperature attainable with the oxy-hydrogen blowpipe is about 2,400° C.; and in actual practice, using the Wanner optical pyrometer upon a mass of magnesite exposed to the heat of the blowpipe jet, a temperature of 2,100° C. is reached. A recent application of the jet is found in the division of heavy steel plates, and it is possible so to concentrate the high temperature that a narrow cut may be fused through a plate with rapidity and smoothness. In practice the best results are obtained by using the oxy-hydrogen blowpipe followed closely by a jet of pure oxygen, this latter completing the operation by burning the metal itself along the line which the blowpipe has already raised to a high temperature.

Still higher temperatures may be reached by the use of acetylene in the blowpipe in place of the hydrogen, and it has been claimed that with the oxy-acetylene blowpipe a heat of 3,600° C. is reached. Pyrometer tests, however, show a temperature of 2,340° C.; but the actual heat of the oxy-acetylene jet is probably somewhere between these two figures. It must be remembered that these extremely high heats are produced within a very limited area, practically only at the point of the jet, and in this fact lies the working value of the apparatus. There are no great radiation losses. The heat can be directed exactly upon the point to be affected and the surrounding parts, and thus a seam can be welded, a hole perforated, or a plate cut with precision and economy. The apparatus can be taken to the work, and much heavy handling avoided, so that the successful solution of a laboratory problem, the commercial production of oxygen, has added a new tool to the workshop.

The organization of a new technical society, devoted to the subject of the production of artificial illumination, calls attention to the enormous growth in recent years of this department of applied science. It is estimated that in the United States alone there is involved for artificial light a yearly expenditure of not less than $200,000,000, of which one-half is for electric lighting, one-sixth for gas, and one-third for oil; not taking into account the limited use of natural gas and acetylene for lighting.

The need for special attention to this department of engineering appears in the fact that probably at least $20,000,000 of this yearly bill for light is wasted. That is to say, fully ten per cent of the light produced is lost through improper application, apart from any of the wastes which may have been incurred in its actual production. In many cases, especially when the electric light is used, more than twenty-five per cent of the illuminating effect is absorbed by the use of unsuitable globes, shades, or reflectors, as well as by improper distribution of the sources of light.

It has often been said that by far the best illumination which is given to public streets is not from the street lamps themselves, but from the brightly lighted shop windows, electric signs, and other private sources of artificial light. This fact in itself indicates the wasteful manner in which the light is thrown out into the highway and, incidentally, into the eyes of the passers-by, instead of being directed upon the objects within, where its effect is really desired. In some advanced manufacturing establishments it is now understood that the maintenance of white walls and ceilings, reflecting and distributing the light which is thrown upon them, while the eyes of the operatives are screened from the glare of the direct rays from the lamps, gives the best results. In like manner the encouragement of the use of light-colored buildings, upon which the rays of powerful and highly efficient electric lamps can be directed, would go a long way toward the improvement of the illumination of public streets.

Much of the inefficiency of modern lighting appliances lies in the use of attachments and methods inherited from the earlier days when more primitive apparatus was necessary. A lamp, requiring the draught of an ascending column of heated air, and fed from a reservoir of "spillable" liquid, necessarily demanded a support beneath it, and the consequent shadow was accepted as inevitable. To-day we see similar designs repeated and imitated for use with lamps capable of being held in any position, and fed with an imponderable supply of energy through a cold and flexible wire. This is but one example of inefficiency in the use of modern lighting appliances. There are many others which will reveal themselves upon inspection. Ample opportunity exists for the illuminating engineer to show what he can do.

Some time ago I called attention to the extensive freight subway system which has been constructed under the streets of Chicago, and spoke of the effectiveness of such a method for relieving the surface congestion. The electric equipment of the system is now about completed, and it is expected that the full service will be inaugurated by the middle of the present year. The capacity of the system is given as 30,000 tons of freight daily. In considering this statement it must be remembered that the subway cannot be compared with an ordinary surface railroad, since it is equipped with small cars, capable of being raised on elevators into the basements and cellars of the establishments served, while the principal purpose of the system is to handle the detailed merchandise of the business establishments of the city, and to constitute a distribution system, practically replacing the work of the teamsters. It is interesting to note that the Chicago subway system cost about $20,000,000, or thirty per cent more than the Simplon tunnel, and about one-seventh the estimated cost of the Panama canal.

One of the important elements of the work of the engineer is the provision of mechanical appliances and methods for doing as much as possible of the work formerly performed by human and animal labor. Thus, in the case of the Chicago freight subways, noted above, much of the handling of merchandise through the streets of the city will be done more expeditiously, cheaply, and unobtrusively by machinery. When, as is too often the case, controversial difficulties arise to add to the unavoidable physical obstructions to be overcome, it is especially the function of the engineer to devise methods and appliances for relieving the strain.

A notable example of such work is seen in the enormous increase in the methods of construction by which brickwork is superseded by concrete. Brickwork masonry involves a large amount of skilled labor of a restricted sort, frequently liable to interruptions and difficulties. With the general introduction of concrete, reinforced by embedded metallic members in the

32

form of rods, lattice-work, netting, and the like, a vast amount of structural work, formerly dependent upon the skill of the bricklayer, becomes possible with a smaller amount of labor furnished from sources readily acessible, and less liable to interruption.   The complated work is generally more satisfactory and more permanent, as well as more rapid of execution, than brickwork, while in most cases the cost of the concrete is far below that of the laid masonry.

An especial application of reinforced concrete, and one which is widely extending, is that of replacing timber as a material in the construction of piles for foundations.   The use of piles of timber, driven firmly into the ground for foundations and supports in soft or sandy soil, is of very ancient date.   Such a method was employed by the Romans, while among many modern nations the system is used to provide foundations for buildings of magnitude.   Practically all the important structures in Venice and in Amsterdam rest upon wooden piles driven into the mud by the impact of falling weights, great masses of masonry thus resting upon buried forests of tree-trunks.   The timber pile is now being extensively replaced by the pile of reinforced concrete.   Such piles are made of several vertical rods of steel, fitted to a pointed metal shoe at the bottom, and wrapped around with a spiral binding of heavy wire, the whole being filled and surrounded with concrete, and forming a pillar of artificial stone in the midst of which is a steel skeleton.   Concrete piles are effectively sunk by the water-jet method, a powerful stream of water being directed upon the mud or sand where the point of the shoe is resting.   A moderate pressure causes the pile to follow the excavation made by the water jet, and thus the concrete pillar is sunk to a depth dependent upon the nature of the soil. In some cases a pipe is embedded in the axis of the pile, thus enabling the water jet to be delivered through the pile itself, and the sinking is rapidly and effectively accomplished.   Such piles have the great advantage of being immune from decay, the alkaline concrete preventing the oxidation of the embedded steel, while the ravages of the teredo, so fatal to timber piles in marine structures, are rendered impossible.

Another important department of engineering work is that which relates to the construction and arrangement of buildings so as to provide against danger or loss of life by fire.   Especially important is it that places of public assembly, theatres, concert halls, auditoriums, and the like, should be constructed with every precaution known to science as applied to fire protection.   In view of the attention at present devoted to the prevention of such dangers in theatres, it is of much interest to note the experimental investigations recently conducted in Vienna by the Austrian Society of Engineers and Architects.   These experiments were made upon á small building, reproducing as nearly as practicable the relative proportions and arrangements of an actual theatre, the building being made of reinforced concrete, so that it might be used for repeated tests without requiring reconstruction. The results of a number of tests showed that practical safety to the audience could be assured if suitable openings were provided above the stage, to give an outlet for the smoke and gases of combustion and permit a strong upward draught to be created. Both in form and action the proscenium arch of a theatre resembles the opening of an ordinary fireplace in a room, the difference being principally one of dimensions. When a chimney is obstructed, the smoke and gases from a newly lighted fire pour out from under the fireplace arch into the room. In like manner, in a theatre the absence of any opening above the stage into the outer air causes the smoke and flames from a fire to roll out under the proscenium arch, to suffocate those in the upper galleries and create panic and disaster below. No fire-proof curtain can hold the pressure of expanding air and gases back upon the stage; whereas, if a free opening exists above, no curtain at all is necessary, since the pressure is converted into suction and the flow is the other way. Many detailed devices have been suggested for the prompt and automatic opening of vents above the stage in case of fire, but the principle has been established beyond possibility of doubt.

Increasing attention is being paid by engineers to the subject of the abatement of noise. The mechanical equivalent of sound does not yet appear to have been determined, in the sense in which we have a mechanical equivalent of heat, for instance; but it is well understood that the production of noise involves the consumption of mechanical energy and that it means a waste of money. The best machinery runs quietly, and any unusual or excessive noise is taken as an indication of wear, of imperfect action, or of loss. The fact that many operations involve the production of noise is simply an evidence of the inefficient manner in which they are conducted. Sometimes it cannot be helped, more often it is simply neglected. When it is really necessary to produce powerful sounds the amount of energy required is better appreciated, as, for instance, when it is found that a steam or gas engine of many horse power is required to operate a coast-signal siren. There is a story told of a certain tug-boat which was fitted with such a large whistle that the engines had to be stopped when the whistle was blown, the boiler being incapable of supplying both at the same time. However this may be, it is interesting to learn that the whole question of the production of noise is becoming a subject for technical study, both for the purpose of economizing mechanical energy, and incidentally for the relief of the strain, already too great, upon the human nervous system.   HENRY HARRISON SUPLEE.

FINANCE.

We saw in the last number of The Forum the rather extraordinary position in which the security and money markets had been left by the events of the autumn. A speculative movement of unusually large proportions, based on borrowed money and involving the virtual cornering of several stocks with an outstanding capital ranging from $25,000,000 to $70,000,-000, had been undertaken at the very time when both home and foreign money markets were beginning to tighten. The rise in stocks and the stringency in money continued simultaneously. The time at length arrived when the twenty-five per cent ratio of reserves to deposit liabilities required by law from the national banks was impaired; a substantial deficit was substituted; and simultaneously the call money rate on Wall Street advanced to figures not reached since the " Boer War panic "in the autumn of 1899. Instead of abandoning the effort to put up stocks, that movement was continued, and in the closing week of the year the remarkable spectacle was witnessed of call money at 125 per cent—and the stock market, nevertheless, advancing steadily. Under such unusual conditions, almost unparalleled in American finance, the new year opened.

The situation at the opening of January was peculiar in many ways. No one denied that the country's commercial and industrial outlook was as bright as it had been pictured by the most enthusiastic optimists of September. In all departments of production and exchange, signs of the wholesome condition were manifest. It is probable that there has not been a time in recent years, with the possible exception of the last months of 1900, when every section of the United States shared so equally in the prosperity of the hour. The same story of material welfare and busy industry came from the iron and steel manufactories of the East, from the wheat district of the Northwest, and from the cotton section of the South. At the opening of the year the aggregate of checks passed through the country's clearing houses surpassed all records. The total of such exchanges for December ran ten per cent beyond 1905, and exceeded by more than $4,000,000,000 any previous December's record in the country's history. Exchanges in the United States during January ran thirty-seven per cent ahead of 1905, and not only exceeded by $5,000,000,000 any other January total, but were actually more than double the January results in 1900, or in any preceding year. But in so far as this active exchange of credits signified exceptionally busy industry and trade, it involved a demand on the country's money supply probably unprecedented in our history; and the question immediately at issue was whether this very activity was not bound to draw so heavily on the general stock of capital as to leave no great margin over for the use of speculators.

It was precisely this difficulty which the wealthy operators had encountered in their manœuvres to put up stocks during the last two months of 1905. It had been argued from the beginning of that movement that once the month of January should be reached, money conditions would be easy and the rise of prices would continue without the assistance of manipulators. This reasoning had done much to retain the support of outside investors and speculators in the anomalous market of November and December. There were, however, two manifestly weak points in the argument — one, that it made no allowance for the extent to which such a condition had, in Wall Street phrase, been discounted by the autumn movement of prices; the other, that it took as little into reckoning the question whether the extreme stringency of money during December did not mean that the strain was bound to continue if the demands of Wall Street were to be as great in subsequent months as they had been in the last months of 1905.

The usual course of events in the money market is that completion of large cash payments incident to the harvest season will release such sums of ready cash that interior banks will ship their surplus back to New York City, thus repleting Eastern bank reserves. Next, after the gathering together of cash for disbursements in the January interest and dividends, it is expected that large sums of cash will come back on deposit from the recipients of such payments. The collection of this dividend money is one reason for the familiar stringency in the last days of December; its disbursement and return explains the ease which usually follows during the opening weeks of January. We have seen that the automatic return of harvest money to the East did not occur at the end of 1905 as had been expected, and we have found the reason to have been that the very activity in Western trade, to which attention has been so frequently called, necessitated retention of a good part of this cash by Western banks.

The January disbursements, however, stood on a somewhat different basis, and it was natural enough that despite the 125 per cent money market in the last days of December the rate should decline perceptibly at the opening of January. And this in fact occurred. On the first business day of January, call loans were made at sixty per cent. On the second day fifty per cent was the highest figure; on the third, the maximum was twenty-two per cent; and, on the fourth, ten per cent was the best rate reached. By the middle of the ensuing week call money had got down to six per cent; by the close of January four per cent was the ruling rate on call, while time loans, which had ended the previous month at a rate equivalent to twelve per cent, fell below five.

With this decline in the money rate, and the simultaneous rise in the surplus reserve of the New York Associated Banks from $571,000 on January 6 — actually the lowest figure reported at the opening of that month in twenty-six years—to $16,764,000 on January 20, came a fresh outburst of speculation for the rise on the Stock Exchange, with some exceedingly violent advances. Following, as this movement did, the extraordinary exhibition of strength in the December market, the first and most common inference drawn from it was that nothing could now stop the rush of prices to a higher level. In this conviction, at the opening of January, the outside public seemed for a time to share. The volume of trading on the New York Stock Exchange rose to extraordinary figures. While 1,000,-000 shares sold in a day was still a high average, the record of January 26 and 27 was, in round figures, 2,000,000 each. But with this the upward movement of speculative prices faltered and a rather remarkable counter-movement ensued. Cool-headed watchers had been steadfastly predicting that the forcing-up of the November and December stock market, in the face of acute money stringency, was a movement so utterly artificial that the penalty for such defiance of financial rule and caution must follow quickly after it. They now began to see their prediction verified. Renewed unsettlement in the money market itself came distinctly into sight.

The question had remained open, even after the return of the money market to comparative ease, at the end of January, whether the remarkable stringency of December was a mere incident of the hour, not destined to trouble financial markets again, or whether, on the other hand, it indicated an underlying situation which was likely to develop again later in the present year. The importance of this question must be judged in connection with the belief prevalent throughout Wall Street at the opening of the year, that this is bound to be a period of very great activity and profit in commercial, industrial, and financial quarters — that, in other words, capital will be in continuous demand, not only for use in an active interior trade, but in connection with large financial operations. This being conceded, it obviously becomes a matter of high importance for the future that markets should know how far they may reckon confidently on the supplies of capital and credit sufficient to finance these various demands without inconvenience.

There had been two lines of reasoning regarding the December stringency. One was that it merely represented the tightening of money incidental to the end of the year, and that the manner in which stock-market values ignored the 100 per cent rate proved that the money-market

episode was of slight concern. The other inference was less agreeable.
Looking, as they had a right to do in making forecasts, at the precedent
for the money stringency around the opening of the present year, it was
found, in the first place, that severe money stringency at that time has
always foreshadowed one of two things — either heavy liquidation and
subsiding of trade activity, or else recurrence of tight money during the
balance of the year. Now, the sixty per cent rate to which call money
rose for a time on Wall Street at the opening of January set a figure for the
month which has been equalled in no January market since the seventies.
The subjoined table, giving the highest rate touched for call money during
January, in a series of years, gives some idea of the exceptional nature of
this year's level. It will be seen that the only years of recent times which
even approached the showing of last January were 1890, 1882, 1880 and
1878:

Year.	Per cent.	Year.	Per cent.
1905	$3\frac{1}{2}$	1887	8
1904	6	1886	5
1903	15	1885	$1\frac{1}{2}$
1902	15	1884	3
1901	6	1883	12
1900	12	1882	51
1899	6	1881	6
1898	6	1880	31
1897	2	1879	6
1896	10	1878	90
1895	$1\frac{1}{2}$	1877	11
1894	$1\frac{1}{2}$	1876	7
1893	7	1875	5
1892	5	1874	11
1891	9	1873	90
1890	45	1872	65
1889	8	1871	90
1888	6	1870	7

As to these years, it may be remarked that the high rate with which 1890
opened was a fair foreshadowing of the ensuing year. In 1890, as in the
present season, rates for call money declined during February to the three
and four per cent levels, and a "boom" occurred on the Stock Exchange;
but by May the stringency returned, and, along with an active movement
of prosperity on the Stock Exchange and in the country at large, bank surplus reserves were speedily exhausted and on six separate weeks between
the middle of August and the middle of December call money rose above
100 per cent in Wall Street. In the other years referred to, such return of
stringency was not a uniform result; but in practically every case — notably in 1882 and 1880 — such return was avoided solely through extensive liquidation on the Stock Exchange, usually combined with a halt
in general trade activity.

The obvious inference, then, would seem to have been, at the opening
of 1906, that chances favored the return of tight money and a strain on bank
resources during the balance of the year unless the demands on capital from

financial and industrial quarters could be reduced. As to how far these demands have shown themselves I shall have more to say later on. For the present, attention may be called to the curious views expressed in substantial Wall Street quarters regarding the money stringency. At the New York Chamber of Commerce meeting, on January 4, Mr. Jacob H. Schiff, in a vigorous address, declared that the high money rates of the period were "a disgrace to a civilized community." Developing that view, Mr. Schiff proceeded as follows:

.There must be a cause for such conditions. It cannot be the condition of the country itself, for wherever you look there is prosperity — prosperity as we never had it before. It is true that our prosperity may be a contributory condition. It cannot be that the speculation which prosperity always brings forward can be the sole reason for the conditions which we have witnessed and are still witnessing. Other countries have had wider speculation than the United States. In France, in Germany, in England, speculation is rampant and has been rampant at all times, at certain periods; and still you have never seen the money market for sixty days in such a condition that rates have varied all the way from ten to 125 per cent. I say that it is a disgrace to a civilized community. There must be a cause for it, and we all know the cause. The cause is in our insufficient circulating medium, or the insufficient elasticity of our circulating medium. I don't like to play the rôle of Cassandra, but mark what I say: If this condition of affairs is not changed, and changed soon, we will get a panic in this country compared with which the three which have preceded it would only be child's play.

This plain assertion, that an inadequate currency was the cause of the money convulsions of last winter, calls for some analysis. In the first place, it should be observed that the country's total money circulation, outside of United States Treasury holdings, footed up to $2,569,600,000 on January 1, 1905; that on September 1, 1905, when the money strain began, the total was $2,621,600,000; and that at the close of 1905, when money was rising to above 100 per cent in Wall Street, this total outstanding circulation was reported by the Government as $2,671,500,000. That is to say, the country's actual money supply had increased nearly $50,-000,000 during the period of stringency and more than $100,000,000 during the twelve months of 1905.

This would seem effectually to dispose of the theory that the currency system was not providing adequate circulating medium. Mr. Schiff's idea, however, it will be observed, goes further, indicating that the inelasticity of the currency prevented its proper adjustment to the needs of one season and another; and on this point he clearly showed his belief that the Treasury should by some arbitrary method have withdrawn money from the market in the summer when commercial needs were slight, and have paid it out again in the winter when demands were urgent. Without passing judgment on the question whether such constant interference with the money market by the officers of the Government would or would not be salutary, the question may be raised again as to whether a system should necessarily be blamed because it is mis-used by experts.

That Wall Street speculators engaged themselves in enormously large commitments during the easy money of the summer, and by that means absorbed the capital which should later on have been at the disposal of legit-imate borrowers, no one can doubt. Nor may it be doubted that this group of speculators included some banking interests that might have been expected to exercise caution on their own account. That they did not do so, the subsequent course of the money market clearly indicated.

The theory which was very prevalent, that the Treasury somehow caused the trouble in the winter, has the slightest imaginable basis. There have been years when a heavy surplus revenue withdrew from the market such enormous sums of money as to deplete the bank reserves at a time when credits were most needed. Nothing of the sort occurred in the pres-ent instance. During August public expenditure exceeded income by $4,600,000; in September excess receipts were $8,900,000; October's ex-cess of expenditure was $5,300,000; and the changes during November and December were of no great importance. In fact the Treasury's deposits with the banks rose from $68,800,000 at the close of August to $70,400,000 on December 31.

This was reasonably clear proof that the Treasury had not been respon-sible for the shrinkage in New York bank reserves. Furthermore, state-ments during the autumn of 1905 showed that the Treasury was not main-taining in its vaults more than its customary "working balance." During November that balance barely exceeded $60,000,000; it has usually been much larger. Secretary Shaw was besieged throughout October and No-vember with the most urgent applications for relief to the money market —by which the applicants meant that the Government ought to place on deposit with the Wall Street banks a good part even of this working bal-ance. The Secretary very properly refused, on the ground that the money stringency in New York was caused not by legitimate trade conditions, but by a rampant Wall Street speculation; and he proved his point by reference to the fact that money rates at interior centres, where bona-fide trade was conspicuously active, had at no time reached the figures quoted in Wall Street during November and December.

Both the Secretary of the Treasury, and bankers who have complained that the currency system did not give proper relief, have advocated that the remedy should be the granting of facilities for bank-note circulation at short notice, and on other than United States Government bonds security. The Secretary himself urged in his annual report that power for what he called an emergency bank-note issue should be conferred on the banks and the government department which supervised them. The Secretary con-cluded in his annual report:

As a means to this end, I suggest the advisability of permitting national banks to issue a volume of additional government guaranteed currency equal in amount to fifty per cent of the bond-secured currency maintained by them, but subject to a tax of five or six per cent until redeemed by the deposit of a like amount in the Treasury. By eliminating the words "secured by United States bonds deposited with the Treasury of the United States" from national bank notes now authorized. the additional currency would be identical in form with that based upon a deposit of bonds, and its presence would not alarm, for it would not be known.

This proposition for an emergency currency, which in some respects imitates that now permitted by the German Government to the Imperial Bank of Germany, was not approved by the Chamber of Commerce itself when it came to consider Mr. Schiff's resolution of January 4. The Chamber's conclusion regarding such an emergency issue was that "standing by itself it would, when availed of, only increase the distrust and difficulties, to allay which ostensibly would be its purpose." But the further point was urged, as regards the Secretary's currency proposal, that, however beneficial such an emergency circulation might conceivably be for general purposes, it could not possibly be of any use in relieving such a situation as that which existed last December. An increase of fifty per cent in an outstanding bank-note circulation might, indeed, increase the total outstanding stock of bank notes by $250,000,000. This is a sufficiently substantial increase; but, on the other hand, it must be remembered that the New York bank situation of November and December had to do with the two considerations of decreasing cash reserves and increasing liabilities. On the liability account, new bank-note issues could have no effect, save possibly to increase them; while, as to the bank reserves, notes of a national bank are, for obvious reasons, not accepted as lawful money for reserve against deposit liabilities.

The inference, therefore, is that no matter what increase might have been made in outstanding bank notes, no increase would have followed in the lawful bank reserves. It has been argued that through such increased bank-note issues, the demand for legal-tender money from the bank reserve, for use in the harvest country or in the city trade, would be so far reduced that city banks might retain their reserve money as it was at the opening of the season. To this contention it must be replied, first, that the Western banks which drew out money from the East were in the same position as the Eastern institutions in that they needed cash to replenish their reserves, and needed, therefore, not bank notes, but government coin or legal tenders.

As for a harvest money, it must also be observed that payments of this sort call for large supplies of what is known as small money — bills of one and two dollars each — whereas, the minimum amount for which a bank note under the law may now be issued is five dollars. In short, viewing the agitation over remedies for the recent money stringency, one is led back directly to the first conclusion, namely, that the situation at December's end clearly resulted from a reckless use of credit by large speculators on the Stock Exchange who pursued their speculations at a time when bank resources were in high demand for legitimate purposes throughout the country. That these speculators played a dangerous game, and that the present year's results will be largely governed by the question whether they attempt the experiment again or not, is now conceded universally by intelligent home and foreign judgment.

The stock markets during the opening weeks of January fulfilled in nearly all respects the prediction of these operators. There was a burst of enthusiasm, prices went rapidly higher, and in the various commission-broker houses, through which the general public deals in the market, there were signs of large participation by such outside interests. Traditionally, the arrival of such outside buyers is the occasion for profit-taking by speculators who had previously bought and advanced the market. Undoubtedly it had been the expectation of the various cliques which had stood behind the November and December market that this public participation would expand to such magnitude as to make perfectly easy the disposal of all such speculative holdings at a continuous advance. It is now in order to inquire exactly how far this happened.

The stock-market situation at the opening of 1906 was frequently compared with that at the opening of 1901. Superficially, there were numerous points of resemblance. The great prosperity of the country, and the reported eagerness of many European markets, notably London and Berlin, to take a hand in our stock-market speculations, provide the main parallel. Whether the general public would make the same use of its accumulative savings as it did five years ago was the question to be decided. That an amount of wealth quite as great as that of 1901 was falling into the hands of the American public no doubt whatever existed. But something more than mere existence of tangible resources is needed to provoke an excited speculation. To people who look back at the episode of 1901, it is perfectly obvious that successful "deals" in corporation finance, each one verifying a sensational rumor which had preceded it, and each being of such nature as apparently to enhance the value of the property, had much to do with the explosion of excitement which came to a head in April of that year. It will be recalled that, during those few months of 1901, the Steel Corporation merger was carried through; two or three coal-carrying railway properties were bought up by other companies at an extravagant advance in price; the Union Pacific Railway bought the $198,000,000 Southern Pacific; Chicago, Burlington, and Quincy's $100,000,000 stock was purchased through issue of bonds at a price of $200 per share, where it had stood at $125 only a month or two before. Finally, there was a general stirring in the market in which nearly all railway stocks advanced, the report in each case being that similar operations were under way for the purchase of these properties also regardless of expense, and the facts being that a seemingly irresistible buying power was in the market.

It is now well understood what was the true basis of that movement in 1901. These various properties were being bought not by individual capitalists for themselves, but by other corporations. The purchasing companies expected later to issue their own securities in an increased amount sufficient to pay the extravagant price for the properties acquired. While waiting to make such arrangements, the purchase money for the extravagant deals was provided by "underwriting syndicates," in which most of the requisite capital was procured from the life-insurance companies, the largest of these institutions being almost invariably interested, directly or indirectly, in the undertakings.

This is an old story; it is worth repeating now, chiefly because of the question raised at the opening of January, as to whether we should not witness this season another such outburst as that of 1901. Keeping in mind the above description of 1901, the first point to occur to the reader will undoubtedly be that the life-insurance companies were by no means likely to play in a "boom" this year the peculiar part which they played five years ago. Companies lately under rigid investigation, and with legislation pending, devised explicitly to forbid such practices as participation in Wall Street syndicates, are not very likely to take the chance of defying public opinion by engaging again in such a venture. There was, therefore, not the slightest reason to suppose that the life companies would lend any tangible assistance to this season's movement.

Just what effect the absence of access to these piles of capital would have on the prospect for company deals such as stirred up the speculative public's imagination at this time in 1901, was, therefore, a question of interest. Before December was fairly ended, it might be said that Wall Street was listening with strained attention for news of the deals which were to start the "bull movement" on its genuine upward course. Of rumors there were plenty, and they had much effect upon the market. We saw last year, however, in reviewing the experience of April, 1905, that rumor and fulfilment are in Wall Street two very different things. We have also seen that in 1901 the main provocation to the speculative outburst was the fact that the rumors promptly and visibly materialized. The experience of that year in this regard has been somewhat singular.

Before the close of January, it was announced that the $52,000,000 Street Railway system of New York and the $35,000,000 Subway system were to be amalgamated. The usual further announcement regarding the purpose of enlisting the aid of a "syndicate" to place the stocks on a higher selling basis accompanied this news. It was also apparent, from the terms of the announcement, that in place of $117,000,000 in various kinds of securities outstanding on the old companies to be merged, new securities in the amount of $225,000,000 were to be put out. Not only was this substantial increase made, but the $35,000,000 Interborough stock, which had just managed to pay eight per cent per annum, was to be turned into $70,000,000 worth of four and one-half per cent bonds — which was, of course, equivalent to an exchange for a security paying nine per cent. This was precisely the sort of announcement which in 1901 drove the stock market into a frenzy of excitement.

Its effect on the market of January, 1906, was different. The announcement was received with dislike and suspicion by the public; it was declared to be a stock-jobbing and stock-watering scheme. When, in response to the searching criticism directed at the merger provisions by the press, it was found that the street-railway shareholders were withholding their assent, it proved necessary for the promoters of the deal to induce respectable Wall Street banking houses to sign their names to circulars urging such shareholders to assent; using the rather singular argument that if the shareholders did not join the merger deal their property would be jeopardized and the seven per cent dividend guaranteed them under the older merger deal of 1902 could probably not be paid. Considering that the people appealing for assents from these shareholders, this year, were in the main exactly the people who asked their assent to the disastrous "deal" of 1902, a sufficiently singular situation was created. In the end the merger plan appeared to achieve a limited success. Its future fortunes need not just now concern us further. The special point to notice is that this deal, instead of exciting the buoyant hopes of 1901, caused suspicion, dislike, and irritation to spread throughout the financial community.

Next in order, following numerous rumors and predictions, came an apparent settlement of the so-called "copper war." Ever since the entry of the Amalgamated Copper Company promoters into the Montana territory, they had been fighting independent copper properties mainly owned by F. A. Heinze. The contest had developed the use of the most disreputable methods. Through the very peculiar performances both of courts and legislatures in the afflicted district, trade and industry in the Montana copper country had been totally disorganized, many productive mines being actually shut off from production through the issuing of injunctions growing out of the copper war and the whole business of the towns becoming precarious. Largely because of urgent efforts of legitimate Montana interests, this struggle was at the close of January settled by compromise, the only tangible announcement being that the law suits would forthwith be discontinned and that eventually all the companies were likely to be united under a single head.

Here, then, was obviously another bit of news suited to influence spéculative feelings like the announcement of 1901.   While the rumor of such a copper settlement was afloat but unconfirmed, stocks of the properties concerned advanced with excessive violence.   When the announcement came, there was a prompt relapse upon the Stock Exchange.   Some part of Wall Street's mercurial contingent declared that the "copper deal" was not as far-reaching as had been promised and expected; another, and the larger part, objected that if the scheme of a new copper "holding company" were to be carried out, another flood of securities must be expected on the market.   Let it be observed that in both lines of reasoning, the market's argument was entirely different from that of five years ago.   These two instances fairly typify the community's general attitude.   When it is added that, except for these two episodes, and for an increase in the dividend rate of several important companies, none of last season's excited Stock Exchange predictions materialized, it will be seen at once that a different situation has arisen from that to which we have been seeking a parallel.

Nevertheless, as we have seen, the markets started off with excited buoyancy in January.   Before the month was over, there were such advances from the earlier prices of the month as thirteen points in Amalgamated Copper; sixty-eight in Anaconda Copper stock; thirteen in Chicago, Milwaukee, and St. Paul Railway; twelve in Union Pacific; and eight to ten in numerous other railway and industrial securities.   While this movement was in progress, the money market seemed to remain unruffled.   It was true, however, that, even in the third week of January, call and time money both held at a figure not paralleled in this season since 1893.   During the third week of February, when an active Stock Exchange market happened to be coincident with the raising of funds for a large new issue of securities, call money suddenly rose to eight per cent.

This was a figure paralleled at that time of year on only three occasions during the past generation — in 1896, when the offer to a public subscription of $100,000,000 United States bonds at inviting prices drew advance bids of $568,000,000; in 1893, when a twelve per cent rate marked the beginning of that year's financial panic, and, in 1890, when, as can now be seen, ten per cent money in February was a sign that the load of securities resting on home and foreign markets really involved something like financial exhaustion.   At the same time as the rise in money last February, each successive bank statement showed a position weaker than any reached in the opening months of a year since 1890.   It is true that during all this period surplus reserves were not impaired, and that, as we have seen, the excess over the legal ratio of reserves rose during January to $16,000,000.

This in itself looked well, but these figures must necessarily be judged

by comparison with the same date in other years. That test applied, it
will be found that, even in the week referred to, the $16,000,000 surplus
reserve was not only much the smallest recorded at that date in sixteen
years, but compared with a surplus of $27,000,000 and $34,000,000, respectively, even in such active Stock Exchange years as 1901 and 1899. The
inference was obvious that as the normal demands on capital and withdrawal of currency during the spring time came about, there was less of
the reserve left to draw upon than in any recent year. Of this situation, the high rate on Wall Street's money market was the truthful
barometer.

During last year's expansion of values on the Stock Exchange, the
point was frequently made that a movement of the sort was justified by
the fact that no very large issues of new securities, such as occurred in
1901, had been brought forth to absorb the reserves of floating capital.
This reasoning was not altogether accurate, because a substantial volume
of securities had been quietly placed even during 1905. To what extent
this movement had progressed, may be judged from the following table
showing the new issues listed on the Stock Exchange during the five past
years, but not including stocks or bonds put out merely to replace other
retired issues:

	First Six Mos.	Whole Year.
1905	$409,594,000	$694,202,000
1904	223,480,000	550,445,000
1903	201,835,000	364,459,000
1902	285,354,000	448,585,000
1901	458,508,000	649,708,000
1900	272,440,000	444,228,000

While these figures of 1905 are large, it will be observed that the greater
part of the new securities came out during the first half of the year. Yet
it was well understood, in the middle of 1905, that nearly all railway corporations had matured plans of such magnitude as to involve large issues of
new stocks and bonds. These issues were not made in the autumn of 1905;
the reason being, as now alleged by the railway officers themselves, that
banking interests had advised them to wait until January. Obedient to
this intimation, the railways kept their securities in general off from the
autumn market. But, as we have seen already, the capital which, in the
normal order of events, should have been devoted to these legitimate
railway purposes, was utilized to the last drop for the huge winter stock
speculation. This fact adds to the absolute discredit into which that
movement has appropriately fallen; but the point to notice now is that
the January date had come, that the railways were now prepared to ask
the markets for the capital required, and that the markets were obviously
in no shape to accede to the request. During January such announcements were made with caution and deliberation; during February they

followed one another with such startling rapidity that the total announce-ment of such issues for the first two months footed up to the remarkable figure of $350,000,000.

This, it will be observed, fell not far short of the record for the full six months at the opening of 1905. It was plain that if all these securities were to seek an immediate sale, there would be some considerable strain on domestic capital. The extent to which the reserves of capital were be-ing held back against such possible demands was made evident on Febru-ary 15, when New York City applied to the market for a $20,000,000 loan. Even last November, it had grown evident that the supply of cap-ital for such conservative investments was diminishing, and as a conse-quence it was found barely possible to float a three and a half per cent city loan at par. While the law requires the city to obtain at least par for the issue of its bonds, it allows the fixing of an interest rate as high as four per cent, but no higher. Accordingly, in last February's loan announcement, the four per cent rate was fixed by the city's finance authorities for the first time in many years. As a result, the bonds brought an average price of 108, which meant an investment yield of three and three-fourths per cent. This was by far the most disadvantageous price to the city at which a New York City bond has been sold in recent years. At the close of 1900, New York bonds were placed at a price netting investors less than three per cent; in the middle of the speculative excitement at the beginning of 1901, its three and one-half per cent bonds were placed at 110½, which meant an interest return of only 3.08 per cent.

No doubt this rapid lowering of the prices during the present year was partly a result of the "municipal-ownership" campaign, with the knowl-edge of the enormous drafts on municipal credit which such a movement, if successful, might involve. The lower price was also a consequence of the very large recent issue of bonds by New York City, which in a sense glutted the more or less restricted market for its securities. But New York City was not alone among municipalities in this decline of prices for its bonds, and the reason clearly lay in the increasingly large demands on capital from others quarters.

This February outcome of a high-grade loan was, therefore, in some respects typical of the general market. It had an unquestionably bad effect on sentiment and, as a matter of fact, it was followed promptly by a down-ward movement on the Stock Exchange. This decline proceeded slowly at first and then with rapidly accelerated speed, until by the opening of March such losses from the high price prevalent in the early days of Febru-ary had been made as fifteen and twenty points. In fact, before the first week of March had reached its end it was growing evident that in the ma-jority of stocks all advances made in the great speculation of last winter had been cancelled. Let it be remembered, also, that these declines had in almost every instance happened during the last two weeks of February. The extent of this upward and downward swing may be judged from the following table showing the prices of typical stocks at the close of August, 1905, the highest subsequently attained — mostly last January — and those at the opening of March:

	August 1905.	High January, 1906.	Prices Opening March.
Amalgamated Copper	83½	118¼	100
American Smelting	126¼	174	150⅜
Anaconda Mining	113	300	245½
Baltimore and Ohio	112	117	108¾
Brooklyn Rapid Transit	69	94⅛	78⅝
Chicago, Milwaukee, and St. Paul	179⅜	193	175½
Chicago and Northwestern	217½	240	223
Federal Mining and Smelting	94¼	199	175
Great Northern	315	348	309½
New York Central	149⅞	156¼	144¾
Northern Pacific	207½	232½	207½
Pennsylvania	143⅜	147½	136¾
Reading	116¼	164	126¾
Union Pacific	131¾	160½	149⅛
United States Steel preferred	103½	113¼	104¼

It will be noticed that many important stocks, especially among the railways, sold in March actually below the price of last summer, before the autumn's great advance began.

The Stock Exchange liquidation probably served to avert a severely stringent money market in the early days of spring. Nevertheless, although the forced liquidation of speculative holdings must have released large amounts in call loans and loans on time, the Wall Street money rate remained extremely close, call money touching seven per cent at the close of February, and the sixty-day rate rising to six per cent at the opening of March — a rate unparalleled for this season of the year save in 1903 and 1893. It was obvious that these high bids for money accommodation had much to do with the large demands on investment capital to which I have referred already. But it was also evident from the industrial news from the country's interior centres that the continued prosperity of the United States and the active business at internal markets were of themselves absorbing a great share of the country's capital.

On January 29, the Comptroller of the Currency called for returns of the 5,900 national banks of the United States. Compiled, these figures showed an increase in loans of $343,000,000 from the preceding January, and in individual deposits of $476,000,000; whereas, the cash reserve held against these expanded liabilities had actually decreased fully $1,000,000.

The extent to which this credit expansion had progressed may be seen from
the subjoined table giving the statements as nearly as possible of the date
corresponding to the January returns this year:

	Loans.	Cash.	Individual Deposits.
1906	$4,071,041,164	$668,303,289	$4,088,420,136
1905	3,728,166,086	669,971,553	3,612,499,598
1904	3,469,195,044	614,626,152	3,300,619,898
1903	3,350,897,744	570,598,719	3,159,534,591
1902	3,128,627,094	561,764,854	2,982,489,201
1901	2,814,388,346	552,342,476	2,753,969,722
1900	2,481,579,945	476,544,317	2,481,847,036
1899	2,299,041,947	508,086,560	2,232,193,157
1898	2,138,078,280	440,893,111	1,982,660,933
1897	1,886,282,264	420,281,715	1,669,219,961
1896	1,951,344,781	337,361,833	1,648,092,869
1895	1,951,846,832	374,644,695	1,667,843,286
1894	1,858,763,803	414,135,407	1,586,800,444

With the continued tightening of the money market, notwithstanding
Stock Exchange liquidation, and with interior banks drawing freely on
New York for purposes of their own, the Eastern markets began to look
to other quarters for relief. The high rate bid, especially for two months'
loans, at the opening of March was in effect an effort to touch the reserves
of Europe on capital. Just as in 1903, when our six per cent bid brought
$40,000,000 or $50,000,000 German capital to the temporary relief of the
New York money market, so during February and March, this year, the
high rate offered from New York resulted in an extremely heavy transfer
of capital from both London and Paris. So great were these remittances
that the announcement of the Treasury on March 2, that $10,000,000
government money would be deposited with the market, passed almost
unnoticed.

It was recognized that the Secretary in this move was merely placing
back on the open market money which had been automatically withdrawn
from it by the Treasury's operations during February. In other words,
the Treasury, which at length during February reached a point where a
surplus revenue had been earned for the fiscal year to date, was now drawing freely on the market, as it had not done in November or December, and
the Secretary was accordingly taking steps to prevent depletion of the outside currency supplies. This was not looked upon as relief of the first importance; at the opening of March the financial community was looking
with most expectancy to Europe.

I have said that large sums of capital had by that time been remitted
by Europe to the New York market. In view of the situation of the American
money market, it was a matter of great interest how far this foreign relief was

likely to be continued. That question in its turn depended naturally on the state of the European banks and the European markets. Now, the great banks of Europe, like the associated banks of New York City, had improved their position since the end of 1905. Return of money from the provinces had in these markets, as in ours, replenished bank reserves, and money rates at such points as London and Berlin had accordingly declined. Responding to these influences, the Imperial Bank of Germany had on January 18 reduced its official discount rate from six to five per cent, and the Bank of England, whose ratio of reserve to liabilities had fallen on December 20 to the very low figure of thirty-six and one-fourth per cent and on January 3 to twenty-nine and seven-eighths, had by the close of January risen to the respectable percentage of forty-two and a half.

Nevertheless, when the same tests as have been applied to our bank showing were applied to these foreign bank returns, it was seen at once that the showing was by no means as strong as might have been desired. On the 1st of March, for instance, while the Bank of England showed forty-three and one-eighth per cent as its proportion of reserves to liabilities, it was necessary to go back to 1892 in order to find a year when the ratio at that date was not higher. So of the German Bank, as to which late in February its president stated that the outlay in discounts and advances was $42,000,000 larger than at the same date a year before, while metallic reserves were $27,000,000 smaller.

The state of affairs at the Bank of Russia threw peculiar interest on this situation. At the close of 1905, fear that the Russian Government was disintegrating had produced an acute panic at the Russian money centres. During the days of uprising by the people, when the Government seemed powerless and the entire Russian community in a state of anarchy, the rush of well-to-do people to take refuge across the border became naturally very great. These people either sent ahead of them for deposit in Paris or Berlin money withdrawn by them from the Russian banks, or else, on arriving at the French and German cities, drew on St. Petersburg or Moscow for the same purposes. In either case the result was to create an extreme demand on Russia's gold reserves for the benefit of outside markets. During December this movement resulted in such complete demoralization of exchange on Russia that the Imperial Russian Bank was forced to ship $25,000,000 gold from St. Petersburg to Berlin. This outflow continued at a moderate rate, its most serious symptom being, however, that at the moment when home gold reserves were being depleted by this drain in the market for exchange, the bank's foreign credit funds were also falling through payments on its debt and the Government's inability to raise further outside loans. At the same time outstanding notes of the Imperial Bank were reaching large proportions. The following table shows the movement in thousands of roubles, the rouble roughly valued at fifty cents

	Home Gold Reserve.	Gold Abroad.	Notes Issued.	Notes Held by Bank.
Feb. 14	732,224	213,826	1,265,000	104,877
Feb. 5	731,135	218,823	1,265,000	91,153
Jan. 29	726,133	185,701	1,290,000	118,732
Jan. 21.........	717,091	193,039	1,290,000	104,273
Jan. 14	713,492	206,069	1,290,000	85,412
Dec. 29	737,038	209,893	1,270,000	76,990
Dec. 21	767,576	222,218	1,230,000	63,926
Dec. 14	822,178	213,925	1,190,000	65,071
Feb., 1905	892,920	129,170	950,000	55,327

On February 14, 1904, the week when war broke out, the bank held 745,700,000 roubles gold at home, and 175,100,000 abroad; its note circulation, less amount of notes held by the bank, being only 509,600,000 roubles.

It will be observed from the above table that, although the results in December and January were distinctly alarming, an improvement of some magnitude began toward the close of January, that home gold reserves increased more than 18,000,000 roubles in three weeks, while note issues were reduced and gold balances on the foreign markets fairly held in hand. Apparently the reason for this better showing was that the Paris market, uneasy over what might ensue if default on the Russian coupon were to be necessitated, had advanced to the Russian Government $50,000,000, but with the stipulation that this fund should not be used save for payment of external coupons on the Russian debt.

The comparative table of the Russian Bank's reserve and note liabilities is of special interest because at its low point of January 14 the reserve for the first time since the adoption of currency reform in 1898 had fallen below the amount prescribed by law to be held against circulation. The law of 1897 provides explicitly that note circulation up to 600,000,000 roubles shall be secured by fifty per cent in gold, but that circulation in excess of the sum prescribed must be secured by gold, rouble for rouble. The December 14 statement shows that home gold reserves alone already failed to provide legal security for outstanding notes. It was, however, answered that by its practice the Imperial Bank had the right to count, among its reserves against note circulation, the gold balances outstanding on other European markets. Had these been added on December 14 to the home reserve, sufficient security to conform with the law of 1897 would have been in hand. On January 14, however, such had been in the interim the decline of cash reserves and the expansion of circulation that home and foreign holdings of the bank combined failed to make up the amount of reserve prescribed by law. As will be seen from the above comparisons, this deficiency was presently repaired. How far it will yet be possible for Russian finances to maintain themselves on an even keel during a somewhat trying money market likely to be encountered later in the year remains, however, an open question.

It will be observed that the Russian Bank disturbances operated in two distinct directions upon the European markets. So long as doubt existed over the payment of the Russian coupons great apprehension was expressed. At the same time, this very depletion of the Imperial Bank's reserves resulted, as we have seen, in an outflow of gold from St. Petersburg to Berlin and Paris. This gold came in very handily for the German market and was a factor of no small importance in strengthening the position of the German Bank.

In other directions Europe's financial situation, though disturbed by passing incidents, did not seem to be in any serious measure jeopardized. The dispute between France and Germany over the paramount influence in Morocco had the usual effect, in depressing security markets, which Europe, pending a diplomatic clash, invariably looks for. The sweeping victory of the Liberal Government in England had another curious effect on which politicians hardly could have reckoned. Sir Henry Campbell-Bannerman, the new Premier, came into office pledged, among other things, for restriction of the use of Chinese labor in the Transvaal gold mines. This story of Chinese labor is by no means without interest and may have an important bearing on the later market. After the war it was found that native labor was not easy to procure in the gold mines on the old-time basis, the Kaffirs having been utterly demoralized by the high wages paid them for use around the camps. The expedient was evolved of importing Chinese coolies under contract, a species of slavery which evoked from Sir William Harcourt and other humanitarian Englishmen a vigorous protest — ignored, however, by the ministry of the day. Permission to import Chinese labor, under such conditions, was granted to the mine owners; and at last year's close, nearly 50,000 coolies were thus at work in the Transvaal mines. On acceding to power, after Mr. Balfour's resignation, the new Liberal Premier promptly announced, on December 21, in a public speech, that the Government had decided "to stop forthwith, as far as it is practicable to do it forthwith, the recruitment and embarkation of coolies in China and their importation into South Africa." It was further explained that the Chinese already in the Transvaal had brought the supply of labor at the mines to the maximum reached before the war, and that prohibition of further contracts with the Chinese purveyors of the coolies would affect only such laborers as, in the undisturbed order of events, would have embarked for South Africa next October.

It should have been reasonably clear from this further information that no intention was entertained of reducing the Transvaal labor problem to the situation which it occupied during or shortly after the Transvaal War. It so happened, however, that the London markets took the Government's move with the greatest seriousness. Whether the situation in the market for gold-mining shares was already made precarious by the excessive speculation of last year, or whether the large proprietors had withdrawn from the speculative market with the view of affecting sentiment and opposing the Government's proposition for the forbidding of Chinese labor, is an open question. The fact was that during the closing days of February the London market for Kaffir shares declined with excessive violence, throwing Stock Exchange operations generally in that market into great demoralization. It will thus appear that the foreign situation of itself was by no means clear. On the whole it was evident that the strong position still maintained by the Paris market, and the restriction of Europe's speculation, tended to aid our markets in their endeavor to procure relief from Europe. In the main the loans thus placed for the account of New York bankers were for a two months' period, which would have brought them to maturity in May. The question how far these foreign markets can be depended on for additional relief around that time, if needed, is another matter.

On February 22 the long-expected report of the Armstrong Insurance Commitee was submitted to the New York State Legislature. Writing in THE FORUM three months ago on the insurance investigation, I summed up the situation as follows:

There are, I think, several definite forms toward which all thinking citizens ought to bend their energies. The size of the insurance company should be limited by law. Its scope of investment should be prudently restricted. Its ownership of subsidiary companies should be wholly prohibited. Its issuance of deferred dividend or "semi-tontine" policies should, if possible, be suppressed. Its officers and trustees should be forbidden by law to engage in any syndicate operation in which they have engaged their company. Fees of soliciting agents should be rigidly limited. Finally, whether by law or by the public's absolute demand, the "dummy director" should be excluded from every life-insurance board

The recommendations of the Armstrong Committee deal in a very thorough manner with each of the points referred to in the above paragraph. Recognizing that the enormous size and stupendous growth of the three largest insurance companies is a danger in itself, the Armstrong Committee recommends that the new business to be written by any insurance company hereafter shall be limited to $150,000,000 per annum. The distinct purpose of this recommendation is to hold the aggregate resources of the three greatest institutions where they stand to-day. The figure given was arrived at on the basis of the total termination of policies by death, maturity, surrender, and other causes during 1904, when it amounted to $129,125,280 for the Mutual Life, $139,513,210 for the Equitable, and $162,326,114 for the New York Life. As regards other companies a percentage limit — reasonably liberal, however — was placed on the writing of new business. As to this recommendation, it is clear that discussion will converge on the wisdom of stopping outright the acceptance of applications for insurance after an arbitrary figure. That the plan proposed would serve the purpose of controlling undue growth, there can be no doubt.

The scope of investment for insurance companies, the Armstrong Committee advised, should be limited by absolute exclusion from the field of stocks and of bonds based solely on collateral of stocks. The committee argued that investment of insurance funds in stocks not only involves the company in a proprietary interest in other business, but "affords ready opportunities to conceal irregular transactions and to hide the malversation of funds." Such investments, the committee concluded, should be prohibited. This prohibition naturally would affect the third point raised above, namely, that ownership of subsidiary companies should be prohibited. The committee made a special point of the evils necessarily arising from control of other banking institutions by insurance companies. They believed this adding of an alien business to the natural purposes of insurance to be mischievous in itself. Their recommendation in this regard merely repeats the decided conclusions of the Frick Committee in the Equitable case and the recommendations of almost every insurance trustee committee which has investigated the question during the last quarter century.

As regards deferred dividend policies, the committee recommended that "no attempt should be made to disturb rights under existing contracts, but the issuing of so-called deferred dividend policies in the future should be forbidden." The committee's ground for this straightforward recommendation was, first, that estimates relied upon when such policies were issued have been invariably falsified by the event, but second, and more important, that the vast accumulations of money permitted by this form of insurance have made possible wasteful financial methods, and have absolved the companies from any check through an annual accounting. "It is the opinion of the committee," the report continued, "that dividends should be distributed annually, being applied either in reduction of premiums, or to the purchase of additional insurance, or paid in cash at the option of the insured." In these conclusions pretty much all unprejudiced students of the question will agree.

In the matter of syndicate participations, the committee recommended that "the Statutes should forbid all syndicate participations," and that "it should also be provided that no officer or director should be pecuniarily interested either as principal, co-principal, agent, or beneficiary in any purchase, sale, or loan made by the corporation except in case of a loan upon his policy." This recommendation hardly needs discussion. As to agents' commissions, the committee advised that all of them should be definitely agreed upon in advance, should bear a fixed percentage to the premium for each thousand dollars of insurance, and that renewal commissions should be limited to four years and to a certain percentage, say ten per cent, of the first year's commissions.

Finally, in the "dummy-director" matter, the report made sweeping recommendations. It advised that the terms of all existing insurance directors be made to expire November 15 next; that all annual meetings be postponed until that date; that existing lists of policy-holders be made accessible; that independent nominations be authorized by any group of 100 policy-holders; that ballots containing names of all candidates be circulated by the company itself. It is clear that, under such a provision, opportunity for changes, wherever necessary and advisable, will occur.

What is to be said of the financial future left open by this extraordinary season? The two patent influences, acting in opposite directions, are the uninterrupted prosperity of the United States and the equally uninterrupted evidence that demands on capital run a close race with increase in supply. As the spring season opens, the temper of the people is altogether optimistic; that of the markets, perplexed and mistrustful. Financial markets in this country are for the time sustained by thirty or forty millions in loans obtained from Europe, whereby our own bank liabilities were reduced.

It is assumed that, with the settlement of the Morocco quarrel, European capital in still greater quantity will be at New York's disposal. The question is, how long will this capital remain in New York's hands? Abundant harvests, with a resultant heavy export trade, should help to liquidate the debit balance; yet it must also be remembered that great harvests will place an added burden on the autumn money market. The prospect is for another tight-money season — if not in the spring, at all events in the autumn. Whether such stringency will, as in 1903, apply a severe check to expansion of values in the markets, or whether, as was the case last winter, speculation will go its way regardless of it, is the problem of the coming season. There is reason to think that financial Europe will be, to a greater extent than in many years, the key to the situation.

ALEXANDER D. NOYES.

MUSIC.

AT the beginning of the season our Metropolitan opera was strongly reminiscent of that good old game of our childhood, "What are you going to give the old bachelor to keep house with?" We all remember that the answer to that query had to be undeviatingly the same. What were the principal operas performed at the Metropolitan? Caruso. Who sang the chief rôles? Caruso. Why was German opera given so late? Caruso. Well, after all, it is a great satisfaction to have a singer of Mr. Caruso's fine ability among us as an exponent of the tenor rôles of Italian operas; and both he and Mme. Sembrich have contributed to the artistic pleasure of thousands of opera-goers this winter.

The repertory of the first week of the season was very promising; the operas performed being "La Gioconda," "The Queen of Sheba," "Rigoletto," "Hänsel und Gretel," and "Tannhäuser." This programme was surely in accordance with the cosmopolitan character of our great city. The first-named production, a full-fledged modern Italian opera, with its conspiracies, daggers, conflagration, and poison-cup, drew an enormous audience. The house was sold out long in advance, and the applicants for admission tickets began to congregate before five o'clock, nearly three hours in advance of the opening of the box office. By seven, the crowd stood four or five abreast in the lobby; and one line extended up Broadway to Fortieth Street, west to Seventh Avenue, and down Seventh Avenue nearly to Thirty-ninth Street.

The "Queen of Sheba," the second opera performed, treats of a Hebraic subject; "Rigoletto," with its mellifluous melodies, is still the delight of the veteran who vividly recalls the good old days of the Grand Opera House and the Academy of Music; "Hänsel und Gretel" is a thoroughly German subject; and "Tannhäuser," finally, may almost be called an American opera, so popular is it, even with our native element. But then, alas! there came a period when we were carried back to the golden age of Louis Philippe and Andrew Jackson, there to abide. "La Sonnambula" and "Lucia di Lammermoor," and other operas of the same description, now dominated the stage, and continued to dominate it pretty well to the close of the season. The revival of old operas is, in itself, commendable; but, unfortunately, the choice, whatever may have been the guiding motive, was not a happy one.

A better trio than that consisting of Messrs. Caruso, Scotti, and Plan-
çon it is difficult to imagine. Yet, while the male contingent of the
Metropolitan was, in the main, excellent, particularly as regards Italian
opera, the female members of the cast did not, as a rule, make a
very good showing. True, there were, from time to time, during the
winter, changes of cast; and, among others, we heard Mme. Rappold, whose Sulamith was accepted with applause by public and critics
alike. But in the case of Mme. Rappold, as of several others, the visits
were so brief that we were almost tempted to ask, with the guest of the
"Red Horse" at Sudbury:

> Would the vision there remain?
> Would the vision come again?

Alas! the vision did not remain, but fled across the bridge to Brooklyn; and long did the New Yorkers gaze in vain across the cruel Helles-
pont which divides us from our better municipal half, waiting for the
return of Mme. Rappold.

The success of Mme. Rappold fully justifies the urgent plea made
in THE FORUM immediately upon the appointment of Mr. Conried as
manager of the Metropolitan, to the effect that American talent should
at last find an opportunity to appear before the footlights. From the
manner in which the press throughout the United States at that time
indorsed this view, it was evident that public sentiment was in favor
of encouraging "home industry" in this field. The Opera School, at
that time likewise recommended in these pages as a valuable adjunct
of an operatic institution in this city, has also been productive of much
good. These and other innovations are deserving of commendation.
The scenery has been greatly improved, and various accessories which
serve to please the eye have been added with advantage. There is no
desire whatever to pick flaws; but it cannot be overlooked that the
chief fault at the Metropolitan this year has been the too frequent
selection of works which are not representative of any school, past or
present, worthy of survival.

While American talent is being encouraged at the opera, foreign talent, in the shape of distinguished orchestral leaders from abroad, is
finding recognition in the concerts given by our prominent New York
orchestras. These visits of foreign conductors, such as Mengelberg
and Fiedler, might be productive of much good, if the orchestras over
which they presided were always sufficiently prepared to respond to
their leadership. Even Richard Strauss could not present his own
compositions satisfactorily in this country, owing to the evident lack
of preparation on the part of the organization whose duty it was to carry

out his musical intentions. The same experience was repeated this year in the case of a celebrated conductor from Frankfort-on-the-Main who had been selected to conduct one of the Philharmonic concerts.

There is altogether too much of this sort of thing; and the worst of it is that not only the conductor, but even the composer of the piece performed, especially if it be a novelty to our public, is held accountable for blunders traceable to entirely different sources. In this connection it is pleasant again to refer to the good work done by the Russian Symphony Society this winter under the leadership of Mr. Altschuler, and temporarily of Mr. Safonoff. Perhaps the most praiseworthy feature of these concerts of Russian music is the frequent performance of compositions new to the American public — a feature which characterizes also the symphony concerts of Mr. Walter Damrosch, who has recently brought out many noteworthy musical numbers by Elgar, Massenet, and other European celebrities. Some of the novelties produced in this way during the past winter deserve to become more popular here.

It is given to but few men to create new forms, or to give an entirely new construction to forms already created, as is the case with Richard Strauss. It is almost equally difficult to endow well-known musical forms with new life, as does Max Reger. The tendency with a large number of composers is to follow the paths of programme music, seeking an interesting poetic fabric as a basis of musical interpretation. Great and heroic themes, such as those chosen by Liszt in his "Dante," "Tasso," "Hunnenschlacht," etc., are less in evidence. The heroic epic is giving place more and more to what may perhaps be designated as the romance; and the process once observable in the field of poetry seems to repeat itself in that of programme music, which is branching out into a great variety of forms.

Together with the growth of programme music in the stricter sense, we have an increasing number of those compositions, vocal and instrumental, which partake of the narrative form and suggest a distinct story. One of these the writer should like to mention here, because it was brought out during the musical season just terminated and was enthusiastically received. It is the charming "Legend of the Sage-Bush," set to music by Massenet and sung by Mr. Campanari at one of the Damrosch concerts. According to the programme, "It tells of the flight of the Holy Family into Egypt during the slaughter of the Innocents, when, overcome by fatigue and anxiety for the child Jesus, the Virgin Mary appeals to the Rose to open its petals in order to make a bed for the child. The Rose proudly refuses, whereupon the humble Sage-Bush offers its shelter, and in its leaves the child slumbers and is hidden from the view of Herod's bloodstained soldiers." Melodramas, such as Schilling's musical setting of the "Witches' Song" by Ernst von Wildenbruch, find favor, and even scenes or musical numbers taken from operas are well received, provided a suitable programme is subjoined.

A unique composition brought out by the Russian Symphony Society this winter goes to show how far the tendency toward descriptive music can be carried. This was the "Hebrew Rhapsody" by Zolotaryoff. We have about twenty Hungarian Rhapsodies, as well as a Spanish one, from the pen of Franz Liszt. We have an Italian and a Scotch Symphony by no less important a composer than Mendelssohn, and a Scandinavian Symphony by Cowen—all of them classics. The idea of adding to these a Hebrew Rhapsody is a clever one; but, unfortunately, the title is misleading. Naturally, the idea suggests itself that the composer would here draw upon a rich fund of noble Oriental melody. Then, too, there is the terse and graphic language of the Old Testament, with its inexhaustible fund of poetry. But the composer has here gone far beyond the ordinary limits to depict a subject which is purely dialect; and this dialect quality in its peculiarity the music unmistakably seeks to imitate, whatever other scenes or ideas the composer may have had in mind. The subject is unique, and, as the instrumentation indicates, is carried out with some degree of ingenuity; but the title of the work does not fit it at all. As we have had Italian, Scotch, Scandinavian, Irish, Welsh, and American symphonies, so we may with equal justice have a Hebrew rhapsody or symphony; for, as already stated, there is abundant musical and poetic material here. But the task should not be undertaken lightly, by one not specially qualified for the task.

"Pianism," that peculiar phase of our modern artistic culture, still finds more and more votaries. The troubadour of the Middle Ages was an "event"; and when he made his appearance before the castle, all flocked to hear his lay. In the palmy days of Franz Liszt, the pianist was greeted with an ovation equally flattering. But the multiplication of pianists has been going on with such alarming rapidity that there is no telling where it will end. And yet, despite this wonderful activity, the instrument of interpretation itself is still very far from perfection. When we gaze upon a grand piano of to-day and compare it with its predecessor of 1850, or even of 1875, we cannot but admire the long list of improvements and additions which have been made to perfect its form, to increase its tone and sonority, and to facilitate its action. As regards strength and durability, also, the piano of to-day is truly a giant as compared with its earlier predecessors. Yet, in some of the most important particulars, but little progress has been made, despite considerable experimentation. Now, wherein lies the deficiency?

The sonatas of Beethoven are in many respects miniature symphonies orchestrally conceived. Under the hands of a Liszt, a Tausig, or a Rubinstein, even the mechanical imperfections of the instrument were in some respects overcome, so great was the genius of these men. Under the spell of Rubinstein's playing, notes were absolutely forgotten; and even single tones — and that not always in rapid but also in slow movements, were so admirably blended into phrases that the sound of a single C sharp or B flat, for example, never even suggested itself. These men aimed at what the Germans would appropriately designate as *gesammteffekte* (general tonal effects).

The writer will never forget the impression produced on him at the first Rubinstein concert which he attended. Beethoven's G Major Concerto was to be played; and, after the fashion of young people, the writer took the pianoforte score along to the performance, in order to be better able to follow it. Not only had he practised this score before, but he had even committed it to memory. Yet he might as well have tried to count the spokes of a wheel in motion as to follow the flight of Rubinstein's genius as he interpreted this masterpiece.

The artists mentioned succeeded in converting the piano into an orchestra. Even the compositions of Chopin, though by no means entitled to the classification of orchestral, generally demand a tone almost vocal in its fulness, and a close connection between notes and chords akin to that produced by the voice or a violin. Now, this fulness and roundness of tone and the power of sustaining it in equal volume or diminishing it at pleasure — true essentials, as we have here seen, of all pianoforte compositions worthy of the name — cannot be secured on instruments as at present constructed. By means of tremendous strength, marvellous technique, and genius of the very highest order, the three before-mentioned pianists forced even the instrument of their day to do their bidding; and numerous were the devices to which they were compelled to resort to overcome in a measure its mechanical deficiencies. What a boon it would therefore be to our pianists — and their number is legion — if they were able at last to overcome the present pronounced asthmatic character of their instruments and to produce the effects intended by our great composers!

It appears that an invention has now been successfully applied abroad whereby the sounding-board of the instrument is so constructed that, while securely fastened and fully supported, it is nevertheless to a far greater extent than at present in suspension; and it is claimed that, by this arrangement, the sound-waves are practically unbroken.

This radical transformation of the sounding-board, it is said, strikes at the very root of the evil, which hitherto has been frequently attributed to other causes. It is not within the province of this article to enter into the technical details underlying the construction of this device. Suffice it to say that the instrument has been publicly tested and that the results are pronounced most satisfactory. In connection with this, it may be interesting to state that a key-board for juvenile performers has also been successfully constructed, which will enable even the youngster of four or five to try his skill. As our youthful violinist starts out with an instrument suitable to his size, so our youthful pianist can now attack his little key-board and start on his upward path to fame.

Fame, indeed! Even our poets have recently begun to glorify in verse the heroes of the key-board. We have poems by Paul Heyse and others glorifying the symphonies of Beethoven. Tributes in verse have been paid to many a distinguished singer and violinist. And now we have a poem from the pen of Richard Watson Gilder, inspired, it is said, by the playing of Mlle. Adèle aus der Ohe. Only the opening lines can here be quoted:

> At the dim end of day
> I heard the great musician play;
> Saw her white hands, now slow, now swiftly pass,
> Where gleamed the polished wood, as in a glass,
> The shadowy hands repeating every motion.

This is the day of light opera — very light opera. In New York, during our recent season, there have been produced, to mention only a few, "The Mayor of Tokio," "Véronique," "Mlle. Modiste," "Moonshine," "The Gingerbread Man," "The Earl and the Girl," "Babes in Toyland," and "The Babes and the Baron." The "babes," we see, are very much in evidence; and to them, it seems, even music must be subservient. We are leading the strenuous life, and during our moments of leisure seek recreation in what are called "light operas." Any music will do, so long as it keeps "a-going." There was a time when the musical features of an operetta were regarded as of some slight importance. It is no exaggeration to say that, to-day, the veriest trash may be pieced together with other remnants of musical "old clothes," and, if only fitted here and there to something of a topical nature, will find acceptance. True, these plays are often designed to be of an ephemeral character; they come and go. But the services which Euterpe is compelled to perform to-day are truly pitiful.

Abroad, also, the humorous *genre* has been very pronounced, and about one-third of the seventy new or revived operas produced last year belonged to the class still known as "opéra comique." One of these was the "Flauto Solo" (Flute Solo) composed by our old friend D'Albert, who long ago reaped his laurels as a pianist and is now obtaining even greater celebrity as a composer, although his exceptional physical strength — so conspicuous a feature of his playing — still enables him to undertake pianistic tours in addition to his other work.

Like Leoncavallo's opera of last year, "Flauto Solo" treats of an episode identified with the history of the Hohenzollerns, though the dramatic fabric itself is, of course, largely fictitious. Louise Mühlbach, whose novels were the perpetual delight of our grandmothers, took us right into the sacred precincts of the abode of kings and queens and made us feel "quite to hum." Under the magic influence of her fluent pen, we came to be on terms of such easy familiarity with Napoleon and Josephine that we could afford to drop their titles and address them by the familiar appellation of "du." In D'Albert's opera the faithful and devoted Brandenburger is conducted into the home of royalty and invited to sit on the best sofa. The following is a somewhat meagre outline of the plot:

The father of Frederick the Great was a military man and loved only the "regimentsmusik." Therefore he discouraged the higher artistic aims of his youthful son Fritz, who loved the flute and preferred Italian music. In the opera, the King's German kapellmeister, Pepusch by name, whose humble talent is only adapted to military music, composes a canon for six bassoons, imitating the grunting of pigs (have we not heard of a similar episode in the life of Louis XI, only that in the latter instance the little pigs were dressed up and danced before His Majesty?). In this piece, Pepusch takes revenge on the young Frederick by including a part for the flute, the favorite instrument of that prince, which part is designed to imitate the squealing of a little suckling. Poor Fritz has to play the part, very much against his inclination, but does it so cleverly that his obdurate old father is completely won over. Lortzing, in "Zar und Zimmermann," has cleverly imitated the braying of a donkey; Strauss, in "Don Quixote," has given voice to the bleating of sheep; and D'Albert has now gone a step farther in the domain of musical zoölogy.

The popularity of Wagner seems to be increasing abroad, judging by the fact that 1,642 performances of his operas were given in Germany alone during the past year — a considerable increase over the previous season. Among the foreigners whose works obtained a hearing in Germany — now the centre of musical activity abroad — for the first time during the past season, the following nationalities were represented: France, Italy, Belgium, Roumania, Sweden, Bohemia, England, and the United States, the last-mentioned finding its representative in Louis Coerne.

Mr. Coerne, quite a number of whose sixty or seventy compositions have already been very favorably received (the symphonic poem "Hiawatha" and the opera "The Girls of Marblehead" being prominent among these), has obtained a distinct success at Bremen, where his opera "Zenobia" was recently performed. Although only thirty-six years of age, the young American seems to have convinced the European critics that we can also produce operatic composers. True, Mr. Coerne was educated at the Munich Conservatory; but otherwise he is wholly identified with the United States, having studied at Harvard prior to his visit abroad. He has held the position of organist in several American cities and is now professor of music at Northampton, Massachusetts. Mr. Arthur Friedheim, also, whom many of us remember as a very gifted pianist, and who at one time seemed disposed to make America his home, has also successfully brought out a new opera. It is entitled "Die Tänzerin" and was performed at Cologne.

A proposed subdivision of this paper into "Music Abroad" and "Music in America" becomes more and more difficult, owing to the fact that the principle of reciprocity is rapidly becoming established in the field of music, even though its application with regard to the tariff would at present appear to be a beautiful dream. While we are importing European conductors from Germany, France, Russia, Holland, England, and elsewhere, the compositions of men like McDowell, Paine, Bartlett, Chadwick, Kelley, and others are gradually acquiring an increasing market in Europe. The career of American singers abroad has from time to time been followed in these pages; and it is gratifying to state that some of our native pianists and violinists are finding ever greater favor with European audiences. Recently, the European press reports concerning the violinist, Karl Klein, for example, the son of that well-known and genial musician, Bruno Oscar Klein, have aroused great hopes of a brilliant future for this youthful master of the bow, who, though only nineteen years of age, has inspired a eulogy in the London "Times" such as that extremely conservative paper rarely gives expression to. It may be interesting to those who believe in the encouragement of our native talent to glance at the following extract:

Although the name of musical executive genius is legion nowadays, when almost every practical musician possesses a command of technique undreamt of except by the very elect five-and-twenty years ago, it is not often that two such fine examples of contemporary ability as Herr Richard Buhlig and Mr. Karl Klein possess are heard on one and the same day. Both these musicians are, it is understood, of American nationality, and both gave concerts on Tuesday, the former at Æolian Hall in the afternoon, the latter in the Queen's Hall in the evening. . . . Of Mr. Klein there can be no two opinions, to judge by his first performance. He is young and exuberant, and his playing is full of the exuberance of youth, and as the works chosen for his first appearance here were Tchaikovsky's concerto, Lalo's "Symphonie Espagnole," Bach's so-called "Air," in Wilhelmj's transcription, and Wieniawski's Polonaise, there was no reason why this quality should not be paramount. Mr. Klein has a fine, broad, and round tone, a splendid technique, and a rare warmth of style, and all of these, combined with his splendid freedom and infectious high spirits, make him an extremely interesting violinist. In fact, his manliness, even in Bach's "Air," which so often is made mawkish, and in the lovely "Canzonetta," from Tchaikovsky's concerto, was superb, and Mr. Klein quite carried his large audience away with him, and made a genuinely successful first appearance here.

The critic of the "Violin Times" calls Mr. Klein "the greatest genius of the rising generation." Let us hope that these reports will be verified upon Mr. Klein's appearance in New York.

While the Metropolitan Opera House has recently had an array of American singers comprising Mmes. Eames, Fremstad, Nordica, Homer, Rappold, Walker, Weed, and Jacobi, and Messrs. Bispham, Rand, Pollock, and Blass, American singers abroad are also reaping laurels, prominent among them being the baritone Mr. Charles W. Clark, whose excellent pronunciation of the German is, by the way, especially lauded in the press reports concerning him. It is somewhat unfortunate that, owing to the difficulties of the German language, even singers of considerable vocal ability should so frequently be guilty of serious lapses in this regard, or, by reason of insufficient familiarity with the language, fail to grasp the meaning of important lines.

Signor Puccini has done us the honor to place our modern naval heroes and our distinguished consuls on the stage of grand opera, taking his cue from an American novel, partly Italianized by him into "Madama Butterfly." Nearly everyone is familiar with John Long's pleasing story, Madam Butterfly, the scene of which is laid in Japan. Therefore the repetition of the plot will not be necessary here. It is said that, in the opera, Eastern and Western elements are well contrasted musically; but it would be interesting to know what motif Signor Puccini has chosen for depicting the American consul in civilian garb. To be sure, our consuls have long been particular favorites on the light-opera stage. They are generally men of so gay and light-hearted a nature as there depicted that their selection appears peculiarly appropriate. It seems all they have to do is to have a good time and to make everybody else happy. But how did Puccini portray our national representative in a Prince Albert? Why will not Mr. Conried give us an opportunity of judging? The opera opened the season at Milan last year; it has been given in England; and, if the writer is not mistaken, it has even made its way to Buenos Ayres. "La Tosca" and "La Bohème" have long been familiar to New York audiences. But that is all we have heard of the composer of the "veritistic school" here.

34

But the great musical event in the operatic field last year was the production of Richard Strauss's "Salome," based upon the story by Oscar Wilde. It has been said that Wilde's drama was inspired by the narrative of Flaubert. Subsequently, it is claimed, the Englishman visited the great art galleries of England, Belgium, France, Germany, and Italy, in order, if possible, to find in the great paintings portraying the subject some suggestion as to the proper historical setting and coloring for his drama. If the writer is not mistaken, it was a painting by Moreau which finally determined the English playwright to give to his awful picture of Roman decadence its present form.

As Bayreuth is the Mecca of the faithful Wagnerite, so Dresden last year was the focal centre to which thronged the admirers of Strauss from every part of the civilized world. Difficult indeed were the obstacles with which Strauss had to contend, both before and after he had found in the manager of the Royal Opera at Dresden a valuable coadjutor. First of all there was the prejudice against the play itself, which had to be overcome. Then there was the musical score, with the almost insuperable tasks it assigned to the principal singers. It is said that the prima-donna, Frau Wittig, several times returned the part assigned to her — that of the daughter of Herodias — stating that it was impossible of performance. Nevertheless, she subsequently superbly went through the artistic ordeal imposed upon her in the climax of the work, where she has to sing steadily for a full quarter of an hour, and then dance uninterruptedly for nearly the same length of time.

The instrumental forces requisite to perform this play were augmented to the extraordinary number of 104 musicians, including sixty strings, an organ, and the celeste, that instrument with which Tchaikovsky was so delighted when he first saw it at Paris shortly after its invention, and which has since been so skilfully employed by his compatriot Rimsky-Korsakoff and other modern composers. The realistic effects which Strauss has here produced are said to transcend anything else that he has yet written; and the bits of humor, which with him are unfailing, however drastic, are said to have been wonderfully effective and convincing. In one passage, for example, he lets three men carry on an exciting conversation, one talking in seven-eighth time and the other two simultaneously in five-eighth and four-quarter, while the orchestra continues its original tempo. Yet the vast audience, as well as the discerning critics who heard the performance of this short play — its duration was only an hour and a half — could not but marvel at the extraordinary power and ingenuity displayed by the composer. Upon the conclusion of the opera, Strauss was recalled twenty-five times before the curtain.

The very possibility of bringing about a performance which is said to have been absolutely convincing is in itself a colossal achievement.

To understand this "realism" of Strauss in its full scope one must first of all understand the great movements of our time, the under-currents which, though all may be setting in the same direction, nevertheless manifest themselves in different ways according to the individual. Were it possible to have really standard performances of Strauss's tremendously difficult works, the writer is convinced that even the man of average musical or general culture would recognize that there is a personality involved here which does not arbitrarily select its material nor aim at specific effects. In all of Strauss's work we notice a steady progression enforced by inward necessity, and in each of them there is a perfectly logical and coördinate sequence of ideas. That they are so frequently rendered in a fragmentary and incomprehensible manner is not the fault of the composer.

Yet this is not the place to enter upon a discussion in detail of the work of the foremost musician of the age. It may be well to point out, however, that the most just critical estimates of the German composer have recently proceeded from English critics. Paul Colberg, for example, well says that "Strauss's music will not stand an analysis by picking it to atoms," while J. W. G. Hatham, in an excellent article entitled "The Abolition of Key," refers to a prominent characteristic of Strauss's work, in the following pertinent passage:

Without abolishing tonality, it may be possible to expand its limits. It is possible to strain the bounds of key-relationship to such a point that it is extremely difficult to point to a certain passage as being in this or that key — and yet how far from outraging our sense of the beautiful! We are enchanted with the results. It was the fashion when Wagner first came to the front to accuse him of not writing melody, and it is probable that in the days when Bach was not understood the same defect was attributed to him. The people say that Strauss cannot write melody. But he is far too clever a man not to understand the value of rhythm, climax, or melody. His climaxes are terrific, his knowledge of all the subtleties of rhythm is endless, and his melodies are full of beauty and charm, though less obvious than in the case of the older writers.

If Strauss's "Salome" carries us back 2,000 years, to the period of Roman decadence, Chenier's "Siberia," which was performed at Paris and received there with tremendous enthusiasm, presents one of the saddest and most tragic phases of contemporaneous history. Thus we see how wide is the scope afforded to the operatic composer, and how varied are the tendencies of opera to-day, at least as regards the selection of subjects. Grand operas dealing with contemporary events are rare. In the case of "Siberia," it is said that it was not the music so much as the *tout-ensemble* which produced so profound an impression at Paris.

One of the principal episodes represents the passage of a group of exiles through the Siberian snows. At first the audience faintly hears a song of the boatmen of the Volga in the far distance. The captives, on hearing the well-known melody, take up the strains in chorus. But fainter and fainter becomes their song, until at last they disappear upon the wide steppe. The effect is said to have been intensely affecting and dramatic.

The small nations of Europe are as proud and jealous of their political independence and historic traditions, and probably even more so, than those of greater extent. Especially is this true of Holland and Belgium. In the latter country, a Flemish opera, "De Vlassgaard," by Joseph Van der Meulen, was performed more than a dozen times at Ghent, and subsequently at Brussels. It can readily be imagined with what enthusiasm a really meritorious work such as this, when sung in the language of the country, is greeted in Belgium, a country so small in area, yet blessed with the largest population per square mile in Europe, and an intensely patriotic population at that. Moreover, there is no country on the Continent where music is more zealously cultivated, every village having its little band, its singing society, and its musical fêtes. And why should it not be so in the land of Orlando di Lasso? Is not the very origin of modern music traced in a great measure to the men of Flanders? What country has had so many political vicissitudes? Yet is it not marvellous that, though France and Spain, England and Austria, Holland and Germany, have to some extent left their impress here, the fundamental characteristics of the people, despite occupations and sieges, and foreign domination and tyranny, should have remained so strongly rooted? Let us therefore welcome those endeavors which seek to perpetuate as long as possible the noble national traditions of Flanders.

As regards quantity, the output in the field of song has this year probably surpassed all previous records; and it is especially the *lied* (song) with orchestral accompaniment, the prominent exponents of which are Strauss, D'Albert, Mahler, and others, which is acquiring greater popularity. Songs of a religious nature, however, are to-day at a very low ebb in Germany, the land in which Protestant church music first acquired its true glory under the influence of Johann Sebastian Bach. And what a host of others, known to-day the world over, followed in his train! Well may we say "*Tempora mutantur.*" Italians and Englishmen to-day seem to dominate this field, and in Germany as elsewhere are heard the compositions of Bossi, Elgar, and Wolf-Ferrari.

In the field of instrumental music the "Sinfonietta" of Max Reger, that most gifted and versatile of all the younger instrumental and lyrical composers abroad, has been the novelty of the winter. It would easily be possible here to write an entire essay on this prolific composer, who, though only thirty-three years of age, has already written about 200 songs and a great variety of other compositions, those for the organ having already earned for him the title of "Classiker der Orgelphantasie" (The Classic of the Organ Fantasy). The piano accompaniment to several of his songs is probably the most complicated ever attempted. Reger is a man of imposing presence, more than six feet tall, and, like Strauss, is said to be gifted with a great fund of humor, of which he occasionally gives his hearers the benefit. In one of his compositions, for example, he has introduced the themes "S-c-h-a-f" (Sheep) and "A-f-f-e" (Monkey), by which terms some unkind persons have said he meant to designate his critics.

Rousseau was a great philosopher; that he was also a musician who compiled one of our famous musical dictionaries and a composer who wrote the delightful opéra comique "Le Devin du Village" is not so well known, perhaps. It is likely that the musical element within him had a more powerful influence on his development than many suppose. Beethoven was a musician; that he was also a philosopher, a thinker of the highest order, is the profound conviction of the present writer. The late Friedrich Nietzsche, the eminent philosopher, was powerfully influenced by music, to the extent that he once composed an orchestral work which he sent to Hans von Bülow, with whom he was on terms of close friendship. From the letters between Nietzsche and Bülow, which were included in the third volume of Nietzsche's correspondence, recently published, it would appear that Bülow did not like Nietzsche's composition very much. This is evident from the following characteristic and somewhat amusing extract from one of these letters, which is here in part translated:

ESTEEMED PROFESSOR: Your kind communication and enclosure have put me in an embarrassment such as I have never experienced before. I ask myself, Shall I remain silent, utter a civilized commonplace, or come out with the true colors? [Here follows the expression of Bülow's high appreciation of Nietzsche as a scientific investigator. In other words, Bülow slightly sugar-coats the pill which he is about to administer in order to effect a cure.] As a musician I am accustomed, like Hansemann, who declared that "in money-matters pleasantry ceases," to follow the principle that "in *materia musica* politeness ceases." But to the point: Your "Manfred Meditation" is the extreme of fantastic extravagance, the most unrefreshing and anti-musical production that my eyes have long encountered in the form of notation on paper. Often I was compelled to ask myself, "Is the whole thing a jest? Did he perhaps intend to pen a parody on the so-called *Music of the Future?*" [Here follows another sweetener, whereupon Bülow resumes:] Once more — do not take it unkindly! — You have yourself designated your music as horrible. It is so in fact — more horrible than you believe; yet not injurious as regards its influence on the public, but worse than that — injurious to yourself, who cannot better kill such leisure as you have at your disposal than to violate Euterpe.

The old Germans were accustomed to giving and taking hard knocks; and the modern representatives of a certain tendency do not hesitate to use the bludgeon and the battle-axe in literature. Well, Nietzsche did not spare, and why should Bülow? And, after all, it has been said that the first condition of true friendship is absolute frankness — a statement exemplified here with a vengeance.

"Davon isst und trinkt man" (That is meat and drink to one), once said a friend to the writer in characterizing a certain literary production. The same may be said of Mr. Henry T. Finck's "Edvard Grieg," in the series entitled "Living Masters of Music."[1] The book is charmingly written, is entertaining from cover to cover, and is sure to become popular with all music-lovers. Mr. Finck has the gift of the true biographer, of nowhere obtruding his own personality. It is Grieg who is constantly before us, now as a student, and again at the conductor's desk, or in the quiet of his home; and the facts that Mr. Finck presents in connection with the career of Grieg — facts presented by means of letters, conversations, authentic anecdotes, etc., — not only afford a vivid picture of the composer himself from a variety of viewpoints, but also bring us in contact with many eminent contemporaries of the distinguished Norwegian, such as Björnson, Ole Bull, Ibsen, and Liszt. Mr. Finck says in his preface: "Before I reached the middle of my manuscript, I had to implore the publisher to allow me 10,000 words more than the 20,000 first asked for, being loath to leave the good things I had found to my successors." It is with regret that the present writer feels constrained to confine himself to the mention of only one of these. "good things."

One of the illustrations to Mr. Finck's little volume is a group-picture representing Mr. and Mrs. Grieg and Mr. and Mrs. Björnson. Grieg and Björnson have always been very close friends. On a certain occasion Grieg played his newly-composed "Vaterlandslied" (Patriotic Song) for Björnson, who was delighted with it, stating that it strongly suggested to him the accents of speech (*Wortklang*). The next day Björnson came to Grieg and said: "It is to be a song for all young Norwegians. But at the beginning there is something that has so far baffled me. . . . I feel that the melody demands verse. Yet it eludes me. But it will come!" Then the two friends parted. The writer presents the sequel in the words of Grieg:

The next morning, while I was sitting in my garret room in Upper Wall Street

[1] New York: John Lane Co.

giving a lesson to a young lady, someone in the street pulled the bell-cord as if he were trying to tear out the whole thing. Then there was a clattering as if a wild horde were breaking in, and a voice shouting "Forward! Forward! Hurrah! I have it! Forward!" My pupil trembled like an aspen leaf. My wife, in the adjoining room, was almost frightened out of her wits. But when, a moment later, the door was opened and Björnson stood there, joyous and beaming like a sun, there was great glee. And then we listened to the beautiful poem just completed:

"Fremad! Fädres höie härtag var.
Fremad! Nordmänd, ogsaa vi det tar!"

Letters are always interesting, especially when they reflect a man's true personality. In the "Life and Letters of Peter Ilich Tchaikovsky," by Modest Tchaikovsky, edited from the Russian by Rosa Newmarch,[1] we have a perfect embarrassment of riches in this regard. Especially noteworthy is the correspondence of the distinguished Russian composer during his American tour in 1891. Upon the whole, the reader gains the impression that Tchaikovsky's life must have been a pretty sad one and that it was pervaded throughout by that strong tinge of melancholy which is said to be characteristic of the Muscovite, and which must have been especially so in the case of the subject of this biography. Tchaikovsky's sensitiveness is almost morbid. Severe, too, almost harsh, are his criticisms of some of the distinguished composers of his day — Rubinstein among others. Yet it cannot but be interesting, especially to the musician, to follow the career of a man whose popularity in several countries of Europe, as well as in the United States, is constantly increasing, and whose splendid artistic endowment is universally conceded.

JOSEPH SOHN.

[1] John Lane Co.: New York.

THE EDUCATIONAL OUTLOOK.

EDUCATIONAL research is a scientific procedure. In the hands of dilettanti it is apt to become an instrument of mischief. The analysis of educational results is the business of technically trained persons. Neither appointment by mayor, comptroller, or school board, nor election by popular vote, can supply the wisdom required for the task. Apparently excellent work may be utterly contemned in the eyes of experts. On the other hand, results over which the amateur investigator pours out the vessels of wrath may in reality be entitled to commendation. Furthermore, tests, in order to establish anything, must be of a comparative nature. Absolutism, in whatever form it may appear, is at best only a subject for discussion. The reasonableness of a test must be proved before its results can be accepted as authoritative. It is well to bear these cautions in mind when reading the findings of educational investigating commissions.

Research is likely to become for a time the ruling fad in the school world. With a zeal and enthusiasm characteristic of converts to a new idea of great magnitude, friends and foes of schools and school systems have undertaken investigations of various kinds. Most of these inquiries bear unmistakable evidences of a desire to prove a point. Not revelations, but confirmations, seem to be wanted. The futility of this sort of affirmatory scrutation ought to be manifest without further argument. Experience shows, however, that while the motives of inquisitors are openly questioned, their assertions, presented as results of an inquest, are commonly accepted as proofs, especially if they are sufficiently startling to appeal to the sensation-mongering newspapers.

Criticism pre-supposes standards. Unfortunately for the schools, the number of standards by which educational results may be measured with some degree of finality is very limited. The work begun by Dr. Rice has not been developed extensively enough as yet to warrant the utterance of positive judgments as to the capabilities of schools. Business men may complain that the graduates of the elementary schools are not as quick and accurate at arithmetical calculations as they ought to be. Standards of seemingly reasonable expectation and standards of possible attainment are not necessarily congruent.

The present interest in examinations of the product of the schools should prove a strong incentive to the scientific development of rational educational standards. Here is a fallow field of immeasurable extent where expert laborers are sadly needed. University schools of pedagogy are really the places where work of this kind should be done. The expense involved in carrying on the investigations is necessarily large. Laboratory methods invariably consume more money than mere book studies, but the results are of all the greater benefit to the world. There ought not to be much difficulty in persuading some wealthy philanthropist that the endowment of a bureau or a university chair of educational research would prove a most satisfactory investment. As matters stand at present, no one can tell absolutely whether the millions expended annually for schools are yielding adequate returns, how much money is wasted in foolish experiments, what are the latent possibilities of public instruction. We have no really effective method of recording educational achievement. Every teacher does the best he can, and takes the greater part of his experience into the grave with him. School journals and teachers' meetings are not sufficient for the task of gathering, systematizing, and spreading abroad the best results of educational thought and practice. A Carnegie who should grasp the great significance of this opportunity might render incalculable service to mankind by coming forward in support of the idea.

The teachers, apparently, are ready to help on the construction of standards for testing the results of their work. Every really significant investigation which is brought to their attention is at once utilized extensively as a basis for comparative self-examination. Thus, the Springfield examination commented upon in the last number of THE FORUM has been repeated in schools over the whole country, with widely differing results, to be sure, but nevertheless confirming fully the conclusions here offered. From the more than 200 tests which have fallen under my notice, the one by Principal Mills of a public school in Brooklyn comes probably nearest to being representative of the findings in the average best schools of the country. The test is described by Dr. William H. Maxwell in his official report to the New York City Board of Education, which was made public last month. Mr. Mills applied the questions to fifty-four girls and forty boys in the eighth year of the elementary school. The Springfield examination of 1846, it will be remembered, was participated in by fifty-six boys and twenty-nine girls of the high school. The returns in arithmetic were as follows:

	Springfield, 1846.	Brooklyn, 1905.
Per cent correct	29.46	71.27
Per cent having first example correct...... Less than	50.	92.55
Per cent having second example correct	58.82	93.61
Per cent having fourth example correct	12.94	72.34
Per cent of boys having sixth example correct......	8.23	46.80
Per cent of girls who failed in fourth example........	100	25.92
Per cent of girls who failed in sixth example	100	46.29
Per cent of girls who solved interest example........	10.34	68.51
Total average of the girls.........................	19	72.69

The results of the spelling test were as follows:

	Springfield, 1846.	Brooklyn, 1905.
Number of pupils	85	94
Per cent of pupils who received 70 per cent or more ..	17.64	35.10
Per cent who missed every word	2.35	
Per cent who spelled but one word	10.58	
Per cent who missed 17 or more words	27.05	11.06

Superintendent Maxwell adds these comments:

The conclusions to be drawn from these results in a Brooklyn school are very positive. Spelling and arithmetic, instead of suffering in a course of study which trains a child to use all of his powers of expression, are actually far better than — in fact, at least twice as good as — they were under a curriculum with endless, brain-tiring, uninteresting drill — and nothing else— on the "three R's." Our schools are still far from having reached the ideal for which all intelligent teachers are striving, but we may at least enjoy the satisfaction of knowing that not only are the "three R's" not neglected, but that the extension of the course of study to embrace execution and expression is steadily improving those attainments that depend chiefly on judgment and memory. The acquisition of skill in any intellectual or bodily function develops a reserve of intellectual power to be drawn upon when occasion requires.

Meanwhile, Cleveland, Ohio, has had an educational investigation of its own, the results of which have stirred up considerable feeling at home and abroad. Proceeding from the not uncommon assumption that any intelligent citizen is able to determine the quality of scholastic results, the school board last year appointed a commission composed almost wholly of laymen to report upon the efficiency of the city's common schools. A sub-committee, headed by President Thwing of the Western Reserve University, prepared a conservative and really excellent statement concerning the conditions and needs of the Cleveland high schools. But the report which caused the sensation was the one by the Committee on Elementary Schools. While apparently intended to be fair and free from prejudice, the desire to prove a point is not entirely concealed. The chief fault of the report is its amateurishness and the consequent rashness in drawing conclusions.

No one can charge the Cleveland Committee on Elementary Schools with not having been painstaking enough. The investigation must have caused Mr. Avery, the chairman, an immense amount of labor. Familiarity with the history of attempts to test the efficiency of schools and school curricula would have saved him and his committee much criticism. Only trained experts can successfully carry on an examination that will actually establish a case. How much weight would be attached to the findings of a committee composed of teachers regarding the efficiency of a garrison or a hospital? The Cleveland committee no doubt meant well, and some of its conclusions are quite sound. But its recommendations very naturally lack authority, except the fictitious importance which official credentials may accord it in its own locality. The committee deplores the inadequacy of results in the so-called essentials, but praises the teachers. It goes on record with this statement:

The great majority of the teachers in our common schools are intelligent and earnest, wholly qualified and fit for the positions they occupy.

It is very interesting to follow the reasoning of the committee, as it reveals misconceptions which are quite prevalent, but which are not often recorded in such a manner that one can show the errors involved. "Intelligent reading" the committee quite correctly understands to mean "the transferring of the thought of the writer to the mind of the reader or the listener." It is also safe in saying that "without such reading, satisfactory progress in school is impossible." But when it comes to account for alleged poor results in reading it fires a blank shot:

It appears that the time allowance provided by the school schedule for this subject covers several things in addition to actual reading by the individual pupils. The testimony of the teachers in our common schools is to the effect that, for such reading, the individual pupil has from five to eleven minutes per week — not that many minutes per day, but that many minutes per week. After this statement it is not surprising that, of the teachers in grades five to eight inclusive, only sixty-two reported that they had enough time for reading, while more reported that they had not enough time for this fundamental study, and that, of the 1,312, not more than three reported in definite terms that the results were satisfactory. In almost every case it was suggested that better results could be secured if the teacher and pupils were relieved of some of the work required for other subjects.

Teachers, parents, and others who appeared in person before the committee were unanimous and emphatic in their statements that the teaching of reading in the Cleveland common schools is the weakest point in our school curriculum. In response to inquiries sent to our high-school principals as to the facts bearing on this subject as developed in their experience, one of them replies: "Intelligent reading seems to be one of the lost arts among the pupils coming to us." The testimony to this effect is so emphatic and so nearly unanimous as to leave no doubt that a radical reform in this respect is needed.

Analysis is bound to weaken somewhat the complaint regarding the time allowance for reading. The committee suggests elsewhere that there are usually more than fifty children in a class. Assigning to each individual pupil "from five to eleven minutes per week—not that many minutes per day, but that many minutes per week"—means that a minimum of 250 to 550 minutes per week is given to reading, or from fifty to 110 minutes a day. The committee thus in effect asserts that even two hours a day is not enough for the teaching of reading. Experts would consider the time allowance amply sufficient for all practical purposes. "Relief of some of the work required for other subjects" is not likely to improve the quality of reading, under the circumstances. The committee's implied suggestion that eleven minutes a day for each individual pupil would be none too much, is simply asking for a time allowance of more than nine hours a day for reading alone.

"Intelligent reading" is a variable performance. It certainly pre-supposes that a pupil knows what he is reading about when he is reading. If this kind of reading is to be counted among "the lost arts" in Cleveland, the conclusion must be that either the pupils have not learned to read thoughtfully, or that they are given something to read which they cannot understand. In the former case the elementary schools are to be blamed: in the latter case, one of "our high-school principals" is wrong. There is no doubt that in the majority of schools I have visited, too little attention is paid to making the reading pupil realize that he ought to try to understand and remember what he is reading. This seems to be more or less true of city schools generally. The Cleveland committee's plan would probably be to let the pupil read aloud a certain number of minutes each day, as no allowance is made for silent reading. Here is exactly the place where much responsibility may be located for the large amount of thoughtless reading. Silent reading for thought-getting would be a much more valuable exercise, especially if an examination follows where an account must be given of the results of the silent-study period.

Prof. Brumbaugh of the University of Pennsylvania illustrated the point at issue very strikingly at the national convention of school superintendents recently held in Louisville. He spoke of the folly of keeping the pupil constantly dependent upon the orders of the teacher. When a child leans back to think over a matter of some interest to himself, the ordinary teacher immediately reproves him for non-attendance to his duties. "John, keep your eye on your work! Lizzie, get busy!" These are reproaches that kill many nascent attempts at thoughtfulness. The example by which Dr. Brumbaugh fixed his point related to his boyhood days on the farm. "My mother told me," he said, "whenever I saw a hen setting on a dozen eggs to let her alone." The child wants to be permitted to think long enough "to hatch out something." Here is a suggestion which is well worth the consideration of teachers.

The spelling "test" of the Cleveland committee proves very little beyond showing that the absurd garb in which many English words appear is not always as well memorized by children as some of their elders would have them do. These were the words used in the "test":

drowsy	elegant	sieve
peninsular	tongue	guardian
excelled	orange	convalesce
diligence	Delaware	hazel
measles	cholera	blamable
stirred	civilize	telegraph
alliance	anxiety	barbarous
opponent	Wednesday	marvel
surviving	veteran	obliged
worthy	military	financial
annoyance	increased	navigator
ratio	chargeable	business
dimmer	possess	collision
wrangle	imagine	seditious
opposed	patriotic	balance
control	abandon	ally
conceal	riddle	

The "test" was applied in four schools. The words were "pronounced by the regular teachers in the usual form, the committee being desirous here, as in every case, to avoid anything that might tend in any way to the embarrassment or confusion of any of the pupils." The examination was given to 144 eight-year pupils. Thirty-six of the fifty words were misspelled in the poorest paper. One paper contained no error. The total number of misspelled words was 1,887, the average thus being about thirteen words per pupil, which would seem to be a comparatively fair showing. The Cleveland committee, however, is scandalized.

In arithmetic the committee confined itself to the eighth year, on the assumption that if the Cleveland schools "are giving their pupils a satisfactory training in this really essential branch of study, the fact would show in the work done by pupils who had most nearly completed the common-school course." So far, so good. But the committee carried its method of selection a little too far when it decided to test only:

(a) Some of the pupils who came from portions of the city that are supposed to be marked, in an especial degree, by the liberally educated class.

(b) Some of the pupils largely representative of the artisan class.

(c) Some of the fairly representative of the foreign-born part of our population.

The following "test," which, the committee had been informed, "would have been perfectly fair for fifth-grade pupils," was applied to the selected eighth-year classes:

NOTE. — Read this printed slip carefully and then wait for the order to begin the work called for.

Name of school.

Number of grade.

Name of pupil.

Fill the blanks above.

Harry Clifton bought of James Armitage goods as indicated below. The clerk who sold the goods and made the memoranda misspelled some of the words. The bookkeeper corrected these errors in making up the account and you are expected to do the same. The memoranda showed the following charges:

1 March, 2 dozzen Orranges at 45 cents a dozzen; 2 March, 2 pecks of aples at 35c a peck; 3 March, 2 cans punkins @ 12 ½c each; 4 Mar. 2 Galons Molassis at 55c a gall and 2 ℔ Butter at 33c a pound; 6 March, 11 yards of callico at 7c per yard; 6 Mar., 2 ℔ coffey at ⅔ of a dollar a pound; 7 Mar. 1 sack sugor, $1.18; 8 Mar, 1 gal sirrup, $1.00; 10 March, Pickels, 33c; next day, Cabbage, 12 cents, 14 Mar, Cheese 75c; 15 Mar., 3 ℔ Rasins at 15c a pound; ditto 2 ton soft cole a $3.75 a ton; 16 March, paid in cash $6.00 on acct; 17 March, 3 rolls wall Paper @ 17c a roll; 20 March, 3 hours plummers Time at 50 cents an hour; 25 March 1 refrigerater, $20.00; 27 March, 1 spunge, 37 cents; last day of the month, 2 doz. Lemons at 16 cents a doz.

Write out, in the form below, the itemized bill for the above, showing the amount due on the account, and receipt the bill.

The form furnished was such a one as is ordinarily used for an itemized statement of sales. The pupils were given five minutes for the study of the problem and for filling in the information items asked for at the head of the paper. Then forty-five minutes by the clock were allowed for the completion of the itemized bill as directed. The "test" was carried into five different schools, and given to 144 pupils; 551 words were misspelled. One pupil who evidently did not know how to spell "refrigerator" substituted therefor the word ice-box. This was not counted an error, because of a feeling that the resourcefulness shown was worth more than the ability to spell the word. Forty-seven of the pupils failed properly to enter the name of the debtor, and only receipted the bill in proper form. The committee understands that bookkeeping is taught in the latter half of the eighth-grade year. The papers handed in by the pupils clearly show that no pupil was handicapped by the form in which the questions were put or the answers written. The most significant result of the test lies in the fact that of the 144 pupils only fifty-seven got the correct answer, and that the school returning the largest proportion of correct answers was the one most distinctively representative of the immigrant class.

The committee calls the "test" one in "simple commercial arithmetic," and says it was disappointing. Other examinations in simple addition, subtraction, multiplication, and division were decided upon. Here stop-watches were used, and other proceedings helped to ordea lze the occasion. Nevertheless, the schools should have done better than they did, if arithmetic had been satisfactorily taught, and the committee is not radical when it ventures the opinion "that nothing it can say would add to the impressiveness of this exhibit." Mental arithmetic is commended to the teachers as a remedy. Unfortunately this form of performing calculations is also subject to human frailty and inefficiency. A method cannot be depended upon for the production of results. The right sort of teachers with the right sort of supervision to hold them to account will solve the problem more surely.

The penmanship of the good old times, anyway of the early seventies, is considered by the committee to have been better than that which the Cleveland schools turn out in the present year of grace. This may be true, because for a certain period the schools of Cleveland made a special feature of chirography. However, no greater mistake can be made than to judge of the efficiency of a school by the character of its penmanship, for the simple reason that the development of artistic penmanship may involve an extremely costly sacrifice of time in all the studies which call for written exercises — a fact not generally taken into account. Indeed, Dr. Rice has noted specific instances in which pupils have consumed a full hour longer than necessary in working out sets of problems in arithmetic, by reason of being compelled by their teachers to write their figures with copper-plate accuracy.

I would like to repeat a suggestion made in these pages once before, which, if carried out, would effectually dispose of a little of the never-ending declamations about the superior excellencies of the schools of the past. Some of the older colleges of the country have in their possession papers supplied in the entrance examinations of years gone by. With the assistance of students, a professor of pedagogy or some other educational expert might readily make comparisons with the papers of recent years. The results of the investigation would be fully worth the time and labor required for the task.

Of course, whatever may be established with reference to the intellectual product of the old schools of former days, a door will still be open for those who mourn the decline of morals and the disappearance of "old-fashioned honesty" from the land. Just now we are right in the midst of lamentations of this sort. Those who incline to optimism have newspapers and frenzied magazines thrust before their eyes, to be converted by reports of investigations into various forms of "graft." We are told that men occupying positions of trust and honor have been found wanting in the virtues which are the very root of manliness and righteousness. All these things are true, alas! But are they the prodncts of the modern school? Look at the men at whom an indignant public is pointing the finger of scorn. Their hair is white and their step is tottering: they were trained in the "thorough" schools of the past, where the schoolmaster's word was law, where "lickin' and larnin'" went hand-in-hand, where the three R's were the supreme anxiety. The investigators of these men are the products of the modern school. Philadelphia was redeemed from political slavery by the young men of the city. Almost everywhere the warfare upon "graft" has had its beginning in the ranks of young men, most of them graduated from college within the last ten or twelve years. These young men had ideals and could not stand idly by while monstrous evils were threatening to corrode the very foundations of democratic institutions. These young men founded good-government clubs, not minding the scoffs of their cynical seniors. They organized vigilance committees to bring to task the betrayers of public trusts, whom a diffident generation had lifted into power.

And why should not the present be an advance over the past? Has not the past been the teacher of the present? By guidance, direction, and prescription, as well as by its mistakes, the past has raised civilization to a higher plane. If this were not true, then human effort would be in vain. We have profited by the achievements and errors of those who have gone this way before us, as they profited by the achievements and errors of their forerunners. If to-day were not better than yesterday, then the teachers of yesterday would stand altogether condemned. It is perfectly fitting that alarming symptoms of moral obliquity in public life should draw attention to the opportunity afforded at school for instilling in the youthful minds right views of human relationships and obligations. There need be no fault-finding. It is more economical for educators to go directly at the study of the needs of the times and then to do the best that can be done to meet these needs.

How prevalent the anxiety for the spiritual welfare of the young is at present, and how desirous educators are to come to a fuller understanding of their duties in this respect, was very evident at the Louisville meeting of the Department of Superintendence of the National Educational Association. No discussion excited greater interest than that occupied with the means afforded in the common schools for moral and religious training and instruction. President Thompson, of the Ohio University, treated one phase of the problem so admirably that there was an immediate demand for printed copies of his paper. One positive suggestion made by him was that pupils should have opportunities for initiative and free choice to develop responsibility. Prescription and direction are poor props for moral conduct. The conscience must get hold of truth and impel the individual to live his convictions. Miss Julia Richman, of New York City, described what the school can do for the moral regeneration of the supposedly "incorrigible" child. Judge Lindsey, of Denver, told about the wonderful work of his juvenile court and the power of faith in boys and girls.

With all the excellent thoughts presented, nothing was said of the really greatest opportunity of the common school, that of training children in social service. This is the key-note of the new education. Social service develops unselfishness, zeal in a brother's cause, a humanitarian attitude, and moral efficiency. Holiness is not the supreme aim, but efficient loving-kindness. One interesting item of information was brought forward by Superintendent Raymond, of South Dakota. He stated that the Teachers' Association of his State had appointed a committee to investigate the subject of moral and religious instruction, with a view of elaborating a series of tenets upon which people of all creeds could agree, and which might then be taught in the schools.

Whether or not there should be specific and systematic instruction in morality supplied to the children in the schools, is with many still an unsettled question. The only real difficulty in the way of a general acceptance of the new subject appears to be the apprehension that teachers will involve themselves more or less in theological discussions giving offence to the community. There is a plan by which this may be overcome. It is the one which South Dakota has evidently decided to try. Guiding principles need to be formulated and illustrative model lessons furnished, something after the fashion of the report on industrial education presented to the National Council of Education last summer. This is really a problem for the National Educational Association to handle.

My personal conviction has been for some years that two or three religious ideas may well be adopted by the common schools of the United States as fundamental in a suitable scheme of teaching morality. Morality, without religion, is devoid of dynamic power. Religion is the heart of morality. In matters pertaining to moral duty the heart speaks louder than the head. Systems of morals have been formulated omitting every reference to the human brotherhood in God and solely occupied with so-called "natural-science laws." They may be interesting and useful pieces of logic, and as such benefit the intellect. But inspiration they have only when the heart speaks, in spite of the care exercised to stifle its voice. It is not profitable to try to teach morals without appeal to the feelings. The problem is before us and is likely to occupy us for

35

some years to come. Oratory will not solve it. There will have to be patient research and wise experiment.

Second in importance to moral training on the programme of the Department of Superintendence was the question of ways and means for improving the efficiency of grammar schools. Prof. Frank McMurry, of Columbia University, argued for the training of children in the art of study. They must be taught how to use maps and charts and reference books. The child needs to learn how to master a new problem without help from anyone. School programmes ordinarily make no provision whatever for this. The result is that many pupils never acquire the art of independent thinking and working.

An interesting point in the paper by Prof. Avery, of Indiana University, on the teaching of arithmetic, was that his State had found by practical experience that whatever results are actually required by law to be produced in school are invariably secured. It is another confirmation of the belief that children are capable of almost anything: they supply what is asked for, providing, of course, that the demands are not too numerous. Wherever the emphasis is placed, there the effort is uniformly greatest.

On the whole, the Louisville meeting was a very satisfactory one, although the programme did not occupy itself as intensely with vital problems of school administration and supervision as it ought to have done. Of late years it has been the tendency of the department to talk about questions of general educational import rather than to discuss those which are specifically in the scope of its purposes. At last a halt has been called to this scattering of effort. A resolution was adopted at Louisville as follows:

Resolved, That we believe that the interest of educational progress and of this department requires specialization with its resultant definite attention to particular problems and conditions. We, therefore, recommend that the programmes of this department be devoted to a discussion of the duties and responsibilities of school administration, management, supervision, and organization.

Now the department may return to its proper sphere of acting. It is all very well for speakers before the National Educational Association to argue for the extension of industrial training, of cooking, and other desirable things, for the increase of teachers' salaries, for broader high-school courses, for school nurses, for a more tasteful decoration of schools, and whatever else may serve to render the education of the people more efficient and place teaching upon the plane it ought justly to occupy. The National Educational Association platform is well suited for the announcement of new problems and the declaration of new creeds. The Department of Superintendence is by the very nature of its constitution bound to consider more particularly the practical administrative questions raised by those new problems. "Where is the money to come from?" is a subject of greater anxiety to ninety-nine per cent of the superintendents than any other. Most fine educational theories are wrecked on the financial rock. Hence no one need be ashamed to place the real problems of administration on the programme of the department. They are vital.

I cannot close my review without at least a brief reference to the passing away of one who for many years took a keen interest in the progress of education in America. The death of Dr. William Rainey Harper, president of the University of Chicago from the inception of the institution in 1891, did not come unexpectedly, yet the sorrow for it is none the less. He was a lovable man, and he worked with an energy that seemed inexhaustible. As an organizer and administrator he had no superior in the field of higher education in America. While he was not, strictly speaking, an educator, and it would be unwise to compare him with those who are, he has been of much help to the cause of education by the espousal of the educational ideas of others. His greater glory, aside from his wonderful business ability, must be looked for in theological scholarship and in his inspirational power as a teacher of theological lore. He was an authority on the Semitic languages, especially Hebrew. To Bible archæology and Assyriology he made valuable contributions. American theology loses in him an erudite scholar, a great inspiring force, and a masterly teacher; Chicago University a never-wearying worker for the enlargement of its scope and efficiency, one who aimed to make it the most comprehensive institution of learning in the world; the country at large, an honored citizen, who by his wonderful personality and labor added to her glory among the nations of the world.

OSSIAN H. LANG.

DR. BIRKBECK HILL AND HIS EDITION OF JOHNSON'S "LIVES OF THE POETS."[1]

THIS is in every sense of the term an Oxford book, indeed, a Pembroke College book, although it includes many a poet who never sang in that famous "nest of singing birds." In the preface to his edition of Boswell's "Life of Johnson" Dr. Birkbeck Hill told us how, when he entered Pembroke, he loved to think that Johnson had been there before him, and how, although he did not then read Boswell, his mind, by "a happy chance," was turned to that eighteenth century of the literature of which he was to become so devoted a student. In Addison and the other classics of the age of prose and reason, he found an "exquisitely clear style," an "admirable common sense," and a freedom from affectation that afforded "a delightful contrast" to many of the eminent authors of his own time. He found also none of "those troublesome doubts, doubts of all kinds, which since the great upheaval of the French Revolution have harassed mankind"; and so he passed from one leisurely writer to another, without knowing that he was steadily preparing himself for what was to be the main work of his life.

At last, in 1869, "a happy day" came for him, "when in an old bookshop, almost under the shadow of a great cathedral," he bought a second-hand copy of a somewhat early edition of Boswell in five volumes. These became his "inseparable companions." He began to note parallel passages and allusions; as a reviewer, he made himself a specialist in works dealing with Boswell and Johnson; and then he offered to edit a Boswell for a publisher who had just engaged another editor. Not discouraged, and despite grievous illness, he continued to study his favorite author, and in 1878 he published "Dr. Johnson: His Friends and His Critics." Then he unearthed and edited some curious letters of the youthful Boswell, and was drawn off into two biographical tasks that took him out of his chosen century; but by 1885 he was ready for the compositors to begin upon his edition of Boswell, and in March, 1887, he signed the preface of what it

---

[1] "Lives of the English Poets." By Samuel Johnson, LL.D. Edited by George Birkbeck Hill, D.C.L., sometime Honorary Fellow of Pembroke College, Oxford. With a brief sketch of Dr. Birkbeck Hill, by his nephew, Harold Spencer Scott, M.A., New College, Oxford. In three volumes. Oxford, at the Clarendon Press MDCCCCV. 8vo, pp. xxvii. 487; iv. 440; iv. 568.

JOHNSON'S "LIVES OF THE POETS."

may be a commonplace but is certainly not an exaggeration to call one of the most monumental works of modern scholarship.

His devotion to Johnson's memory did not slacken, however, when he had corrected the proofs of the enormous index that almost fills the sixth volume of his Boswell. He edited Johnson's letters, and his essays, and his "Rasselas," and he gathered notes for the most enduring of the Doctor's works, "The Lives of the Poets." Death came to him before this task, his greatest after the Boswell, could be entirely completed; but lovers of the eighteenth century and its literature were reassured when they learned that he had left his edition of the Lives in such a shape that, with some attention from a sympathetic and competent hand, it could be given to the world without injustice to his memory. The three portly volumes just published under the supervision of his nephew, Mr. Scott, are amply worthy to stand, not only as a practically final edition of one of the best known of English classics, but as the crowning work of a life of singular devotion to a beneficent task, and of a scholarship as broad and humane as it was accurate and painstaking.

After a brief prefatory note, which tells us that the text is that of the edition of 1783, with modernized punctuation, Mr. Scott gives a slight memoir of his uncle, the main points of which shall be reproduced here, since they are concerned with a personality decidedly more interesting and important than not a few of the poets whose lives follow in stately succession, with all the formality of eighteenth-century style, and the somewhat overpowering paraphernalia of nineteenth and twentieth century erudition.

George Birkbeck Norman Hill came of a Birmingham family who were followers of Priestley and enthusiasts for social and educational reform. One of his uncles was Rowland Hill, the postal reformer. The family was well known for founding and practising the Hazelwood system of education, which gave pupils a considerable measure of self-government and emphasized the importance of sympathetic instruction. Birkbeck Hill, whose name recalls that of the founder of mechanics' institutes, was born on June 7, 1835, at Bruce Castle, Tottenham, in Middlesex, where his father, Arthur Hill, was head-master of a new school. His mother died early, but his father lived to be an old man, whose perennial interest in literature could not have been without its influence upon his son. The boy seems to have inherited much of the utilitarian fervor of his ancestors — their zeal for improvements, their hatred of shams — but he was apparently more alive to the poetry and romance of life than utilitarians are supposed to be.

He was well educated at his father's school, though suffering some neglect on the side of the classics, and, when nearly twenty, he matriculated at Pembroke College, Oxford. He had been brought up to revere the writers of the preceding generation, especially those favored by "The Edinburgh Review"; now he was thrown with young men who were quoting Tennyson. He was soon introduced to the coterie of which Burne-Jones and William Morris were leaders, and for awhile he seemed in danger of becoming an admirer of Wordsworth and a contemner of Pope. Fortunately, as he tells us in the preface to his Boswell, the college authorities required him every week to turn into some sort of Latin a passage from "The Spectator." He naturally preferred to loiter over the clear English, and sighed when he had to abandon that for his own attempts at Latin. Perhaps it was through this weekly communion with Addison that he was finally saved, as by fire — for he had learned to know Rossetti and Swinburne — to become the editor of the author of the famous injunction: "Whoever wishes to attain an English style, familiar but not coarse, and elegant but not ostentatious, must give his days and nights to the volumes of Addison."

As he had been thrown back by illness, Birkbeck Hill, when he graduated in 1858, did not take a very distinguished degree. Eight years later he took a B.C.L., and three years after that a D.C.L. Meanwhile, on leaving Oxford, he had begun to teach in his father's school and had made an early marriage. Seven children were born to him during the nineteen years he remained at the Tottenham school, and this important period of his life must doubtless be regarded as successful, although he chafed against his profession, and finally gave it up after he had been sole headmaster for nine years. He was interested in teaching and in athletics — he was a great walker — but his nephew thinks that his temperament was too sensitive for his calling. Before he abandoned it, some of his energy had been diverted to literature; for in 1869 — rather late, it would seem — he became a regular contributor to "The Saturday Review," during the editorship of his friend Philip Harwood. To use his own words, he made havoc among the minor poets and novelists. But after awhile amusement turned to dejection and he gave up the poets; then the novelists proved too much for him. He became totally incapacitated for reading any novels save the favorites of his youth. "All in vain," he declared, "friends have urged me to read the works of Black, Blackmore, Hardy, Howells, Henry James, Stevenson, and Kipling. Not a single story of any one of these writers have I ever read or am I ever likely to read." Some such honest confession might probably relieve the souls of many professional reviewers and publishers' readers.

Meanwhile the Johnsonian studies already briefly described had begun to relieve the tedium of school teaching and reviewing. In 1877 he suffered a complete breakdown in health, and was never afterward strong.

He had to resign his head-mastership and spend several winters abroad. Thenceforth his life was that of a quiet scholar; and when one considers how much he accomplished, despite his painful asthma and other physical drawbacks, one is disposed to extend to him much the same sort of admiration that is spontaneously given to heroic workers like Prescott and Parkman. Between 1878, when, as we have seen, he published his first book, "Dr. Johnson: His Friends and His Critics," and 1900, he wrote or edited twenty books. Nine of these dealt primarily with Johnson or Boswell. Five were concerned with other eighteenth-century authors, Goldsmith, Hume, Lord Chesterfield, Swift, and Gibbon. He collaborated also in the biography of his uncle, Sir Rowland Hill, and edited "Colonel Gordon in Central Africa," as well as the correspondence of Dante Gabriel Rossetti with William Allingham. Besides these he wrote " Writers and Readers," "Talks About Autographs" — titles that are sufficiently descriptive — and "Harvard College, by an Oxonian." The last-named book was the result of a visit to this country, made with his wife in 1893 to see their eldest daughter, the wife of Prof. W. J. Ashley, then holding a chair in Harvard. Another result of this and of a succeeding visit in 1896 was a series of contributions to "The Atlantic Monthly"—in the main gathered into volumes already enumerated. It may be suspected, too, that without this New-World connection Dr. Hill might never have included in his notes to the "Lives of the Poets" citations from a book lying so far outside his chief lines of interest as Oliver Wendell Holmes's biography of Ralph Waldo Emerson. Yet, after all, Holmes was a true child of the eighteenth century, and there is thus a certain appropriateness in his being quoted in this edition of a great classic dealing with the masters of the couplet he loved so well.

Little more need be gleaned here from Mr. Scott's sketch, which might have been made longer without risk of lapse from the good taste that characterizes it. We learn that Dr. Hill was very sympathetic with children, as befitted one trained as he had been, and that his temperament was genial, as one somehow imagines should be the case with born lovers of the eighteenth century—witness, at least, Thackeray. His attitude toward religious matters is not brought into relief; but we are given to understand that his views on such subjects were very different from those of General Gordon, and it may well be that in this respect also he was by nature competent to sympathize with certain marked characteristics of many of the writers of his favorite century.

It is pleasant to find him, after the publication of his Boswell in 1887, living for nearly six years at Oxford, mingling with brother scholars and continuing to add to his own scholarly equipment and output. Then, finding that the climate did not suit him, he spent his winters abroad, keeping up his work as well as he could away from the Bodleian and the British Museum. The two volumes of "Johnsonian Miscellanies," which appeared five years after the edition of Johnson's Letters of 1892, were considerably delayed by the state of his health. Yet his miscellaneous tasks seemed to grow upon him rather than to decrease, and during the last three years of his life he labored systematically upon the noble volumes that have just given us a fresh reminder of how large is the debt of gratitude we owe him for his life of devoted literary service during years when a less brave and conscientious man might have thought himself well entitled to play the part of an idle valetudinarian. Finally, in the spring of 1902, his wife, who for some years had been in precarious health, began to sink, and his own last months were rendered more anxious through his ministrations to her. She died in October, 1902, and he followed her speedily, dying on February 27, 1903, at his daughter's house at Hampstead.

In a sense his epitaph must inevitably be summed up in the superlative he employed in dedicating his Boswell to Jowett — "Johnsonianissimus"; but, although to be the greatest Johnsonian of his time, and to bid fair to be the greatest for many a year, if not for ages to come, is sufficient honor for any scholar who, like Birkbeck Hill, is capable of appreciating how great Samuel Johnson really was; nevertheless one feels that Dr. Hill's character and culture were so broad and deep and individual that one scarcely cares to apply to him an epithet which involves an overshadowing of his personality. Perhaps one can salve one's conscience by giving him the place of past-master in the goodly fellowship of those who love and study the eighteenth century. Or, perhaps, one can best leave him to his fame and his rest from the ills of life with the simple statement that he was a true scholar and lover of literature.

Reference was made on a previous page to a sort of honest confession that might relieve the soul of a professional reviewer. The present reviewer will apply his own words to himself, and confess that it is much easier to abridge and comment on Mr. Scott's sketch of Dr. Hill than to appraise in an adequate fashion the three volumes that are the result of their joint labors. The extent of those labors is fairly indicated by the facts that the index occupies ninety-five large double-column pages in small type, and that the "Titles of Many of the Works Quoted in the Notes" fill nearly ten more. The Lives themselves number exactly fifty-two, several of them, like those of Pope and Savage, having the dimensions of a little book; and it is a rare page that does not yield a quarter of its space to annotations, while the chief lives provoke or encourage the annotator to flow over into appendices that apparently amount to ninety-five in number. These, in their best estate, are only somewhat long notes, hence they are not so formidable as the figures just given might lead a timorous reader to suppose. They represent, however, with the annotations, an enormous amount of labor on the part of Dr. Hill, as well as of Mr. Scott, who has "verified in the proofs by a comparison with the original authority almost every quotation and reference in the notes." They can accordingly furnish a scrupulous reviewer with just as much material for the dry-as-dust occupation of collating and testing as the most meticulously accurate of mortals could possibly desire.

Such testing is not needed here, for two very good reasons. In the first place, Dr. Hill's reputation for accuracy is already established, and it is therefore to be presumed that such errors as have slipped into his volumes are of the sort that "creep and intrude and climb into the fold," no matter how many proof-readers brandish their blue pencils. In the second place, to annotate annotations, so to speak, in these days when the leisurely lovers of foot-notes — to say nothing of leisurely lovers of any sort of reading — are supposed to be on the wane rather than on the increase, would plainly be but a questionable mode of attempting to secure consideration for a new edition of an old-fashioned classic. While, however, a systematic examination of the scholarly apparatus so generously furnished seems scarcely necessary, or even advisable, some discursive comments upon it may perhaps prove not uninteresting, and may serve to illustrate its scope and its qualities. But it should be remembered that although foot-notes, to their lovers, are readable in and for themselves, the true way to make them helpful and enjoyable is to take them along with the text in sips of contentment rather than in gulps of haste. Annotated editions such as those of Dr. Birkbeck Hill have their true place rather in the simple than in the strenuous life. Whether either of these factitious — or fictitious — modes of existence is likely to inspire the creation of books worthy of foot-notes is, of course, another matter.

One does not have to proceed far in one's examination either of the notes or of the list of books quoted before one perceives that in this posthumous work Dr. Hill cast his nets almost as frequently and as widely as he did in his Boswell, and caught almost as many fish, large and small, common and strange, in the shape of apposite and illuminating quotations from all manner of books and writers. Omitting to consider works specifically pertaining to the fifty-two poets treated by Johnson, we find, nevertheless, a goodly number of volumes left to represent the editor's reading around his subject. Such a list of names, as Jowett, Algarotti, John Wilkes, Matthew Arnold, Bishop Atterbury, Lord Bacon, Baretti, Beattie, Bentham, Richard Bentley, Bishop Berkeley and his son George Monck Berkeley, Thomas Birch, Blackstone, Boileau, Borrow, Vincent Bourne, Abel Boyer, Bishop Burnet, Burke, Dr. Burney, Lord Byron,

Campbell, Alexander and two more famous Carlyles, Mrs. Carter, Lord Chesterfield, Colley Cibber — names some of which are still as fresh as ever, and some are fading, and some are practically dead — ought to give a fair idea of the magnitude of Dr. Hill's task, when it is stated that they do not exhaust the more or less outside reading indicated on two pages of his index of titles.

Among the authors who yield him the most numerous and the choicest quotations are Addison, Arbuthnot, Boswell — as a matter of course, and Johnson himself from other works than the Lives — Bolingbroke, Burke, Burnet, Lord Chesterfield, Coleridge, Cowper, Dennis, Dryden, Fielding, Edward FitzGerald, Gibbon, Goldsmith, Gray, Hume, Lamb, Landor, Macaulay, Malone, Lady Mary Wortley Montagu, Mark Pattison, Pepys, Pope, Sir Walter Scott, Southey, Steele, Swift, Tennyson, Voltaire, Horace Walpole, Warburton, Joseph Warton, and Wordsworth. As one of the most illustrious and copious of this extraordinary group exclaimed with regard to Chaucer's Prologue — "Here is God's plenty." It is a little surprising, however, to find so few quotations from as prolific and appreciative a writer upon all that pertains to the poetry of the seventeenth and eighteenth centuries as Mr. Edmund Gosse. Can it be that Dr. Birkbeck Hill, disenchanted by his contact with modern poetry and fiction, felt inclined to dispense with the aid of latter-day criticism?

We answer at once in the negative, when we find him quoting from our own Prof. Phelps's excellent "Beginnings of the English Romantic Movement," and utilizing editions of poets prepared by such scholars as Mr. Aitken, Mr. Austin Dobson, and Mr. Tovey. The absence of Ward's "English Poets," however, from the list of works quoted, the failure to cite Matthew Arnold on Gray's sterility and Mr. Swinburne on the lyrical quality of Collins, the apparent ignoring of such excellent editions as those of Butler and Prior by Mr. R. B. Johnson and of Gay by the late Mr. Underhill — all this induces in one the suspicion that the aging scholar, as was natural, preferred to use the tools with which he was most familiar.

It would be difficult, nevertheless, to show that in many important, or indeed, unimportant, places he failed to be as full and accurate in his annotations as any reasonable critic could desire. A few careless slips, such as assigning 1605, instead of 1606, as the date of Waller's birth, have been caught in the list of errata. Occasionally a note leaves matters too much in the air, as, for example, that on Parnell's Posthumous Works, which might easily, it would seem, be interpreted to lend countenance to the idea that they are spurious. In the note to Johnson's meagre list of the predecessors of "The Spectator," a reference to Tutchin's "Observator" and Defoe's "Review" would have been helpful. Indeed, Defoe might have furnished Dr. Hill with a much larger number of good citations than

he obtained from that voluminous writer. Sometimes the notes do not
give sufficient information. For example, that on Charles Davenant, son
of the dramatist, does not bring out the fact that he was prominent as a
writer on economic and political topics ; and that on the American, James
Ralph, the friend of Franklin, would lead no reader to suspect that that
butt of Pope's satire was of the slightest importance among the historians
of his day.

A rare instance of Dr. Hill's letting a good thing slip is his failure to
point out that the Duchess of Queensberry, Prior's " Kitty, beautiful and
young," who had been banished from the court because she solicited subscriptions for Gay's prohibited opera "Polly," within "the very precincts
of St. James's itself," lived to be present at the first representation of that
worthless piece in 1777. One somewhat wonders, too, at apparently
finding no mention of the not very acute controversy over the authorship of "Rule Britannia."

It is probably impossible not to smile at Dr. Hill's grim humor when
he protested that it was not his duty to edit Sir Herbert Croft, who furnished the larger part of the sketch of Young; but Croft's pages are in
Dr. Hill's book, and it was hardly sufficient for Dr. Hill's nephew to state
within square brackets that Sir Leslie Stephen in "The Dictionary of
National Biography" had corrected several of Croft's errors. At the
very beginning of Croft's narrative the old date of Young's birth stands
uncorrected, 1681 instead of 1683; nor does the reader seem anywhere
to be referred to the admirable study by Dr. W. Thomas, "Le Poète
Edward Young." But these and similar points are obviously trifles.
It is much better to comment on the careful bit of investigation Mr.
Scott has made with regard to "Thomson and the Surveyor-Generalship
of the Leeward Islands"—a clear proof of the unsparing pains with
which these volumes were prepared for the press—and to collect a few
of Dr. Hill's choicest annotations as samples of what the appreciative
reader will find in abundance.

As we should expect, some of the best quotations are taken over from
a storehouse of such good things of which Dr. Hill was the lawful proprietor, his own Boswell. As characteristic as any of these is Johnson's
reply to Hannah More, who had "expressed a wonder that the poet who
had written 'Paradise Lost' should write such poor sonnets." "Milton,
madam," replied the great lexicographer, "was a genius that could cut
a Colossus from a rock, but could not carve heads upon cherry stones."
Much less familiar is Johnson's delightful statement to Malone, that there
had been "too many honey-suckle lives of Milton, and that his should be
in another strain." It was so emphatically in another strain, that the
amiable poet Cowper wanted to "thresh his old jacket" in consequence.

Holding in our own tempers, we need not grow excited over the information that " Dr. Birkbeck Hill left an unfinished note in which he points out that 'Lycidas' can be read without emotion." Of course it can be, except, perhaps, by recalcitrant schoolboys. The question is, whether it ought to be. But there are better things in these volumes than either Dr. Johnson's or Dr. Birkbeck Hill's opinion on the subject of Milton's famous elegy.

Such is George II's question, why Milton did not write his "Paradise Lost" in prose. One sympathizes more with Stephen Duck, the peasant poet, who read the great epic over "twice or thrice with a dictionary before he could understand the language." We find ourselves somewhat at a loss to understand the language in which the fulsome panegyrists of the late seventeenth century couched their compliments. Dr. Hill selects two which it would be hard to surpass. The first is Dryden's to Roscommon:—

> " How will sweet Ovid's ghost be pleased to hear
> His fame augmented by a British peer ! "

Cant goes almost farther in the second, and blasphemy a good deal farther. It is Halifax's lament for Charles II !

> " In Charles, so good a man and King, we see
> A double image of the Deity.
> Oh! had he more resembled it! Oh! why
> Was He not still more like, and could not die? "

This seems unsurpassable; yet if Dr. Hill had been concerned with the poems of Mr. Richard Duke, he would doubtless have secured an almost equally startling couplet in memory of a monarch whose wit has been more often extolled than his virtue: —

> " Good Titus could, but Charles could never say,
> Of all his royal life he lost a day! "

Less amusing but more interesting than the notes embodying extravagancies of this sort are those that group together or contrast characteristics and opinions of famous men. Thus, in connection with Milton's idea that he wrote best between the "autumnall æquinoctiall" and "the vernall," it is not amiss for the annotator to give us quotations which show that Crabbe thought he composed best in the fall, while Tennyson worked best in the early spring. A typically useful collection of citations is the appendix to the life of Hughes, which contains a number of early attacks upon the fashionable Italian opera. An entertaining note is made up of the views of Pope, Johnson, Gray, Gibbon, and Tennyson with regard to the worthlessness or the worth of critics in general. The historian and the laureate were much less severe than their fellow men of letters.   Perhaps it is less instructive, but it is more interesting, to be told that Swift apparently thought that "The Wife of Bath" was a play by Shakespeare, and that his friend Gay had borrowed the title of his comedy from the greater dramatist.   And, to put an end to this picking of plums, how admirably Arbuthnot, whom Cowper seems to have considered the only real man he encountered in the first eight volumes of the Lives, got the best of the painter Jervas, who "piqued himself on total infidelity"! "Come, Jervas," said the Doctor, "this is all an air and affectation; nobody is a sounder believer than you."   "I!" said Jervas; "I believe nothing."   "Yes, but you do," replied the Doctor; "nay, you not only believe, but practise; you are so scrupulous an observer of the Commandments that you never make the likeness of anything that is in heaven above, or in the earth beneath."

With this anecdote from the fastidious Horace Walpole we may turn, in conclusion, from annotations to text and at the same time to a sturdy personage, who, whatever his faults, has never been accused of being a dilettante.   Probably few readers at all capable of appreciating Johnson's singularly mixed but essentially noble character have ever put down the sixth volume of Dr. Hill's Boswell without thinking or ejaculating — "What a man!"   It is to be hoped that just as few will put down the third volume of this edition of the Lives without confessing that they have been in the presence of a critic who, with all his limitations, has never yet been surpassed among Englishmen in those two prime requisites — sound feeling and sound judgment.

It sometimes seems to be assumed that Johnson's fame is really the creation of Boswell.   In a sense this is partly true, and it is surely a mistake to follow Macaulay's lead and treat as though he were also a thorough-going fool the little Scotch toady and sot whom Lowell truly declared to be "quite as unique as Shakespeare."   But it is equally a mistake, as Dr. Hill made clear through his thirty or more years of devotion to Johnson, not to emphasize the part a great man takes in his own biography.   If Johnson had not been a great man, had not possessed a uniquely salient personality, even the biographical genius of Boswell would have produced a portrait which, while it might have won and retained the admiration of the critics, would surely have failed to hold the admiration of the public at large.

On much the same lines of argument one can successfully defend Johnson's fame as a critic.   "The Lives of the Poets" would not have taken its place with the best English classics if the man that wrote it had not been both a biographer and a critic of great and abiding excellence.

His importance in the evolution of English biographical writing is at once revealed when we compare his "Life of Savage" with the formal and stiff attempts at biography made by Defoe and other writers of the preceding generation.   In criticism, Johnson had in Addison a forerunner far more graceful than himself; but in weight of learning, in poise of judgment, in broad, healthy common sense, he plainly surpassed his critical predecessors and contemporaries.   Far more subtle critics have since arisen among us, yet none more robust, more impartial, more essentially sane.   He did lay violent hands on "Lycidas"; but it is better to use hands than to scratch with claws or to peck with beaks.

And in his "Lives of the Poets" Johnson was at his best.   In preparation for his Dictionary he had done much reading in English poetry from the Restoration to his own day.   He was fairly in touch, by means of a not very long-continued literary tradition, with nearly all the poets with whom he had to deal.   He had a large fund of gossip about them, and he was in sympathy with most of them.   If he had had to begin with Chaucer instead of with Cowley, we should have had many more faults to lay at his door.   As it is, we have not a great many faults to put there. A very different sort of critic, Matthew Arnold, was right when he pointed out in his introduction to the chief Lives that Johnson was a great man and that his criticism, even of poetry, often has value, because of his character as a man.   It often has value, too, because of the terse, sensible, sometimes grimly humorous fashion in which it is expressed, as any teacher who, dealing with the eighteenth century, makes a habit of quoting Johnson will soon discover from the way his hearers brighten up when the great Doctor's periods begin to roll in upon their ears.

The lives selected by Matthew Arnold were those of Milton, Dryden, Swift, Addison, Pope, and Gray; for he was aiming to cover in a somewhat connected manner the history of English poetry for a century.   The poor account of Gray was the only one that was out of place; and, if the lives of Cowley and Savage had been added, Johnson would have been excellently represented.   The last-named is not only famous for the picture it gives of the struggles of men of letters in the London of Johnson's youth, but is furthermore notable as containing more sympathetic feeling than is usual with Johnson in his rôle of biographer.   It is feeling also that redeems the very inadequate sketch of Collins.

Among other important lives are those of Waller, of the long-forgotten Edmund or "Rag" Smith, of Sir Richard Blackmore, whose "Creation" deserved at least a little of the charity Johnson showed its much-ridiculed author; of Congreve, and of Prior.   Thomson is not adequately treated, but few readers will quarrel with the brief notices accorded many of the poetasters whom Johnson's bookseller employers chose to reissue.   A light is thrown on the critic's free-and-easy methods of research by the famous remark he made when he handed over the manuscript of his life of the dramatist Nicholas Rowe. He said he thought he had done pretty well, in view of the fact that he had not read Rowe for thirty years. He certainly had; and it is a proof of his great powers to find a work dealing with so many unimportant and so few thoroughly popular poets, not only demanding the annotations of several generations of scholars, but also ranking among the books that every catholic reader is expected to have read in whole or in part.

Probably the main idea such a reader should carry away from "The Lives of the Poets" is that it is the work of a man much larger than most of the writers whose careers he described — of a man who had read and heard and seen much; whose judgments, however biassed and unintelligent, were always honest; who rarely or never failed to show common sense in his opinions, though he was sometimes lacking in the uncommon sense of high poetic feeling and comprehension; who withheld his praise from everything that did not square with his ideas of what was decent and right; who filled his post of judge with dignity, if not always with entire fairness; who, finally, was keenly concerned for the honor of literature and sound learning and for the welfare of his fellow-men. But this is only to say that the man Johnson is seen in his chief book, and that the man Johnson was truly great.　　　W. P. TRENT.

AN EFFORT TO SUPPRESS NOISE.

That which the world torments me in most is the awful confusion of noise. It is the devil's own infernal din all the blessed day long, confounding God's works and His creatures. A trulV awful hell-like combination, and the worst of it is a railwaV whistle like the screech of ten thousand cats and everV cat of them all as big as a cathedral.—CARLYLE.

IT is a far cry back along the eighteen centuries that separate Pompeii of the year 79 from Gotham of to-day, and yet we experience a delightful sense of nearness in reading a graffito traced long ago on a Pompeian houseside: "Macerior begs the ædile to prevent the people from making a noise, disturbing the good folks who are asleep." Dear old Macerior! May his task of anti-noise agitator have been easier than that of his successors of the present day! At least, in fair Pompeii, his quest of jurisdiction, in order to abate the nuisance, could not have been extended, and he ran no danger of being tossed back and forth from department to board, and then from board to bureau, nor of being whirled dizzily from municipal to state authorities, from state to federal authorities, and then back again and around again, as would be his lot to-day. Furthermore, the ills from which he sought relief were less grievous than those under which we sigh to-day; for instead of shrieking whistles and clanging gongs and thundering flat-wheeled trolleys, he only suffered from the noisy merriment of homeward bound, rose-crowned roysterers, chanting the praises of Venus Physica.

The anti-noise crusader of to-day, in starting out on his weary way, must be prepared for the fact that he will certainly meet with many who are not in sympathy with his aims. In substance, Carlyle says, in another place, that civilization, however much respect it has developed for noses, has not yet come to respect for ears; that olfactory sensitiveness is regarded in a great body of laws against smells, but auditory sensitiveness, when it complains, is told to toughen itself. And Schopenhauer says:

There are people, it is true — nay, a great many people — who smile at such things, because they are not sensitive to noise; but they are just the very people who are also not sensitive to argument, or thought, or poetry, or art; in a word, to any kind of intellectual influence. . . . Noise is the most impertinent of all forms of interruption. It is not only an interruption, but also a disruption of thought. Of course, where there is nothing to interrupt, noise will not be so particularly painful.

As for myself, I met with disapproval, but scarcely with discouragement, on the part of five persons whom I interviewed in my recent efforts to suppress the unnecessary blowing of whistles along the water front of Manhattan Island: a policeman, a steamboat official, a physician, an army officer, and a real-estate owner. "What about the blowin' of whistles?" inquired the first, indignantly. "Aw! anybody who objects to whistles don't know what they're talkin' about." The same sentiment was expressed by the steamboat official. "I don't believe it!" he exclaimed, when shown a few whistling records; "I don't believe it," he repeated, and then added: "Oh! well, I suppose you *did* hear them, but then you folks hear the noise from the Bay, and from almost all of the East River, and from the Harlem, as well as from the North River. And *why* do you people object to whistling? Why, I hear the whistles from the harbor way off in —— (naming a place about thirteen miles away in an air line), and I don't mind them. Anybody who objects to whistles doesn't know what he is talking about." The third, the doctor, was equally positive. "Whistles disturb hospital patients? Perfectly ridiculous! People don't hear noise unless it has been suggested to them, or unless they want to hear it. Nobody can be awakened by telephones or alarm clocks unless he desires to be disturbed. Will I not make inquiries about it of the hospital resident staff? No, I won't. What do I care about the resident staff? I am sure there is nothing to complain of."

The military officer spoke like the others. "I shall not protest against the blowing of whistles, for I am never disturbed by any noise," said he. "Even a cannon which goes off every morning, just outside my door, cannot awaken me, unless I retire very early. Nothing awakens me, and I shall make no complaint, nor shall I permit any to be made here." The fifth, and last, was the owner of a house on the river front, who was very angry that any agitation should have been started, fearing lest it might cause depreciation of real-estate values. Poor, human ostrich! his head was buried so deep in the sand that he *would* not know that values were already absurdly low just on account of the noise and not because of the agitation. "There is no noise of whistles," he reiterated; "it is all absurd!"

On the other hand, the worker for peace and quiet will probably meet with such gratitude from a long-suffering public, and such hearty encouragement from a sympathetic press, that he will feel well repaid for any efforts he may make, even though the struggle with official apathy be wearisome.

But all this by way of preface. Let me now narrate the steps in my effort to abate the tooting nuisance which has caused so much misery in the Borough of Manhattan.

36

Last summer it was noticed by many that the tooting of tugs at night, which had always been annoying, had suddenly become much worse. Just why this was so, nobody could explain; yet persons living near the river front were unanimous in declaring that the toots were more numerous, more prolonged, and more piercing in quality than ever before. It is possible that some new tugs with strident sirens had been added, or that some old ones had been fitted up with larger whistles, and that then perhaps a spirit of emulation urged those members of the river brotherhood who were unsupplied with such shrieking horrors to practise even more assiduously than ever on their whistle-cords, so as to make good, by vigor and endurance, on their part, what was lacking in the calibre of their whistles. Who knows? At any rate, sleep in the homes along the river front and even far back from the water-line was reduced to the minimum: people suffered, but then after all it was "nobody's business" to stop it, and so it went on. Truly has it been said: "It is the worst sign of all when men submit to a torture because it is general and not particular. Everybody is in the same boat. That idea consoles and soothes them."

These signals varied, ranging from the shrillest of shrieks to the deepest of booming sounds; some were short, others long; some were single, others in series of twenty or thirty toots. They were endless in variety, and each was worse than any of the others. Sometimes an individual solo, in this infernal concert, would consist of seven, fifteen, seventeen, or even thirty short blasts, followed by one long ear-splitting shriek, and then, before the echoes had died away on the Jersey shore, it would all immediately be repeated. That the number of toots was astonishingly large was shown by careful records (duly sworn to) taken by second-year and third-year students in the Columbia University Law School. These records placed the average at not much less than 3,000 a night.

And yet, less suffering was caused by the multiplicity of signals than by the large calibre of the whistles used. For instance, many sedate, little toots such as were given by a few of the boats could certainly be better borne than even one of the mad shrieks that rang out again and again on the night air. These shrieks lacked none of the qualities of noise which are held by Sully to be the most disagreeable. They were protracted, sometimes lasting almost forty seconds, excessive in volume, high or sharp, sudden or explosive, and, above all, uneven or irregular. As Sully says: "When the sequence is wholly disorderly or arhythmic, the mind is kept, so to speak, in a state of tip-toe expectation of every succeeding moment," in a sort of "imaginative preoccupation of the attention."

What made this signaling so much more annoying was the knowledge that it was not called for either by statute or emergency requirements, but was given by the tugs to inform the crew of the waiting scows of their approach, and could have been almost entirely dispensed with by having watchmen on the piers, by arranging a system of light signals, and by having some alarm clocks, set for the change of tide.   And then the question arises in one's mind: Why should a captain be allowed to draw up a boat near shore and there continue with perfect impunity to assault the silence of the night with a most maddening of sirens, when a mere citizen who might attempt to blow even a moderately small whistle on the river bank would be immediately apprehended?·

The testimony of scow captains and others whose occupation confined them to the water front, who were interviewed by the above-mentioned law students, showed how unnecessary this whistling was.   One scow captain stated:

At times the tugs do a lot of unnecessary signaling; they commence whistling for the scow captains when distant from one-half to two miles, and keep it up until they arrive at the dock.   Sometimes the tugs keep on whistling even after the captain answers.   Some of the captains seem to try to see how much noise they can make, and are at their worst in the middle of the night.   If the captain does not answer quickly, even though he may be up and in sight, the tug keeps on blowing. Some of the tug captains belong to a brotherhood, and, as members of this brotherhood meet, they give the fraternal signal.   It is the customary thing to signal for members of the crew who have left the tugs to go into the city.

An inspector at one of the dumps gave the following statement:

At the docks the captains of the scows go down into their cabins and go to sleep. The tugs keep on signalling till the captain appears.   Then, too, the captains use their whistles to wake up their own crews.   The deck hands on tugs go to saloons when the tugs are at the docks, and the captains of the tugs call them back by means of the whistle.

Another scow captain said:

When the tugs approach the dock, they signal the captain of the scows so that he may have the scows ready when the tug reaches the dock.   Not content with one signal, they keep up a whistling until the captain comes upon the deck.   I think that many of the tugs whistle just for fun.   I am sure that much of the whistling is unnecessary.   When one or more of the crew leave the tug to go into the city, it is a regular rule to blow the whistle for them to come back.   If the captain of a scow is away, they signal in the same manner for him.   Sometimes the captain of a barge has had no notice that the tug is coming for him, and goes out into the town for groceries, etc.   A tug then has to call him.

This captain was also of the opinion that tugs often blow much more loudly than is necessary.   The proprietor of a boat-house on the river front stated:

There is more whistling done at night than in the daytime.   Much of this is unnecessary.   A specific instance of unnecessary whistling is the case of the tug-boat "——" which signals to call the attention of its captain, who lives in the vicinity of —— street.   This noise has been complained of frequently.   Very often, also, the captains of the tugs blow particular signals to attract the attention of servant girls on the Drive.

Finally, the noise became so annoying that I notified the Department of Health of the nuisance, and cited the case of the Mount Vernon Board of Health, which had absolutely suppressed all noises from 10 A.M. to 6 P.M. "Yes, we know that the trouble exists," came the answer over the 'phone, "but then the case is different here from what it is in Mount Vernon. You see, the Hudson is a federal waterway." "Well then," I replied, "the tooting is a federal nuisance, but nevertheless it most certainly ought to be suppressed. Won't you move in the matter?" "Well, we'll see what can be done." [And here let me say that the word *federal* seemed to cast terror into the heart of everyone whom I interviewed on the matter. *Federal* courts, *federal* authorities, *federal* waterways, *federal* jurisdiction, all were uttered with bated breath, while a *federal* nuisance was held by all to be something beyond all hope of remedy, indeed something almost sacrosanct.[1]] Weeks came and weeks went, but the tooting was ever with us. Repeated appeals to the Department of Health elicited only the information that my statements had all been verified by their inspectors, but there the matter rested.

Thinking that the Dock Department might be able to abate the nuisance, I called on the Dock Commissioner, but was informed that his jurisdiction did not extend to any boat that was not actually tied up to a dock. After that I visited the Wardens of the Port and the U. S. Local Steamboat Inspectors, both of whom declared that they also were unable to move in the matter, owing to lack of jurisdiction.

Next the Collector's Office was appealed to and the matter referred to the Law Division. Here most able efforts were made, both by the Solicitor to the Collector, Mr. Francis Hamilton, and by his first assistant, Mr. E. H. Barnes, to ascertain what could be done to abate the nuisance. It appeared to them that "Section 4450 seems to vest in the Local Board of Steamboat Inspectors all necessary powers to punish by suspension or revocation of license the commission of any act on the part of a licensed officer which they adjudge to be 'misconduct' or 'negligence' or 'unskilfulness.'" But the U. S. Local Steamboat Inspectors, when the question was referred to them, decided that the point was not well taken.

[1] An instance in point is the statement of the late Dr. Dent, at the meeting held in the Collector's Office. He said:

"Three years ago the noise on the river became so annoying that patients and employés throughout the entire institution complained and asked for relief. I took the matter up with our counsel, and was informed that this question belonged to the federal courts. I was discouraged and dropped the matter, and let my patients suffer."

The aid of the Police Department was next invoked, and Commissioner McAdoo assured me of his willingness to act provided that authorization to do so could be obtained from the office of the Corporation Counsel. At his suggestion that I should secure the signatures of some residents of the Drive, protesting against this nuisance, I promised to bring him a petition signed by poor and rich alike, by the dwellers in the crowded tenements of the lower East Side as well as by the occupants of Riverside mansions, and I also stated that I would make a special feature of our municipal institutions.

The response to my inquiries was prompt. Among those who willingly collected signatures for me was a well-known real-estate agent who sent me almost 700; while a policeman gladly offered to bring me a list of those living in his down-town district, who, although distant four blocks from the river front, slept but little, owing to the incessant din. Clubs and associations and private individuals sent me signatures, until, having received over 3,000, I thought that no more were necessary.

The hospital feature had always seemed to me of special interest, and I therefore determined to ascertain if I was mistaken in supposing that the tug$_8$ caused serious suffering among the city's sick and unfortunate charges. Dr. S. T. Armstrong, of Bellevue and Gouverneur hospitals, who was first visited, declared:

Unnecessary signalling by tugs and other steam vessels in the East River has been a matter of long-standing annoyance to the sick who are treated in Gouverneur and Bellevue hospitals, both of which institutions are on the river front.

Mr. Lamb, Superintendent of the City Hospital at Blackwell's Island, stated:

The almost constant blowing of whistles contiguous to the hospital is not only distressing to the patients, physicians, and employés of the City Hospital on Blackwell's Island, but also exceedingly harmful to them.

Dr. Charles Hornby, Superintendent of the Flower Hospital, wrote as follows :

I am glad that the subject of whistle tooting by tug-boats, etc., on the river front is receiving attention. Flower Hospital is situated near the East River, and its patients suffer from the noises. There is a garbage dump at 61st Street and East River. . . . The barges are taken away every morning about two o'clock. There is a watchman who evidently is seldom there or else is sleeping. When the tug-boat comes, it blows its whistle in a manner which wakes up every patient — not a single blast or two, but a continued stream of hoarse toots. After this has continued for a long time, the boatmen and the watchmen commence to swear and abuse each other. Although we are two blocks away, the oaths and shouted recriminations penetrate the hospital. The whole nightly occurrence is a disgrace to the neighborhood.

A very strong indorsement of the agitation against nocturnal noises was made by Dr. M. S. Gregory, resident alienist of Bellevue Hospital, who said:

I think that the hundreds of employés of Bellevue as well as of the Gouverneur Hospital who are obliged to reside on the premises would be unanimous in declaring that their sleep is frequently disturbed at night by the incessant whistling of passing steamers on the river. It is quite important that these employés, whose work is arduous and trying, should secure an adequate amount of undisturbed sleep, in order to render proper services to the patients under their care. I am quite sure, however, that we physicians, nurses, and employés would hardly complain of such annoyances if we did not feel that this whistling was of more serious harm to the patients in the hospital. Picture to yourself a patient in the agony of death who is suddenly startled by the shrill noise of prolonged whistles! Then again, many patients suffering from typhoid, meningitis, and other serious illness will become annoyed by the least noise or disturbance. To these, restful sleep is of paramount importance, and frequently such disturbances may cause a relapse or turn the scale against them. In many delirious patients an hour's rest or sleep may mean life. You can readily imagine the disappointment of the doctor and nurse who have struggled to bring about the much-desired quiet and sleep, when suddenly all their efforts are frustrated as a result of the disturbing whistles. Coming to the department immediately under my charge — that of the Psychopathic Wards, where the disturbed and restless insane patients are cared for — I can only say from personal experience that the whistling from the boats does a great deal of injury to the patients and makes our work more trying and difficult. As you know, no doubt, the insane as a class are most suspicious, and I have often observed that an apprehensive patient would go into a state of frenzy as a result of these annoying noises. They often imagine that this incessant whistling is meant for them and that it means their death-knell. Of course, such a patient will disturb all the other patients in the ward, and, as already stated, makes the work of the nurses most trying and difficult. Moreover, in the treatment of some forms of mental affections, due to mental and physical exhaustion, restful sleep is a most important factor, and frequent disturbance of the same may permanently endanger the future mental welfare of the patient. Heretofore, we have been compelled to endure this disturbance without a murmur, as we would thunder from the clouds or a pestilential visitation of Providence. We earnestly hope, however, that something can be done at least to lessen this annoyance and abate the danger to the poor unfortunate sick of this great city.

The following letter was written by the late Dr. E. C. Dent, but a few hours before his sudden death:

In the Manhattan State Hospital, on Ward's Island, we have about 4,500 patients and about 1,000 employés, making a total of 5,500 individuals living on this island. Our patients are all insane. Many of them are very nervous and excitable and are easily disturbed by the loud whistling of the boats on the river. Tug-boats often tie up on the New York side opposite the hospital, and frequently do a great deal of signalling by whistling which, it seems to me, is unnecessary. In fact it frequently occurs that persons conversing in the office are obliged to suspend conversation until the boats are through with their whistling. It has been quite often observed that tug-boats' captains appear to carry on conversation among themselves by a series of tootings. It must be apparent to everyone that these unnecessary, shrill noises are not calculated to soothe a disordered or an irritable nervous system. . . .

I sincerely wish for your success in abating this nuisance so that signalling and whist- ling on the rivers will be reduced to the actual necessities required by law. I shall be pleased to coöperate in any way possible to attain this end.

A certain pathetic interest attaches to this letter, as is shown by the fol- lowing extract from a note written to me, a few days later, by Mr. Lewis M. Farrington, Secretary to the late Dr. Dent:

When this letter was taken to Dr. Dent for signature, he called me in and dic- tated the little personal note which accompanied the letter. I wrote the note hur- riedly, and when he signed it he had on his overcoat, ready to leave the office, as it proved, forever. It seems peculiarly fitting that his last official act should be an effort to make more endurable the lot of these unfortunates whose care and treatment had been his life-work. I would add that Dr. Dent was deeply interested in the efforts you are making to abate the unnecessary whistling nuisance, and he many times ex- pressed the wish that he could be of more service to you.

Dr. S. L. Cash, resident physician of the Willard Parker Hospital, stated:

Often the whistling is as loud as it is long, and seems to jar the hospital build- ing, [and] the tugs that tie up at the piers during all hours of the night signal with their whistles to an alarming extent.

It is impossible to quote from all the letters which were received from superintendents of hospitals and allied institutions, indorsing the move- ment. Among the names, however, may be mentioned: Dr. J. B. Mickle, Superintendent of the Metropolitan Hospital, Blackwell's Island; Mr. Robert Roberts, Superintendent of the City Home, Blackwell's Island (containing about 2,500 old and infirm inmates); Mr. M. C. Dunphy, Superintendent of the New York City Children's Hospital and Schools, Randall's Island; Mr. Joseph P. Byers, Superintendent of the New York House of Refuge, at Randall's Island; and Warden Fallon, Superin- tendent of the Penitentiary.

Outside of the Borough of Manhattan, the Long Island College Hospital, through Richard E. Shaw, Superintendent, added its protest against the nuisance of steamboat whistles, and the danger that is caused, in certain cases, "by the unearthly and prolonged shrieking which occurs nightly at the different docks in the neighborhood." From Washington, D. C., too, came a similar protest, written by Dr. William A. White, Superintendent of the Government Hospital for the Insane:

We who deal with the insane and with the highly nervous appreciate perhaps better than most people how acutely painful a noise may be, and would welcome any legislation that would secure its abatement. We can only feel that the useless shrieking of whistles is a demonstration which belongs to the age of savagery with its war-paint and tom-toms, and hope that our modern civilization may be relieved from it.

Backed by practically every municipal institution. I then returned to the Board of Health and begged it, even if it could not take an active part in suppressing the noise, through a lack of jurisdiction, at least to help on the movement by sending me a strong indorsement. In answer to this appeal, I received the following statement from Hermann M. Biggs, M.D., General Medical Officer of the Department of Health:

Your communication, with complaints attached, referring to the nuisance created by the unnecessary whistling of tug-boats and transfer boats on the waters of the East and North Rivers was duly received, and the facts therein stated were verified by our inspectors. I would say further in reference to this matter that the subject had previously been brought to the attention of the Department of Health through a similar complaint, and especially through the complaints of the medical staff and nurses of its own hospitals situated at the foot of East 16th Street and on North Brother Island. Sometimes, as it is stated in the communication sent to the Department, the nuisance created in this way is almost unbearable, and, in the opinion of the officers of this Board, absolutely without reason or justification. We do not refer at all in this matter to the signalling necessary to the ordinary navigation of the waters around New York, but to the prolonged use of whistles for arousing watchmen and similar purposes which are unnecessary, and which constitute the chief source of this nuisance. The question of the jurisdiction of the Department of Health over this matter has been submitted, at the direction of the Board, to the Corporation Counsel for decision. I would only add that the Board of Health and its medical officers are thoroughly in sympathy with you and the attempt you are making to abate a nuisance which is, in our opinion, a serious menace to the health and comfort of the inhabitants of New York City.

After the array of evidence and indorsement cited, there could be no denying the fact that this unnecessary whistling was not only a general public nuisance, but also a grave menace to health; and the most natural conclusion, therefore, was that it ought to be dealt with by the Department of Health. However, since the Department seemed unable to decide the question as to whether it had jurisdiction or not, I appealed to the Police Department again and received, a few days later, the following letter from Commissioner McAdoo:

Following up our interview, I beg to say that I will be glad, so far as the law permits, to coöperate with the federal authorities with reference to the matter of abating the nuisance of tug-boat whistling on the North and East Rivers and adjacent waters, and that you are at liberty so to state to them. I acknowledge in this connection the receipt of the admirably arranged testimony presented by you, with reference to the matter in question.

This was encouraging, but the chief difficulty that was encountered was not the apprehension, but primarily the detection, of the elusive tooters, shrouded as they were in the darkness of the night. Of course, if we could only obtain a revenue cutter, matters would be simplified; but then, alas! revenue cutters are things that cannot easily be borrowed. However, I returned to the Law Division of the Collector's Office, with a request for a boat and for the presentation of the matter to the federal authorities at Washington. It was then that a meeting, to be held at the Collector's Office, was arranged between the U. S. Local Steamboat Inspectors and those interested in the movement. With the exception of threshing out the matter in public, however, and the rallying to the support of the movement of the entire press, not much was gained; for at the meeting, as both before and afterward, the U. S. Local Inspectors simply listened and promised nothing. The unanimous opinion of those present seemed to be that the best way of abating the nuisance would be to obtain evidence against the tug men through the assistance of a revenue cutter, and that the Secretary of the Treasury should be addressed for permission to use a boat for that purpose. Of the sympathy of Secretary Shaw we felt assured; for although he had been unable to wait over for the meeting, he had expressed himself as being in favor of taking steps to stop the whistling, and had characterized the movement as a proper one. Great was our disappointment, therefore, when a few days later we were informed that the whole matter had been referred to the Department of Commerce and Labor, while no information was vouchsafed us as to the assignment of a cutter.

While this quest of jurisdiction was going on, the leading papers from the Atlantic to the Pacific were rendering us most valuable assistance. From the very first, the press had pointed out that "indiscriminate signalling is an interference with the signals that are necessary to the safety of traffic"; and also that continuous whistling "no longer has any significance for purposes of signalling." Many expressed the hope that this "movement against the boat whistles might develop into a much more comprehensive one and come to be a general suppression of a thousand inexcusable assaults upon urban ears." Still another looked forward to what might soon be a "general triumph over the steam whistle. That triumph, in turn, should be a part of a universal crusade against unnecessary noise. . . . All in all, there is no vice in New York so thoroughly ripe for squads and crusaders as that of noise production." From Seattle, Washington, to Jamaica, Long Island, and from Maine to Alabama, there seemed to be a general hunting up of old noise ordinances and a desire to abate the suffering caused by unnecessary sounds. Papers of twenty-three States and territories published approving accounts of this attempt at noise reform.

The only opposition that we encountered was when, for two consecutive days, one of our dailies printed interviews with tug captains on the subject. They, of course, declared that whistles were a necessity, in fact the "only means of safety for river craft," and that the "commerce of the port hangs on the use of signals to regulate the shipping." One steamboat man indignantly exclaimed: "You might as well try to abolish

steamboats altogether as try to prevent them from blowing their whistles
— you might as well try to abolish commerce." We, who were only protesting against the *unnecessary* use of steam whistles, were accused of
"crass ignorance and sentimentality" and of heaven only knows what
else! Nevertheless, this defence of whistling by the tug captains was,
perhaps, the strongest argument that was brought forward in our behalf;
for it was therein unconsciously admitted, from beginning to end, that
this whistling, that caused so much suffering, was not required for purposes of navigation, but was simply used as a means of long-distance
communication with the crews of the waiting scows. One captain declared: "There is no use discussing that subject. If the whistles of the
tugs to signal those on the piers be done away with, it would necessitate
an extra deck hand to act as a messenger to notify the pier hands, besides all the time that would be lost." Another states: "We run the risk
of losing a whole tide if we do not rouse the crew on the barge." Still another said: "It is absolutely imperative that we notify those on shore
that we have arrived." While a fourth declared: "You must whistle to
wake up the crew, which you cannot expect to stay on watch day and
night. The boats are not of sufficient importance to keep two watchers
employed."

The "Marine Journal" almost from the first took up the cudgels in
our support and assured us of its "loyalty to the cause you have espoused
in regard to unnecessary whistle blowing, which is certainly a laudable one
and will, beyond a doubt, meet with success, as you have the sympathy,
and will evidently get the coöperation, of everyone but those who blow
whistles for personal, not official, reasons." It was also the editor of the
"Marine Journal," Captain George L. Norton, who was instrumental in
getting passed by the National Board of Steam Navigation the following
resolutions:

Whereas, The attention of the members of the National Board of Steam Navigation has been called to reports in the public prints in regard to unnecessary whistle
blowing by masters and pilots, causing annoyance to citizens residing along the rivers
of this harbor, especially during the night, it is hereby

Resolved, By the members of the National Board of Steam Navigation that they
will instruct the masters and pilots of their tug-boats and other steam craft to blow
their whistles only when absolutely necessary and in conformity with the law.

But, alas! this resolution, passed by those who represented nearly
the entire tug-boat and ferry-boat interests of the city, was productive
of no lasting good. For a few nights there was comparative quiet, and
then the hubbub broke forth afresh. It was thus evident to all that,
to secure any lasting benefit, the power of the law must be recognized
as being behind any measures that might be taken by marine interests

to abate the nuisance. The tug men evidently felt they both could and would whistle if they desired to do so, in spite of the instructions issued to them by their superiors.

Early in January it was announced, in a despatch from Washington, that Secretary Metcalf, of the Department of Commerce and Labor, had decided that the Board of Supervising Inspectors of Steam Vessels were alone capable of dealing with the question. The telegram then went on to state:

> There is some question in the minds of the Commerce and Labor officials whether the Government can control the use of steamboat whistles, no matter whether unnecessary signals are given or not. The rule against " misbehavior" on the part of steamboat captains has never been applied in a case of this kind, and at present the statute is not specific enough to cover such violation. It is believed that the steamboat inspectors at their annual meeting will deem the matter of sufficient importance to draw up a special rule by which the unnecessary use of whistles may be punishable under the general charge of " misbehavior." This, if signed by the Secretary of the Department of Commerce and Labor, will become a law.

Having been invited to attend the annual meeting of Supervising Inspectors in Washington, I decided to ascertain, beforehand, whether the captains of larger craft were of the same opinion as the tug men regarding the *necessity* of *unnecessary* whistling. The answers to the letters that I sent out to the captains of our largest river passenger boats were most gratifying, and proved what I had always believed to be the fact, that this indiscriminate whistling and the use of powerful sirens constituted a menace to navigation as well as to health. One of the first letters I received came from Mr. George A. White, Assistant General Manager of the Hudson River Day Line, captain of the steamboat *Albany*, and also Chairman of the Association of Passenger Steamboat Lines, who wrote:

> I am in full sympathy with the whistling crusade now under way, both from the standpoint of a resident of the pestered district and as one whose life and business are all connected with steamboats, and who deplores the confusion caused by the unwarranted blowing of very large whistles on very small boats. The enormous whistles of many of the small tugs which carry high steam pressure (150 to 200 pounds) are blown probably eighty or ninety per cent more frequently than necessary, a fact which can only be classified, in its offensiveness, as rowdyism. It is simply a case of the smallest boy making the most noise. In fog or snow storm, constant warning signals are necessary and compulsory; but, in any case, the volume of sound need be no more in New York Harbor than on the Thames in London or on the Mersey at Liverpool.

Another letter came from Captain M. I. Brightman, of the steamer *Boston*, who said:

> I think that there should be not only a law to abate the unnecessary blowing of whistles, but also one to abolish entirely all the hideous-sounding inventions that are used by many crafts in the harbor. It has been proved to me by years of experience

that a whistle with a somewhat pleasing tone is fully as effective in thick weather as the freaks that make such horrible noises in use by several boats around the city.

A third letter was written by Samuel Crocker, captain of the steamer *Mohegan*, and read as follows:

There is a great deal of whistling done and sometimes it is a menace to the people going up and down the rivers, and I think that a great deal of it is unnecessary and uncalled for.

Mr. H. Nickerson, Superintendent of the New England Navigation Company, sent me the following:

I believe, in fact I know, that a great deal of the whistling done by tow-boats and lighters in New York Harbor is unnecessary, and if all vessels confined themselves to just what is needed in that line, the whistling would be so small in comparison with the past that you would not be annoyed to any great extent.

Mr. H. H. Webber, captain of the steamer *City of Fall River*, stated:

I am in most hearty sympathy and accord with you and your purpose to stop useless whistling. When for any cause we lay over for a night at a dock in this city, it is almost impossible to get a good night's rest on account of tooting whistles. None but regular whistles should ever be given, as all others are uncalled for.

The testimony, then, that I had collected to submit to the Board of Supervising Inspectors was of two kinds: one kind, from superintendents of hospitals and allied institutions, which claimed it was a menace to health; the other, from captains and those whose occupation confined them to the river front, all of which showed that the indiscriminate whistling was not only unnecessary, but even a menace to navigation.

The only requests that we submitted to the Board were these: (1) that whistling be restricted to statute and emergency requirements; (2) that watchmen be placed on each pier, to receive light signals from approaching tugs and transmit them to the crews of the waiting scows; (3) that every vessel carry two whistles, one small and light for clear weather, and one of larger calibre for times of fog or tempest; and (4) that there be stationed here a representative of the Department of Labor and Commerce, to whom complaints could be referred and whose duty it should be to have the waterways properly patrolled just as the streets are policed.

The Supervising Inspectors, in turn, decided, however, that they had no jurisdiction in the matter. They apparently could regulate nothing, recommend nothing, decide on nothing, have control over nothing. They could not stop "hoodlum whistling," or substitute a whistle of a reasonable size for a shrieking siren, or even advise that unnecessary signals be omitted.

The next day Mr. Edward W. Sims, solicitor to the department, handed down an opinion on the subject, from which I quote:

With reference to the unnecessary sounding of steam whistles in the vicinity of New York, there is no existing federal law or regulation which prohibits the whistling complained of or authorizes the punishment of the alleged offenders. . . . Title 52 of the Revised Statutes of the United States, above referred to, includes laws "for the regulation of steam vessels," and laws governing "the transportation of passengers and merchandise," and thus embraces what, for the sake of convenience, is called "The Steamboat Inspection Laws." The purpose of these laws is primarily the protection of the passengers, crew, and property on vessels propelled by steam; and also the protection of the lives and property of persons on other boats and at the wharves (Hartranft v. Du Pont, 118 U. S. 126). None of the provisions of law show any intent to legislate upon, or provide for, the protection of persons and property on land. It follows, therefore, that the Board of Supervising Inspectors is without authority to prohibit whistling solely because it disturbs the local peace. . . . While a State statute or a municipal ordinance could not, of course, affect or interfere with whistling required by federal laws or regulations, it would, in my opinion, be a valid local police regulation, in so far as it prohibited useless and unnecessary whistling.

And thus the vicious circle was completed. The question of jurisdiction was still unsettled, and, after having been shuffled from municipal to federal authorities, was again sent back to New York for settlement.

The trip to Washington was not in vain, however, for it was there that the matter was taken up by the National Association of Masters, Mates, and Pilots. This association, numbering about 10,000 men, was holding its annual meeting at that time and requested me to bring the matter before them. After my address, the following resolutions were read and then unanimously carried. These resolutions and a letter, also given below, from the same association, constitute unanswerable arguments as to the urgency of suppressing indiscriminate and, above all, noisy signalling:

AMERICAN ASSOCIATION OF MASTERS, MATES, AND PILOTS,
NATIONAL EXECUTIVE COMMITTEE.
WASHINGTON, D. C., January 24, 1906.

Whereas, It has come to the knowledge of the Grand Harbor that many complaints have been entered by Mrs. Rice, Commissioner Darlington of the Health Department of New York City, and many other people connected with the various hospitals, both private and public, against the unnecessary blowing of whistles, especially the so-called siren whistle;

And Whereas, We consider this unnecessary noise detrimental to the safe navigation of steam vessels of the port of New York and detrimental to the patients in the different institutions on the water front;

And Whereas, We fully realize that the city, state, or federal authorities have not got the proper jurisdiction in these cases; therefore be it

Resolved, That this Grand Harbor shall request all subordinate harbors under their jurisdiction, especially those situated in New York City, to issue a circular letter requesting our members to abstain from this practice.

(Signed) JOHN C. SILVA, *President.*
(Signed) LUTHER B. DOW, *Gen. Counsel and Treas.*

The letter read as follows:

My dear Mrs. Rice: Referring again to the hearing held this day before Assistant Secretary Murray of the Department of Commerce and Labor, and the Board of
U. S. Supervising Inspectors of Steam Vessels, and after carefully looking over many
of the complaints, letters, and evidences in your possession, I am of the firm belief that
this excessive blowing of steam whistles by the various steam vessels in the port of
New York, by which many patients in the different hospitals and other people are annoyed, can be greatly lessened if it were possible for the Board of Supervising Inspectors to make a regulation so that the whistles would be more uniform as to size and
tone of same. I am convinced that the many complaints about the whistles are not
for the reason that they blow so many times, but it is for the reason that the tone of
the whistles is of such a shrieking nature and is made so powerful that it is heard at
an unnecessary distance. Assuring you that myself and the Association will aid you
in abating any nuisance of this kind, I am,

Respectfully,

(Signed) Luther B. Dow, *General Counsel.*

And these resolutions have borne fruit; for whereas formerly the
whistling was almost incessant, it is not unusual now to have nights of
comparative tranquillity along the river front. Of course there are still
some captains who apparently wish to show their contemptuous disapproval of these resolutions by shrieking just as loudly as ever, but they
are decidedly in the minority. As regards the improvement noticed, I
should like to quote from the letter sent to me by Mr. James D. Lamb,
Superintendent of the City Hospital, Blackwell's Island. Speaking of
the whistling, he says:

It has been very materially decreased, and I wish to thank you, in behalf of the
patients and employés, for your earnest efforts to abate this nuisance which has been
so detrimental to the health and comfort of all the patients and employés in this
hospital. I will report later to you where your inspector can do good in further abating this nuisance.

And I should also like to quote from a letter written to me by Captain White, because it shows strongly the interest that is taken in the
movement by many of those who were at first supposed to be antagonistic to it:

I feel that you are to be congratulated and complimented on the results which
you have accomplished, and that overwrought New Yorkers owe you a debt of gratitude for the possibility of more quiet rest. The war cry of your enemies seems to
have been " Hoot, mon!" while your war cry has been decency and order. It seemed
to me rather a hopeless task at the start, but I frankly confess that I am amazed at
your results.

Naturally there is danger that these measures, adopted voluntarily by
the marine interests and river-men, will, in the future, tend to become
a dead letter unless followed up by new legislation or by the passage of
new ordinances.

And now the question is, what shall the next step be? It does seem as if the Department of Commerce and Labor, in view of the attitude taken by the Association of Masters, Mates, and Pilots, at their annual meeting in January, ought seriously to take up the question of abolishing sirens and "hoodlum whistling." And even as recently as March 2, the following strong letter was sent me by Captain Luther B. Dow, General Counsel and Treasurer of the Association:

If it were possible to have the Department of Commerce and Labor regulate the tone of whistles so that they might be a little more uniform, and abolish the siren whistle altogether, I believe from actual experience that it would be better for the masters and pilots in command of boats plying on the waters of New York Harbor. I am not alone in this belief. The use of any kind of a whistle for anything except what is absolutely necessary I claim is a detriment to the navigation of all kinds of steam craft; navigation would be much safer and whistles would be paid more attention to if a little more care were taken. . . . If necessary I could get quite a number of masters who would sign a statement to this effect.

Of course, it is needless to reiterate how firmly I am in accord with the sentiment of the Association's conclusion that the large calibre of whistles causes even more suffering than does the constant signalling, and that a blast from a whistle loud enough, apparently, to jar a hospital building, as well as "the unearthly and prolonged shrieking which occurs nightly at the different docks," can scarcely be required to warn a boat, a quarter of a mile away, that a ferry-boat is leaving its pier. I also believe, since the purpose of the "Steamboat-Inspection Laws" is primarily the protection of the passengers, crew, and property on vessels, that it is the duty of the Supervising Inspectors to abate a nuisance that is considered by all concerned to be a menace to navigation by masking or rendering inaudible the signals that should properly be given, by rendering extremely difficult the docking of vessels, and by gravely interfering with the repose of the crews of all kinds of craft, from the poorest and dingiest scow up to that of the finest ocean steamship, tied up at its dock.[1]

On the other hand, it is both hoped and believed that the New York Board of Health will see its way clear to doing its utmost to abate this nuisance, especially in view of the important additions that, since my return from Washington, I have made to the mass of material already submitted to it. First and foremost are the extracts from the Report of the Bay Pollution Commission (recently brought to my attention), in which

---

[1] Just as this article is going to press, it is announced from Washington that Representative Bennet of New York, after consultation with officers of the Department of Commerce and Labor, has prepared a bill to prevent the unnecessary blowing of steamboat whistles in New York harbor. I take this opportunity of acknowledging the valuable aid that our movement has already received from Congressmen Bennet and J. Van Vlechten Olcott.

the police jurisdiction of New York State for sanitary purposes over the waters of the Hudson River is settled.   Next, the strong letters from a number of prominent physicians regarding the necessity of rest to health and life.

As regards the character of the jurisdiction of New York State the report says:

It was to be a police jurisdiction of and over all vessels, ships, boats, or craft of every kind that did or might float upon the surface of said waters, and over all the elements and agents or instruments of commerce, while the same were afloat in or upon the waters of said bay and river for quarantine and health purposes, and to secure the observance of all the rules and regulations for the protection of passengers and property, and all fit governmental control designed to secure the interests of trade and commerce in said port of New York, and preserve thereupon the public peace. . . . "From a perusal of these two causes, it will be seen that the jurisdiction of the State of New York in and to all the waters of the Hudson River and New York Bay is primarily a police jurisdiction for sanitary and quarantine purposes; and the right of the State of New Jersey to erect wharves, piers, bulkheads, and improvements from its shores into such waters is especially upheld in the Central Railroad case, from which I have above quoted.   Over and above the rights of the two contiguous States is the right of the federal Government in the navigable waters of New York Bay and the Hudson River, in so far as the protection of navigation is concerned " (see State of Pennsylvania vs. Wheeling Bridge Company, et al., 13 Howard, 518).

Professor William H. Thompson stated:

I am heartily in favor of any measures being adopted which will lessen the effects of unnecessary noises. . . . The injurious effect of noise as such on many persons is too well demonstrated to need argument; but when the effects are felt by whole collections of the sick with nervous diseases, it becomes not a general but a very particular concern of medical men. . . . I unhesitatingly pronounce the constant whistles of passing steam craft as extremely injurious to the inmates of the hospitals for the insane and would urge the adoption of the most stringent regulations to suppress this evil.

Dr. Charles L. Dana, President of the Academy of Medicine, said:

I am only too glad to add my voice in protest against noises of this city.   I can hear now practically a continuous tooting of horns from the North River [Dr. Dana lives between Fifth and Sixth Avenues, about in the middle of the city], and I can understand how serious and distressing this must be to the population living nearer than I do. . . . There is an enormous lot of preventable noise, and I hope your energetic attack on river tooting noises will be made to include other things.

Dr. John Winters Brannan, President of the Hospital Board, wrote:

You notice what Dr. Cash says of the especial annoyance to the patients in the wards nearest the river.   This is important, as these wards are considered the best in the hospital, and in our new Bellevue Hospital we are planning to place as many wards as possible close to the river, in order that the patients may have the benefit of the freshness and breeze from the water.   For the sake of the sick and helpless poor of New York, I hope your efforts will meet with success.

Dr. George W. Jacoby stated:

Cell exhaustion — fatigue — cannot be avoided, but recuperation is a right of nature, the wanton interference with which constitutes an infringement on the personal right of the individual and which should be protected by law. . . . The case which you have made out certainly shows that the incessant whistling of steamers upon our rivers does disturb the rest of the inmates of our hospitals, of the employés of our benevolent institutions, and of the community at large and, by so much, interferes with their natural right to recuperation. I am heartily in favor of the agitation which you have begun, and hope that the abolition of these river noises by ordinance will be but the initiative to the legislative abolition of many other unnecessary and unwarrantable street noises.

From Dr. John H. Girdner I received the following:

City noises exert a deleterious effect on the human system; this is especially marked in the case of invalids and children. Noise is a most potent factor in producing functional diseases of the brain and nervous system, not alone by its direct action, but by destroying sound, refreshing sleep. A very large percentage of the noises of New York City are wholly unnecessary and should be suppressed as a sanitary measure. Unnecessary blowing of whistles on the rivers and in the harbor of New York is particularly nerve-racking and sleep-destroying.

Dr. William Hirsch wrote:

Permit me to assure you of my sincerest sympathy in the noble fight which you have undertaken against the intolerable nuisance of unnecessary noises on the river. I have a considerable number of patients whose night-rest is disturbed by the incessant whistling, and who, therefore, suffer great agony, their recovery naturally being retarded. I heartily wish you a complete success in your crusade against these outrages, and hope that eventually this may lead to the suppression of unnecessary street noises, which are equally injurious to the nervous system, and which form a disgrace in any civilized community.

Dr. S. Weir Mitchell stated:

We are just waking up enough to battle with the noise nuisance in this city [Philadelphia]. Years ago there was an interesting suit brought against St. Mark's Church obliging them to limit the ringing of their bells to within certain hours, on account of the offensive character of the noise made. Any movement of this kind has my full sympathy. I presume I am not to return these papers. If you say that I am not to do so I shall forward them to the health officer here.

Unfortunately the limited space of a magazine article will not admit of the barest enumeration of all the preventable noises that beat upon the tortured ear in our great city.   They order these things better in Europe, where the steam whistle has been largely suppressed. We are indeed a wonderful nation, but have much to learn from the Old World as regards the simple, sane commonplaces of ordinary life, of which protection from unreasonable noise is one of the most obvious. Considering the strenuous life that we live in America and the enormous stress under which we labor, sleep is, for us, of exceptional importance if we are not to become

37

a nation of neuræsthenics. It is certainly within the power of the people to procure it for themselves; and associations ought to be formed in every city of the Union with the object of impressing upon the authorities, especially the boards of health, the absolute obligations which they are under to use their police powers in this direction as vigorously as in any other. Oh! for a few more earnest workers like Professor Morse of Salem, Dr. Girdner of New York, and Dr. Kempster of Milwaukee, who have, for years, striven so patiently to secure for suffering fellow-mortals

> "Sleep, that knits up the ravell'd sleave of care,
> The death of each day's life, sore labour's bath,
> Balm of hurt minds, great nature's second course,
> Chief nourisher in life's feast."

Mrs. Isaac L. Rice.

JAPAN'S POLICY IN KOREA.

It is not a question of ambition, but a matter of necessity, that Japan should become a great power on the Asiatic continent. Should she fail in that, there is but one thing left for her — national death. Our very existence depends upon her attainment of this object. It is forced upon us as a means of self-defence. As for our relation with Korea, that is not a matter of a single day. From the most remote period we have always been more or less together. A number of anthropologists are to-day gathering evidence proving that the race peopling the southern part of the peninsula of Korea is of the same stock as that whence we of Japan have sprung. Dr. Betz, in particular, spent a long time in Korea; and, as a result of his scientific investigations, he tells us of the radical difference between the people of southern and those of northern Korea. They differ in their bony structure, for example; those of northern Korea being similar to the Tartar family, while those of the south are kin to our own race.

In ancient times, the famous chieftain of Kyushu, called Kumaso, raised the standard of revolt against the imperial house. He was in sympathy with Korea, whose cause he endeavored to serve. This it was which animated our heroic Empress Jingo to tear out the rebellion by the roots, declaring that the Kyushu rebels must be fought in Korea; and the famous punitive expedition of Shinra, as a portion of the Korean peninsula was then called, has become one of our most cherished historical traditions. Our relations with Korea are therefore the inheritance of fifteen centuries. When the Tartars conceived the idea of conquering Japan, they began their process of subjugation with the Tartar tribes on the northern borders of the Korean peninsula, and thence proceeded southward. When their conquest over Korea was complete, they took offensive measures against the Kyushu coast. This, the Tartar expedition of the period of Tokimune, in the Hojo Shogunate, fell short of its object. Japan did not fail to retaliate the insult of the Tartar; and her first step was an expedition for the subjugation of Korea. For us as for the Tartar, Korea was the highway by which the goal of military glory was to be reached.

Happily for Korea and the Mongol Empire, and unfortunately for us, the downfall of the Hojo Shogunate rang down the curtain upon this expedition, which might have been of far-reaching historic importance. Although the dream of that age failed to materialize, it was revived after three hundred years. Under the leadership of the great military genius Toyotomi Hideyoshi, the Japanese army then made a victorious march through Korea, which, however, was arrested by the death of the great commander. Japan was also at that time rent by constant feuds at home. Everywhere military chieftains divided the Empire and struggled for the mastery. At last the unification of feudal Japan was brought about under Togugawa Isyasu, who founded the Togugawa Shogunate, which inaugurated nearly three hundred years of peace. In the tranquillity and ease of a fenced-in land, Japan troubled herself but little concerning affairs beyond the seas.

Then came the present régime. In the early days of the restoration the old attitude on the Korean question was resumed. Kido wished to send a punitive expedition to the peninsula, as did Saigo in the sixth year of Meiji (1873). Thus we see that, despite the changes wrought by time, the spirit remained the same. In the month of March of the ninth year of Meiji (1876), we concluded a treaty of amity with the government of Korea, and so came into the relationship of a treaty power with her.

Now, this, the famous treaty of Ko-Kwa, was the first treaty that Korea had ever concluded with any independent foreign state, with the single exception of China. A few years later, in 1882, Seoul saw riotous outbreaks. The mob attacked our legation and burnt it. Our minister, Mr. Hanabusa, was forced to flee for his life, and by means of a surveying vessel of the British government off the coast managed to make his escape to Japan. Our government, greatly surprised, summoned a council to meet before the throne. Opinions were divided. While some of the members of this conference were for war, others declared for peace. Finally the peace party won the day. Yet it was impossible to ignore the whole affair. Our government therefore landed forces at Chemulpo as an armed escort to our minister, Mr. Hanabusa. Thereupon China also sent soldiers. For a time the whole world anxiously watched these proceedings. In the end, however, through the treaty of Saibutsuko, a peaceful settlement of the affair was reached.

Two years later, in 1884, a difference arose between our minister, Takezoe, and the Chinese minister to Korea; and the soldiers of China and of Japan crossed swords in the very palace of the Korean king. This misunderstanding was adjusted by the treaty of Tien-Tsin, which enabled us to exact from China the admission that Korea was an independent state. It further stipulated that neither China nor Japan was to send soldiers into Korea without cause, and that, should the inevitable happen, both of the high contracting parties should notify each other of the movement of troops. The treaty was concluded through Marquis Ito, who acted as our envoy.

A matter of great significance in connection with the Tien-Tsin treaty is that here, for the first time in two thousand years, Japan changed her policy toward Korea.   Prior to the treaty of Ko-Kwa, we had looked upon Korea as our enemy.   We were ever on the alert for a favorable opportunity and justifiable cause for taking revenge upon her.   After the conclusion of the treaty, however, the policy of revenge and invasion was entirely out of the question.   For the first time the policy of Japan toward Korea changed in the direction of developing Korea and of leading her in the path of enlightenment.   The first concrete expression of a radical change of policy, therefore, was the treaty of Tien-Tsin.   In that treaty Japan forced China — always savage in her attitude toward Korea and always looking down upon that country as one of her dependencies — to recognize the independence of the peninsula.   Moreover, the treaty debarred China from carrying out at will rigorous measures of repression and of spoliation.   There is no question as to the sincerity and uprightness of Japan in this regard.

In 1894, however, there arose, hornet-like, a band of men who styled themselves the Tong-haku party. Desolation, devastation, and bloodshed seemed to them mere pastime.   Acts of positive savagery multiplied rapidly, and the Korean government seemed powerless.   Indeed, it looked as if that government itself was encouraging this mad lawlessness of the Tong-haku.   China at once found in this disturbance an excuse to send a large armed force into Korea.   We also despatched troops, according to our right.   This was the beginning of the war between Japan and China.   Happily, in the following year, after gaining a complete victory, we saw the restoration of peace by the treaty of Shimonoseki.

The peace secured by that treaty was, however, of a very temporary nature.   The occupation of the Liao-tong peninsula by Japan was not at all favorable to the wild ambition of Russia and the realization of her dream of a Far Eastern empire.   Evidently she felt that a protest proceeding from herself alone would prove ineffectual.   She therefore sought to bring to her assistance two powers who had no great interests in that portion of the Far East, namely, France and Germany.   As these powers could find no valid reason for protesting, they hit upon the idea of spreading the report that the occupation of the Liao-tong peninsula by Japan would be injurious to the peace of the Far East.   As for Japan, she was powerless against this triple alliance.   The Liao-tong peninsula, which she had bought with the blood and tears of her people, was restored to China.

It is true that, in the treaty of Tien-Tsin, China had acknowledged the independence of Korea.   But that was merely the text of a treaty. The fact is that China subsequently dealt with Korea precisely as if that country were still one of her dependencies. After the war with Japan, however, China definitely recognized the independence of Korea in deed as formerly by letter. Yet, after all these services rendered in her behalf, did Korea show the slightest gratitude toward or confidence in Japan? During the war with China, and for some time after the successful termination of that war, Korea did appear to be friendly toward us. Immediately upon the restoration of the Liao-tong peninsula, however, through the coercion of the triple alliance before referred to, there came a sudden and complete change in the attitude of the Korean government and its people toward Japan. Instead of putting their trust in Japan, instead of being friendly to her, they looked upon her with suspicion, indeed, with decided disfavor.

Hardly had we relieved Korea from the domination of China, and that, too, at great cost, when the peninsula was invaded by another power, much more remorseless and cruel, and naturally more dangerous. Russia now took the place of China at the court of Seoul. The ambition of Russia was not to be compared with that of China. Such was its madness that it was not only bent on conquering Korea, but its purpose was to extend its policy of aggression against Japan as well. For ten years we exhausted every means to bring about a happy settlement in order to avoid a crisis and to persuade Russia to change her mind. We tried commercial treaties and numerous other methods of pacification in vain. Finally, in February, 1904, diplomatic relations between the two countries were severed, and the world witnessed one of the greatest wars of modern times.

It is evident, therefore, that the cause both of the Chino-Japanese and of the Russo-Japanese war was the independence of Korea. The two wars differ, so far as we are concerned, in details only. With China we had cultivated pleasant relations for two thousand years; as regards Russia, hatred of one hundred years' standing had been nurtured.

After this brief historic review, I wish to say something of the geographical position of Korea. Judged by her area, Korea is not a great country. Being a peninsula, her coastline is exceedingly long. The climate of her northeastern borders, in the two provinces of Ham-Kyong, is extremely cold because of the Arctic tides which wash the coast at that point. There the climate is something like that of our Hokkaido, or of Karafuto. The southern and western shores of the country, however, receive the benefit of the equatorial current, as does our own favored coast of Kyushu. In the fisheries there is a source of great wealth. Moreover, the small islands that dot the seas here like stepping-stones contribute to the convenience of her fishermen. Along her northeastern littoral the marine products are much like those of our northern waters, and herring and salmon abound. Along her southern and western coast, the waters teem with fish similar to those which exist in the waters of Kyushu. During the recent war, a large number of people derived a considerable income from the fishery enterprises in the Korean waters and in the Yellow Sea, with the product of which they supplied the navy and army. It has been reported that, in this section of the seas, there are also great schools of whales. At all events, none can deny the wealth of the marine products of the Korean waters. With the introduction of modern methods and appliances, a great revenue could be derived from this source.

Although a small country, Korea on land has the advantage of being connected with a great continent. Her rivers, for example, are large. Owing to the absence of industrial education, the Koreans, at present, are not deriving as much benefit from their navigable streams as they otherwise might. By the application of enterprise and intelligent effort, the Korean streams can be converted into a valuable system of communication; and the numerous harbors, situated as they are on an extensive coastline, may in time become valuable centres of commerce. With the establishment of transportation facilities, both by sea and on land, Korea will see the advent of a new day.

Some have declared the soil of Korea to be sterile, and the yield but half of that of Japan. I have not found reason to put any faith in this statement. It may be that the yield of the Korean farms is scanty at present as compared with that produced on a similar area in our own land. At the same time, it must always be kept in mind that agriculture in Korea is still primitive. I am of the opinion that it is not so much to the soil itself, but to waste and carelessness, as well as the absence of scientific methods, that the present agricultural conditions must be attributed. As soon as suitable improvements, both in implements and methods of agriculture, shall have been secured, it will be seen that, after all, the difference between the Korean and Japanese soils is not so great as at present supposed.

I have learned indeed, from a number of people who have come home from their investigations in Korea, that, in a large part of the peninsula, the soil is much richer than in Japan. It should also be borne in mind that the neglected and uncultivated area is very extensive. Perhaps, therefore, one is justified in saying that the yield of the Korean soil should be about the same as that of Japan. Taking the present population of Korea at 10,000,000, the country should be able to support about 30,000,000 additional population. Placing the annual increase of our population at half a million, Korea should therefore be able to absorb our surplus population for fifty or sixty years to come.

Placer mining in Korea is yielding much profit. In this field there is large room for the introduction of modern methods and machinery; and there can be no question as to the vast increase of production that would follow such improvements. Forestry, like agriculture, is not developed in Korea. The timber business has not been very prosperous of late. Still, there are many forests in the peninsula which have not seen an axe in a hundred, or perhaps a thousand, years, because of the lack of transportation facilities. Korea is in the position of the miser who hoards his treasure, fearing to put it to use. Should the waterway transportation facilities of Yalu once become an established fact, we should no doubt hear of the opening of the great treasure-house in the thickly wooded stretch of northern Korea.

On the plains of Korea, cattle raising has been tried. The methods, as in other industrial activities, are quite elementary, and, of course, the stock is not very select. Yet, notwithstanding these obstacles, the Koreans raise cattle for export, although they themselves consume considerable meat. As for minerals, the fame of the Korean mines has travelled far. The country is especially rich in coal and iron; and these two minerals are an acknowledged factor in the civilization of a people. Besides, a great majority of the iron works of Japan are in Kyushu, that portion of our country which is nearest to the peninsula. To us, therefore, the development of these minerals in Korea would prove very advantageous. Altogether, the work to be performed here is one of great promise.

Since the beginning of the recent war, owing to the unbroken series of victories which Japan gained over Russia, the influence and prestige of the latter country, so far as Korea is concerned, are things of the past. And now, what is our own policy toward Korea? What should that policy be? Younger men would say: Conquer Korea and occupy her territory at once. They neither understand the national policy of Japan, nor do they appreciate what she has learned in the past. For many years, the failure and impotency of the Korean government have been the root of all the political troubles in the Far East. The neighbors of Korea have always been the victims of her lamentable weakness, the sufferers from her abuses and blunders. This is true particularly of our own country. We have been forced to take up arms against China and against Russia — all because of her. It is plain, then, that the work of superintending and guiding into the path of righteousness and health the sadly tangled affairs of Korea, both domestic and international, is more than a mere measure of self-defence on the part of Japan; it is a matter of world-wide significance. Should Japan succeed in the task of cleansing the Far-East of its political sins, she will be entitled to the respect and gratitude of the world, for permanent peace in this portion of the globe will thereby be established. Korea will then, in truth, become an independent state. This is the only policy for Japan to pursue with regard to the troublesome Korean question. Indeed, it is a positive duty imposed upon the power which has taken up the guardianship of the Far Eastern balance of affairs.

Of the many and varied problems which call for solution, the economic one is of paramount importance. To-day almost all else depends upon the economic health of a state. If, therefore, we should fail to solve this problem, all our efforts toward a settlement of Korean politics and the establishment of order in the military and foreign affairs of the peninsula would end in failure. Korea would fail, just as Spain and Portugal have failed.

To conquer another land through the might of arms is a very temporary affair. If successful, it is the success of an hour, and very far from an achievement of ages. On the other hand, success in the upbuilding of the economic affairs of a land is not at all of a temporary nature: it exerts a long and permanent influence. All history shows this. If our policy toward Korea is to be attended with permanent results, it must be carried out first of all along the lines of economic advancement. Nothing else would be able to place Korea in the position of maintaining her independence, and nothing else would permit us to hope for the permanence of peace in the Far East. Her gain is our gain. Truly profitable dealings between individuals are always mutual; and this is true also of nations. In a deeper sense, and looking at it from the larger aspect of things, we can never achieve greatness for our own country at the expense of our neighbors, especially of Korea. As we keenly study the interests of Japan, we must necessarily at the same time recognize the rights and interest of the peninsula.

In this particular, the first question which confronts us is that of colonization. Now, there are people who would have you believe that the Japanese are not at all successful as colonizers. They submit as proof the Hokkaido colonization scheme, which failed in spite of every encouragement offered by the government. They also point to the fact that America, Hawaii, and Mexico are trying to exclude our laboring classes from their shores.

It is undeniable that the colonization work in Hokkaido was not very successful. But why? The question may be easily answered. The densest population of Japan is in the southwest. As one goes north, the population decreases in density. Now, the only colonists who could have made the Hokkaido colonization work successful would have been people accustomed to similar climatic conditions — the people of northern Japan, for instance. But in that portion of our country there was no need for emigration; there was plenty of room at home. Moreover, the question of travelling expenses entailed by a journey from the southern portion of our empire to the extreme northern corner would naturally have been a serious one for the colonists.

So much for Hokkaido. The hostile attitude of the nations of North America is not due to the fact that our laboring classes are lacking in the qualities which go to make the successful colonist: it is due to an entirely different cause. It is feared there that the presence of Japanese laborers would bring about a competition between these and the working classes of the respective countries involved, to the financial detriment of these latter. This hostility against Japanese immigrants furnishes a rather eloquent commentary on the superior endowment of the Japanese laborer, which enables him to stand out as the fittest in a keen competition.

The distance between Japan and Korea is such that a person standing on a certain point on our coast can discern the outline of our neighbor's domain through a fairly powerful telescope. From Karatsu, Kyushu, to Fusan, Korea, is only six or seven hours' steaming. Karatsu, in the distant days of Hideyoshi, was the base of operations which that chieftain chose when he made his famous invasion of Korea. It stands in the centre of dense populations. It is situated in that southwestern district where, from time immemorial, could always be found a large number of fishermen. When the fisheries in the Korean waters shall be developed, Karatsu will, in all probability, become a large depot and distributing centre for marine products, commanding the markets of Korea.

Colonization work in Korea will confer a twofold benefit. On the one hand, it will provide a home and a field of activity for the ever increasing population of our own country, and thus lessen among us the number of idlers, those parasites of human society. On the other hand, it will help materially to develop the resources of Korea, and so increase the wealth of that country. Moreover, with the increase of the Japanese population there, our foreign trade with the peninsula will of necessity become more extensive and more prosperous.

Nor is this all. Our industrious farmers and skilful fishermen cannot fail to exert a favorable influence upon the Koreans themselves, who are over fond of idleness and ease. The example of our frugal race may lead the Koreans in the direction of work and of economy, and encourage them to save their earnings. When the administration is corrupt, it naturally comes about that the officials also become more and more avaricious and lawless. Under such circumstances, the question of saving earnings on the part of the workingmen is a mere farce. What little money they may be able to put by is taken away from them as soon as their savings are discovered by the officials. Let the old order of things once be removed, and the corrupt officials will have no opportunity for further spoliation at pleasure; and let the property rights of the people be respected and their persons held sacred in the eyes of the law, and a new era in the economic conditions of the Korean people will have dawned.

The economic salvation of Korea depends much upon the establishment of transportation facilities and the installation of better means of communication. Nature has been partial to her. The sea surrounds her on three sides; and, as if that were not enough, the Yalu covers with its waters a large portion of the territory which adjoins Manchuria. Therefore steamship lines are of paramount importance with her. As for railways, one line starts from Fusan and runs to Seoul; the other line runs westward from Seoul to Wiji. The Seoul and Fusan Railway, which covers about 274 miles, was completed on the 10th of November, 1904, and on the 1st of January, 1905, it was opened for traffic. The line was undertaken by a private company at first, which did not expect to have it in operation until 1907. Upon the outbreak of the Russo-Japanese War, however, the requirements of military transportation hastened its completion.

By means of this railroad line, the distance between Tokio and Seoul has been materially shortened. There are 1,118 miles between the two capitals. Before the construction of the railway, it took nearly a week to make the journey. To-day, it can be made in two days and eight hours. When everything shall be in perfect running order, the time can be shortened to fifty hours. One hardly realizes how much this will affect the economic condition of Korea and our industrial enterprises there. Nor should the political and diplomatic significance of having Seoul within fifty hours of Tokio be overlooked.

After all, however, the Seoul-Fusan line, with its steamship connections, is but one of many lines which will have to be established. From Tokio, through Fusan, Seoul, and Chemulpo, the line is extending its way to Wiji. But it must not stop there. From Wiji, it must cross the Yalu to Yinkan. It should be in touch with the East China Railway, and so come into direct connection with Vladivostock and St. Petersburg on the north. At the same time it may be brought into direct connection with Peking via the the Tien-Tsin Railway. I am of the opinion that Peking is to be a great railway centre in the future. A European railway, such as the Central-Asiatic line proposed by Russia, or one which, coming through Constantinople, would pass through Persia and India, or a railway built in connection with and beyond the present Bagdad line — any or all of such roads could run to Peking as a terminus. When our Korean line shall have a direct connection with Siberia and Europe to the north, and with Peking on the south, the port of Fusan will find itself one of the principal gateways of eastern Asia.

As for the island empire of Japan, that country would find in Fusan the connecting link between her own territories and the two great continents of Asia and Europe. The Korean Railway will in this way become part and parcel of the machinery of world-communication.   Although it differs materially from our lines at home, the men in charge of our administration virtually regard it as one of these.   They have, however, unfortunately permitted it to become partly a private line.   The fact that the East China Railway, ceded by Russia, is government property, whereas the Korean Railway is to some extent a private enterprise, presents a very anomalous condition, which may lead to considerable confusion.   And the fact that the Korean Railway is semi-governmental property makes matters still more complicated.   Here then, in the very centre of a system, world-wide in its ramifications, we have a line governed partly by private interests and partly by governmental policy.   As the state has a vital interest in maintaining unity of management and control, I earnestly hope that the trans-Korean railway will become a government line, fitly commemorating our recent victorious campaign against Russia.

COUNT OKUMA.

CPSIA information can be obtained
at www.ICGtesting.com
Printed in the USA
BVHW081503061118
532319BV00009B/319/P